DATABASE CONCEPTS

NINTH EDITION

David M. Kroenke

David J. Auer
Western Washington University

Scott L. Vandenberg
Siena College

Robert C. Yoder
Siena College

Vice President of Courseware Portfolio Management: Andrew Gilfillan
Executive Portfolio Manager: Samantha Lewis
Team Lead, Content Production: Laura Burgess
Content Producer: Faraz Sharique Ali
Portfolio Management Assistant: Bridget Daly
Director of Product Marketing: Brad Parkins
Director of Field Marketing: Jonathan Cottrell
Product Marketing Manager: Heather Taylor
Field Marketing Manager: Bob Nisbet
Product Marketing Assistant: Liz Bennett
Field Marketing Assistant: Derrica Moser
Senior Operations Specialist: Diane Peirano

Senior Art Director: Mary Seiner
Interior and Cover Design: Pearson CSC
Cover Art: Artwork by Donna Auer
Senior Product Model Manager: Eric Hakanson
Manager, Digital Studio: Heather Darby
Course Producer, MyLab MIS: Jaimie Noy
Digital Studio Producer: Tanika Henderson
Full-Service Project Manager: Gowthaman Sadhanandham
Full Service Vendor: Integra Software Service Pvt. Ltd.
Manufacturing Buyer: LSC Communications, Maura Zaldivar-Garcia
Text Printer/Bindery: LSC Communications
Cover Printer: LSC Communications

Credits and acknowledgments borrowed from other sources and reproduced, with permission, in this textbook appear on the appropriate page within text.

Microsoft and/or its respective suppliers make no representations about the suitability of the information contained in the documents and related graphics published as part of the services for any purpose. All such documents and related graphics are provided "as is" without warranty of any kind. Microsoft and/or its respective suppliers hereby disclaim all warranties and conditions with regard to this information, including all warranties and conditions of merchantability, whether express, implied or statutory, fitness for a particular purpose, title and non-infringement. In no event shall Microsoft and/or its respective suppliers be liable for any special, indirect or consequential damages or any damages whatsoever resulting from loss of use, data or profits, whether in an action of contract, negligence or other tortious action, arising out of or in connection with the use or performance of information available from the services.

The documents and related graphics contained herein could include technical inaccuracies or typographical errors. Changes are periodically added to the information herein. Microsoft and/or its respective suppliers may make improvements and/or changes in the product(s) and/or the program(s) described herein at any time. Partial screen shots may be viewed in full within the software version specified.

Microsoft® Windows®, and Microsoft Office® are registered trademarks of the Microsoft Corporation in the U.S.A. and other countries. This book is not sponsored or endorsed by or affiliated with the Microsoft Corporation.

MySQL®, the MySQL Command Line Client®, the MySQL Workbench®, and the MySQL Connector/ODBC® are registered trademarks of Sun Microsystems, Inc./Oracle Corporation. Screenshots and icons reprinted with permission of Oracle Corporation. This book is not sponsored or endorsed by or affiliated with Oracle Corporation.

Oracle Database XE 2016 by Oracle Corporation. Reprinted with permission.

PHP is copyright The PHP Group 1999–2012, and is used under the terms of the PHP Public License v3.01 available at **http://www.php.net/license/3_01.txt.** This book is not sponsored or endorsed by or affiliated with The PHP Group.

ArangoDB is a copyright of ArangoDB GmbH.

Library of Congress Cataloging-in-Publication Data

Names: Kroenke, David M., author. | Auer, David J., author. |
    Vandenberg, Scott L., author. | Yoder, Robert C., author.
Title: Database concepts/David M. Kroenke, David J. Auer, Western
    Washington University, Scott L. Vandenberg, Siena College, Robert C.
    Yoder, Siena College.
Description: Ninth edition. | New York, NY : Pearson, [2020] | Includes
    index.
Identifiers: LCCN 2018052988 | ISBN 9780135188149 | ISBN 0135188148
Subjects: LCSH: Database management. | Relational databases.
Classification: LCC QA76.9.D3 K736 2020 | DDC 005.74—dc23 LC record available at
    https://lccn.loc.gov/2018052988

1 19

 Pearson

ISBN 10:   0-13-518814-8
ISBN 13: 978-0-13-518814-9

Brief Contents

ONLINE EXTENSIONS: SEE PAGE 517 FOR INSTRUCTIONS

Contents

ONLINE EXTENSIONS: SEE PAGE 517 FOR INSTRUCTIONS

A Working with MySQL
SECTION 1—INSTALLING MYSQL COMMUNITY SERVER 8.0
SECTION 2—CREATING AND USING A MYSQL DATABASE
SECTION 3—USING SQL IN MYSQL
SECTION 4—IMPORTING MICROSOFT EXCEL DATA INTO A MYSQL DATABASE
SECTION 5—CREATING A DATABASE DESIGN ON MYSQL WORKBENCH
SECTION 6—DATABASE ADMINISTRATION IN MYSQL
SECTION 7—BUSINESS INTELLIGENCE SYSTEMS USING MYSQL
SECTION B—ADVANCED SQL IN MYSQL

Summary • *Key Terms* • *Review Questions* • *Exercises* • *Marcia's Dry Cleaning Case Questions* • *Garden Glory Project Questions* • *James River Jewelry Project Questions* • *The Queen Anne Curiosity Shop Project Questions*

B Advanced SQL
EXTENDING THE WP DATABASE
USING THE SQL ALTER TABLE STATEMENT
USING THE SQL MERGE STATEMENT
EXTENSIONS TO SQL QUERY TECHNIQUES
USING SQL SET OPERATORS
CREATING AND WORKING WITH SQL VIEWS
USING SQL VIEWS
SQL PERSISTENT STORED MODULES (SQL/PSM)
WORKING WITH MICROSOFT ACCESS SECTION B—ADVANCED SQL IN MICROSOFT ACCESS AND IMPORTING MICROSOFT EXCEL DATA

Summary • *Key Terms* • *Review Questions* • *Exercises* • *Working with Microsoft Access Key Terms* • *Working with Microsoft Access Exercises* • *Heather Sweeney Designs Case Questions* • *Garden Glory Project Questions* • *James River Jewelry Project Questions* • *The Queen Anne Curiosity Shop Project Questions*

C Advanced Business Intelligence and Big Data
REPORTING SYSTEMS
DATA MINING
WHAT IS BIG DATA?
EXTENSIBLE MARKUP LANGUAGE (XML)
NOSQL DATABASE MANAGEMENT SYSTEMS
USING THE RELATIONAL DATABASE FEATURES OF MICROSOFT AZURE
WORKING WITH MICROSOFT ACCESS SECTION C—CREATING MICROSOFT ACCESS SWITCHBOARDS

Summary • *Key Terms* • *Review Questions* • *Exercises* • *Working with Microsoft Access Key Terms* • *Working with Microsoft Access Exercises* • *Marcia's Dry Cleaning Case Questions* • *Garden Glory Project Questions* • *James River Jewelry Project Questions* • *The Queen Anne Curiosity Shop Project Questions*

Preface

Colin Johnson is a production supervisor for a small manufacturer in Seattle. Several years ago, Colin wanted to build a database to keep track of components in product packages. At the time, he was using a spreadsheet to perform this task, but he could not get the reports he needed from the spreadsheet. Colin had heard about Microsoft Access, and he tried to use it to solve his problem. After several days of frustration, he bought several popular Microsoft Access books and attempted to learn from them. Ultimately, he gave up and hired a consultant who built an application that more or less met his needs. Over time, Colin wanted to change his application, but he did not dare try.

Colin was a successful businessperson who was highly motivated to achieve his goals. A seasoned Windows user, he had been able to teach himself how to use Microsoft Excel, Microsoft PowerPoint, and a number of production-oriented application packages. He was flummoxed at his inability to use Microsoft Access to solve his problem. "I'm sure I could do it, but I just don't have any more time to invest," he thought. This story is especially remarkable because it has occurred tens of thousands of times over the past decade to many other people.

Microsoft, Oracle, IBM, and other database management system (DBMS) vendors are aware of such scenarios and have invested millions of dollars in creating better graphical interfaces, hundreds of multi-panel wizards, and many sample applications. Unfortunately, such efforts treat the symptoms and not the root of the problem. In fact, most users have no clear idea what the wizards are doing on their behalf. As soon as these users require changes to database structure or to components such as forms and queries, they drown in a sea of complexity for which they are unprepared. With little understanding of the underlying fundamentals, these users grab at any straw that appears to lead in the direction they want. The consequence is poorly designed databases and applications that fail to meet the users' requirements.

Why can people like Colin learn to use a word processor or a spreadsheet product yet fail when trying to learn to use a DBMS product? First, the underlying database concepts are unnatural to most people. Whereas everyone knows what paragraphs and margins are, no one knows what a *relation* (also called a *table*) is. Second, it seems as though using a DBMS product ought to be easier than it is. "All I want to do is keep track of something. Why is it so hard?" people ask. Without knowledge of the *relational model*, breaking a sales invoice into five separate tables before storing the data is mystifying to business users.

This book is intended to help people like Colin understand, create, and use databases in a DBMS product, whether they are individuals who found this book in a bookstore or students using this book as their textbook in a class.

NEW TO THIS EDITION

Students and other readers of this book will benefit from new content and features in this edition. These include the following:

- The structure of the book has been reorganized to provide more emphasis on the essential concepts of databases and their use, and on the newest developments in Business Intelligence (BI) Systems, Cloud Computing, Big Data, and nonrelational (NoSQL) databases. Much material previously found in online extensions has been reintegrated into the book itself or reorganized into one of three online Extensions.

- Microsoft Office 2019, and particularly Microsoft Access 2019, is now the basic software used in the book and is shown running on Microsoft Windows 10.[1]
- The sections in each chapter previously called "The Access Workbench" have been reorganized as "Working with Microsoft Access," and now integrate material on using Microsoft Visio 2019 for data modeling and database design.
- DBMS software coverage has been updated to include MySQL Community Server 8.0 and MySQL Workbench 8.0. MySQL is now the example DBMS used throughout the book (instead of Microsoft SQL Server), and all SQL output in the book is shown as displayed in MySQL Workbench.[2]
- Detailed coverage of MySQL is in the online Extension "Working with MySQL," which now includes coverage equivalent to "Working with Microsoft Access." There is a separate section of "Working with MySQL" for each chapter in the book, so that work on MySQL can be done in conjunction with the topics covered in the book.
- Support for Oracle and Microsoft SQL Server is continued in the text of Chapter 3 and online Extension B (SQL and Advanced SQL) by indicating the major syntactic differences and in the instructor solutions to those sections.
- The continuing discussion of SQL in DBC e08 Appendix E, "Advanced SQL," is retained as the online Extension "Advanced SQL." The extension contains a discussion of the SQL ALTER statement, SQL set operators (UNION, etc.), SQL correlated subqueries, SQL views, and SQL/Persistent Stored Modules (SQL/PSM).
- A short introduction to physical database design and related considerations has been added to Chapter 6 ("Database Administration"), along with an example of using MySQL database security using roles.
- The NoSQL introduction in Chapter 7 has been expanded to include coverage of the CAP theorem and a more detailed description of document databases, using examples from the ArangoDB NoSQL database management system. This description is continued and deepened in the Extension "Advanced Business Intelligence and Big Data."
- Updated material on cloud computing, virtualization using containers, and the new Hadoop processing model is now in Chapter 7.
- Updated material for the former Appendices J, "Business Intelligence Systems" and K, "Big Data," is now available in the online Extension "Advanced Business Intelligence and Big Data." This material includes enhanced coverage of NoSQL DBMSs, with additional examples of NoSQL graph databases from an actual system (ArangoDB) and an expansion of the NoSQL document database coverage from Chapter 7 (again using ArangoDB). Some of the database features of the Microsoft Azure cloud platform are also covered in this extension.
- The James River Jewelry project questions have been reintegrated into the book chapters to make it easier to use this material when assigning projects.
- Videos demonstrating many tasks described in the "Working with Microsoft Access" and "Working with MySQL" sections of the book will be available online to users of the e-text version of the book.

---

[1]Microsoft recommends installing and using the 32-bit version of Microsoft Office 2019, even on 64-bit versions of the Microsoft Windows operating system. We also recommend that you install and use the 32-bit version.

[2]While we still like and use Microsoft SQL Server, it has simply become too complex for use as our example DBMS in Database Concepts. MySQL is much easier to install and use when introducing students to relational databased DBMS products in a concepts book like this one. We still use Microsoft SQL Server as our example DBMS in our book Database Processing: Fundamentals, Design, and Implementation, 15th ed. (Upper Saddle River, NJ: Pearson, 2019) where it is discussed in depth.

THE NEED FOR ESSENTIAL CONCEPTS

With today's technology, it is impossible to utilize a DBMS successfully without first learning fundamental concepts. After years of developing databases with business users, we believe that the following database concepts are essential:

- Fundamentals of the relational model
- Structured Query Language (SQL)
- Data modeling
- Database design
- Database administration

And because of the increasing use of the Internet, the World Wide Web, commonly available analysis tools, and the emergence of the NoSQL movement, four more essential concepts need to be added to the list:

- Data warehouse structures
- Business intelligence (BI) systems
- Cloud computing and virtualization
- Nonrelational structured data storage (Big Data and NoSQL systems)

Users like Colin—and students who will perform jobs similar to his—need not learn these topics to the same depth as future information systems professionals. Consequently, this textbook presents only essential concepts—those that are necessary for users like Colin who want to create and use small databases. Many of the discussions in this book are rewritten and simplified explanations of topics that you will find fully discussed in David M. Kroenke, David J. Auer, Scott L. Vandenberg, and Robert C. Yoder's *Database Processing: Fundamentals, Design, and Implementation.*[3] However, in creating the material for this text, we have endeavored to ensure that the discussions remain accurate and do not mislead. Nothing here will need to be unlearned if students take more advanced database courses.

TEACHING CONCEPTS INDEPENDENT OF DBMS PRODUCTS

This book does not assume that students will use any particular DBMS product. The book does illustrate database concepts with Microsoft Access and MySQL Community Server so that students can use these products as tools and actually try out the material, but all the concepts are presented in a DBMS-agnostic manner. When students learn the material this way, they come to understand that the fundamentals pertain to any database, from the smallest Microsoft Access database to the largest MySQL, Microsoft SQL Server, or Oracle Database database. Moreover, this approach avoids a common pitfall. When concepts and products are taught at the same time, students frequently confound concepts with product features and functions. For example, consider referential integrity constraints. When they are taught from a conceptual standpoint, students learn that there are times when the values of a column in one table must always be present as values of a column in a second table. Students also learn how this constraint arises in the context of relationship definition and how either the DBMS or the application must enforce this constraint. If taught in the context of a DBMS—say, in the context of Microsoft Access—students will only learn that in some cases you check a check box and in other cases you do not. The danger is that the underlying concept will be lost in the product feature.

---

[3]David M. Kroenke, David J. Auer, Scott L. Vandenberg, and Robert C. Yoder, *Database Processing: Fundamentals, Design, and Implementation,* 15th ed. (Upper Saddle River, NJ: Pearson, 2019).

All this is not to say that a DBMS should not be used in this class. On the contrary, students can best master these concepts by applying them using a commercial DBMS product. This edition of the book was written to include enough basic information about Microsoft Access and MySQL so that you can use these products in your class without the need for a second book or other materials. Microsoft Access is covered in some depth because of its popularity as a personal database and its inclusion in the Microsoft Office Professional suite of applications. However, if you want to cover a particular DBMS in depth or use a DBMS product not discussed in the book, you need to supplement this book with another text or additional materials. Pearson provides a number of books for Microsoft Access and other DBMS products, and many of them can be packaged with this text.

WORKING WITH MICROSOFT ACCESS

This new edition of the text renames "The Access Workbench" to "Working with Microsoft Access," and continues to feature Microsoft Access as our introductory DBMS. Because Microsoft Access is widely used in introductory database classes, we feel it is important to include specific information on using Microsoft Access. Each chapter has an accompanying section of "Working with Microsoft Access," which illustrates the chapter's concepts and techniques using Microsoft Access. The "Working with…" topics start with creating a database and a single table in Chapter 1 and move through various topics, finishing with using Microsoft Access (together with Microsoft Excel) to produce PivotTable OLAP reports in Chapter 7. We have also integrated the Microsoft Visio material formerly found in Appendix G into the book itself to demonstrate the use of Visio for creating data models as described in Chapter 4. This material is not intended to provide comprehensive coverage of Microsoft Access, but all the necessary basic Microsoft Access topics are covered so that your students can learn to effectively build and use Microsoft Access databases.

WORKING WITH MYSQL

This new edition adds support for MySQL Community Server 8.0 at a level equivalent to "Working with Microsoft Access." This allows us to fully integrate an Enterprise class DBMS into the text. This material is found in online Extension A, "Working with MySQL." Topics include some previously found in Appendix C, in particular using the MySQL Workbench to create database designs as discussed in Chapter 5. Because MySQL is an Enterprise class DBMS widely used in introductory database classes, we feel it is important to include specific information on using MySQL. There is a section in "Working with MySQL" that aligns with each chapter in the book and with online Extension B, "Advanced SQL." While, like "Working with Microsoft Access," this material is not intended to provide comprehensive coverage of MySQL, all of the necessary basic MySQL topics are covered.[4]

KEY TERMS, REVIEW QUESTIONS, EXERCISES, CASES, AND PROJECTS

Because it is important for students to apply the concepts they learn, each chapter concludes with sets of key terms, review questions, exercises (including exercises tied to "Working with Microsoft Access"), Case Question sets, and three projects that run throughout the book. Students should know the meaning of each of the key terms and be able to answer the review questions if they have read and understood the chapter material. Each of the exercises requires students to apply the chapter concepts to a small problem or task.

---

[4]Note that while we have increased our support of MySQL in this edition, we have dropped the material on Microsoft SQL Server and Oracle XE formerly found in Appendices A and B, respectively. We still include some basic discussion of Microsoft SQL Server and Oracle Database XE in the text, but if you need more complete coverage of either Microsoft SQL Server or Oracle Database, please see David M. Kroenke, David J. Auer, Scott L. Vandenberg, and Robert C. Yoder, *Database Processing: Fundamentals, Design, and Implementation,* 15th ed. (Upper Saddle River, NJ: Pearson, 2019).

The first of the projects, Garden Glory, concerns the development and use of a database for a partnership that provides gardening and yard maintenance services to individuals and organizations. The second project, James River Jewelry, addresses the need for a database to support a frequent-buyer program for a retail store. The third project, The Queen Anne Curiosity Shop, concerns the sales and inventory needs of a retail business. These three projects appear in all of the book's chapters. In each instance, students are asked to apply the project concepts from the chapter. Instructors will find more information on the use of these projects in the instructor's manual and can obtain databases and data from the password-protected instructor's portion of this book's Web site (**www.pearsonhighered.com/kroenke**).

SOFTWARE USED IN THE BOOK

Just as we have treated our discussions in a DBMS-agnostic way, whenever possible we have selected software to be as operating system independent as possible. It is amazing how much excellent software is available online. Many major DBMS vendors provide free versions of their premier products (for example, Microsoft's SQL Server Developer edition and Express edition, Oracle Corporation's Oracle Database Express Edition (Oracle Database XE), and MySQL Community Server). In this text, we will be using Microsoft Access 2019, Microsoft Excel 2019, and MySQL Community Edition 8.0.

Over the past 30-plus years, we have found the development of databases and database applications to be an enjoyable and rewarding activity. We believe that the number, size, and importance of databases will increase in the future and that the field will achieve even greater prominence. It is our hope that the concepts, knowledge, and techniques presented in this book will help students to participate successfully in database projects now and for many years to come.

CHANGES FROM THE EIGHTH EDITION

This edition represents a restructuring of Database Concepts to reemphasize the basic concepts of database systems and database development in today's mobile environment. We have streamlined the content and presentation to make it easier for instructors to cover the essentials of database systems. We frame database topic discussions within today's Internet- and mobile applications–based networked environment and economy. Today, databases are no longer isolated entities found somewhere in obscure server rooms, but rather are ubiquitous parts of websites and tablet and smartphone apps. We are literally dependent upon databases in our lives, whether exchanging email messages, posting to our Facebook pages, or shopping online. To this end, we have reintegrated material formerly in several appendices back into the book itself, and reduced online material to three extensions:

- Online extension A—Working with MySQL. This extension provides detailed coverage of MySQL Community Server 8.0 and the MySQL Workbench similar to the coverage of Microsoft Access in the "Working with Microsoft Access" sections.
- Online extension B—Advanced SQL. This extension provides the same material to supplement the SQL material in Chapter 3 that was previously found in Appendix E. This material should meet the needs of those classes that want to go beyond basic SQL without the need for an additional textbook.
- Online extension C—Advanced Business Intelligence and Big Data. This extension provides coverage of how to use BI, Big Data, Azure Cloud, and nonrelational database tools so that you can have your students experience these tools in action.

BOOK OVERVIEW

This textbook consists of seven chapters and three online extensions (all of which are readily available online at **www.pearsonhighered.com/kroenke**). Chapter 1 explains why databases are used, what their components are, and how they are developed. Students will learn the purpose of databases and their applications as well as how databases differ from and improve on lists in spreadsheets. Chapter 2 introduces the relational model and defines basic relational terminology. It also introduces the fundamental ideas that underlie normalization and describes the normalization process.

Chapter 3 presents fundamental SQL statements. Basic SQL statements for data definition are described, as are SQL SELECT and data modification statements. No attempt is made to present advanced SQL statements; only the essential statements are described. Online Extension B, "Advanced SQL," adds coverage of advanced SQL topics, such as the SQL ALTER TABLE statement, SQL set operators (e.g., UNION), SQL views, and SQL/Persistent Stored Modules (SQL/PSM).

The next two chapters consider database design. Chapter 4 addresses data modeling using the entity-relationship (E-R) model. This chapter describes the need for data modeling, introduces basic E-R terms and concepts, and presents a short case application (Heather Sweeney Designs) of E-R modeling. Chapter 5 describes database design and revisits normalization as a step in database design. The data model from the case example in Chapter 4 is transformed into a relational design in Chapter 5.

In this edition, we continue to use the prescriptive procedure for normalizing relations through the use of a four-step process. This approach not only makes the normalization task easier, it also makes normalization principles easier to understand. For instructors who want a bit more detail on normal forms, short definitions of most normal forms are included in Chapter 2.

The last two chapters consider database management and the uses of databases in applications. Chapter 6 provides an overview of database administration. The case example database is built as a functioning database, and it serves as the example for a discussion of the need for database administration. The chapter surveys concurrency control, security, and backup and recovery techniques. Database administration is an important topic because it applies to all databases, even personal, single-user databases. In fact, in some ways this topic is more important for those smaller databases because no professional database administrator is present to ensure that critical tasks are performed.

Chapter 7 discusses the emerging world of Big Data and the NoSQL movement, including under this umbrella business intelligence (BI) systems and the data warehouse architectures that support them, which often involve Big Data and NoSQL concepts. Chapter 7 also provides a discussion of distributed databases, object-relational databases, virtualization, and cloud computing as they relate to the continuing evolution of NoSQL systems and Big Data. Many details of BI and NoSQL systems can be found in online Extension C, "Advanced Business Intelligence and Big Data." More specifically, Chapter 7 discusses dimensional databases as an example of a data warehouse architecture, walking through how to build a dimensional database for Heather Sweeney Designs and then using it to produce a PivotTable online analytical processing (OLAP) report as an example of BI reporting. This chapter also includes a brief introduction to NoSQL databases in general and document databases in particular, using the ArangoDB NoSQL DBMS.

Online Extension A introduces MySQL Community Server 8.0 and the MySQL Workbench. There is a section to match each chapter in the book and online Extension B, "Advanced SQL." This allows students to gradually learn the capabilities of an Enterprise class DBMS.

Online Extension B provides additional coverage of SQL topics to allow instructors to teach advanced SQL topics without the need of an additional textbook. This includes material on SQL programming via SQL/Persistent Stored Modules (SQL/PSM).

Online Extension C describes some data analysis techniques, including report systems, data mining, market basket analysis, and decision trees. An introduction to XML and JSON provides context for more details on document databases and other NoSQL database systems, using ArangoDB to illustrate both graph databases and more advanced features of document databases. We present a case study of using Microsoft SQL Server Management Studio to create an account and connect to Microsoft's Azure cloud to migrate a SQL database from a personal computer to Azure. Lastly, we show how to create switchboards in our "Working with Microsoft Access" section.

KEEPING CURRENT IN A RAPIDLY CHANGING WORLD

In order to keep *Database Concepts* up to date between editions, we post updates on the book's Web site at **www.pearsonhighered.com/kroenke** as needed. Instructor resources and student materials are also available on the site, so be sure to check it from time to time.

ACKNOWLEDGMENTS

We would like to thank the following reviewers for their insightful and helpful comments:

Arthur Lee, Lord Fairfax Community College
Behrooz Saghafi, Ph.D., Chicago State University
Betsy Page Sigman, Georgetown University
Bijoy Bordoloi, Southern Illinois University, Edwardsville
Carolyn Carvalho, Kent State University at Ashtabula
David Chou, Eastern Michigan University
David L. Olson, University of Nebraska
Fen Wang, Central Washington University
Gabriel Peterson, North Carolina Central University
Jeffrey Burton, Daytona State College
Jim Pierson, Forsyth Technical Community College
Jing Wang, University of New Hampshire
Jose Nieves, Lord Fairfax Community College
Joshua S. White, PhD, State University of New York Polytechnic Institute
Julie Lewis, Baker College
June Lane, Bucks County Community College
Kui Du, University of Massachusetts Boston
Manuel Rossetti, University of Arkansas
Matt Hightower, Cerro Coso Community College
Maya Tolappa, Waubonscc Community College
Meg Murray, Kennesaw State University
Norman Hahn, Thomas Nelson Community College
Patrick Appiah-Kubi, Indiana State University
Paul Pennington, University of Houston
Paul Tallon, Loyola University Maryland
Richard Grant, Seminole State College of Florida
Richard T. Evans, South Suburban College
Robert Demers, University of Massachusetts - Lowell
Stephen Larson, Slippery Rock University

We would like to thank Donna Auer for letting us use one of her cold wax paintings as the cover art for this book. This artwork was also the basis for design elements within the book.

We would like to thank Samantha Lewis, our editor; Faraz Sharique Ali, our content producer, and Gowthaman Sadhanandham, our project manager, for their professionalism, insight, support, and assistance in the development of this project. We would also like to thank William Morris for his comments on the text and Harold Wise for his work on the supplements. Finally, David Kroenke would like to thank his wife, Lynda; David Auer would like to thank his wife, Donna; Scott Vandenberg would like to thank his wife, Kristin; and Robert Yoder would like to thank Diane, Rachael, and Harrison Yoder for their love, encouragement, and patience while this project was being completed.

David Kroenke
Langley, Washington

David Auer
Clinton, Washington

Scott Vandenberg
Loudonville, New York

Robert Yoder
Loudonville, New York

About the Authors

David M. Kroenke entered the computing profession as a summer intern at the RAND Corporation in 1967. Now retired, his career spanned education, industry, consulting, and publishing.

He has taught at the University of Washington, Colorado State University, and Seattle University. Over the years, he has led dozens of teaching seminars for college professors. In 1991 the International Association of Information Systems named him Computer Educator of the Year.

In industry, Kroenke has worked for the U.S. Air Force and Boeing Computer Services, and he was a principal in the startup of three companies. He was also vice president of product marketing and development for the Microrim Corporation and was chief technologist for the database division of Wall Data, Inc. He is the father of the semantic object data model. Kroenke's consulting clients include IBM Corporation, Microsoft, Computer Sciences Corporation, and numerous other companies and organizations.

His text *Database Processing: Fundamentals, Design, and Implementation*, first published in 1977, is now in its 14th edition (coauthored with David Auer for the 11th, 12th, 13th, and 14th editions, and with David Auer, Scott Vandenberg, and Robert Yoder for the 15th [40th anniversary] edition). He introduced *Database Concepts* (now in the 9th edition that you are reading) in 2003 (coauthored with David Auer for the 3rd, 4th, 5th, 6th, and 7th editions, and coauthored with David Auer, Scott Vandenberg, and Robert Yoder for the 8th and 9th editions). Kroenke has published many other textbooks, including the classic *Business Computer Systems* (1981). Recently, he has authored *Using MIS* (8th edition), *Experiencing MIS* (6th edition), *MIS Essentials* (4th edition), *Processes, Systems and Information: An Introduction to MIS* (2nd edition) (coauthored with Earl McKinney), and *Essentials of Processes, Systems and Information* (coauthored with Earl McKinney).

An avid sailor, Kroenke also wrote *Know Your Boat: The Guide to Everything That Makes Your Boat Work*. Kroenke lives on Whidbey Island in Washington state. He has two children and three grandchildren.

David J. Auer is a Senior Instructor Emeritus at the College of Business (CBE) of Western Washington University in Bellingham, WA. He served as the director of Information Systems and Technology Services at CBE from 1994 to 2014 and taught in CBE's Department of Decision Sciences from 1981 to 2015. He has taught CBE courses in quantitative methods, production and operations management, statistics, finance, and management information systems. Besides managing CBE's computer, network, and other technology resources, he also teaches management information systems courses. He has taught the Principles of Management Information Systems and Business Database Development courses, and he was responsible for developing CBE's network infrastructure courses, including Computer Hardware and Operating Systems, Telecommunications, and Network Administration.

He has coauthored several MIS-related textbooks, including *Database Processing: Fundamentals, Design, and Implementation*, first published in 1977, and now in its 15th edition (coauthored with David Kroenke for the 11th, 12th, 13th, and 14th editions, and with David Kroenke, Scott Vandenberg, and Robert Yoder for the 15th [40th anniversary] edition), and *Database Concepts*, now in the 9th edition that you are reading (coauthored with David Kroenke for the 3rd, 4th, 5th, 6th, and 7th editions, and coauthored with David Kroenke, Scott Vandenberg, and Robert Yoder for the 8th and 9th editions).

Auer holds a bachelor's degree in English literature from the University of Washington, a bachelor's degree in mathematics and economics from Western Washington University, a master's degree in economics from Western Washington University, and a master's degree in counseling psychology from Western Washington University. He served as a commissioned officer in the U.S. Air Force, and he has also worked as an organizational development specialist and therapist for an employee assistance program (EAP).

Auer and his wife, Donna, live on Whidbey Island in Washington state. He has two children and four grandchildren.

Scott L. Vandenberg has been on the Computer Science faculty at Siena College since 1993, where he regularly teaches three different database courses at several levels to both computer science and business majors. Prior to arriving at Siena, he taught undergraduate and graduate courses in database systems at the University of Massachusetts–Amherst. Since arriving at Siena, he has also taught graduate and undergraduate database courses at the University of Washington–Seattle. He has developed five different database courses over this time. His other teaching experience includes introductory computer science, introductory programming, data structures, management information systems, and three years teaching Siena's required interdisciplinary freshman writing course.

Vandenberg's recent research publications are mainly in the areas of computer science education and data science applications, with earlier work on query optimization and algebraic query languages. He holds a bachelor's degree in mathematics and computer science from Cornell University and master's and PhD degrees in computer science from the University of Wisconsin–Madison. Medieval history and playing hockey are two things that can tear him away from a database. Vandenberg lives in Averill Park, NY, with his wife, Kristin, and has two children.

Robert C. Yoder began his professional career at the University at Albany as a systems programmer managing mainframes and Unix servers. He became the Assistant Director of Systems Programming, gaining over 25 years' experience as a programmer and technical manager. Yoder has research experience working on 3-D geographic information systems. Yoder holds BS and MS degrees in computer science and a PhD in information science, all from the University at Albany.

Yoder joined the Computer Science department at Siena College in 2001 and teaches business database, management information systems, geographic information systems, data structures, networks, and operating systems courses. Yoder lives in Niskayuna, NY, with his wife, Diane, and has two children. He enjoys traveling, hiking, and walking his dog.

1

Database Fundamentals

Part 1 introduces fundamental concepts and techniques of database management. Chapter 1 explains database technology, discusses why databases are used, and describes the components of a database system. Chapter 2 introduces the relational model and defines key relational database terms. It also presents basic principles of relational database design. Chapter 3 presents Structured Query Language (SQL), an international standard for creating and processing relational databases.

After you have learned these fundamental database concepts, we will focus on database modeling, design, and implementation in Part 2. Finally, we will discuss database management, data warehouses, business intelligence (BI) systems, cloud computing, virtualization, Big Data, and nonrelational "NoSQL" database management systems in Part 3.

Getting Started

- Understand the importance of databases in Internet Web applications and mobile apps
- Understand the nature and characteristics of databases
- Understand the potential problems with lists
- Understand the reasons for using a database
- Understand how using related tables helps you avoid the problems of using lists
- Know the components of a database system

- Learn the elements of a database
- Learn the purpose of a database management system (DBMS)
- Understand the functions of a database application
- Introduce Web database applications
- Introduce data warehouses and business intelligence (BI) systems
- Introduce Big Data and cloud computing

Knowledge of database technology increases in importance every day. Databases are used everywhere: They are key components of e-commerce and other Web-based applications. They lay at the heart of organization-wide operational and decision support applications. Databases are also used by thousands of work groups and millions of individuals. It is estimated that there are more than 10 million active databases in the world today.

The purpose of this book is to teach you the essential relational database concepts, technology, and techniques that you need to begin a career as a database developer. This book does not teach everything of importance in relational database technology, but it will give you sufficient background to be able to create your own personal databases and to participate as a member of a team in the development of larger, more complicated databases. You will also be able to ask the right questions to learn more on your own.

This chapter discusses the importance of databases in the Internet world and then introduces database processing concepts. We will investigate the reasons for using a relational database. We begin by describing some of the problems that can occur when using lists. Using a series of examples, we illustrate how using sets of related tables helps you to avoid those problems. Next, we describe the components of a database system and explain the elements of a database, the purpose of a database management system (DBMS), and the functions of a database application. Finally, we introduce nonrelational databases.

THE IMPORTANCE OF DATABASES IN THE INTERNET AND MOBILE APP WORLD

Let's stop for a moment and consider the incredible information technology available for our use today.

The **personal computer (PC)** became widely available with the introduction of the **Apple II** in 1977 and the **IBM Personal Computer (IBM PC)** in 1981. PCs were networked into **Local Area Networks (LANs)** using the **Ethernet networking technology**, which was developed at the **Xerox Palo Alto Research Center (Xerox PARC)**[1] in the early 1970s and adopted as a national standard in 1983.

The **Internet**—the global computer network of networks—was created as the Department of Defense **Advanced Research Projects Agency Network (ARPANET)** in 1969 and then grew and was used to connect all the LANs (and other types of networks). The Internet became widely known and used when the **World Wide Web**[2] (or **the Web**, or **WWW**) became easily accessible in 1993. Everyone got a computer software application called a **Web browser** and starting *browsing* **Web sites**. Online retail Web sites such as **Amazon.com** (online since 1995) and "brick-and-mortar" stores with an online presence such as Best Buy appeared, and people started extensively *shopping online*.

In the early 2000s, **Web 2.0**[3] Web sites started to appear—allowing users to add content to Web sites that had previously held static content. Web applications such as Facebook, Wikipedia, and Twitter appeared and flourished.

In a parallel development, the **mobile phone** or **cell phone** was demonstrated and developed for commercial use in the 1970s. After decades of mobile phone and cell phone network infrastructure development, the **smartphone** appeared. Apple brought out the **iPhone** in 2007. Google created the **Android operating system**, and the first Android-based smartphone entered the market in 2008. Ten years later, in 2018 (as this is being written), smartphones and **tablet computers (tablets)** are widely used, and thousands of application programs known as **apps** are widely available and in daily use. Most Web applications now have corresponding smartphone and tablet apps (you can "tweet" from either your computer or your smartphone)!

The latest development is the **Internet of Things (IoT)**,[4] where devices such as smart speakers, smart home devices (smoke detectors and thermostats), and even appliances such as refrigerators connect to the Internet and are network accessible. In particular, **smart speakers** such as the Amazon Echo series, Apple HomePod, the Google Home series, and Harmon Kardon INVOKE enable users to interact by voice with network-accessible apps via virtual assistants such as Amazon Alexa, Apple's Siri, Google Assistant, and Microsoft Cortana.

What many people do not understand is that in today's Web application, smartphone app, and IoT app environment, most of what they do depends upon databases.

We can define **data** as recorded facts and numbers. We can initially define a *database* (we will give a better definition later in this chapter) as the structure used to hold or store

---

[1]The mouse and the multi-window graphical user interface commonly used in computer operating systems today were also developed at Xerox PARC. From there, they were adapted and popularized by Apple and Microsoft. For more information, see the Wikipedia article **PARC (company)** (accessed June 2018) at https://en.wikipedia.org/wiki/PARC_(company).

[2]The World Wide Web and the first Web browser were created by Tim Berners-Lee in 1989 and 1990, respectively. For more information, see the Wikipedia article **World Wide Web** (accessed June 2018) at https://en.wikipedia.org/wiki/World_Wide_Web and the World Wide Web Consortium (W3C) Web site (accessed June 2018) at https://www.w3.org/Consortium/.

[3]Web 2.0 was originated by Darcy DiNucci in 1999 and introduced to the world at large in 2004 by publisher Tim O'Reilly. See the Wikipedia article **Web 2.0** (accessed June 2018) at https://en.wikipedia.org/wiki/Web_2.0.

[4]For more information, see the Wikipedia article **Internet of Things** (accessed June 2018) at https://en.wikipedia.org/wiki/Internet_of_things. The article states that there were 8.4 billion network-capable IoT devices in 2017, with an expected 30 billion IoT devices by 2020!

that data. We process that data to provide *information* (which we also define in more detail later in this chapter) for use in Web applications and smartphone apps.

Do you have a Facebook account? If so, all your posts, your comments, your "likes," and other data you provide to Facebook (such as photos) are stored in a *database*. When your friend posts an item, it is initially stored in the *database* and then displayed to you.

Do you have a Twitter account? If so, all your tweets are stored in a *database*. When your friend tweets something, it is initially stored in the *database* and then displayed to you.

Do you shop at **Amazon.com**? If so, how do you find what you are looking for? You enter some words in a search text window on the Amazon home Web page (if you are using a Web browser) and click the Go button. Amazon's computers then search Amazon's *databases* and return a formatted on-screen report of items that match what you searched for.

The search process is illustrated in Figure 1-1, where we search the Pearson Higher Education Web site for books authored by *David Kroenke*. Figure 1-1(a) shows the upper portion of the Pearson Higher Education Web site home page. While many Web sites (including Amazon.com, REI, and Best Buy) have a text box for entering search keywords on the home page itself for immediate use, at the Pearson site we have to click on a Search catalog button to access the search function on the *Advanced Catalog Search* page shown in Figure 1-1(b). On this page, we enter the author name *Kroenke* in the Author text box, and then click the Search button. The Pearson catalog database is searched, and the Web application returns a *Search Results* page containing a listing of books authored by David Kroenke, as shown in Figure 1-1(c).

The use of databases by Web applications and smartphone apps is illustrated in Figure 1-2. In this figure, people have computers (desktop or notebook), smartphones, and smart speakers, which are examples of **devices** used by people, who are referred to as **users**.

FIGURE 1-1

Searching a Database in a Web Browser

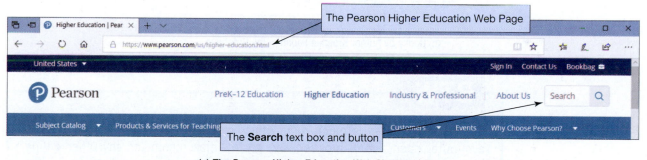

(a) The Pearson Higher Education Web Site Home Page

Courtesy of Pearson Education.

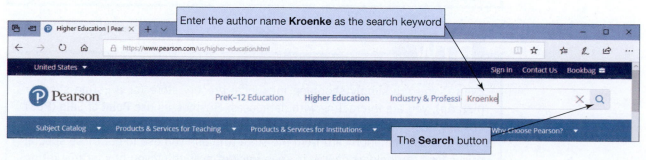

(b) Entering Author Name *Kroenke* as the Search Keyword

Courtesy of Pearson Education.

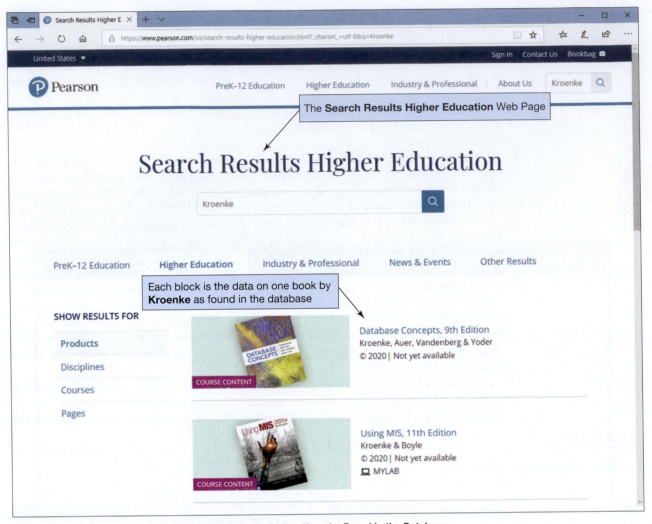

(c) Books by Author Kroenke Found in the Database

Courtesy of Pearson Education.

BTW

Seeing this process is much more effective than just reading about it. Take a minute, open a Web browser, and go to Amazon.com (or any other online retailer, such as Best Buy, L.L.Bean, or REI). Search for something you are interested in, and watch the database search results be displayed for you. You just used a *database*.

BTW

Even if you are simply shopping in a local grocery store (or a coffee shop or pizzeria), you are interacting with databases. Businesses use **Point of Sale (POS) systems** to record every purchase in a database, to monitor inventory, and, if you have a sales promotion card from the store (the one you use to get those special prices for "cardholders only"), to keep track of everything you buy for marketing purposes. All the data POS systems gather is stored in, of course, a *database*.

FIGURE 1-2

The Internet and Mobile Device World

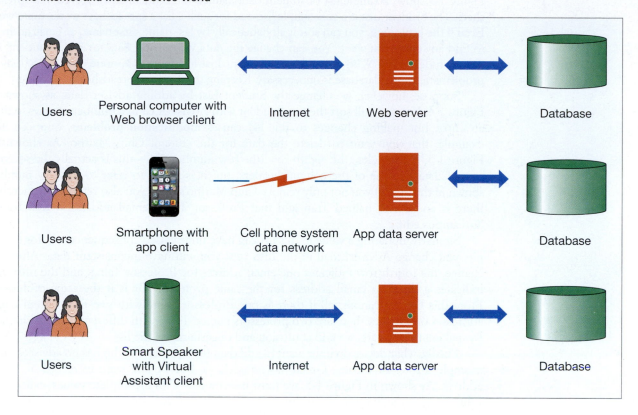

On these devices are **client** applications (Web browsers, apps, virtual assistants) used by people to obtain **services** such as searching, browsing, online purchasing, and tweeting over the Internet or cell phone networks. These services are provided by **server** computers, and these computers hold the databases containing the data needed by the client applications.

This structure is known as **client-server architecture**, and it supports most of the Web applications in use today. The simple fact is that without databases, we could not have the ubiquitous Web applications and apps that are currently used by so many people.

WHY USE A DATABASE?

A database is used to help people keep track of things, and the most commonly used type of database is the *relational database*, although *nonrelational databases* (which are used extensively in online applications such as Facebook and Twitter) are now also widely used. We will discuss the relational database model in depth in Chapter 2, and nonrelational databases are discussed in Chapter 7. For now, you just need to understand a few basic facts about how a relational database helps people track things of interest to them.

You might wonder why we need a special term (and course) for such technology when a simple **list** could serve the same purpose. Many people do keep track of things by using lists, and sometimes such lists are valuable. In other cases, however, simple lists lead to data inconsistencies and other problems.

In this section, we examine several different lists and show some of these problems. As you will see, we can solve the problems by splitting lists into tables of data. Such tables are the key components of a relational database. A majority of this text concerns the design of such tables and techniques for manipulating the data they contain.

WHAT ARE THE PROBLEMS WITH USING LISTS?

Figure 1-3 shows a simple list of student data, named the Student List,[5] stored in a spreadsheet. The Student List is a very simple list, and for such a list a spreadsheet works quite well. Even if the list is long, you can sort it alphabetically by last name, first name, or email address to find any entry you want. You can change the data values, add data for a new student, or delete student data. With a list like the Student List in Figure 1-3, none of these actions is problematic, and a database is unnecessary. Keeping this list in a spreadsheet is just fine.

Suppose, however, we change the Student List by adding adviser data, as shown in Figure 1-4. You can still sort the new Student with Adviser List in a number of ways to find an entry, but making changes to this list causes **modification problems**. Suppose, for example, that you want to delete the data for the student Chip Marino. As shown in Figure 1-5, if you delete the eighth row (the row numbered 8—this is actually the seventh row of data because of the column headers, but it is easier to refer to the row number shown in the figure) you not only remove Chip Marino's data, you also remove the fact that there is an adviser named Tran and that Professor Tran's email address is Ken.Tran@ ourcampus.edu.

Similarly, updating a value in this list can have unintended consequences. If, for example, you change AdviserEmail in the fifth row, you will have inconsistent data. After the change, the fourth row indicates one email address for Professor Taing, and the fifth row indicates a different email address for the same professor. Or is it the same professor? From this list, we cannot tell if there is one Professor Taing with two inconsistent email addresses or whether there are two professors named Taing with different email addresses. By making this update, we add confusion and uncertainty to the list.

Finally, what do we do if we want to add data for a professor who has no advisees? For example, Professor George Green has no advisees, but we still want to record his email address. As shown in Figure 1-5, we must insert a row with incomplete values, called **null values**, in the database field. In this case, the term *null value* means a missing value, but there are other meanings of the term *null value* that are used when working with databases. We will discuss the problems of null values in detail in Chapter 2, where we will show that null values are always problematic and that we want to avoid them whenever possible.

FIGURE 1-3

The Student List in a Spreadsheet

	A	B	C	D
1	SID	StudentLastName	StudentFirstName	StudentEmail
2	S0023	Andrews	Matthew	Matthew.Andrews@ourcampus.edu
3	S0065	Fischer	Douglas	Douglas.Fisher@ourcampus.edu
4	S0083	Hwang	Terry	Terry.Hwang@ourcampus.edu
5	S0132	Thompson	James	James.Thompson@ourcampus.edu
6	S0154	Brisbon	Lisa	Lis.Brisbon@ourcampus.edu
7	S0167	Lai	Tzu	Tzu.Lai@ourcampus.edu
8	S0212	Marino	Chip	Chip.Marino@ourcampus.edu

Excel 2019, Windows 10, Microsoft Corporation.

FIGURE 1-4

The Student with Adviser List

	A	B	C	D	E	F
1	SID	StudentLastName	StudentFirstName	StudentEmail	AdviserLastName	AdviserEmail
2	S0023	Andrews	Matthew	Matthew.Andrews@ourcampus.edu	Baker	Linda.Baker@ourcampus.edu
3	S0065	Fischer	Douglas	Douglas.Fisher@ourcampus.edu	Baker	Linda.Baker@ourcampus.edu
4	S0083	Hwang	Terry	Terry.Hwang@ourcampus.edu	Taing	Susan.Taing@ourcampus.edu
5	S0132	Thompson	James	James.Thompson@ourcampus.edu	Taing	Susan.Taing@ourcampus.edu
6	S0154	Brisbon	Lisa	Lis.Brisbon@ourcampus.edu	Valdez	Richard.Valdez@ourcampus.edu
7	S0167	Lai	Tzu	Tzu.Lai@ourcampus.edu	Valdez	Bill.Yeats@ourcampus.edu
8	S0212	Marino	Chip	Chip.Marino@ourcampus.edu	Tran	Ken.Tran@ourcampus.edu

Excel 2019, Windows 10, Microsoft Corporation.

[5]In order to easily identify and reference the lists being discussed, we capitalize the first letter of each word in the list names in this chapter. Similarly, we capitalize the names of the database tables associated with the lists.

Now, what exactly happened in these two examples? We had a simple list with four columns, added two more columns to it, and thereby created several problems. The problem is not just that the list has six columns instead of four. Consider a different list that has six columns: the Student with Residence List shown in Figure 1-6. This list has five columns, yet it suffers from none of the problems of the Student with Adviser List in Figure 1-5.

In the Student with Residence List in Figure 1-6, we can delete the data for student Chip Marino and lose only data for that student. No unintended consequences occur. Similarly, we can change the value of Residence for student Tzu Lai without introducing any inconsistency. Finally, we can add data for student Garret Ingram and not have any null values.

An essential difference exists between the Student with Adviser List in Figure 1-5 and the Student with Residence List in Figure 1-6. Looking at those two figures, can you determine the difference? The essential difference is that the Student with Residence List in Figure 1-6 is all about a *single thing*: All the data in that list concern *students.* In contrast, the Student with Adviser List in Figure 1-5 is about *two things*: Some of the data concern *students,* and some of the data concern *advisers.* In general, whenever a list has data about two or more different things, modification problems will result.

To reinforce this idea, examine the Student with Adviser and Department List in Figure 1-7. This list has data about three different things: *students, advisers,* and *departments.* As you can see in the figure, the problems with inserting, updating, and deleting data just get worse. A change in the value of AdviserLastName, for example, might necessitate a change in only AdviserEmail, or it might require a change in AdviserEmail, Department, and AdminLastName. As you can imagine, if this list is long—for example, if the list has thousands of rows—and if several people process it, the list will be a mess in a very short time.

FIGURE 1-5

Modification Problems in the Student with Adviser List

Excel 2019, Windows 10, Microsoft Corporation.

FIGURE 1-6

The Student with Residence List

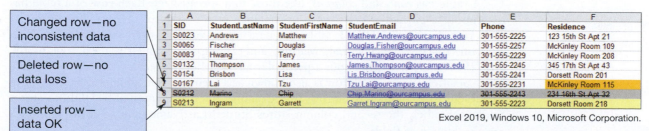

Excel 2019, Windows 10, Microsoft Corporation.

FIGURE 1-7

The Student with Adviser and Department List

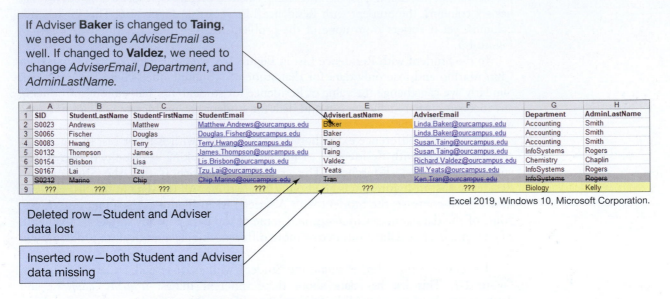

Excel 2019, Windows 10, Microsoft Corporation.

USING RELATIONAL DATABASE TABLES

The problems of using lists were first identified in the 1960s, and a number of different techniques were developed to solve them. Over time, a methodology called the **relational model** emerged as the leading solution, and today most commercial databases are still based on the relational model. We examine the relational model in detail in Chapter 2. Here, however, we introduce the basic ideas of the relational model by showing how it solves the modification problems of lists.

Remember your eighth-grade English teacher? He or she said that a paragraph should have a single theme. If you have a paragraph with more than one theme, you need to break it up into two or more paragraphs, each with a *single theme*. That idea is the foundation of the design of relational databases. A **relational database** contains a collection of separate tables. A **table** holds data about one and only one theme in most circumstances. If a table has two or more themes, we break it up into two or more tables.

A Relational Design for the Student with Adviser List

The Student with Adviser List in Figures 1-4 and 1-5 has two themes: *students* and *advisers*. If we put this data into a relational database, we place the student data in one table named STUDENT and the adviser data in a second table named ADVISER.

A database usually has multiple tables, and each table contains data about a different type of thing. For example, Figure 1-8 shows a database with two tables: The STUDENT table holds data about students, and the ADVISER table holds data about advisers.

A table has *rows* and *columns*, like those in a spreadsheet. Each **row** of a table has data about a particular occurrence or **instance** of the thing of interest. For example, each row of the STUDENT table has data about one of seven students: Andrews, Brisbon, Fischer, Hwang, Lai, Marino, and Thompson. Similarly, each row of the ADVISER table has data about a particular adviser. Because each row *records* the data for a specific instance, each row is also known as a **record**. Each **column** of a table stores a characteristic common to all rows. For example, the first column of STUDENT stores StudentNumber, the second column stores StudentLastName, and so forth. Columns are also known as **fields**.

FIGURE 1-8

The Adviser and Student Tables

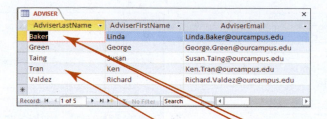

STUDENT data linked to ADVISER data via **AdviserLastName**

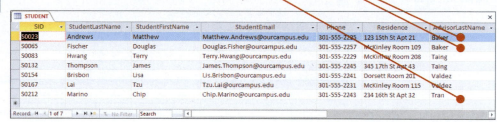

Access 2019, Windows 10, Microsoft Corporation.

> **BTW**
>
> A table and a *spreadsheet* (also known as a *worksheet*) are very similar in that you can think of both as having rows, columns, and cells. The details that define a table as something different from a spreadsheet are discussed in Chapter 2. For now, the main differences you see are that tables have column names instead of identifying letters (for example, *Name* instead of *A*) and that the rows are not necessarily numbered.
>
> Although, in theory, you could switch the rows and columns by putting instances in the columns and characteristics in the rows, this is never done. Every database in this text and 99.999999 percent of all databases throughout the world store instances in rows and characteristics in columns.

> **BTW**
>
> In this book, table names appear in all capital, or uppercase, letters (STUDENT, ADVISER). Column names have initial capitals (Phone, Address), and where column names consist of more than one word, the initial letter of each word is capitalized (LastName, AdviserEmail).

We still want to show which students have which advisers, however, so we leave AdviserLastName in the STUDENT table. As shown in Figure 1-8, the values of AdviserLastName now let us link rows in the two tables to each other.

Now consider possible modifications to these tables. As you saw in the last section, three basic **modification actions** are possible: **insert**, **update**, and **delete**. To evaluate a design, we need to consider each of these three actions. As shown in Figure 1-9, we can insert, update, and delete in these tables with no modification problems.

FIGURE 1-9

Modifying the Adviser and Student Tables

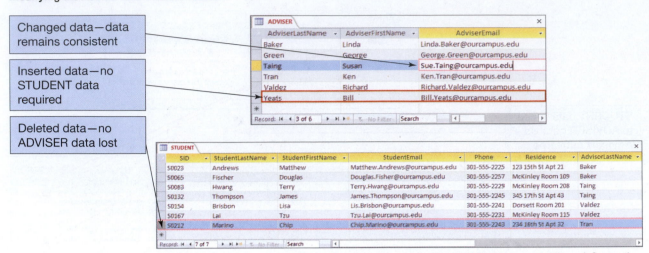

Access 2019, Windows 10, Microsoft Corporation.

For example, we can insert the data for Professor Bill Yeats by just adding his data to the ADVISER table. No student references Professor Yeats, but this is not a problem. Perhaps a student will have Professor Yeats as an adviser in the future. We can also update data values without unintended consequences. The email address for Professor Susan Taing can be changed to Sue.Taing@ourcampus.edu, and no inconsistent data will result because Professor Taing's email address is stored just once in the ADVISER table. Finally, we can delete data without unintended consequences. For example, if we delete the data for student Chip Marino from the STUDENT table, we lose no adviser data.

A Relational Design for the Student with Adviser and Department List

We can use a similar strategy to develop a relational database for the Student with Adviser and Department List shown in Figure 1-7. This list has three themes: *students, advisers,* and *departments.* Accordingly, we create three tables, one for each of these three themes, as shown in Figure 1-10.

As illustrated in Figure 1-10, we can use AdviserLastName and Department to link the tables. Also, as shown in this figure, this set of tables does not have any modification problems. We can insert new data without creating null values, we can modify data without creating inconsistencies, and we can delete data without unintended consequences. Notice in particular that when we add a new row to DEPARTMENT, we can add rows in ADVISER, if we want, and we can add rows in STUDENT for each of the new rows in ADVISER, if we want. However, all these actions are independent. None of them leaves the tables in an inconsistent state.

Similarly, when we modify an AdviserLastName in a row in STUDENT, we automatically pick up the adviser's correct first name, email address, and department. If we change AdviserLastName in the first row of STUDENT to Taing, it will be connected to the row in ADVISER that has the correct AdviserFirstName, AdviserEmail, and Department values. If we want, we can also use the value of Department in ADVISER to obtain the correct DEPARTMENT data. Finally, notice that we can delete the row for student Marino without a problem.

As an aside, the design in Figure 1-10 has removed the problems that occur when modifying a list, but it has also introduced a new problem, this time in the ADVISER table.

FIGURE 1-10

The Department, Adviser, and Student Tables

Can insert DEPARTMENT data as needed— no ADVISER or STUDENT data required

Can change STUDENT Adviser name as needed— new value is linked to its own data

Can delete STUDENT data as needed—no DEPARTMENT or ADVISER data lost

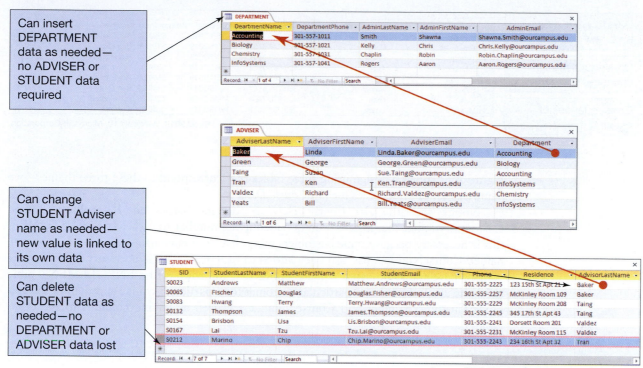

Access 2019, Windows 10, Microsoft Corporation.

Specifically, what would happen if we deleted the first row in ADVISER? Students Andrews and Fischer would have an invalid value of AdviserLastName because Professor Baker would no longer exist in the ADVISER table. To prevent this problem, we can design the database so that a deletion of a row is not allowed if other rows depend on it, or we can design it so that the dependent rows are deleted as well. Also, with the current table design we can't have two or more advisers with the same last name! We are skipping way ahead here, however, and we will discuss such issues in later chapters.

A Relational Design for Art Course Enrollments

To fix in your mind the ideas we have been examining, consider the Art Course List in Figure 1-11, which is used by an art school that offers art courses to the public. This list has modification problems. For example, suppose we change the value of CourseDate in the first row. This change might mean that the date for the course is changing, in which case the CourseDate values should be changed in other rows as well. Alternatively, this change could mean that a new Advanced Pastels (Adv Pastels) course is being offered. Either is a possibility.

As with the previous examples, we can remove the problems and ambiguities by creating a separate table for each theme. However, in this case the themes are more difficult to determine. Clearly, one of the themes is *customer* and another one is *art course*. However, a third theme exists that is more difficult to bring to light. The customer has paid a certain amount toward a course. The amount paid is not a property of the customer because it varies depending on which course the customer is taking. For example, customer Ariel Johnson paid $250 for the Advanced Pastels (Adv Pastels) course and $350 for the Intermediate Pastels (Int Pastels) course. Similarly, the amount paid is not a property of the course because it varies with which customer has taken the course. Therefore, the third theme of this list must concern the *enrollment* of a particular student in a particular class.

FIGURE 1-11

The Art Course List with Modification Problems

	A	B	C	D	E	F	G
1	CustomerLastName	CustomerFirstName	Phone	CourseDate	AmountPaid	Course	Fee
2	Johnson	Ariel	206-567-1234	10/1/2019	$250.00	Adv Pastels	$500.00
3	Green	Robin	425-678-8765	9/15/2019	$350.00	Beg Oils	$350.00
4	Jackson	Charles	360-789-3456	10/1/2019	$500.00	Adv Pastels	$500.00
5	Johnson	Ariel	206-567-1234	3/15/2019	$350.00	Int Pastels	$350.00
6	Pearson	Jeffery	206-567-2345	10/1/2019	$500.00	Adv Pastels	$500.00
7	Sears	Miguel	360-789-4567	9/15/2019	$350.00	Beg Oils	$350.00
8	Kyle	Leah	425-678-7654	11/15/2019	$250.00	Adv Pastels	$500.00
9	Myers	Lynda	360-789-5678	10/15/2019	$0.00	Beg Oils	$350.00

How to enter the fee for a new course?

Consequences of changing this date?

Consequences of deleting this row?

Excel 2019, Windows 10, Microsoft Corporation.

Figure 1-12 shows a design using three tables that correspond to these three themes—we name this set of three tables the *Art Course Database*.

Notice that the *Art Course Database* design assigns an **ID column** named CustomerNumber that assigns a unique identifying number to each row of CUSTOMER; this is necessary because some customers might have the same name. Another ID column, named CourseNumber, has also been added to COURSE. This is necessary because some courses have the same name. Finally, notice that the rows of the ENROLLMENT table show the amount paid by a particular customer for a particular course and that the ID columns CustomerNumber and CourseNumber are used as linking columns to the other tables.

FIGURE 1-12

The Art Course Database Tables

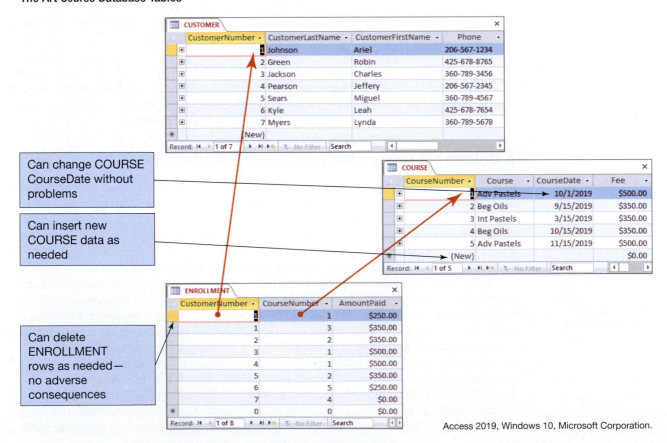

Can change COURSE CourseDate without problems

Can insert new COURSE data as needed

Can delete ENROLLMENT rows as needed— no adverse consequences

Access 2019, Windows 10, Microsoft Corporation.

A Relational Design for Parts and Prices

Now let's consider a more complicated example. Figure 1-13 shows a spreadsheet that holds the Project Equipment List used by a housing contractor named Carbon River Construction to keep track of the parts that it buys for various construction projects.

The first problem with this list concerns modifications to the existing data. Suppose your job is to maintain the Project Equipment List, and your boss tells you that customer Elizabeth Barnaby changed her phone number. How many changes would you need to make to this spreadsheet? For the data in Figure 1-13, you would need to make this change 10 times. Now suppose the spreadsheet has 5,000 rows. How many changes might you need to make? The answer could be dozens, and you need to worry not only about the time this will take but also about the possibility of errors—you might miss her name in a row or two and fail to properly update her phone number in these rows.

Consider a second problem with this list. In this business, each supplier agrees to a particular discount for all parts it supplies. For example, in Figure 1-13 the supplier NW Electric has agreed to a 25 percent discount. With this list, every time you enter a new part quotation, you must enter the supplier of that part along with the correct discount. If dozens or hundreds of suppliers are used, there is a chance that you will sometimes enter the wrong discount. If you do, the list will have more than one discount for one supplier—a situation that is incorrect and confusing.

A third problem occurs when you enter data correctly but inconsistently. The first row has a part named 200 Amp panel, whereas the fifteenth row has a part named Panel, 200 Amp. Are these two parts the same item, or are they different? It turns out that they are the same item, but they were named differently.

FIGURE 1-13

The Project Equipment List as a Spreadsheet

	A	B	C	D	E	F	G	H	I	J
1	**ProjectName**	**OwnerContact**	**Phone**	**Category**	**Quantity**	**ItemDescription**	**UnitPrice**	**ExtendedPrice**	**Supplier**	**Discount**
2	Highland House	Elizabeth Barnaby	555-444-8899	Electrical	1	200 Amp Panel	$170.00	$170.00	NW Electric	25.00%
3	Highland House	Elizabeth Barnaby	555-444-8899	Electrical	3	50 Watt Breaker	$60.00	$180.00	NW Electric	25.00%
4	Highland House	Elizabeth Barnaby	555-444-8899	Electrical	7	20 Watt Breaker	$35.00	$245.00	NW Electric	25.00%
5	Highland House	Elizabeth Barnaby	555-444-8899	Electrical	15	15 Watt Breaker	$35.00	$525.00	NW Electric	25.00%
6	Highland House	Elizabeth Barnaby	555-444-8899	Electrical	200	12 ga, 3 Wire, per foot	$1.50	$300.00	EB Supplies	15.00%
7	Highland House	Elizabeth Barnaby	555-444-8899	Electrical	300	14 ga, 3 Wire, per foot	$1.25	$375.00	EB Supplies	15.00%
8	Baker Remodel	John Stanley	555-787-8392	Exterior	35	Siding, 4x8 feet	$22.50	$787.50	Contractor, Inc.	35.00%
9	Highland House	Elizabeth Barnaby	555-444-8899	Electrical	10	15 Watt Breaker	$35.00	$350.00	EB Supplies	15.00%
10	Baker Remodel	John Stanley	555-787-8392	Exterior	28	1x4 - 8 feet	$4.75	$133.00	Contractor, Inc.	35.00%
11	Baker Remodel	John Stanley	555-787-8392	Exterior	100	Cedar Shingles, bundle	$65.00	$6,500.00	Contractor, Inc.	35.00%
12	Highland House	Elizabeth Barnaby	555-444-8899	Interior	15	Door	$275.00	$4,125.00	Interior, Inc.	15.00%
13	Highland House	Elizabeth Barnaby	555-444-8899	Interior	15	Door Hinge Set	$29.95	$449.25	Interior, Inc.	15.00%
14	Highland House	Elizabeth Barnaby	555-444-8899	Interior	15	Door Handle Set	$52.50	$787.50	Interior, Inc.	15.00%
15	Hew Remodel	Ralph Hew	555-298-4244	Electrical	1	Panel, 200 Amp	$170.00	$170.00	NW Electric	25.00%
16	Hew Remodel	Ralph Hew	555-298-4244	Electrical	2	50 Watt Breaker	$60.00	$120.00	NW Electric	25.00%
17	Hew Remodel	Ralph Hew	555-298-4244	Electrical	5	20 Watt Breaker	$35.00	$175.00	NW Electric	25.00%
18	Hew Remodel	Ralph Hew	555-298-4244	Electrical	20	15 Watt Breaker	$35.00	$700.00	NW Electric	25.00%
19	Hew Remodel	Ralph Hew	555-298-4244	Electrical	150	12 ga, 3 Wire, per foot	$1.50	$225.00	NW Electric	25.00%
20	Hew Remodel	Ralph Hew	555-298-4244	Electrical	300	14 ga, 3 Wire, per foot	$1.25	$375.00	NW Electric	25.00%
21										

Excel 2019, Windows 10, Microsoft Corporation.

FIGURE 1-14

The Project Equipment Database Tables

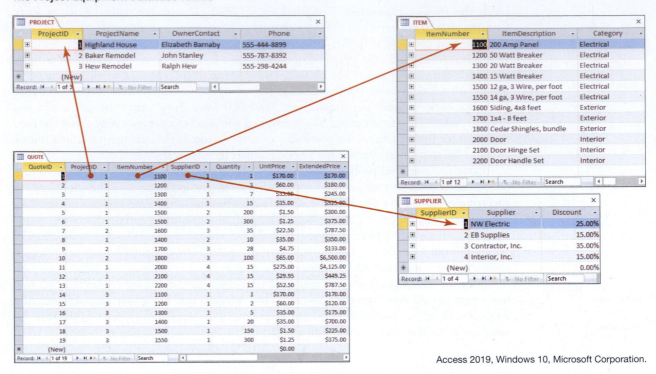

Access 2019, Windows 10, Microsoft Corporation.

A fourth problem concerns partial data. Suppose you know that a supplier offers a 20 percent discount, but Carbon River has not yet ordered from the supplier. Where do you record the 20 percent discount?

Just as we did for the previous examples, we can fix the Project Equipment List by breaking it up into separate tables. Because this list is more complicated, we need to use more tables. When we analyse the Project Equipment List, we find data about four themes: *projects, items, price quotations*, and *suppliers.* Accordingly, we create a database with four tables and relate those four tables using linking values, as before. Figure 1-14 shows our four tables and their relationships—we will name this set of tables the *Project Equipment Database*.

In Figure 1-14, note that the QUOTE table holds a unique quote identifier (QuoteID), a quantity, a unit price, an extended price (which is equal to [quantity * unit price]), and three ID columns as linking values: ProjectID for PROJECT, ItemNumber for ITEM, and SupplierID for SUPPLIER.

Now if Elizabeth Barnaby changes her phone number we need to make that change only once—in the PROJECT table. Similarly, we need to record a supplier discount only once—in the SUPPLIER table.

HOW DO I PROCESS RELATIONAL TABLES USING SQL?

By now, you may have a burning question: It may be fine to tear the lists into pieces to eliminate processing problems, but what if the users want to view their data in the format of the original list? With the data separated into different tables, the users will have to jump from one table to another to find the information they want, and this jumping around will become tedious.

This is an important question and one that many people addressed in the 1970s and 1980s. Several approaches were invented for combining, querying, and processing sets of tables. Over time, one of those approaches, a language called **Structured Query Language (SQL)**, emerged as the leading technique for data definition and manipulation. Today, SQL is an international standard. Using SQL, you can reconstruct lists from their

FIGURE 1-15

Results of the SQL Query to Recreate the Art Course List Data

CustomerLastName	CustomerFirstName	Phone	CourseDate	AmountPaid	Course	Fee
Johnson	Ariel	206-567-1234	10/1/2019	$250.00	Adv Pastels	$500.00
Johnson	Ariel	206-567-1234	3/15/2019	$350.00	Int Pastels	$350.00
Green	Robin	425-678-8765	9/15/2019	$350.00	Beg Oils	$350.00
Jackson	Charles	360-789-3456	10/1/2019	$500.00	Adv Pastels	$500.00
Pearson	Jeffery	206-567-2345	10/1/2019	$500.00	Adv Pastels	$500.00
Sears	Miguel	360-789-4567	9/15/2019	$350.00	Beg Oils	$350.00
Kyle	Leah	425-678-7654	11/15/2019	$250.00	Adv Pastels	$500.00
Myers	Lynda	360-789-5678	10/15/2019	$0.00	Beg Oils	$350.00

Record: 14 1 of 8 ▶ ▶I ▶ No Filter   Search

Access 2019, Windows 10, Microsoft Corporation.

underlying tables; you can query for specific data conditions; you can perform computations on data in tables; and you can insert, update, and delete data.

You will learn how to code SQL statements in Chapter 3. However, to give you an idea of the structure of such statements, let's look at an SQL statement that joins the three tables in Figure 1-12 to produce the original Art Course List. Do not worry about understanding the syntax of this statement; just realize that it produces the result shown in Figure 1-15, which contains all the Art Course List data (although in a slightly different row order). As you will learn in Chapter 3, it is also possible to select rows, to order them, and to make calculations on row data values.

```
SELECT    CUSTOMER.CustomerLastName,
          CUSTOMER.CustomerFirstName, CUSTOMER.Phone,
          COURSE.CourseDate, ENROLLMENT.AmountPaid,
          COURSE.Course, COURSE.Fee
FROM      CUSTOMER, ENROLLMENT, COURSE
WHERE     CUSTOMER.CustomerNumber =
              ENROLLMENT.CustomerNumber
   AND    COURSE.CourseNumber = ENROLLMENT.CourseNumber;
```

The next SQL statement joins the Art Course Database tables together, computes the difference between the course Fee and the AmountPaid, and stores this result in a new column named AmountDue. The SQL statement then selects only rows for which AmountDue is greater than zero and presents the results sorted by CustomerLastName. Compare the data in Figure 1-15 with the results in Figure 1-16 to ensure that the results are correct.

```
SELECT    CUSTOMER.CustomerLastName,
          CUSTOMER.CustomerFirstName, CUSTOMER.Phone,
          COURSE.Course, COURSE.CourseDate, COURSE.Fee,
          ENROLLMENT.AmountPaid,
          (COURSE.Fee-ENROLLMENT.AmountPaid) AS AmountDue
FROM      CUSTOMER, ENROLLMENT, COURSE
WHERE     CUSTOMER.CustomerNumber =
              ENROLLMENT.CustomerNumber
   AND    COURSE.CourseNumber = ENROLLMENT.CourseNumber
   AND    (COURSE.Fee ENROLLMENT.AmountPaid) > 0
ORDER BY  CUSTOMER.CustomerLastName;
```

FIGURE 1-16

Results of the SQL Query to Compute Amount Due

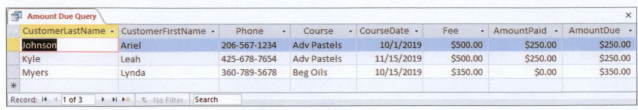

CustomerLastName	CustomerFirstName	Phone	Course	CourseDate	Fee	AmountPaid	AmountDue
Johnson	Ariel	206-567-1234	Adv Pastels	10/1/2019	$500.00	$250.00	$250.00
Kyle	Leah	425-678-7654	Adv Pastels	11/15/2019	$500.00	$250.00	$250.00
Myers	Lynda	360-789-5678	Beg Oils	10/15/2019	$350.00	$0.00	$350.00

Record: 1 of 3   No Filter   Search

Access 2019, Windows 10, Microsoft Corporation.

WHAT IS A DATABASE SYSTEM?

As shown in Figure 1-17, a **database system** has four components: users, the database application, the database management system (DBMS), and the database.

Starting from the right of Figure 1-17, the **database** is a collection of related tables and other structures. The **database management system (DBMS)** is a computer program used to create, process, and administer the database. The DBMS receives requests encoded in SQL and translates those requests into actions on the database. The DBMS is a large, complicated program that is licensed from a software vendor; companies almost never write their own DBMS programs.

A **database application** is a set of one or more computer programs that serves as an intermediary between the user and the DBMS. Application programs read or modify database data by sending SQL statements to the DBMS. Application programs also present data to users in the format of forms and reports. Application programs can be acquired from software vendors, and they are also frequently written in-house. The knowledge you gain from this text will help you write database applications.

Users, the fourth component of a database system, employ a database application to keep track of things. They use forms to read, enter, and query data, and they produce reports.

Of these components, we will consider the database, the DBMS, and database applications in more detail.

The Database

In the most general case, a database is defined as a self-describing collection of related records. For all relational databases (still the majority of databases today and the primary type considered in this book), this definition can be modified to indicate that a database is a self-describing collection of related tables.

The two key terms in this definition are **self-describing** and **related tables**. You already have a good idea of what we mean by *related tables.* One example of related tables consists of the ADVISER and STUDENT tables, which are related by the common column AdviserName. We build on this idea of relationships further in Chapter 2.

Self-describing means that a description of the structure of the database is contained within the database itself. Because this is so, the contents of a database can always be

FIGURE 1-17

Components of a
Database System

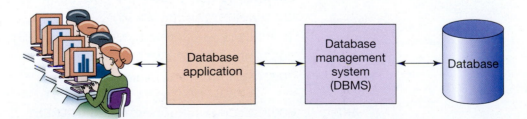

Users

FIGURE 1-18

Example Metadata: A
Relationship Diagram
for the Art Course
Tables in Figure 1-12

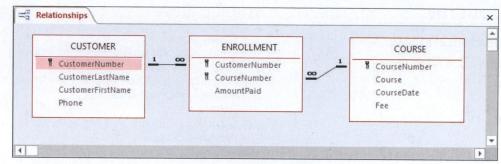

Access 2019, Windows 10, Microsoft Corporation.

FIGURE 1-19

Database Contents

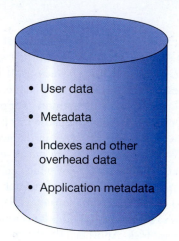

- User data
- Metadata
- Indexes and other overhead data
- Application metadata

determined just by looking inside the database itself. Looking anywhere else is not necessary. This situation is akin to that at a library, where you can tell what is in the library by examining the catalog that resides within the library.

Data about the structure of a database are called **metadata**. Examples of metadata are the names of tables, the names of columns and the tables to which they belong, properties of tables and columns, and so forth.

All DBMS products provide a set of tools for displaying the structure of their databases. For example, Figure 1-18 shows a diagram produced by Microsoft Access that displays the relationships between the Art Course database tables shown in Figure 1-12. Other tools describe the structure of the tables and other components.

The contents of a database are illustrated in Figure 1-19. A database has user data and metadata, as just described. A database also has indexes and other structures that exist to improve database performance, and we discuss such structures in later chapters. Finally, some databases contain application metadata; these data describe application elements, such as forms and reports. For example, Microsoft Access carries application metadata as part of its databases.

The DBMS

The purpose of a DBMS is to create, process, and administer databases. A DBMS is a large, complicated product that is almost always licensed from a software vendor. One DBMS product is Microsoft Access. Other commercial DBMS products are:

- Microsoft SQL Server
- Oracle Corporation's MySQL
- Oracle Corporation's Oracle Database
- IBM's DB2

Dozens of other DBMS products exist, but these five have the lion's share of the market.

FIGURE 1-20

Functions of a DBMS

- Create database
- Create tables
- Create supporting structures (e.g., indexes)
- Read database data
- Modify (insert, update, or delete) database data
- Maintain database structures
- Enforce rules
- Control concurrency
- Provide security
- Perform backup and recovery

Figure 1-20 lists the functions of a DBMS. A DBMS is used to create a database and to create tables and other supporting structures inside that database. As an example of the latter, suppose that we have an EMPLOYEE table with 10,000 rows and that this table includes a column, DepartmentName, that records the name of the department in which an employee works. Furthermore, suppose that we frequently need to access employee data by DepartmentName. Because this is a large database, searching through the table to find, for example, all employees in the accounting department would take a long time. To improve performance, we can create an index (akin to the index at the back of a book) for DepartmentName to show which employees are in which departments. Such an index is an example of a supporting structure that is created and maintained by a DBMS.

The next two functions of a DBMS are to read and modify database data. To do this, a DBMS receives SQL and other requests and transforms those requests into actions on the database files. Another DBMS function is to maintain all the database structures. For example, from time to time it might be necessary to change the format of a table or another supporting structure. Developers use a DBMS to make such changes.

With most DBMS products, you can declare rules about data values and have a DBMS enforce them. For example, in the Art Course database tables in Figure 1-12, what would happen if a user mistakenly entered a value of 9 for CustomerNumber in the ENROLLMENT table? No such customer exists, so such a value would cause numerous errors. To prevent this situation, you can tell the DBMS that any value of CustomerNumber in the ENROLLMENT table must already be a value of CustomerNumber in the CUSTOMER table. If no such value exists, the insert or update request should be disallowed. The DBMS then enforces these rules, which are called **referential integrity constraints**.

The last three functions of a DBMS listed in Figure 1-20 have to do with database administration. A DBMS controls **concurrency** by ensuring that one user's work does not inappropriately interfere with another user's work. This important (and complicated) function is discussed in Chapter 6. Also, a DBMS contains a security system that is used to ensure that only authorized users perform authorized actions on the database. For example, users can be prevented from seeing certain data. Similarly, users' actions can be confined to making only certain types of data changes on specified data.

Finally, a DBMS provides facilities for backing up database data and recovering it from backups when necessary. The database, as a centralized repository of data, is a valuable organizational asset. Consider, for example, the value of a book database to a company such as Amazon.com. Because the database is so important, steps must be taken to ensure that no data will be lost in the event of errors, hardware or software problems, or natural or human catastrophes.

Application Programs

Figure 1-21 lists the functions of database application programs. First, an application program creates and processes forms. Figure 1-22 shows a typical form for entering and processing customer data for the Art Course application.

FIGURE 1-21

Functions of Database
Application Programs

- Create and process forms
- Process user queries
- Create and process reports
- Execute application logic
- Control application

Notice that this form hides the structure of the underlying tables from the user. By comparing the tables and data in Figure 1-12 to the form in Figure 1-22, we can see that data from the CUSTOMER table appear at the top of the form, whereas data from the ENROLLMENT and the COURSE tables are combined and presented in a tabular section labelled Course Enrollment Data.

The goal of this form, like that for all data entry forms, is to present the data in a format that is useful for the users, regardless of the underlying table structure. Behind the form, the application processes the database in accordance with the users' actions. The application generates an SQL statement to insert, update, or delete data for any of the three tables that underlie this form.

The second function of application programs is to process user queries. The application program first generates a query request and sends it to the DBMS. Results are then formatted and returned to the user. Figure 1-23 illustrates this process in a query of the Art Course database in Figure 1-12.

In Figure 1-23(a), the application obtains the name or part of a name of a course. Here the user has entered the characters *pas*. When the user clicks OK, the application constructs an SQL query statement to search the database for any course containing these characters. The result of this SQL query is shown in Figure 1-23(b). In this particular case, the application queried for the relevant course and then joined the ENROLLMENT and

FIGURE 1-22

Example Data Entry Form

Customer Data Entry Form

CustomerNumber	1
CustomerLastName	Johnson
CustomerFirstName:	Ariel
Phone	206-567-1234

Course Enrollment Data

Course	CourseDate	Fee	AmountPaid	AmountDue
Int Pastels	3/15/2019	$350.00	$350.00	$0.00
Adv Pastels	10/1/2019	$500.00	$250.00	$250.00

Record: 1 of 2   No Filter   Search

Record: 1 of 7   No Filter   Search

Access 2019, Windows 10, Microsoft Corporation.

FIGURE 1-23

Example Query

(a) Query Parameter Form

(b) Query Results

Access 2019, Windows 10, Microsoft Corporation.

CUSTOMER data to the qualifying COURSE rows. Observe that the only rows shown are those with a course name that includes the characters *pas*.

The third function of an application is to create and process reports. This function is somewhat similar to the second because the application program first queries the DBMS for data (again using SQL). The application then formats the query results as a report. Figure 1-24 shows a report that displays all the Art Course database enrollment data in order by course. Notice that the report, like the form in Figure 1-22, is structured according to the users' needs and not according to the underlying table structure.

FIGURE 1-24

Example Report

Course Enrollment Report

Course	CourseDate	CustomerLastName	CustomerFirstName	Phone	Fee	AmountPaid	AmountDue
Adv Pastels							
	10/1/2019						
		Jackson	Charles	360-789-3456	$500.00	$500.00	$0.00
		Johnson	Ariel	206-567-1234	$500.00	$250.00	$250.00
		Pearson	Jeffery	206-567-2345	$500.00	$500.00	$0.00
	11/15/2019						
		Kyle	Leah	425-678-7654	$500.00	$250.00	$250.00
Beg Oils							
	9/15/2019						
		Green	Robin	425-678-8765	$350.00	$350.00	$0.00
		Sears	Miguel	360-789-4567	$350.00	$350.00	$0.00
	10/15/2019						
		Myers	Lynda	360-789-5678	$350.00	$0.00	$350.00
Int Pastels							
	3/15/2019						
		Johnson	Ariel	206-567-1234	$350.00	$350.00	$0.00

Access 2019, Windows 10, Microsoft Corporation.

In addition to generating forms, queries, and reports, the application program takes other actions to update the database in accordance with application-specific logic. For example, suppose a user using an order entry application requests 10 units of a particular item. Suppose further that when the application program queries the database (via the DBMS) it finds that only eight units are in stock. What should happen? It depends on the logic of that particular application. Perhaps no units should be removed from inventory and the user should be notified, or perhaps the eight units should be removed and two more placed on back order. Perhaps some other action should be taken. Whatever the case, the application program's job is to execute the appropriate logic.

Finally, the last function of application programs listed in Figure 1-21 is to control the application. This is done in two ways. First, the application needs to be written so that only logical options are presented to the user. For example, the application may generate a menu with user choices. In this case, the application needs to ensure that only appropriate choices are available. Second, the application needs to control data activities with the DBMS. The application might direct the DBMS, for example, to make a certain set of data changes as a unit. The application might tell the DBMS to either make all these changes or none of them. You will learn about such control topics in Chapter 6.

PERSONAL VERSUS ENTERPRISE-CLASS DATABASE SYSTEMS

Database technology can be used in a wide array of applications. On one end of the spectrum, a researcher might use database technology to track the results of experiments performed in a lab. Such a database might include only a few tables, and each table would have, at most, several hundred rows. The researcher would be the only user of this application. This is a typical use of a **personal database system**.

At the other end of the spectrum, some enormous databases support international organizations. Such databases have hundreds of tables with millions of rows of data and support thousands of concurrent users. These databases are in use 24 hours a day, 7 days a week. Just making a backup of such a database is a difficult task. These databases are typical uses of **enterprise-class database systems**.

Figure 1-25 shows the four components of a personal database application. As you can see from this figure, Microsoft Access (or another personal DBMS product) takes on the role of both the database application and the DBMS. Microsoft designed Microsoft Access this way to make it easier for people to build personal database systems. Using Microsoft Access, you can switch between DBMS functions and application functions and never know the difference.

By designing Microsoft Access this way, Microsoft has hidden many aspects of database processing. For example, behind the scenes Microsoft Access uses SQL just as all other relational DBMS products do. You have to look hard, however, to find it. Figure 1-26 shows the SQL statement that Microsoft Access used for the query in Figure 1-15. As you examine this figure, you might be thinking, "I'm just as glad they hid it—it looks complicated and hard." In fact, it looks harder than it is, but we will leave that topic for Chapter 3.

FIGURE 1-25

Personal Database System

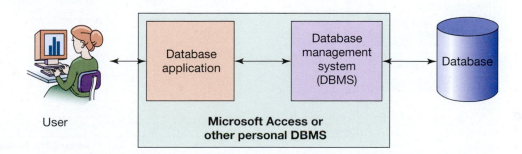

User

Microsoft Access or other personal DBMS

FIGURE 1-26

SQL Generated by Microsoft Access Query

The SQL has been arranged to make it easy to read

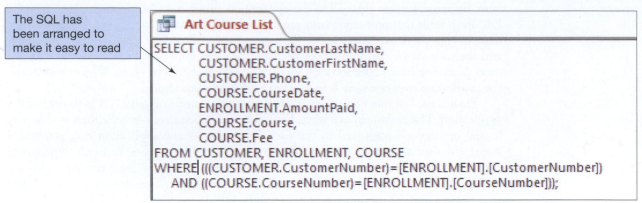

```
Art Course List

SELECT CUSTOMER.CustomerLastName,
       CUSTOMER.CustomerFirstName,
       CUSTOMER.Phone,
       COURSE.CourseDate,
       ENROLLMENT.AmountPaid,
       COURSE.Course,
       COURSE.Fee
FROM CUSTOMER, ENROLLMENT, COURSE
WHERE ((((CUSTOMER.CustomerNumber)=[ENROLLMENT].[CustomerNumber])
   AND ((COURSE.CourseNumber)=[ENROLLMENT].[CourseNumber]));
```

Access 2019, Windows 10, Microsoft Corporation.

Figure 1-27 shows the Microsoft Access query results (the same results shown in Figure 1-15) in Microsoft Access 2019. Microsoft Access 2019 is a commonly used personal DBMS and is available as part of the Microsoft Office 2019 suite. We introduce you to Microsoft Access 2019 in this book using a section in each chapter called "Working with Microsoft Access." By the time you have completed all the sections of "Working with Microsoft Access," you will have a solid understanding of how to use Microsoft Access 2019 to create and use databases.

The problem with database technology being hidden (and with using lots of *wizards* to accomplish database design tasks) is that you do not understand what is being done on your behalf. As soon as you need to perform some function that the Microsoft Access team did not anticipate, you are lost. Therefore, to be even an average database developer you have to learn what is behind the scenes.

Furthermore, such products are useful only for personal database applications. When you want to develop larger database systems, you need to learn all the hidden technology. For

FIGURE 1-27

Microsoft Access 2019

The database name **Art-Course-Database**

The table object **CUSTOMER** is displayed under the **Tables** section of All Access Objects

The query object **Art Course List** stores the query itself

The query results in table format

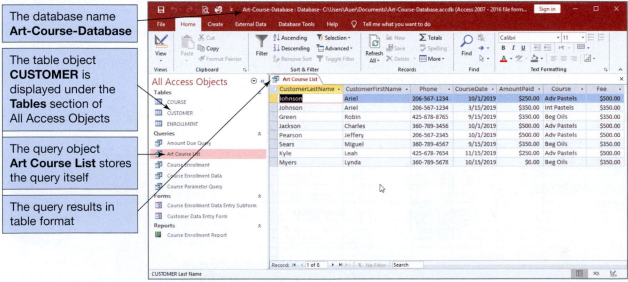

Access 2019, Windows 10, Microsoft Corporation.

FIGURE 1-28

Enterprise-Class
Database System

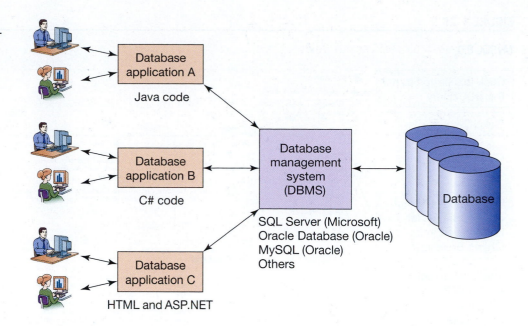

example, Figure 1-28 shows an enterprise-class database system that has three different applications, each of which has many users. The storage of the database itself is spread over many different disks—perhaps even over different specialized computers known as *database servers*.

Notice that in Figure 1-28 the applications are written in three different languages: Java, C#, and a blend of HTML and ASP.NET. These applications call on an industrial-strength DBMS product to manage the database. No wizards or simple design tools are available to develop a system like this; instead, the developer writes program code using standard tools, such as those in integrated development environments. To write such code, you need to know SQL and other data access standards.

Although hidden technology and complexity are good in the beginning, business requirements will soon take you to the brink of your knowledge, and then you will need to know more. To be a part of a team that creates such a database application, you will need to know everything in this book. Over time, you will need to add to your skills. We will close this chapter with three examples of enterprise-class DBMS products.

MySQL Community Server 8.0

Figure 1-29 shows the same SQL query used to produce the query results in Figure 1-15 and the associated query results when the SQL is executed in Oracle's **MySQL Community Server 8.0** DBMS. We are actually running the query in the user client interface to MySQL 8.0, which is the **MySQL Workbench**.

MySQL Community Server 8.0 edition can be downloaded for free, is a standard, full-strength edition of MySQL, and may be used in production environments. However, if you want the full product support package, you have to purchase MySQL 8.0 Enterprise Edition from Oracle. MySQL is a popular open-source product and is widely used for Web database applications. This version is a great learning tool, and more information can be found in online Extension A, "Working with MySQL."

Note that in Figure 1-29 we are again using exactly the same SQL statement we used previously, but now you can see how it is entered into a text editor window in the MySQL Workbench and which button to click to run the SQL query against the art_course_database (note that MySQL uses all lowercase letters in object names) tables. You can also see how the query results, which match those shown in Figure 1-15 but are sorted in a different order, are displayed in a separate Results window.

FIGURE 1-29

MySQL 8.0

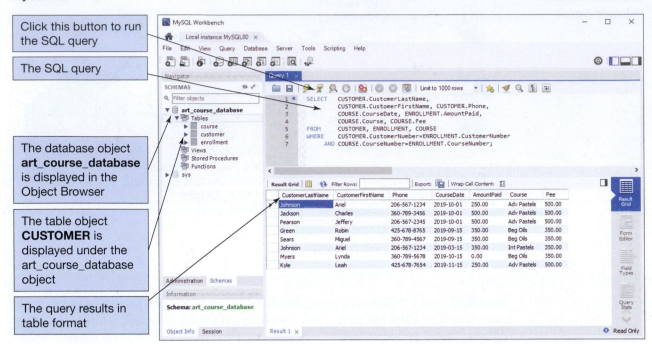

MySQL Community Server 8.0, MySQL Workbench, Oracle Corporation.

Microsoft SQL Server 2017

Figure 1-30 shows the same SQL query used to produce the query results in Figure 1-15 and the associated query results when the SQL is executed in the **Microsoft SQL Server 2017** DBMS. We are actually running the query in the **Microsoft SQL Server Management Studio**, which is the user client interface to Microsoft SQL Server 2017.

We are using the freely downloadable **Microsoft SQL Server 2017 Developer Edition**. This version is a great learning tool, but can only be used in a single-user development environment. Microsoft also has the freely downloadable **Microsoft SQL Server 2017 Express Edition**, which in addition to being used as a learning tool can also be used for smaller production databases.[6]

Note that in Figure 1-30 we are using exactly the same SQL statement we used previously, but now you can see how it is entered into a text editor window in Microsoft SQL Server Management Studio and how the Execute button is used to execute the SQL statement against the Art_Course_Database tables. You can also see how the query results, which match those shown in Figure 1-15 but are sorted in a different order, are displayed in a separate Results window. This illustrates the importance of SQL—it is essentially the same in all DBMS products, and thus it is vendor and product independent (although some differences in SQL syntax exist between various DBMS products).

Oracle Database XE

Figure 1-31 shows the same SQL query used to produce the query results in Figure 1-15 and the associated query results when the SQL is executed in the **Oracle Database 18c**

---

[6]For more information on Microsoft SQL Server 2017, see David M. Kroenke, David J. Auer, Scott L. Vandenberg, and Robert C. Yoder, *Database Processing: Fundamentals, Design, and Implementation (15th ed)*. Upper Saddle River, NJ: Pearson, 2019.

FIGURE 1-30

Microsoft SQL Server 2017

Click this button to run the SQL query

The database object **Art_Course _Database** is displayed in the Object Explorer

The table object **CUSTOMER** is displayed under the Art_Course _Database object

The SQL query

The query results in table format

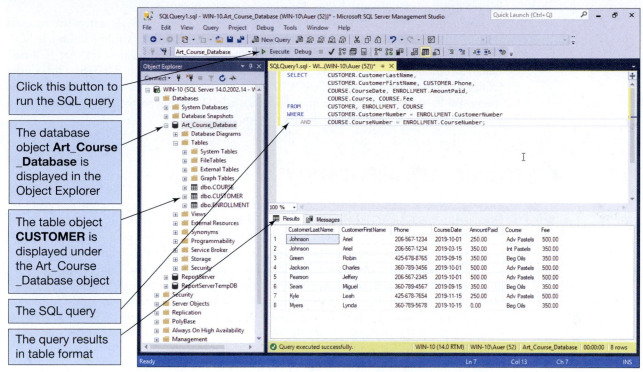

SQL Server 2017, SQL Server Management Studio, Microsoft Corporation.

FIGURE 1-31

Oracle Database XE

The database object **Art_Course_Database** is displayed in the Oracle Connections browser

Click this button to run the SQL query

The table object **CUSTOMER** is displayed in the Tables objects

The SQL query

The query results in table format

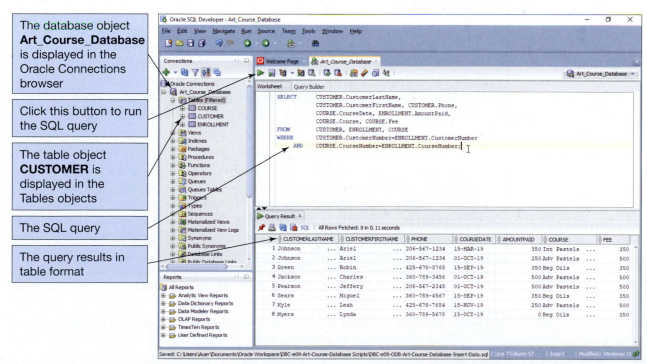

Oracle Database XE, SQL Developer 18.4, Oracle Corporation.

Express Edition (XE) DBMS, which is commonly referred to as **Oracle Database XE**. We are using **Oracle SQL Developer** as the user client interface to Oracle Database XE.[7]

Oracle Database XE is available for free download. Oracle Database XE is a great learning tool, and it can also be used for smaller production databases.

Note that in Figure 1-31 we are again using exactly the same SQL statement we used previously, but now you can see how it is entered into a text editor window in Oracle SQL Developer and how to click a button to run the SQL statement against the Art_Course_ Database (note that specific naming conventions exist for each DBMS) tables (the COURSE, CUSTOMER, and ENROLLMENT table objects). You can also see how the query results, which match those shown in Figure 1-15 but are sorted in a different order, are displayed in a separate Query Result window.

WHAT IS A WEB DATABASE APPLICATION?

As we discussed earlier in this chapter, today's Internet and mobile device world relies on the user having (1) a Web browser or (2) a mobile app to access an application powered by data in a database. Figure 1-2 illustrated this environment.

The Web browser user interface is now commonly used on PCs. When an application with a Web user interface, such as the Web application that lets you shop at amazon.com, is dependent on a database to store the data needed by the application, we call this a **Web database application**. Figure 1-32 illustrates a Web database application for the Wedgewood Pacific (WP) company, which manufactures and sells consumer drones.[8] We will build the database for WP in Chapter 3. While Web processing is beyond the scope of this book, note that applications and Web pages use an **application programming interface (API)** in a programming language such as PHP or JavaScript to connect to a DBMS. This allows then to send SQL commands to the DBMS and receive results back.

> ### BTW
>
> Of these three enterprise-class DBMS products, Oracle Database, while perhaps the most powerful DBMS product of the three, is the most difficult to master. If you are studying Oracle Database in a class, your instructor will know how to introduce Oracle Database topics to you to ease the learning process as well as the appropriate order of topics to make sure you learn the material in an orderly fashion. Oracle Database is widely used in industry, and your efforts to learn about it will be a good investment.
>
> However, if you are working through this book on your own, we believe you will find is easier to start with Microsoft SQL Server 2017 or Oracle MySQL Community Server 8.0 (which is the DBMS we use to illustrate most topics in the text). Both of these products are relatively easy to download, install, and start using. Both are also widely used and will be good investments of your time and energy. However, we strongly recommend that you start with MySQL because we support it in depth in this book.

[7]For more information on Oracle Database and Oracle Database XE, see David M. Kroenke, David J. Auer, Scott L. Vandenberg, and Robert C. Yoder, *Database Processing: Fundamentals, Design, and Implementation (15th ed)*. Upper Saddle River, NJ: Pearson, 2019.

[8]The technical term is **unmanned aerial vehicle** (UAV). See the Wikipedia article **Unmanned aerial vehicle** (accessed December 2018) at https://en.wikipedia.org/wiki/Unmanned_aerial_vehicle.

FIGURE 1-32

The WP Web Page

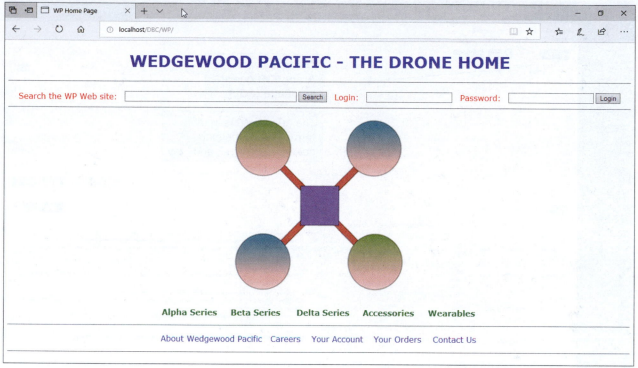

Microsoft Edge, Windows 10, Microsoft Corporation.

WHAT ARE DATA WAREHOUSES AND BUSINESS INTELLIGENCE (BI) SYSTEMS?

When you buy a product online, your purchase becomes a **transaction** that is recorded in the company's database. Specifically, it is recorded in an **online transaction processing (OLTP)** database. These databases maintain current production data for the company.

Another type of database is used for **data analysis** by the company. Data analysis work should *not* be done on the production database—we do not want any chance of breaking the production database while we are doing our analysis of company data! Therefore, we create another place to store the data for data analysis, and this is called a **data warehouse**. We use the data warehouse for such work as **online analytical processing (OLAP)**. OLAP is an example of a **business intelligence (BI) system**. BI systems are tools used to analyze and report on company data. Data warehouses and BI systems are introduced in Chapter 7, with an extension of the discussion in Extension C, "Advanced Business Intelligence and Big Data."

WHAT IS BIG DATA?

Big Data is the current term for the enormous datasets generated by Web and mobile applications such as search tools (for example, Google and Bing), Web 2.0 social networks (for example, Facebook, LinkedIn, and Twitter), and scientific data collection tools.[9]

Big Data datasets are often stored in **nonrelational databases**, which are often referred to as **NoSQL** databases. The term *NoSQL*, however, is really a bit of a misnomer. It means,

---

[9]See the Wikipedia article **Big data** (accessed December 2018—note the alternative spelling of the term with lowercase first letters) at https://en.wikipedia.org/wiki/Big_data.

FIGURE 1-33

ArangoDB

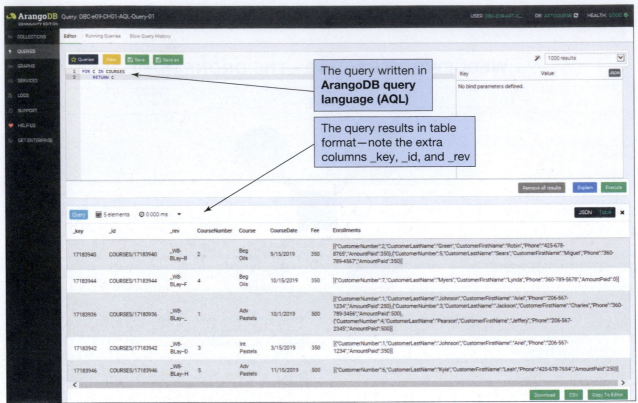

Courtesy of ArangoDB GmbH.

literally, a database that doesn't use SQL. What it really means, however, is a nonrelational database, regardless of what query language is used.

The need for nonrelational databases arose out of the development of Web 2.0 applications that allowed users to create and store data that would be subsequently displayed on a Web page. These applications required a database with different capabilities (specifically the ability to quickly create and store massive amounts of data), and nonrelational databases were created to handle this data. For example, both Facebook and Twitter use the Apache Software Foundation's Cassandra database. In this book, we will use **ArangoDB** from the German company triAGENS GmgH. Figure 1-33 shows a query in **ArangoDB query language (AQL)**, which is ArangoDB's equivalent of SQL, to obtain the same results we got with the SQL query we used in Figures 1-26, 1-29, 1-30, and 1-31. Note that although the same data is returned, it is structured and formatted very differently. Also be aware of some column names generated by ArangoDB, but not found in our relational databases—_key, _id, and _rev.

We introduce Big Data and nonrelational databases in Chapter 7, and extend the discussion in online Extension C, "Advanced Business Intelligence and Big Data." For now, simply understand that the components of a database system shown in Figure 1-17 apply regardless of whether the DBMS is working with relational or nonrelational databases.

WHAT IS CLOUD COMPUTING?

Until recently, companies bought their computer and networking hardware (server computers, routers, switches, and so on), and kept them in-house on the business premises. Currently, however, many companies are opting to use hardware owned and operated by

FIGURE 1-34

Microsoft Azure Cloud Service

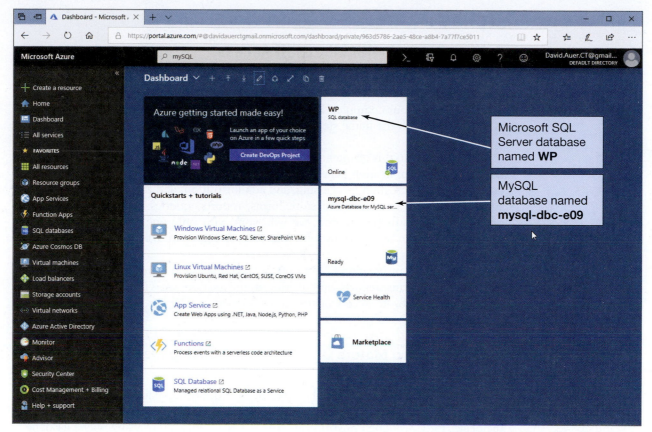

Azure, Microsoft Edge, Microsoft Corporation.

another company. This can result in lower business costs for companies because they do not incur the costs of buying, housing, and maintaining computer hardware and the software that runs on the hardware. So, for example, a company may decide to use a product such as **Microsoft Office 365 for Business** or **Microsoft Azure** as the platform to host their email services or Web server. In this case, we say that the company's computing resources are **"in the cloud"** and that the company is using **cloud computing**.[10] Figure 1-34 shows the Microsoft Azure cloud services dashboard page. Note that we are hosting two databases here—a Microsoft SQL Server database named WP, and also a MySQL 8.0 version of the WP database. The list of options in the left-hand column gives a good idea of the services available in cloud computing.

Basically, if you actually know where your company's servers are, you are *not* using cloud computing. If the servers are off site somewhere, and you only know they are at somebody else's **data center** (a facility that houses many servers and their associated infrastructure), you *are* using cloud computing. Many companies besides Microsoft offer cloud computing services. For example, Amazon offers **Amazon Web Services (AWS)**, and Google offers the **Google Cloud Platform**. We discuss cloud computing and the associated topic of **virtual machines** in Chapter 7 and demonstrate working with Microsoft Azure in online Extension C, "Advanced Business Intelligence and Big Data."

---

[10]See the Wikipedia article **Cloud Computing** (accessed December 2018) at https://en.wikipedia.org/wiki/Cloud_computing.

WORKING WITH MICROSOFT ACCESS

SECTION 1

Getting Started with Microsoft Access

The sections of "Working with Microsoft Access" are designed to reinforce the concepts you learn in each chapter. In addition, you will learn many Microsoft Access skills by following along on your computer. In this chapter's section, we review some database basics as we walk through the initial steps necessary to build and use Microsoft Access database applications.

As discussed in this chapter, Microsoft Access is a personal database that combines a DBMS with an application generator. The DBMS performs the standard DBMS functions of database creation, processing, and administration, and the application generator adds the abilities to create and store forms, reports, queries, and other application-related functions. In this section, we will work with only one table in a database; in Chapter 2's section of "Working with Microsoft Access" you will expand this to include two or more tables.

We will begin by creating a Microsoft Access database to store the database tables and the application forms, reports, and queries. In this section, we will work with basic forms and reports. Microsoft Access queries are discussed in Chapter 3's section of "Working with Microsoft Access."

The Wallingford Motors Customer Relationship Management System

Our Microsoft Access database will be used by a car dealership named Wallingford Motors, which is located in the Wallingford district of Seattle, Washington. Wallingford Motors is the dealer for a new line of hybrid cars named Gaia.[11] Instead of using only a gasoline or diesel engine, hybrid cars are powered by a combination of energy sources, such as gasoline and electricity. Gaia produces the following four models:

1. **SUHi:** The sport-utility hybrid (Gaia's answer to the SUV)
2. **HiLuxury:** A luxury-class four-door sedan hybrid
3. **HiStandard:** A basic four-door sedan hybrid
4. **HiElectra:** A variant of the HiStandard that uses a higher proportion of electrical power

Interest in hybrid cars—and specifically in the Gaia product line—is increasing. The sales staff at Wallingford Motors needs a way to track its customer contacts. Therefore, our database application will be a simple example of what is known as a **customer relationship management (CRM) system**. A CRM is used by sales staff to track current, past, and potential customers as well as the sales staff's contacts with these customers (among other uses). We will start out with a personal CRM used by one salesperson and expand it into a companywide CRM in later sections.[12]

Creating a Microsoft Access Database

We will name our Microsoft Access application and its associated database **WMCRM**. Our first step is to create a new Microsoft Access database.

---

[11]Gaia, or Gaea, was the Greek goddess of the earth. Previous editions of *Database Concepts* have used the spelling *Gaea*, but we are now switching to the more common spelling *Gaia*. For more information, see the Wikipedia article **Gaia** (accessed June 2018) at https://en.wikipedia.org/wiki/Gaia.

[12]Many CRM applications are available in the marketplace. In fact, Microsoft has one: Microsoft Dynamics CRM.

Creating the Microsoft Access Database WMCRM

1. For Windows 10, select **Start | Access** as shown in Figure WA-1-1. The Start button is the Windows icon at the left side of the Windows Desktop Taskbar.

   ■ **NOTE:** For Windows 8 and Windows 8.1, click the Access tile on the Start screen.

   ■ **NOTE:** For Windows 7, select **Start | All Programs | Microsoft Office | Microsoft Access 2019**.

   ■ **NOTE:** We recommend that you pin a Microsoft Access 2019 button to the Windows Desktop Taskbar for ease of use. To do this, right-click the **Microsoft Access 2019 icon** in the Start menu to open a shortcut menu, then click **More**, and then click the **Pin to Taskbar** command. The result is shown in Figure WA-1-1.

   ■ **NOTE:** The menu commands, icon locations, and file locations used in "Working with Microsoft Access" are those found when using Microsoft Access 2019 in the Microsoft Windows 10 operating system. If you are using the Microsoft **Windows 8.1** or the **Microsoft Windows 7** operating systems, the exact operating system terminology may vary somewhat, but these variations will not change the required actions.

   ■ **NOTE:** Microsoft Access 2019 is used in these sections, and the wording of the steps and appearance of the screenshots reflect its use. If you have a different version of Microsoft Access, there will be some differences in the step details and in what you see onscreen. However, the basic functionality is the same, and you can complete "Working with Microsoft Access" operations using any version of Microsoft Access.

FIGURE WA-1-1

Starting Microsoft Access 2019

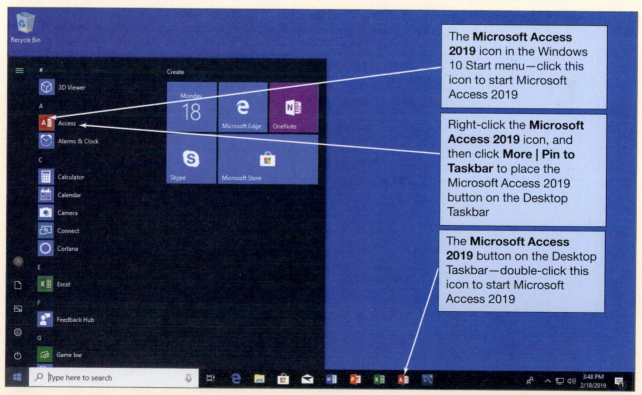

Access 2019, Windows 10, Microsoft Corporation.

(Continued)

FIGURE WA-1-2

The Microsoft Access 2019 Splash Screen

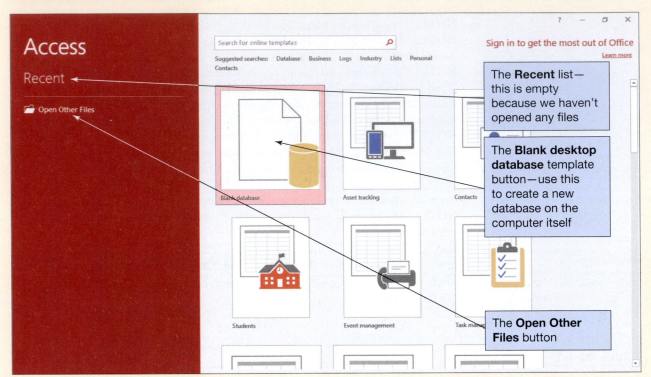

Access 2019, Windows 10, Microsoft Corporation.

2. The Microsoft Access 2019 Splash Screen appears, as shown in Figure WA-1-2. This screen displays the names of database files that have been recently used, an Open Other Files command, and template buttons for various types of databases and database applications.

3. Click the **Blank desktop database** template button to open the Blank desktop database dialog box as shown in Figure WA-1-3.

   ■ **NOTE:** By default, in Windows 10 and Windows 8.1 the database will be created in the *Documents* folder on This PC. Note that this is a major difference introduced in Windows 8.1. In Windows 8, Windows 7, and Windows XP, the database will be created in the *My Documents* folder in the *Documents* library folder. The *Documents* library folder contains both a *My Documents* folder and a *Public Documents* folder.

4. Type in the database name **WMCRM** in the **File Name** text box, and then click the **Create** button.

   ■ **NOTE:** If you clicked the Open button (as shown in Figure WA-1-3) to browse to a different file location, use the File New Database dialog box to create the new database file. After you have browsed to the correct folder, type the database name in the File Name text box of the File | New Database dialog box, and then click the OK button to create the new database.

5. The new database appears, as shown in Figure WA-1-4. The Microsoft Access window itself is now named (in full—only part may be visible) **WMCRM: Database – C:\Users\Auer\ Documents\WMCRM.accdb (Access 2007-2016 file format) – Access** to include the database name.

   ■ **NOTE:** The reference to Microsoft Access 2007–2016 in the window name indicates that the database is stored as an **.accdb* file, which is the Microsoft Access database file format introduced with Microsoft Access 2007. Prior versions of Microsoft Access used the **.mdb* file format. Microsoft Access 2019 does not introduce a new database file format but continues to use the Microsoft Access 2007 **.accdb* file format.

FIGURE WA-1-3

The Blank Desktop Database Dialog Box

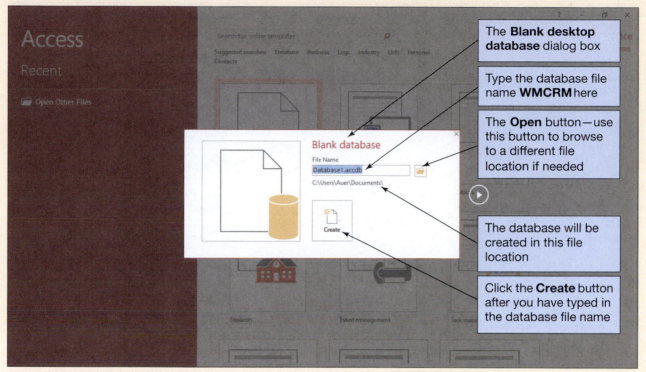

The **Blank desktop database** dialog box

Type the database file name **WMCRM** here

The **Open** button—use this button to browse to a different file location if needed

The database will be created in this file location

Click the **Create** button after you have typed in the database file name

Access 2019, Windows 10, Microsoft Corporation.

FIGURE WA-1-4

The New Microsoft Access Database

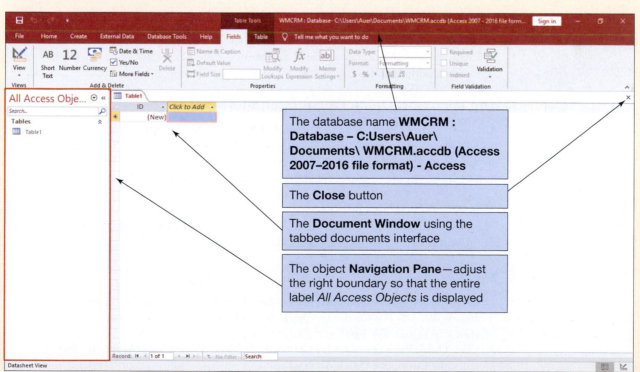

The database name **WMCRM : Database – C:\Users\Auer\ Documents\ WMCRM.accdb (Access 2007–2016 file format) - Access**

The **Close** button

The **Document Window** using the tabbed documents interface

The object **Navigation Pane**—adjust the right boundary so that the entire label *All Access Objects* is displayed

Access 2019, Windows 10, Microsoft Corporation.

(Continued)

FIGURE WA-1-5

The Microsoft Office Fluent User Interface

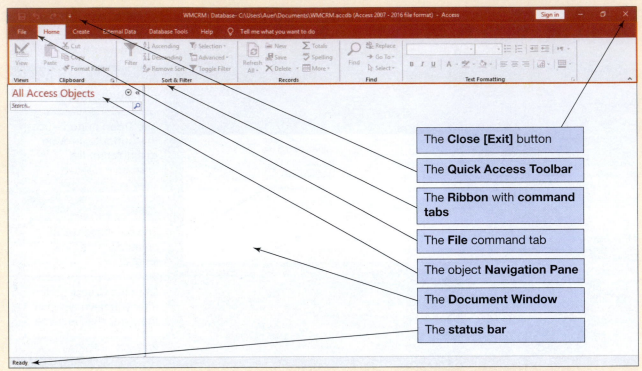

Access 2019, Windows 10, Microsoft Corporation.

6. Note that because this is a new database, Microsoft Access has assumed that you will want to immediately create a new table. Therefore, a new table named **Table1** is displayed in Datasheet view in the document window. We do *not* want this table open at this time, so click the **Close Table** button in the document window shown in Figure WA-1-4.

7. The Microsoft Access 2019 window with the new database appears, as shown in Figure WA-1-5. You can see most of the features of the Microsoft Office Fluent user interface in this window.

The Microsoft Office Fluent User Interface

Microsoft Access 2019 uses the **Microsoft Office Fluent user interface** found in most (but not all) of the Microsoft Office 2007, Office 2010, Office 2013, Office 2016, and Office 2019 applications. The major features of the interface can be seen in Figure WA-1-5. To illustrate its use, we will modify some of the default settings of the Microsoft Access database window.

The Quick Access Toolbar

First, we will modify the Quick Access Toolbar shown in Figure WA-1-5 to include a Quick Print button and a Print Preview button.

Modifying the Microsoft Access Quick Access Toolbar

1. Click the **Customize Quick Access Toolbar** drop-down arrow button shown in Figure WA-1-5. The Customize Quick Access Toolbar drop-down list appears, as shown in Figure WA-1-6.
2. Click **Quick Print**. The Quick Print button is added to the Quick Access Toolbar.
3. Click the **Customize Quick Access Toolbar** drop-down button again. The Customize Quick Access Toolbar drop-down list appears.
4. Click **Print Preview**. The Print Preview button is added to the Quick Access Toolbar.

FIGURE WA-1-6

The Quick Access Toolbar

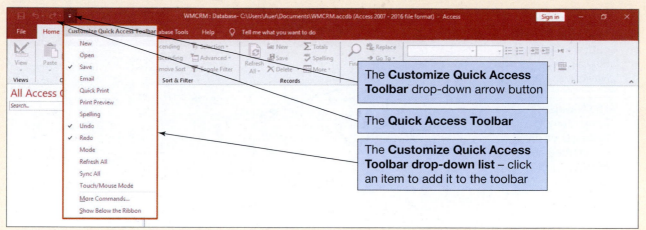

Access 2019, Windows 10, Microsoft Corporation.

FIGURE WA-1-7

The Navigation Pane Drop-Down List

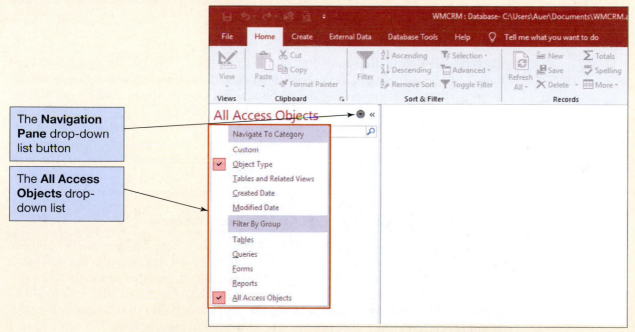

Access 2019, Windows 10, Microsoft Corporation.

The added buttons are visible in the figures shown later in this section of "The Access Workbench," such as Figure WA-1-7.

Database Objects and the Navigation Pane

Microsoft uses the term **object** as a general name for the various parts of a Microsoft Access database. Thus, a *table* is an object, a *report* is an object, a *form* is an object, and so on. Microsoft Access objects are displayed in the Microsoft Access **Navigation Pane**, as shown in Figure WA-1-4. However, because you have not created any objects in the WMCRM database, the Navigation Pane is currently empty.

The Navigation Pane is currently labeled as *All Access Objects*, which is what we want to see displayed. We can, however, select exactly which objects will be displayed by using

(Continued)

FIGURE WA-1-8

The Empty Navigation Pane

Use the **Shutter Bar Open/Close** button to hide or display the Navigation Pane

The Navigation Pane is empty because we have not created any objects for this database

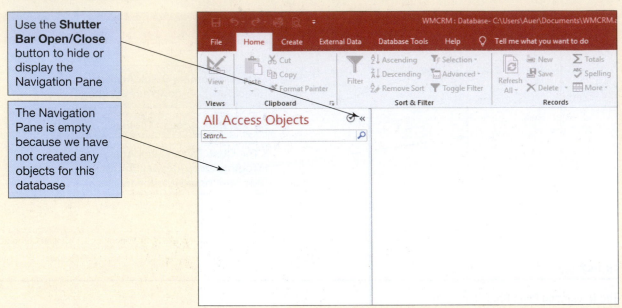

Access 2019, Windows 10, Microsoft Corporation.

the **Navigation Pane drop-down list**. As shown in Figure WA-1-7, the Navigation Pane drop-down list is controlled by the **Navigation Pane drop-down list button**. Figure WA-1-8 shows the empty Navigation Pane and the **Shutter Bar Open/Close button**. We can hide the Navigation Pane if we want to by clicking the Shutter Bar Open/Close button, which is displayed as a left-facing double-chevron button on the upper-right corner of the Navigation Pane in Figure WA-1-8. If we click the button, the Navigation Pane shrinks to a small band labeled *Navigation Pane* on the left side of the Microsoft Access 2019 window. The band will then display the Shutter Bar Open/Close button as a right-facing double-chevron button that we can click to restore the Navigation Pane when we want to use it again.

Closing a Database and Exiting Microsoft Access

The *Close* button shown in Figure WA-1-5 is actually a *close and exit button*. You can click it to close the active database and then exit Microsoft Access. Note that Microsoft Access actively saves most changes to a database, and it prompts you with *Save* command requests when they are needed. For example, when you close a table with modified column widths Microsoft Access asks whether you want to save the changes in the table layout. Therefore, you do not need to save Microsoft Access databases the way you save Microsoft Word documents and Microsoft Excel workbooks. You can simply close a database, knowing that Microsoft Access has already saved all critical changes since you opened it.

Closing a Database and Exiting Microsoft Access

1. Click the **Close** button. The database closes, and you exit Microsoft Access.

Opening an Existing Microsoft Access Database

Earlier in this section of "Working with Microsoft Access" we created a new Microsoft Access database for the Wallingford Motors CRM (WMCRM.accdb), modified some Microsoft Access settings, and closed the database and exited Microsoft Access. Before we can continue building this database, we need to start Microsoft Access and open the WMCRM.accdb database.

Instead of clicking the Close button, you can simultaneously close the database and exit Microsoft Access by clicking the File command tab, and then clicking the Exit command. To close just the database while leaving Microsoft Access open, select the File command tab, and then click the Close Database command.

When we open an existing database, Microsoft Access 2019 (like Microsoft Access 2007, 2010, 2013 and 2016 before it) gives us the option of using Microsoft Access security options to shut down certain Microsoft Access 2019 features in a database to protect ourselves against harm not only from viruses but also from other possible problems. Unfortunately, the Microsoft Access 2019 security options also shut down significant and needed operational features of Microsoft Access. Therefore, we will normally enable the features that the Microsoft Access 2019 security warning warns us about when we open an existing database.

Opening a Recently Opened Microsoft Access Database

1. Open Microsoft Access 2019 by using the **Start | Access** command on the Windows Desktop screen (or click the Microsoft Access 2019 icon on the Windows Taskbar if you pinned it there as suggested). Microsoft Access 2019 is displayed with the splash screen open, as shown in Figure WA-1-9.
2. The **Recent list** is displayed on the splash screen, and the database file WMCRM is now listed there.
   - **NOTE:** By default, Microsoft Windows hides the file extension for known file types such as the Microsoft Access 2019 *.accdb* files. To change this setting (which we

FIGURE WA-1-9

The Recent File List

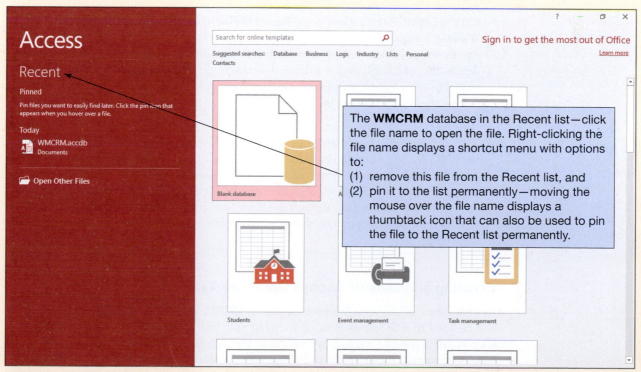

The **WMCRM** database in the Recent list—click the file name to open the file. Right-clicking the file name displays a shortcut menu with options to:
(1) remove this file from the Recent list, and
(2) pin it to the list permanently—moving the mouse over the file name displays a thumbtack icon that can also be used to pin the file to the Recent list permanently.

Access 2019, Windows 10, Microsoft Corporation.

(Continued)

FIGURE WA-1-10

The Security Warning Bar

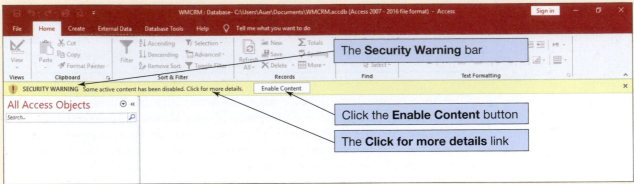

Access 2019, Windows 10, Microsoft Corporation.

prefer to do), open **File Explorer**, click the **View** tab, and then click the **Options** button to display the **Folder Options** dialog box. In the **Folder Options** dialog box, click the **View** tab. In the **Advanced** settings, uncheck the **Hide extensions of known file types** checkbox. Click the **Apply** button, and then click the **OK** button to close the **Folder Options** dialog box. Finally, close File Explorer itself. When Microsoft Access 2019 is closed and reopened, file names will be shown with the *.accdb file extension visible.

3. Note that if the database has been used very recently it will be available in the Recent file list. You may make the file a permanent part of the Recent file list by right-clicking the file name to display a shortcut menu, and then clicking the *Pin to list* command (or by clicking the *thumbtack icon* that is displayed when the mouse pointer is moved over the file name). Similarly, you can remove a file from the Recent list by using the *Remove from list* command on the shortcut menu.

4. Click the **WMCRM** file name in the **Recent file list** to open the database. A **Security Warning** bar appears with the database, as shown in Figure WA-1-10.

5. At this point, we have the option of clicking the Security Warning bar's **Click for more details** link, which will display a detailed version of the warning together with security options. However, for our purposes in this text, we simply need to enable the active content, so click the **Enable Content** button.

   ■ **NOTE:**   At some point, you should select the **Click for more details** link and explore the available security settings.

   ■ **NOTE:**   In Microsoft Access 2007, the Security Warning bar appeared every time the database was reopened (although from a *nontrusted location*—see Chapter 6's section of "Working with Microsoft Access" for a discussion of *trusted locations*). In Microsoft Access 2010 through 2019, the Security Warning bar is only displayed the first time you reopen a database, and your choice of options is remembered from that point on.

Creating a Microsoft Access Database Table

At this point in the development of the WMCRM database application, the database will be used by one salesperson, so we need only two tables in the WMCRM database— CUSTOMER and CONTACT. We will create the CUSTOMER table first. The CUSTOMER table will contain the columns and characteristics shown in the table in Figure WA-1-11. The column characteristics are type, key, required, and remarks.

FIGURE WA-1-11

Database Column Characteristics for the CUSTOMER Table

Column Name	Type	Key	Required	Remarks
CustomerID	AutoNumber	Primary Key	Yes	Surrogate Key
LastName	Short Text (25)	No	Yes	
FirstName	Short Text (25)	No	Yes	
Address	Short Text (35)	No	No	
City	Short Text (35)	No	No	
State	Short Text (2)	No	No	
ZIP	Short Text (10)	No	No	
Phone	Short Text (12)	No	Yes	
Fax	Short Text (12)	No	No	
EmailAddress	Short Text (100)	No	No	

FIGURE WA-1-12

Microsoft Access 2019 Data Types

Name	Type of Data	Size
Short Text	Characters and numbers	Maximum 255 characters
Long Text	Large text	Maximum 65,535 characters
Number	Numeric data	Varies with Number type
Date/Time	Dates and times from the year 100 to the year 9999	Stored as 8-byte double–precision integers
Currency	Numbers with decimal places	One to four decimal places
AutoNumber	A unique sequential number	Incremented by one each time
Yes/No	Fields that can contain only two values	Yes/No, On/Off, True/False, etc.
OLE Object	An object embedded in or linked to a Microsoft Access table	Maximum 1 GB
Hyperlink	A hyperlink address	Maximum 2,048 characters in each of three parts of the hyperlink address
Attachment	Any supported type of file may be attached to a record	Independent of Microsoft Access
Calculated	Results of a calculation based on data in other cells	Varies depending on values used in calculation
Lookup Wizard...	A list of possible data values located in a value list	Varies depending on the values in the value list

Type refers to the kind of data the column will store. Some possible Microsoft Access data types are shown in Figure WA-1-12. For CUSTOMER, most data are stored as **short text** data, which can store up to 255 characters (also commonly called **character** data, this data type was previously called just **text**, and **long text** now refers to a data type previously called **memo**, which can store up to 65,535 characters), which means we can enter strings of letters, numbers, and symbols (a space is considered a symbol). The number behind the words *Short Text* indicates how many characters can

(Continued)

be stored in the column. For example, customer last names may be up to 25 characters long. The only **number**, or **numeric**, data column in the CUSTOMER table is CustomerID, which is listed as **AutoNumber**. This indicates that Microsoft Access will automatically provide a sequential number for this column for each new customer that is added to the table.

Key refers to table identification functions assigned to a column. These are described in detail in Chapter 2. At this point, you simply need to know that a **primary key** is a column value used to identify each row; therefore, the values in this column must be unique. This is the reason for using the AutoNumber data type, which automatically assigns a unique number to each row in the table as it is created.

Required refers to whether the column must have a data value. If it must, a value must be present in the column. If not, the column may be blank (which is called a NULL value). Note that because CustomerID is a primary key used to identify each row it *must* have a value.

Remarks contains comments about the column or how it is used. For CUSTOMER, the only comment is that CustomerID is a **surrogate key**. Surrogate keys are discussed in Chapter 2. At this point, you simply need to know that surrogate keys are usually computer-generated unique numbers used to identify rows in a table (that is, a primary key). This is done by using the Microsoft Access AutoNumber data type.

Creating the CUSTOMER Table

1. Click the **Create** command tab to display the **Create** command groups.
2. Click the **Table Design** button, as shown in Figure WA-1-13. The **Table1** tabbed document window is displayed in **Design** view, as shown in Figure WA-1-14. Note that along with the **Table1** window a contextual tab grouping named **Table Tools** is displayed and that this tab grouping adds a new command tab named **Design** to the set of command tabs displayed.
   - **NOTE:** It seems like now would be a good time to name the new table CUSTOMER. With Microsoft Access, however, you do not name a table until you save it the first time, and you cannot save a table until you have at least one column defined. So, we will define the columns, and then we will save and name the table. If you want, save the table after you have defined just one column. This will close the table, so you will have to reopen it to define the remaining columns.
3. In the **Field Name** column text box of the first line, type the column name **CustomerID**, and then press the **Tab** key to move to the **Data Type** column. (You can also click the Data Type column to select it.)
   - **NOTE:** The terms *column* and *field* are considered synonyms in database work. The term *attribute* is also considered to be equivalent to these two words.
4. Select the **AutoNumber** data type for CustomerID from the **Data Type** drop-down list, as shown in Figure WA-1-15.

FIGURE WA-1-13

The Table Design Button

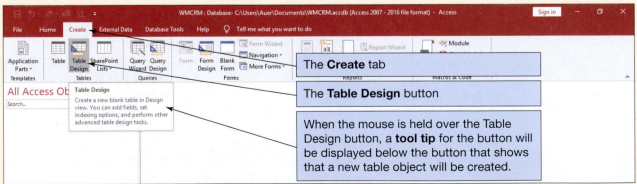

Access 2019, Windows 10, Microsoft Corporation.

FIGURE WA-1-14

The Table1 Tabbed Document Window

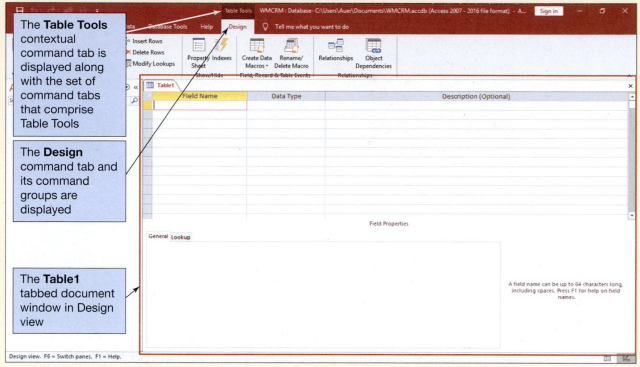

The **Table Tools** contextual command tab is displayed along with the set of command tabs that comprise Table Tools

The **Design** command tab and its command groups are displayed

The **Table1** tabbed document window in Design view

Access 2019, Windows 10, Microsoft Corporation.

FIGURE WA-1-15

Selecting the Data Type

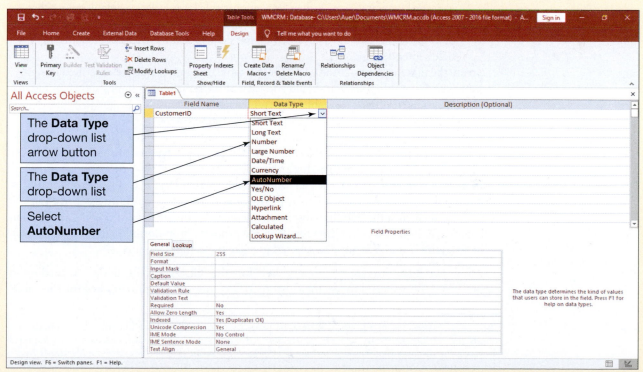

The **Data Type** drop-down list arrow button

The **Data Type** drop-down list

Select **AutoNumber**

Access 2019, Windows 10, Microsoft Corporation.

(Continued)

FIGURE WA-1-16

The Completed CustomerID Column

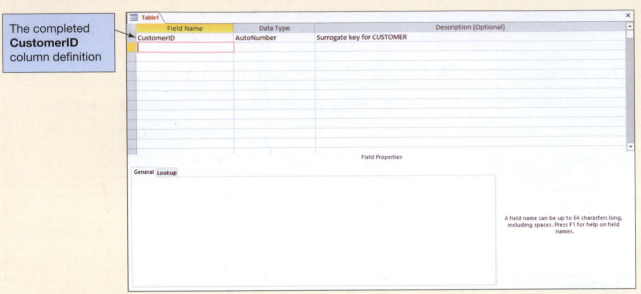

The completed **CustomerID** column definition

Access 2019, Windows 10, Microsoft Corporation.

5. If you like, you may store an optional comment in the Description column. To do so, move to the Description column by pressing the **Tab** key or clicking in the **Description** text box. Type the text **Surrogate key for CUSTOMER**, and then press the **Tab** key to move to the next row. The **Table1** tabbed document window now looks as shown in Figure WA-1-16.

- **NOTE:** The Remarks column in the set of database column characteristics shown in Figure WA-1-11 is *not* the same as the table Description column shown in Figure WA-1-16. Be careful not to confuse them. The Remarks column is used to record technical data, such as facts about table keys and data default values that are necessary for building the table structure. The Description column is used to describe to the user the data stored in that field so that the user understands the field's intended use.

6. Create the other columns of the CUSTOMER table using the sequence described in steps 3 through 5—at this point you should add each of the remaining columns shown in Figure WA-1-11 to the CUSTOMER table while following those steps.

- **NOTE:** See Figure WA-1-19 for the Description entries.

7. To set the number of characters in text columns, edit the Data Type Field Properties **Field Size** property text box, as shown in Figure WA-1-17. The default value for Field Size is 255, which is also the maximum value for a Short Text field.

8. To make a column required, click anywhere in the column Data Type Field Properties **Required** property text box to display the **Required** property drop-down list arrow button, and then click the button to display the Required property drop-down list, as shown in Figure WA-1-18. Select Yes from the Required property drop-down list. The default is No (not required), and **Yes** must be selected to make the column required.[13]

Now we need to set a primary key for the CUSTOMER table. According to Figure WA-1-11, we need to use the CustomerID column as the primary key for this table.

[13]Microsoft Access has an additional Data Type property named Allow Zero Length. This property confounds the settings necessary to truly match the SQL constraint NOT NULL discussed in Chapter 3. However, the discussion of Allow Zero Length is beyond the scope of this book. See the Microsoft Access Help system for more information.

FIGURE WA-1-17

The Completed CustomerID Column

Edit this number to set the number of characters

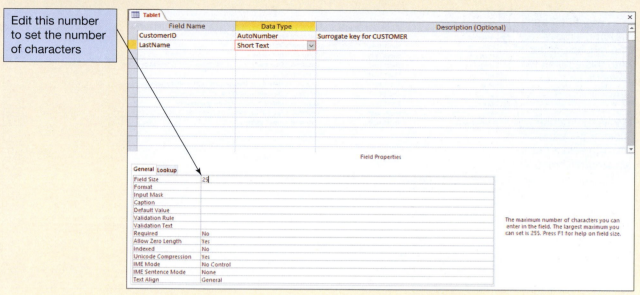

Access 2019, Windows 10, Microsoft Corporation.

FIGURE WA-1-18

Setting the Column Required Property Value

Click anywhere in the Required text box to display the **Required property** drop-down list arrow button

Select **Yes** from the Required property drop-down list

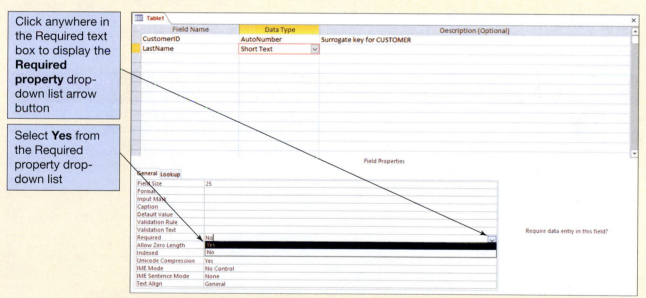

Access 2019, Windows 10, Microsoft Corporation.

Setting the CUSTOMER Table Primary Key

1. Move the mouse pointer to the **row selector column** of the row containing the CustomerID properties, as shown in Figure WA-1-19. Click to select the row.
2. Click the **Primary Key** button in the Tools group of the Design tab, as shown in Figure WA-1-20, to set CustomerID as the primary key for the CUSTOMER table.

We have finished building the CUSTOMER table. Now we need to name, save, and close the table.

(Continued)

FIGURE WA-1-19

Selecting the CustomerID Row

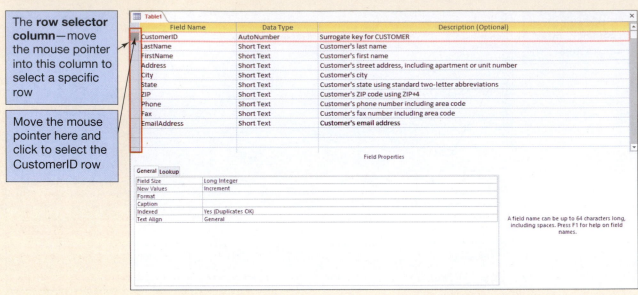

The **row selector column**—move the mouse pointer into this column to select a specific row

Move the mouse pointer here and click to select the CustomerID row

Access 2019, Windows 10, Microsoft Corporation.

FIGURE WA-1-20

Setting the Primary Key

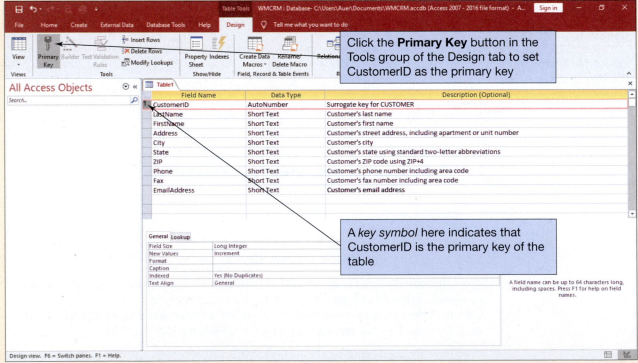

Click the **Primary Key** button in the Tools group of the Design tab to set CustomerID as the primary key

A *key symbol* here indicates that CustomerID is the primary key of the table

Access 2019, Windows 10, Microsoft Corporation.

FIGURE WA-1-21

Naming and Saving the CUSTOMER Table

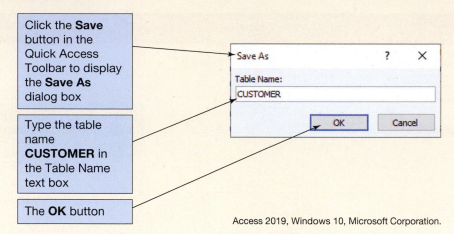

Click the **Save** button in the Quick Access Toolbar to display the **Save As** dialog box

Type the table name **CUSTOMER** in the Table Name text box

The **OK** button

Access 2019, Windows 10, Microsoft Corporation.

Naming, Saving, and Closing the CUSTOMER Table

1. To name and save the CUSTOMER table, click the **Save** button (the one that looks like a floppy disk) in the Quick Access Toolbar. The **Save As** dialog box appears, as shown in Figure WA-1-21.
2. Type the table name **CUSTOMER** into the **Save As** dialog box's Table Name text box, and then click **OK**. The table is named and saved. The table name CUSTOMER now appears on the document tab, and the CUSTOMER table object is displayed in the Navigation Pane, as shown in Figure WA-1-22.

FIGURE WA-1-22

The Named CUSTOMER Table

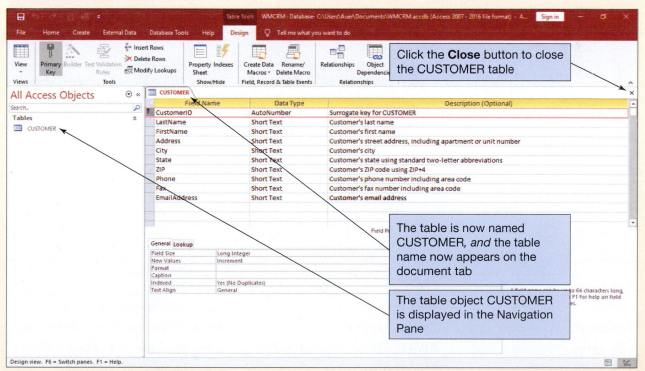

Click the **Close** button to close the CUSTOMER table

The table is now named CUSTOMER, *and* the table name now appears on the document tab

The table object CUSTOMER is displayed in the Navigation Pane

Access 2019, Windows 10, Microsoft Corporation.

(Continued)

FIGURE WA-1-23

The CUSTOMER Table Object

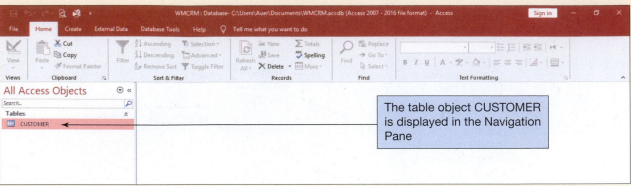

Access 2019, Windows 10, Microsoft Corporation.

3. To close the CUSTOMER table, click the **Close** button in the upper-right corner of the tabbed documents window, as shown in Figure WA-1-22. After the table is closed, the CUSTOMER table object remains displayed in the Navigation Pane, as shown in Figure WA-1-23.

Inserting Data into Tables: The Datasheet View

There are three commonly used methods for adding data to a table. First, we can use a table as a **datasheet**, which is visually similar to and works like a Microsoft Excel worksheet. When we do this, the table is in **Datasheet view**, and we enter the data cell by cell. Second, we can build a **data entry form** for the table and then use the form to add data. Third, we can use SQL to insert data. This section covers the first two of these methods; we will use the SQL method in Chapter 3's section of "Working with Microsoft Access."

In Microsoft Access 2019, we can also use Datasheet view to create and modify table characteristics. When we open a table in Datasheet view, the Table Tools contextual tab includes a Datasheet command tab and ribbon with tools to do this. We do *not* recommend this; using Design view is better, as previously discussed in this section, for creating and modifying table structures.

However, at this point we do not need to modify the table structure—we simply need to put some data into the CUSTOMER table. Figure WA-1-24 shows some data for

FIGURE WA-1-24

Wallingford Motors CUSTOMER Data

LastName	FirstName	Address	City	State	Zip
Griffey	Ben	5678 25th NE	Seattle	WA	98178
Christman	Jessica	3456 36th SW	Seattle	WA	98189
Christman	Rob	4567 47th NW	Seattle	WA	98167
Hayes	Judy	234 Highland Place	Edmonds	WA	98210

LastName	FirstName	Phone	Fax	EmailAddress
Griffey	Ben	206-456-2345		Ben.Griffey@somewhere.com
Christman	Jessica	206-467-3456		Jessica.Christman@somewhere.com
Christman	Rob	206-478-4567	206-478-9998	Rob.Christman@somewhere.com
Hayes	Judy	425-354-8765		Judy.Hayes@somewhere.com

FIGURE WA-1-25

The CUSTOMER Table in Datasheet View

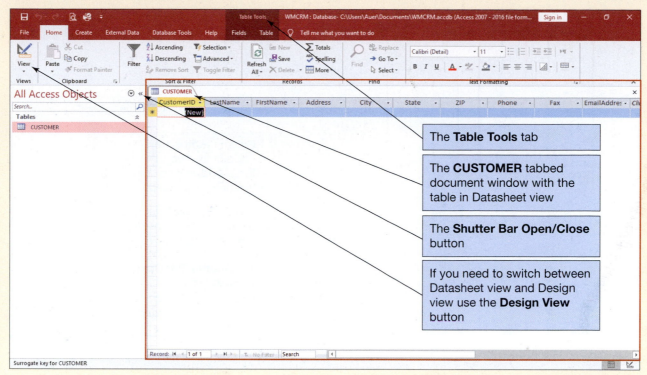

The **Table Tools** tab

The **CUSTOMER** tabbed document window with the table in Datasheet view

The **Shutter Bar Open/Close** button

If you need to switch between Datasheet view and Design view use the **Design View** button

Access 2019, Windows 10, Microsoft Corporation.

Wallingford Motors customers (note that the LastName and FirstName data is repeated for proper alignment of the continued data).

Adding Data to the CUSTOMER Table in Datasheet View

1. In the Navigation Pane, double-click the **CUSTOMER** table object. The CUSTOMER table window appears in a tabbed document window in Datasheet view, as shown in Figure WA-1-25. Note that some columns on the right side of the datasheet do not appear in the window, but you can access them by scrolling the document pane or by minimizing the Navigation Pane.
    - **NOTE:** As in a worksheet, the intersection of a row and column in a datasheet is called a *cell*.
2. Click the **Shutter Bar Open/Close** button to collapse the Navigation Pane. This makes more of the CUSTOMER datasheet visible, as shown in Figure WA-1-26.
3. Click the **CUSTOMER** document tab to select the CUSTOMER table in Datasheet view.
4. Click the cell in the CustomerID column with the phrase **(New)** in it to select that cell in the new row of the CUSTOMER datasheet.
5. Press the **Tab** key to move to the LastName cell in the new row of the CUSTOMER datasheet. For customer Ben Griffey, type **Griffey** in the LastName cell. Note that as soon as you do this, the AutoNumber function puts the number 1 in the CustomerID cell and a new row is added to the datasheet, as shown in Figure WA-1-27.
6. Using the **Tab** key to move from one column to another in the CUSTOMER datasheet, enter the rest of the data values for Ben Griffey.
    Figure WA-1-28 shows the final result. Note that the width of the Email column was expanded using the mouse to move the border of the column—just as you would in a Microsoft Excel worksheet.

(*Continued*)

FIGURE WA-1-26

The Collapsed Navigation Pane

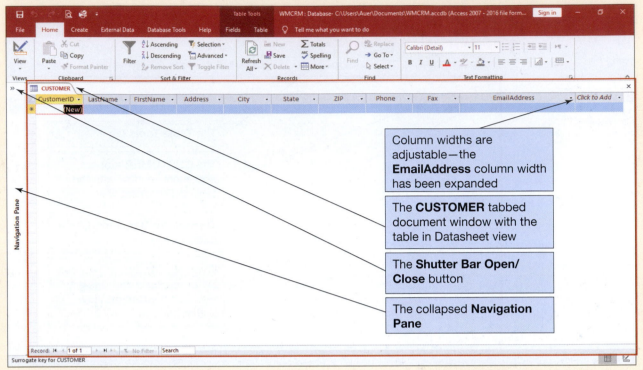

Access 2019, Windows 10, Microsoft Corporation.

FIGURE WA-1-27

Entering Data Values for Ben Griffey

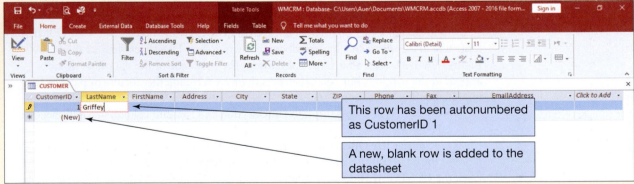

Access 2019, Windows 10, Microsoft Corporation.

- **NOTE:** If you make a mistake and need to return to a cell, click the cell to select it and Microsoft Access will automatically shift into Edit mode. Alternatively, you can use **Shift+Tab** to move to the left in the datasheet, and then press **F2** to edit the contents of the cell.

- **NOTE:** Remember that LastName, FirstName, and Phone *require* a data value. You will not be able to move to another row or close the table window until you have a value in each of these cells.

- **NOTE:** Figure WA-1-28 shows a column labeled *Click to Add* to the right of the Email column. This is a table tool in Datasheet view that you can use to create or modify table structures. We do not recommend using these tools—we prefer to use Design view instead!

FIGURE WA-1-28

The Completed Row of Data Values

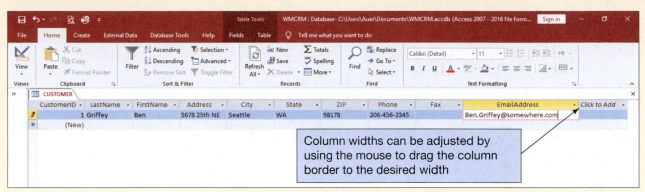

Access 2019, Windows 10, Microsoft Corporation.

7. Use the **Tab** key to move to the next row of the CUSTOMER datasheet and enter the data for Jessica Christman, as shown in Figure WA-1-29.
8. Adjust the datasheet column widths so that you can see the contents of the datasheet in one screen. Figure WA-1-29 shows the final result.
9. We are adding only the data for Jessica Christman at this point, and we will add the remaining CUSTOMER data later in this section of "Working with Microsoft Access." Click the **Close** button in the upper-right corner of the document window to close the CUSTOMER datasheet. A dialog box appears that asks whether you want to save the changes you made to the layout (column widths). Click the **Yes** button.
10. Click the **Shutter Bar Open/Close** button to expand the Navigation Pane. This makes the objects in the Navigation Pane visible.

Modifying Data in Tables: The Datasheet View

After entering data into a table, you can modify or change the data by editing the data values in the Datasheet view. To illustrate this, we will temporarily change Jessica Christman's phone number to 206-467-9876.

FIGURE WA-1-29

The Completed CUSTOMER Datasheet

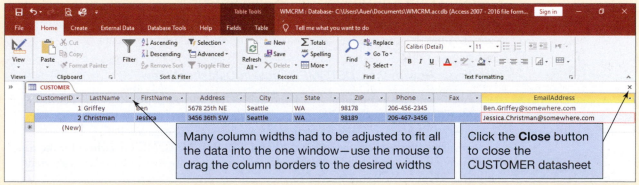

Access 2019, Windows 10, Microsoft Corporation.

(Continued)

FIGURE WA-1-30

The Modified CUSTOMER Datasheet

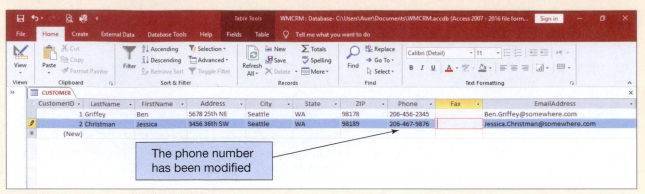

Access 2019, Windows 10, Microsoft Corporation.

Modifying Data in the CUSTOMER Table in Datasheet View

1. In the Navigation Pane, double-click the **CUSTOMER** table object. The CUSTOMER table window appears in a tabbed document window in Datasheet view.
2. Click the **Shutter Bar Open/Close** button to collapse the Navigation Pane.
3. Click the **cell** that contains Jessica Christman's phone number to select it. Microsoft Access automatically puts the cell into Edit mode.
   - **NOTE:** If you instead use the **Tab** key (or **Shift-Tab** to move to the left in the datasheet) to select the cell, press the **F2** key to edit the contents of the cell.
4. Change the phone number to **206-467-9876**.
   - **NOTE:** Remember that Phone has a field size of 12 characters. You have to delete characters before you can enter new ones.
5. Press the **Enter** key or otherwise move to another cell to complete the edit. The CUSTOMER datasheet appears as shown in Figure WA-1-30.
6. Because we really do not want to change Jessica Christman's phone number, edit the Phone value back to its original value of **206-467-3456**. Complete the edit and click the **Save** button on the Quick Access Toolbar to save the changes.
7. Click the **Close** button in the upper-right corner of the document window to close the CUSTOMER datasheet.
8. Click the **Shutter Bar Open/Close** button to expand the Navigation Pane.

Deleting Rows in Tables: The Datasheet View

After the data have been entered into a table, you can delete an entire row in Datasheet view. To illustrate this, we will temporarily delete Jessica Christman's data.

Deleting a Row in the CUSTOMER Table in Datasheet View

1. In the Navigation Pane, double-click the **CUSTOMER** table object. The CUSTOMER table window appears in a tabbed document window in Datasheet view.
2. Click the **Shutter Bar Open/Close** button to collapse the Navigation Pane.
3. Right-click the **row selector cell** on the left side of the CUSTOMER datasheet for the row that contains Jessica Christman's data. This selects the entire row and displays a shortcut menu, as shown in Figure WA-1-31.
   - **NOTE:** The terms *row* and *record* are synonymous in database usage.

FIGURE WA-1-31

Deleting a Row in the CUSTOMER Datasheet

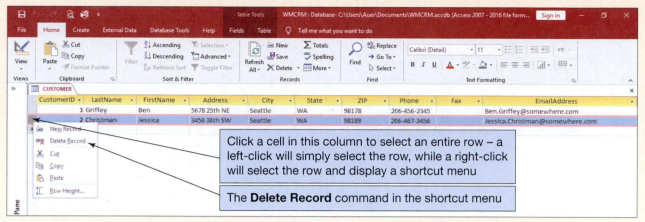

Access 2019, Windows 10, Microsoft Corporation.

4. Click the **Delete Record** command in the shortcut menu. As shown in Figure WA-1-32, a Microsoft Access dialog box appears, warning you that you are about to permanently delete the record.

- **NOTE:** As also shown in Figure WA-1-32, Microsoft Access 2019 with default settings performs the visual trick of actually removing the row! However, the row is not permanently deleted until you click the **Yes** button in the Microsoft Access dialog box. If you click the **No** button, the row reappears.

5. Click the **Yes** button to complete the deletion of the row.

- **NOTE:** Alternatively, you can delete the row by clicking the **row selector cell** and then pressing the **Delete** key. The same Microsoft Access dialog box shown in Figure WA-1-32 then appears.

6. Because we do not want to really lose Jessica Christman's data at this point, add a new row to the CUSTOMER datasheet and reenter Jessica's data. As shown in Figure WA-1-33, the CustomerID number for Jessica Christman is now 3 instead of 2. In an autonumbered column, each number is used only once.

FIGURE WA-1-32

The Microsoft Access Deletion Warning Dialog Box

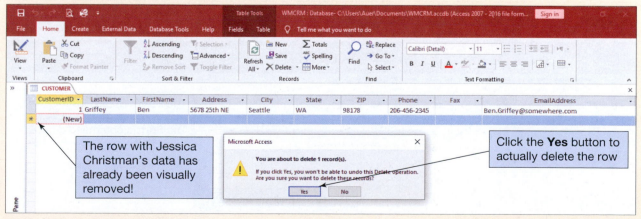

Access 2019, Windows 10, Microsoft Corporation.

(Continued)

FIGURE WA-1-33

The New CustomerID Number

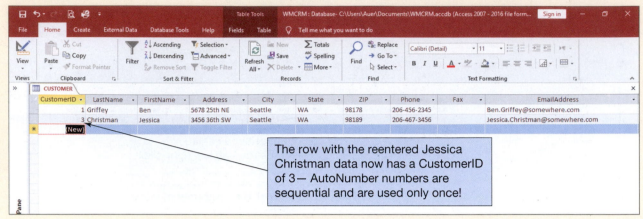

The row with the reentered Jessica Christman data now has a CustomerID of 3— AutoNumber numbers are sequential and are used only once!

Access 2019, Windows 10, Microsoft Corporation.

7. Click the **Close** button in the upper-right corner of the document window to close the CUSTOMER datasheet.
8. Click the **Shutter Bar Open/Close** button to expand the Navigation Pane.

Inserting Data into Tables: Using a Form

Now, we will create and use a **form** to insert data into a table. A form provides a visual reference for entering data into the various data columns, and Microsoft Access has a form generator as part of its application generator functions. We could build a form manually in Form Design view, but instead we can take the easy route and use the **Form Wizard**, which will take us through a step-by-step process to create the form we want.

Creating a Data Entry Form for the CUSTOMER Table

1. Click the **Create** command tab to display the Create command tab and its command groups, as shown in Figure WA-1-34.
2. Click the **Form Wizard** button shown in Figure WA-1-34. The Form Wizard appears, as shown in Figure WA-1-35.

FIGURE WA-1-34

The Create Command Tab and Form Wizard Button

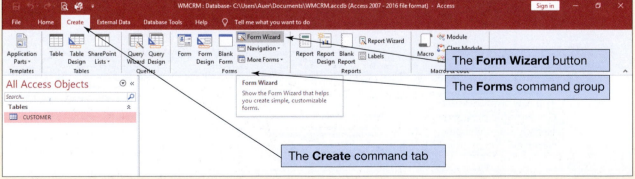

Access 2019, Windows 10, Microsoft Corporation.

FIGURE WA-1-35

The Form Wizard

The **Form Wizard**

The CUSTOMER table is already selected

The **right-facing single chevron** button

Click the **right-facing double chevron** button to select all of the fields in the table

The **Next** button

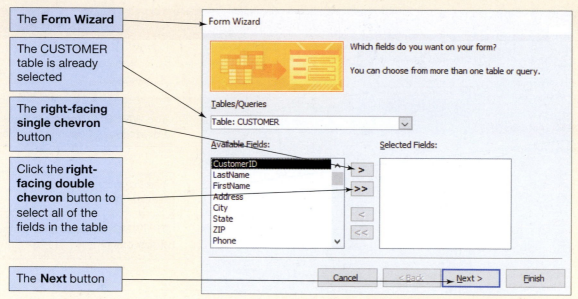

Access 2019, Windows 10, Microsoft Corporation.

3. The CUSTOMER table is already selected as the basis for the form, so we only have to select which columns we want to include on the form. We can choose columns one at a time by highlighting a column name and clicking the right-facing single-chevron button. Or we can choose all the columns at once by clicking the right-facing double-chevron button. We want to add all the columns in this case, so click the **right-facing double-chevron** button to add all the columns, and then click the **Next** button.
    - **NOTE:** In a real-world situation, we might not want to display the CustomerID value. In that case, we would deselect it by highlighting it and clicking the left-facing single-chevron button.
4. When asked, "What layout would you like for your form?" click the **Next** button to select the default **Columnar** layout.
5. When asked, "What title do you want for your form?" type the form title **WMCRM Customer Data Form** into the text box and then click the **Finish** button. As shown in Figure WA-1-36, the completed form appears in a tabbed document window and a WMCRM Customer Data Form object is added to the Navigation Pane.
    - **NOTE:** The WMCRM Customer Data Form is properly constructed and sized for our needs. Sometimes, however, we might need to make adjustments to the form design. We can make form design changes by switching to form Design view. To switch to form Design view, click the **Design View** button in the View gallery.

Now that we have the form we need, we can use the form to add some data to the CUSTOMER table.

Inserting Data into the CUSTOMER Table Using a Form

1. Click the **New Record** button. A blank form appears.
2. Click the **LastName** text box to select it. Enter the data for Rob Christman as shown in Figure WA-1-24. You can either use the **Tab** key to move from text box to text box or you can click the text box you want to edit.

(Continued)

FIGURE WA-1-36

The Completed WMCRM Customer Data Form

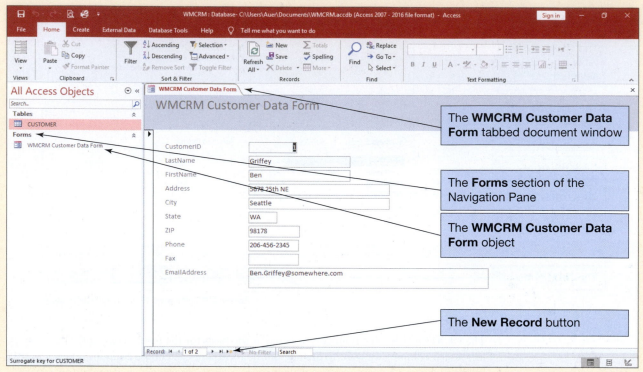

Access 2019, Windows 10, Microsoft Corporation.

3. When you are done entering the data for Rob Christman, enter the data for Judy Hayes as shown in Figure WA-1-24. After you have entered the data for Judy Hayes, your form will look as shown in Figure WA-1-37.
4. Click the **Close** button in the upper-right corner of the document window to close the WMCRM Customer Data Form.

FIGURE WA-1-37

The WMCRM Customer Data Form for Customer Judy Hayes

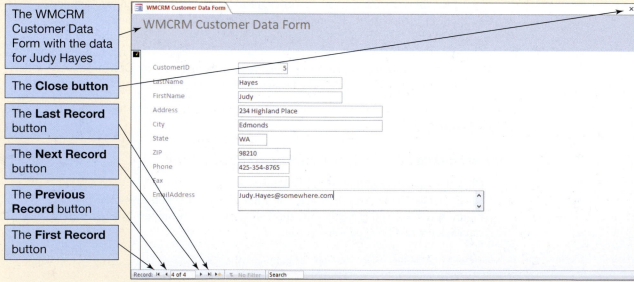

Access 2019, Windows 10, Microsoft Corporation.

FIGURE WA-1-38

The Delete Record Button

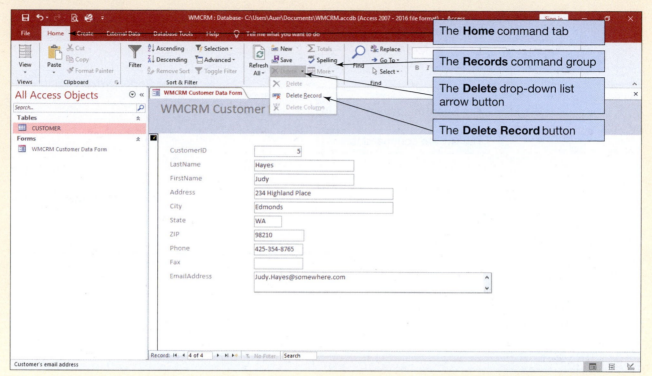

Access 2019, Windows 10, Microsoft Corporation.

Modifying Data and Deleting Records: Using a Form

Just as we can modify data and delete rows in Datasheet view, we can edit data and delete records by using a form. Editing data is simple: Move to the record you want to edit by using the **record navigation buttons** (First Record, Previous Record, and so on) shown in Figure WA-1-37, click the appropriate field text box, and then edit the contents. Deleting a record is also simple: Move to the record you want to edit by using the record navigation buttons and then click the *Delete Record* button in the Delete drop-down list of the Records group of the Home command tab, as shown in Figure WA-1-38. However, you will not use these capabilities at this time.

Creating Single-Table Microsoft Access Reports

One common function of an application is to generate printed reports. Microsoft Access 2019 has a report generator as part of its application generator functions. Just as with forms, we could build a form manually, or we can take the easy route and use the **Report Wizard**.

Creating a Report for the CUSTOMER Table

1. Click the **Create** command tab to display the Create command groups, as shown in Figure WA-1-39.
2. Click the **Report Wizard** button shown in Figure WA-1-39. The Report Wizard appears, as shown in Figure WA-1-40.
3. The CUSTOMER table is already selected as the basis for the report, so we only have to select which columns we want on the report. Just as with the Form Wizard, we can choose columns one at a time by highlighting the column name and clicking the right-facing

(Continued)

FIGURE WA-1-39

The Create Command Tab and Report Wizard Button

Access 2019, Windows 10, Microsoft Corporation.

FIGURE WA-1-40

The Report Wizard

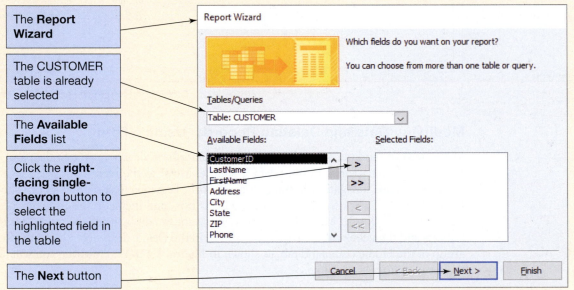

Access 2019, Windows 10, Microsoft Corporation.

single-chevron button. We can also choose all the columns at once by clicking the right-facing double-chevron button. In this case, we want to use only the columns **LastName, FirstName, Phone, Fax**, and **Email**. Click each column name in the Available Fields list to select it, and then click the **right-facing single-chevron** button to move each column to Selected Fields. The completed selection looks as shown in Figure WA-1-41.

- **NOTE:**   You can select only one column at a time. The usual technique of selecting more than one column name at a time by pressing and holding the **Ctrl** key while clicking each additional column name does *not* work in this case.

4. Click the **Next** button.
5. Microsoft Access now asks, "Do you want to add any grouping levels?" Grouping can be useful in complex reports, but we do not need any groupings for this simple report that lists customers. Instead, we can use the default nongrouped column listing, so click the **Next** button.

FIGURE WA-1-41

The Completed Column Selection

The **Selected Fields** list

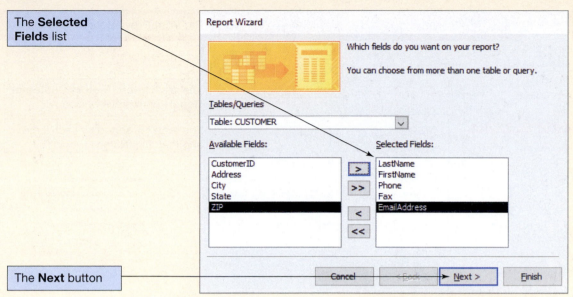

The **Next** button

Access 2019, Windows 10, Microsoft Corporation.

6. As shown in Figure WA-1-42, we are now asked, "What sort order do you want for your records?" The most useful sorting order in this case is by last name, with sorting by first name for identical last names. For both sorts, we want an *ascending* sort (from A to Z). Click the **sort field 1** drop-down list arrow and select **LastName**. Leave the sort order button set to **Ascending**.
7. Click the **sort field 2** drop-down list arrow and select **FirstName**, leave the sort order button set to **Ascending**, and click the **Next** button.

FIGURE WA-1-42

Choosing the Sort Order

The **sort field 1** drop-down list arrow button

Select **LastName** from the drop-down list

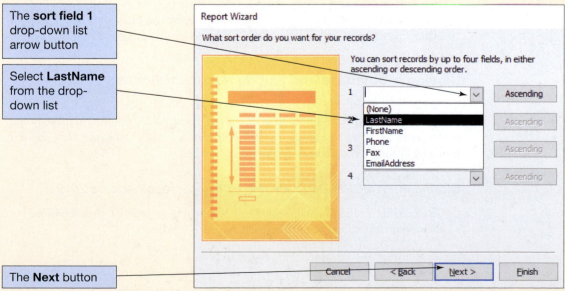

The **Next** button

Access 2019, Windows 10, Microsoft Corporation.

(Continued)

FIGURE WA-1-43

The Finished Report

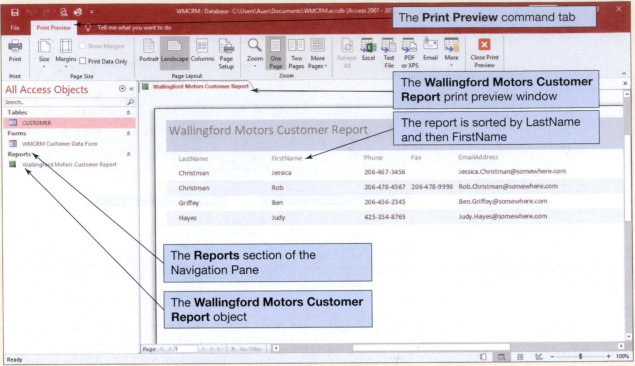

The **Print Preview** command tab

The **Wallingford Motors Customer Report** print preview window

The report is sorted by LastName and then FirstName

The **Reports** section of the Navigation Pane

The **Wallingford Motors Customer Report** object

Access 2019, Windows 10, Microsoft Corporation.

8. We are now asked, "How would you like to lay out your report?" We will use the default setting of **Tabular Layout**, but click the **Landscape Orientation** radio button to change the report orientation to landscape. Click the **Next** button.

9. Access then asks, "What title do you want for your report?" Edit the report title to read **Wallingford Motors Customer Report**. Leave the **Preview the report** radio button selected. Click the **Finish** button. As shown in Figure WA-1-43, the completed report appears in a tabbed document window, a Reports section has been added to the Navigation Pane, and the Wallingford Motors Customer Report object appears in this section.

10. Click the **Close** button in the upper-right corner of the document window.

Closing a Database and Exiting Microsoft Access 2019

We have finished all the work we need to do in this chapter's "Working with Microsoft Access." We have learned how to create a database; how to build database tables, forms, and reports; and how to populate a table with data by using Datasheet view and a form. We finish by closing the database and Microsoft Access.

Closing the WMCRM Database and Exiting Microsoft Access 2019

1. To close the WMCRM database and exit Microsoft Access 2019, click the **Close** button in the upper-right corner of the Microsoft Access 2019 window.

SUMMARY

The importance of database processing increases every day because databases are used in information systems everywhere—and increasingly so. The purpose of this book is to teach you essential database concepts and to help you get started using and learning database technology.

Today's Internet and smartphone world depends on databases. Personal computers use Web clients to browse, shop, and communicate online. Smartphones use apps over cell phone data networks to do the same. The Internet of Things (IoTs) uses devices such as smart speakers with virtual assistants to access apps over the Internet. All these applications rely on databases.

The purpose of a database is to help people keep track of things. Lists can be used for this purpose, but if a list involves more than one theme, modification problems will occur when data are inserted, updated, or deleted.

Relational databases store data in the form of tables. Almost always, the tables are designed so that each table stores data about a single theme. Lists that involve multiple themes need to be broken up and stored in multiple tables, one for each theme. When this is done, a column needs to be added to link the tables to each other so that the relationship from a row in one table to a row in another table can be shown.

Structured Query Language (SQL) is an international language for processing tables in relational databases. You can use SQL to join together and display data stored in separate tables, create new tables, and query data from tables in many ways. You can also use SQL to insert, update, and delete data.

The components of a database system are the database, the database management system (DBMS), one or more database applications, and users. A database is a self-describing collection of related records. A relational database is a self-describing collection of related tables. A database is self-describing because it contains a description of its contents within itself, which is known as metadata. Tables are related by storing linking values of a common column. The contents of a database are user data; metadata; supporting structures, such as indexes; and sometimes application metadata.

A database management system (DBMS) is a large, complicated program used to create, process, and administer a database. DBMS products are almost always licensed from software vendors. Specific functions of a DBMS are summarized in Figure 1-20.

The functions of database applications are to create and process forms, to process user queries, and to create and process reports. Application programs also execute specific application logic and control the application. Users provide data and data changes and read data in forms, queries, and reports.

DBMS products for personal database systems provide functionality for application development and database management. They hide considerable complexity, but at a cost: Requirements unanticipated by DBMS features cannot be readily implemented. Enterprise-class database systems include multiple applications that might be written in multiple languages. These systems may support hundreds or thousands of users.

An example of a personal database system is Microsoft Access 2019, which is discussed in this book in chapter sections titled "Working with Microsoft Access." These sections cover all the basic knowledge that you need to create and use databases in Microsoft Access 2019.

Examples of enterprise-class DBMS products Oracle MySQL 8.0, Microsoft SQL Server 2017, and Oracle Database XE. We discuss MySQL 8.0 in this book, and detailed information on installing and using MySQL Community Server 8.0 can be found in Extension A, "Working with MySQL."

Web sites that interact with the user by displaying data stored in a database are known as Web database applications. Online transaction data is stored in an online transaction processing (OLTP) database. Companies build data warehouses to store data needed for data analysis in a business intelligence (BI) system, which includes tools such as online analytical processing (OLAP) systems. BI systems are discussed in Chapter 7 and Extension C, "Advanced Business Intelligence and Big Data."

The term *Big Data* refers to the extremely large datasets generated by Web 2.0 applications such as Facebook and Twitter. Big Data datasets are often stored in nonrelational DBMSs. The term *NoSQL* refers to nonrelational databases used in Web 2.0 applications. NoSQL databases, and specifically ArangoDB, are discussed in Chapter 7, and Extension C, "Advanced Business Intelligence and Big Data."

The term *cloud computing* is used to denote applications run on hardware and network resources located at a hosted data center instead of owned and operated by the company itself. Cloud computing is discussed in Chapter 7, and using cloud computing is illustrated in Extension C, "Advanced Business Intelligence and Big Data."

KEY TERMS

Amazon.com
Amazon Web Services
Android operating system
Apple II
apps
ArangoDB
ArangoDB query language (AQL)
Advanced Research Projects Agency
   Network (ARPANET)
Big Data
business intelligence (BI) system
cell phone
client (applications)
client-server architecture
cloud computing
column
concurrency
data
data analysis
data center
data warehouse
database
database application
database management system
   (DBMS)
database system
delete
devices
enterprise-class database system
Ethernet networking technology
fields
Google Cloud Platform

IBM Personal Computer (IBM PC)
ID column
in the cloud
insert
instance
Internet
Internet of Things (IoTs)
iPhone
list
Local Area Networks (LANs)
metadata
Microsoft Azure
Microsoft Office 365 for Business
Microsoft SQL Server
   Management Studio
Microsoft SQL Server 2017
Microsoft SQL Server 2017
   Developer Edition
Microsoft SQL Server 2017 Express
   Edition
mobile phone
modification action
modification problems
MySQL Community Server 8.0
MySQL Workbench
nonrelational databases
NoSQL
null values
online analytical processing (OLAP)
online transaction processing
   (OLTP)
Oracle Database XE

Oracle Database 18c Express
   Edition (XE)
Oracle SQL Developer
personal computer (PC)
personal database system
Point of Sale (POS) system
record
referential integrity constraints
related tables
relational database
relational model
row
self-describing
server
services
smart speakers
smartphone
Structured Query Language (SQL)
table
tablet computers (tablets)
transaction
update
virtual machines
user
Web 2.0
Web browser
Web database application
Web sites
World Wide Web (the Web, or
   WWW)
Xerox Palo Alto Research Center
   (Xerox PARC)

REVIEW QUESTIONS

1.1   Describe the historic development of Internet and smartphone technology from the early days of personal computers (PCs) to today's Internet Web application and smartphone app–based information systems environment.

1.2   Why do today's Internet Web applications and smartphone apps need databases?

FIGURE 1-35

The Veterinary Office List—Version One

	A	B	C	D	E	F	G	H
1	PetName	PetType	PetBreed	PetDOB	OwnerLastName	OwnerFirstName	OwnerPhone	OwnerEmail
2	King	Dog	Std. Poodle	27-Feb-16	Downs	Marsha	201-823-5467	Marsha.Downs@somewhere.com
3	Teddy	Cat	Cashmier	1-Feb-15	James	Richard	201-735-9812	Richard.James@somewhere.com
4	Fido	Dog	Std. Poodle	17-Jul-17	Downs	Marsha	201-823-5467	Marsha.Downs@somewhere.com
5	AJ	Dog	Collie Mix	5-May-17	Frier	Liz	201-823-6578	Liz.Frier@somewhere.com
6	Cedro	Cat	Unknown	6-Jun-14	James	Richard	201-735-9812	Richard.James@somewhere.com
7	Woolley	Cat	Unknown	???	James	Richard	201-735-9812	Richard.James@somewhere.com
8	Buster	Dog	Border Collie	11-Dec-13	Trent	Miles	201-634-7865	Miles.Trent@somewhere.com
9	Jiddah	Cat	Abyssinian	1-Jul-10	Evans	Hilary	201-634-2345	Hilary.Evans@somewhere.com

Excel 2019, Windows 10, Microsoft Corporation.

1.3 Read the description of the search process on the Pearson Web site in this chapter. Using your own computer, find another retailer Web site (other than those discussed or mentioned in this chapter), and search for something of interest to you. Write up a description (with screen shots if possible) of your search.

1.4 Why is the study of database technology important?

1.5 What is the purpose of this book?

1.6 Describe the purpose of a database.

1.7 What is a modification problem? What are the three possible types of modification problems?

1.8 Figure 1-35 shows a list that is used by a veterinary office. Describe three modification problems that are likely to occur when using this list.

1.9 Name the two themes in the list in Figure 1-35.

1.10 What is an ID column?

1.11 Break the list in Figure 1-35 into two tables, each with data for a single theme. Assume that owners have a unique phone number but that pets have no unique column. Create an ID column for pets like the one created for customers and courses for the Art Course database tables in Figure 1-12.

1.12 Show how the tables you created for question 1.11 solve the problems you described in question 1.8.

1.13 What does *SQL* stand for, and what purpose does it serve?

1.14 Another version of the list used by the veterinary office is shown in Figure 1-36. How many themes does this list have? What are they?

1.15 Break the list in Figure 1-36 into tables, each with a single theme. Create ID columns as you think necessary.

1.16 Show how the tables you created for question 1.15 solve the three problems of lists identified in this chapter.

1.17 Describe in your own words and illustrate with tables how relationships are represented in a relational database.

1.18 Name the four components of a database system.

1.19 Define the term *database*.

FIGURE 1-36

The Veterinary Office List—Version Two

	A	B	C	D	E	F	G	H	I	J	K
1	PetName	PetType	PetBreed	PetDOB	OwnerLastName	OwnerFirstName	OwnerPhone	OwnerEmail	Service	Date	Charge
2	King	Dog	Std. Poodle	27-Feb-16	Downs	Marsha	201-823-5467	Marsha.Downs@somewhere.com	Ear Infection	17-Aug-18	$ 65.00
3	Teddy	Cat	Cashmier	1-Feb-15	James	Richard	201-735-9812	Richard.James@somewhere.com	Nail Clip	5-Sep-18	$ 27.50
4	Fido	Dog	Std. Poodle	17-Jul-17	Downs	Marsha	201-823-5467	Marsha.Downs@somewhere.com			
5	AJ	Dog	Collie Mix	5-May-17	Frier	Liz	201-823-6578	Liz.Frier@somewhere.com	One-year Shots	5-May-18	$ 42.50
6	Cedro	Cat	Unknown	6-Jun-14	James	Richard	201-735-9812	Richard.James@somewhere.com	Nail Clip	5-Sep-18	$ 27.50
7	Woolley	Cat	Unknown	???	James	Richard	201-735-9812	Richard.James@somewhere.com	Skin Infection	3-Oct-18	$ 35.00
8	Buster	Dog	Border Collie	11-Dec-13	Trent	Miles	201-634-7865	Miles.Trent@somewhere.com	Laceration Repair	5-Oct-18	$ 127.00
9	Jiddah	Cat	Abyssinian	1-Jul-10	Evans	Hilary	201-634-2345	Hilary.Evans@somewhere.com	Booster Shots	4-Nov-18	$ 111.00

Excel 2019, Windows 10, Microsoft Corporation.

1.20   Why do you think it is important for a database to be self-describing?

1.21   List the contents of a database.

1.22   Define the term *metadata*, and give some examples of metadata.

1.23   Describe the use of an index.

1.24   Define the term *application metadata*, and give some examples of application metadata.

1.25   What is the purpose of a DBMS?

1.26   List the specific functions of a DBMS.

1.27   Define the term *referential integrity constraint.* Give an example of a referential integrity constraint for the tables you created for question 1.11.

1.28   Explain the difference between a DBMS and a database.

1.29   List the functions of a database application.

1.30   Explain the differences between a personal database system and an enterprise-class database system.

1.31   What is the advantage of hiding complexity from the user of a DBMS? What is the disadvantage?

1.32   Summarize the differences between the database systems in Figures 1-25 and 1-28.

1.33   What is a *Web database application*? Why are Web database applications important in today's Web and mobile computing environment?

1.34   What is online transaction processing (OLTP), and what is online analytical processing (OLAP)? What is a business intelligence (BI) system, and where is the data used by a BI system stored?

1.35   What is *Big Data*? What is a *NoSQL* database? What are *Web 2.0* applications, how are they related to Big Data, and why can't these applications use a relational database?

1.36   What is *cloud computing*? Where are the hardware and network resources used in cloud computing located?

EXERCISES

The following spreadsheets form a set of named spreadsheets with the indicated column headings. Use these spreadsheets to answer exercises 1.37 through 1.39.

A. **Name of spreadsheet**: EQUIPMENT
   Column headings:
   Number, Description, AcquisitionDate, AcquisitionPrice

B. **Name of spreadsheet**: COMPANY
   Column headings:
   Name, IndustryCode, Gross Sales, OfficerName, OfficerTitle

C. **Name of spreadsheet**: COMPANY
   Column headings:
   Name, IndustryCode, Gross Sales, NameOfPresident

D. **Name of spreadsheet**: COMPUTER
   Column headings:
   SerialNumber, Make, Model, DiskType, DiskCapacity

E. **Name of spreadsheet**: PERSON
   Column headings:
   Name, DateOfHire, DeptName, DeptManager, ProjectID, NumHours, ProjectManager

1.37 For each of the spreadsheets provided, indicate the number of themes you think the spreadsheet includes and give an appropriate name for each theme. For some of them, the answer may depend on the assumptions you make. In these cases, state your assumptions.

1.38 For any spreadsheet that has more than one theme, show at least one modification problem that will occur when inserting, updating, or deleting data.

1.39 For any spreadsheet that has more than one theme, break up the columns into tables such that each table has a single theme. Add ID columns if necessary, and add a linking column (or columns) to maintain the relationship between the themes.

WORKING WITH MICROSOFT ACCESS

Key Terms

AutoNumber (data type)
character (data type)
customer relationship management (CRM) system
data entry form
datasheet
Datasheet view
form
Form Wizard
key
long text (data type)
memo (data type)
Microsoft Office Fluent user interface
Navigation Pane
Navigation Pane drop-down list

Navigation Pane drop-down list button
number (data type)
numeric (data type)
object
primary key
record navigation buttons
remarks
Report Wizard
required
short text (data type)
Shutter Bar Open/Close button
surrogate key
text (data type)
type

Exercises

The Wedgewood Pacific (WP) company, founded in 1987 in Seattle, Washington, manufactures and sells consumer drone aircraft. This is an innovative and rapidly developing market. In January 2018, the FAA said that 181,000 drones (out of the approximately 700,000 drones that may have been sold during the 2015 Christmas season) had been registered under the new FAA drone registration rules.[14]

WP currently produces three drone models: the Alpha III, the Bravo III, and the Delta IV. These products are created by WP's Research and Development group, and produced at WP's production facilities. WP manufactures some of the parts used in the drones, but also purchases some parts from other suppliers.

The company is located in two buildings. One building houses the Administration, Legal, Finance, Accounting, Human Resources, and Sales and Marketing departments, and the second houses the Information Systems, Research and Development, and Production departments. The company database contains data about employees; departments; projects; assets, such as finished goods inventory, parts inventory, and computer equipment; and other aspects of company operations.

[14]See https://www.transportation.gov/briefing-room/faa-drone-registry-tops-one-million (accessed January, 2019).

FIGURE 1-37

Database Column Characteristics for the WP EMPLOYEE Table

EMPLOYEE

Column Name	Type	Key	Required	Remarks
EmployeeNumber	AutoNumber	Primary Key	Yes	Surrogate Key
FirstName	Short Text (25)	No	Yes	
LastName	Short Text (25)	No	Yes	
Department	Short Text (35)	No	Yes	
Position	Short Text (35)	No	No	
Supervisor	Number	No	No	Long Integer
OfficePhone	Short Text (12)	No	No	
EmailAddress	Short Text (100)	No	Yes	

FIGURE 1-38

Wedgewood Pacific EMPLOYEE Data

Employee Number	FirstName	LastName	Department	Position	Supervisor	OfficePhone	EmailAddress
1	Mary	Jacobs	Administration	CEO		360-285-8110	Mary.Jacobs@WP.com
2	Rosalie	Jackson	Administration	Admin Assistant	1	360-285-8120	Rosalie.Jackson@WP.com
3	Richard	Bandalone	Legal	Attorney	1	360-285-8210	Richard.Bandalone@WP.com
4	George	Smith	Human Resources	HR3	1	360-285-8310	George.Smith@WP.com
5	Alan	Adams	Human Resources	HR1	4	360-285-8320	Alan.Adams@WP.com
6	Ken	Evans	Finance	CFO	1	360-285-8410	Ken.Evans@WP.com
7	Mary	Abernathy	Finance	FA3	6	360-285-8420	Mary.Abernathy@WP.com
8	Tom	Caruthers	Accounting	FA2	6	360-285-8430	Tom.Caruthers@WP.com
9	Heather	Jones	Accounting	FA2	6	360-285-8440	Heather.Jones@WP.com
10	Ken	Numoto	Sales and Marketing	SM3	1	360-285-8510	Ken.Numoto@WP.com
11	Linda	Granger	Sales and Marketing	SM2	10	360-285-8520	Linda.Granger@WP.com
12	James	Nestor	InfoSystems	CIO	1	360-285-8610	James.Nestor@WP.com
13	Rick	Brown	InfoSystems	IS2	12		Rick.Brown@WP.com
14	Mike	Nguyen	Research and Development	CTO	1	360-285-8710	Mike.Nguyen@WP.com
15	Jason	Sleeman	Research and Development	RD3	14	360-285-8720	Jason.Sleeman@WP.com
16	Mary	Smith	Production	OPS3	1	360-285-8810	Mary.Smith@WP.com
17	Tom	Jackson	Production	OPS2	16	360-285-8820	Tom.Jackson@WP.com
18	George	Jones	Production	OPS2	17	360-285-8830	George.Jones@WP.com
19	Julia	Hayakawa	Production	OPS1	17		Julia.Hayakawa@WP.com
20	Sam	Stewart	Production	OPS1	17		Sam.Stewart@WP.com

A. Create a Microsoft Access database named WP in a Microsoft Access file named WP.accdb.

B. Figure 1-37 shows the column characteristics for the WP EMPLOYEE table. Using the column characteristics, create the EMPLOYEE table in the WP database.

C. Figure 1-38 shows the data for the WP EMPLOYEE table. Using Datasheet view, enter the data for the first three rows of data in the EMPLOYEE table shown in Figure 1-38 into your EMPLOYEE table.

D. Create a data input form for the EMPLOYEE table and name it WP Employee Data Form. Make any adjustments necessary to the form so that all data display properly. Use this form to enter the rest of the data in the EMPLOYEE table shown in Figure 1-38 into your EMPLOYEE table.

E. Create a report named Wedgewood Pacific Employee Report that presents the data contained in your EMPLOYEE table sorted first by employee last name and second by employee first name. Make any adjustments necessary to the report so that all headings and data display properly. Print a copy of this report.

CASE QUESTIONS

SAN JUAN SAILBOAT CHARTERS

San Juan Sailboat Charters (SJSBC) is an agency that leases (charters) sailboats. SJSBC does not own the boats. Instead, SJSBC leases boats on behalf of boat owners who want to earn income from their boats when they are not using the boats themselves, and SJSBC charges the owners a fee for this service. SJSBC specializes in boats that can be used for multiday or weekly charters. The smallest sailboat available is 28 feet in length, and the largest is 51 feet in length.

Each sailboat is fully equipped at the time it is leased. Most of the equipment is provided at the time of the charter. The majority of the equipment is provided by the owners, but some is provided by SJSBC. Some of the owner-provided equipment is attached to the boat, such as radios, compasses, depth indicators and other instrumentation, stoves, and refrigerators. Other owner-provided equipment is not physically attached to the boat, such as sails, lines, anchors, dinghies, life preservers, and equipment in the cabin (dishes, silverware, cooking utensils, bedding, and so on). SJSBC provides consumable supplies such as charts, navigation books, tide and current tables, soap, dish towels, toilet paper, and similar items. The consumable supplies are treated as equipment by SJSBC for tracking and accounting purposes.

Keeping track of equipment is an important part of SJSBC's responsibilities. Much of the equipment is expensive, and those items not physically attached to the boat can be easily damaged, lost, or stolen. SJSBC holds the customers responsible for all of the boat's equipment during the period of their charter.

SJSBC likes to keep accurate records of its customers and charters, and customers are required to keep a log during each charter. Some itineraries and weather conditions are more dangerous than others, and the data from these logs provides information about the customer experience. This information is useful for marketing purposes, as well as for evaluating a customer's ability to handle a particular boat and itinerary.

Sailboats need maintenance (two definitions of *boat* are: (1) "break out another thousand" and (2) "a hole in the water into which one pours money"). SJSBC is required by its contracts with the boat owners to keep accurate records of all maintenance activities and costs.

A. Create a sample list of owners and boats. Your list will be similar in structure to that in Figure 1-35, but it will concern owners and boats rather than owners and pets. Your list should include, at a minimum, owner name, phone, and billing address, as well as boat name, make, model, and length.

B. Describe modification problems that are likely to occur if SJSBC attempts to maintain the list in a spreadsheet.

C. Split the list into tables such that each has only one theme. Create appropriate ID columns. Use a linking column to represent the relationship between a boat and an owner. Demonstrate that the modification problems you identified in part B have been eliminated.

D. Create a sample list of owners, boats, and charters. Your list will be similar to that in Figure 1-36. Your list should include the data items from part A as well as the charter date, charter customer, and the amount charged for each charter.

E. Illustrate modification problems that are likely to occur if SJSBC attempts to maintain the list from part D in a spreadsheet.

F. Split the list from part D into tables such that each has only one theme. Create appropriate ID columns. Use linking columns to represent relationships. Demonstrate that the modification problems you identified in part E have been eliminated.

GARDEN GLORY PROJECT QUESTIONS

Garden Glory is a partnership that provides gardening and yard maintenance services to individuals and organizations. Garden Glory is owned by two partners. They employ two office administrators and a number of full- and part-time gardeners. Garden Glory will provide one-time garden services, but it specializes in ongoing service and maintenance. Many of its customers have multiple buildings, apartments, and rental houses that require gardening and lawn maintenance services.

A. Create a sample list of owners and properties. Your list will be similar in structure to that in Figure 1-35, but it will concern owners and properties rather than owners and pets. Your list should include, at a minimum, owner name, phone, and billing address, as well as property name, type, and address.

B. Describe modification problems that are likely to occur if Garden Glory attempts to maintain the list in a spreadsheet.

C. Split the list into tables such that each has only one theme. Create appropriate ID columns. Use a linking column to represent the relationship between a property and an owner. Demonstrate that the modification problems you identified in part B have been eliminated.

D. Create a sample list of owners, properties, and services. Your list will be similar to that in Figure 1-36. Your list should include the data items from part A as well as the date, description, and amount charged for each service.

E. Illustrate modification problems that are likely to occur if Garden Glory attempts to maintain the list from part D in a spreadsheet.

F. Split the list from part D into tables such that each has only one theme. Create appropriate ID columns. Use linking columns to represent relationships. Demonstrate that the modification problems you identified in part E have been eliminated.

JAMES RIVER JEWELRY PROJECT QUESTIONS

James River Jewelry is a small jewelry shop. While James River Jewelry does sell typical jewelry purchased from jewelry vendors, including such items as rings, necklaces, earrings, and watches, it specializes in hard-to-find Asian jewelry. Although some Asian jewelry is manufactured jewelry purchased from vendors in the same manner as the standard jewelry is obtained, many of the Asian jewelry pieces are often unique single items purchased directly from the artisan who created the piece (the term *manufactured* would be an inappropriate description of these pieces). James River Jewelry has a small but loyal clientele, and it wants to further increase customer loyalty by creating a frequent buyer program. In this program, after every 10 purchases, a customer will receive a credit equal to 50 percent of the average of his or her 10 most recent purchases. This credit must be applied to the next (or 11th) purchase.

A. Create a sample list of customers and purchases and a second list of customers and credits. Your lists should include customer data you think would be important to James River along with typical purchase data. Credit data should include the date of the credit, the total amount of the 10 purchases used as the basis of the credit, and the credit amount.

B. Describe modification problems that are likely to occur if James River attempts to maintain the lists in a spreadsheet.

C. Split the lists into tables such that each has only a single theme. Create appropriate ID columns. Use one ID to represent the relationship between a purchase and a customer and use another ID to represent the relationship between a credit and a customer.

D. Attempt to combine the two lists you created in part A into a single list. What problems occur as you try to do this? Look closely at Figure 1-36. An essential difference exists between a list of the three themes customer, purchase, and credit and a list of the three themes PetName, Owner, and Service in Figure 1-36. What do you think this difference is?

E. Change the tables from part C so that the purchase list has not only the ID of Customer but also the ID of Credit. Compare this arrangement to the tables in your answer to question 1.15. What is the essential difference between these two designs?

THE QUEEN ANNE CURIOSITY SHOP PROJECT QUESTIONS

The Queen Anne Curiosity Shop sells both antiques and current-production household items that complement or are useful with the antiques. For example, the store sells antique dining room tables and new tablecloths. The antiques are purchased from both individuals and wholesalers, and the new items are purchased from distributors. The store's customers include individuals, owners of bed-and-breakfast operations, and local interior designers who work with both individuals and small businesses. The antiques are unique, although some multiple items, such as dining room chairs, may be available as a set (sets are never broken). The new items are not unique, and an item may be reordered if it is out of stock. New items are also available in various sizes and colors (for example, a particular style of tablecloth may be available in several sizes and in a variety of colors).

A. Create a sample list of purchased inventory items and vendors and a second list of customers and sales. The first list should include inventory data, such as a description, manufacturer and model (if available), item cost, and vendor identification and contact data you think should be recorded. The second list should include customer data you think would be important to the Queen Anne Curiosity Shop, along with typical sales data.

B. Describe problems that are likely to occur when inserting, updating, and deleting data in these spreadsheets.

C. Attempt to combine the two lists you created in part A into a single list. What problems occur as you try to do this?

D. Split the spreadsheets you created in part A into tables such that each has only one theme. Create appropriate ID columns.

E. Explain how the tables in your answer to part D will eliminate the problems you identified in part B.

F. What is the relationship between the tables you created from the first spreadsheet and the tables you created from the second spreadsheet? If your set of tables does not already contain this relationship, how will you add it into your set of tables?

2

The Relational Model

CHAPTER OBJECTIVES

- Learn the conceptual foundation of the relational model
- Understand how relations differ from nonrelational tables
- Learn basic relational terminology
- Learn the meaning and importance of keys, foreign keys, and related terminology

- Understand how foreign keys represent relationships
- Learn the purpose and use of surrogate keys
- Learn the meaning of functional dependencies
- Learn to apply a process for normalizing relations

This chapter explains the relational model, the single most important standard in database processing today. This model, which was developed and published in 1970 by Edgar Frank Codd, commonly referred to as E. F. Codd,[1] then an employee at IBM, was founded on the theory of relational algebra. The model has since found widespread practical application, and today it is used for the design and implementation of every commercial relational database worldwide. This chapter describes the conceptual foundation of this model.

---

[1]E. F. Codd, "A Relational Model of Data for Large Shared Databanks," *Communications of the ACM* (June 1970): 377–387. A downloadable copy of this paper in PDF format is available at **http://dl.acm.org/ citation.cfm?id=362685**.

RELATIONS

Chapter 1 states that databases help people keep track of things and that relational DBMS products store data in the form of tables. Here we need to clarify and refine those statements. First, the formal name for a "thing" that is being tracked is **entity**, which is defined as something of importance to the user that needs to be represented in the database. Further, it is not entirely correct to say that DBMS products store data in tables. DBMS products store data in the form of relations, which are a special type of table. Specifically, a **relation** is a two-dimensional **table** consisting of **rows** and **columns** that has the following characteristics:

1. Each row of the table holds data that pertain to some entity or a portion of some entity.
2. Each column of the table contains data that represent an attribute of the entity. For example, in an EMPLOYEE relation, each row would contain data about a particular employee, and each column would contain data that represented an attribute of that employee, such as LastName, Phone, or EmailAddress.
3. The cells of the table must hold a single value, and thus no repeating elements are allowed in a cell.
4. All the entries in any column must be of the same kind. For example, if the third column in the first row of a table contains EmployeeNumber, then the third column in all other rows must contain EmployeeNumber as well.
5. Each column must have a unique name.
6. The order of the columns within the table is unimportant.
7. The order of the rows is unimportant.
8. The set of data values in each row must be unique—no two rows in the table may hold identical sets of data values.

The characteristics of a relation are summarized in Figure 2-1.

Note that in our definition of a relation, all the values in a column are of the same kind. If, for example, the second column of the first row of a relation has FirstName, then the second column of every row in the relation has FirstName. This is an important requirement that is known as the **domain integrity constraint**, where the term **domain** means a grouping of data that meets a specific type definition. For example, FirstName would have a domain of names such as *Albert, Bruce, Cathy, David, Edith*, and so forth, and all values of FirstName *must* come from the names in that domain.

In Figure 2-1 and in this discussion, we use the term *entity* to mean some identifiable thing. A customer, a salesperson, an order, a part, and a lease are all examples of what we mean by an entity. When we introduce the entity-relationship model in Chapter 4, we will make the definition of entity more precise. For now, just think of an entity as some identifiable thing that users want to track.

FIGURE 2-1

Characteristics of a Relation

1. Rows contain data about an entity
2. Columns contain data about attributes of the entity
3. Cells of the table hold a single value
4. All entries in a column are of the same kind
5. Each column has a unique name
6. The order of the columns is unimportant
7. The order of the rows is unimportant
8. No two rows may hold identical sets of data values

A Sample Relation and Two Nonrelations

Figure 2-2 shows a sample EMPLOYEE table. Consider this table in light of the characteristics discussed earlier. First, each row is about an EMPLOYEE entity, and each column represents an attribute of employees, so those two conditions are met. Each cell has only one value, and all entries in a column are of the same kind. Column names are unique, and we could change the order of either the columns or the rows and not lose any information. Finally, no two rows are identical—each row holds a different set of data values. Because this table meets all requirements of the definition of *relation*, we can classify it as a relation.

Now, consider the tables shown in Figures 2-3 and 2-4. Neither of these tables is a relation. The EMPLOYEE table in Figure 2-3 is not a relation because the Phone column has cells with multiple entries. For example, George Smith has three values for phone, and Mary Abernathy has two values. Multiple entries per cell are not permitted in a relation.

The table in Figure 2-4 is not a relation for two reasons. First, the order of the rows is important. Because the row under George Smith contains his fax number, we may lose track of the correspondence between his name and his fax number if we rearrange the rows. The second reason this table is not a relation is that not all values in the EmailAddress column are of the same kind. Some of the values are email addresses, and others are types of phone numbers.

Although each cell can have only one value, that value can vary in length. Figure 2-5 shows the table from Figure 2-2 with an additional variable-length Comment attribute. Even though a comment can be lengthy and varies in length from row to row, there is still only one comment per cell. Thus, the table in Figure 2-5 is a relation.

FIGURE 2-2

Sample EMPLOYEE Relation

EmployeeNumber	FirstName	LastName	Department	EmailAddress	Phone
101	Mary	Jacobs	Administration	Mary.Jacobs@ourcompany.com	360-285-8110
102	Rosalie	Jackson	Administration	Rosalie.Jackson@ourcompany.com	360-285-8120
103	Richard	Bandalone	Legal	Richard.Bandalone@ourcompany.com	360-285-8210
104	George	Smith	Human Resources	George.Smith@ourcompany.com	360-285-8310
105	Alan	Adams	Human Resources	Alan.Adams@ourcompany.com	360-285-8320
106	Ken	Evans	Finance	Ken.Evans@ourcompany.com	360-285-8410
107	Mary	Abernathy	Finance	Mary.Abernathy@ourcompany.com	360-285-8420

FIGURE 2-3

Nonrelational Table— Multiple Entries per Cell

EmployeeNumber	FirstName	LastName	Department	EmailAddress	Phone
101	Mary	Jacobs	Administration	Mary.Jacobs@ourcompany.com	360-285-8110
102	Rosalie	Jackson	Administration	Rosalie.Jackson@ourcompany.com	360-285-8120
103	Richard	Bandalone	Legal	Richard.Bandalone@ourcompany.com	360-285-8210
104	George	Smith	Human Resources	George.Smith@ourcompany.com	360-285-8310, 360-285-8391, 206-723-8392
105	Alan	Adams	Human Resources	Alan.Adams@ourcompany.com	360-285-8320
106	Ken	Evans	Finance	Ken.Evans@ourcompany.com	360-285-8410
107	Mary	Abernathy	Finance	Mary.Abernathy@ourcompany.com	360-285-8420, 360-285-8491

FIGURE 2-4

Nonrelational Table— Order of Rows Matters and Kind of Column Entries Differs in Email

EmployeeNumber	FirstName	LastName	Department	EmailAddress	Phone
101	Mary	Jacobs	Administration	Mary.Jacobs@ourcompany.com	360-285-8110
102	Rosalie	Jackson	Administration	Rosalie.Jackson@ourcompany.com	360-285-8120
103	Richard	Bandalone	Legal	Richard.Bandalone@ourcompany.com	360-285-8210
104	George	Smith	Human Resources	George.Smith@ourcompany.com	360-285-8310
				Fax:	360-285-8391
				Home:	206-723-8392
105	Alan	Adams	Human Resources	Alan.Adams@ourcompany.com	360-285-8320
106	Ken	Evans	Finance	Ken.Evans@ourcompany.com	360-285-8410
107	Mary	Abernathy	Finance	Mary.Abernathy@ourcompany.com	360-285-8420
				Fax:	360-285-8491

FIGURE 2-5

Relation with Variable-
Length Column Values

EmployeeNumber	FirstName	LastName	Department	EmailAddress	Phone	Comments
101	Mary	Jacobs	Administration	Mary.Jacobs@ourcompany.com	360-285-8110	Company CEO. Completed her MBA in June, 2015.
102	Rosalie	Jackson	Administration	Rosalie.Jackson@ourcompany.com	360-285-8120	
103	Richard	Bandalone	Legal	Richard.Bandalone@ourcompany.com	360-285-8210	Partner at Able, Bandalone and Conerstone. Company counsel on a retainer basis.
104	George	Smith	Human Resources	George.Smith@ourcompany.com	360-285-8310	
105	Alan	Adams	Human Resources	Alan.Adams@ourcompany.com	360-285-8320	
106	Ken	Evans	Finance	Ken.Evans@ourcompany.com	360-285-8410	
107	Mary	Abernathy	Finance	Mary.Abernathy@ourcompany.com	360-285-8420	

A Note on Presenting Relation Structures

Throughout this book, when we write out the relation structure of a relation that we are discussing, we use the following format:

RELATION_NAME (Column01, Column02,…, LastColumn)

The relation name is written first, and it is written in all capital (uppercase) letters (for example, EMPLOYEE), and the name is singular, not plural (EMPLOYEE, not EMPLOYEES). If the relation name is a combination of two or more words, we join the words with an underscore (for example, EMPLOYEE_PROJECT_ASSIGNMENT). Column names are contained in parentheses and are written with an initial capital letter followed by lowercase letters (for example, Department). If the column name is a combination of two or more words, the first letter of each word is capitalized (for example, EmployeeNumber and LastName). Thus, the EMPLOYEE relation shown in Figure 2-2 would be written as:

EMPLOYEE (EmployeeNumber, FirstName, LastName, Department,
   EmailAddress, Phone)

Relation structures, such as the one shown earlier, are part of a database schema. A **database schema** is the design on which a database and its associated applications are built.

A Note on Terminology

In the database world, people generally use the terms *table* and *relation* interchangeably. Accordingly, from now on this book does the same. Thus, any time we use the term *table* we mean a table that meets the characteristics required for a relation. Keep in mind, however, that, strictly speaking, some tables are not relations.

Sometimes, especially in traditional data processing, people use the term **file** instead of *table*. When they do so, they use the term **record** for *row* and the term **field** for *column*. To further confound the issue, database theoreticians sometimes use yet another set of terms: Although they do call a table a *relation*, they call a *row* a **tuple** (rhymes with *couple*) and a *column* an **attribute**. These three sets of terminology are summarized in Figure 2-6.

To make matters even more confusing, people often mix up these sets of terms. It is not unusual to hear someone refer to a relation that has rows and fields. As long as you know what is intended, this mixing of terms is not important.

We should discuss one other source of confusion. According to Figure 2-1, a table that has duplicate rows is not a relation. However, in practice this condition is often ignored.

FIGURE 2-6

Equivalent Sets of
Terms

Table	Row	Column
File	Record	Field
Relation	Tuple	Attribute

Sometimes when manipulating relations with a DBMS, we may end up with a table that has duplicate rows. To make that table a relation, we should eliminate the duplicates. On a large table, however, checking for duplication can be time-consuming. Therefore, the default behavior for DBMS products is not to check for duplicate rows. Hence, in practice, tables might exist with duplicate (nonunique) rows that are still called relations. You will see examples of this situation in the next chapter.

TYPES OF KEYS

A **key** is one or more columns of a relation that is used to identify a row. A key can be **unique** or **nonunique**. For example, for the EMPLOYEE relation in Figure 2-2, EmployeeNumber is a *unique key* because a data value of EmployeeNumber identifies a unique row. Thus, a query to display all employees having an EmployeeNumber of 200 will produce a single row. In contrast, Department is a *nonunique key*. It is a key because it is used to identify a row, but it is nonunique because a data value of Department potentially identifies more than one row. Thus, a query to display all rows having a Department value of Accounting will produce several rows.

From the data in Figure 2-2, it appears that EmployeeNumber, LastName, and EmailAddress are all unique identifiers. However, to decide whether this is true, database developers must do more than examine sample data. Instead, they must ask the users or other subject-matter experts whether a certain column is unique. The column LastName is an example where this is important. It might turn out that the sample data just happen to have unique values for LastName. The users, however, might say that LastName is not always unique.

Composite Keys

A key that contains two or more attributes is called a **composite key**. For example, suppose that we are looking for a unique key for the EMPLOYEE relation, and the users say that although LastName is not unique, the combination of LastName and Department is unique. Thus, for some reason the users know that two people with the same last name will never work in the same department. Two Johnsons, for example, will never work in accounting. If that is the case, then the combination (LastName, Department) is a unique composite key.

Alternatively, the users may know that the combination (LastName, Department) is not unique but that the combination (FirstName, LastName, Department) is unique. The latter combination, then, is a composite key with three attributes.

Composite keys, like one-column keys, can be unique or nonunique.

Candidate and Primary Keys

Candidate keys are keys that uniquely identify each row in a relation. Candidate keys can be single-column keys, or they can be composite keys. The **primary key** is the candidate key that is chosen as the key that the DBMS will use to uniquely identify each row in a relation. For example, suppose that we have the following EMPLOYEE relation:

EMPLOYEE (EmployeeNumber, FirstName, LastName, Department, EmailAddress, Phone)

The users tell us that EmployeeNumber is a unique key, that EmailAddress is a unique key, and that the composite key (FirstName, LastName, DepartmentName) is a unique key. Therefore, we have three candidate keys. When designing the database, we choose one of the candidate keys to be the primary key. In this case, for example, we use EmployeeNumber as the primary key.

> **BTW**
>
> It may help you to understand why the unique keys that could be used as the main identifier for the relation are referred to as candidate keys if you think of them as the "candidates" in the running to be elected "primary key"—but remember that only one candidate will win the election. Any "losing" candidate keys will still be present in the relation, and each will be known as an **alternate key**.

The primary key is important not only because it can be used to identify unique rows but also because it can be used to represent rows in relationships. Although we did not indicate it in the Art Course Database tables in Figure 1-12 in Chapter 1, CustomerNumber was the primary key of CUSTOMER. As such, we used CustomerNumber to represent the relationship between CUSTOMER and ENROLLMENT by placing CustomerNumber as a column in the ENROLLMENT table to create the link between the two tables. In addition, many DBMS products use values of the primary key to organize storage for the relation. They also build indexes and other special structures for fast retrieval of rows using primary key values.

In this book, we indicate primary keys by underlining them. Because EmployeeNumber is the primary key of EMPLOYEE, we write the EMPLOYEE relation as:

EMPLOYEE (EmployeeNumber, FirstName, LastName, Department, EmailAddress, Phone)

To function properly, a primary key, whether it is a single column or a composite key, must have unique data values inserted into every row of the table. While this fact may seem obvious, it is significant enough to be named the **entity integrity constraint** and is a fundamental requirement for the proper functioning of a relational database.

> **BTW**
>
> What do you do if a table has no candidate keys? In that case, define the primary key as the collection of all the columns in the table. Because there are no duplicate rows in a stored relation, the combination of all the columns of the table will always be unique. Again, although tables generated by SQL manipulation may have duplicate rows, the tables that you design to be stored should never be constructed to have data duplication. Thus, the combination of all columns is always a candidate key.

Each DBMS program has its own way of creating and indicating a primary key. In the section "Working with Microsoft Access" of Chapter 1, we briefly discussed primary keys and explained

FIGURE 2-7

Defining a Primary Key in Microsoft Access 2019

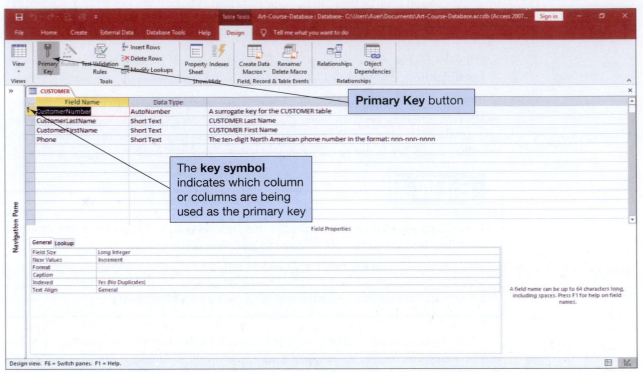

Access 2019, Windows 10, Microsoft Corporation.

how to set a primary key in Microsoft Access 2019. Figure 2-7 shows the CUSTOMER table from the Art Course database in Figure 1-12 in the Microsoft Access table Design view. In table Design view, we can spot the primary key of the table by finding the key symbol next to the names of the columns in the primary key. In this case, a key symbol is located next to CustomerNumber, which means that the developer has defined CustomerNumber as the primary key for this table.

Figure 2-8 shows the same CUSTOMER table in Oracle's MySQL Community Server 8.0,[2] as seen in the MySQL Workbench graphical utility program. This display is more complex than Microsoft Access, but we can spot the primary key of the table by finding the key symbol next to the name(s) of the primary key column(s) in the Column Name list. For a complete discussion of primary keys in MySQL, see Extension A, "Working with MySQL."

In Figure 2-8, the table names are often listed with *dbo* preceding the table name, as in dbo.CUSTOMER. The dbo stands for *database owner*, and it occurs frequently in SQL Server.

---

[2]On February 26, 2008, Sun Microsystems acquired MySQL from MySQL AB. On April 29, 2009, Oracle Corporation made an offer to buy Sun Microsystems, and on January 27, 2010, Oracle completed its acquisition of Sun Microsystems. For more details, see www.oracle.com/us/sun/index.htm. This makes Oracle the owner of both the Oracle Database and the MySQL DBMS. As of this writing, MySQL 8.0 is the latest production version of the popular MySQL DBMS. The free MySQL Community Server edition and the MySQL Workbench can be downloaded from the MySQL Web site at http://dev.mysql.com/downloads/. If you are running a Microsoft Windows OS, you should download and use the MySQL Installer for Windows available at **http://dev.mysql.com/downloads/windows/installer/**. MySQL is an enterprise-class DBMS and, as such, is much more complex than Microsoft Access. Also, like other enterprise-class DBMS products, MySQL does not include application development tools, such as form and report generators. For more information and an in-depth introduction to MySQL, see Extension A, "Working with MySQL."

FIGURE 2-8

Defining a Primary Key in MySQL 8.0

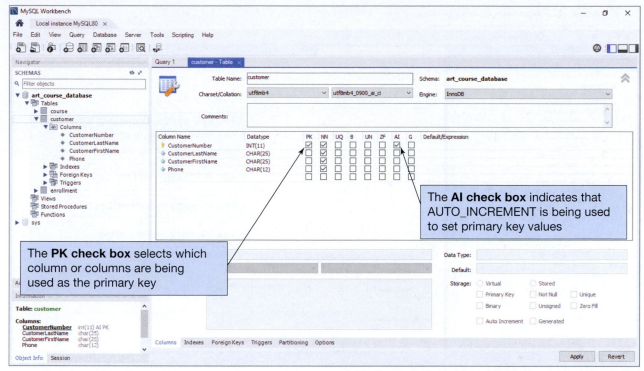

MySQL Community Server 8.0, MySQL Workbench, Oracle Corporation.

Figure 2-9 shows the same CUSTOMER table in Microsoft SQL Server 2017,[3] as it appears in the Microsoft SQL Server Management Studio graphical utility program. This display is more complex, but again we can spot the primary key of the table by finding the key symbol next to the names of the columns in the primary key. Again, there is a key symbol next to CustomerNumber, indicating that CustomerNumber is the primary key for this table.

Figure 2-10 shows the same CUSTOMER table in Oracle's Oracle Database XE (also known as Oracle Database 18c Express Edition),[4] as seen in the Oracle SQL Developer

---

[3]Microsoft has released various versions of SQL Server, and the latest version is SQL Server 2017. We recommend using the now freely downloadable SQL Server 2017 Developer Edition, which is for single user, non-production use. SQL Server 2017 Express is the least powerful version available, but it is intended for general production use and can be downloaded for free from the Microsoft SQL Server 2017 Express homepage at **www.microsoft.com/en-us/server-cloud/products/sql-server/#fbid=LO4TSseuGs9**. SQL Server is an enterprise-class DBMS and, as such, is much more complex than Microsoft Access. And like most enterprise-class DBMS products, SQL Server does not include application development tools, such as form and report generators. For more information and an in-depth introduction to Microsoft SQL Server, see David M. Kroenke, David J. Auer, Scott L. Vandenberg, and Robert C. Yoder, *Database Processing: Fundamentals, Design, and Implementation,* 15th ed. (Upper Saddle River, NJ: Pearson, 2019).

[4]Originally just referred to as *Oracle*, the database product is now known as Oracle Database because Oracle Corporation has grown far beyond its database product roots and now owns and sells a large range of products. These can be seen at **www.oracle.com**. As of this writing, Oracle Database 12c Release 2 is the latest production version. The freely downloadable Oracle Database XE (Oracle Database Express Edition 11g Release 2) is available at **www.oracle.com/technetwork/database/database-technologies/express-edition/downloads/index.html?ssSourceSiteId=ocomen**. Oracle Database XE is an enterprise-class DBMS and, as such, is much more complex than Microsoft Access. And like most enterprise-class DBMS products, Oracle Database does not include application development tools, such as form and report generators. For more information and an in-depth introduction to Oracle Database, see David M. Kroenke, David J. Auer, Scott L. Vandenberg, and Robert C. Yoder, *Database Processing: Fundamentals, Design, and Implementation,* 15th ed. (Upper Saddle River, NJ: Pearson, 2019).

FIGURE 2-9

Defining a Primary Key in Microsoft SQL Server 2017

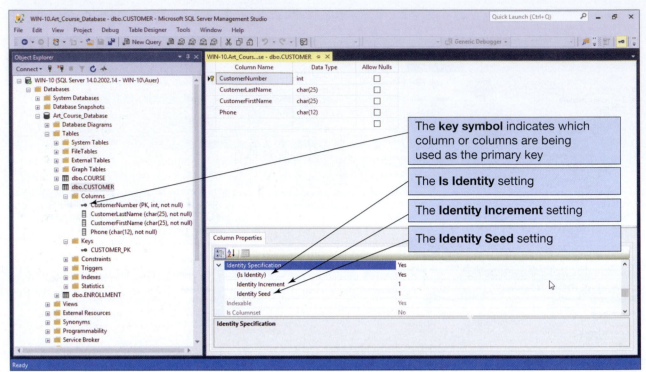

SQL Server 2017, SQL Server Management Studio, Microsoft Corporation.

FIGURE 2-10

Defining a Primary Key in Oracle Database XE

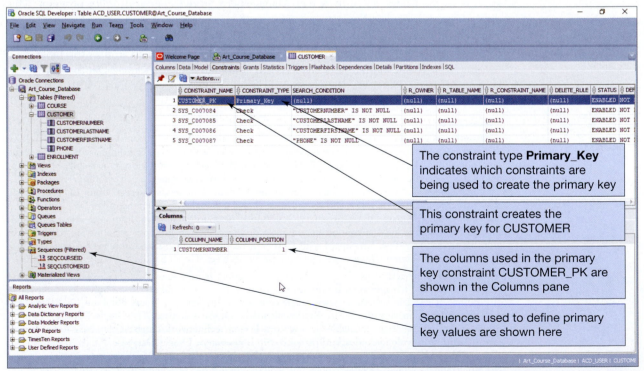

Oracle Database XE, SQL Developer 18.4, Oracle Corporation.

graphical utility program. This display is more complex than Microsoft Access, but we can spot the primary key of the table by finding the row with the term Primary_Key in the CONSTRAINT_TYPE column, and then selecting that row. When we do so, the set of primary key columns is displayed in the tabbed Columns pane.

A common method of specifying primary keys is to use SQL, which we briefly introduced in Chapter 1. We will see how SQL is used to designate primary keys in Chapter 3.

Surrogate Keys

A **surrogate key** is a column with a unique, DBMS-assigned identifier that has been added to a table to be the primary key. The unique values of the surrogate key are assigned by the DBMS each time a row is created, and the values never change.

An ideal primary key is short and numeric and never changes. Sometimes one column in a table will meet these requirements or come close to them. For example, EmployeeNumber in the EMPLOYEE relation should work very well as a primary key. But in other tables, the primary key does not come close to being ideal. For example, consider the relation PROPERTY:

PROPERTY (Street, City, State, ZIP, OwnerID)

The primary key of PROPERTY is (Street, City, State, ZIP), which is long and nonnumeric (although it probably will not change). This is not an ideal primary key. In cases like this, the database designer will add a surrogate key, such as PropertyID:

PROPERTY (PropertyID, Street, City, State, ZIP, OwnerID)

Surrogate keys are short and numeric and never change—they are ideal primary keys. Because the values of the surrogate primary key will have no inherent meaning to users, they are often hidden on forms, query results, and reports.

Surrogate keys have been used in the databases we have already discussed. For example, in the Art Course Database tables shown in Figure 1-12 we added the surrogate keys CustomerNumber to the CUSTOMER table and CourseNumber to the COURSE table.

Most DBMS products have a facility for automatically generating key values. In Figure 2-7, we can see how surrogate keys are defined with Microsoft Access 2019. In Microsoft Access, Data Type is set to AutoNumber. With this specification, Microsoft Access assigns a value of 1 to CustomerNumber for the first row of CUSTOMER, a value of 2 to CustomerNumber for the second row, and so forth.

Enterprise-class DBMS products, such as MySQL, Microsoft SQL Server, and Oracle Database, offer more capability. For example, MySQL uses the **AUTO_INCREMENT** function to automatically assign surrogate key numbers. In AUTO_INCREMENT, the starting value can be any value (the default is 1), but the increment will always be 1. Figure 2-8 shows that CustomerNumber is a surrogate key for CUSTOMER that uses AUTO_INCREMENT (AI) to set the value of the column.

With SQL Server, the developer can specify the starting value of the surrogate key as well as the amount by which to increment the key for each new row. Figure 2-9 shows how this is done for the definition of the surrogate key CustomerNumber for the CUSTOMER table. In the Column Properties window, which is below the dbo.CUSTOMER table column details window, there is a set of **identity** specifications that have been set to indicate to SQL Server that a surrogate key column exists. The **is identity** value for CustomerNumber is set to Yes to make CustomerNumber a surrogate key. The starting value of the surrogate key is called the **identity seed**. For CustomerNumber, it is set to 1. Furthermore, the amount that is added to each key value to create the next key value is called the **identity increment**. In this example, it is set to 1. These settings mean that when the user creates the first row of the CUSTOMER table, SQL Server will give the value 1 to CustomerNumber. When the second row of CUSTOMER is created, SQL Server will give the value 2 to CustomerNumber, and so forth.

Oracle Database uses a **SEQUENCE** function to define automatically increasing sequences of numbers that can be used as surrogate key numbers. When using a SEQUENCE, the starting value can be any value (the default is 1), but the increment will always be 1. Figure 2-10 shows the existing sequences in the Art Course Database.

Foreign Keys and Referential Integrity

As described in Chapter 1, we place values from one relation into a second relation to represent a relationship. The values we use are the primary key values (including composite primary key values, when necessary) of the first relation. When we do this, the attribute in the second relation that holds these values is referred to as a **foreign key**. For example, in the Art Course database shown in Figure 1-12 we represent the relationship between customers and the art courses they are taking by placing CustomerNumber, the primary key of CUSTOMER, into the ENROLLMENT relation. In this case, CustomerID in ENROLLMENT is referred to as a foreign key. This term is used because CustomerNumber is the primary key of a relation that is foreign to the table in which it resides.

Consider the following two relations, where besides the EMPLOYEE relation, we now have a DEPARTMENT relation to hold data about departments:

EMPLOYEE (<u>EmployeeNumber</u>, FirstName, LastName, Department,
   EmailAddress, Phone)

and:

DEPARTMENT (<u>DepartmentName</u>, BudgetCode, OfficeNumber,
   DepartmentPhone)

where EmployeeNumber and DepartmentName are the primary keys of EMPLOYEE and DEPARTMENT, respectively.

Now, suppose that Department in EMPLOYEE contains the names of the departments in which employees work and that DepartmentName in DEPARTMENT also contains these names. In this case, Department in EMPLOYEE is said to be a foreign key to DEPARTMENT. In this book, we denote foreign keys by displaying them in italics. Thus, we would write these two relation descriptions as follows:

EMPLOYEE (<u>EmployeeNumber</u>, FirstName, LastName, *Department*,
   EmailAddress, Phone)

and:

DEPARTMENT (<u>DepartmentName</u>, BudgetCode, OfficeNumber,
   DepartmentPhone)

Note that the primary key and the foreign key do not need to have the same column name. The only requirement is that they have the same set of values.

In most cases, ensuring that every value of a foreign key matches a value of the primary key is important. In the previous example, the value of Department in every row of EMPLOYEE should match a value of DepartmentName in DEPARTMENT. If this is the case (and it usually is), then we declare the following rule:

Department in EMPLOYEE must exist in DepartmentName in DEPARTMENT

Such a rule is called a **referential integrity constraint**. Whenever you see a foreign key, you should always look for an associated referential integrity constraint.

Consider the Art Course database shown in Figure 1-12. The structure of this database is:

CUSTOMER (<u>CustomerNumber</u>, CustomerLastName, CustomerFirstName, Phone)

COURSE (<u>CourseNumber</u>, Course, CourseDate, Fee)

ENROLLMENT (<u>*CustomerNumber*</u>, <u>*CourseNumber*</u>, AmountPaid)

The ENROLLMENT table has a composite primary key of (CustomerNumber, CourseNumber), where CustomerNumber is a foreign key linking to CUSTOMER and CourseNumber is a foreign key linking to COURSE. Therefore, two referential integrity constraints are required:

CustomerNumber in ENROLLMENT must exist in CustomerNumber in
    CUSTOMER

and:

CourseNumber in ENROLLMENT must exist in CourseNumber in COURSE

Just as DBMS products have a means of specifying primary keys, they also have a way to set up foreign key referential integrity constraints. We discuss the details of setting up referential integrity constraints in this chapter's section of "Working with Microsoft Access." Figure 2-11 shows the tables from the Art Course database in Figure 1-12 in the Microsoft Access Relationships window and with the Edit Relationships dialog box showing the details of the relationship between CUSTOMER and ENROLLMENT. Notice that the Enforce Referential Integrity check box is checked, so the referential integrity constraint

FIGURE 2-11

Enforcing Referential Integrity in Microsoft Access 2019

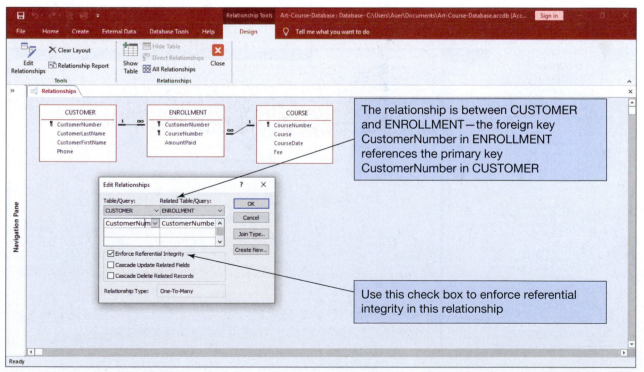

Access 2019, Windows 10, Microsoft Corporation.

FIGURE 2-12

Enforcing Referential Integrity in MySQL 8.0

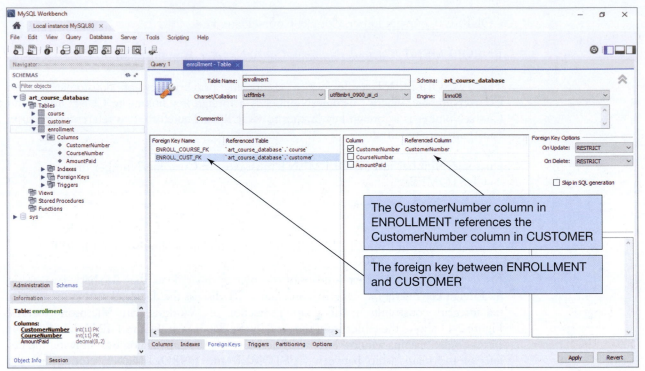

MySQL Community Server 8.0, MySQL Workbench, Oracle Corporation.

FIGURE 2-13

Enforcing Referential Integrity in Microsoft SQL Server 2017

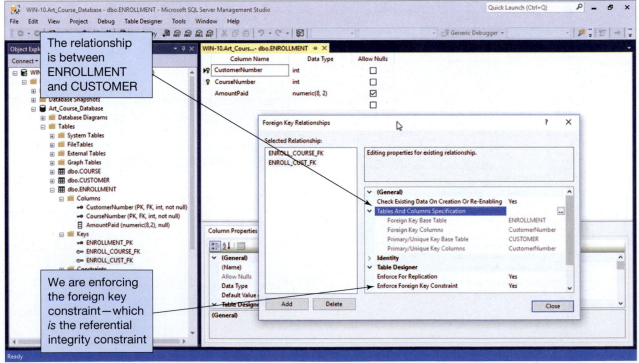

SQL Server 2017, SQL Server Management Studio, Microsoft Corporation.

FIGURE 2-14

Enforcing Referential Integrity in Oracle Database XE

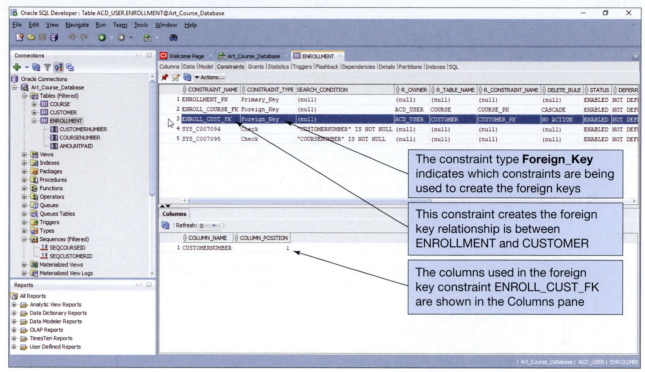

Oracle Database XE, SQL Developer 18.4, Oracle Corporation.

between CustomerNumber in ENROLLMENT (the foreign key) and CustomerNumber in CUSTOMER (the primary key) is being enforced.

Figure 2-12 shows foreign keys in MySQL 8.0 Community Server. Here the Foreign Keys tab in the MySQL Workbench utility displays the properties of each foreign key.

Figure 2-13 shows the same foreign key relationship between CUSTOMER and ENROLLMENT in the Microsoft SQL Server Management Studio program. Again, this display is more complex, but notice that the property Table Designer: Enforce Foreign Key Constraint is set to Yes. This means that the referential integrity constraint between CustomerNumber in ENROLLMENT (the foreign key) and CustomerNumber in CUSTOMER (the primary key) is being enforced.

Figure 2-14 shows foreign keys in Oracle Database XE. Here the Constraints tab in the Oracle SQL Developer utility displays the properties of each foreign key.

Just as SQL can be used to specify primary keys, it can also be used to set referential integrity constraints. We will look at how to use SQL to do this in the next chapter.

THE PROBLEM OF NULL VALUES

Before we leave the discussion of relations and the relationships between them, we need to discuss a subtle but important topic: null values. A **null value** is a missing value in a cell in a relation. Consider the following relation, which is used to track finished goods for an apparel manufacturer:

ITEM (<u>ItemNumber</u>, ItemName, Color, Quantity)

FIGURE 2-15

Sample ITEM Relation
and Data

ItemNumber	ItemName	Color	Quantity
110	T-shirt, Small	Red	15
111	T-shirt, Small	Blue	25
115	T-shirt, Small	Green	22
120	T-shirt, Medium	Red	45
125	T-shirt, Medium	Green	52
310	Baseball Cap, Fits All	Red	38
311	Baseball Cap, Fits All	Blue	54
400	Spring Hat		120

Figure 2-15 shows sample data for this table. Notice that in the last row of data—the row with ItemNumber 400 and ItemName Spring Hat—there is no value for Color. The problem with null values is that they are ambiguous; we do not know how to interpret them because three possible meanings can be construed. First, it might mean that no value of Color is appropriate; Spring Hats do not come in different colors. Second, it might mean that the value is known to be blank; that is, Spring Hats have a color, but the color has not yet been decided. Maybe the color is established by placing ribbons around the hats, but this is not done until an order arrives. Finally, the null value might mean that the hats' color is simply unknown; the hats have a color, but no one has checked yet to see what it is.

You can eliminate null values by requiring an attribute value. DBMS products allow you to specify whether a null value can occur in a column. We discussed how to do this for Microsoft Access in the section "Working with Microsoft Access" of Chapter 1. For Microsoft SQL Server 2017, notice the column in the dbo.CUSTOMER table column details window labeled *Allow Nulls* in Figure 2-8. A check box without a check mark means that null values are not allowed in this column. Note that, in Figure 2-9, the Oracle SQL Developer utility for Oracle Database XE is showing the data on the Constraints tab, and this tab does not indicate null values. If, however, we looked at the Columns tab, we would see whether null values are allowed in each column. For MySQL 8.0 Community Server, note that in Figure 2-10 the Column Details tab in the MySQL Table Editor shows an NN (NOT NULL) check box that indicates whether null values are allowed in the column. Regardless of the DBMS being used, if nulls are not allowed, then some value must be entered for each row in the table. If the attribute is a text value, users can be allowed to enter values such as "not appropriate," "undecided," or "unknown," when necessary. If the attribute is not text, then some other coding system can be developed.

For now, be aware that null values can occur and that they always carry some ambiguity. Chapter 3 will show another, possibly more serious, problem of null values.

TO KEY OR NOT TO KEY—THAT IS THE QUESTION!

Again, as defined by Codd, the rows of a relation must be unique (no two rows may be identical), but there is no requirement for a designated *primary* key in the relation. Recall that we described a *primary key* as a column (or columns) with a set of values that uniquely identify each row.

However, the requirement that no two rows be identical *implies* that a primary key can be defined for the relation. Further, in the "real world" of databases, every relation (or table as it is more often referred to in daily use) *does* have a defined primary key.

To understand how to designate or assign a primary key for a relation, we need to learn about the different types of keys used in relational databases, and this means we need to learn about functional dependencies, which are the foundation upon which keys are built. We will then discuss specifically how to assign primary keys in relations.

We have defined three constraints so far in our discussion:

- The *domain integrity constraint*
- The *entity integrity constraint*
- The *referential integrity constraint*

The purpose of these three constraints, taken as a whole, is to create **database integrity**, which means that the data in our database will be useful, meaningful data.[5]

FUNCTIONAL DEPENDENCIES AND NORMALIZATION

This section introduces some of the concepts used for relational database design; these concepts are used in the next several chapters and expanded upon in Chapter 5. This book presents only the essentials. To learn more, you should consult other, more comprehensive references.[6]

Functional Dependencies

To get started, let us take a short excursion into the world of algebra. Suppose you are buying boxes of cookies, and someone tells you that each box costs $5. Knowing this fact, you can compute the cost of several boxes with the formula:

$$CookieCost = NumberOfBoxes \times \$5$$

A more general way to express the relationship between CookieCost and NumberOfBoxes is to say that CookieCost depends on NumberOfBoxes. Such a statement tells the character of the relationship between CookieCost and NumberOfBoxes, even though it doesn't give the formula. More formally, we can say that CookieCost is **functionally dependent** on NumberOfBoxes. Such a statement, which is called a **functional dependency**, can be written as follows:

$$NumberOfBoxes \rightarrow CookieCost$$

This expression says that NumberOfBoxes determines CookieCost. The term on the left, NumberOfBoxes, is called the **determinant**.

Using another example, we can compute the extended price of a part order by multiplying the quantity of the item by its unit price:

$$ExtendedPrice = Quantity \times UnitPrice$$

---

[5]For more information and discussion, see the Wikipedia article on **data integrity** at **http://en.wikipedia.org/wiki/Data_integrity** and the articles linked to that article.

[6]See David M. Kroenke, David J. Auer, Scott L. Vandenberg, and Robert C. Yoder, *Database Processing: Fundamentals, Design, and Implementation*, 15th ed. (Upper Saddle River, NJ: Prentice Hall, 2019), and C. J. Date, *An Introduction to Database Systems*, 8th ed. (Boston: Addison-Wesley, 2004).

FIGURE 2-16

Sample OBJECT
Relation and Data

Object Color	Weight	Shape
Red	5	Ball
Blue	5	Cube
Yellow	7	Cube

In this case, we would say that ExtendedPrice is functionally dependent on Quantity and UnitPrice, or:

(Quantity, UnitPrice) → ExtendedPrice

The composite (Quantity, UnitPrice) is the determinant of ExtendedPrice.

Now, let us expand these ideas. Suppose you know that a sack contains either red, blue, or yellow objects. Further suppose you know that the red objects weigh 5 pounds each, the blue objects weigh 5 pounds each, and the yellow objects weigh 7 pounds each. If a friend looks into the sack, sees an object, and tells you the color of the object, you can tell the weight of the object. We can formalize this in the same way as in the previous example:

ObjectColor → Weight

Thus, we can say that Weight is functionally dependent on ObjectColor and that ObjectColor determines Weight. The relationship here does not involve an equation, but this functional dependency is still true. Given a value for ObjectColor, you can determine the object's weight.

In addition, if we know that the red objects are balls, the blue objects are cubes, and the yellow objects are cubes, then:

ObjectColor → Shape

Thus, ObjectColor also determines Shape. We can put these two together and state:

ObjectColor → (Weight, Shape)

Thus, ObjectColor determines Weight and Shape.

Another way to represent these facts is to put them into a table, as shown in Figure 2-16. Note that this table meets all the conditions in our definition of a relation, as listed in Figure 2-1, so we can refer to it as a relation. If we call it the OBJECT relation and use ObjectColor as the primary key, we can write this relation as:

OBJECT (ObjectColor, Weight, Shape)

Now, you may be thinking that we have just performed some trick or sleight of hand to arrive at a relation, but one can make the argument that the only reason for having relations is to store instances of functional dependencies. Consider a relation such as the CUSTOMER relation from the Art Course database in Figure 1-12:

CUSTOMER (CustomerNumber, CustomerLastName, CustomerFirstName, Phone)

Here we are simply storing facts that express the following functional dependency:

CustomerNumber → (CustomerLastName, CustomerFirstName, Phone)

Perhaps the easiest way to understand functional dependencies is:

If I tell you one specific fact, can you respond with a unique associated fact?

Using the OBJECT relation in Figure 2-16, if I tell you that the ObjectColor is Red, can you uniquely tell me the associated Shape? Yes, you can, and it is Ball. Therefore, ObjectColor determines Shape, and a functional dependency exists with ObjectColor as the determinant.

Now, if I tell you that the Shape is Cube, can you uniquely tell me the associated ObjectColor? No, you cannot because it could be either Blue or Yellow. Therefore, Shape *does not determine* ObjectColor, and ObjectColor is not functionally dependent on Shape.

Primary and Candidate Keys Revisited

Now that we have discussed the concept of functional dependency, we can define primary and candidate keys more formally. Specifically, a primary key of a relation can be defined as "one or more attributes that functionally determine all the other attributes of the relation." The same definition holds for candidate keys as well.

Recall the EMPLOYEE relation from Figure 2-2 (shown without primary or foreign keys indicated):

EMPLOYEE (EmployeeNumber, FirstName, LastName, Department, EmailAddress, Phone)

As previously discussed, based on information from users, this relation has three candidate keys: EmployeeNumber, EmailAddress, and the composite (FirstName, LastName, Department). Because this is so, we can state the following:

EmployeeNumber → (FirstName, LastName, Department, EmailAddress, Phone)

Equivalently stated in words, if we are given a value for EmployeeNumber, we can determine FirstName, LastName, Department, EmailAddress, and Phone. Similarly, we can state that:

EmailAddress → (EmployeeNumber, FirstName, LastName, Department, Phone)

That is, if we are given a value for EmailAddress, we can determine EmployeeNumber, FirstName, LastName, Department, and Phone. Finally, we also can state that:

(FirstName, LastName, Department) → (EmployeeNumber, EmailAddress, Phone)

This means that if we are given values of FirstName, LastName, and Department, we can determine EmployeeNumber, EmailAddress, and Phone.

These three functional dependencies express the reason the three candidate keys are candidate keys. When we choose a primary key from the candidate keys, we are choosing which functional dependency we want to define as the one that is most meaningful or important to us.

Normalization

The concepts of functional dependencies and determinants can be used to help in the design of relations. Recalling the concept from Chapter 1 that a table or relation should have only one theme, we can define **normalization** as the process of (or set of steps for) breaking a table or relation with more than one theme into a set of tables such that each has only one theme. Normalization is a complex topic, and it consumes one or more chapters of more theoretically oriented database books. Here we reduce this topic to a few ideas that capture the essence of the process. After this discussion, if you are interested in the topic, you should consult the references mentioned earlier for more information.

The problem that normalization addresses is as follows: A table can meet all the characteristics listed in Figure 2-1 and still have the modification problems we identified for lists in Chapter 1. Specifically, consider the following ADVISER_LIST relation:

ADVISER_LIST (AdviserID, AdviserName, Department, Phone, Office, StudentNumber, StudentName)

What is the primary key of this relation? Given the definitions of candidate key and primary key, it has to be an attribute that determines all the other attributes. The only attribute that has this characteristic is StudentNumber. Given a value of StudentNumber, we can determine the values of all the other attributes:

StudentNumber → (AdviserID, AdviserName, Department, Phone, Office, StudentName)

We can then write this relation as follows:

ADVISER_LIST (AdviserID, AdviserName, Department, Phone, Office, <u>StudentNumber</u>, StudentName)

However, this table has modification problems. Specifically, an adviser's data are repeated many times in the table, once for each advisee. This means that updates to adviser data might need to be made multiple times. If, for example, an adviser changes offices, that change will need to be completed in all the rows for the person's advisees. If an adviser has 20 advisees, that change will need to be entered 20 times.

Another modification problem can occur when we delete a student from this list. If we delete a student who is the only advisee for an adviser, we will delete not only the student's data but also the adviser's data. Thus, we will unintentionally lose facts about two entities while attempting to delete one.

If you look closely at this relation, you will see a functional dependency that involves the adviser's data. Specifically:

AdviserID → (AdviserName, Department, Phone, Office)

Now, we can state the problem with this relation more accurately—in terms of functional dependencies. Specifically, this relation is poorly formed because it has a functional dependency that does not involve the primary key. Stated differently, AdviserID is a determinant of a functional dependency, but it is not a candidate key and thus cannot be the primary key under any circumstances.

Relational Design Principles

From the discussion so far, we can formulate the following design principles for what we can call a **well-formed relation**:

1. For a relation to be considered well formed, every determinant must be a candidate key.
2. Any relation that is not well formed should be broken into two or more relations that are well formed.

These two principles are the heart of normalization—the process of examining relations and modifying them to make them well formed. This process is called *normalization* because you can categorize the problems to which relations are susceptible into different types called *normal forms*.

There are many defined normal forms. Technically, our well-formed relations are those that are said to be in **Boyce-Codd Normal Form (BCNF)**. Another example of a normal form, a relation is in **first normal form (1NF)** if it:

- has the characteristics listed in Figure 2-1, and
- has a defined primary key, and
- no **repeating groups**.

The statement that 1NF has "no repeating groups" refers to what are known as *multivalued dependencies*, and this occurs when there are multiple values of a data item such as the multiple phone numbers shown in Figure 2-3.

To simplify the discussion of normal forms, we will put off our discussion of multivalued dependencies until later in this chapter. Thus, in our initial 1NF examples, there are no "repeating groups" that we have to worry about. After our discussion of multivalued dependencies and the associated **multivalue, multicolumn problem**, you will have no trouble spotting and dealing with repeating groups and 1NF.

Besides first normal form and Boyce-Codd normal form, other normal forms exist, such as second, third, fourth, fifth, and domain/key normal form. We further describe normal forms later in this chapter.

However, if we simply follow the aforementioned BCNF design principles we will avoid almost all the problems associated with non-normalized tables. In some rare instances, these principles do not address the problems that arise (see Exercises 2.40 and 2.41), but if you follow these principles, you will be safe most of the time.

The Normalization Process

We can apply the principles just described to formulate the following **normalization process** for normalizing relations:

1. Identify all the candidate keys of the relation.
2. Identify all the functional dependencies in the relation.

FIGURE 2-17

Sample PRESCRIPTION Relation and Data

PrescriptionNumber	Date	Drug	Dosage	CustomerName	CustomerPhone	CustomerEmailAddress
P10001	10/17/2019	DrugA	10mg	Smith, Alvin	575-523-2233	ASmith@somewhere.com
P10003	10/17/2019	DrugB	35mg	Rhodes, Jeff	575-645-3455	JRhodes@somewhere.com
P10004	10/17/2019	DrugA	20mg	Smith, Sarah	575-523-2233	SSmith@somewhere.com
P10007	10/18/2019	DrugC	20mg	Frye, Michael	575-645-4566	MFrye@somewhere.com
P10010	10/18/2019	DrugB	30mg	Rhodes, Jeff	575-645-3455	JRhodes@somewhere.com

3. Examine the determinants of the functional dependencies. If any determinant is not a candidate key, the relation is not well formed. In this case:
   a. Place the columns of the functional dependency in a new relation of their own.
   b. Make the determinant of the functional dependency the primary key of the new relation.
   c. Leave a copy of the determinant as a foreign key in the original relation.
   d. Create a referential integrity constraint between the original relation and the new relation.
4. Repeat step 3 as many times as necessary until every determinant of every relation is a candidate key.

To understand this process, consider the following relation:

PRESCRIPTION (PrescriptionNumber, Date, Drug, Dosage, CustomerName, CustomerPhone, CustomerEmailAddress)

Sample data for the PRESCRIPTION relation are shown in Figure 2-17.

Step 1 of the Normalization Process   According to the normalization process, we first identify all candidate keys. PrescriptionNumber clearly determines Date, Drug, and Dosage. If we assume that a prescription is for only one person, then it also determines CustomerName, CustomerPhone, and CustomerEmailAddress. By law, prescriptions must be for only one person, so PrescriptionNumber is a candidate key.

Does this relation have other candidate keys? Date, Drug, and Dosage do not determine PrescriptionNumber because many prescriptions can be written on a given date, many prescriptions can be written for a given drug, and many prescriptions can be written for a given dosage.

What about customer columns? If a customer had only one prescription, then we could say that some identifying customer column—for example, CustomerEmailAddress—would determine the prescription data. However, people can have more than one prescription, so this assumption is invalid.

Given this analysis, the only candidate key of PRESCRIPTION is PrescriptionNumber.

Step 2 of the Normalization Process   In step 2 of the normalization process, we now identify all functional dependencies. PrescriptionNumber determines all the other attributes, as just described. If a drug had only one dosage, then we could state that:

Drug → Dosage

But this is not true because some drugs have several dosages. Therefore, Drug is not a determinant. Furthermore, Dosage is not a determinant because the same dosage can be given for many different drugs.

However, examining the customer columns, we do find a functional dependency:

CustomerEmailAddress → (CustomerName, CustomerPhone)

To know whether a functional dependency is true for a particular application, we need to look beyond the sample data in Figure 2-17 and ask the users. For example, it is possible that some customers share the same email address, and it is also possible that some

CustomerEmailAddress	CustomerName	CustomerPhone
ASmith@somewhere.com	Smith, Alvin	575-523-2233
JRhodes@somewhere.com	Rhodes, Jeff	575-645-3455
MFrye@somewhere.com	Frye, Michael	575-645-4566
SSmith@somewhere.com	Smith, Sarah	575-523-2233

PrescriptionNumber	Date	Drug	Dosage	CustomerEmailAddress
P10001	10/17/2019	DrugA	10mg	ASmith@somewhere.com
P10003	10/17/2019	DrugB	35mg	JRhodes@somewhere.com
P10004	10/17/2019	DrugA	20mg	SSmith@somewhere.com
P10007	10/18/2019	DrugC	20mg	MFrye@somewhere.com
P10010	10/18/2019	DrugB	30mg	JRhodes@somewhere.com

customers do not have email. For now, we can assume that the users say that CustomerEmailAddress is a determinant of the customer attributes.

Step 3 of the Normalization Process   In step 3 of the normalization process, we ask whether there is a determinant that is *not* a candidate key. In this example, CustomerEmailAddress is a determinant and not a candidate key. Therefore, PRESCRIPTION has normalization problems and is not well formed. According to step 3, we split the functional dependency into a relation of its own:

CUSTOMER (<u>CustomerEmailAddress</u>, CustomerName, CustomerPhone)

We make the determinant of the functional dependency, CustomerEmailAddress, the primary key of the new relation.

We leave a copy of CustomerEmailAddress in the original relation as a foreign key. Thus, PRESCRIPTION is now:

PRESCRIPTION (<u>PrescriptionNumber</u>, Date, Drug, Dosage, *CustomerEmailAddress*)

Finally, we create the referential integrity constraint:

CustomerEmailAddress in PRESCRIPTION must exist in CustomerEmailAddress, in
    CUSTOMER

At this point, if we move through the three steps, we find that neither of these relations has a determinant that is not a candidate key, and we can say that the two relations are now normalized. Figure 2-18 shows the result for the sample data.

Normalization Examples

We now illustrate the use of the normalization process with four examples.

Normalization Example 1   The relation in Figure 2-19 shows a table of student residence data named STU_DORM. The first step in normalizing it is to identify all candidate keys. Because StudentNumber determines each of the other columns, it is a candidate key. LastName cannot be a candidate key because two students have the last name Smith. None of the other columns can be a candidate key, either, so StudentNumber is the only candidate key.

Next, in step 2, we look for the functional dependencies in the relation. Besides those for StudentNumber, a functional dependency appears to exist between DormName and DormCost. Again, we would need to check this out with the users. In this case, assume that the functional dependency:

DormName → DormCost

is true and assume that our interview with the users indicates that no other functional dependencies exist.

FIGURE 2-19

Sample STU_DORM
Relation and Data

StudentNumber	LastName	FirstName	DormName	DormCost
100	Smith	Terry	Stephens	3,500.00
200	Johnson	Jeff	Alexander	3,800.00
300	Abernathy	Susan	Horan	4,000.00
400	Smith	Susan	Alexander	3,800.00
500	Wilcox	John	Stephens	3,500.00
600	Webber	Carl	Horan	4,000.00
700	Simon	Carol	Stephens	3,500.00

In step 3, we now ask whether any determinants exist that are not candidate keys. In this example, DormName is a determinant, but it is not a candidate key. Therefore, this relation is not well formed and has normalization problems.

To fix those problems, we place the columns of the functional dependency (DormName, DormCost) into a relation of their own and call that relation DORM. We make the determinant of the functional dependency the primary key. Thus, DormName is the primary key of DORM. We leave the determinant DormName as a foreign key in STU_DORM. Finally, we find the appropriate referential integrity constraint. The result is:

STU_DORM (<u>StudentNumber</u>, LastName, FirstName, *DormName*)

DORM (<u>DormName</u>, DormCost)

with the constraint:

DormName in STU_DORM must exist in DormName in DORM

The data for these relations appear as shown in Figure 2-20.

Normalization Example 2   Now, consider the EMPLOYEE table in Figure 2-21. First, we identify the candidate keys in EMPLOYEE. From the data, it appears that EmployeeNumber and EmailAddress each identify all the other attributes. Hence, they are candidate keys (again, with the proviso that we cannot depend on sample data to show all cases; we must verify this assumption with the users).

In step 2, we identify other functional dependencies. From the data, it appears that there are two other functional dependencies:

Department → DepartmentPhone

and

DepartmentPhone → Department

FIGURE 2-20

Normalized STU_DORM
and DORM Relations
and Data

StudentNumber	LastName	FirstName	DormName
100	Smith	Terry	Stephens
200	Johnson	Jeff	Alexander
300	Abernathy	Susan	Horan
400	Smith	Susan	Alexander
500	Wilcox	John	Stephens
600	Webber	Carl	Horan
700	Simon	Carol	Stephens

DormName	DormCost
Alexander	3,800.00
Horan	4,000.00
Stephens	3,500.00

FIGURE 2-21

Sample EMPLOYEE
Relation and Data

EmployeeNumber	FirstName	LastName	Department	EmailAddress	DepartmentPhone
101	Mary	Jacobs	Administration	Mary.Jacobs@ourcompany.com	360-285-8100
102	Rosalie	Jackson	Administration	Rosalie.Jackson@ourcompany.com	360-285-8100
103	Richard	Bandalone	Legal	Richard.Bandalone@ourcompany.com	360-285-8200
104	George	Smith	Human Resources	George.Smith@ourcompany.com	360-285-8300
105	Alan	Adams	Human Resources	Alan.Adams@ourcompany.com	360-285-8300
106	Ken	Evans	Finance	Ken.Evans@ourcompany.com	360-285-8400
107	Mary	Abernathy	Finance	Mary.Abernathy@ourcompany.com	360-285-8400

EmployeeNumber	FirstName	LastName	Department	EmailAddress
101	Mary	Jacobs	Administration	Mary.Jacobs@ourcompany.com
102	Rosalie	Jackson	Administration	Rosalie.Jackson@ourcompany.com
103	Richard	Bandalone	Legal	Richard.Bandalone@ourcompany.com
104	George	Smith	Human Resources	George.Smith@ourcompany.com
105	Alan	Adams	Human Resources	Alan.Adams@ourcompany.com
106	Ken	Evans	Finance	Ken.Evans@ourcompany.com
107	Mary	Abernathy	Finance	Mary.Abernathy@ourcompany.com

Department	DepartmentPhone
Administration	360-285-8100
Finance	360-285-8400
Human Resources	360-285-8300
Legal	360-285-8200

Assuming that this is true, then according to step 3 we have two determinants, Department and DepartmentPhone, that are not candidate keys. Thus, EMPLOYEE has normalization problems.

To fix those problems, we generally simply place the columns in the extra functional dependencies in tables of their own and make the determinants the primary keys of the new tables. We leave the determinants as foreign keys in the original table.

However, note that the two extraneous functional dependencies are simply the reverse of each other. This often occurs when two columns are functionally dependent on each other. In such a case, we only need to move *one* of the functional dependencies into a new table. The other dependency will be removed as well when we do this. Which one should we move? It really doesn't matter, and we can choose to create the new table based on either functional dependency. Our choice becomes a matter of reasonableness, and in this case it seems more reasonable to make Department the primary key of a new table named DEPARTMENT.

The result is the two tables:

EMPLOYEE (EmployeeNumber, FirstName, LastName, *Department*, EmailAddress)
DEPARTMENT (Department, DepartmentPhone)

with the referential integrity constraint:

Department in EMPLOYEE must exist in Department in DEPARTMENT

The result for the sample data is shown in Figure 2-22.

Normalization Example 3 Now, consider the MEETING table in Figure 2-23. We begin by looking for candidate keys. No column by itself can be a candidate key. Attorney determines different sets of data, so it cannot be a determinant. The same is true for ClientNumber, ClientName, and MeetingDate. In the sample data, the only column that does not determine different sets of data is Duration, but this uniqueness is accidental. It is easy to imagine that two or more meetings would have the same duration.

The next step is to look for combinations of columns that can be candidate keys. (Attorney, ClientNumber) is one combination, but the values (Boxer, 1000) determine two different sets of data. They cannot be a candidate key. The combination (Attorney, ClientName) fails for the same reason. The only combinations that can be candidate keys of this relation are (Attorney, ClientNumber, MeetingDate) and (Attorney, ClientName, MeetingDate).

Let us consider those possibilities further. The name of the relation is MEETING, and we are asking whether (Attorney, ClientNumber, MeetingDate) or (Attorney, ClientName, MeetingDate) can be a candidate key. Do these combinations make sense as identifiers of a meeting? They do unless more than one meeting of the same attorney and client occurs on the same day. In that case, we need to add a new column, MeetingTime, to the relation and

Attorney	ClientNumber	ClientName	Date	Duration
Boxer	1000	ABC, Inc	11/5/2019	2.00
Boxer	2000	XYZ Partners	11/5/2019	5.50
James	1000	ABC, Inc	11/7/2019	3.00
Boxer	1000	ABC, Inc	11/9/2019	4.00
Wu	3000	Malcomb Zoe	11/11/2019	7.00

make this new column part of the candidate key. In this example, we assume that this is not the case and that (Attorney, ClientNumber, MeetingDate) and (Attorney, ClientName, MeetingDate) are the candidate keys.

The second step is to identify other functional dependencies. Here two exist:

ClientNumber → ClientName

and:

ClientName → ClientNumber

Each of these determinants is part of one of the candidate keys. For example, ClientNumber is part of (Attorney, ClientNumber, MeetingDate). However, being part of a candidate key is not enough. The determinant must be the same as the entire candidate key. Thus, the MEETING table is not well formed and has normalization problems.

When you are not certain whether normalization problems exist, consider the three modification operations discussed in Chapter 1: insert, update, and delete. Do problems exist with any of them? For example, in Figure 2-23 if you change ClientName in the first row to ABC, Limited, do inconsistencies arise in the data? The answer is *yes* because ClientNumber 1000 would have two different names in the table. This and any of the other problems that were identified in Chapter 1 when inserting, updating, or deleting data are sure signs that the table has normalization problems.

To fix the normalization problems, we create a new table, CLIENT, with columns ClientNumber and ClientName. Both of these columns are determinants; thus, either can be the primary key of the new table. However, whichever one is selected as the primary key also should be made the foreign key in MEETING. Thus, two correct designs are possible. First, we can use:

MEETING (<u>Attorney</u>, <u>*ClientNumber*</u>, <u>MeetingDate</u>, Duration)
CLIENT (<u>ClientNumber</u>, ClientName)

with the referential integrity constraint:

ClientNumber in MEETING must exist in ClientNumber in CLIENT

Second, we can use:

MEETING (<u>Attorney</u>, <u>*ClientName*</u>, <u>MeetingDate</u>, Duration)
CLIENT (ClientNumber, <u>ClientName</u>)

with the referential integrity constraint:

ClientName in MEETING must exist in ClientName in CLIENT

Data for the first design are shown in Figure 2-24.

Notice in these two designs that either the attribute ClientNumber or ClientName is both a foreign key and also part of the primary key of MEETING. This illustrates that foreign keys can be part of a composite primary key.

FIGURE 2-24

Normalized MEETING and CLIENT Relations and Data

Attorney	ClientNumber	Date	Duration
Boxer	1000	11/5/2019	2.00
Boxer	2000	11/5/2019	5.50
James	1000	11/7/2019	3.00
Boxer	1000	11/9/2019	4.00
Wu	3000	11/11/2019	7.00

ClientNumber	ClientName
1000	ABC, Inc
2000	XYZ Partners
3000	Malcomb Zoe

Note that when two attributes, such as ClientNumber and ClientName, each determine one another they are **synonyms**. They both must appear in a relation to establish their equivalent values. Given that equivalency, the two columns are interchangeable; one can take the place of the other in any other relation. All things being equal, however, the administration of the database will be simpler if one of the two is used consistently as a foreign key. This policy is just a convenience, however, and not a logical requirement for the design.

Normalization Example 4   For our last example, let us consider a relation that involves student data. Specifically:

GRADE (ClassName, Section, Term, Grade, StudentNumber, StudentName,
   ProfessorName, Department, ProfessorEmailAddress)

Given the confused set of columns in this table, it does not seem well formed, and it appears that the table will have normalization problems. We can use the normalization process to find what they are and to remove them.

First, what are the candidate keys of this relation? No column by itself is a candidate key. One way to approach this is to realize that a grade is a combination of a class and a student. In this table, which columns identify classes and students? A particular class is identified by (ClassName, Section, Term), and a student is identified by StudentNumber. Possibly, then, a candidate key for this relation is:

(ClassName, Section, Term, StudentNumber)

This statement is equivalent to saying:

(ClassName, Section, Term, StudentNumber) → (Grade, StudentName,
   ProfessorName, Department, ProfessorEmailAddress)

This is a true statement as long as only one professor teaches a class section. For now, we will make that assumption and consider the alternate case later. If only one professor teaches a section, then (ClassName, Section, Term, StudentNumber) is the one and only candidate key.

Second, what are the additional functional dependencies? One involves student data, and another involves professor data, specifically:

StudentNumber → StudentName

and:

ProfessorName → ProfessorEmailAddress

We also need to ask if ProfessorName determines Department. It will if a professor teaches in only one department. In that case, we have:

ProfessorName → (Department, ProfessorEmailAddress)

Otherwise, Department must remain in the GRADE relation.

We will assume that professors teach in just one department, so we can confirm the following functional dependencies from our earlier discussion:

StudentNumber → StudentName

and:

ProfessorName → (Department, ProfessorEmailAddress)

If we examine the GRADE relation a bit further, however, we can find one other functional dependency. If only one professor teaches a class section, then:

(ClassName, Section, Term) → ProfessorName

Thus, according to step 3 of the normalization process, GRADE has normalization problems because the determinants StudentNumber, ProfessorName, and (ClassName, Section, Term) are not candidate keys. Therefore, we form a table for each of these functional dependencies. As a result, we have a STUDENT table, a PROFESSOR table, and a CLASS_PROFESSOR table. After forming these tables, we then take the appropriate columns out of GRADE and put them into a new version of the GRADE table, which we will name GRADE_1. We now have the following design:

STUDENT (StudentNumber, StudentName)
PROFESSOR (ProfessorName, Department, ProfessorEmailAddress)
CLASS_PROFESSOR (ClassName, Section, Term, *ProfessorName*)
GRADE_1 (*ClassName*, *Section*, *Term*, Grade, *StudentNumber*)

with the referential integrity constraints:

StudentNumber in GRADE_1 must exist in StudentNumber in STUDENT

ProfessorName in CLASS_PROFESSOR must exist in ProfessorName in PROFESSOR

(ClassName, Section, Term) in GRADE_1 must exist in (ClassName, Section, Term) in CLASS_PROFESSOR

Next, consider what happens if more than one professor teaches a section of a class. In that case, the only change is to make ProfessorName part of the primary key of CLASS_PROFESSOR. Thus, the new relation is:

CLASS_PROFESSOR_1 (ClassName, Section, Term, *ProfessorName*)

Class sections that have more than one professor will have multiple rows in this table—one row for each of the professors.

This example shows how normalization problems can become more complicated than simple examples might indicate. For large commercial applications that potentially involve hundreds of tables, such problems can sometimes consume days or weeks of design time.

Eliminating Anomalies from Multivalued Dependencies

In the interest of full disclosure, if professors can teach more than one class in the previous example, then GRADE has what is called a **multivalued dependency**. When modification problems are due to functional dependencies and we then normalize relations to BCNF, we eliminate these anomalies. However, anomalies can also arise from another kind of dependency—the multivalued dependency. A *multivalued dependency* occurs when a determinant is matched with a particular *set* of values.

Examples of multivalued dependencies are (note the use of the double arrows to indicate a multivalued dependency):

EmployeeName → → EmployeeDegree
EmployeeName → → EmployeeSibling
PartKitName → → Part

In each case, the determinant is associated with a set of values, and example data for each of these multivalued dependencies are shown in Figure 2-25. Such expressions are

FIGURE 2-25

Examples of
Multivalued
Dependencies

EMPLOYEE_DEGREE

EmployeeName	EmployeeDegree
Chau	BS
Green	BS
Green	MS
Green	PhD
Jones	AA
Jones	BA

EMPLOYEE_SIBLING

EmployeeName	Employee Sibling
Chau	Eileen
Chau	Jonathan
Green	Nikki
Jones	Frank
Jones	Fred
Jones	Sally

PARTKIT_PART

PartKitName	Part
Bike Repair	Screwdriver
Bike Repair	Tube Fix
Bike Repair	Wrench
First Aid	Aspirin
First Aid	Bandaids
First Aid	Elastic Bands
First Aid	Ibuprofin
Toolbox	Drill and drill bits
Toolbox	Hammer
Toolbox	Saw
Toolbox	Screwdriver
Toolbox	Wrench

read as "EmployeeName multidetermines EmployeeDegree" and "EmployeeName multi-determines EmployeeSibling" and "PartKitName multidetermines Part." Note that multi-determinants are shown with a double arrow rather than a single arrow.

Employee Jones, for example, has degrees AA and BA. Employee Green has degrees BS, MS, and PhD. Employee Chau has just one degree, BS. Similarly, employee Jones has siblings (brothers and sisters) Fred, Sally, and Frank. Employee Green has sibling Nikki, and employee Chau has siblings Jonathan and Eileen. Finally, PartKitName Bike Repair has parts Wrench, Screwdriver, and Tube Fix. Other kits have parts as shown in Figure 2-25.

Unlike functional dependencies, the determinant of a multivalued dependency can never be the primary key. In all three of the tables in Figure 2-25, the primary key consists of the composite of the two columns in each table. For example, the primary key of the EMPLOYEE_DEGREE table is the composite key (EmployeeName, EmployeeDegree).

Multivalued dependencies pose no problem as long as they exist in tables of their own. None of the tables in Figure 2-25 has modification anomalies. Notice that when you put multivalued dependencies into a table of their own, they disappear. The result is just a table with two columns, and the primary key (and sole candidate key) is the composite of those two columns. When multivalued dependencies have been isolated in this way, the table is said to be in **fourth normal form (4NF)**.

The hardest part of multivalued dependencies is finding them. And if A $\rightarrow\rightarrow$ B, then any relation that contains A, B, and one or more additional columns will have modification anomalies. The modified original table will now have its repeating group eliminated and will be in at least 1NF. The moved data will be in 4NF.

Whenever you encounter tables with odd anomalies, especially anomalies that require you to insert, modify, or delete different numbers of rows to maintain integrity, check for multivalued dependencies. You are likely to encounter the multivalue, multicolumn problem when creating databases from nondatabase data. It is particularly common in spreadsheet and text data files. Fortunately, the preferred two-table design is easy to create, and the SQL for moving the data to the new design is easy to write.

BTW

A few years ago, people argued that only three phone number columns were needed per person: Home, Office, and Fax. Later they said, "Well, okay, maybe we need four: Home, Office, Fax, and Mobile." Today, who would want to guess the maximum number of phone numbers a person might have? Rather than guess, just store Phone in a separate table; such a design will allow each person to have from none to an unlimited number of phone numbers.

BTW

If you have a table in 4NF and add additional columns that are dependent on the original composite key in the 4NF table, the revised table must now be put into BCNF. Consider the 4NF table PHONE_NUMBER:

PHONE_NUMBER (<u>CustomerNumber</u>, <u>PhoneNumber</u>)

If we now include a PhoneType column, which will be dependent on the composite primary key, we now have a table that is in BCNF instead of 4NF:

PHONE_NUMBER (<u>CustomerNumber</u>, <u>PhoneNumber</u>, PhoneType)

Note that while we created this table to resolve a multivalue, multicolumn problem, that problem is *still* solved, and any repeating group problem has also been resolved.

BTW

You will get a chance to work with multivalued dependencies and 4NF in exercises 2.40 and 2.41. If you want to learn about them, see one of the more advanced texts mentioned in the footnote on page 85. In general, you should normalize your relationships so that they are in either BCNF or 4NF.

NORMAL FORMS: ONE STEP AT A TIME

Instead of normalizing directly to BCNF, some people prefer to take a step-by-step approach, starting at 1NF and then moving through successive normal forms until BCNF. Here is a brief discussion of the successive normal forms, and how to reach them.

A table and a spreadsheet are very similar to one another in that we can think of both as having rows, columns, and cells. Edgar Frank (E. F.) Codd, the originator of the relational model, defined three normal forms in an early paper on the relational model. He defined any table that meets the definition of a relation (see Figure 2-1 on page 71) as being in first normal form (1NF).

This definition, however, brings us back to the "To Key or Not to Key" discussion. Codd's set of conditions for a relation does not require a primary key, but one is clearly implied by the condition that all rows must be unique. Thus, there are various opinions on whether a relation has to have a defined primary key to be in 1NF.[7]

For practical purposes, we will define 1NF as it is used in this book as a table that:

1. Meets the set of conditions for a relation, and
2. Has a defined primary key, and
3. No repeating groups.

For 1NF, ask yourself: Does the table meet the definition in Figure 2-1 such that there are no repeating groups, and does it have a defined primary key? If the answer is *yes*, then the table is in 1NF.

Codd pointed out that such tables can have anomalies (which are referred to elsewhere in the text as *normalization problems*), and he defined a **second normal form (2NF)** that eliminated some of those anomalies. A relation is in 2NF if and only if (1) it is in 1NF and (2) all nonkey attributes are determined by the entire primary key. This means that if the primary key is a composite primary key, no nonkey attribute can be determined by an attribute or attributes that make up only part of the key. Thus, if you have a relation (**A, B, N, O, P**) with the composite key (**A, B**), then none of the nonkey attributes—**N, O,** or **P**—can be determined by *just* **A** or *just* **B**.

For 2NF, ask yourself: (1) Is the table in 1NF, and (2) are all nonkey attributes determined by *only* the *entire* primary key rather than *part* of the primary key? If the answers are *yes* and *yes*, then the table is in 2NF. Note that the problem solved by 2NF can *only occur* in a table with a *composite primary key*—if the table has a single column primary key, then this problem *cannot occur* and if the table is in 1NF it will also be in 2NF.

However, the conditions of 2NF did not eliminate all the anomalies, so Codd defined **third normal form (3NF)**. A relation is in 3NF if and only if (1) it is in 2NF and (2) there are no nonkey attributes determined by another nonkey attribute. Technically, the situation described by the preceding condition is called a **transitive dependency**. Thus, in our relation (**A, B, N, O, P**) *none* of the nonkey attributes—**N, O,** or **P**—can be determined by **N, O,** or **P** or any combination of them.

For 3NF, ask yourself: (1) Is the table in 2NF, and (2) are there any nonkey attributes determined by *another* nonkey attribute or attributes? If the answers are *yes* and *no*, then the table is in 3NF.

Not long after Codd published his paper on normal forms, it was pointed out to him that even relations in 3NF could have anomalies. As a result, he and R. Boyce defined the **Boyce-Codd Normal Form (BCNF)**, which eliminated the anomalies that had been found with 3NF. As stated earlier, a relation is in BCNF if and only if every determinant is a candidate key.

For BCNF, ask yourself: (1) Is the table in 3NF, and (2) are all *determinants* also *candidate keys*? If the answers are *yes* and *yes*, then the table is in BCNF.

1NF through BCNF are summed up in a widely known phrase:

I swear to construct my tables so that all nonkey columns are dependent on the key, the whole key, and nothing but the key, so help me Codd!

This phrase actually is a very good way to remember the order of the normal forms:

I swear to construct my tables so that all nonkey columns are dependent on

- *the key,* [This is 1NF]
- *the whole key,* [This is 2NF]
- *and nothing but the key,* [This is 3NF and BCNF]

so help me Codd!

---

[7]For a review of some of the discussion, see the Wikipedia article **First normal form** at **http://en.wikipedia.org/wiki/First_normal_form**.

Also note that all these definitions were made in such a way that a relation in a higher normal form is defined to be in all lower normal forms. Thus, a relation in BCNF is automatically in 3NF, a relation in 3NF is automatically in 2NF, and a relation in 2NF is automatically in 1NF.

There the matter rested until others discovered another kind of dependency, called a **multivalued dependency**, which is discussed earlier in this chapter and is illustrated in exercise 2.40 and exercise 2.41. To eliminate multivalued dependencies, fourth normal form (4NF) was defined. To put tables into 4NF, the initial table must be split into tables such that the multiple values of any multivalued attribute are moved into the new tables. These are then accessed via 1:N relationships between the original table and the tables holding the multiple values.

For 4NF, ask yourself: (1) Have the multiple values determined by any multivalued dependency been moved into a separate table? If the answer is *yes*, then the tables are in 4NF.

A little later, another kind of anomaly involving tables that can be split apart but not correctly joined back together was identified, and **fifth normal form (5NF)** was defined to eliminate that type of anomaly. A discussion of 5NF is beyond the scope of this book.

You can see how the knowledge evolved: None of these normal forms was perfect—each one eliminated certain anomalies, and none asserted that it was vulnerable to no anomaly at all. At this stage, in 1981, R. Fagin took a different approach and asked why, rather than just chipping away at anomalies, we do not look for conditions that would have to exist in order for a relation to have no anomalies at all. He did just that and, in the process, defined **domain/key normal form (DK/NF)**, and, no, that is not a typo—the name has the slash between *domain* and *key*, while the acronym places it between *DK* and *NF*! Fagin proved that a relation in DK/NF can have no anomalies, and he further proved that a relation that has no anomalies is also in DK/NF.

For some reason, DK/NF never caught the fancy of the general database population, but it should have. As you can tell, no one should brag that their relations are in BCNF—instead we should all brag that our relations are in DK/NF. But for some reason (perhaps because there is fashion in database theory, just as there is fashion in clothes), it just is not done.

You are probably wondering what the conditions of DK/NF are. Basically, DK/NF requires that all the constraints on data values be logical implications of the definition of domains and keys. To the level of detail of this text, and to the level of detail experienced by 99 percent of all database practitioners, this can be restated as follows: Every determinant of a functional dependency must be a candidate key. This is exactly where we started and what we have defined as BCNF.

You can broaden this statement a bit to include multivalued dependencies and say that every determinant of a functional or multivalued dependency must be a candidate key. The trouble with this is that as soon as we constrain a multivalued dependency in this way, it is transformed into a functional dependency. Our original statement is fine. It is like saying that good health comes to overweight people who lose weight until they are of an appropriate weight. As soon as they lose their excess weight, they are no longer overweight. Hence, good health comes to people who have appropriate weight.

For DK/NF, ask yourself: Is the table in BCNF? For our purposes in this book, the two terms are synonymous, so if the answer is *yes*, we will consider that the table is also in DK/NF.

So, as Paul Harvey used to say, "Now you know the rest of the story." Just ensure that every determinant of a functional dependency is a candidate key (BCNF), and you can claim that your relations are fully normalized. You do not want to say they are in DK/NF until you learn more about it, though, because someone might ask you what that means. However, for most practical purposes your relations are in DK/NF as well.

Note: For more information on normal forms, see David M. Kroenke, David J. Auer, Scott L. Vandenberg, and Robert C. Yoder, *Database Processing: Fundamentals, Design, and Implementation*, 15th ed. (Upper Saddle River, NJ: Prentice Hall, 2019): 161–181.[8]

---

[8]For another view of normalization see Marc Rettig's 5 *Rules of Data Normalization* presented in poster form at **http://www.databaseanswers.org/downloads/Marc_Rettig_5_Rules_of_Normalization_Poster.pdf**.

WORKING WITH MICROSOFT ACCESS

Section 2

Working with Multiple Tables in Microsoft Access

In the section "Working with Microsoft Access" of Chapter 1, we learned how to create Microsoft Access 2019 databases, tables, forms, and reports. However, we were limited to working with only one table. In this section, we will:

- See examples of the modification problems discussed in Chapter 1 and 2.
- Work with multiple tables.

We will continue to use the WMCRM database we created in Chapter 1's section "Working with Microsoft Access." At this point, you have created and populated (which means you have inserted the data into) the CUSTOMER table. Figure WA-2-1 shows the contacts that have been made with each customer. Note that there is no customer with CustomerID 2—this is because we deleted and re-entered the data for Jessica Christman.

FIGURE WA-2-1

CONTACT Data

CustomerID	Date	Type	Remarks
1	7/7/2018	Phone	General interest in a Gaia.
1	7/7/2018	Email	Sent general information.
1	7/12/2018	Phone	Set up an appointment.
1	7/14/2018	Meeting	Bought a HiStandard.
3	7/19/2018	Phone	Interested in a SUHi, set up an appointment.
1	7/21/2018	Email	Sent a standard follow-up message.
4	7/27/2018	Phone	Interested in a HiStandard, set up an appointment.
3	7/27/2018	Meeting	Bought a SUHi.
4	8/2/2018	Meeting	Talked up to a HiLuxury. Customer bought one.
3	8/3/2018	Email	Sent a standard follow-up message.
4	8/10/2018	Email	Sent a standard follow-up message.
5	8/15/2018	Phone	General interest in a Gaia.

Possible Modification Problems in the WMCRM Database

We know from the topics covered in this chapter that we really need a separate table to store the CONTACT data, but to illustrate the modification problems discussed in Chapter 1, let us combine it into one table with the data already in CUSTOMER. This table is available in the file WMCRM-Combined-Data.accdb, which is available at the Web site for this book (**www.pearsonhighered.com/kroenke**). We will use this database to see modification problems in non-normalized tables and then build the correctly normalized tables in the actual WMCRM database.

We will need to start Microsoft Access 2019, open the WMCRM-Combined-Data. accdb file, and take a look at the WMCRM-Combined-Data database.

(Continued)

FIGURE WA-2-2

The Microsoft Access 2019 Splash Screen

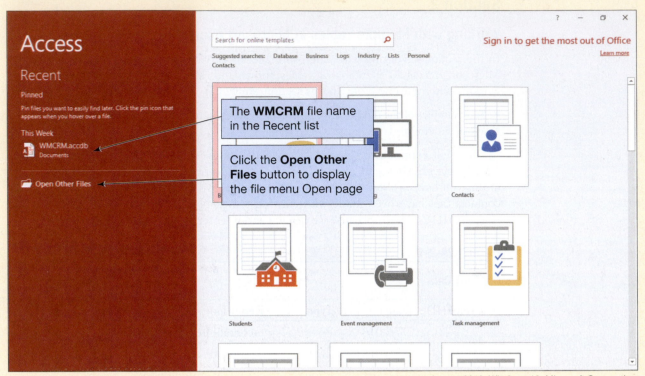

Access 2019, Windows 10, Microsoft Corporation.

Opening an Existing Microsoft Access Database

1. Select the **Start | Access** command, or click the **Microsoft Access 2019** button on the Taskbar if you pinned it there. The Microsoft Access 2019 splash screen window appears, as shown in Figure WA-2-2.
   - **NOTE:** The menu command or icon location used to start Microsoft Access 2019 may vary, depending on the operating system and how Microsoft Office is installed on the computer you are using.
2. Click the **Open Other Files** button on the Microsoft Access 2019 splash screen to open the File | Open page, as shown in Figure WA-2-3.
3. Click the **This PC** button to open the Open | This PC pane, as shown in Figure WA-2-4.
4. Click the **Browse** button to open the Open dialog box, as shown in Figure WA-2-5.
5. Browse to the **WMCRM-Combined-Data.accdb file**, click the file name to highlight it, and then click the **Open** button.
6. The **Security Warning** bar appears with the database. Click the Security Warning bar's **Enable Content** button to select this option.
7. In the Navigation Pane, double-click the **CUSTOMER_CONTACT** table object to open it.
8. If a Field List pane is displayed on the right side of the tabbed document window, click the **Field List Close** button to close this pane.
9. Click the **Shutter Bar Open/Close** button to minimize the Navigation Pane.
10. The CUSTOMER_CONTACT table appears in Datasheet view, as shown in Figure WA-2-6. Note that there is one line for each contact, which has resulted in the duplication of basic customer data. For example, there are five sets of basic data for Ben Griffey.
11. Close the CUSTOMER_CONTACT table by clicking the document window's **Close** button.
12. Click the **Shutter Bar Open/Close** button to expand the Navigation Pane.

FIGURE WA-2-3

The Microsoft Access 2019 File | Open Page

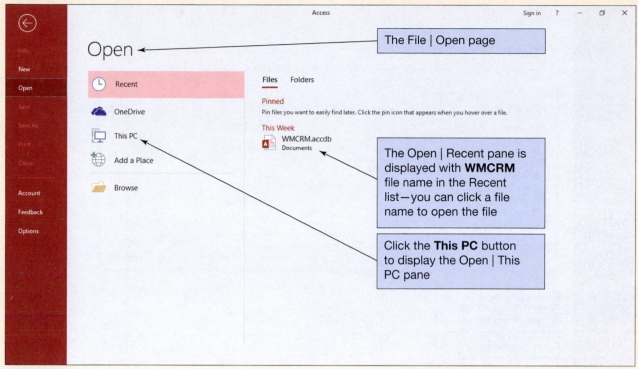

The File | Open page

The Open | Recent pane is displayed with **WMCRM** file name in the Recent list—you can click a file name to open the file

Click the **This PC** button to display the Open | This PC pane

Access 2019, Windows 10, Microsoft Corporation.

FIGURE WA-2-4

The Microsoft Access 2019 Open | This PC Pane

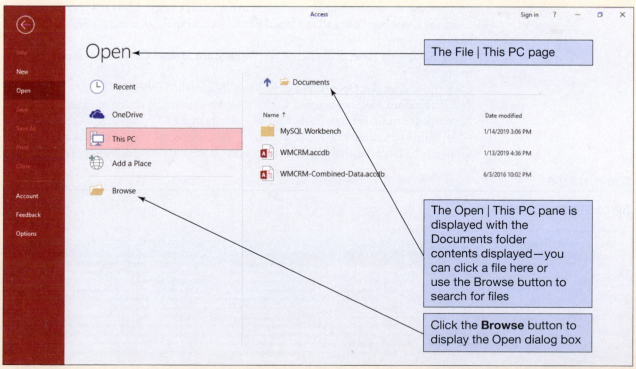

The File | This PC page

The Open | This PC pane is displayed with the Documents folder contents displayed—you can click a file here or use the Browse button to search for files

Click the **Browse** button to display the Open dialog box

Access 2019, Windows 10, Microsoft Corporation.

(Continued)

FIGURE WA-2-5

The Open Dialog Box

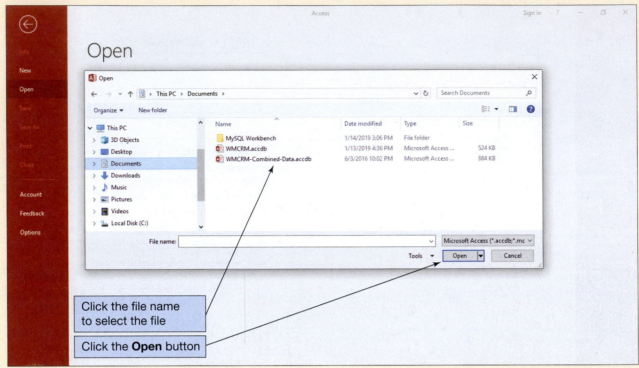

Access 2019, Windows 10, Microsoft Corporation.

13. In the Navigation Pane, double-click the **Customer Contact Data Input Form** object to open it. The Customer Contact Data Input Form appears, as shown in Figure WA-2-7. Note that the form displays all the data for one record in the CUSTOMER_CONTACT table.

14. Close the Customer Contact Data Input Form by clicking the document window's **Close** button.

15. In the Navigation Pane, double-click the **Wallingford Motors Customer Contact Report** to open it.

16. Click the **Shutter Bar Open/Close** button to minimize the Navigation Pane.

17. The Wallingford Motors Customer Contact Report appears, as shown in Figure WA-2-8. Note that the form displays the data for all contacts in the CUSTOMER_CONTACT table, sorted by CustomerNumber and Date. For example, all the contact data for Ben Griffey (who has a CustomerID of 1) is grouped at the beginning of the report.

FIGURE WA-2-6

The CUSTOMER_CONTACT Table

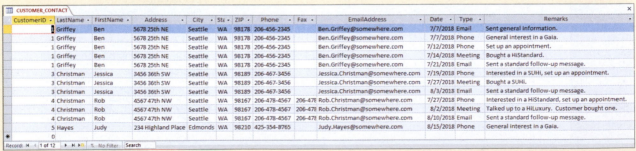

Access 2019, Windows 10, Microsoft Corporation.

FIGURE WA-2-7

The Customer Contact Data Input Form

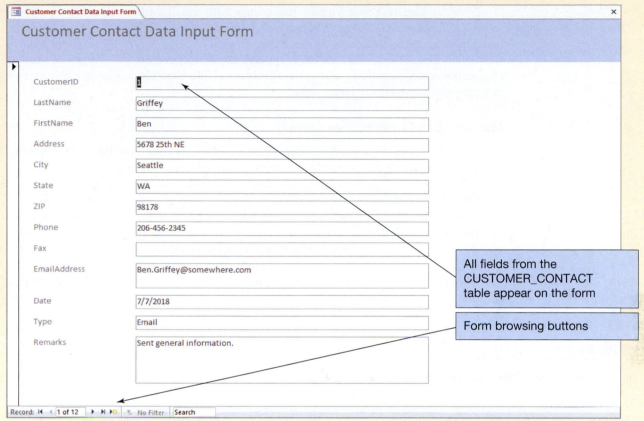

Access 2019, Windows 10, Microsoft Corporation.

FIGURE WA-2-8

The Wallingford Motors Customer Contact Report

Access 2019, Windows 10, Microsoft Corporation.

(Continued)

18. Close the Wallingford Motors Customer Contact Report by clicking the document window's **Close** button.
19. Click the **Shutter Bar Open/Close** button to expand the Navigation Pane.

Now, assume that Ben Griffey has changed his email address from *Ben.Griffey@ somewhere.com* to *Ben.Griffey@elsewhere.com*. In a well-formed relation, we would have to make this change only once, but a quick examination of Figures WA-2-6 through WA-2-8 shows that Ben Griffey's email address appears in multiple records. We therefore have to change it in every record to avoid update problems. Unfortunately, it is easy to miss one or more records, especially in large tables.

Updating Ben Griffey's Email Address

1. In the Navigation Pane, double-click the **Customer Contact Data Input Form** object to open it. Because Ben Griffey is the customer in the first record, his data is already in the form.
2. Edit the Email address to read Ben.Griffey@elsewhere.com, as shown in Figure WA-2-9.
3. Click the **Next Record** button to move to the next record in the table. Again, the record shows Ben Griffey's data, so again edit the **Email** address to read *Ben.Griffey@elsewhere.com.*
4. Click the **Next Record** button to move to the next record in the table. For the third time, the record shows Ben Griffey's data, so again edit the **Email** address to read *Ben.Griffey@ elsewhere.com*.
5. Click the **Next Record** button to move to the next record in the table. For the fourth time, the record shows Ben Griffey's data, so again edit the **Email** address to read *Ben.Griffey@ elsewhere.com*.

FIGURE WA-2-9

The Customer Contact Data Input Form with the Updated Email Address

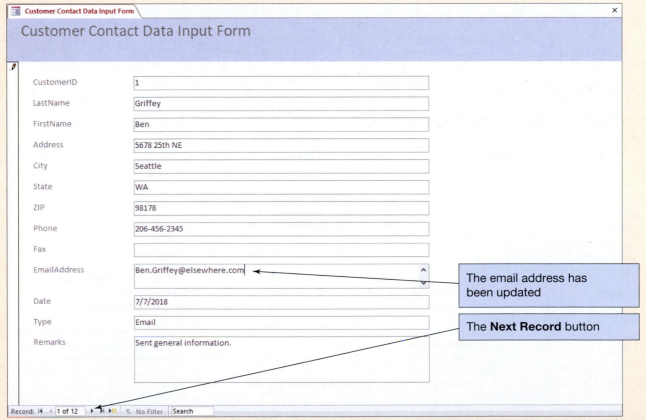

FIGURE WA-2-10

The Updated Wallingford Motors Customer Contact Report

Wallingford Motors Customer Contact Report						
CustomerID	Date	LastName	FirstName	EmailAddress	Type	Remarks
1						
	7/7/2018	Griffey	Ben	Ben.Griffey@elsewhere.com	Phone	General interest in a Gaia.
	7/7/2018	Griffey	Ben	Ben.Griffey@elsewhere.com	Email	Sent general information.
	7/12/2018	Griffey	Ben	Ben.Griffey@elsewhere.com	Phone	Set up an appointment.
	7/14/2018	Griffey	Ben	Ben.Griffey@elsewhere.com	Meeting	Bought a HiStandard.
	7/21/2018	Griffey	Ben	Ben.Griffey@somewhere.com	Email	Sent a standard follow-up message.
3						
	7/19/2018	Christman	Jessica	Jessica.Christman@somewhere.com	Phone	Interested in a SUHi, set up an appointment.
	7/27/2018	Christman	Jessica	Jessica.Christman@somewhere.com	Meeting	Bought a SUHi.
	8/3/2018	Christman	Jessica	Jessica.Christman@somewhere.com	Email	Sent a standard follow-up message.
4						
	7/27/2018	Christman	Rob	Rob.Christman@somewhere.com	Phone	Interested in a HiStandard, set up an appointment.
	8/2/2018	Christman	Rob	Rob.Christman@somewhere.com	Meeting	Talked up to a HiLuxury. Customer bought one.
	8/10/2018	Christman	Rob	Rob.Christman@somewhere.com	Email	Sent a standard follow-up message.
5						
	8/15/2018	Hayes	Judy	Judy.Hayes@somewhere.com	Phone	General interest in a Gaia.

A modification problem has occurred. Not all records were updated with the new email address, and the database records are now inconsistent

Access 2019, Windows 10, Microsoft Corporation.

6. Assume that we have made all the necessary updates to the database records. Close the Customer Contact Data Input form by clicking the document window's **Close** button.
7. In the Navigation Pane, double-click the report **Wallingford Motors Customer Contact Report** to open it.
8. Click the **Shutter Bar Open/Close** button to minimize the Navigation Pane. The Wallingford Motors Customer Contact Report now looks as shown in Figure WA-2-10. Note that the email addresses shown for Ben Griffey are inconsistent—we missed one record when we updated the table, and now we have inconsistent data. A modification error—in this case an update error—has occurred.
9. Close the Wallingford Motors Customer Contact Report by clicking the document window's **Close** button.
10. Click the **Shutter Bar Open/Close** button to expand the Navigation Pane.

This simple example shows how easily modification problems can occur in tables that are not normalized. With a set of well-formed, normalized tables, this problem would not have occurred.

Closing the WMCRM-Combined-Data Database

1. Click the **Close** button to close the database and exit Microsoft Access.

Working with Multiple Tables

The table structure for the CUSTOMER_CONTACT table in the WMCRM-Combined-Data database is:

CUSTOMER_CONTACT (CustomerID, LastName, FirstName, Address, City, State, ZIP, Phone, Fax, EmailAddress, Date, Type, Remarks)

(Continued)

FIGURE WA-2-11

Database Column Characteristics for the WMCRM CONTACT Table

Column Name	Type	Key	Required	Remarks
ContactID	AutoNumber	Primary Key	Yes	Surrogate Key
CustomerID	Number	Foreign Key	Yes	Long Integer
ContactDate	Date/Time	No	Yes	Short Date
ContactType	Short Text (10)	No	Yes	Allowed values are Phone, Fax, Email, and Meeting
Remarks	Long Text	No	No	

Applying the normalization process discussed in this chapter, we will have the following set of tables:

CUSTOMER (<u>CustomerID</u>, LastName, FirstName, Address, City, State, ZIP, Phone, Fax, EmailAddress)
CONTACT (<u>ContactID</u>, *CustomerID*, ContactDate, ContactType, Remarks)

with the referential integrity constraint:

CustomerID in CONTACT must exist in CustomerID in CUSTOMER

Note that we have modified a couple of column names in the CONTACT table—we are using ContactDate instead of Date and ContactType instead of Type. We discuss the reason for this later in this section. Our task now is to build and populate the CONTACT table and then to establish the relationship and referential integrity constraint between the two tables.

First, we need to create and populate (insert data into) the CONTACT table, which will contain the columns and column characteristics shown in the table in Figure WA-2-11.[9] The CustomerID column appears again in CONTACT, this time designated as a foreign key. As discussed in this chapter, the term *foreign key* designates this column as the link to the CUSTOMER table. The value in the CustomerID column of CONTACT tells which customer was contacted. All we have to do is look up the value of CustomerID in the CUSTOMER table.

Note that when we build the CONTACT table there is no "foreign key" setting. We will set up the database relationship between CUSTOMER and CONTACT after we have finished building the CONTACT table.

Note the following:

- Some new data types are being used: Number, Date/Time, and Long Text.
- CustomerID must be set as a Number data type and specifically as a Long Integer data type to match the data type Microsoft Access creates for the AutoNumber data type in the CUSTOMER table.
- The ContactType column has only four allowed values: Phone, Fax, Email, and Meeting. For now, we can simply input only these data values. You will learn how to enforce the data restriction for this column in Chapter 3.

---

[9]Although we are using it for simplicity in this example, a column such as Remarks (also often called Comments or Notes) can cause problems in a database. For a complete discussion, see David M. Kroenke, David J. Auer, Scott L. Vandenberg, and Robert C. Yoder, *Database Processing: Fundamentals, Design, and Implementation*, 15th ed. (Upper Saddle River, NJ: Pearson, 2019).

FIGURE WA-2-12

The Reserved Word Warning

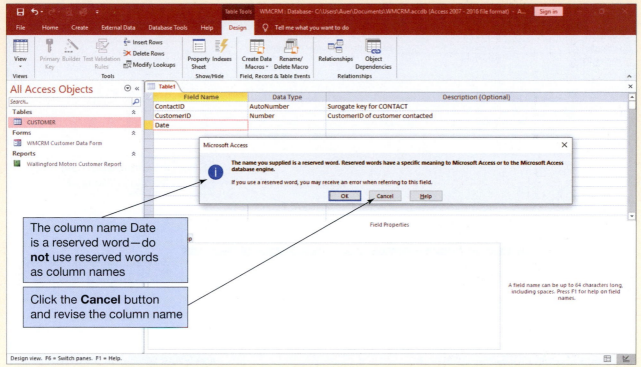

The column name Date is a reserved word—do **not** use reserved words as column names

Click the **Cancel** button and revise the column name

Access 2019, Windows 10, Microsoft Corporation.

Creating the CONTACT Table

1. Open Microsoft Access 2019.
2. In the Recent list of database files, click **WMCRM.accdb**. The database file opens in Microsoft Access.
3. Click the **Create** command tab.
4. Click the **Table Design** button.
   The Table1 tabbed document window is displayed in Design view. Note that along with the Table1 window a contextual tab named Table Tools is displayed and that this tab adds a new command tab and ribbon, named Design, to the set of command tabs displayed.
5. Using the steps we followed to create the CUSTOMER table in Chapter 1's section "Working with Microsoft Access," begin to create the CONTACT table. The following steps detail only new information that you need to know to complete the CONTACT table.
   - **NOTE:** When creating the CONTACT table, be sure to enter appropriate comments in the Description field for the column in the Design view.
6. When creating the CustomerID column, set the data type to **Number**. Note that the default Field Size setting for Number is Long Integer, so no change is necessary. Be sure to set the Required property to **Yes**.
7. After creating the ContactID column, set it as the primary key of the table.
8. When creating the ContactDate column, start by using the column name *Date*. As soon as you enter the column name and try to move to the Data Type column, Microsoft Access displays a dialog box, warning you that Date is a reserved word, as shown in Figure WA-2-12. Click the **Cancel** button, and change the column name to **ContactDate**.
   - **NOTE:** Normally, you should avoid reserved words such as Date and Time. Generally, column names such as ContactDate are preferred, both to avoid reserved words and to clarify exactly which date you are referring to, and that is why we changed the column names in the CONTACT table.

(Continued)

FIGURE WA-2-13

Setting the Date Format

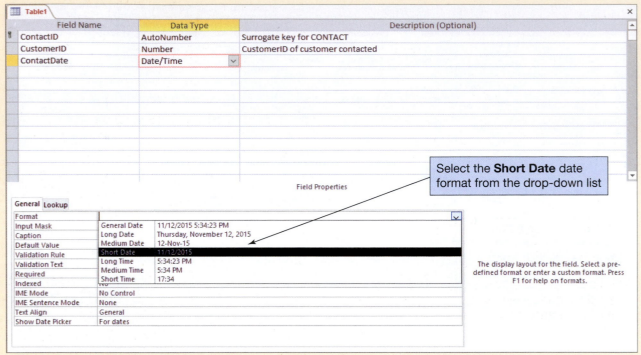

Access 2019, Windows 10, Microsoft Corporation.

9. When creating the ContactDate column, set the data type to **Date/Time** and set the format to **Short Date**, as shown in Figure WA-2-13. Be sure to set the Required property to **Yes**.
10. When creating the ContactType column, be sure to set the Required property to **Yes.** It is also a good idea to note the list of values for this column in the Description field.
11. When creating the Remarks columns, be sure to set the data type to **Long Text**.
12. To name and save the CONTACT table, click the **Save** button in the Quick Access Toolbar.
13. Type the table name **CONTACT** into the Save As dialog box text box, and then click the **OK** button. The table is named and saved, and it now appears with the table name CONTACT.
14. To close the CONTACT table, click the **Close** button in the upper-right corner of the tabbed document window. The CONTACT table now appears as a table object in the Navigation Pane.

Creating Relationships Between Tables

In Microsoft Access, you build relationships between tables by using the **Relationships window**, which you access by using the **Database Tools | Relationships** command. After a relationship is created in the Relationships window, referential integrity constraints are set in the **Edit Relationships dialog box** within that window by using the **Enforce Referential Integrity check box**.

Creating the Relationship Between the CUSTOMER and CONTACT Tables

1. Click the **Database Tools** command tab to display the Database Tools command groups, as shown in Figure WA-2-14.
2. Click the **Relationships** button in the Relationships group. As shown in Figure WA-2-15, the Relationships tabbed document window appears, together with the Show Table dialog box. Note that along with the Relationships window, a contextual tab named Relationship

FIGURE WA-2-14

The Database Tools Command Tab

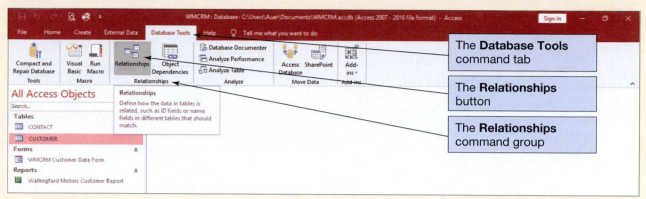

FIGURE WA-2-15

The Relationships Window

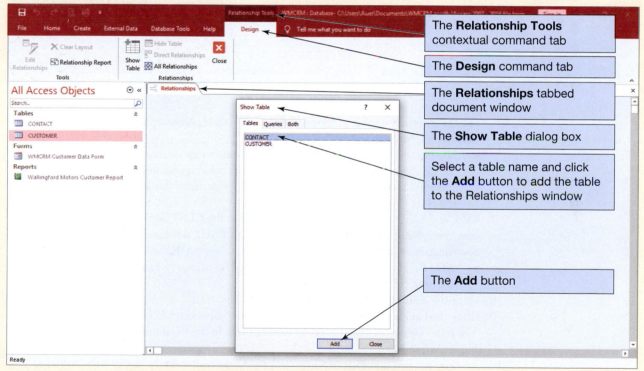

Tools is displayed and that this tab adds a new command tab named Design to the set of command tabs displayed.

3. In the Show Table dialog box, the CONTACT table is already selected. Click the **Add** button to add CONTACT to the Relationships window.

4. In the Show Table dialog box, click the **CUSTOMER** table to select it. Click the **Add** button to add CUSTOMER to the Relationships window.

5. In the Show Table dialog box, click the **Close** button to close the dialog box.

6. Rearrange and resize the table objects in the Relationships window using standard Windows drag-and-drop techniques. Rearrange the CUSTOMER and CONTACT table

(Continued)

FIGURE WA-2-16

The Table Objects in the Relationships Window

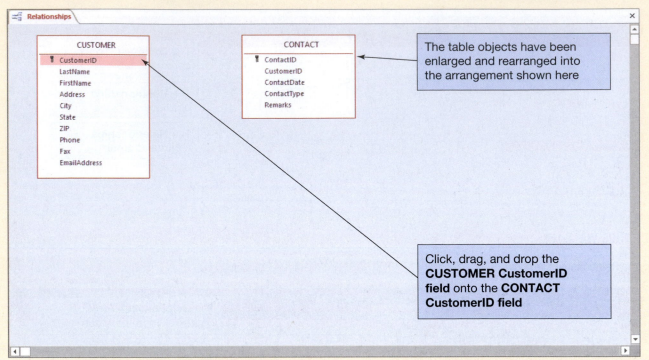

Access 2019, Windows 10, Microsoft Corporation.

objects until they appear as shown in Figure WA-2-16. Now we are ready to create the relationship between the tables.

■ **NOTE:** A formal description of how to create a relationship between two tables is "In the Relationships window, drag a primary key column and drop it on top of the corresponding foreign key column." It is easier to understand this after you have actually done it.

7. Click and hold the column name **CustomerID in the CUSTOMER table**, and then drag it over the **column name CustomerID in the CONTACT table**. Release the mouse button, and the Edit Relationships dialog box appears, as shown in Figure WA-2-17.

■ **NOTE:** In CUSTOMER, CustomerID is the primary key, and in CONTACT, CustomerID is the foreign key.

8. Click the **Enforce Referential Integrity** check box.

9. Click the **Create** button to create the relationship between CUSTOMER and CONTACT. The relationship between the tables now appears in the Relationships window, as shown in Figure WA-2-18.

10. To close the Relationships window, click the **Close** button in the upper-right corner of the document window. A Microsoft Access warning dialog box appears, asking whether you want to save changes to the layout of relationships. Click the **Yes** button to save the changes and close the window.

At this point, we need to add data on customer contacts to the CONTACT table. Using the CONTACT table in Datasheet view, as discussed earlier, we enter the data shown in Figure WA-2-1 into the CONTACT table. Again, note that there is *no* customer with CustomerID of 2—this is because we deleted and re-entered the data for Jessica Christman in Chapter 1's section "Working with Microsoft Access." Also note that because referential integrity is enabled, we *cannot* enter a CustomerID that does not already exist in the CUSTOMER table. The CONTACT table with the data inserted looks as shown in Figure WA-2-19. Be sure to close the table after the data have been entered.

FIGURE WA-2-17

The Edit Relationships Dialog Box

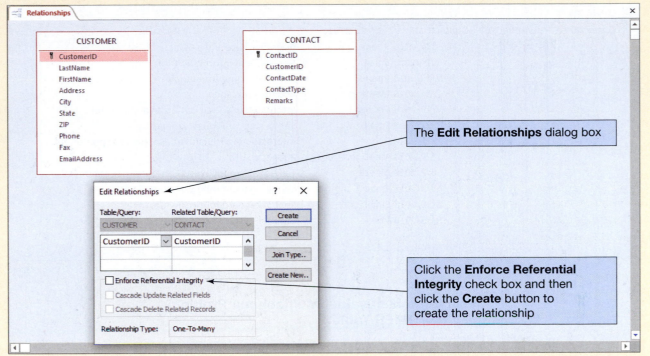

Access 2019, Windows 10, Microsoft Corporation.

FIGURE WA-2-18

The Completed Relationship

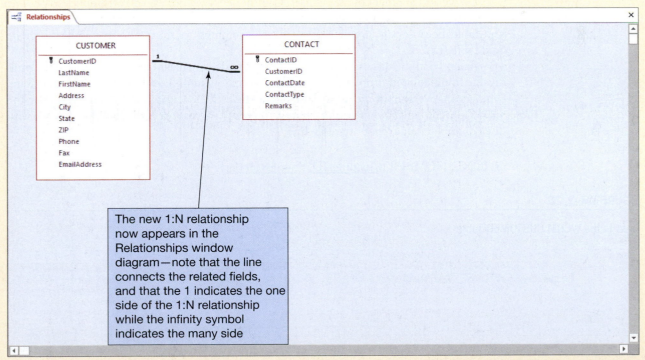

Access 2019, Windows 10, Microsoft Corporation.

(*Continued*)

FIGURE WA-2-19

Data in the CONTACT Table

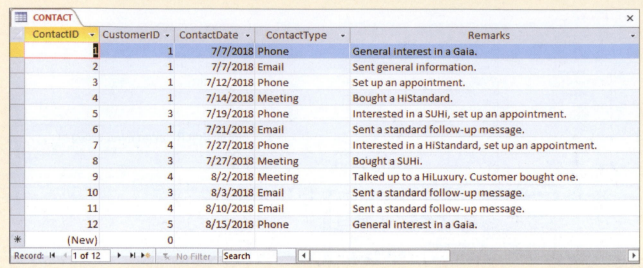

Access 2019, Windows 10, Microsoft Corporation.

Resolving the Multivalue, Multicolumn Problem in the CUSTOMER Table

Wallingford Motors customer Ben Griffey has just called give the sales staff his new cell phone number. This phone number does not replace the current phone number we have for Ben—he has now told us that that is his home phone—so we want to add the new cell phone number to his record in the CUSTOMER table. However, as can be seen in Figure WA-2-20, we already have his home phone number in the table. So, where do we put the cell phone number?

Do we add another column labeled CellPhone? If we do, we will create the *multivalue, multicolumn problem* discussed earlier in this chapter. If fact, this problem *already exists* in the table because we already have multiple columns to store phone numbers: Phone and Fax!

As noted in the discussion of normal forms and normalization, the solution to the multivalue, multicolumn problem is to create a new table in 4NF to hold the multivalue data. This means we should create the following table. We created a data entry form for the CUSTOMER table. Now we will create a Microsoft Access form that will let us work with the combined data from both tables:

PHONE_NUMBER (CustomerID, PhoneNumber)

FIGURE WA-2-20

Data in the WCRM CUSTOMER Table

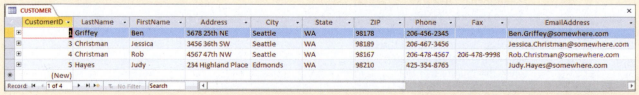

Access 2019, Windows 10, Microsoft Corporation.

with the referential integrity constraint:

CustomerID in PHONE_NUMBER must exist in CustomerID in CUSTOMER

Note that in a 4NF table, the two columns together form a composite primary key. However, adding a column named PhoneType makes sense so that we know which phone number is which. This puts our new table into BCNF instead of 4NF, but still solves the problem and gives us:

PHONE_NUMBER (<u>CustomerID</u>, <u>PhoneNumber</u>, PhoneType)

with the referential integrity constraint:

CustomerID in PHONE_NUMBER must exist in CustomerID in CUSTOMER

We must then remove the Phone and Fax columns from CUSTOMER, and our final schema is:

CUSTOMER (<u>CustomerID</u>, LastName, FirstName, Address, City, State, ZIP, EmailAddress)
CONTACT (<u>ContactID</u>, *CustomerID*, ContactDate, ContactType, Remarks)
PHONE_NUMBER (*<u>CustomerID</u>*, <u>PhoneNumber</u>, PhoneType)

with the referential integrity constraint:

CustomerID in CONTACT must exist in CustomerID in CUSTOMER
CustomerID in PHONE_NUMBER must exist in CustomerID in CUSTOMER

The column characteristics for the new PHONE_NUMBER table are shown in Figure WA-2-21, and the WMCRM PHONE_NUMBER table data (including Ben's new cell phone number) are shown in Figure WA-2-22. Using the techniques we have covered in this section of "Working with Microsoft Access," we need to create the PHONE_NUMBER table, create the foreign key link to the CUSTOMER table, populate the PHONE_NUMBER table, and finally drop the Phone and Fax columns from the CUSTOMER table.

FIGURE WA-2-21

Database Column Characteristics for the WMCRM PHONE_NUMBER Table

PHONE_NUMBER

Column Name	Type	Key	Required	Remarks
CustomerID	Number	Primary Key, Foreign Key	Yes	Long Integer
PhoneNumber	Short Text (12)	Primary Key	Yes	
PhoneType	Short Text (25)	No	No	

(Continued)

FIGURE WA-2-22

WMCRM PHONE_NUMBER Table Data

CustomerID	PhoneNumber	PhoneType
1	206-456-2345	Home
1	206-765-5678	Cell
3	206-467-3456	
4	206-478-4567	
4	206-478-9998	Fax
5	425-354-8765	

Creating, Linking, and Populating the PHONE_NUMBER Table

1. Using the techniques you have learned to create a table in Microsoft Access 2019, create the PHONE_NUMBER table as specified in Figure WA-2-21.
2. The only new step here is setting a composite primary key. To do this select the **CustomerID** row as you normally would to set a primary key. Hold down the **CRTL** key and click the **PhoneNumber** row. When both rows are selected, as shown in Figure WA-2-23, click the **Primary Key** button to set the composite primary key.
3. Save the new table as PHONE_NUMBER.
4. Using the techniques you have learned to link two tables by using a foreign key, create a relationship to link the PHONE_NUMBER table CustomerID column to the **CUSTOMER** table CustomerID column. Enforce referential integrity on the relationship. When you are done, the relationships between the tables will appear as shown in Figure WA-2-24.

FIGURE WA-2-23

Setting the Composite Primary Key in the PHONE_NUMBER Table

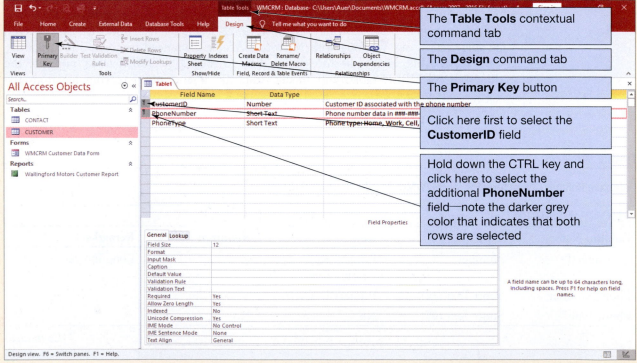

Access 2019, Windows 10, Microsoft Corporation.

FIGURE WA-2-24

The WMCRM Relationships with the PHONE_NUMBER Table

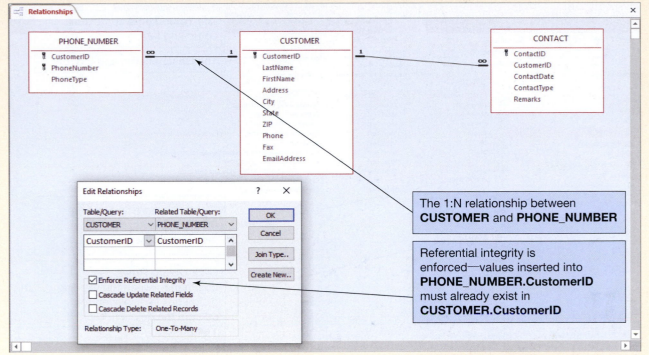

Access 2019, Windows 10, Microsoft Corporation.

5. Using the techniques you have learned, populate the PHONE_NUMBER table with the data shown in Figure WA-2-22. When you are done, the PHONE_NUMBER table data will appear as shown in Figure WA-2-25.

6. To remove the Phone column from the CUSTOMER table, first open the CUSTOMER table in Design view. Next, select the row that contains the Phone column specifications by right-clicking on the row boundary. This also opens the shortcut menu shown in Figure WA-2-26. Click the **Delete Rows** command to delete the Phone columns. A warning dialog box will be displayed—click the **Yes** button in this dialog box to confirm the deletion.

7. To remove the Fax column from the CUSTOMER table, repeat the process in step 6 (except for opening the CUSTOMER table—it is already open in Design view).

FIGURE WA-2-25

Data in the WMCRM PHONE_NUMBER Table

Access 2019, Windows 10, Microsoft Corporation.

(Continued)

FIGURE WA-2-26

Deleting the Phone Column in the WMCRM CUSTOMER Table

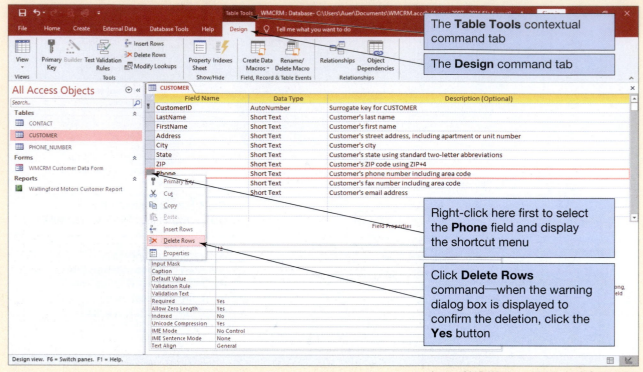

Access 2019, Windows 10, Microsoft Corporation.

8. Save the changes to the CUSTOMER table, and switch to Datasheet view. The data in the CUSTOMER table now appears as shown in Figure WA-2-27.
9. Close the **CUSTOMER** table.

Closing the Database and Exiting Microsoft Access

We have finished the work we need to do in this chapter's "Working with Microsoft Access." As usual, we finish by closing the database and Microsoft Access.

Closing the WMCRM Database and Exiting Microsoft Access

1. To close the WMCRM database and exit Microsoft Access 2019, click the **Close** button in the upper-right corner of the Microsoft Access 2019 window.

FIGURE WA-2-27

Data in the Altered WMCRM CUSTOMER Table

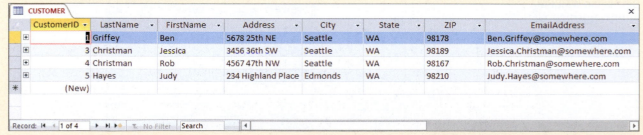

Access 2019, Windows 10, Microsoft Corporation.

SUMMARY

The relational model is the most important standard in database processing today. It was first published by E. F. Codd in 1970. Today, it is used for the design and implementation of almost every commercial database.

An entity is something of importance to a user that needs to be represented in a database. A relation is a two-dimensional table that has the characteristics listed in Figure 2-1. In this book, and in the database world in general, the term *table* is used synonymously with the term *relation*. Three sets of terminology are used for relational structures. The terms *table, row*, and *column* are used most commonly, but *file, record*, and *field* are sometimes used in traditional data processing. Theorists also use the terms *relation, tuple*, and *attribute* for the same three constructs. Sometimes these terms are mixed and matched. Strictly speaking, a relation may not have duplicate rows; however, sometimes this condition is relaxed because eliminating duplicates can be a time-consuming process.

A key is one or more columns of a relation that is used to identify a row. A unique key identifies a single row; a nonunique key identifies several rows. A composite key is a key that has two or more attributes. A relation has one primary key, which must be a unique key. A relation may also have additional unique keys, called candidate keys. A primary key is used to represent the table in relationships, and many DBMS products use values of the primary key to organize table storage. In addition, an index normally is constructed to provide fast access via primary key values. An ideal primary key is short and numeric and never changes.

A surrogate key is a unique numeric value that is included in a relation to serve as the primary key. Surrogate key values have no meaning to the user and are normally hidden on forms, query results, and reports.

A foreign key is an attribute that is placed in a relation to represent a relationship. A foreign key is the primary key of a table that is different from (foreign to) the table in which it is placed. Primary and foreign keys may have different names, but they must use the same data types and sets of values. A referential integrity constraint specifies that the values of a foreign key must be present in the primary key.

A null value occurs when no value has been given to an attribute. The problem with a null value is that its meaning is ambiguous. It can mean that no value is appropriate, that a value is appropriate but has not yet been chosen, or that a value is appropriate and has been chosen but is unknown to the user. It is possible to eliminate null values by requiring attribute values. Another problem with null values will be discussed in Chapter 3.

A functional dependency occurs when the value of one attribute (or set of attributes) determines the value of a second attribute (or set of attributes). The attribute on the left side of a functional dependency is called the determinant. One way to view the purpose of a relation is to say that the relation exists to store instances of functional dependencies. Another way to define a primary (and candidate) key is to say that such a key is an attribute (or set of attributes) that functionally determines all the other attributes in a relation.

Normalization is the process of evaluating a relation and, when necessary, breaking the relation into two or more relations that are better designed and said to be well formed. According to normalization theory, a relation is poorly structured if it has a functional dependency that does not involve the primary key. Specifically, in a well-formed relation, every determinant is a candidate key.

The multivalue, multicolumn design sets a fixed number of repeating values and stores each in a column of its own (for example, storing home phone and cell phone numbers in separate columns). Such a design limits the number of items allowed and results in awkward Structured Query Language (SQL) query statements (SQL queries are discussed in Chapter 3). A better design results from putting multiple values in a table of their own.

A process for normalizing relations into BCNF is shown on page 89–90, and a discussion of multivalued dependencies and 4NF is found on pages 96–98. According to this process, relations that have normalization problems are divided into two or more relations that do not have such problems. Foreign keys are established between the old and new relations, and referential integrity constraints are created. For reference, a brief discussion of all normal forms is presented on pages 99–100.

KEY TERMS

alternate key	fifth normal form (5NF)	primary key
attribute	first normal form (1NF)	record
AUTO_INCREMENT	fourth normal form (4NF)	referential integrity constraint
Boyce-Codd Normal Form (BCNF)	foreign key	relation
candidate key	functional dependency	repeating groups
column	functionally dependent	row
composite key	identity	second normal form (2NF)
database integrity	identity increment	SEQUENCE
database schema	identity seed	surrogate key
determinant	is identity	synonyms
domain	key	table
domain integrity constraint	multivalue, multicolumn problem	third normal form (3NF)
domain/key normal form (DK/NF)	multivalued dependency	transitive dependency
entity	nonunique key	tuple
entity integrity constraint	normalization	unique key
field	normalization process	well-formed relation
file	null value	

REVIEW QUESTIONS

2.1 Why is the relational model important?

2.2 Define the term *entity,* and give an example of an entity (other than the one from this chapter).

2.3 List the characteristics a table must have to be considered a relation. Define the term *domain*, and explain the significance of the *domain integrity constraint* to a relation.

2.4 Give an example of a relation (other than one from this chapter).

2.5 Give an example of a table that is not a relation (other than one from this chapter).

2.6 Under what circumstances can an attribute of a relation be of variable length?

2.7 Explain the use of the terms *file, record*, and *field*.

2.8 Explain the use of the terms *relation, tuple*, and *attribute*.

2.9 Under what circumstances can a relation have duplicate rows?

2.10 Define the term *unique key* and give an example.

2.11 Define the term *nonunique key* and give an example.

2.12 Give an example of a relation with a unique composite key.

2.13 Define the terms *candidate key* and *primary key*. Explain the difference between a primary key and a candidate key. Explain the significance of the *entity integrity constraint* to a primary key

2.14 Describe four uses of a primary key.

2.15 What is a *surrogate key*, and under what circumstances would you use one?

2.16 How do surrogate keys obtain their values?

2.17   Why are the values of surrogate keys normally hidden from users on forms, queries, and reports?

2.18   Explain the term *foreign key,* and give an example.

2.19   Explain how primary keys and foreign keys are denoted in this book.

2.20   Define the term *referential integrity constraint,* and give an example of one. How does the referential integrity constraint contribute to database integrity?

2.21   Explain three possible interpretations of a null value.

2.22   Give an example of a null value (other than one from this chapter), and explain each of the three possible interpretations for that value.

2.23   Define the terms *functional dependency* and *determinant* using an example not from this book.

2.24   In the following equation, name the functional dependency and identify the determinant(s):

$$Area = Length \times Width$$

2.25   Explain the meaning of the following expression:

$$A \rightarrow (B, C)$$

Given this expression, tell if it is also true that:

$$A \rightarrow B$$

and:

$$A \rightarrow C$$

2.26   Explain the meaning of the following expression:

$$(D, E) \rightarrow F$$

Given this expression, tell if it is also true that:

$$D \rightarrow F$$

and:

$$E \rightarrow F$$

2.27   Explain the differences in your answers to questions 2.25 and 2.26.

2.28   Define the term *primary key* in terms of functional dependencies.

2.29   If you assume that a relation has no duplicate data, how do you know there is always at least one primary key?

2.30   How does your answer to question 2.29 change if you allow a relation to have duplicate data?

2.31   In your own words, describe the nature and purpose of the normalization process.

2.32   Examine the data in the Veterinary Office List—Version One in Figure 1-35 (see page 63), and state assumptions about functional dependencies in that table. What is the danger of making such conclusions on the basis of sample data?

2.33   Using the assumptions you stated in your answer to question 2.32, what are the determinants of this relation? What attribute(s) can be the primary key of this relation?

2.34   Describe a modification problem that occurs when changing data in the relation in question 2.32 and a second modification problem that occurs when deleting data in this relation.

2.35   Examine the data in the Veterinary Office List—Version Two in Figure 1-36 (see page 63), and state assumptions about functional dependencies in that table.

2.36   Using the assumptions you stated in your answer to question 2.35, what are the determinants of this relation? What attribute(s) can be the primary key of this relation?

2.37   Explain a modification problem that occurs when changing data in the relation in question 2.35 and a second modification problem that occurs when deleting data in this relation.

EXERCISES

2.38   Apply the normalization process to the Veterinary Office List—Version One relation shown in Figure 1-35 (see page 63) to develop a set of normalized relations. Show the results of each of the steps in the normalization process.

2.39   Apply the normalization process to the Veterinary Office List—Version Two relation shown in Figure 1-36 (see page 63), to develop a set of normalized relations. Show the results of each of the steps in the normalization process.

2.40   What is the multivalue, multicolumn problem? What is a multivalued dependency, and how is it resolved by 4NF? To answer these questions, consider the following relation:

STUDENT(StudentNumber, StudentName, SiblingName, Major)

Assume that the values of SiblingName are the names of all of a given student's brothers and sisters; also assume that students have at most one major.

A.   Define and discuss the *multivalue, multicolumn problem*. Define and discuss a *multivalued dependency*.

B.   Show an example of this relation for two students, one of whom has three siblings and the other of whom has only two siblings.

C.   List the candidate keys in this relation.

D.   State the functional dependencies in this relation.

E.   Explain why this relation does not meet the relational design criteria set out in this chapter (that is, why this is not a well-formed relation).

F.   Define and discuss 4NF and how 4NF can be used to allow a set of well-formed relations.

G.   Divide this relation into a set of relations that meet the relational design criteria (that is, that are well formed). Specify the type of final normal form for each the final relations.

2.41   What is the *multivalue, multicolumn problem*? What is a *multivalued dependency*, and how is it resolved by 4NF? To answer these questions, alter exercise 2.40 to allow students to have multiple majors. In this case, the relational structure is:

STUDENT (StudentNumber, StudentName, SiblingName, Major)

A.   Define and discuss the *multivalue, multicolumn problem*. Define and discuss a *multivalued dependency*.

B.   Show an example of this relation for two students, one of whom has three siblings and the other of whom has one sibling. Assume that each student has a single major.

C.   Show the data changes necessary to add a second major for only the first student.

D. Based on your answer to part C, show the data changes necessary to add a second major for the second student.

E. Explain the differences in your answers to parts C and D. Comment on the desirability of this situation.

F. Define and discuss 4NF, and how 4NF can be used to allow a set of well-formed relations.

G. Divide this relation into a set of well-formed relations. Specify the type of normal form for each of the final relations.

2.42 The text states that you can argue that "the only reason for having relations is to store instances of functional dependencies." Explain, in your own words, what this means.

2.43 Consider a table named ORDER_ITEM, with data as shown in Figure 2-26. The schema for ORDER_ITEM is:

ORDER_ITEM (OrderNumber, SKU, Quantity, Price)

where SKU is a "Stock Keeping Unit" number, which is similar to a part number. Here it indicates which product was sold on each line of the table. Note that one OrderNumber must have at least one SKU associated with it and may have several. Use this table and the detailed discussion of normal forms on pages 99–100 to answer the following questions.

A. Define 1NF. Is ORDER_ITEM in 1NF? If not, why not, and what would have to be done to put it into 1NF? Make any changes necessary to put ORDER_ITEM into 1NF. If this step requires you to create an additional table, make sure that the new table is also in 1NF.

B. Define 2NF. Now that ORDER_ITEM is in 1NF, is it also in 2NF? If not, why not, and what would have to be done to put it into 2NF? Make any changes necessary to put ORDER_ITEM into 2NF. If this step requires you to create an additional table, make sure that the new table is also in 2NF.

C. Define 3NF. Now that ORDER_ITEM is in 2NF, is it also in 3NF? If not, why not, and what would have to be done to put it into 3NF? Make any changes necessary to put ORDER_ITEM into 3NF. If this step requires you to create an additional table, make sure that the new table and any other tables created in previous steps are also in 3NF.

D. Define BCNF. Now that ORDER_ITEM is in 3NF, is it also in BCNF? If not, why not, and what would have to be done to put it into BCNF? Make any changes necessary to put ORDER_ITEM into BCNF. If this step requires you to create an additional table, make sure that the new table and any other tables created in previous steps are also in BCNF.

FIGURE 2-26

The ORDER_ITEM Table

OrderNumber	SKU	Quantity	Price
1000	201000	1	300.00
1000	202000	1	130.00
2000	101100	4	50.00
2000	101200	2	50.00
3000	100200	1	300.00
3000	101100	2	50.00
3000	101200	1	50.00

WORKING WITH MICROSOFT ACCESS

Key Terms

Edit Relationships dialog box   Relationships window
Enforce Referential Integrity check box

Exercises

In the Exercises for the section of "Working with Microsoft Access" in Chapter 1, we created a database for the Wedgewood Pacific (WP) company of Seattle, Washington, and created and populated the EMPLOYEE table. In this exercise, we will build the rest of the tables needed for the database, create the referential integrity constraints between them, and populate them.

The full set of normalized tables for the WP database is as follows:

DEPARTMENT (<u>DepartmentName</u>, BudgetCode, OfficeNumber, DepartmentPhone)

EMPLOYEE (<u>EmployeeNumber</u>, FirstName, LastName, *Department*, Position, Supervisor, OfficePhone, EmailAddress)

PROJECT (<u>ProjectID</u>, ProjectName, *Department*, MaxHours, StartDate, EndDate)

ASSIGNMENT (<u>*ProjectID*</u>, <u>*EmployeeNumber*</u>, HoursWorked)

The primary key of DEPARTMENT is DepartmentName, the primary key of EMPLOYEE is EmployeeNumber, and the primary key of PROJECT is ProjectID. Note that the EMPLOYEE table is the same as the table we have created, except that Department is now a foreign key. In EMPLOYEE and PROJECT, Department is a foreign key that references DepartmentName in DEPARTMENT. Note that a foreign key does not need to have the same name as the primary key to which it refers. The primary key of ASSIGNMENT is the composite (ProjectID, EmployeeNumber). ProjectID is also a foreign key that references ProjectID in PROJECT, and EmployeeNumber is a foreign key that references EmployeeNumber in EMPLOYEE.

The referential integrity constraints are:

Department in EMPLOYEE must exist in DepartmentName in DEPARTMENT

Department in PROJECT must exist in DepartmentName in DEPARTMENT

ProjectID in ASSIGNMENT must exist in ProjectID in PROJECT

EmployeeNumber in ASSIGNMENT must exist in EmployeeNumber in EMPLOYEE

A. Figure 2-27 shows the column characteristics for the WP DEPARTMENT table. Using the column characteristics, create the DEPARTMENT table in the WP.accdb database.

B. For the DEPARTMENT table, create a data input form named WP Department Data Form. Make any necessary adjustments to the form so that all data display properly. Use this form to enter into your DEPARTMENT table the data in the DEPARTMENT table shown in Figure 2-28.

C. Create the relationship and referential integrity constraint between DEPARTMENT and EMPLOYEE. Enable enforcing of referential integrity and enable cascading of data updates, but do *not* enable cascading of deletions.

FIGURE 2-27

Column Characteristics for the WP DEPARTMENT Table

Column Name	Type	Key	Required	Remarks
DepartmentName	Short Text (35)	Primary Key	Yes	
BudgetCode	Short Text (30)	No	Yes	
OfficeNumber	Short Text (15)	No	Yes	
DepartmentPhone	Short Text (12)	No	Yes	

FIGURE 2-28

WP DEPARTMENT Table Data

DepartmentName	BudgetCode	OfficeNumber	DepartmentPhone
Administration	BC-100-10	BLDG01-210	360-285-8100
Legal	BC-200-10	BLDG01-220	360-285-8200
Human Resources	BC-300-10	BLDG01-230	360-285-8300
Finance	BC-400-10	BLDG01-110	360-285-8400
Accounting	BC-500-10	BLDG01-120	360-285-8405
Sales and Marketing	BC-600-10	BLDG01-250	360-285-8500
InfoSystems	BC-700-10	BLDG02-210	360-285-8600
Research and Development	BC-800-10	BLDG02-250	360-285-8700
Production	BC-900-10	BLDG02-110	360-285-8800

D. Figure 2-29 shows the column characteristics for the WP PROJECT table. Using the column characteristics, create the PROJECT table in the WP.accdb database.

E. Create the relationship and referential integrity constraint between DEPARTMENT and PROJECT. Enable enforcing of referential integrity and enable cascading of data updates, but do *not* enable cascading of deletions.

F. For the PROJECT table, create a data input form named WP Project Data Form. Make any necessary adjustments to the form so that all data display properly. Use this form to enter into your PROJECT table the data in the PROJECT table shown in Figure 2-30.

FIGURE 2-29

Column Characteristics for the WP PROJECT Table

Column Name	Type	Key	Required	Remarks
ProjectID	Number	Primary Key	Yes	Long Integer
ProjectName	Short Text (50)	No	Yes	
Department	Short Text (35)	Foreign Key	Yes	
MaxHours	Number	No	Yes	Double, fixed, 2 decimal places
StartDate	Date/Time	No	No	Medium date
EndDate	Date/Time	No	No	Medium date

(Continued)

FIGURE 2-30

WP PROJECT Table Data

ProjectID	ProjectName	Department	MaxHours	StartDate	EndDate
1000	2019 Q3 Production Plan	Production	100.00	05/10/19	06/15/19
1100	2019 Q3 Marketing Plan	Sales and Marketing	135.00	05/10/19	06/15/19
1200	2019 Q3 Portfolio Analysis	Finance	120.00	07/05/19	07/25/19
1300	2019 Q3 Tax Preparation	Accounting	145.00	08/10/19	10/15/19
1400	2019 Q4 Production Plan	Production	100.00	08/10/19	09/15/19
1500	2019 Q4 Marketing Plan	Sales and Marketing	135.00	08/10/19	09/15/19
1600	2019 Q4 Portfolio Analysis	Finance	140.00	10/05/19	

FIGURE 2-31

Column Characteristics for the WP ASSIGNMENT Table

Column Name	Type	Key	Required	Remarks
ProjectID	Number	Primary Key, Foreign Key	Yes	Long Integer
EmployeeNumber	Number	Primary Key, Foreign Key	Yes	Long Integer
HoursWorked	Number	No	No	Double, fixed, 1 decimal places

G. During creation and population of the DEPARTMENT table, the data were entered into the table before the referential integrity constraint with EMPLOYEE was created, but during creation and population of the PROJECT table, the referential integrity constraint was created before the data were entered. Why did the order of the steps differ? Which order is normally the correct order to use?

H. Figure 2-31 shows the column characteristics for the WP ASSIGNMENT table. Using the column characteristics, create the ASSIGNMENT table in the WP.accdb database.

I. Create the relationship and referential integrity constraint between ASSIGNMENT and PROJECT and between ASSIGNMENT and EMPLOYEE. When creating both relations, enable enforcing of referential integrity, but do *not* enable cascading of data updates or cascading of data from deleted records.

J. For the ASSIGNMENT table, create a data input form named WP Assignment Data Form. Make any necessary adjustments to the form so that all data display properly. Use this form to enter into your ASSIGNMENT table the data in the ASSIGNMENT table shown in Figure 2-32.

K. When creating the relationships between the database tables, we allowed the cascading of data changes between some tables but not between others. (*Cascading* means that changes to data in one table are also made to the other table in the relationship.) The value of a primary key changes in this case, and that change is then made in the values of the matching foreign key. Why did we enable

FIGURE 2-32

WP ASSIGNMENT Table Data

ProjectID	EmployeeNumber	HoursWorked
1000	1	30.00
1000	6	50.00
1000	10	50.00
1000	16	75.00
1000	17	75.00
1100	1	30.00
1100	6	75.00
1100	10	55.00
1100	11	55.00
1200	3	20.00
1200	6	40.00
1200	7	45.00
1200	8	45.00
1300	3	25.00
1300	6	40.00
1300	8	50.00
1300	9	50.00
1400	1	30.00
1400	6	50.00
1400	10	50.00
1400	16	75.00
1400	17	75.00
1500	1	30.00
1500	6	75.00
1500	10	55.00
1500	11	55.00
1600	3	20.00
1600	6	40.00
1600	7	45.00
1600	8	45.00

cascading of related field values between (1) DEPARTMENT and EMPLOYEE and (2) DEPARTMENT and PROJECT but not for (3) EMPLOYEE and ASSIGNMENT and (4) PROJECT and ASSIGNMENT?

L. Does the multivalue, multicolumn problem exist in the current set of WP tables? If so, how would you fix it? If not, what modifications to the EMPLOYEE table would create the problem, and how would you then fix this problem?

REGIONAL LABS

Regional Labs is a company that conducts research and development work on a contract basis for other companies and organizations. Figure 2-33 shows data that Regional Labs collects about projects and the employees assigned to them.

This data is stored in a relation (table) named PROJECT:

PROJECT (ProjectID, EmployeeName, EmployeeSalary)

A. Assuming that all functional dependencies are apparent in this data, which of the following are true?

ProjectID → EmployeeName

ProjectID → EmployeeSalary

(ProjectID, EmployeeName) → EmployeeSalary

EmployeeName → EmployeeSalary

EmployeeSalary → ProjectID

EmployeeSalary → (ProjectID, EmployeeName)

B. What is the primary key of PROJECT?

C. Are all the nonkey attributes (if any) dependent on the primary key?

D. In what normal form is PROJECT?

E. Describe two modification anomalies that affect PROJECT.

F. Is ProjectID a determinant? If so, based on which functional dependencies in part A?

G. Is EmployeeName a determinant? If so, based on which functional dependencies in part A?

H. Is (ProjectID, EmployeeName) a determinant? If so, based on which functional dependencies in part A?

I. Is EmployeeSalary a determinant? If so, based on which functional dependencies in part A?

J. Does this relation contain a transitive dependency? If so, what is it?

K. Redesign the relation to eliminate modification anomalies.

FIGURE 2-33

Sample Data for Regional Labs

ProjectID	EmployeeName	Employee Salary
100-A	Eric Jones	64,000.00
100-A	Donna Smith	70,000.00
100-B	Donna Smith	70,000.00
200-A	Eric Jones	64,000.00
200-B	Eric Jones	64,000.00
200-C	Eric Parks	58,000.00
200-C	Donna Smith	70,000.00
200-D	Eric Parks	58,000.00

GARDEN GLORY PROJECT QUESTIONS

Figure 2-34 shows data that Garden Glory collects about properties and services.

A. Using these data, state assumptions about functional dependencies among the columns of data. Justify your assumptions on the basis of these sample data and also on the basis of what you know about service businesses.

B. Given your assumptions in part A, comment on the appropriateness of the following designs:

1. PROPERTY (<u>PropertyName</u>, PropertyType, Street, City, ZIP, ServiceDate, Description, Amount)

2. PROPERTY (PropertyName, PropertyType, Street, City, ZIP, <u>ServiceDate</u>, Description, Amount)

3. PROPERTY (<u>PropertyName</u>, PropertyType, Street, City, ZIP, <u>ServiceDate</u>, Description, Amount)

4. PROPERTY (<u>PropertyID</u>, PropertyName, PropertyType, Street, City, ZIP, ServiceDate, Description, Amount)

5. PROPERTY (<u>PropertyID</u>, PropertyName, PropertyType, Street, City, ZIP, <u>ServiceDate</u>, Description, Amount)

6. PROPERTY (<u>PropertyID</u>, PropertyName, PropertyType, Street, City, ZIP, *ServiceDate*)

   and:

   SERVICE (<u>ServiceDate</u>, Description, Amount)

7. PROPERTY (<u>PropertyID</u>, PropertyName, PropertyType, Street, City, ZIP, ServiceDate)

   and:

   SERVICE (<u>ServiceID</u>, *ServiceDate*, Description, Amount)

8. PROPERTY (<u>PropertyID</u>, PropertyName, PropertyType, Street, City, ZIP, *ServiceDate*)

   and:

   SERVICE (<u>ServiceID</u>, ServiceDate, Description, Amount, *PropertyID*)

FIGURE 2-34

Sample Data for Garden Glory

PropertyName	PropertyType	Street	City	ZIP	ServiceDate	Description	Amount
Eastlake Building	Office	123 Eastlake	Seattle	98119	5/5/2018	Lawn Mow	$ 42.50
Elm St Apts	Apartment	4 East Elm	Lynnwood	98223	5/8/2018	Lawn Mow	$ 123.50
Jeferson Hill	Office	42 West 7th St	Bellevue	98040	5/8/2018	Garden Service	$ 53.00
Eastlake Building	Office	123 Eastlake	Seattle	98119	5/10/2018	Lawn Mow	$ 42.50
Eastlake Building	Office	123 Eastlake	Seattle	98119	5/12/2018	Lawn Mow	$ 42.50
Elm St Apts	Apartment	4 East Elm	Lynnwood	98223	5/15/2018	Lawn Mow	$ 123.50
Eastlake Building	Office	123 Eastlake	Seattle	98119	5/19/2018	Lawn Mow	$ 42.50

9. PROPERTY (PropertyID, PropertyName, PropertyType, Street, City, ZIP)

and:

SERVICE (ServiceID, ServiceDate, Description, Amount, *PropertyID*)

C. Suppose Garden Glory decides to add the following table:

SERVICE_FEE (PropertyID, ServiceID, Description, Amount)

Add this table to what you consider to be the best design in your answer to part B. Modify the tables from part B as necessary to minimize the amount of data duplication. Will this design work for the data in Figure 2-34? If not, modify the design so that this data will work. State the assumptions implied by this design.

JAMES RIVER JEWELRY PROJECT QUESTIONS

James River Jewelry is a small jewelry shop. While James River Jewelry does sell typical jewelry purchased from jewelry vendors, including such items as rings, necklaces, earrings, and watches, it specializes in hard-to-find Asian jewelry. Although some Asian jewelry is manufactured jewelry purchased from vendors in the same manner as the standard jewelry is obtained, many of the Asian jewelry pieces are often unique single items purchased directly from the artisan who created the piece (the term *manufactured* would be an inappropriate description of these pieces). James River Jewelry has a small but loyal clientele, and it wants to further increase customer loyalty by creating a frequent buyer program. In this program, after every 10 purchases, a customer will receive a credit equal to 50 percent of the average of his or her 10 most recent purchases. This credit must be applied to the next (or 11th) purchase. Figure 2-35 shows data that James River Jewelry collects for its frequent buyer program.

A. Using these data, state assumptions about functional dependencies among the columns of data. Justify your assumptions on the basis of these sample data and also on the basis of what you know about retail sales.

B. Given your assumptions in part A, comment on the appropriateness of the following designs:

1. CUSTOMER (Name, Phone, EmailAddress, InvoiceNumber, InvoiceDate, PreTaxAmount)

2. CUSTOMER (Name, Phone, EmailAddress, InvoiceNumber, InvoiceDate, PreTaxAmount)

3. CUSTOMER (Name, Phone, EmailAddress, InvoiceNumber, InvoiceDate, PreTaxAmount)

4. CUSTOMER (CustomerID, Name, Phone, EmailAddress, InvoiceNumber, InvoiceDate, PreTaxAmount)

FIGURE 2-35

Sample Data for James River Jewelry

Name	Phone	EmailAddress	InvoiceNumber	InvoiceDate	PreTaxAmount
Elizabeth Stanley	555-236-7789	Elizabeth.Stanley@somewhere.com	1001	5/5/2019	$ 155.00
Fred Price	555-236-0091	Fred.Price@somewhere.com	1002	5/7/2019	$ 203.00
Linda Becky	555-236-0392	Linda.Becky@somewhere.com	1003	5/11/2019	$ 75.00
Pamela Birch	555-236-4493	Pamela.Birch@somewhere.com	1004	5/15/2019	$ 67.00
Richardo Romez	555-236-3334	Richard.Romez@somewhere.com	1005	5/15/2019	$ 330.00
Elizabeth Stanley	555-236-7789	Elizabeth.Stanley@somewhere.com	1006	5/16/2019	$ 25.00
Linda Becky	555-236-0392	Linda.Becky@somewhere.com	1007	5/25/2019	$ 45.00
Elizabeth Stanley	555-236-7789	Elizabeth.Stanley@somewhere.com	1008	6/6/2019	$ 445.00
Samantha Jackson	555-236-1095	Samantha.Jackson@somewhere.com	1009	6/7/2019	$ 72.00

5. CUSTOMER (<u>Name</u>, Phone, EmailAddress)

    and:

    PURCHASE (<u>InvoiceNumber</u>, InvoiceDate, PreTaxAmount)

6. CUSTOMER (Name, Phone, <u>EmailAddress</u>)

    and:

    PURCHASE (<u>InvoiceNumber</u>, InvoiceDate, PreTaxAmount, *EmailAddress*)

7. CUSTOMER (Name, Phone, <u>EmailAddress</u>)

    and:

    PURCHASE (<u>InvoiceNumber</u>, Phone, InvoiceDate, PreTaxAmount, *EmailAddress*)

C. Modify what you consider to be the best design in part B to include a column called AwardPurchaseAmount. The purpose of this column is to keep a balance of the customers' purchases for award purposes. Assume that returns will be recorded, with invoices having a negative PreTaxAmount.

D. Add a new AWARD table to your answer to part C. Assume that the new table will hold data concerning the date and amount of an award that is given after a customer has purchased 10 items. Ensure that your new table has appropriate primary and foreign keys.

THE QUEEN ANNE CURIOSITY SHOP PROJECT QUESTIONS

Figure 2-36 shows typical sales data for the Queen Anne Curiosity Shop, and Figure 2-37 shows typical purchase data.

A. Using these data, state assumptions about functional dependencies among the columns of data. Justify your assumptions on the basis of these sample data and also on the basis of what you know about retail sales.

FIGURE 2-36

Sample Sales Data for the Queen Anne Curiosity Shop

LastName	FirstName	Phone	InvoiceDate	InvoiceItem	Price	Tax	Total
Shire	Robert	206-524-2433	14-Dec-18	Antique Desk	3,000.00	249.00	3,249.00
Shire	Robert	206-524-2433	14-Dec-18	Antique Desk Chair	500.00	41.50	541.50
Goodyear	Katherine	206-524-3544	15-Dec-18	Dining Table Linens	1,000.00	83.00	1,083.00
Bancroft	Chris	425-635-9788	15-Dec-18	Candles	50.00	4.15	54.15
Griffith	John	206-524-4655	23-Dec-18	Candles	45.00	3.74	48.74
Shire	Robert	206-524-2433	5-Jan-19	Desk Lamp	250.00	20.75	270.75
Tierney	Doris	425-635-8677	10-Jan-19	Dining Table Linens	750.00	62.25	812.25
Anderson	Donna	360-538-7566	12-Jan-19	Book Shelf	250.00	20.75	270.75
Goodyear	Katherine	206-524-3544	15-Jan-19	Antique Chair	1,250.00	103.75	1,353.75
Goodyear	Katherine	206-524-3544	15-Jan-19	Antique Chair	1,750.00	145.25	1,895.25
Tierney	Doris	425-635-8677	25-Jan-19	Antique Candle Holders	350.00	29.05	379.05

FIGURE 2-37

Sample Purchase Data for the Queen Anne Curiosity Shop

PurchaseItem	PurchasePrice	PurchaseDate	Vendor	Phone
Antique Desk	1,800.00	7-Nov-18	European Specialties	206-325-7866
Antique Desk	1,750.00	7-Nov-18	European Specialties	206-325-7866
Antique Candle Holders	210.00	7-Nov-18	European Specialties	206-325-7866
Antique Candle Holders	200.00	7-Nov-18	European Specialties	206-325-7866
Dining Table Linens	600.00	14-Nov-18	Linens and Things	206-325-6755
Candles	30.00	14-Nov-18	Linens and Things	206-325-6755
Desk Lamp	150.00	14-Nov-18	Lamps and Lighting	206-325-8977
Floor Lamp	300.00	14-Nov-18	Lamps and Lighting	206-325-8977
Dining Table Linens	450.00	21-Nov-18	Linens and Things	206-325-6755
Candles	27.00	21-Nov-18	Linens and Things	206-325-6755
Book Shelf	150.00	21-Nov-18	Harrison, Denise	425-746-4322
Antique Desk	1,000.00	28-Nov-18	Lee, Andrew	425-746-5433
Antique Desk Chair	300.00	28-Nov-18	Lee, Andrew	425-746-5433
Antique Chair	750.00	28-Nov-18	New York Brokerage	206-325-9088
Antique Chair	1,050.00	28-Nov-18	New York Brokerage	206-325-9088

B. Given your assumptions in part A, comment on the appropriateness of the following designs:

1. CUSTOMER (<u>LastName</u>, FirstName, Phone, InvoiceDate, InvoiceItem, Price, Tax, Total)

2. CUSTOMER (<u>LastName</u>, <u>FirstName</u>, Phone, InvoiceDate, InvoiceItem, Price, Tax, Total)

3. CUSTOMER (LastName, FirstName, <u>Phone</u>, InvoiceDate, InvoiceItem, Price, Tax, Total)

4. CUSTOMER (<u>LastName</u>, <u>FirstName</u>, Phone, <u>InvoiceDate</u>, InvoiceItem, Price, Tax, Total)

5. CUSTOMER (<u>LastName</u>, <u>FirstName</u>, Phone, InvoiceDate, <u>InvoiceItem</u>, Price, Tax, Total)

6. CUSTOMER (<u>LastName</u>, <u>FirstName</u>, Phone)

   and:

   SALE (<u>InvoiceDate</u>, InvoiceItem, Price, Tax, Total)

7. CUSTOMER (<u>LastName</u>, <u>FirstName</u>, Phone, *InvoiceDate*)

   and:

   SALE (<u>InvoiceDate</u>, InvoiceItem, Price, Tax, Total)

8. CUSTOMER (<u>LastName</u>, <u>FirstName</u>, Phone)

   and:

   SALE (<u>InvoiceDate</u>, <u>InvoiceItem</u>, Price, Tax, Total, *LastName, FirstName*)

C. Modify what you consider to be the best design in part B to include surrogate ID columns called CustomerID and SaleID. How does this improve the design?

D. Modify the design in part C by breaking SALE into two relations named SALE and SALE_ITEM. Modify columns and add additional columns as you think necessary. How does this improve the design?

E. Given your assumptions, comment on the appropriateness of the following designs:

1. PURCHASE (<u>PurchaseItem</u>, PurchasePrice, PurchaseDate, Vendor, Phone)

2. PURCHASE (<u>PurchaseItem</u>, <u>PurchasePrice</u>, PurchaseDate, Vendor, Phone)

3. PURCHASE (<u>PurchaseItem</u>, PurchasePrice, <u>PurchaseDate</u>, Vendor, Phone)

4. PURCHASE (<u>PurchaseItem</u>, PurchasePrice, PurchaseDate, <u>Vendor</u>, Phone)

5. PURCHASE (<u>PurchaseItem</u>, PurchasePrice, <u>PurchaseDate</u>)

   and:

   VENDOR (<u>Vendor</u>, Phone)

6. PURCHASE (<u>PurchaseItem</u>, <u>PurchasePrice</u>, PurchaseDate, *Vendor*)

   and:

   VENDOR (<u>Vendor</u>, Phone)

7. PURCHASE (<u>PurchaseItem</u>, PurchasePrice, <u>PurchaseDate</u>, *Vendor*)

   and:

   VENDOR (<u>Vendor</u>, Phone)

F. Modify what you consider to be the best design in part E to include surrogate ID columns called PurchaseID and VendorID. How does this improve the design?

G. The relations in your design from part D and part F are not connected. Modify the database design so that sales data and purchase data are related.

3 Structured Query Language

- Learn basic SQL statements for creating database structures
- Learn basic SQL statements for adding data to a database
- Learn basic SQL SELECT statements and options for processing a single table
- Learn basic SQL SELECT statements for processing multiple tables with subqueries

- Learn basic SQL SELECT statements for processing multiple tables with joins
- Learn basic SQL statements for modifying and deleting data from a database
- Learn basic SQL statements for modifying and deleting database tables and constraints

This chapter describes and discusses **Structured Query Language (SQL)**. SQL is not a complete programming language; rather, it is a **data sublanguage**. SQL consists only of constructs for defining and processing a database. To obtain a full programming language, SQL statements must be embedded in scripting languages, such as VBScript, or in programming languages, such as Java or C#. SQL statements also can be submitted interactively, using a DBMS-supplied command prompt.

SQL was developed by the IBM Corporation in the late 1970s, and successive versions were endorsed as national standards by the **American National Standards Institute (ANSI)** in 1986, 1989, and 1992. The 1992 version is sometimes referred to as SQL-92 or sometimes ANSI-92 SQL. In 1999, SQL:1999 (also referred to as SQL3), which incorporated some object-oriented concepts, was released. This was followed by the release of SQL:2003 in 2003, SQL:2006 in 2006, SQL:2008 in 2008, SQL:2011 in 2011, and, most recently, SQL:2016 in 2016. Each of these added new features or extended existing SQL features, including SQL support for the SQL TRUNCATE TABLE and SQL MERGE statements in SQL:2008; support for **Extensible Markup Language (XML)** (XML is discussed in Chapter 7 and online Extension C) in SQL:2008; and support for **JavaScript Object Notation (JSON)** (JSON is discussed in Chapter 7 and the online Extension C) in SQL:2016. SQL has also been endorsed as a standard by the **International Organization for Standardization (ISO)** (and, no, that's not a typo—the acronym is *ISO*, not *IOS*!). Our discussion here focuses on common language features that have been in SQL since SQL-92 but does include some features from SQL:2003 and SQL:2008.[1]

SQL is text-oriented. It was developed long before the **graphical user interface (GUI)** became common and requires only a text processor. Today, Microsoft Access, Microsoft SQL Server, Oracle Database, MySQL, and other DBMS products provide GUI tools for performing many of the tasks that are performed using SQL. However, the key phrase in that last sentence is *many of*. You cannot do everything with graphical tools that you can do with SQL. Furthermore, to generate SQL statements dynamically in program code, you must use SQL.

You will learn how to use SQL with Microsoft Access in this chapter's section of "Working with Microsoft Access." Access uses SQL but hides it behind the scenes, presenting a variant of the **Query by Example (QBE)** GUI for general use. Although knowledge of SQL is not a requirement for using Access, you will be a stronger and more effective Access developer if you know SQL.

SQL statements are commonly divided into categories, five of which are of interest to us here:

- **Data definition language (DDL)** statements, which are used for creating tables, relationships, and other structures.
- **Data manipulation language (DML)** statements, which are used for querying, inserting, modifying, and deleting data. One component of SQL DML is SQL views. Views are used to create predefined queries.[2]
- **SQL/Persistent stored modules (SQL/PSM)** statements, which extend SQL by adding procedural programming capabilities, such as variables and flow-of-control statements, that provide some programmability within the SQL framework.
- **Transaction control language (TCL)** statements, which are used to mark transaction boundaries and control transaction behavior.
- **Data control language (DCL)** statements, which are used to grant database permissions (or to revoke those permissions) to users and groups so that the users or groups can perform various operations on the data in the database.

In this chapter, we discuss the basic components of SQL DDL and DML. Additional SQL DML (SQL views) and SQL/PSM are discussed in Extension B, "Advanced SQL." and SQL TCL and DCL are discussed in Chapter 6.

---

[1]For more information about the history and development of SQL, see the Standardization section of the Wikipedia article on **SQL** at https://en.wikipedia.org/wiki/SQL. Wikipedia also has articles on some of the named versions of SQL. For example, see the article on **SQL:2008** at https://en.wikipedia.org/wiki/SQL:2008 for a discussion of the features added to SQL:2008.

[2]Queries by themselves are sometimes considered to be another major category of SQL commands, but we do not make that distinction in this book. For more details, see the Wikipedia article on **SQL** at https://en.wikipedia.org/wiki/SQL.

WEDGEWOOD PACIFIC

The Wedgewood Pacific (WP) company, founded in 1957 in Seattle, Washington, manufactures and sells consumer drone aircraft. This is an innovative and rapidly developing market. In January 2018, the FAA said that over 1 million drones had been registered under the new FAA drone registration rules.[3]

WP currently produces three drone models, the Alpha III, the Bravo III, and the Delta IV. These products are created by WP's Research and Development group, and produced at WP's production facilities. WP manufactures some of the parts used in the drones, but also purchases some parts from other suppliers.

The company is located in two buildings. One building houses the Administration, Legal, Finance, Accounting, Human Resources, and Sales and Marketing departments, and the second houses the Information Systems, Research and Development, and Production departments. The company database contains data about *employees, departments, projects, assets* (such as finished goods inventory, parts inventory, and computer equipment), and other aspects of company operations.

In this chapter, we use an example database for WP that has the following four relations:

DEPARTMENT (<u>DepartmentName</u>, BudgetCode, OfficeNumber, DepartmentPhone)

EMPLOYEE (<u>EmployeeNumber</u>, FirstName, LastName, *Department*, Position, *Supervisor*, OfficePhone, EmailAddress)

PROJECT (<u>ProjectID</u>, ProjectName, *Department*, MaxHours, StartDate, EndDate)

ASSIGNMENT (*<u>ProjectID</u>*, *<u>EmployeeNumber</u>*, HoursWorked)

The primary key of DEPARTMENT is DepartmentName, the primary key of EMPLOYEE is EmployeeNumber, and the primary key of PROJECT is ProjectID. In EMPLOYEE and PROJECT, Department is a foreign key that references DepartmentName in DEPARTMENT. Remember that a foreign key does not need to have the same name as the primary key to which it refers. The primary key of ASSIGNMENT is the composite (ProjectID, EmployeeNumber). ProjectID is also a foreign key that references ProjectID in PROJECT, and EmployeeNumber is a foreign key that references EmployeeNumber in EMPLOYEE.

Finally, note the foreign key Supervisor in EMPLOYEE, which references EmployeeNumber in the same EMPLOYEE table. When a foreign key links to the primary key of the *same table*, this forms what is called a **recursive relationship**. We discuss recursive relationships in detail in Chapter 4 and Chapter 5, and in online Extension B, "Advanced SQL." In this case, we use the recursive relationship to enforce a constraint that a number entered into the Supervisor column must already exist as an EmployeeNumber.

The referential integrity constraints are:

Department in EMPLOYEE must exist in DepartmentName in DEPARTMENT

Supervisor in EMPLOYEE must exist in EmployeeNumber in EMPLOYEE

Department in PROJECT must exist in DepartmentName in DEPARTMENT

ProjectID in ASSIGNMENT must exist in ProjectID in PROJECT

EmployeeNumber in ASSIGNMENT must exist in EmployeeNumber in EMPLOYEE

An illustration of these tables in Microsoft Access 2019, and the database column characteristics for these tables are shown in Figure 3-1. Note that the tables and relationships shown in Figure 3-1(a) do *not* include the recursive relationship in EMPLOYEE—the creation of recursive relationships in Microsoft Access 2019 is discussed in online Extension B, "Advanced SQL." Sample data for these relations are shown in Figure 3-2.

---

[3]See https://flightsafety.org/1-million-drones/ (accessed January, 2019).

FIGURE 3-1

Database Column Characteristics for the WP Database

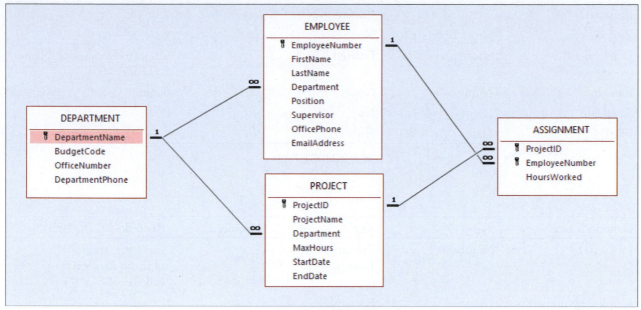

Access 2019, Windows 10, Microsoft Corporation.

(a) The WP Tables in Microsoft Access 2019

Column Name	Type	Key	Required	Remarks
DepartmentName	Short Text (35)	Primary Key	Yes	
BudgetCode	Short Text (30)	No	Yes	
OfficeNumber	Short Text (15)	No	Yes	
DepartmentPhone	Short Text (12)	No	Yes	

(b) DEPARTMENT Table

Column Name	Type	Key	Required	Remarks
EmployeeNumber	AutoNumber	Primary Key	Yes	Surrogate Key
FirstName	Short Text (25)	No	Yes	
LastName	Short Text (25)	No	Yes	
Department	Short Text (35)	Foreign Key	Yes	Links to DepartmentName in DEPARTMENT
Position	Short Text (35)	No	No	
Supervisor	Number	Foreign Key	No	Long Integer. Links to EmployeeNumber in EMPLOYEE
OfficePhone	Short Text (12)	No	No	
EmailAddress	Short Text (100)	No	Yes	

(c) EMPLOYEE Table   (*Continued*)

FIGURE 3-1 Continued

ColumnName	Type	Key	Required	Remarks
ProjectID	Number	Primary Key	Yes	Long Integer
ProjectName	Short Text (50)	No	Yes	
Department	Short Text (35)	Foreign Key	Yes	Links to DepartmentName in DEPARTMENT
MaxHours	Number	No	Yes	Double
StartDate	Date	No	No	
EndDate	Date	No	No	

(d) PROJECT Table

Column Name	Type	Key	Required	Remarks
ProjectID	Number	Primary Key, Foreign Key	Yes	Long Integer Links to ProjectID in PROJECT
EmployeeNumber	Number	Primary Key, Foreign Key	Yes	Long Integer Links to EmployeeNumber in EMPLOYEE
HoursWorked	Number	No	No	Double

(e) ASSIGNMENT Table

FIGURE 3-2

Sample Data for the WP Database

DepartmentName	BudgetCode	OfficeNumber	DepartmentPhone
Administration	BC-100-10	BLDG01-210	360-285-8100
Legal	BC-200-10	BLDG01-220	360-285-8200
Human Resources	BC-300-10	BLDG01-230	360-285-8300
Finance	BC-400-10	BLDG01-110	360-285-8400
Accounting	BC-500-10	BLDG01-120	360-285-8405
Sales and Marketing	BC-600-10	BLDG01-250	360-285-8500
InfoSystems	BC-700-10	BLDG02-210	360-285-8600
Research and Development	BC-800-10	BLDG02-250	360-285-8700
Production	BC-900-10	BLDG02-110	360-285-8800

(a) DEPARTMENT Table Data

FIGURE 3-2 Continued

Employee Number	FirstName	LastName	Department	Position	Supervisor	OfficePhone	EmailAddress
1	Mary	Jacobs	Administration	CEO		360-285-8110	Mary.Jacobs@WP.com
2	Rosalie	Jackson	Administration	Admin Assistant	1	360-285-8120	Rosalie.Jackson@WP.com
3	Richard	Bandalone	Legal	Attorney	1	360-285-8210	Richard.Bandalone@WP.com
4	George	Smith	Human Resources	HR3	1	360-285-8310	George.Smith@WP.com
5	Alan	Adams	Human Resources	HR1	4	360-285-8320	Alan.Adams@WP.com
6	Ken	Evans	Finance	CFO	1	360-285-8410	Ken.Evans@WP.com
7	Mary	Abernathy	Finance	FA3	6	360-285-8420	Mary.Abernathy@WP.com
8	Tom	Caruthers	Accounting	FA2	6	360-285-8430	Tom.Caruthers@WP.com
9	Heather	Jones	Accounting	FA2	6	360-285-8440	Heather.Jones@WP.com
10	Ken	Numoto	Sales and Marketing	SM3	1	360-285-8510	Ken.Numoto@WP.com
11	Linda	Granger	Sales and Marketing	SM2	10	360-285-8520	Linda.Granger@WP.com
12	James	Nestor	InfoSystems	CIO	1	360-285-8610	James.Nestor@WP.com
13	Rick	Brown	InfoSystems	IS2	12		Rick.Brown@WP.com
14	Mike	Nguyen	Research and Development	CTO	1	360-285-8710	Mike.Nguyen@WP.com
15	Jason	Sleeman	Research and Development	RD3	14	360-285-8720	Jason.Sleeman@WP.com
16	Mary	Smith	Production	OPS3	1	360-285-8810	Mary.Smith@WP.com
17	Tom	Jackson	Production	OPS2	16	360-285-8820	Tom.Jackson@WP.com
18	George	Jones	Production	OPS2	17	360-285-8830	George.Jones@WP.com
19	Julia	Hayakawa	Production	OPS1	17		Julia.Hayakawa@WP.com
20	Sam	Stewart	Production	OPS1	17		Sam.Stewart@WP.com

(b) EMPLOYEE Table Data

(Continued)

FIGURE 3-2   Continued

ProjectID	ProjectName	Department	MaxHours	StartDate	EndDate
1000	2019 Q3 Production Plan	Production	100.00	05/10/19	06/15/19
1100	2019 Q3 Marketing Plan	Sales and Marketing	135.00	05/10/19	06/15/19
1200	2019 Q3 Portfolio Analysis	Finance	120.00	07/05/19	07/25/19
1300	2019 Q3 Tax Preparation	Accounting	145.00	08/10/19	10/15/19
1400	2019 Q4 Production Plan	Production	100.00	08/10/19	09/15/19
1500	2019 Q4 Marketing Plan	Sales and Marketing	135.00	08/10/19	09/15/19
1600	2019 Q4 Portfolio Analysis	Finance	140.00	10/05/19	

(c) PROJECT Table Data

ProjectID	EmployeeNumber	HoursWorked
1000	1	30.00
1000	6	50.00
1000	10	50.00
1000	16	75.00
1000	17	75.00
1100	1	30.00
1100	6	75.00
1100	10	55.00
1100	11	55.00
1200	3	20.00
1200	6	40.00
1200	7	45.00
1200	8	45.00
1300	3	25.00
1300	6	40.00
1300	8	50.00
1300	9	50.00
1400	1	30.00
1400	6	50.00
1400	10	50.00
1400	16	75.00
1400	17	75.00
1500	1	30.00
1500	6	75.00
1500	10	55.00
1500	11	55.00
1600	3	20.00
1600	6	40.00
1600	7	45.00
1600	8	45.00

(d) ASSIGNMENT Table Data

In this database, each row of DEPARTMENT is potentially related to many rows of EMPLOYEE and PROJECT. Similarly, each row of PROJECT is potentially related to many rows of ASSIGNMENT, and each row of EMPLOYEE is potentially related to many rows of ASSIGNMENT.

Finally, assume the following rules, which are called **business rules**:

- If an EMPLOYEE row is to be deleted and that row is connected to any ASSIGNMENT, the EMPLOYEE row deletion will be disallowed.
- If a PROJECT row is deleted, then all the ASSIGNMENT rows that are connected to the deleted PROJECT row will also be deleted.

The business sense of these rules is as follows:

- If an EMPLOYEE row is deleted (for example, if the employee is transferred), then someone must take over that employee's assignments. Thus, the application needs someone to reassign assignments before deleting the employee row.
- If a PROJECT row is deleted, then the project has been canceled, and maintaining records of assignments to that project is unnecessary.

These rules are typical business rules. You will learn more about such rules in Chapter 5.

"Does Not Work with Microsoft Access ANSI-89 SQL"

If you have completed the end-of-chapter "Working with Microsoft Access" for Chapters 1 and 2, you will recognize the database we're using in this chapter as the Wedgewood Pacific database from those exercises. You can use that database to try out the SQL commands in this chapter. However, be warned that not all standard SQL syntax works in Access.

As mentioned previously, our discussion of SQL is based on SQL features present in SQL standards since the ANSI SQL-92 standard (which Microsoft refers to as ANSI-92 SQL). Unfortunately, Microsoft Access defaults to the earlier SQL-89 version—Microsoft calls it ANSI-89 SQL or Microsoft Jet SQL (after the Microsoft Jet DBMS used by Access). ANSI-89 SQL differs significantly from SQL-92, and therefore some features of the SQL-92 language will not work in Access.

Microsoft Access 2019 (and the earlier Microsoft Access 2003, 2007, 2010, and 2016 versions) does contain a setting that allows you to use SQL-92 instead of the default ANSI-89 SQL. Microsoft included this option to allow Access tools such as forms and reports to be used in application development for Microsoft SQL Server, which supports newer SQL standards. To set the option, after you have opened Microsoft Access 2019, click the **File** command tab and then click the **Options** command to open the Access Options dialog box. In the Access Options dialog box, click the **Object Designers** button to display the Access Options Object Designers page, as shown in Figure 3-3.

As shown in Figure 3-3, the **SQL Server Compatible Syntax (ANSI 92)** options control which version of SQL is used in an Access 2019 database. If you check the **This database** check box, you will use SQL-92 syntax in the current database (if you open Microsoft Access without opening a database, this option is grayed out and not available). Or you can check the **Default for new databases** check box to make SQL-92 syntax the default for all new databases you create.

Unfortunately, very few Access users or organizations using Access are likely to set the Access SQL version to the SQL-92 option, and in this chapter, we assume that Access is running in the default ANSI-89 SQL mode. One advantage of doing so is that it will help you understand the limitations of Access ANSI-89 SQL and how to cope with them.

In the discussion that follows, we use "Does Not Work with Microsoft Access ANSI-89 SQL" boxes to identify SQL commands and clauses that do not work in Access ANSI-89 SQL. We also identify any workarounds that are available. Remember that the one *permanent* workaround is to choose to use the SQL-92 syntax option in the databases you create!

FIGURE 3-3

The Microsoft Access 2019 Options Object Designers Page

The **Object Designers** button

The **SQL Server Compatible Syntax (ANSI 92)** option controls the use of SQL-89 versus SQL-92 syntax in Access queries

Use this check box to use SQL-92 syntax in just the open database

Use this check box to use SQL-92 syntax when new databases are created

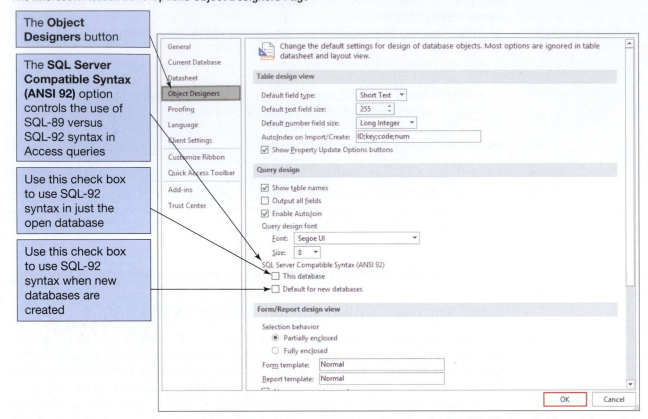

Access 2019, Windows 10, Microsoft Corporation.

> ## BTW
>
> Different DBMS products implement SQL in slightly different ways. The SQL statements in this chapter run on MySQL (MySQL 8.0 Community Edition was used to obtain the output shown in this chapter) and also run on Microsoft Access with exceptions as noted. If you are running the SQL statements on a different DBMS, you may need to make adjustments—consult the documentation for the DBMS you are using. Most of the SQL in this chapter will also work with SQL Server 2017 and Oracle Database XE with minor syntactic adjustments.

SQL FOR DATA DEFINITION (DDL)—CREATING TABLES AND RELATIONSHIPS

The SQL DDL is used to create and alter database structures, such as tables, and to insert, modify, and delete data in the tables.

Before creating tables, you must create a database. Although there is an SQL statement for creating a database, most developers use GUI tools to create databases. The tools are DBMS specific. Creating a database in Microsoft Access is demonstrated in Chapter 1's section of "Working with Microsoft Access." For instructions on how to create a database in MySQL 8.0, see online Extension A, "Working with MySQL." For all other DBMS products, consult the documentation.[4]

The **SQL CREATE TABLE statement** is used to create table structures. The essential format of this statement is:

```
CREATE TABLE NewTableName (
     three-part column definition,
     three-part column definition,
     three-part column definition,
     optional table constraints
     ...
     );
```

The parts of the three-part column definition are the column name, the column data type, and, optionally, one or more constraints on column values. Thus, we can restate the CREATE TABLE format as:

```
CREATE TABLE NewTableName (
     ColumnName   DataType   OptionalColumnConstraints,
     ColumnName   DataType   OptionalColumnConstraints,
     ColumnName   DataType   OptionalColumnConstraints,
     optional table constraints
     ...
     );
```

The column constraints we consider in this text are PRIMARY KEY, FOREIGN KEY, NOT NULL, NULL, and UNIQUE. In addition to these, there is also a CHECK column constraint, which is discussed with the ALTER statement in online Extension B, "Advanced SQL", in this chapter's section of "Working with Microsoft Access", and in the case questions at the end of this chapter. Finally, the **DEFAULT keyword** (DEFAULT is not considered a column constraint) can be used to set initial values.

Does Not Work with Microsoft Access ANSI-89 SQL

Microsoft Access ANSI-89 SQL does not support the UNIQUE and CHECK column constraints nor the DEFAULT keyword.

Solution: Equivalent constraints and initial values can be set in the table Design view. See the discussion in this chapter's section of "Working with Microsoft Access."

Consider the SQL CREATE TABLE statements for the DEPARTMENT and EMPLOYEE tables shown in Figure 3-4 (which includes the DEPARTMENT, EMPLOYEE, and PROJECT tables but intentionally omits the ASSIGNMENT table at this point in the discussion).

---

[4]Also see David M. Kroenke, David J. Auer, Scott L. Vandenberg, and Robert C. Yoder, *Database Processing: Fundamentals, Design, and Implementation*, 15th ed. (Upper Saddle River, NJ: Pearson, 2019), online Chapter 10A, for information on creating databases in SQL Server 2017, and online Chapter 10B for information on creating databases in Oracle Database XE.

FIGURE 3-4

SQL CREATE TABLE Statements

```
CREATE  TABLE DEPARTMENT(
     DepartmentName       Char(35)          PRIMARY KEY,
     BudgetCode           Char(30)          NOT NULL,
     OfficeNumber         Char(15)          NOT NULL,
     DepartmentPhone      Char(12)          NOT NULL
     );

CREATE  TABLE EMPLOYEE(
     EmployeeNumber       Int               PRIMARY KEY,
     FirstName            Char(25)          NOT NULL,
     LastName             Char(25)          NOT NULL,
     Department           Char(35)          NOT NULL DEFAULT 'Human Resources',
     Position             Char(35)          NULL,
     Supervisor           Int               NULL,
     OfficePhone          Char(12)          NULL,
     EmailAddress         VarChar(100)      NOT NULL UNIQUE
     );

CREATE  TABLE PROJECT (
     ProjectID            Int               PRIMARY KEY,
     ProjectName          Char(50)          NOT NULL,
     Department           Char(35)          NOT NULL,
     MaxHours             Numeric(8,2)      NOT NULL DEFAULT 100,
     StartDate            Date              NULL,
     EndDate              Date              NULL
     );
```

Whereas Figure 3-1 shows column data types as used in Microsoft Access 2019, Figure 3-4 shows SQL data types. Although the two are basically the same, SQL uses some different terms and syntax to denote the SQL data types.

The EMPLOYEE column EmployeeNumber has an Integer (abbreviated Int) data type and a PRIMARY KEY column constraint. The next column, FirstName, uses a Character (signified by Char) data type and is 25 characters in length. The **NOT NULL constraint** indicates that a value must be supplied when a new row is created. The seventh column, OfficePhone, uses a Char(12) data type (to store separators between the area code, prefix, and number) with a **NULL constraint**. NULL indicates that null values are allowed, which means that a row can be created without a value for this column.

The fourth column, Department, uses the Char(35) data type, a NOT NULL column constraint, and the DEFAULT keyword to set the department value to the human resources department if no department value is entered when a new row is created.

The eighth and final column, EmailAddress, uses the VarChar(100) data type and the NOT NULL and UNIQUE column constraints. VarChar means a variable-length character data type. Thus, EmailAddress contains character data values that vary in length from row to row, and the maximum length of an EmailAddress value is 100 characters. However, if an EmailAddress value has only 14 characters, then only 14 characters will be stored.

As implied by the existence of VarChar, Char values are of fixed length. The Char(25) definition for FirstName means that 25 characters will be stored for every value of FirstName, regardless of the length of the value entered. FirstNames will be padded with blanks to fill the 25 spaces when necessary.

You might wonder, given the apparent advantage of VarChar, why it isn't used all the time. The reason is that extra processing is required for VarChar columns. A few extra bytes are required to store the length of the value, and the DBMS must go to some trouble to arrange variable-length values in memory and on disk. Vendors of DBMS products usually provide guidelines for when to use which type, and you should check the documentation for your specific DBMS product for more information.

The **UNIQUE constraint** for EmailAddress means that there cannot be any duplicated values in the EmailAddress column. This ensures that each person has a different email address.

In the PROJECT table, the MaxHours column uses the Numeric (8,2) data type. This means that MaxHours values consist of up to eight decimal digits, with two digits assumed to the right of the decimal point. The decimal point is not stored and does not count as one of the eight digits. Thus, the DBMS would display the stored value 12345 as 123.45, and the stored value of 12345678 (which uses all eight of the allowed digits) as 123456.78.

In the EMPLOYEE and PROJECT tables, the SQL DEFAULT keyword is used. Although technically not a constraint, DEFAULT appears in the constraints column in our three-column CREATE TABLE structure, and it is used to specify the data value that will be used if no specific value is inserted into a row of data. For example, DEFAULT 100 means that when a new row is created in the PROJECT table, if no value is provided for MaxHours, the DBMS is to provide the value 100.00. Note that the input value does not assume that the last two numbers are to the right of the decimal place.

Does Not Work with Microsoft Access ANSI-89 SQL

Although Microsoft Access supports a Number data type, it does not support the (*m, n*) extension to specify the number of digits and the number of digits to the right of the decimal place.

Solution: You can set these values in the table Design view after the column is created. See the discussion in this chapter's section of "Working with Microsoft Access."

Also in the PROJECT table, the StartDate column uses the Date data type. This means that StartDate values will consist of dates (there is a Time data type for use with times). Various DBMS products handle date and time values in different ways, and, again, you should consult the documentation for your specific DBMS product. According to the SQL standard and as shown in Figure 3-4, every SQL statement should end with a semicolon. Although some DBMS products do not require the semicolon, learning to provide it is good practice. Also, as a matter of style, we place the ending parenthesis and the semicolon on a line of their own. This style blocks out the table definitions for easy reading.

The five data types shown in Figure 3-4 are the basic SQL data types, but DBMS vendors have added others to their products. Figure 3-5(a), Figure 3-5(b), and Figure 3-5(c) show some of the data types allowed by MySQL 8.0, SQL Server 2017, and Oracle Database XE respectively.

Even when Microsoft Access reads standard SQL, the results of running an SQL statement may be a bit different in Access. For example, Microsoft Access reads SQL statements containing both Char and VarChar data types but converts both these data types to a fixed Text data type in the Access database.

Defining Primary Keys with Table Constraints

Although primary keys can be defined as shown in Figure 3-4, we prefer to define primary keys using a table constraint. Table constraints are identified by the **CONSTRAINT keyword** and can be used to implement various constraints. Consider the CREATE TABLE statements shown in Figure 3-6, with the ASSIGNMENT table now included, which shows how to define the primary key of a table by using a table constraint.

First, the columns of the table are defined as usual, except that the column that will be the primary key must be given the column constraint NOT NULL. After the table columns are defined, a table constraint, identified by the word CONSTRAINT, is used to create the primary key. Every table constraint has a name followed by the definition of the constraint. Note that in the DEPARTMENT table the DepartmentName column is now labeled as NOT NULL and a CONSTRAINT clause has been added at the end of the table

FIGURE 3-5

Data Types for Widely Used DBMS Products

NumericData Type	Description
BIT (M)	M = 1 to 64.
TINYINT	Range is from −128 to 127.
TINYINT UNSIGNED	Range is from 0 to 255.
BOOLEAN	0 = FALSE; 1 = TRUE. Synonym for TINYINT(1).
SMALLINT	Range is from −32,768 to 32,767.
SMALLINT UNSIGNED	Range is from 0 to 65,535.
MEDIUMINT	Range is from −8,388,608 to 8,388,607.
MEDIUMINT UNSIGNED	Range is from 0 to 16,777,215.
INT or INTEGER	Range is from −2,147,483,648 to 2,147,483,647.
INT UNSIGNED or INTEGER UNSIGNED	Range is from 0 to 4,294,967,295.
BIGINT	Range is from −9,223,372,036,854,775,808 to 9,223,372,036,854,775,807.
BIGINT UNSIGNED	Range is from 0 to 18,446,744,073,709,551,616.
FLOAT (P)	P = Precision; Range is from 0 to 53.
FLOAT or REAL (M, D)	Small (single-precision) 4-byte floating-point number: M = Display width D = Number of digits after the decimal point
DOUBLE (M, D)	Normal (double-precision) 8-byte floating-point number: M = Display width D = Number of digits after decimal point
DEC (M[,D]) or DECIMAL (M[,D]) or FIXED (M[,D]) or NUMERIC (M[,D])	Fixed-point number: M = Total number or digits D = Number of digits after the decimal point.
Date and Time Data Types	**Description**
DATE	YYYY-MM-DD : Range is from 1000-01-01 to 9999-12-31.
DATETIME	YYYY-MM-DD HH:MM:SS. Range is from 1000-01-01 00:00:00 to 9999-12-31 23:59:59.
TIMESTAMP	Range is from 1970-01-01 00:00:01 to 2038-01-19 03:14:07.
TIME	HH:MM:SS : Range is from −838:59:59:000000 to 838:59:59:000000.
YEAR (M)	Range is from 1901 to 2155.
String Data Types	**Description**
CHAR (M)	Fixed length character string. M = 0 to 255 bytes.
VARCHAR (M)	Variable length character string. M = 0 to 65,535 bytes.
BLOB (M)	BLOB = Binary Large Object: maximum 65,535 characters.

(a) Common MySQL 8.0 Data Types

FIGURE 3-5   Continued

String Data Types	Description
TEXT (M)	Maximum 65,535 characters.
TINYBLOB, TINYTEXT	See documentation.
MEDIUMBLOB, MEDIUMTEXT	See documentation.
LONGBLOB, LONGTEXT	See documentation.
ENUM ('value1', 'value2', . . .)	An enumeration. Only one value, but chosen from list. See documentation.
SET ('value1', 'value2', . . .)	A set. Zero or more values, all chosen from list. See documentation.

(a) Common MySQL 8.0 Data Types (continued)

Numeric Data Types	Description
Bit	1-bit integer. Values of only **0, 1,** or **NULL**.
Tinyint	1-byte integer. Range is from **0** to **255**.
Smallint	2-byte integer. Range is from $-2^{(15)}$ (**−32,768**) to $+2^{(15)}$ **−1** (**+32,767**).
Int	4-byte integer. Range is from $-2^{(31)}$ (**−2,147,483,468**) to $+2^{(31)}$ **−1** (**+2,147,483,467**).
Bigint	8-byte integer. Range is from $-2^{(63)}$ (**−9,223,372,036,854,775,808**) to $+2^{(63)}$ **−1** (**+9,223,372,036,854,775,807**).
Decimal (p[,s])	Fixed precision (p) and scale (s) numbers. Range is from -10^{38} **+1** to 10^{38} **−1** with maximum precision (p) of 38. Precision ranges from 1 to 38, and default precision is 18. Scale (s) indicates the number of digits to the right of the decimal place. Default scale value is 0, and scale values range from 0 to p, where 0 <= s <= p.
Numeric (p[,s])	Numeric works identically to Decimal.
Smallmoney	4-byte money. Range is from **−214,748.3648** to **+214,748.3647** with accuracy of one ten-thousandth of a monetary unit. Use decimal point to separate digits.
Money	9-byte money. Range is from **−922,337,203,685,477.5808** to **+922,337,203,685,477.5807** with accuracy of one ten-thousandth of a monetary unit. Use decimal point to separate digits.
Float (n)	n-bit storage of the mantissa in scientific floating-point notation. The value of n ranges from 1 to 53, and the default is 53.
Real	Equivalent to Float (24).
Date and Time Data Types	**Description**
Date	3-bytes fixed. Default format YYYY-MM-DD. Range is from **January 1, 1** (0001-01-01) to **December 31, 9999** (9999-12-31).
Time	5-bytes fixed is default with 100 nanosecond precision (.0000000). Default format is HH:MM:SS.NNNNNNN. Range is from **00:00:00.0000000** to **23:59:59.9999999**.
Smalldatetime	4-bytes fixed. Restricted date range and rounds time to nearest second. Range is from **January 1, 1900 00:00:00 AM** (1900-01-01 00:00:00) to **June 6, 2079 23:59.59 PM** (2079-06-06 23:59.59).

(b) Common Microsoft SQL Server 2017 Data Types

(Continued)

FIGURE 3-5   Continued

Date and Time Data Types	Description
Datetime	8-bytes fixed. Basically combines Date and Time, but spans fewer dates and has less time precision (rounds to .000, .003, or .007 seconds). Use DATETIME2 for more precision. Date range is from **January 1, 1753** (1753-01-01) to **December 31, 9999** (9999-12-31).
Datetime2	8-bytes fixed. Combines Date and Time with full precision. Use instead of DATETIME. Range is from **January 1, 1 00:00:00.0000000 AM** (0001-01-01 00:00:00.0000000) to **December 31, 9999 23:59.59.9999999 PM** (9999-12-31 23:59.59.9999999).
Datetimeoffset	10-byte fixed-length default with 100 nanosecond precision (.0000000). Uses 24-hour clock, based on Coordinated Universal Time (UTC). UTC is a refinement of Greenwich Mean Time (GMT), based on the prime meridian at Greenwich, England, which defines when midnight (00:00:00.0000000) occurs. Offset is the time zone difference from the Greenwich time zone. Default format is YYYY-MM-DD HH:MM:SS.NNNNNNN (+|−)HH:MM. Range is from **January 1, 1 00:00:00.0000000 AM** (0001-01-01 00:00:00.0000000) to **December 31, 9999 23:59.59.9999999 PM** (9999-12-31 23:59.59.9999999) with an **offset of −14:59 to +14:59**. Use for 24-hour time.
Timestamp	See documentation.
String Data Types	**Description**
Char (n)	n-byte fixed-length string data (non-Unicode). Range of n is from **1** to **8000**.
Varchar (n | max)	n-byte variable-length string data (non-Unicode). Range of n is from **1** to **8000**. Max creates a maximum $+2^{(31)} -1$ bytes (2 GBytes).
Text	Use VARCHAR(max). See documentation.
Nchar (n)	(n x 2)-byte fixed-length **Unicode** string data. Range of n is from **1** to **4000**.
Nvarchar (n | max)	(n x 2)-byte variable-length **Unicode** string data. Range of n is from **1** to **4000**. Max creates a maximum $+2^{(31)} -1$ bytes (2 GBytes).
Ntext	Use NVARCHAR(max). See documentation.
Binary (n)	n-byte fixed-length binary data. Range of n is from **1** to **8000**.
Other Data Types	**Description**
Varbinary (n | max)	Variable-length binary data. Range of n is from **1** to **8000**. Max creates a maximum $+2^{(31)} -1$ bytes (2 GBytes).
Image	Use VARBINARY(max). See documentation.
Uniqueidentifier	16-byte Globally Unique Identifier (GUID). See documentation.
hierarchyid	See documentation.
Cursor	See documentation.
Table	See documentation.
XML	Use for storing XML data. See documentation.
Sql_variant	See documentation.

(b) Common Microsoft SQL Server 2017 Data Types (continued)

FIGURE 3-5 Continued

Numeric Data Types	Description
SMALLINT	Synonym for INTEGER, implemented as NUMBER(38,0).
INT	Synonym for INTEGER, implemented as NUMBER(38,0).
INTEGER	When specified as a data type, it is implemented as NUMBER(38,0).
NUMBER (p[,s])	1 to 22 bytes. Fixed precision (p) and scale (s) numbers. Range is from $-10^{38}+1$ to $10^{38}-1$ with maximum precision (p) of 38. Precision ranges from 1 to 38, and default precision is 18. Scale (s) indicates the number of digits to the right of the decimal place. Default scale value is 0, and scale values range from -84 to 127, where s can be greater than p.
FLOAT (p)	1 to 22 bytes. Implemented as NUMBER(p). The value of p ranges from 1 to 126 bits.
BINARY_FLOAT	5-byte 32-bit floating-point number.
BINARY_LONG	9-byte 64-bit floating-point number.
RAW (n)	n-byte fixed-length raw binary data. Range of n is from 1 to 2000.
LONG RAW	Raw variable-length binary data. Maximum is 2 GBytes.
BLOB	Maximum [(4-GByte – 1)x(database block size)] binary large object.
BFILE	See documentation.
Date and Time Data Types	**Description**
DATE	7-bytes fixed. Default format is set explicitly with the NLS_DATE_FORMAT parameter. Range is from January 1, 4712 BC to December 31, 9999 AD. It contains the fields YEAR, MONTH, DAY, HOUR, MINUTE, and SECOND (no fractional seconds). It does not include a time zone.
TIMESTAMP (p)	Includes fractional seconds based on a precision of p. Default of p is 6, and the range is 0 to 9. 7 to 11-bytes fixed, based on precision. Default format is set explicitly with the NLS_TIMESTAMP_FORMAT parameter. Range is from January 1, 4712 BC to December 31, 9999 AD. It contains the fields YEAR, MONTH, DAY, HOUR, MINUTE, and SECOND. It contains fractional seconds. It does not include a time zone.
TIMESTAMP (p) WITH TIME ZONE	Includes fractional seconds based on a precision of p. Default of p is 6, and the range is 0 to 9. 13-bytes fixed. Default format is set explicitly with the NLS_TIMESTAMP_FORMAT parameter. Range is from January 1, 4712 BC to December 31, 9999 AD. It contains the fields YEAR, MONTH, DAY, TIMEZONE_HOUR, TIMEZONE_MINUTE, and TIMEZONE_SECOND. It contains fractional seconds. It includes a time zone.
TIMESTAMP (p) WITH LOCAL TIME ZONE	Basically the same as TIMESTAMP WITH TIME ZONE, with the following modifications: (1) data is stored with times based on the database time zone when stored, and (2) users view data in session time zone.
INTERVAL YEAR [p(year)] TO MONTH	See documentation.
INTERVAL DAY [p(day)] TO SECOND [p(seconds)]	See documentation.
String Data Types	**Description**
CHAR (n[BYTE | CHAR])	n-byte fixed-length string data (non-Unicode). Range of n is from 1 to **2000**. BYTE and CHAR refer to the semantic usage. See documentation.

(c) Common Oracle Database XE Data Types

(Continued)

FIGURE 3-5   Continued

String Data Types	Description
VARCHAR2 (n[BYTE | CHAR])	n–byte variable-length string data (non-Unicode). Range of n is from 1 to **4000** BYTEs or CHARACTERs. BYTE and CHAR refer to the semantic usage. See documentation.
NCHAR (n)	(n x 2)-byte fixed-length **Unicode** string data. Up to (n x 3)-bytes for UTF8 encoding. Maximum size is **2000** bytes.
NVARCHAR2 (n)	Variable-length **Unicode** string data. Up to (n x 3)-bytes for UTF8 encoding. Maximum size is **4000** bytes.
LONG	Variable-length string data (non-Unicode) with maximum a maximum $2^{(31-1)}$ bytes (2 GBytes). See documentation.
CLOB	Maximum [(4-GByte – 1)x(database block size)] character large object (non-Unicode). Supports fixed-length and variable-length character sets.
NCLOB	Maximum [(4-GByte – 1)x(database block size)] **Unicode** character large object. Supports fixed-length and variable-length character sets.

Other Data Types	Description
ROWID	See documentation.
UROWID	See documentation.
HTTPURIType	See documentation.
XMLType	Use for storing XML data. See documentation.
SDO_GEOMETRY	See documentation.

(c) Common Oracle Databse XE Data Types (continued)

definition. This is a **PRIMARY KEY constraint**, and is named DEPARTMENT_PK, and it is defined by the keywords PRIMARY KEY(DepartmentName). The constraint name is selected by the developer, and the only naming restriction is that the constraint name must be unique in the database. Usually a standard naming convention is used. In this text, we name primary PRIMARY KEY constraints using the name of the table followed by an underscore and the letters P and K:

```
CONSTRAINT  TABLENAME_PK  PRIMARY KEY({PrimaryKeyColumns})
```

Defining primary keys using table constraints offers three advantages. First, it is required for defining composite keys because the PRIMARY KEY column constraint cannot be used on more than one column. We previously excluded the ASSIGNMENT table from Figure 3-4 because it is not possible to declare the primary key of the ASSIGNMENT table using the technique in Figure 3-4, but Figure 3-6 now includes the ASSIGNMENT table and illustrates the declaration of the primary key ASSIGNMENT_PK as a composite key using the SQL phrase PRIMARY KEY (ProjectID, EmployeeNumber). The second advantage is that by using table constraints you can choose the name of the constraint that defines the primary key. Controlling the name of the constraint has advantages for administering the database, as you will see later when we discuss the SQL DROP statement.

Finally, using a table constraint to define the primary key allows us to easily define surrogate keys in some DBMS products. Notice that in Figure 3-6 the EmployeeNumber column definition in EMPLOYEE now includes the **AUTO_INCREMENT property**. This illustrates how surrogate keys are defined in MySQL. The keyword AUTO_INCREMENT indicates that this is a surrogate key that will start at 1 (although this starting number may be modified after the AUTO_INCREMENT is created) for the first row created and increase by 1 (this is the only increment allowed by

FIGURE 3-6

Creating Primary Keys with SQL Table Constraints

```
CREATE   TABLE DEPARTMENT(
    DepartmentName      Char(35)        NOT NULL,
    BudgetCode          Char(30)        NOT NULL,
    OfficeNumber        Char(15)        NOT NULL,
    DepartmentPhone     Char(12)        NOT NULL,
    CONSTRAINT          DEPARTMENT_PK   PRIMARY KEY(DepartmentName)
    );

CREATE   TABLE EMPLOYEE(
    EmployeeNumber      Int             NOT NULL AUTO_INCREMENT,
    FirstName           Char(25)        NOT NULL,
    LastName            Char(25)        NOT NULL,
    Department          Char(35)        NOT NULL DEFAULT 'Human Resources',
    Position            Char(35)        NULL,
    Supervisor          Int             NULL,
    OfficePhone         Char(12)        NULL,
    EmailAddress        VarChar(100)    NOT NULL UNIQUE,
    CONSTRAINT          EMPLOYEE_PK     PRIMARY KEY(EmployeeNumber)
    );

CREATE   TABLE PROJECT (
    ProjectID           Int             NOT NULL,
    ProjectName         Char(50)        NOT NULL,
    Department          Char(35)        NOT NULL,
    MaxHours            Numeric(8,2)    NOT NULL DEFAULT 100,
    StartDate           Date            NULL,
    EndDate             Date            NULL,
    CONSTRAINT          PROJECT_PK      PRIMARY KEY (ProjectID)
    );

CREATE   TABLE ASSIGNMENT (
    ProjectID           Int             NOT NULL,
    EmployeeNumber      Int             NOT NULL,
    HoursWorked         Numeric(6,2)    NULL,
    CONSTRAINT          ASSIGNMENT_PK   PRIMARY KEY (ProjectID, EmployeeNumber)
    );
```

MySQL—Microsoft SQL Server and Oracle Database allow you to set your own increment value), as each additional row is created. Thus, EmployeeNumber will start with the number 1 and increase by an increment of 1 (that is, 1, 2, 3, 4, 5,....). Note that ProjectID, which will start with the number 1000 and increase by 100 (that is, 1000, 1100, 1200,....), *cannot* use AUTO_INCREMENT because of the increment value of 100. We will have to insert the values of ProjectID ourselves. The exact techniques used to define surrogate key sequences vary extensively from DBMS to DBMS, so consult the documentation for your specific product.

Does Not Work with Microsoft Access ANSI-89 SQL

Although Microsoft Access does support an AutoNumber data type, it *always* starts at 1 and increments by 1. Further, AutoNumber *cannot* be used as an SQL data type.

Solution: For a surrogate primary key that starts at 1 and increments by 1, set the AutoNumber data type manually after the table is created but before any data is inserted into the table. For any surrogate primary key that either does not start at 1 or does not increment by 1 (or both), create the primary key column as a long integer data type, and enter the primary key data manually (or by application code) after the table is created.

Defining Foreign Keys with the Table Constraints

You may have noticed that none of the tables in Figure 3-4 or Figure 3-6 include any foreign key columns. You can use table **FOREIGN KEY constraints** to define foreign keys and their associated referential integrity constraints. Figure 3-7 shows the final SQL code for our tables, complete with the needed FOREIGN KEY constraints.

EMPLOYEE has a table constraint named EMP_DEPART_FK that defines the foreign key relationship between the Department column in EMPLOYEE and the DepartmentName column in DEPARTMENT.

Notice the phrase ON UPDATE CASCADE. The **ON UPDATE phrase** shows what action should be taken if a value of the primary key DepartmentName in DEPARTMENT

FIGURE 3-7

Creating Foreign Keys with SQL Table Constraints

```
CREATE   TABLE DEPARTMENT(
        DepartmentName       Char(35)        NOT NULL,
        BudgetCode           Char(30)        NOT NULL,
        OfficeNumber         Char(15)        NOT NULL,
        DepartmentPhone      Char(12)        NOT NULL,
        CONSTRAINT           DEPARTMENT_PK   PRIMARY KEY(DepartmentName)
        );

CREATE   TABLE EMPLOYEE(
        EmployeeNumber       Int             NOT NULL AUTO_INCREMENT,
        FirstName            Char(25)        NOT NULL,
        LastName             Char(25)        NOT NULL,
        Department           Char(35)        NOT NULL DEFAULT 'Human Resources',
        Position             Char(35)        NULL,
        Supervisor           Int             NULL,
        OfficePhone          Char(12)        NULL,
        EmailAddress         VarChar(100)    NOT NULL UNIQUE,
        CONSTRAINT           EMPLOYEE_PK     PRIMARY KEY(EmployeeNumber),
        CONSTRAINT           EMP_DEPART_FK   FOREIGN KEY(Department)
                                REFERENCES DEPARTMENT(DepartmentName)
                                     ON UPDATE CASCADE,
        CONSTRAINT           EMP_SUPER_FK    FOREIGN KEY(Supervisor)
                                REFERENCES EMPLOYEE(EmployeeNumber)
        );

CREATE   TABLE PROJECT (
        ProjectID            Int             NOT NULL,
        ProjectName          Char(50)        NOT NULL,
        Department           Char(35)        NOT NULL,
        MaxHours             Numeric(8,2)    NOT NULL DEFAULT 100,
        StartDate            Date            NULL,
        EndDate              Date            NULL,
        CONSTRAINT           PROJECT_PK      PRIMARY KEY (ProjectID),
        CONSTRAINT           PROJ_DEPART_FK  FOREIGN KEY(Department)
                                REFERENCES DEPARTMENT(DepartmentName)
                                     ON UPDATE CASCADE
        );

CREATE   TABLE ASSIGNMENT (
        ProjectID            Int          NOT NULL,
        EmployeeNumber       Int          NOT NULL,
        HoursWorked          Numeric(6,2) NULL,
        CONSTRAINT           ASSIGNMENT_PK   PRIMARY KEY (ProjectID, EmployeeNumber),
        CONSTRAINT           ASSIGN_PROJ_FK  FOREIGN KEY (ProjectID)
                                REFERENCES PROJECT (ProjectID)
                                     ON UPDATE NO ACTION
                                     ON DELETE CASCADE,
        CONSTRAINT           ASSIGN_EMP_FK   FOREIGN KEY (EmployeeNumber)
                                REFERENCES EMPLOYEE (EmployeeNumber)
                                     ON UPDATE NO ACTION
                                     ON DELETE NO ACTION
        );
```

changes. The **CASCADE keyword** means that the same change should be made to the related Department column in EMPLOYEE. This means that if a department named *Sales and Marketing* is changed to *Sales/Marketing*, then the foreign key values should be updated to reflect this change. Because DepartmentName is not a surrogate key, the values could be changed, and setting ON UPDATE CASCADE is reasonable. Note that we also establish the recursive relationship with the EMPLOYEE table by adding a FOREIGN KEY constraint. We discuss using SQL in recursive relationships in the "Advanced SQL" extension.

The PROJECT table has a similar foreign key relationship with DEPARTMENT, and the same logic applies, except that here there will be two types of project: completed and in-process. The business rules dealing with this situation are explored in the end-of-chapter exercises.

For the ASSIGNMENT table, there are two foreign key constraints: one to EMPLOYEE and one to PROJECT. The first one defines the constraint ASSIGN_PROJ_FK (the name is up to the developer, as long as it is unique) that specifies that ProjectID in ASSIGNMENT references the ProjectID column in PROJECT. Here the ON UPDATE phrase is set to **NO ACTION**. Recall that ProjectID is a surrogate key and thus will never change. In this situation, there is no need to cascade updates to the referenced primary key, so updates to PROJECT.ProjectID values that have employees assigned to them are disallowed.

Notice that there is also an **ON DELETE phrase**, which shows what action should be taken if a row in PROJECT is deleted. Here the phrase ON DELETE CASCADE means that when a PROJECT row is deleted, all rows in ASSIGNMENT that are connected to the deleted row in PROJECT also should be deleted. Thus, when a PROJECT row is deleted, all ASSIGNMENT rows for that PROJECT row will be deleted as well. This action implements the second business rule on page 141.

The second foreign key table constraint defines the foreign key constraint ASSIGN_EMP_FK. This constraint indicates that the EmployeeNumber column references the EmployeeNumber column of EMPLOYEE. Again, the referenced primary key is a surrogate key, so ON UPDATE NO ACTION is appropriate for this constraint. The phrase ON DELETE NO ACTION indicates to the DBMS that no EMPLOYEE row deletion should be allowed if that row is connected to an ASSIGNMENT row. This declaration implements the first business rule on page 141.

Because ON DELETE NO ACTION is the default, you can omit the ON DELETE expression, and the declaration will default to no action. However, specifying it makes better documentation.[5]

Table constraints can be used for purposes other than creating primary and foreign keys. One of the most important purposes is to define constraints on data values, and we explore the SQL **CHECK constraint** in the end-of-chapter case questions, in Extension B, "Advanced SQL", and in this chapter's section of "Working with Microsoft Access." As always, see the documentation for your DBMS for more information on this topic.

Does Not Work with Microsoft Access ANSI-89 SQL

Microsoft Access does not completely support foreign key CONSTRAINT phrases. Although the basic referential integrity constraint can be created using SQL, the ON UPDATE and ON DELETE clauses are not supported.

Solution: ON UPDATE and ON DELETE actions can be set manually after the relationship is created. See the discussion in this chapter's section of "Working with Microsoft Access."

---

[5]You may be wondering why we don't use the ON DELETE phrase with the foreign key constraints between DEPARTMENT and EMPLOYEE and between DEPARTMENT and PROJECT. After all, there will probably be business rules defining what should be done with employees and projects if a department is deleted. However, enforcing those rules will be more complex than simply using an ON DELETE statement, and this topic is beyond the scope of this book. For a full discussion, see David M. Kroenke, David J. Auer, Scott L. Vandenberg, and Robert C. Yoder, *Database Processing: Fundamentals, Design, and Implementation*, 15th ed. (Upper Saddle River, NJ: Pearson, 2019), Chapter 7.

Submitting SQL to the DBMS

After you have developed a text file with SQL statements like those in Figure 3-4, Figure 3-6, and Figure 3-7, you can submit them to the DBMS. The means by which you do this varies from DBMS to DBMS. With MySQL 8.0, you can type them into a query window in the MySQL Workbench (for a complete discussion, see Extension A, "Working with MySQL"). For MySQL, you can also enter the statements via the MySQL Shell or the MySQL Command Line. Microsoft SQL Server 2017 and Oracle Database XE use similar techniques. How to do this in Microsoft Access is discussed in this chapter's section of "Working with Microsoft Access."

Figure 3-8 shows the MySQL Workbench window after the SQL statements in Figure 3-7 have been processed in MySQL. The SQL code appears in a tabbed script window on the right, and the object icons representing the newly created tables can be seen in the Navigator window on the left. The green check marks next to the commands in the Output window on the lower right indicate that the SQL statements were processed correctly.

Figure 3-9 shows the Microsoft SQL Server Management Studio window after the SQL statements in Figure 3-7 [slightly modified to conform to SQL Server syntax—note the use of the IDENTITY (1,1) keyword instead of AUTO_INCREMENT] have been entered and processed in SQL Server 2017 Developer Edition. The SQL code itself appears in a query window on the upper right, and the message "Command(s) completed successfully" in the Messages window on the lower right indicates that the SQL statements were processed correctly. The object icons representing the tables can be seen in the Object Explorer window on the left, where the name of each table is prefixed with *dbo*, which SQL Server uses for *database owner*.

Figure 3-10 shows the Oracle SQL Developer window after the SQL statements in Figure 3-7 (slightly modified to conform to Oracle Database syntax—note that there is

FIGURE 3-8

Processing the SQL CREATE TABLE Statements Using MySQL 8.0

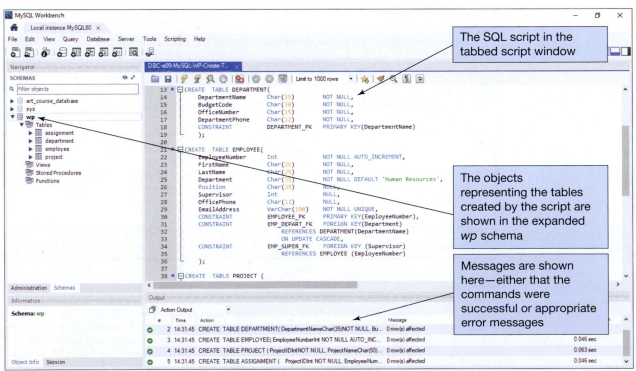

MySQL Community Server 8.0, MySQL Workbench, Oracle Corporation.

FIGURE 3-9

Processing the SQL CREATE TABLE Statements Using Microsoft SQL Server 2017

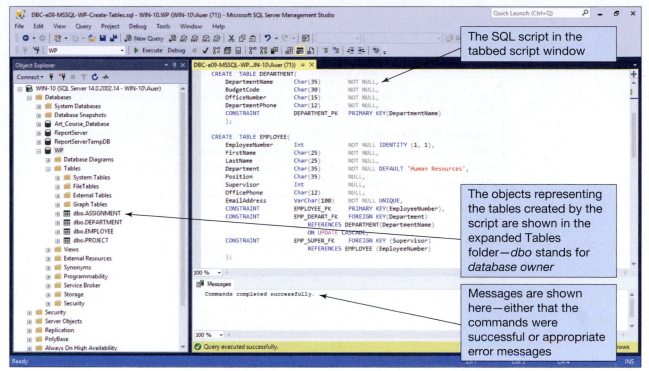

SQL Server 2017, SQL Server Management Studio, Microsoft Corporation.

FIGURE 3-10

Processing the SQL CREATE TABLE Statements Using Oracle Database XE

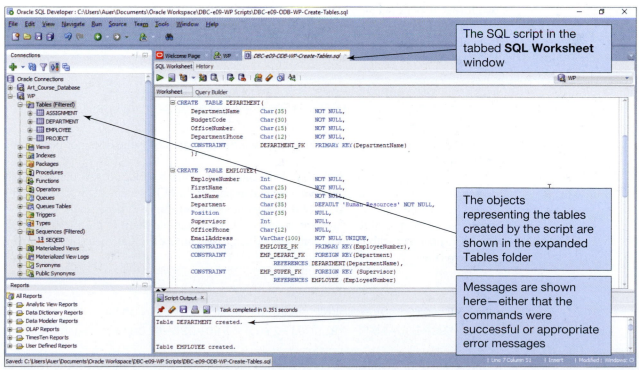

Oracle Database XE, SQL Developer 18.4, Oracle Corporation.

no keyword to create a surrogate key in this code) have been processed in Oracle Database XE. The SQL code appears in a tabbed script window on the right, and object icons representing the newly created tables can be seen in the tabbed Connections window on the left.

Does Not Work with Microsoft Access ANSI-89 SQL

Unlike MySQL 8.0, SQL Server 2017, and Oracle Database XE, Microsoft Access does not support SQL scripts.

Solution: You can still create tables by using the SQL CREATE command and inserting data by using the SQL INSERT command (discussed later in this chapter), but you must do so one command at a time. See the discussion in this chapter's section of "Working with Microsoft Access."

SQL FOR DATA MANIPULATION (DML)—INSERTING DATA

The SQL DML is used to query databases and to modify data in the tables. In this section, we discuss how to use SQL to insert data into a database. The following sections describe how to query the data, and how to change and delete the data.

There are three possible data modification operations: insert, update, and delete. Because we need to populate our database tables, we discuss how to insert data at this time. We will wait until later in the chapter, after we've discussed some other useful SQL syntax, to consider updating and deleting data.

Inserting Data

Data can be added to a relation by using the **SQL INSERT statement**. This statement has two forms, depending on whether data are supplied for all of the columns.

We'll put the data shown in Figure 3-2(a) into the DEPARTMENT table. If the data for all columns are supplied, such as for the administration department, then the following INSERT can be used:

```
INSERT INTO DEPARTMENT VALUES('Administration',
     'BC-100-10', 'BLDG01-210', '360-285-8100');
```

If the DBMS is providing a surrogate key, then the primary key value does not need to be specified.

SQL statements can also include an **SQL comment**, which is a block of text that is used to document the SQL statement but not executed as part of the SQL statement. SQL comments are enclosed in between **/* and */ (SQL comment symbols)**. Any text between these symbols is ignored when the SQL statement is executed. For example, here is the previous SQL INSERT statement with an SQL comment added to document the statement by including a statement label:

```
/* *** SQL-INSERT-CH03-01 *** */
INSERT INTO DEPARTMENT VALUES('Administration',
     'BC-100-10', 'BLDG01-210, '360-285-8100');
```

Because the SQL comment is ignored when the SQL statement is executed, the result of running this statement will be identical to the result of running the statement without the comment. We will use similar comments to label the SQL statements in this chapter as an easy way to reference a specific SQL statement in the text.

The data shown in Figure 3-2(b) will be put in the EMPLOYEE table. Because EmployeeNumber is a surrogate key—specified as AUTO_INCREMENT in MySQL—the same type of INSERT statement can usually (there are exceptions for some DBMS products) be used when data are supplied for all other columns. For example, to insert the data for Rosalie Jackson, the following INSERT can be used:

```
/* *** SQL-INSERT-CH03-02 *** */
INSERT INTO EMPLOYEE VALUES(
     'Rosalie', 'Jackson', 'Administration', 'Admin Assistant', 1,
     '360-285-8120', 'Rosalie.Jackson@WP.com');
```

Note that numbers such as Integer and Numeric values are not enclosed in single quotes, but Char, VarChar, and Date values are.

> **BTW**
>
> SQL is very fussy about single quotes. It wants the plain, nondirectional quotes found in basic text editors. The fancy directional quotes produced by many word processors will produce errors. For example, the data value 'Rosalie' is correctly stated, but 'Rosalie' is not. Do you see the difference?

Although the previous INSERT statements follow standard SQL syntax and should work in most DBMS products that uses SQL, the process that a DBMS uses for generating surrogate keys can require modifications to these statements. For example, MySQL treats the AUTO_INCREMENT value as a missing value, so that your INSERT statement has to list all the column names where data is being inserted *except the AUTO_INCREMENT column*, or use NULL values as inserted values *including a null value for the AUTO_INCREMENT column*. Thus, SQL-INSERT-CH03-02 (which is the INSERT statement to insert the second set of values in our data set) needs to be rewritten as:

```
/* *** SQL-INSERT-CH03-03 *** */
INSERT INTO EMPLOYEE VALUES(
     NULL, 'Rosalie', 'Jackson', 'Administration', 'Admin
     Assistant', 1, '360-285-8120', 'Rosalie.Jackson@WP.com');
```

> **BTW**
>
> SQL Server and Oracle Database handle surrogate keys in their own unique ways. SQL Server uses an IDENTITY function (see SQL Server 2017 documentation), and Oracle Database uses sequences (see Oracle Database XE documentation).

If data for some columns are missing, then the names of the columns for which data are provided must be listed. For example, consider the data for Mary Jacobs which does not have a Supervisor value. The correct INSERT statement for this data is:

```
/* *** SQL-INSERT-CH03-04 *** */
INSERT INTO EMPLOYEE(FirstName, LastName, Department,
     Position, OfficePhone, EmailAddress)
     VALUES(
     'Mary', 'Jacobs', 'Administration', 'CEO',
     '360-285-8110', 'Mary.Jacobs@WP.com');
```

A NULL value will be inserted for Supervisor.

Let's consider three points regarding the this version of the INSERT command. First, the order of the column names must match the order of the values. In the preceding example, the order of the column names is FirstName, LastName, Department, Position, OfficePhone, and EmailAddress, so the order of the values must also be FirstName, LastName, Department, Position, OfficePhone, and EmailAddress.

Second, although the order of the data must match the order of the column names, the order of the column names does not have to match the order of the columns in the table. For example, the following INSERT, where EmailAddress is placed at the beginning of the column list, would also work:

```
/* *** SQL-INSERT-CH03-05 *** */
INSERT INTO EMPLOYEE(EmailAddress, FirstName, LastName,
     Department, Position, OfficePhone)
     VALUES(
     'Mary.Jacobs@WP.com', 'Mary', 'Jacobs',
     'Administration', 'CEO', '360-285-8110');
```

Finally, for the INSERT to work, values for all NOT NULL columns must be provided. You can omit Supervisor only because this column is defined as NULL.

Further, DBMS products vary a lot on how they want to see Date values. To insert the first row of PROJECT Data in MySQL, we will use the following syntax for date values:

```
/* *** SQL-INSERT-CH03-06 *** */
INSERT INTO PROJECT VALUES(
     1000, '2019 Q3 Production Plan', 'Production', 100.00,
     '2019-05-10', '2019-06-15');
```

Microsoft SQL Server prefers to see dates follows:

```
/* *** SQL-INSERTCH03-06-MSSQL *** */
INSERT INTO PROJECT VALUES(
     1000, '2019 Q3 Production Plan', 'Production', 100.00,
     '05-MAY-19', '15-JUN-19');
```

Oracle Database has the most complex date formatting, and wants to see:

```
/* *** SQL-INSERTCH03-06-ODB *** */
INSERT INTO PROJECT VALUES(
     1000, '2019 Q3 Production Plan', 'Production', 100.00,
     TO_DATE('05-MAY-19', 'DD-MON-YY'),
     TO_DATE('15-JUN-19', 'DD-MON-YY'));
```

Figure 3-11 shows the SQL INSERT statements needed to populate the WP database tables created by the SQL CREATE TABLE statements in Figure 3-7. Note that the order in which the tables are populated does matter because of the foreign key referential integrity constraints.

FIGURE 3-11

SQL INSERT Statements

```
/*****    DEPARTMENT DATA    ***********************************************************/

INSERT INTO DEPARTMENT VALUES(
    'Administration', 'BC-100-10', 'BLDG01-210', '360-285-8100');
INSERT INTO DEPARTMENT VALUES(
    'Legal', 'BC-200-10', 'BLDG01-220', '360-285-8200');
INSERT INTO DEPARTMENT VALUES(
    'Human Resources', 'BC-300-10', 'BLDG01-230', '360-285-8300');
INSERT INTO DEPARTMENT VALUES(
    'Finance', 'BC-400-10', 'BLDG01-110', '360-285-8400');
INSERT INTO DEPARTMENT VALUES(
    'Accounting', 'BC-500-10', 'BLDG01-120', '360-285-8405');
INSERT INTO DEPARTMENT VALUES(
    'Sales and Marketing', 'BC-600-10', 'BLDG01-250', '360-285-8500');
INSERT INTO DEPARTMENT VALUES(
    'InfoSystems', 'BC-700-10', 'BLDG02-210', '360-285-8600');
INSERT INTO DEPARTMENT VALUES(
    'Research and Development', 'BC-800-10', 'BLDG02-250', '360-285-8700');
INSERT INTO DEPARTMENT VALUES(
    'Production', 'BC-900-10', 'BLDG02-110', '360-285-8800');


/*****    EMPLOYEE DATA    ***********************************************************/
/*    Note that MySQL allows NULL in the AUTO_INCREMENT                             */
/*    field to generate the next value                                             */

INSERT INTO EMPLOYEE
    (FirstName, LastName, Department, Position, OfficePhone, EmailAddress)
    VALUES(
    'Mary', 'Jacobs', 'Administration', 'CEO',
    '360-285-8110', 'Mary.Jacobs@WP.com');
INSERT INTO EMPLOYEE VALUES(
    NULL,'Rosalie', 'Jackson', 'Administration', 'Admin Assistant', 1,
    '360-285-8120', 'Rosalie.Jackson@WP.com');
INSERT INTO EMPLOYEE VALUES(
    NULL,'Richard', 'Bandalone', 'Legal', 'Attorney', 1,
    '360-285-8210', 'Richard.Bandalone@WP.com');
INSERT INTO EMPLOYEE VALUES(
    NULL,'George', 'Smith', 'Human Resources', 'HR3', 1,
    '360-285-8310', 'George.Smith@WP.com');
INSERT INTO EMPLOYEE VALUES(
    NULL,'Alan', 'Adams', 'Human Resources', 'HR1', 4,
    '360-285-8320', 'Alan.Adams@WP.com');
INSERT INTO EMPLOYEE VALUES(
    NULL,'Ken', 'Evans', 'Finance', 'CFO', 1,
    '360-285-8410', 'Ken.Evans@WP.com');
INSERT INTO EMPLOYEE VALUES(
    NULL,'Mary', 'Abernathy', 'Finance', 'FA3', 6,
    '360-285-8420', 'Mary.Abernathy@WP.com');
INSERT INTO EMPLOYEE VALUES(
    NULL,'Tom', 'Caruthers', 'Accounting', 'FA2', 6,
    '360-285-8430', 'Tom.Caruthers@WP.com');
INSERT INTO EMPLOYEE VALUES(
    NULL,'Heather', 'Jones', 'Accounting', 'FA2', 6,
    '360-285-8440', 'Heather.Jones@WP.com');
INSERT INTO EMPLOYEE VALUES(
    NULL,'Ken', 'Numoto', 'Sales and Marketing', 'SM3', 1,
    '360-285-8510', 'Ken.Numoto@WP.com');
INSERT INTO EMPLOYEE VALUES(
    NULL,'Linda', 'Granger', 'Sales and Marketing', 'SM2', 10,
    '360-285-8520', 'Linda.Granger@WP.com');
INSERT INTO EMPLOYEE VALUES(
    NULL,'James', 'Nestor', 'InfoSystems', 'CIO', 1,
    '360-285-8610', 'James.Nestor@WP.com');
INSERT INTO EMPLOYEE
    (FirstName, LastName, Department, Position, Supervisor, EmailAddress)
    VALUES(
    'Rick', 'Brown', 'InfoSystems', 'IS2', 12, 'Rick.Brown@WP.com');
```

(Continued)

FIGURE 3-11   Continued

```sql
INSERT INTO EMPLOYEE VALUES(
    NULL,'Mike', 'Nguyen', 'Research and Development', 'CTO', 1,
    '360-285-8710', 'Mike.Nguyen@WP.com');
INSERT INTO EMPLOYEE VALUES(
    NULL,'Jason', 'Sleeman', 'Research and Development', 'RD3', 14,
    '360-285-8720', 'Jason.Sleeman@WP.com');
INSERT INTO EMPLOYEE VALUES(
    NULL,'Mary', 'Smith', 'Production', 'OPS3', 1,
    '360-285-8810', 'Mary.Smith@WP.com');
INSERT INTO EMPLOYEE VALUES(
    NULL,'Tom', 'Jackson', 'Production', 'OPS2', 16,
    '360-285-8820', 'Tom.Jackson@WP.com');
INSERT INTO EMPLOYEE VALUES(
    NULL,'George', 'Jones', 'Production', 'OPS2', 17,
    '360-285-8830', 'George.Jones@WP.com');
INSERT INTO EMPLOYEE
    (FirstName, LastName, Department, Position, Supervisor, EmailAddress)
    VALUES(
    'Julia', 'Hayakawa', 'Production', 'OPS1', 17, 'Julia.Hayakawa@WP.com');
INSERT INTO EMPLOYEE
    (FirstName, LastName, Department, Position, Supervisor, EmailAddress)
    VALUES(
    'Sam', 'Stewart', 'Production', 'OPS1', 17, 'Sam.Stewart@WP.com');


/*****    PROJECT DATA    ***********************************************************/

INSERT INTO PROJECT VALUES(
    1000,'2019 Q3 Production Plan', 'Production', 100.00,
    '2019-05-10','2019-06-15');
INSERT INTO PROJECT VALUES(
    1100,'2019 Q3 Marketing Plan', 'Sales and Marketing', 135.00,
    '2019-05-10','2019-06-15');
INSERT INTO PROJECT VALUES(
    1200,'2019 Q3 Portfolio Analysis', 'Finance', 120.00,
    '2019-07-05','2019-07-25');
INSERT INTO PROJECT VALUES(
    1300,'2019 Q3 Tax Preparation', 'Accounting', 145.00,
    '2019-08-10','2019-10-15');
INSERT INTO PROJECT VALUES(
    1400,'2019 Q4 Production Plan', 'Production', 100.00,
    '2019-08-10','2019-09-15');
INSERT INTO PROJECT VALUES(
    1500,'2019 Q4 Marketing Plan', 'Sales and Marketing', 135.00,
    '2019-08-10','2019-09-15');
INSERT INTO PROJECT(ProjectID, ProjectName, Department, MaxHours, StartDate)
    VALUES(
    1600,'2019 Q4 Portfolio Analysis', 'Finance', 140.00,
    '2019-10-05');


/*****    ASSIGNMENT DATA    ***********************************************************/

INSERT INTO ASSIGNMENT VALUES(1000, 1, 30.0);
INSERT INTO ASSIGNMENT VALUES(1000, 6, 50.0);
INSERT INTO ASSIGNMENT VALUES(1000, 10, 50.0);
INSERT INTO ASSIGNMENT VALUES(1000, 16, 75.0);
INSERT INTO ASSIGNMENT VALUES(1000, 17, 75.0);
INSERT INTO ASSIGNMENT VALUES(1100, 1, 30.0);
INSERT INTO ASSIGNMENT VALUES(1100, 6, 75.0);
INSERT INTO ASSIGNMENT VALUES(1100, 10, 55.0);
INSERT INTO ASSIGNMENT VALUES(1100, 11, 55.0);
INSERT INTO ASSIGNMENT VALUES(1200, 3, 20.0);
INSERT INTO ASSIGNMENT VALUES(1200, 6, 40.0);
INSERT INTO ASSIGNMENT VALUES(1200, 7, 45.0);
INSERT INTO ASSIGNMENT VALUES(1200, 8, 45.0);
INSERT INTO ASSIGNMENT VALUES(1300, 3, 25.0);
INSERT INTO ASSIGNMENT VALUES(1300, 6, 40.0);
INSERT INTO ASSIGNMENT VALUES(1300, 8, 50.0);
INSERT INTO ASSIGNMENT VALUES(1300, 9, 50.0);
```

FIGURE 3-11 **Continued**

```
INSERT INTO ASSIGNMENT VALUES(1400, 1, 30.0);
INSERT INTO ASSIGNMENT VALUES(1400, 6, 50.0);
INSERT INTO ASSIGNMENT VALUES(1400, 10, 50.0);
INSERT INTO ASSIGNMENT VALUES(1400, 16, 75.0);
INSERT INTO ASSIGNMENT VALUES(1400, 17, 75.0);
INSERT INTO ASSIGNMENT VALUES(1500, 1, 30.0);
INSERT INTO ASSIGNMENT VALUES(1500, 6, 75.0);
INSERT INTO ASSIGNMENT VALUES(1500, 10, 55.0);
INSERT INTO ASSIGNMENT VALUES(1500, 11, 55.0);
INSERT INTO ASSIGNMENT VALUES(1600, 3, 20.0);
INSERT INTO ASSIGNMENT VALUES(1600, 6, 40.0);
INSERT INTO ASSIGNMENT VALUES(1600, 7, 45.0);
INSERT INTO ASSIGNMENT VALUES(1600, 8, 45.0);

/**************************************************************************/
```

SQL FOR DATA MANIPULATION (DML)—SINGLE TABLE QUERIES

After the tables have been defined and populated, you can use SQL DML to query data in many ways. You can also use it to change and delete data, but the SQL statements for these activities will be easier to learn if we begin with the query statements. In the following discussion, assume that the sample data shown in Figure 3-2 have been entered into the database.

The SQL SELECT/FROM/WHERE Framework

This section introduces the fundamental statement framework for SQL query statements. After we discuss this basic structure, you will learn how to submit SQL statements to Microsoft Access, MySQL, SQL Server, and Oracle Database. If you choose, you can then follow along with the text and process additional SQL statements as they are explained in the rest of this chapter. The basic form of SQL queries uses the **SQL SELECT/FROM/ WHERE framework**. In this framework:

- The **SQL SELECT clause** specifies which *columns* are to be listed in the query results.
- The **SQL FROM clause** specifies which *tables* are to be used in the query.
- The **SQL WHERE clause** specifies which *rows* are to be listed in the query results.

We will use and expand this framework as we work through examples in the following sections. All the examples use the data in Figure 3-2 and the INSERT statements for that data in Figure 3-11 as the basis for the results of the queries.

Reading Specified Columns from a Single Table

We begin very simply. Suppose we want to obtain the values that are in the PROJECT table. To do this, we write an SQL SELECT statement that contains all the column names in the table. An SQL statement to read that data is the following:

```
/* *** SQL-Query-CH03-01 *** */
SELECT     ProjectID, ProjectName, Department, MaxHours,
           StartDate, EndDate
FROM       PROJECT;
```

Using the data in Figure 3-11, when the DBMS processes this statement the result will be:

ProjectID	ProjectName	Department	MaxHours	StartDate	EndDate
1000	2019 Q3 Production Plan	Production	100.00	2019-05-10	2019-06-15
1100	2019 Q3 Marketing Plan	Sales and Marketing	135.00	2019-05-10	2019-06-15
1200	2019 Q3 Portfolio Analysis	Finance	120.00	2019-07-05	2019-07-25
1300	2019 Q3 Tax Preparation	Accounting	145.00	2019-08-10	2019-10-15
1400	2019 Q4 Production Plan	Production	100.00	2019-08-10	2019-09-15
1500	2019 Q4 Marketing Plan	Sales and Marketing	135.00	2019-08-10	2019-09-15
1600	2019 Q4 Portfolio Analysis	Finance	140.00	2019-10-05	NULL
NULL	NULL	NULL	NULL	NULL	NULL

MySQL Community Server 8.0, MySQL Workbench, Oracle Corporation.

The SQL results output shown in this book are as they appear in MySQL Workbench in the **Result Grid** (See Figure 3-12). MySQL Workbench includes a row of NULL values at the end of query results when *every column* in the table is selected in the query. This is not typical of other DBMS products, but MySQL includes this row because you can edit the output and insert additional rows of data in Result Grid window. Therefore, we will *not* include this row in subsequent SQL results screen shots.

When SQL statements are executed, the statements transform tables. SQL query statements start with a table, process that table in some way, and then place the results in another table structure. Even if the result of the processing is just a single number, that number is considered to be a table with one row and one column. As you will learn at the end of this chapter, some SQL statements process multiple tables. Regardless of the number of input tables, though, the result of every SQL statement is a single table.

SQL provides a shorthand notation for querying all the columns of a table. The shorthand is to use an **SQL asterisk (*) wildcard character** to indicate that we want all the columns to be displayed:

```
/* *** SQL-Query-CH03-02 *** */
SELECT    *
FROM      PROJECT;
```

The result will again be a table with all rows and all six of the columns in PROJECT:

ProjectID	ProjectName	Department	MaxHours	StartDate	EndDate
1000	2019 Q3 Production Plan	Production	100.00	2019-05-10	2019-06-15
1100	2019 Q3 Marketing Plan	Sales and Marketing	135.00	2019-05-10	2019-06-15
1200	2019 Q3 Portfolio Analysis	Finance	120.00	2019-07-05	2019-07-25
1300	2019 Q3 Tax Preparation	Accounting	145.00	2019-08-10	2019-10-15
1400	2019 Q4 Production Plan	Production	100.00	2019-08-10	2019-09-15
1500	2019 Q4 Marketing Plan	Sales and Marketing	135.00	2019-08-10	2019-09-15
1600	2019 Q4 Portfolio Analysis	Finance	140.00	2019-10-05	NULL

MySQL Community Server 8.0, MySQL Workbench, Oracle Corporation.

In the SQL SELECT statement, the SELECT clause and the FROM clause are the only required clauses in the statement. We will have a complete query by simply telling SQL which columns should be read from which table. In the rest of this chapter, we will discuss other clauses, such as the WHERE clause, that can be used as part of an SQL SELECT statement. All of these other clauses, however, are optional.

Specifying Column Order in SQL Queries from a Single Table

Suppose we want to obtain just the values of the ProjectName, Department, and MaxHours columns of the PROJECT table. In this case, we specify only the column names ProjectName, Department, and MaxHours, and an SQL SELECT statement to display that data is the following:

```
/* *** SQL-Query-CH03-03 *** */
SELECT     ProjectName, Department, MaxHours
FROM       PROJECT;
```

Using the data in Figure 3-11, the result of this statement is:

ProjectName	Department	MaxHours
2019 Q3 Production Plan	Production	100.00
2019 Q3 Marketing Plan	Sales and Marketing	135.00
2019 Q3 Portfolio Analysis	Finance	120.00
2019 Q3 Tax Preparation	Accounting	145.00
2019 Q4 Production Plan	Production	100.00
2019 Q4 Marketing Plan	Sales and Marketing	135.00
2019 Q4 Portfolio Analysis	Finance	140.00

MySQL Community Server 8.0, MySQL Workbench, Oracle Corporation.

The order of the column names after the keyword SELECT determines the order of the columns in the resulting table. Thus, if you change the order of columns in the previous SELECT statement to:

```
/* *** SQL-Query-CH03-04 *** */
SELECT     ProjectName, MaxHours, Department
FROM       PROJECT;
```

The result will be:

ProjectName	MaxHours	Department
2019 Q3 Production Plan	100.00	Production
2019 Q3 Marketing Plan	135.00	Sales and Marketing
2019 Q3 Portfolio Analysis	120.00	Finance
2019 Q3 Tax Preparation	145.00	Accounting
2019 Q4 Production Plan	100.00	Production
2019 Q4 Marketing Plan	135.00	Sales and Marketing
2019 Q4 Portfolio Analysis	140.00	Finance

MySQL Community Server 8.0, MySQL Workbench, Oracle Corporation.

SUBMITTING SQL STATEMENTS TO THE DBMS

Before continuing the explanation of SQL, learning how to submit SQL statements to specific DBMS products will be useful for you. That way, you can work along with the text by keying and running SQL statements as you read the discussion. The particular means by which you submit SQL statements depends on the DBMS.

To show you how the results look in actual DBMS management tools, Figure 3-12 shows query SQL-Query-CH03-03 as executed in MySQL 8.0 using MySQL Workbench, Figure 3-13 shows the query as executed in Microsoft SQL Server 2017 using Microsoft SQL Server Management Studio (SSMS), and Figure 3-14 shows the query as executed in Oracle Database XE using Oracle SQL Developer. For more details, see online Extension A, "Working with MySQL" for a discussion of using MySQL 8.0 and MySQL Workbench. See *Database Processing: Fundamentals, Design and Implementation* by Kroenke, Auer, Vandenberg and Yoder[6] online chapters 10A and 10B for a discussion of Microsoft SQL Server and Oracle Database respectively. Use of Microsoft Access 2019 query facilities is covered in this chapter's section of "Working with Microsoft Access."

FIGURE 3-12

SQL Query Results in the MySQL Workbench

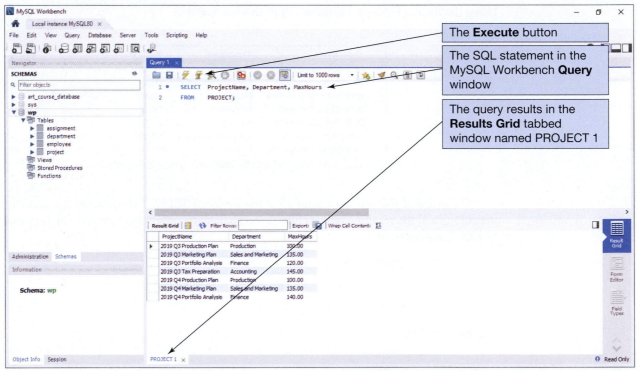

MySQL Community Server 8.0, MySQL Workbench, Oracle Corporation.

---

[6]David M. Kroenke, David J. Auer, Scott L. Vandenberg, and Robert C. Yoder, *Database Processing: Fundamentals, Design, and Implementation*, 15th ed. (Upper Saddle River, NJ: Pearson, 2019). Note that online Chapter 10C on MySQL also includes a discussion of executing SQL queries from the MySQL Command Line Client and the MySQL Shell..

Chapter 3 Structured Query Language 165

FIGURE 3-13

SQL Query Results in the Microsoft SQL Server Management Studio

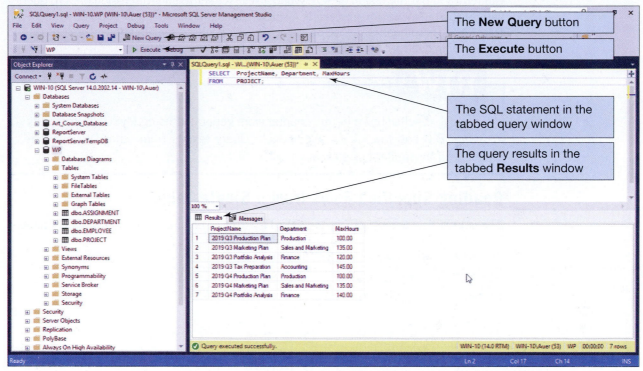

SQL Server 2017, SQL Server Management Studio, Microsoft Corporation.

FIGURE 3-14

SQL Query Results in the Oracle SQL Developer

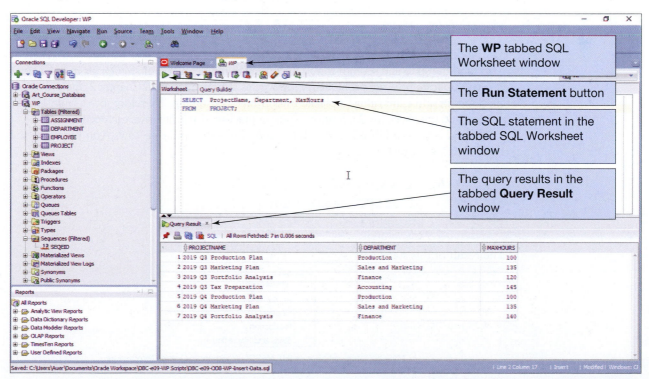

Oracle Database XE, SQL Developer 18.4, Oracle Corporation.

SQL ENHANCEMENTS FOR SINGLE TABLE QUERIES

Now that we know how to run SQL queries in the DBMS product that we are using, we can return to our discussion of SQL syntax itself. We started our discussion of SQL queries with SQL statements for processing a single table, and now we will add additional SQL features to those queries. As we proceed, you will begin to see how powerful SQL can be for querying databases and for creating information from existing data.

The SQL results shown in this chapter were generated using MySQL Community Server 8.0 and the MySQL Workbench. Query results from other DBMS products will be similar but may vary a bit.

Reading Specified Rows from a Single Table

The next SQL statement obtains only the Department column from the PROJECT table:

```
/* *** SQL-Query-CH03-05 *** */
SELECT      Department
FROM        PROJECT;
```

The result is:

Department
▶ Accounting
Finance
Finance
Production
Production
Sales and Marketing
Sales and Marketing

MySQL Community Server 8.0, MySQL Workbench, Oracle Corporation.

Notice that the second and third rows of this table are duplicates, as are the fourth and fifth rows (and the sixth and seventh rows). According to the definition of *relation* given in Chapter 2, such duplicate rows are prohibited. However, as also mentioned in Chapter 2, the process of checking for and eliminating duplicate rows is time-consuming. Therefore, by default, DBMS products do not check for duplication. Thus, in practice, duplicate rows can occur.

If you want the DBMS to check for and eliminate duplicate rows, you must use the **DISTINCT keyword**, as follows:

```
/* *** SQL-Query-CH03-06 *** */
SELECT      DISTINCT Department
FROM        PROJECT;
```

The result of this statement is:

Department
▶ Accounting
Finance
Production
Sales and Marketing

MySQL Community Server 8.0, MySQL Workbench, Oracle Corporation.

The duplicate rows have been eliminated, as desired.

In the previous SQL statements, we selected certain columns for all rows of a table. SQL statements can also be used for the reverse; that is, they can be used to select all the columns for certain rows. The rows to be selected are specified by using the SQL WHERE clause. For example, the following SQL statement will obtain all the columns of the PROJECT table for projects sponsored by the finance department:

```
/* *** SQL-Query-CH03-07 *** */
SELECT    *
FROM      PROJECT
WHERE     Department = 'Finance';
```

The result is:

	ProjectID	ProjectName	Department	MaxHours	StartDate	EndDate
▶	1200	2019 Q3 Portfolio Analysis	Finance	120.00	2019-07-05	2019-07-25
	1600	2019 Q4 Portfolio Analysis	Finance	140.00	2019-10-05	NULL

MySQL Community Server 8.0, MySQL Workbench, Oracle Corporation.

The specific treatment of date and time values varies widely among DBMS products. Most DBMSs have a specific default date format, but allow other date formats to be specified and allowed via built-in functions. As always, see the documentation for your DBMS product.

As previously stated, the pattern SELECT/FROM/WHERE is the fundamental pattern of SQL queries. Many different conditions can be placed in a WHERE clause. These conditions are expressed using the **SQL comparison operators** shown in Figure 3-15. The equal sign (=) that appears in the WHERE clause of SQL-Query-CH03-07 is an SQL comparison operator.

In an SQL WHERE clause, if the column contains text or date data, the comparison values must be enclosed in single quotation marks ('*{text or date data}*'). For example, in the

FIGURE 3-15

SQL Comparison Operators

SQL Comparison Operators	
Operator	**Meaning**
=	Is equal to
<>	Is NOT Equal to
<	Is less than
>	Is greater than
<=	Is less than OR equal to
>=	Is greater than OR equal to
IN	Is equal to one of a set of values
NOT IN	Is NOT equal to any of a set of values
BETWEEN	Is within a range of numbers (includes the end points)
NOT BETWEEN	Is NOT within a range of numbers (includes the end points)
LIKE	Matches a set of characters
NOT LIKE	Does NOT match a set of characters
IS NULL	Is equal to NULL
IS NOT NULL	Is NOT equal to NULL

PROJECT table, we can find projects with a start date of May 10, 2019 by using the following query:

```
/* *** SQL-Query-CH03-08 *** */
SELECT     *
FROM       PROJECT
WHERE      StartDate = '2019/05/10';
```

The results are:

	ProjectID	ProjectName	Department	MaxHours	StartDate	EndDate
▶	1000	2019 Q3 Production Plan	Production	100.00	2019-05-10	2019-06-15
	1100	2019 Q3 Marketing Plan	Sales and Marketing	135.00	2019-05-10	2019-06-15

MySQL Community Server 8.0, MySQL Workbench, Oracle Corporation.

BTW

When using a date in the WHERE clause, you can usually enclose it in single quotes just as you would a character string as shown in SQL-Query-CH03-08. However, when using Microsoft Access 2019, you must enclose dates within the # symbol. For example:

```
/* *** SQL-Query-CH03-08-Access *** */
SELECT     *
FROM       PROJECT
WHERE      StartDate = #05/10/2019#;
```

Microsoft SQL Server and Oracle Database XE also use the single quotes, but they can have other idiosyncrasies when using date data in SQL statements. See the appropriate documentation.

If the column contains numeric data, however, the comparison values need not be in quotes. Thus, to find all the PROJECT rows with a MaxHours value greater than 135, we would use the following SQL statement (also note that no comma is included in the numeric value code when working with large numbers).

For example, the query:

```
/* *** SQL-Query-CH03-09 *** */
SELECT     *
FROM       PROJECT
WHERE      MaxHours > 135;
```

selects all columns from PROJECT where the value of the MaxHours column *is greater than* 135. The result is:

	ProjectID	ProjectName	Department	MaxHours	StartDate	EndDate
▶	1300	2019 Q3 Tax Preparation	Accounting	145.00	2019-08-10	2019-10-15
	1600	2019 Q4 Portfolio Analysis	Finance	140.00	2019-10-05	NULL

MySQL Community Server 8.0, MySQL Workbench, Oracle Corporation.

Values placed in quotation marks may be case sensitive. For example, WHERE Department = 'Finance' and WHERE Department = 'FINANCE' may not be considered the same—check your DBMS documentation (or experiment with some data).

Reading Specified Columns and Rows from a Single Table

So far, we have generally selected certain columns and all rows, or we have selected all columns and certain rows (the exceptions being our discussion of the DISTINCT function). However, we can combine these operations to select certain columns and certain rows by naming the columns we want and then using the SQL WHERE clause. For example, to obtain the FirstName, LastName, and OfficePhone of employees in the accounting department from the EMPLOYEE table, we use the SQL query:

```
/* *** SQL-Query-CH03-10 *** */
SELECT     FirstName, LastName, Department, OfficePhone
FROM       EMPLOYEE
WHERE      Department = 'Accounting';
```

The result is:

FirstName	LastName	Department	OfficePhone
Tom	Caruthers	Accounting	360-285-8430
Heather	Jones	Accounting	360-285-8440

MySQL Community Server 8.0, MySQL Workbench, Oracle Corporation.

Sorting the Results of a Query

The order of rows in the result of a SELECT statement is somewhat arbitrary. If this is undesirable, we can use the **ORDER BY clause** to sort the rows. For example, the following will display the names, phone numbers, and departments of all employees, sorted by Department:

```
/* *** SQL-Query-CH03-11 *** */
SELECT      FirstName, LastName, Department, OfficePhone
FROM        EMPLOYEE
ORDER BY    Department;
```

The result is:

FirstName	LastName	Department	OfficePhone
Tom	Caruthers	Accounting	360-285-8430
Heather	Jones	Accounting	360-285-8440
Mary	Jacobs	Administration	360-285-8110
Rosalie	Jackson	Administration	360-285-8120
Ken	Evans	Finance	360-285-8410
Mary	Abernathy	Finance	360-285-8420
George	Smith	Human Resources	360-285-8310
Alan	Adams	Human Resources	360-285-8320
James	Nestor	InfoSystems	360-285-8610
Rick	Brown	InfoSystems	NULL
Richard	Bandalone	Legal	360-285-8210
Mary	Smith	Production	360-285-8810
Tom	Jackson	Production	360-285-8820
George	Jones	Production	360-285-8830
Julia	Hayakawa	Production	NULL
Sam	Stewart	Production	NULL
Mike	Nguyen	Research and Development	360-285-8710
Jason	Sleeman	Research and Development	360-285-8720
Ken	Numoto	Sales and Marketing	360-285-8510
Linda	Granger	Sales and Marketing	360-285-8520

MySQL Community Server 8.0, MySQL Workbench, Oracle Corporation.

By default, SQL sorts in ascending order. The **ASC keyword** and **DESC keyword** can be used to specify ascending and descending order when necessary. Thus, to sort employees in descending order by Department, use:

```
/* *** SQL-Query-CH03-12 *** */
SELECT     FirstName, LastName, Department, OfficePhone
FROM       EMPLOYEE
ORDER BY   Department DESC;
```

The result is:

FirstName	LastName	Department	OfficePhone
Ken	Numoto	Sales and Marketing	360-285-8510
Linda	Granger	Sales and Marketing	360-285-8520
Mike	Nguyen	Research and Development	360-285-8710
Jason	Sleeman	Research and Development	360-285-8720
Mary	Smith	Production	360-285-8810
Tom	Jackson	Production	360-285-8820
George	Jones	Production	360-285-8830
Julia	Hayakawa	Production	NULL
Sam	Stewart	Production	NULL
Richard	Bandalone	Legal	360-285-8210
James	Nestor	InfoSystems	360-285-8610
Rick	Brown	InfoSystems	NULL
George	Smith	Human Resources	360-285-8310
Alan	Adams	Human Resources	360-285-8320
Ken	Evans	Finance	360-285-8410
Mary	Abernathy	Finance	360-285-8420
Mary	Jacobs	Administration	360-285-8110
Rosalie	Jackson	Administration	360-285-8120
Tom	Caruthers	Accounting	360-285-8430
Heather	Jones	Accounting	360-285-8440

MySQL Community Server 8.0, MySQL Workbench, Oracle Corporation.

Two or more columns can be used for sorting purposes. To sort the employee names and departments first in descending value of Department and then within Department by ascending value of LastName, you specify:

```
/* *** SQL-Query-CH03-13 *** */
SELECT     FirstName, LastName, Department, OfficePhone
FROM       EMPLOYEE
ORDER BY   Department DESC, LastName ASC;
```

The result is:

FirstName	LastName	Department	OfficePhone
Linda	Granger	Sales and Marketing	360-285-8520
Ken	Numoto	Sales and Marketing	360-285-8510
Mike	Nguyen	Research and Development	360-285-8710
Jason	Sleeman	Research and Development	360-285-8720
Julia	Hayakawa	Production	NULL
Tom	Jackson	Production	360-285-8820
George	Jones	Production	360-285-8830
Mary	Smith	Production	360-285-8810
Sam	Stewart	Production	NULL
Richard	Bandalone	Legal	360-285-8210
Rick	Brown	InfoSystems	NULL
James	Nestor	InfoSystems	360-285-8610
Alan	Adams	Human Resources	360-285-8320
George	Smith	Human Resources	360-285-8310
Mary	Abernathy	Finance	360-285-8420
Ken	Evans	Finance	360-285-8410
Rosalie	Jackson	Administration	360-285-8120
Mary	Jacobs	Administration	360-285-8110
Tom	Caruthers	Accounting	360-285-8430
Heather	Jones	Accounting	360-285-8440

MySQL Community Server 8.0, MySQL Workbench, Oracle Corporation.

SQL WHERE Clause Options

SQL includes a number of SQL WHERE clause options that greatly expand SQL's power and utility. In this section, we consider three options: compound clauses, ranges, and wildcards.

Compound SQL WHERE Clauses Using Logical Operators   You can place more than one condition in a WHERE clause by using the **SQL logical operators**, which include the AND, OR, and NOT operators and which are shown in Figure 3-16.

If the **SQL AND operator** is used, only rows meeting *all* the conditions will be selected.

For example, the following query uses the AND operator to ask for employees who work in accounting *and* have the phone number 360-285-8430:

```
/* *** SQL-Query-CH03-14 *** */
SELECT    FirstName, LastName, Department, OfficePhone
FROM      EMPLOYEE
WHERE     Department = 'Accounting'
   AND    OfficePhone = '360-285-8430';
```

The result is:

FirstName	LastName	Department	OfficePhone
Tom	Caruthers	Accounting	360-285-8430

MySQL Community Server 8.0, MySQL Workbench, Oracle Corporation.

If the **SQL OR operator** is used, then rows that meet *any* of the conditions will be selected.

For example, the following query uses the OR operator to ask for employees who work in accounting *or* have the phone number 360-285-8410:

```
/* *** SQL-Query-CH03-15 *** */
SELECT    FirstName, LastName, Department, OfficePhone
FROM      EMPLOYEE
WHERE     Department = 'Accounting'
    OR    OfficePhone = '360-285-8410';
```

The result is:

FirstName	LastName	Department	OfficePhone
Ken	Evans	Finance	360-285-8410
Tom	Caruthers	Accounting	360-285-8430
Heather	Jones	Accounting	360-285-8440

MySQL Community Server 8.0, MySQL Workbench, Oracle Corporation.

FIGURE 3-16

SQL Logical Operators

SQL Logical Operators

Operator	Meaning
AND	Both arguments are TRUE
OR	One or the other or both of the arguments are TRUE
NOT	Negates the associated operator

The **SQL NOT operator** negates or reverses a condition set by a comparison or by an AND or OR operator. For example, to find all the rows in EMPLOYEE that have a Department named Accounting but not an office phone number of 360-285-8430, we can use the SQL NOT operator in our query code. The following query uses the AND keyword to ask for employees who work in accounting *and* do *not* have the phone number 360-285-8430:

```
/* *** SQL-Query-CH03-16 *** */
SELECT      FirstName, LastName, Department, OfficePhone
FROM        EMPLOYEE
WHERE       Department = 'Accounting'
  AND NOT   OfficePhone = '360-285-8430';
```

The result is:

FirstName	LastName	Department	OfficePhone
Heather	Jones	Accounting	360-285-8440

MySQL Community Server 8.0, MySQL Workbench, Oracle Corporation.

Three or more AND and OR conditions can be combined, but in such cases it is often easiest to use SQL IN and NOT IN comparison operators.

SQL WHERE Clauses Using Sets of Values   When we want to include a set of values in the SQL WHERE clause, we use the SQL IN operator or the SQL NOT IN operator (Figure 3-15). For example, suppose we want to obtain all the rows in EMPLOYEE for the employees in the set of departments Administration, Finance, and Accounting. We could construct a WHERE clause with two OR conditions, but an easier way to do this is to use the **IN comparison operator**, which specifies the set of values to be used in the SQL query:

```
/* *** SQL-Query-CH03-17 *** */
SELECT      FirstName, LastName, Department, OfficePhone
FROM        EMPLOYEE
WHERE       Department IN ('Administration', 'Finance',
            'Accounting');
```

In this query, a row will be displayed if it has a Department value equal to Administration, Finance, or Accounting. The result is:

FirstName	LastName	Department	OfficePhone
Tom	Caruthers	Accounting	360-285-8430
Heather	Jones	Accounting	360-285-8440
Mary	Jacobs	Administration	360-285-8110
Rosalie	Jackson	Administration	360-285-8120
Ken	Evans	Finance	360-285-8410
Mary	Abernathy	Finance	360-285-8420

MySQL Community Server 8.0, MySQL Workbench, Oracle Corporation.

To select rows that do *not* have any of these Department values, you would use the **NOT logical operator** in the **NOT IN comparison operator**, as follows:

```
/* *** SQL-Query-CH03-18 *** */
SELECT      FirstName, LastName, Department, OfficePhone
FROM        EMPLOYEE
WHERE       Department NOT IN ('Administration', 'Finance',
            'Accounting');
```

The result of this query is:

FirstName	LastName	Department	OfficePhone
Richard	Bandalone	Legal	360-285-8210
George	Smith	Human Resources	360-285-8310
Alan	Adams	Human Resources	360-285-8320
Ken	Numoto	Sales and Marketing	360-285-8510
Linda	Granger	Sales and Marketing	360-285-8520
James	Nestor	InfoSystems	360-285-8610
Rick	Brown	InfoSystems	NULL
Mike	Nguyen	Research and Development	360-285-8710
Jason	Sleeman	Research and Development	360-285-8720
Mary	Smith	Production	360-285-8810
Tom	Jackson	Production	360-285-8820
George	Jones	Production	360-285-8830
Julia	Hayakawa	Production	NULL
Sam	Stewart	Production	NULL

MySQL Community Server 8.0, MySQL Workbench, Oracle Corporation.

Observe an important difference between the IN and NOT IN operators:

- A row qualifies for an IN condition if the column is *equal to any* of the values in the parentheses.
- A row qualifies for a NOT IN condition if it is *not equal to all* of the items in the parentheses.

SQL WHERE Clauses Using Ranges of Values

WHERE clauses can refer to ranges of values and partial values. When we want to include or exclude a range of numerical values in the SQL WHERE clause, we use the **SQL BETWEEN operator** or the **SQL NOT BETWEEN operator** (Figure 3-15). For example, if we want to see data on the employees with EmployeeNumber values from 2 to 5, we could use the following SQL query:

```
/* *** SQL-Query-CH03-19 *** */
SELECT    FirstName, LastName, Department, OfficePhone
FROM      EMPLOYEE
WHERE     EmployeeNumber >= 2
   AND    EmployeeNumber <= 5;
```

The result is:

FirstName	LastName	Department	OfficePhone
Rosalie	Jackson	Administration	360-285-8120
Richard	Bandalone	Legal	360-285-8210
George	Smith	Human Resources	360-285-8310
Alan	Adams	Human Resources	360-285-8320

MySQL Community Server 8.0, MySQL Workbench, Oracle Corporation.

However, rather than specifying the range of values by using a compound SQL WHERE clause, we can accomplish the same results by using the SQL BETWEEN operator. Note how the SQL BETWEEN operator is used to create a simple, one-line WHERE clause in the following SQL-Query-CH03-20. Note that the SQL BETWEEN comparison operator *includes* the end points, and thus SQL-Query-CH03-20 is equivalent to SQL-Query-CH03-19, which uses the SQL comparison operators **>= (greater than or equal to)** and **<= (less than or equal to)**:

```
/* *** SQL-Query-CH03-20 *** */
SELECT    FirstName, LastName, Department, OfficePhone
FROM      EMPLOYEE
WHERE     EmployeeNumber BETWEEN 2 AND 5;
```

SQL-Query-CH03-20 produces the following result, which is identical to the result for SQL-Query-CH03-19:

FirstName	LastName	Department	OfficePhone
Rosalie	Jackson	Administration	360-285-8120
Richard	Bandalone	Legal	360-285-8210
George	Smith	Human Resources	360-285-8310
Alan	Adams	Human Resources	360-285-8320

MySQL Community Server 8.0, MySQL Workbench, Oracle Corporation.

SQL WHERE Clauses That Use Character String Patterns

There are times when we want to use the SQL WHERE clause to find matching sets or patterns of character strings. **Character strings** include the data that we store in a CHAR or VARCHAR data–type column (*CHAR* columns use a fixed number of bytes to store the data, while *VARCHAR* columns adjust the number of bytes used to fit the actual length of the data) and are composed of letters, numbers, and special characters. For example, the name *Smith* is a character string, as are *360-567-9876* and *Joe#34@elsewhere.com*. To find rows with values that match or do not match specific character string patterns, we use the **SQL LIKE comparison operator** and the **SQL NOT LIKE comparison operator** (Figure 3-15).

To help specify character string patterns, we use two **SQL wildcard characters**:

- The SQL **underscore symbol (_) wildcard character**, which represents a single, unspecified character in a specific position in the character string.
- The SQL **percent sign (%) wildcard character**, which represents any sequence of zero or more contiguous, unspecified characters (including spaces) in a specific position in the character string.

In the following query, the LIKE operator is used with the underscore symbol to find values that fit the pattern *2019 Q_ Portfolio Analysis*:

```
/* *** SQL-Query-CH03-21 *** */
SELECT    *
FROM      PROJECT
WHERE     ProjectName LIKE '2019 Q_ Portfolio Analysis';
```

The underscore means that any character can occur in the spot occupied by the underscore. The result of this statement is:

ProjectID	ProjectName	Department	MaxHours	StartDate	EndDate
1200	2019 Q3 Portfolio Analysis	Finance	120.00	2019-07-05	2019-07-25
1600	2019 Q4 Portfolio Analysis	Finance	140.00	2019-10-05	NULL

MySQL Community Server 8.0, MySQL Workbench, Oracle Corporation.

One underscore is used for each unknown character. To find all employees who have a Phone value that begins with 360-287-88, you can use two underscores to represent any last two digits, as follows:

```
/* *** SQL-Query-CH03-22 *** */
SELECT    *
FROM      EMPLOYEE
WHERE     OfficePhone LIKE '360-285-88__';
```

The result is:

EmployeeNumber	FirstName	LastName	Department	Position	Supervisor	OfficePhone	EmailAddress
16	Mary	Smith	Production	OPS3	1	360-285-8810	Mary.Smith@WP.com
17	Tom	Jackson	Production	OPS2	16	360-285-8820	Tom.Jackson@WP.com
18	George	Jones	Production	OPS2	17	360-285-8830	George.Jones@WP.com

MySQL Community Server 8.0, MySQL Workbench, Oracle Corporation.

While our example in SQL-Query-CH03-22 is correct, it does oversimplify this type of wildcard search a bit. If we are using wildcards with an INTEGER valued column (with the values automatically converted by the DBMS to character strings during the query), there will be no problem. And if we are using a VARCHAR column, again there will be no problem.

But OfficePhone is a CHAR column, and the query could have problems because there would be extra spaces to the right of the characters used as padding to completely fill the CHAR length. For example, if we store the value "four" in a CHAR(8) column named Number, the DBMS will actually store "four_____" ("four" plus four spaces). Most DBMSs will automatically remove trailing spaces when a column value is compared using equality, but when LIKE is used instead, some will not. To deal with these extra spaces, we use the RTRIM function:

```
WHERE RTRIM (Number) LIKE 'four';
```

Because the percent sign represents zero or one or more unknown characters, another way to write the query for employees who have a phone number that starts with 360-287-88 is:

```
/* *** SQL-Query-CH03-23 *** */
SELECT      *
FROM        EMPLOYEE
WHERE       OfficePhone LIKE '360-285-88%';
```

The result is the same as in the previous example:

EmployeeNumber	FirstName	LastName	Department	Position	Supervisor	OfficePhone	EmailAddress
16	Mary	Smith	Production	OPS3	1	360-285-8810	Mary.Smith@WP.com
17	Tom	Jackson	Production	OPS2	16	360-285-8820	Tom.Jackson@WP.com
18	George	Jones	Production	OPS2	17	360-285-8830	George.Jones@WP.com

MySQL Community Server 8.0, MySQL Workbench, Oracle Corporation.

If you want to find all the employees who work in departments that end in *ing*, you can use the % character as follows:

```
/* *** SQL-Query-CH03-24 *** */
SELECT      *
FROM        EMPLOYEE
WHERE       Department LIKE '%ing';
```

The result is:

EmployeeNumber	FirstName	LastName	Department	Position	Supervisor	OfficePhone	EmailAddress
8	Tom	Caruthers	Accounting	FA2	6	360-285-8430	Tom.Caruthers@WP.com
9	Heather	Jones	Accounting	FA2	6	360-285-8440	Heather.Jones@WP.com
10	Ken	Numoto	Sales and Marketing	SM3	1	360-285-8510	Ken.Numoto@WP.com
11	Linda	Granger	Sales and Marketing	SM2	10	360-285-8520	Linda.Granger@WP.com

MySQL Community Server 8.0, MySQL Workbench, Oracle Corporation.

The NOT logical operator, which we used previously as part of the NOT IN comparison operator, can also be used with the LIKE comparison operator to form the SQL NOT

LIKE comparison operator. For example, if you want to find all the employees who work in departments that do *not* end in *ing*, you can use the following SQL query:

```
/* *** SQL-Query-CH03-25 *** */
SELECT    *
FROM      EMPLOYEE
WHERE     Department NOT LIKE '%ing';
```

The result is:

EmployeeNumber	FirstName	LastName	Department	Position	Supervisor	OfficePhone	EmailAddress
1	Mary	Jacobs	Administration	CEO	NULL	360-285-8110	Mary.Jacobs@WP.com
2	Rosalie	Jackson	Administration	Admin Assistant	1	360-285-8120	Rosalie.Jackson@WP.com
3	Richard	Bandalone	Legal	Attorney	1	360-285-8210	Richard.Bandalone@WP.com
4	George	Smith	Human Resources	HR3	1	360-285-8310	George.Smith@WP.com
5	Alan	Adams	Human Resources	HR1	4	360-285-8320	Alan.Adams@WP.com
6	Ken	Evans	Finance	CFO	1	360-285-8410	Ken.Evans@WP.com
7	Mary	Abernathy	Finance	FA3	6	360-285-8420	Mary.Abernathy@WP.com
12	James	Nestor	InfoSystems	CIO	1	360-285-8610	James.Nestor@WP.com
13	Rick	Brown	InfoSystems	IS2	12	NULL	Rick.Brown@WP.com
14	Mike	Nguyen	Research and Development	CTO	1	360-285-8710	Mike.Nguyen@WP.com
15	Jason	Sleeman	Research and Development	RD3	14	360-285-8720	Jason.Sleeman@WP.com
16	Mary	Smith	Production	OPS3	1	360-285-8810	Mary.Smith@WP.com
17	Tom	Jackson	Production	OPS2	16	360-285-8820	Tom.Jackson@WP.com
18	George	Jones	Production	OPS2	17	360-285-8830	George.Jones@WP.com
19	Julia	Hayakawa	Production	OPS1	17	NULL	Julia.Hayakawa@WP.com
20	Sam	Stewart	Production	OPS1	17	NULL	Sam.Stewart@WP.com

MySQL Community Server 8.0, MySQL Workbench, Oracle Corporation.

BTW

While our examples in SQL-Query-CH03-23 and SQL-Query-CH03-24 are correct, they again oversimplify this type of wildcard search a bit, as previously discussed in the By the Way box on page 175. In MySQL, for example, one might think SQL-Query-CH03-24 should not work since all the department names actually end with several spaces in the database: none ends in "ing". MySQL, however, stores the spaces but automatically trims them on retrieval. Not all DBMS products work exactly like this, so the safest approach for SQL-Query-CH03-24 would be to use the following in the WHERE clause:

```
RTRIM(Department) LIKE '%ing'
```

Does Not Work with Microsoft Access ANSI-89 SQL

Microsoft Access ANSI-89 SQL uses wildcards but not the SQL-92 standard wildcards. Microsoft Access uses a **question mark (?)** instead of an underscore to represent single characters and an **asterisk (*)** instead of a percent sign to represent multiple characters. These symbols have their roots in the SQL-89 standard, where they are the correct standard.

Furthermore, Microsoft Access can sometimes be fussy about stored trailing spaces in a text field. You may have problems with a WHERE clause like this:

```
WHERE  ProjectName LIKE '2019 Q? Portfolio Analysis';
```

Solution: Use the appropriate Microsoft Access wildcard characters, and use an RTRIM function to eliminate trailing spaces:

```
WHERE  RTRIM(ProjectName) LIKE '2019 Q? Portfolio
       Analysis';
```

SQL WHERE Clauses That Use NULL Values

As we discussed earlier in this chapter, a missing data value is called a null value. In relational databases, null values are indicated with the special marker **NULL** (written as shown in uppercase letters). When we want to include or exclude rows that contain NULL values, we use the **SQL IS NULL comparison operator** or the **SQL IS NOT NULL comparison operator** (Figure 3-15). Note that in this situation the **SQL IS keyword** is equivalent to an *is equal to* comparison operator. However, the *is equal to* comparison operator is *never* used with NULL values, and the IS NULL and IS NOT NULL operators are never used with values other than NULL.

The following SQL will find the names and departments of all employees who have a NULL value for OfficePhone:

```
/* *** SQL-Query-CH03-26 *** */
SELECT    FirstName, LastName, Department, OfficePhone
FROM      EMPLOYEE
WHERE     OfficePhone IS NULL;
```

The result of this query is:

FirstName	LastName	Department	OfficePhone
Rick	Brown	InfoSystems	NULL
Julia	Hayakawa	Production	NULL
Sam	Stewart	Production	NULL

MySQL Community Server 8.0, MySQL Workbench, Oracle Corporation.

The NOT logical operator can also be used with the IS NULL comparison operator to form the IS NOT NULL comparison operator. For example, if you want to find all the employees who do have phone numbers, you can use the following SQL query:

```
/* *** SQL-Query-CH03-27 *** */
SELECT    FirstName, LastName, Department, OfficePhone
FROM      EMPLOYEE
WHERE     OfficePhone IS NOT NULL;
```

FirstName	LastName	Department	OfficePhone
Mary	Jacobs	Administration	360-285-8110
Rosalie	Jackson	Administration	360-285-8120
Richard	Bandalone	Legal	360-285-8210
George	Smith	Human Resources	360-285-8310
Alan	Adams	Human Resources	360-285-8320
Ken	Evans	Finance	360-285-8410
Mary	Abernathy	Finance	360-285-8420
Tom	Caruthers	Accounting	360-285-8430
Heather	Jones	Accounting	360-285-8440
Ken	Numoto	Sales and Marketing	360-285-8510
Linda	Granger	Sales and Marketing	360-285-8520
James	Nestor	InfoSystems	360-285-8610
Mike	Nguyen	Research and Development	360-285-8710
Jason	Sleeman	Research and Development	360-285-8720
Mary	Smith	Production	360-285-8810
Tom	Jackson	Production	360-285-8820
George	Jones	Production	360-285-8830

MySQL Community Server 8.0, MySQL Workbench, Oracle Corporation.

SQL QUERIES THAT PERFORM CALCULATIONS

Performing certain types of calculations is possible in SQL query statements. One group of calculations involves the use of SQL built-in functions. Another group involves simple arithmetic operations on the columns in the SELECT statement. We consider each in turn.

Using SQL Built-in Aggregate Functions

SQL allows you to calculate values based on the data in the tables. There are five standard **SQL built-in aggregate functions**. As shown in Figure 3-17, SQL includes five built-in aggregate functions: **COUNT**, **SUM**, **AVG**, **MAX**, and **MIN**. Some DBMS products extend these standard functions, but here we focus only on the five standard SQL built-in aggregate functions. These functions operate on the results of a SELECT statement. COUNT, MAX, and MIN work regardless of column data type, but SUM and AVG operate only on integer, numeric, and other number-oriented columns.

COUNT and SUM sound similar but are different. COUNT counts the number of rows in the result, whereas SUM totals the set of values of a numeric column. Thus, the following SQL statement counts the number of rows in the PROJECT table:

```
/* *** SQL-Query-CH03-28 *** */
SELECT    COUNT(*)
FROM      PROJECT;
```

The result of this statement is the following relation:

MySQL Community Server 8.0, MySQL Workbench, Oracle Corporation.

As stated earlier, the result of an SQL SELECT statement is always a relation. If, as is the case here, the result is a single number, that number is considered to be a relation that has only a single row and a single column.

Note that the preceding result has no column name. You can assign a column name to the result by using the **SQL AS keyword**:

```
/* *** SQL-Query-CH03-29 *** */
SELECT    COUNT(*) AS NumberOfProjects
FROM      PROJECT;
```

FIGURE 3-17

SQL Built-in Aggregate Functions

SQL Built-in Aggregate Functions	
Function	Meaning
COUNT(*)	Count the number of rows in the table
COUNT ({Name})	Count the number of rows in the table where column {Name} IS NOT NULL
SUM	Calculate the sum of all values (numeric columns only)
AVG	Calculate the average of all values (numeric columns only)
MIN	Calculate the minimum value of all values
MAX	Calculate the maximum value of all values

Now the resulting number is identified by the column title:

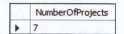

Consider the following two SELECT statements:

```
/* *** SQL-Query-CH03-30 *** */
SELECT    COUNT(Department) AS NumberOfDepartments
FROM      PROJECT;
```

and:

```
/* *** SQL-Query-CH03-31 *** */
SELECT    COUNT(DISTINCT Department) AS NumberOfDepartments
FROM      PROJECT;
```

The result of SQL-Query-CH03-30 is the relation:

	NumberOfDepartments
▶	7

and the result of SQL-Query-CH03-31 is:

	NumberOfDepartments
▶	4

Why do we get two different numbers? Because the first query counts some departments more than once. For example, the Accounting department is counted twice. The second query eliminates the duplicate rows in the count of the departments.

Does Not Work with Microsoft Access ANSI-89 SQL

Microsoft Access does not support the DISTINCT keyword as part of the COUNT expression, so while the SQL command with COUNT (Department) will work, the SQL command with COUNT (DISTINCT Department) will fail.

Solution: Use an SQL subquery structure (discussed later in this chapter) with the DISTINCT keyword in the subquery itself. The following SQL query works:

```
/* *** SQL-Query-CH03-31-Access *** */
SELECT    COUNT(*) AS NumberOfDepartments
FROM      (SELECT DISTINCT Department
           FROM   PROJECT) AS DEPT;
```

Note that this query is a bit different from the other queries using subqueries we show in this text because the preceding subquery is in the FROM clause instead of (as you'll see) the WHERE clause. Basically, this subquery builds a new temporary table named DEPT containing only distinct Department values, and the query counts the number of those values.

We can use multiple SQL built-in aggregate functions in the same query. The following is an example of using four built-in functions that operate on numerical data:

```
/* *** SQL-Query-CH03-32 *** */
SELECT    SUM(MaxHours) AS TotalMaxHours,
          AVG(MaxHours) AS AverageMaxHours,
          MIN(MaxHours) AS MinimumMaxHours,
          MAX(MaxHours) AS MaximumMaxHours
FROM      PROJECT
WHERE     ProjectID <= 1200;
```

The result is:

TotalMaxHours	AverageMaxHours	MinmumMaxHours	MaximumMaxHours
▶ 355.00	118.333333	100.00	135.00

MySQL Community Server 8.0, MySQL Workbench, Oracle Corporation.

You should be aware of two limitations to SQL built-in functions. First, except for grouping (defined later), you should not (and in most DBMS products you *cannot*) combine table column names with an SQL built-in aggregate function. For example, what happens if we run the following SQL query?

```
/* *** SQL-Query-CH03-33 *** */
SELECT    ProjectName, COUNT(*)
FROM      PROJECT;
```

The result in MySQL 8.0 is:

ProjectName	COUNT(*)
▶ 2019 Q3 Production Plan	7

MySQL Community Server 8.0, MySQL Workbench, Oracle Corporation.

Most DBMSs will return an error message from this query, because they cannot determine which of the 7 project names to return. MySQL, unfortunately, processes the query and returns one of the project name values (there is no guarantee as to which one it will return). This problem also arises in the context of GROUP BY queries, discussed later in this chapter.

The second problem with the SQL built-in aggregate functions that you should understand is that you cannot use them in an SQL WHERE clause. This is because the SQL WHERE clause operates on rows (choosing which rows will be displayed), whereas the aggregate functions operate on *columns* (each function calculates a single value based on all the attribute values stored in a column). Thus, you cannot use the following SQL statement:

```
/* *** SQL-Query-CH03-34 *** */
SELECT    *
FROM      PROJECT
WHERE     MaxHours > AVG(MaxHours);
```

An attempt to use such a statement will also result in an error statement from the DBMS:

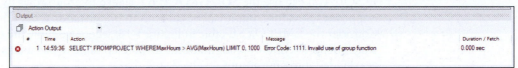

This is the specific MySQL 8.0 error message, but other DBMS products will give you an equivalent error message. The desired result of the preceding query can be computed using an SQL subquery (discussed later in this chapter). The desired result can also be obtained using a sequence of SQL views, which are discussed in online Extension B, "Advanced SQL."

Using SQL Expressions in SQL SELECT Statements

Standard mathematical calculations can also be done in SQL. For example, suppose that all employees at Wedgewood Pacific are paid $24.50 per hour. Given that each project has a MaxHours value, you might want to calculate a *maximum project cost* value for each project that is equal to MaxHours multiplied by the hourly wage rate. You can calculate the needed numbers by using the following query:

```
/* *** SQL-Query-CH03-35 *** */
SELECT    ProjectID, ProjectName, MaxHours,
          (24.50 * MaxHours) AS MaxProjectCost
FROM      PROJECT;
```

The result of the query, which now shows the maximum project cost for each project, is:

ProjectID	ProjectName	MaxHours	MaxProjectCost
1000	2019 Q3 Production Plan	100.00	2450.0000
1100	2019 Q3 Marketing Plan	135.00	3307.5000
1200	2019 Q3 Portfolio Analysis	120.00	2940.0000
1300	2019 Q3 Tax Preparation	145.00	3552.5000
1400	2019 Q4 Production Plan	100.00	2450.0000
1500	2019 Q4 Marketing Plan	135.00	3307.5000
1600	2019 Q4 Portfolio Analysis	140.00	3430.0000

An **SQL expression** is basically a formula or set of values that determines the exact results of an SQL query. We can think of an SQL expression as anything that follows an actual or implied *is equal to* (=) comparison operator (or any other comparison operator, such as *greater than* (>), *less than* (<), and so on) or that follows certain SQL comparison operator keywords, such as LIKE and BETWEEN. Thus, in the WHERE clause

```
WHERE    Department IN ('Administration', 'Finance',
         'Accounting')
```

the SQL expression consisting of the three text values following the IN keyword.

Another use for SQL expressions in SQL statements is to perform character string manipulation. For example, we may want to combine the EMPLOYEE FirstName and LastName columns into a single output column named EmployeeName. This use of SQL expressions is discussed in online Extension B, "Advanced SQL."

GROUPING ROWS USING SQL SELECT STATEMENTS

In SQL, you can use the **SQL GROUP BY clause** to group rows by common values. This is a powerful feature, but it can be difficult to understand. What do we mean by a group? Consider the EMPLOYEE table in Figure 3-18, where we show the employees grouped by which department they work in. Because there are nine departments, we have the employees divided into nine groups.

One use of grouping is to increase the utility of SQL built-in aggregate functions, because you can apply them to groups of rows. For example, SQL-Query-CH03-36 counts the number of employees in each department. To do this, it uses syntax similar to SQL-Query-CH03-33, which returned meaningless data in MySQL and will fail to run in most DBMSs! What is the difference in the two queries? It is the GROUP BY clause that has been added to SQL-Query-CH03-36:

```
/* *** SQL-Query-CH03-36 *** */
SELECT      Department, Count(*) AS NumberOfEmployees
FROM        EMPLOYEE
GROUP BY    Department;
```

The result is:

Department	NumberOfEmployees
▶ Accounting	2
Administration	2
Finance	2
Human Resources	2
InfoSystems	2
Legal	1
Production	5
Research and Development	2
Sales and Marketing	2

MySQL Community Server 8.0, MySQL Workbench, Oracle Corporation.

FIGURE 3-18

Department Groups in the EMPLOYEE Table

This group of rows is employees in the **Administration** department

This group of rows is employees in the **Production** department

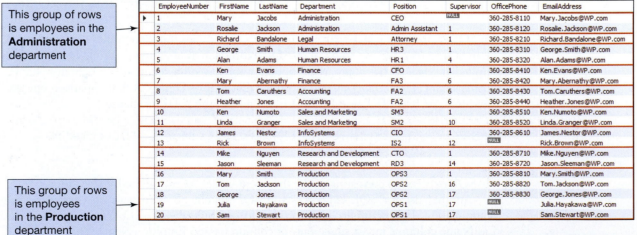

EmployeeNumber	FirstName	LastName	Department	Position	Supervisor	OfficePhone	EmailAddress
▶ 1	Mary	Jacobs	Administration	CEO	NULL	360-285-8110	Mary.Jacobs@WP.com
2	Rosalie	Jackson	Administration	Admin Assistant	1	360-285-8120	Rosalie.Jackson@WP.com
3	Richard	Bandalone	Legal	Attorney	1	360-285-8210	Richard.Bandalone@WP.com
4	George	Smith	Human Resources	HR3	1	360-285-8310	George.Smith@WP.com
5	Alan	Adams	Human Resources	HR1	4	360-285-8320	Alan.Adams@WP.com
6	Ken	Evans	Finance	CFO	1	360-285-8410	Ken.Evans@WP.com
7	Mary	Abernathy	Finance	FA3	6	360-285-8420	Mary.Abernathy@WP.com
8	Tom	Caruthers	Accounting	FA2	6	360-285-8430	Tom.Caruthers@WP.com
9	Heather	Jones	Accounting	FA2	6	360-285-8440	Heather.Jones@WP.com
10	Ken	Numoto	Sales and Marketing	SM3	1	360-285-8510	Ken.Numoto@WP.com
11	Linda	Granger	Sales and Marketing	SM2	10	360-285-8520	Linda.Granger@WP.com
12	James	Nestor	InfoSystems	CIO	1	360-285-8610	James.Nestor@WP.com
13	Rick	Brown	InfoSystems	IS2	12	NULL	Rick.Brown@WP.com
14	Mike	Nguyen	Research and Development	CTO	1	360-285-8710	Mike.Nguyen@WP.com
15	Jason	Sleeman	Research and Development	RD3	14	360-285-8720	Jason.Sleeman@WP.com
16	Mary	Smith	Production	OPS3	1	360-285-8810	Mary.Smith@WP.com
17	Tom	Jackson	Production	OPS2	16	360-285-8820	Tom.Jackson@WP.com
18	George	Jones	Production	OPS2	17	360-285-8830	George.Jones@WP.com
19	Julia	Hayakawa	Production	OPS1	17	NULL	Julia.Hayakawa@WP.com
20	Sam	Stewart	Production	OPS1	17	NULL	Sam.Stewart@WP.com

MySQL Community Server 8.0, MySQL Workbench, Oracle Corporation.

The GROUP BY keyword tells the DBMS to sort the table by the named column and then to apply the built-in function to groups of rows that have the same value for the named column. When GROUP BY is used, the name of the grouping column and built-in functions *may appear* in the SELECT clause. This is the *only* time that a column name and a built-in function can appear together.

We can further restrict the results by using the **SQL HAVING clause** to apply conditions to the groups that are formed. For example, if you want to consider only groups with at least two members, you could specify:

```
/* *** SQL-Query-CH03-37 *** */
SELECT      Department, Count(*) AS NumberOfEmployees
FROM        EMPLOYEE
GROUP BY    Department
HAVING      COUNT(*) > 1;
```

The result of this SQL statement is:

Department	NumberOfEmployees
▶ Accounting	2
Administration	2
Finance	2
Human Resources	2
InfoSystems	2
Production	5
Research and Development	2
Sales and Marketing	2

MySQL Community Server 8.0, MySQL Workbench, Oracle Corporation.

Adding WHERE clauses when using GROUP BY is possible. However, an ambiguity can arise when this is done. If the WHERE condition is applied before the groups are formed, we obtain one result. If, however, the WHERE condition is applied after the groups are formed, we get a different result. To resolve this ambiguity, the SQL standard specifies that when WHERE and GROUP BY occur together, the WHERE condition will be applied first. For example, consider the following query:

```
/* *** SQL-Query-CH03-38 *** */
SELECT      Department, Count(*) AS NumberOfEmployees
FROM        EMPLOYEE
WHERE       EmployeeNumber <= 10
GROUP BY    Department
HAVING      COUNT(*) > 1;
```

In this expression, first the WHERE clause is applied to select employees with an EmployeeNumber less than or equal to 10. Then the groups are formed. Finally, the HAVING condition is applied. The result is:

Department	NumberOfEmployees
▶ Administration	2
Human Resources	2
Finance	2
Accounting	2

MySQL Community Server 8.0, MySQL Workbench, Oracle Corporation.

Note that SQL built-in aggregate functions can be used in the SQL HAVING clause because they are working on the *set of column values in each group*. Earlier we noted that those functions *cannot* be used in the WHERE clause because the WHERE clause is applied to each *single row*. Getting confused between the SQL WHERE clause and the SQL HAVING clause is easy to do. The best way to understand the difference is to remember that:

- The SQL WHERE clause specifies which *rows* will be used to determine the groups.
- The SQL HAVING clause specifies which *groups* will be used in the final result.

SQL FOR DATA MANIPULATION (DML)—MULTIPLE TABLE QUERIES

The queries considered so far have involved data from a single table. However, at times, more than one table must be processed to obtain the desired information.

SQL provides two different techniques for querying data from multiple tables:

- The SQL subquery
- The SQL join

As you will learn, although both work with multiple tables, they are used for slightly different purposes.

Querying Multiple Tables with Subqueries

For example, suppose we want to know the names of all employees who have worked more than 50 hours on any single assignment. The names of employees are stored in the EMPLOYEE table, but the hours they have worked are stored in the ASSIGNMENT table.

If we knew that employees with EmployeeNumber 6, 10, 11, 16, and 17 have worked more than 50 hours on an assignment (which is true), we could obtain their names with the following expression:

```
/* *** SQL-Query-CH03-39 *** */
SELECT     FirstName, LastName
FROM       EMPLOYEE
WHERE      EmployeeNumber IN (6, 10, 11, 16, 17);
```

The result is:

FirstName	LastName
Ken	Evans
Ken	Numoto
Linda	Granger
Mary	Smith
Tom	Jackson

MySQL Community Server 8.0, MySQL Workbench, Oracle Corporation.

But, according to the problem description, we are not given the employee numbers. We can, however, obtain the appropriate employee numbers with the following query:

```
/* *** SQL-Query-CH03-40 *** */
SELECT     DISTINCT EmployeeNumber
FROM       ASSIGNMENT
WHERE      HoursWorked > 50;
```

The result is:

EmployeeNumber
16
17
6
10
11

MySQL Community Server 8.0, MySQL Workbench, Oracle Corporation.

Is there some way to obtain the results of SQL-Query-CH03-40, and then feed them into the WHERE clause in SQL-Query-CH03-39? Yes, there is, and we can combine these two SQL statements by using an SQL **subquery** as follows:

```
/* *** SQL-Query-CH03-41 *** */
SELECT    FirstName, LastName
FROM      EMPLOYEE
WHERE     EmployeeNumber IN
          (SELECT   DISTINCT EmployeeNumber
          FROM      ASSIGNMENT
          WHERE     HoursWorked > 50);
```

The result of this expression is:

FirstName	LastName
Ken	Evans
Ken	Numoto
Linda	Granger
Mary	Smith
Tom	Jackson

MySQL Community Server 8.0, MySQL Workbench, Oracle Corporation.

These are indeed the names of the employees who have worked more than 50 hours on any single assignment. In SQL-Query-CH03-41, the second SELECT statement, the one enclosed in parentheses, is called the SQL subquery. An SQL subquery is an SQL query statement used to determine a set of values that are provided (or returned) to the SQL query (often referred to as the top-level query) that used (or called) the subquery. A subquery is often described as a nested query or a query within a query. The subquery is usually indented, as shown in the earlier SQL-Query-CH03-41, to make the entire query statement easier to read.

It is important to note that SQL queries using subqueries still function like a single table query in the sense that only the columns of the top-level query can be displayed in the query results. For example, in SQL-Query-CH03-41, because the HoursWorked column is in the ASSIGNMENT table (the table used in the subquery itself), the values of the HoursWorked column cannot be displayed in the final results.

Subqueries can be extended to include three, four, or even more levels. Suppose, for example, that you need to know the names of employees who have worked more than 40 hours on an assignment sponsored by the accounting department. You can obtain the project IDs of projects sponsored by accounting with:

```
/* *** SQL-Query-CH03-42 *** */
SELECT    DISTINCT ProjectID
FROM      PROJECT
WHERE     Department = 'Accounting';
```

The result is:

You can obtain the employee numbers of employees working more than 40 hours on those projects with:

```
/* *** SQL-Query-CH03-43 *** */
SELECT    DISTINCT EmployeeNumber
FROM      ASSIGNMENT
WHERE     HoursWorked > 40
          AND        ProjectID IN
          (SELECT    ProjectID
          FROM       PROJECT
          WHERE      Department = 'Accounting');
```

The result is:

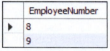

Finally, you can obtain the names of the employees in the preceding SQL statement with:

```
/* *** SQL-Query-CH03-44 *** */
SELECT    FirstName, LastName
FROM      EMPLOYEE
WHERE     EmployeeNumber IN
          (SELECT    DISTINCT EmployeeNumber
          FROM       ASSIGNMENT
          WHERE      HoursWorked > 40
               AND        ProjectID IN
               (SELECT    ProjectID
               FROM       PROJECT
               WHERE      Department = 'Accounting'));
```

The final result is:

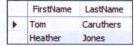

Querying Multiple Tables with Joins

Subqueries are effective for processing multiple tables, as long as the results come from a single table. If, however, we need to display data from two or more tables, subqueries do not work. We need to use an **SQL join operation** instead.

The basic idea of a join is to form a new relation by connecting the contents of two or more other relations. In an SQL join operation, the **SQL JOIN operator** is used to combine two or more tables by concatenating (sticking together) the rows of one table with the rows of another table. If the JOIN operator is actually used as part of the SQL statement syntax, we refer to the join operation as an **explicit join**. If the JOIN operator itself does not appear in the SQL statement, we refer to the join operation as an **implicit join**.

Consider how we might combine data in the EMPLOYEE and ASSIGNMENT tables. We can concatenate the rows of one table with the rows of the second table with the following SQL statement, where we simply list the names of the tables we want to combine:

```
/* *** SQL-Query-CH03-45 *** */
SELECT    FirstName, LastName, ProjectID, HoursWorked
FROM      EMPLOYEE, ASSIGNMENT;
```

This is known as a **CROSS JOIN**, and the result is what is mathematically known as the **Cartesian product** of the rows in the tables, which means that this statement will just stick every row of one table together with every row of the second table. For the EMPLOYEE and ASSIGNMENT tables, there are 20 rows in EMPLOYEE and 30 rows in ASSIGNMENT, so this results in a table with 600 rows! We are not going to show that table here, so if you want to see that result, run SQL-Query-CH03-45 yourself!

This is clearly not what we had in mind. What we really need to do is to select only those rows for which the EmployeeNumber of EMPLOYEE (primary key) matches the EmployeeNumber in ASSIGNMENT (foreign key). This is known as an **inner join**, and this is easy to do—we simply add an SQL WHERE clause to the query requiring that the values in the two columns are equal to each other as follows, as shown in Figure 3-19.

We now use this SQL statement as our query:

```
/* *** SQL-Query-CH03-46 *** */
SELECT FirstName, LastName, ProjectID, HoursWorked
FROM   EMPLOYEE, ASSIGNMENT
WHERE  EMPLOYEE.EmployeeNumber = ASSIGNMENT.EmployeeNumber;
```

The function of this statement is to create a new table having the four columns FirstName, LastName, ProjectID, and HoursWorked. Those columns are to be taken from the EMPLOYEE and ASSIGNMENT tables, under the condition that EmployeeNumber in EMPLOYEE (written in the format *TABLENAME.ColumnName* as EMPLOYEE.EmployeeNumber) equals EmployeeNumber in ASSIGNMENT (written as ASSIGNMENT.EmployeeNumber). Whenever there is ambiguity about which table the column data are coming from, the column name is always preceded with the table name in the format *TABLENAME.ColumnName*.

FIGURE 3-19

Using Primary Key and Foreign Key Values in the SQL WHERE Clause in an Implicit SQL Join

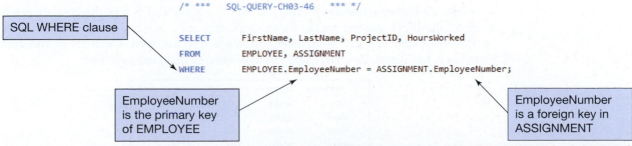

MySQL Community Server 8.0, MySQL Workbench, Oracle Corporation.

> **BTW**
>
> This ambiguity about which table the column data are coming from often happens (as in this case) because the primary key and foreign key column names are the same, but it can happen in other situations.

You can think of the join operation working as follows: Start with the first row in EMPLOYEE. Using the value of EmployeeNumber in this first row (1 for the data in Figure 3-2(b)), examine the rows in ASSIGNMENT. When you find a row in ASSIGNMENT where EmployeeNumber is also equal to 1, join FirstName and LastName of the first row of EMPLOYEE with ProjectID and HoursWorked from the row you just found in ASSIGNMENT.

For the data in Figure 3-2(c), the first row of ASSIGNMENT has EmployeeNumber equal to 1, so you join FirstName and LastName from the first row of EMPLOYEE with ProjectID and HoursWorked from the first row in ASSIGNMENT to form the first row of the join. The result is:

FirstName	LastName	ProjectID	HoursWorked
Mary	Jacobs	1000	30.00

MySQL Community Server 8.0, MySQL Workbench, Oracle Corporation.

Now, still using the EmployeeNumber value of 1, look for a second row in ASSIGNMENT that has EmployeeNumber equal to 1. For our data, the sixth row of ASSIGNMENT has such a value. So, join FirstName and LastName from the first row of EMPLOYEE to ProjectID and HoursWorked in the sixth row of ASSIGNMENT to obtain the second row of the join, as follows:

FirstName	LastName	ProjectID	HoursWorked
Mary	Jacobs	1000	30.00
Mary	Jacobs	1100	30.00

MySQL Community Server 8.0, MySQL Workbench, Oracle Corporation.

Continue in this way, looking for matches for the EmployeeNumber value of 1. There is another in the 18th row, and finally one more in the 23rd row, and you would add the data for that match to obtain the result:

FirstName	LastName	ProjectID	HoursWorked
Mary	Jacobs	1000	30.00
Mary	Jacobs	1100	30.00
Mary	Jacobs	1400	30.00
Mary	Jacobs	1500	30.00

MySQL Community Server 8.0, MySQL Workbench, Oracle Corporation.

At this point, no more EmployeeNumber values of 1 appear in the sample data, so now you move to the second row of EMPLOYEE, obtain the new value of EmployeeNumber (2), and begin searching for matches for it in the rows of ASSIGNMENT. In this case, there are no ASSIGNMENT matches for the EmployeeNumber of 2. Next, you look for rows with an EmployeeNumber value of 3. Now, the tenth row has such a match, so you add FirstName, LastName, ProjectID, and HoursWorked to the result to obtain:

FirstName	LastName	ProjectID	HoursWorked
Mary	Jacobs	1000	30.00
Mary	Jacobs	1100	30.00
Mary	Jacobs	1400	30.00
Mary	Jacobs	1500	30.00
Richard	Bandalone	1200	20.00

MySQL Community Server 8.0, MySQL Workbench, Oracle Corporation.

FIGURE 3-20

Final SQL Join Results
for SQL-Query-CH03-47

FirstName	LastName	ProjectID	HoursWorked
Mary	Jacobs	1000	30.00
Mary	Jacobs	1100	30.00
Mary	Jacobs	1400	30.00
Mary	Jacobs	1500	30.00
Richard	Bandalone	1200	20.00
Richard	Bandalone	1300	25.00
Richard	Bandalone	1600	20.00
Ken	Evans	1000	50.00
Ken	Evans	1100	75.00
Ken	Evans	1200	40.00
Ken	Evans	1300	40.00
Ken	Evans	1400	50.00
Ken	Evans	1500	75.00
Ken	Evans	1600	40.00
Mary	Abernathy	1200	45.00
Mary	Abernathy	1600	45.00
Tom	Caruthers	1200	45.00
Tom	Caruthers	1300	50.00
Tom	Caruthers	1600	45.00
Heather	Jones	1300	50.00
Ken	Numoto	1000	50.00
Ken	Numoto	1100	55.00
Ken	Numoto	1400	50.00
Ken	Numoto	1500	55.00
Linda	Granger	1100	55.00
Linda	Granger	1500	55.00
Mary	Smith	1000	75.00
Mary	Smith	1400	75.00
Tom	Jackson	1000	75.00
Tom	Jackson	1400	75.00

MySQL Community Server 8.0, MySQL Workbench, Oracle Corporation.

You continue until all rows of EMPLOYEE have been examined. The final result is shown in Figure 3-20.

Actually, that is the theoretical result—remember that row order in an SQL query can be arbitrary. To ensure that you get the result shown in Figure 3-20, you need to add an ORDER BY clause to the query:

```
/* *** SQL-Query-CH03-47 *** */
SELECT    FirstName, LastName, ProjectID, HoursWorked
FROM      EMPLOYEE, ASSIGNMENT
WHERE     EMPLOYEE.EmployeeNumber =
              ASSIGNMENT.EmployeeNumber
ORDER BY  EMPLOYEE.EmployeeNumber, ProjectID;
```

The actual result when the SQL-Query-CH03-46 is run in MySQL has the same data results, but the row order is definitely different!

The SQL JOIN ON Syntax

Our SQL join examples so far have used the original, but older, form of the SQL join syntax. Although it can still be used, today most SQL users prefer to use the **SQL JOIN ON syntax**. Consider our query example SQL-Query-CH03-46 as modified with an ORDER BY clause to become SQL-Query-CH03-47. This query uses a join in the WHERE clause:

```
/* *** SQL-Query-CH03-47 *** */
SELECT      FirstName, LastName, HoursWorked
FROM        EMPLOYEE, ASSIGNMENT
WHERE       EMPLOYEE.EmployeeNumber =
                ASSIGNMENT.EmployeeNumber
ORDER BY    EMPLOYEE.EmployeeNumber, ProjectID;
```

Using the JOIN ON syntax, SQL-Query-CH-47 would be modified as follows to become SQL-Query-CH03-48:

```
/* *** SQL-Query-CH03-48 *** */
SELECT      FirstName, LastName, ProjectID, HoursWorked
FROM        EMPLOYEE JOIN ASSIGNMENT
        ON  EMPLOYEE.EmployeeNumber =
                ASSIGNMENT.EmployeeNumber
ORDER BY    EMPLOYEE.EmployeeNumber, ProjectID;
```

The result of SQL-Query-CH03-48 is shown in Figure 3-21, and is, as you would expect, identical to the results for SQL-Query-CH03-47 shown in Figure 3-20.

FIGURE 3-21

Final SQL Join Results
for SQL-Query-CH03-48

FirstName	LastName	HoursWorked
Mary	Jacobs	30.00
Mary	Jacobs	30.00
Mary	Jacobs	30.00
Mary	Jacobs	30.00
Richard	Bandalone	20.00
Richard	Bandalone	25.00
Richard	Bandalone	20.00
Ken	Evans	50.00
Ken	Evans	75.00
Ken	Evans	40.00
Ken	Evans	40.00
Ken	Evans	50.00
Ken	Evans	75.00
Ken	Evans	40.00
Mary	Abernathy	45.00
Mary	Abernathy	45.00
Tom	Caruthers	45.00
Tom	Caruthers	50.00
Tom	Caruthers	45.00
Heather	Jones	50.00
Ken	Numoto	50.00
Ken	Numoto	55.00
Ken	Numoto	50.00
Ken	Numoto	55.00
Linda	Granger	55.00
Linda	Granger	55.00
Mary	Smith	75.00
Mary	Smith	75.00
Tom	Jackson	75.00
Tom	Jackson	75.00

MySQL Community Server 8.0, MySQL Workbench, Oracle Corporation.

Although these two join syntaxes are functionally equivalent, the implicit join syntax is early SQL standard syntax and is considered to have been replaced by the explicit SQL JOIN ON join syntax as of the 1992 SQL-92 standard. Most people think that the SQL JOIN ON syntax is easier to understand than the first. Note that when using the SQL JOIN ON syntax:

- The **SQL JOIN keyword** is placed between the table names in the SQL FROM clause, where it replaces the comma that previously separated the two table names, and
- The **SQL ON keyword** now leads into an **SQL ON clause**, which includes the statement of matching key values that was previously in an SQL WHERE clause.
- The SQL WHERE clause is no longer used as part of the join, which makes it easier to read the actual restrictions on the rows in the query in the WHERE clause itself.

Note that the JOIN ON syntax still requires a statement of primary key to foreign key equivalence, as shown in Figure 3-22. Also note that the SQL ON clause does not replace the SQL WHERE clause, which can still be used to determine which rows will be displayed.

A join is just another table, so all the earlier SQL SELECT commands are available for use. We could, for example, group the rows of the join by employee using a GROUP BY clause, and sum the hours they worked using the SUM built-in aggregate function. The following is the SQL for such a query:

```
/* *** SQL-Query-CH03-49 *** */
SELECT      FirstName, LastName,
            SUM(HoursWorked) AS TotalHoursWorked
FROM        EMPLOYEE AS E JOIN ASSIGNMENT AS A
      ON    E.EmployeeNumber = A.EmployeeNumber
GROUP BY    LastName, FirstName
ORDER BY    LastName, FirstName;
```

Note another use for the SQL AS keyword, which is now used to assign aliases to table names so that we can use these aliases in the ON and other clauses. This makes it much easier to write queries with long table names. The result of this query is:

FirstName	LastName	TotalHoursWorked
Mary	Abernathy	90.00
Richard	Bandalone	65.00
Tom	Caruthers	140.00
Ken	Evans	370.00
Linda	Granger	110.00
Tom	Jackson	150.00
Mary	Jacobs	120.00
Heather	Jones	50.00
Ken	Numoto	210.00
Mary	Smith	150.00

MySQL Community Server 8.0, MySQL Workbench, Oracle Corporation.

FIGURE 3-22

Using Primary Key and Foreign Key Values in the SQL ON Clause in an Explicit SQL Join

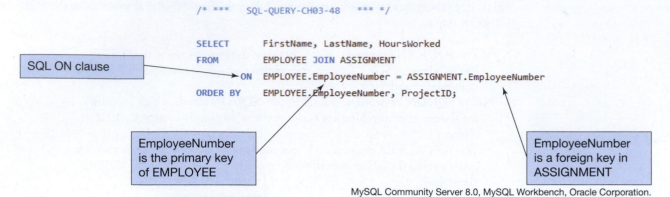

```
/* ***   SQL-QUERY-CH03-48   *** */

SELECT      FirstName, LastName, HoursWorked
FROM        EMPLOYEE JOIN ASSIGNMENT
ON          EMPLOYEE.EmployeeNumber = ASSIGNMENT.EmployeeNumber
ORDER BY    EMPLOYEE.EmployeeNumber, ProjectID;
```

SQL ON clause

EmployeeNumber is the primary key of EMPLOYEE

EmployeeNumber is a foreign key in ASSIGNMENT

MySQL Community Server 8.0, MySQL Workbench, Oracle Corporation.

> **BTW**
>
> Microsoft SQL Server and Oracle Database create table aliases in a similar manner, but Oracle Database does not allow use of the SQL AS keyword. In Oracle Database, the table name is just followed immediately by the alias to be used (this will also work in Microsoft SQL Server). This is shown in SQL-Query-CH03-49-Oracle:
>
> ```
> /* *** SQL-Query-CH03-49-Oracle *** */
> SELECT    FirstName, LastName,
>           SUM(HoursWorked) AS TotalHoursWorked
> FROM      EMPLOYEE E JOIN ASSIGNMENT A
>   ON      E.EmployeeNumber = A.EmployeeNumber
> GROUP BY  LastName, FirstName
> ORDER BY  LastName, FirstName;
> ```

We could apply a WHERE clause during the process of creating the join as follows:

```
/* *** SQL-Query-CH03-50 *** */
SELECT      FirstName, LastName, ProjectID, HoursWorked
FROM        EMPLOYEE AS E JOIN ASSIGNMENT AS A
     ON     E.EmployeeNumber = A.EmployeeNumber
WHERE       HoursWorked > 50
ORDER BY    LastName, FirstName, ProjectID;
```

The result of this join is:

FirstName	LastName	ProjectID	HoursWorked
Ken	Evans	1100	75.00
Ken	Evans	1500	75.00
Linda	Granger	1100	55.00
Linda	Granger	1500	55.00
Tom	Jackson	1000	75.00
Tom	Jackson	1400	75.00
Ken	Numoto	1100	55.00
Ken	Numoto	1500	55.00
Mary	Smith	1000	75.00
Mary	Smith	1400	75.00

MySQL Community Server 8.0, MySQL Workbench, Oracle Corporation.

Our first examples used only two tables, but we can also use the implicit join syntax or the JOIN ON syntax for joins of more than two tables. Here is a three-table query to combine data for EMPLOYEE, PROJECT, and ASSIGNMENT rewritten using the JOIN ON style:

```
/* *** SQL-Query-CH03-51 *** */
SELECT      ProjectName, FirstName, LastName, HoursWorked
FROM        EMPLOYEE AS E JOIN ASSIGNMENT AS A
       ON   E.EmployeeNumber = A.EmployeeNumber
            JOIN PROJECT AS P
                ON   A.ProjectID = P.ProjectID
ORDER BY    P.ProjectID, A.EmployeeNumber;
```

Note how the additional table is added into the query by the additional JOIN ON construction. For each new table added to the query, we simply add another JOIN ON phrase. The results of SQL-Query-CH03-51 are shown in Figure 3-23.

Comparing Subqueries and Joins

Subqueries and joins both process multiple tables, but they differ slightly. As mentioned earlier, a subquery can be used only to retrieve data from the top table, whereas a join can be used to obtain data from any number of tables. Thus, a join can do everything a

FIGURE 3-23

Final SQL Join Results
for SQL-Query-CH03-51

ProjectName	FirstName	LastName	HoursWorked
2019 Q3 Production Plan	Mary	Jacobs	30.00
2019 Q3 Production Plan	Ken	Evans	50.00
2019 Q3 Production Plan	Ken	Numoto	50.00
2019 Q3 Production Plan	Mary	Smith	75.00
2019 Q3 Production Plan	Tom	Jackson	75.00
2019 Q3 Marketing Plan	Mary	Jacobs	30.00
2019 Q3 Marketing Plan	Ken	Evans	75.00
2019 Q3 Marketing Plan	Ken	Numoto	55.00
2019 Q3 Marketing Plan	Linda	Granger	55.00
2019 Q3 Portfolio Analysis	Richard	Bandalone	20.00
2019 Q3 Portfolio Analysis	Ken	Evans	40.00
2019 Q3 Portfolio Analysis	Mary	Abernathy	45.00
2019 Q3 Portfolio Analysis	Tom	Caruthers	45.00
2019 Q3 Tax Preparation	Richard	Bandalone	25.00
2019 Q3 Tax Preparation	Ken	Evans	40.00
2019 Q3 Tax Preparation	Tom	Caruthers	50.00
2019 Q3 Tax Preparation	Heather	Jones	50.00
2019 Q4 Production Plan	Mary	Jacobs	30.00
2019 Q4 Production Plan	Ken	Evans	50.00
2019 Q4 Production Plan	Ken	Numoto	50.00
2019 Q4 Production Plan	Mary	Smith	75.00
2019 Q4 Production Plan	Tom	Jackson	75.00
2019 Q4 Marketing Plan	Mary	Jacobs	30.00
2019 Q4 Marketing Plan	Ken	Evans	75.00
2019 Q4 Marketing Plan	Ken	Numoto	55.00
2019 Q4 Marketing Plan	Linda	Granger	55.00
2019 Q4 Portfolio Analysis	Richard	Bandalone	20.00
2019 Q4 Portfolio Analysis	Ken	Evans	40.00
2019 Q4 Portfolio Analysis	Mary	Abernathy	45.00
2019 Q4 Portfolio Analysis	Tom	Caruthers	45.00

MySQL Community Server 8.0, MySQL Workbench, Oracle Corporation.

Does Not Work with Microsoft Access ANSI-89 SQL

Microsoft Access supports the JOIN ON syntax only with a keyword specifying a standard (INNER) or nonstandard (OUTER) JOIN. OUTER joins are discussed next in the text.

Solution: The Microsoft Access JOIN ON queries run when written with the INNER keyword as:

```
/* *** SQL-Query-CH03-48-Access *** */
SELECT      FirstName, LastName, ProjectID, HoursWorked
FROM        EMPLOYEE INNER JOIN ASSIGNMENT
       ON   EMPLOYEE.EmployeeNumber =
                  ASSIGNMENT.EmployeeNumber
ORDER BY    EMPLOYEE.EmployeeNumber, ProjectID;
```

Further, Microsoft Access requires that the joins be grouped using parentheses when three or more tables are joined:

```
/* *** SQL-Query-CH03-51-Access *** */
SELECT      ProjectName, FirstName, LastName,
            HoursWorked
FROM        (EMPLOYEE AS E INNER JOIN ASSIGNMENT AS A
       ON   E.EmployeeNumber = A.EmployeeNumber)
            INNER JOIN PROJECT AS P
                  ON    A.ProjectID = P.ProjectID
ORDER BY    P.ProjectID, A.EmployeeNumber;
```

Note that these versions of the queries will also work in MySQL 8.0, Microsoft SQL Server 2017, and Oracle Database XE.

---

subquery can do and more. So why learn subqueries? For one, if you just need data from a single table, you might use a subquery because it is easier to write and understand. This is especially true when processing multiple tables.

There is, however, a type of subquery called a **correlated subquery** that can do work that is not possible with joins. Correlated subqueries are discussed in online Extension B, "Advanced, it is important for you to learn about both joins and subqueries, even though right now it appears that joins are uniformly superior.

Inner Joins and Outer Joins

Let's add a new project, the 2019 Q4 Tax Preparation project run by the accounting department, to the PROJECT table as follows:

```
/* *** SQL-INSERT-CH03-05 *** */
INSERT INTO PROJECT
    (ProjectID, ProjectName, Department, MaxHours, StartDate)
    VALUES(1700, '2019 Q4 Tax Preparation, 'Accounting',
    175.00, '2019-12-10');
```

To see the updated PROJECT table, we use the query:

```
/* *** SQL-Query-CH03-52 *** */
SELECT * FROM PROJECT;
```

The results are:

	ProjectID	ProjectName	Department	MaxHours	StartDate	EndDate
▶	1000	2019 Q3 Production Plan	Production	100.00	2019-05-10	2019-06-15
	1100	2019 Q3 Marketing Plan	Sales and Marketing	135.00	2019-05-10	2019-06-15
	1200	2019 Q3 Portfolio Analysis	Finance	120.00	2019-07-05	2019-07-25
	1300	2019 Q3 Tax Preparation	Accounting	145.00	2019-08-10	2019-10-15
	1400	2019 Q4 Production Plan	Production	100.00	2019-08-10	2019-09-15
	1500	2019 Q4 Marketing Plan	Sales and Marketing	135.00	2019-08-10	2019-09-15
	1600	2019 Q4 Portfolio Analysis	Finance	140.00	2019-10-05	NULL
	1700	2019 Q4 Tax Preparation	Accounting	175.00	2019-12-10	NULL

MySQL Community Server 8.0, MySQL Workbench, Oracle Corporation.

Now, with the new project added to PROJECT, we'll rerun the previous query on EMPLOYEE, ASSIGNMENT, and PROJECT but here relabeled as SQL-Query-CH03-53:

```
/* *** SQL-Query-CH03-53 *** */
SELECT      ProjectName, FirstName, LastName, HoursWorked
FROM        EMPLOYEE AS E JOIN ASSIGNMENT AS A
      ON    E.EmployeeNumber = A.EmployeeNumber
            JOIN  PROJECT AS P
                ON    A.ProjectID = P.ProjectID
ORDER BY    P.ProjectID, A.EmployeeNumber;
```

The results of SQL-Query-CH03-53 are shown in Figure 3-24.

The results shown here are correct, but a surprising result occurs. What happened to the new 2019 Q4 Tax Preparation project? The answer is that it does not appear in the join results because its ProjectID value of 1700 had no match in the ASSIGNMENT table. Nothing is wrong with this result; you just need to be aware that unmatched rows do not appear in the result of a join. The join operation discussed in the previous sections is sometimes referred to as an **SQL equijoin** or **SQL inner join**. An inner join only displays data from the rows that match based on join conditions, and as you saw in the last query in the previous section, data can be lost (or at least appear to be lost) when you perform an inner join. In particular, if a row has a value that does not match the WHERE clause condition, that row will not be included in the join result. The 2019 Q4 Tax Preparation project did not appear in the previous join because no row in ASSIGNMENT matched its ProjectID value. This kind of loss is not always desirable, so a special type of join, called an **SQL outer join**, was created to avoid it.

Consider the STUDENT and LOCKER tables in Figure 3-25(a), where we have drawn two tables to highlight the relationships between the rows in each table. The STUDENT table shows the StudentPK (student number) and StudentName of students at a university. The LOCKER table shows the LockerPK (locker number) and LockerType (full size or half size) of lockers at the recreation center on campus. If we run a join between these two tables as shown in SQL-Query-CH03-54, we get a table of students who have lockers assigned to them together with their assigned locker. This result is shown in Figure 3-25(b).

FIGURE 3-24

The Results for
SQL-Query-CH03-53

ProjectName	FirstName	LastName	HoursWorked
2019 Q3 Production Plan	Mary	Jacobs	30.00
2019 Q3 Production Plan	Ken	Evans	50.00
2019 Q3 Production Plan	Ken	Numoto	50.00
2019 Q3 Production Plan	Mary	Smith	75.00
2019 Q3 Production Plan	Tom	Jackson	75.00
2019 Q3 Marketing Plan	Mary	Jacobs	30.00
2019 Q3 Marketing Plan	Ken	Evans	75.00
2019 Q3 Marketing Plan	Ken	Numoto	55.00
2019 Q3 Marketing Plan	Linda	Granger	55.00
2019 Q3 Portfolio Analysis	Richard	Bandalone	20.00
2019 Q3 Portfolio Analysis	Ken	Evans	40.00
2019 Q3 Portfolio Analysis	Mary	Abernathy	45.00
2019 Q3 Portfolio Analysis	Tom	Caruthers	45.00
2019 Q3 Tax Preparation	Richard	Bandalone	25.00
2019 Q3 Tax Preparation	Ken	Evans	40.00
2019 Q3 Tax Preparation	Tom	Caruthers	50.00
2019 Q3 Tax Preparation	Heather	Jones	50.00
2019 Q4 Production Plan	Mary	Jacobs	30.00
2019 Q4 Production Plan	Ken	Evans	50.00
2019 Q4 Production Plan	Ken	Numoto	50.00
2019 Q4 Production Plan	Mary	Smith	75.00
2019 Q4 Production Plan	Tom	Jackson	75.00
2019 Q4 Marketing Plan	Mary	Jacobs	30.00
2019 Q4 Marketing Plan	Ken	Evans	75.00
2019 Q4 Marketing Plan	Ken	Numoto	55.00
2019 Q4 Marketing Plan	Linda	Granger	55.00
2019 Q4 Portfolio Analysis	Richard	Bandalone	20.00
2019 Q4 Portfolio Analysis	Ken	Evans	40.00
2019 Q4 Portfolio Analysis	Mary	Abernathy	45.00
2019 Q4 Portfolio Analysis	Tom	Caruthers	45.00

MySQL Community Server 8.0, MySQL Workbench, Oracle Corporation.

```
* *** EXAMPLE CODE - DO NOT RUN *** */
/* *** SQL-Query-CH03-54 *** */
SELECT      StudentPK, StudentName, LockerFK, LockerPK,
            LockerType
FROM        STUDENT INNER JOIN LOCKER
     ON     STUDENT.LockerFK = LOCKER.LockerPK
ORDER BY    StudentPK;
```

The type of SQL join shown in SQL-Query-CH03-54 is an SQL inner join using an SQL JOIN ON syntax that uses the **INNER keyword**. Note that the result would be the same *without* the INNER keyword, as shown in prior JOIN ON syntax queries.

Now, suppose we want to show all the rows already in the join, but also want to show any rows (students) in the STUDENT table that are not included in the inner join. This means that we want to see all students, including those who have not been assigned a locker. To do this, we use the SQL outer join, which is designed for this very purpose. And because the table we want is listed first in the query and is thus on the left side of the table listing, we specifically use an **SQL left outer join**, which uses the **SQL LEFT JOIN syntax**. This is shown in SQL-Query-CH03-55, which produces the results shown in Figure 3-25(c).

FIGURE 3-25

Types of SQL JOINS

STUDENT

StudentPK	StudentName	LockerFK
1	Adams	NULL
2	Buchanan	NULL
3	Carter	10
4	Ford	20
5	Hoover	30
6	Kennedy	40
7	Roosevelt	50
8	Truman	60

LOCKER

LockerPK	LockerType
10	Full
20	Full
30	Half
40	Full
50	Full
60	Half
70	Full
80	Full
90	Half

(a) The STUDENT and LOCKER Tables Aligned to Show Row Relationships

Only the rows where LockerFK=LockerPK are shown—Note that some StudentPK and some LockerPK values are not in the results

StudentPK	StudentName	LockerFK	LockerPK	LockerType
3	Carter	10	10	Full
4	Ford	20	20	Full
5	Hoover	30	30	Half
6	Kennedy	40	40	Full
7	Roosevelt	50	50	Full
8	Truman	60	60	Half

(b) INNER JOIN of the STUDENT and LOCKER Tables

All rows from STUDENT are shown, even where there is no matching LockerFK=LockerPK value

StudentPK	StudentName	LockerFK	LockerPK	LockerType
1	Adams	NULL	NULL	NULL
2	Buchanan	NULL	NULL	NULL
3	Carter	10	10	Full
4	Ford	20	20	Full
5	Hoover	30	30	Half
6	Kennedy	40	40	Full
7	Roosevelt	50	50	Full
8	Truman	60	60	Half

(c) LEFT OUTER JOIN of the STUDENT and LOCKER Tables

All rows from LOCKER are shown, even where there is no matching LockerFK=LockerPK value

StudentPK	StudentName	LockerFK	LockerPK	LockerType
3	Carter	10	10	Full
4	Ford	20	20	Full
5	Hoover	30	30	Half
6	Kennedy	40	40	Full
7	Roosevelt	50	50	Full
8	Truman	60	60	Half
NULL	NULL	NULL	70	Full
NULL	NULL	NULL	80	Full
NULL	NULL	NULL	90	Half

(d) RIGHT OUTER JOIN of the STUDENT and LOCKER Tables

```
/* *** EXAMPLE CODE - DO NOT RUN *** */
/* *** SQL-Query-CH03-55 *** */
SELECT      StudentPK, StudentName, LockerFK, LockerPK,
                LockerType
FROM        STUDENT LEFT OUTER JOIN LOCKER
        ON  STUDENT.LockerFK = LOCKER.LockerPK
ORDER BY    StudentPK;
```

In the results shown in Figure 3-25(c), note that all the rows from the STUDENT table are now included and that rows that have no match in the LOCKER table are shown with NULL values for locker data. Looking at the output, we can see that the students Adams and Buchanan have no linked rows in the LOCKER table. This means that Adams and Buchanan have not been assigned a locker in the recreation center.

If we want to show all the rows already in the join, but now also any rows in the LOCKER table that are not included in the inner join, we specifically use an **SQL right outer join**, which uses the **SQL RIGHT JOIN syntax** because the table we want is listed second in the query and is thus on the right side of the table listing. This means that we want to see all lockers, including those that have not been assigned to a student. This is shown in SQL-Query-CH03-56, which produces the results shown in Figure 3-25(d).

```
/* *** EXAMPLE CODE - DO NOT RUN *** */
/* *** SQL-Query-CH03-56 *** */
SELECT      StudentPK, StudentName, LockerFK, LockerPK,
                LockerType
FROM        STUDENT RIGHT OUTER JOIN LOCKER
        ON  STUDENT.LockerFK = LOCKER.LockerPK
ORDER BY    LockerPK;
```

In the results shown in Figure 3-25(d), note that all the rows from the LOCKER table are now included and that rows that have no match in the STUDENT table are shown with NULL values for student data. Looking at the output, we can see that the lockers numbered 70, 80, and 90 have no linked rows in the STUDENT table. This means that these lockers are currently unassigned to a student and are available for use. DBMS products today support outer joins, but the specific SQL syntax for the outer join varies by DBMS product. Be sure to consult the documentation for the DBMS product you are using.

The SQL outer join is an important topic, and we will continue our discussion, including examples for our WP database, in online Extension B, "Advanced SQL."

Using SQL Set Operators

Mathematicians use the term **set theory** to describe mathematical operations on sets, where a **set** is defined as a group of distinct items. A relational database table meets the definition of a set, so it is little wonder that SQL includes a group of **SQL set operators** for use with SQL queries. SQL set operators are discussed in online Extension B, "Advanced SQL."

SQL FOR DATA MANIPULATION (DML)—DATA MODIFICATION AND DELETION

The SQL DML contains commands for the three possible data modification operations: insert, modify, and delete. We have already discussed inserting data, and now we consider modifying and deleting data.

Modifying Data

You can modify the values of existing data by using the **SQL UPDATE... SET statement**. However, this powerful command needs to be used with care. Consider the EMPLOYEE table. We can see the current data and who does not yet have an office phone number by using the command:

```
/* *** SQL-Query-CH03-57 *** */
SELECT     *
FROM       EMPLOYEE
WHERE      OfficePhone IS NULL;
```

The results of this query on the EMPLOYEE table look like this:

EmployeeNumber	FirstName	LastName	Department	Position	Supervisor	OfficePhone	EmailAddress
13	Rick	Brown	InfoSystems	IS2	12	NULL	Rick.Brown@WP.com
19	Julia	Hayakawa	Production	OPS1	17	NULL	Julia.Hayakawa@WP.com
20	Sam	Stewart	Production	OPS1	17	NULL	Sam.Stewart@WP.com

MySQL Community Server 8.0, MySQL Workbench, Oracle Corporation.

Note that Rick Brown (EmployeeNumber = 13) has a NULL value for his phone number. Suppose that he has just gotten a phone with phone number 360-287-8620. We can change the value of the OfficePhone column for his data row by using the SQL UPDATE... SET statement, as shown in the following SQL command:

```
/* *** SQL-UPDATE-CH03-01 *** */
UPDATE     EMPLOYEE
   SET     OfficePhone = '360-285-8620'
  WHERE    EmployeeNumber = 13;
```

To see the result, we use the command:

```
/* *** SQL-Query-CH03-58 *** */
SELECT     *
  FROM     EMPLOYEE
  WHERE    EmployeeNumber = 13;
```

The revised data in the EMPLOYEE table for Rick with his new phone number now looks like this:

EmployeeNumber	FirstName	LastName	Department	Position	Supervisor	OfficePhone	EmailAddress
13	Rick	Brown	InfoSystems	IS2	12	360-285-8620	Rick.Brown@WP.com

MySQL Community Server 8.0, MySQL Workbench, Oracle Corporation.

Now consider why this command is dangerous. Suppose that while intending to make this update, we make an error and forget to include the WHERE clause. Thus, we submit the following to the DBMS:

```
/* *** EXAMPLE CODE - DO NOT RUN *** */
/* *** SQL-UPDATE-CH03-02 *** */
UPDATE     EMPLOYEE
   SET     OfficePhone = '360-285-8620';
```

After this command has executed, we would again use a SELECT command to display the contents of the EMPLOYEE relation:

```
/* *** SQL-Query-CH03-59 *** */

SELECT * FROM EMPLOYEE;
```

The EMPLOYEE relation will appear as follows where *all* the OfficePhone values are now the same!

EmployeeNumber	FirstName	LastName	Department	Position	Supervisor	OfficePhone	EmailAddress
1	Mary	Jacobs	Administration	CEO	NULL	360-285-8620	Mary.Jacobs@WP.com
2	Rosalie	Jackson	Administration	Admin Assistant	1	360-285-8620	Rosalie.Jackson@WP.com
3	Richard	Bandalone	Legal	Attorney	1	360-285-8620	Richard.Bandalone@WP.com
4	George	Smith	Human Resources	HR3	1	360-285-8620	George.Smith@WP.com
5	Alan	Adams	Human Resources	HR1	4	360-285-8620	Alan.Adams@WP.com
6	Ken	Evans	Finance	CFO	1	360-285-8620	Ken.Evans@WP.com
7	Mary	Abernathy	Finance	FA3	6	360-285-8620	Mary.Abernathy@WP.com
8	Tom	Caruthers	Accounting	FA2	6	360-285-8620	Tom.Caruthers@WP.com
9	Heather	Jones	Accounting	FA2	6	360-285-8620	Heather.Jones@WP.com
10	Ken	Numoto	Sales and Marketing	SM3	1	360-285-8620	Ken.Numoto@WP.com
11	Linda	Granger	Sales and Marketing	SM2	10	360-285-8620	Linda.Granger@WP.com
12	James	Nestor	InfoSystems	CIO	1	360-285-8620	James.Nestor@WP.com
13	Rick	Brown	InfoSystems	IS2	12	360-285-8620	Rick.Brown@WP.com
14	Mike	Nguyen	Research and Development	CTO	1	360-285-8620	Mike.Nguyen@WP.com
15	Jason	Sleeman	Research and Development	RD3	14	360-285-8620	Jason.Sleeman@WP.com
16	Mary	Smith	Production	OPS3	1	360-285-8620	Mary.Smith@WP.com
17	Tom	Jackson	Production	OPS2	16	360-285-8620	Tom.Jackson@WP.com
18	George	Jones	Production	OPS2	17	360-285-8620	George.Jones@WP.com
19	Julia	Hayakawa	Production	OPS1	17	360-285-8620	Julia.Hayakawa@WP.com
20	Sam	Stewart	Production	OPS1	17	360-285-8620	Sam.Stewart@WP.com

MySQL Community Server 8.0, MySQL Workbench, Oracle Corporation.

This is clearly not what we intended to do. If you did this at a new job where there are 10,000 rows in the EMPLOYEE table, you would experience a sinking feeling in the pit of your stomach and make plans to update your résumé (unless you have mastered how to roll back transactions in your DBMS to restore lost data as we will discuss in Chapter 6, which just might save your job)! The message here: The SQL UPDATE… SET statement is powerful and easy to use, but it is also capable of causing disasters.

BTW

MySQL includes a **Safe Updates** setting which prevents this type of mistake. Be default Safe Updates is enabled, and prevents any UPDATE or DELETE statement from being executed unless it include a WHERE clause to restrict the action. While you can change this setting (which we did to actually run SQL-UPDATE-CH03-02 to get the output shown for SQL-Query-CH03-59), it is best to leave Safe Updates enabled.

The SQL UPDATE… SET statement can modify more than one column value at a time, as shown in the following statement. For example, if Heather Jones (EmployeeNumber = 9) is transferred to the finance department from accounting and given a new finance phone number, you can use the following command to update her data:

```
/* *** EXAMPLE CODE - DO NOT RUN *** */
/* *** SQL-UPDATE-CH03-03 *** */
UPDATE   EMPLOYEE
    SET   Department = 'Finance', OfficePhone = '360-285-8420'
  WHERE   EmployeeNumber = 9;
```

This command changes the values of Phone and Department for the indicated employee.

SQL:2003 introduced the **SQL MERGE statement**, which essentially combines the INSERT and UPDATE statements into one statement that can either insert or update data depending upon whether some condition is met. Thus, the MERGE statement requires some rather complex SQL code, and you should concentrate on thoroughly understanding both the INSERT and UPDATE statements at this point. The SQL MERGE statement is discussed in the online extension "Advanced SQL."

Deleting Data

You can eliminate rows with the **SQL DELETE statement**. However, the same warnings pertain to DELETE as to UPDATE. DELETE is deceptively simple to use and easy to apply in unintended ways. The following, for example, deletes all projects sponsored by the marketing department:

```
/* *** EXAMPLE CODE - DO NOT RUN *** */
/* *** SQL-DELETE-CH03-01 *** */
DELETE
FROM      PROJECT
WHERE     Department = 'Sales and Marketing';
```

Given that we created an ON DELETE CASCADE referential integrity constraint, this DELETE operation not only removes PROJECT rows, it also removes any related ASSIGNMENT rows. For the WP data in Figure 3-2, this DELETE operation removes the projects with ProjectID 1100 (2019 Q3 Marketing Plan) and 1500 (2019 Q4 Marketing Plan) and eight rows (rows 6, 7, 8, and 9 for ProjectID 1100 and rows 23, 24, 25, and 26 for ProjectID 1500) of the ASSIGNMENT table.

As with the SQL UPDATE... SET statement, if you forget to include the WHERE clause, disaster ensues. For example, the SQL code:

```
/* *** EXAMPLE CODE - DO NOT RUN *** */
/* *** SQL-DELETE-CH03-02 *** */
DELETE
FROM      PROJECT;
```

deletes *all* the rows in PROJECT (and because of the ON DELETE CASCADE constraint, *all* the ASSIGNMENT rows as well). This truly would be a disaster!

Again, MySQL includes a **Safe Updates** setting which prevents this type of mistake for any UPDATE or DELETE statement that does not include a WHERE clause to restrict the action.

Observe how the referential integrity constraint differs with the EMPLOYEE table. Here, if we try to process the command:

```
/* *** EXAMPLE CODE - DO NOT RUN *** */
/* *** SQL-DELETE-CH03-03 *** */
DELETE
FROM       EMPLOYEE
WHERE      EmployeeNumber = 1;
```

the DELETE operation fails because rows in ASSIGNMENT depend on the EmployeeNumber value of 1 in EMPLOYEE:

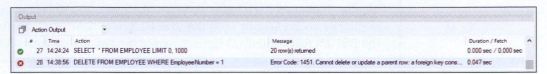

MySQL Community Server 8.0, MySQL Workbench, Oracle Corporation.

If you want to delete the row for this employee, you must first reassign or delete his or her rows in ASSIGNMENT.

SQL FOR DATA DEFINITION (DDL)—TABLE AND CONSTRAINT MODIFICATION AND DELETION

There are many data definition SQL statements that we have not yet described. Two of the most useful are the SQL DROP TABLE and SQL ALTER TABLE statements.

The SQL DROP TABLE Statement

The **SQL DROP TABLE statement** is also one of the most dangerous SQL statements because it drops the table's structure along with all the table's data. For example, to drop the ASSIGNMENT table and all of its data, you use the following SQL statement:

```
/* *** EXAMPLE CODE - DO NOT RUN *** */
/* *** SQL-DROP-TABLE-CH03-01 *** */
DROP TABLE ASSIGNMENT;
```

The SQL DROP TABLE statement does not work if the table contains or could contain values needed to fulfill referential integrity constraints. EMPLOYEE, for example, contains values of EmployeeNumber needed by the foreign key constraint ASSIGN_EMP_FK. In this case, an attempt to issue the statement DROP TABLE EMPLOYEE fails, and an error message is generated.

The SQL ALTER TABLE Statement

To drop the EMPLOYEE table, you must first drop the ASSIGNMENT table or at least delete the foreign key constraint ASSIGN_EMP_FK. This is one place where the ALTER TABLE command is useful. You use the **SQL ALTER TABLE statement** to add, modify, and drop columns and constraints. For example, you can use it to drop the ASSIGN_EMP_FK constraint with the statement:

```
/* *** EXAMPLE CODE - DO NOT RUN *** */
/* *** SQL-ALTER-TABLE-CH03-01 *** */
ALTER TABLE ASSIGNMENT
    DROP CONSTRAINT ASSIGN_EMP_FK;
```

After either dropping the ASSIGNMENT table or the ASSIGN_EMP_FK foreign key constraint, you can then successfully drop the EMPLOYEE table.

We will discuss the SQL ALTER TABLE statement in more detail in online Extension B, "Advanced. SQL," and we illustrate another use of the SQL ALTER TABLE statement in this chapter's section of "Working with Microsoft Access."

Now you know why it is an advantage to control constraint names by using the CONSTRAINT syntax. Because we created the foreign key constraint name ASSIGN_EMP_FK ourselves, we know what it is. This makes it easy to use when we need it.

The SQL TRUNCATE TABLE Statement

The **SQL TRUNCATE TABLE statement** was added in the SQL:2008 standard, so it is one of the latest additions to SQL. Like the SQL DELETE statement, it is used to remove all data from a table while leaving the table structure itself in the database. However, unlike the SQL DELETE statement, the SQL TRUNCATE TABLE statement also *resets any surrogate primary key values* back to the starting point. The SQL TRUNCATE TABLE statement does not use an SQL WHERE clause to specify conditions for the data deletion—*all* the data in the table are *always* removed when the TRUNCATE TABLE statement is used.

The following statement could be used to remove all the data in the PROJECT table:

```
/* *** EXAMPLE CODE - DO NOT RUN *** */
/* *** SQL-TRUNCATE-TABLE-CH03-01 *** */
TRUNCATE TABLE PROJECT;
```

The TRUNCATE TABLE statement *cannot* be used with a table that is referenced by a foreign key constraint because this could result in foreign key values that have no corresponding primary key value. Thus, while we can use TRUNCATE TABLE with the ASSIGNMENT table, we cannot use it with the DEPARTMENT table.

SQL VIEWS

SQL contains a powerful tool known as an SQL view. An **SQL view** is a virtual table created by a DBMS-stored SELECT statement and thus can combine access to data in multiple tables and even in other views. SQL views are discussed in online Extension B, "Advanced SQL," where we show how to create and use SQL views and discuss several specific uses of SQL views in database applications. This is important material that you will find very useful when building databases and database applications, and we will use SQL views in our discussion of online analytical processing (OLAP) reporting systems in Chapter 7.

WORKING WITH MICROSOFT ACCESS

Section 3

Working with Queries in Microsoft Access

In the previous sections of "Working with Microsoft Access," you learned to create Microsoft Access databases, tables, forms, and reports in multiple-table databases. In this section, you will:

- Learn how to use Microsoft Access SQL
- Learn how to run queries on single and multiple tables using both SQL and Query by Example (QBE)
- Learn how to manually set table and relationship properties not supported by Microsoft Access SQL

In this section, we will continue to use the WMCRM database you've been using. At this point, we've created and populated (that is, inserted the data into) the CUSTOMER, PHONE_NUMBER, and CONTACT tables and set the referential integrity constraints between them.

Working with Microsoft Access SQL

You work with Microsoft Access SQL in the SQL view of a query window. The following simple query shows how this works:

```
/* *** SQL-Query-WA-03-01 *** */
SELECT      *
FROM        CUSTOMER;
```

Opening a Microsoft Access Query Window in Design View

1. Start Microsoft Access 2019.
2. Click the **File** command tab to display the File menu and then click the **WMCRM.accdb** database file name in the quick access list to open the database.
3. Click the **Create** command tab to display the Create command groups, as shown in Figure WA-3-1.
4. Click the **Query Design** button.
   The Query1 tabbed document window is displayed in Design view, along with the Show Table dialog box, as shown in Figure WA-3-2.
5. Click the **Close** button on the Show Table dialog box. The Query1 document window now looks as shown in Figure WA-3-3. This window is used for creating and editing Access queries in Design view and is used with Access QBE, as discussed later in this section.

Note that in Figure WA-3-3 the Select button is selected in the Query Type group on the Design tab. You can tell this is so because active or selected buttons are always highlighted in darker gray on the Ribbon. This indicates that we are creating a query that is the equivalent of an SQL SELECT statement.

Also note that in Figure WA-3-3, the View gallery is available in the Results group of the Design tab. We can use this gallery to switch between Design view and SQL view. However, we can also just use the displayed SQL View button to switch to SQL view, which is being displayed because Access considers that to be the view you would most likely choose in the gallery if you used it. Access always presents a "most likely needed" view choice as a button above the View gallery.

FIGURE WA-3-1

The Create Command Tab

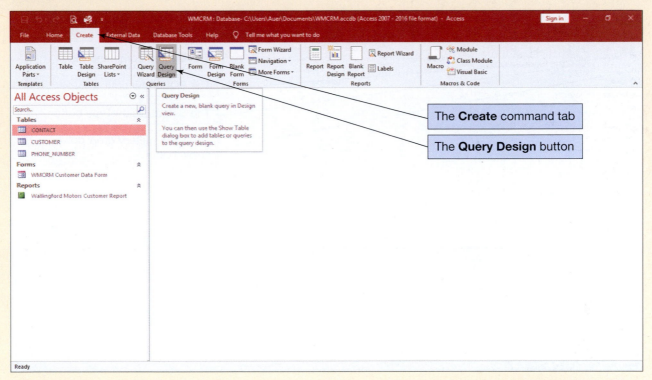

Access 2019, Windows 10, Microsoft Corporation.

FIGURE WA-3-2

The Show Table Dialog Box

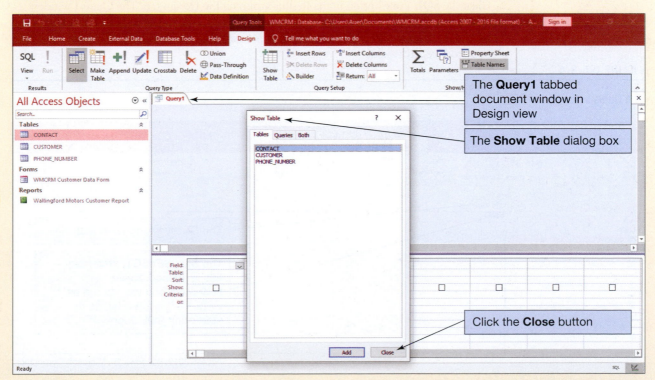

Access 2019, Windows 10, Microsoft Corporation.

(Continued)

FIGURE WA-3-3

The Query Tools Contextual Command Tab

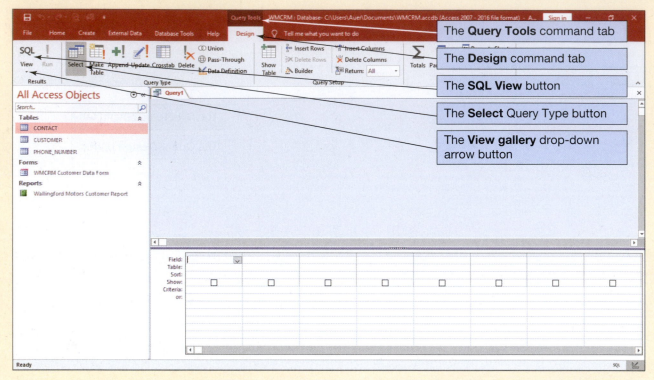

Access 2019, Windows 10, Microsoft Corporation.

Opening a Microsoft Access SQL Query Window and Running a Microsoft Access SQL Query

1. Click the **SQL View** button in the Results group on the Design tab. The Query1 window switches to the SQL view, as shown in Figure WA-3-4. Note the basic SQL command **SELECT;** that's shown in the window. This is an incomplete command, and running it will not produce any results.

FIGURE WA-3-4

The Query1 Window in SQL View

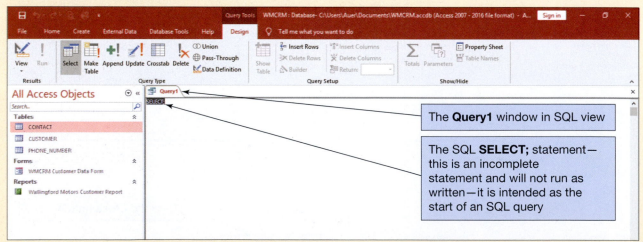

Access 2019, Windows 10, Microsoft Corporation.

FIGURE WA-3-5

The SQL Query

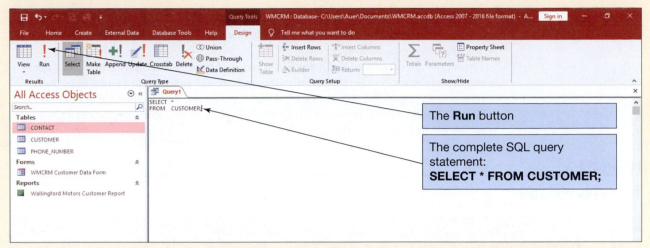

Access 2019, Windows 10, Microsoft Corporation.

2. Edit the SQL SELECT command to read

```
SELECT      *
FROM        CUSTOMER;
```

as shown in Figure WA-3-5.

3. Click the **Run** button on the Design tab. The query results appear, as shown in Figure WA-3-6.

FIGURE WA-3-6

The SQL Query Results

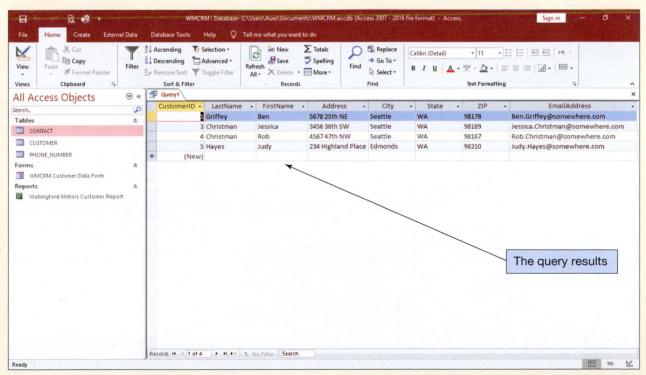

Access 2019, Windows 10, Microsoft Corporation.

(Continued)

Just as we can save Access objects such as tables, forms, and reports, we can save Access queries for future use.

Saving a Microsoft Access SQL Query

1. To save the query, click the **Save** button on the Quick Access Toolbar. The Save As dialog box appears, as shown in Figure WA-3-7.
2. Type in the query name **SQL-Query-WA-03-01,** and then click the **OK** button. The query is saved, and the window is renamed with the query name, as shown in Figure WA-3-8.
3. As shown in Figure WA-3-8, the query document window is now named SQL-Query-WA-03-01, and a newly created SQL-Query-WA-03-01 query object appears in a Queries section of the Navigation Pane.

FIGURE WA-3-7

The Save As Dialog Box

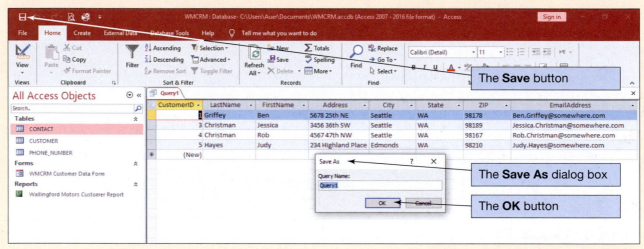

Access 2019, Windows 10, Microsoft Corporation.

FIGURE WA-3-8

The Named and Saved Query

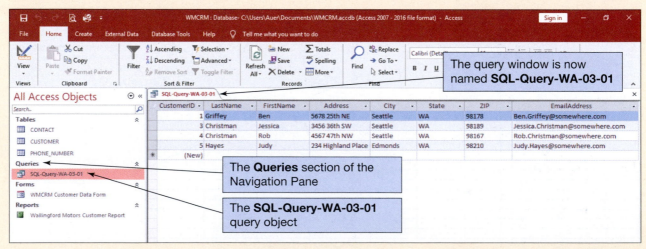

Access 2019, Windows 10, Microsoft Corporation.

4. Close the Query-WA-03-01 window by clicking the document window's **Close** button.
5. If Access displays a dialog box asking whether you want to save changes to the design of the query SQL-Query-WA-03-01, click the **Yes** button.

Working with Microsoft Access QBE

By default, Microsoft Access does not use the SQL interface. Instead, it uses a version of Query by Example (QBE), which uses the Access GUI to build queries. To understand how this works, we'll use QBE to recreate the SQL query we just created using SQL.

Creating and Running a Microsoft Access QBE Query

1. Click the **Create** command tab to display the Create command groups.
2. Click the **Query Design** button.
3. The Query1 tabbed document window is displayed in Design view, along with the Show Table dialog box, as shown in Figure WA-3-2.
4. Click **CUSTOMER** to select the CUSTOMER table. Click the **Add** button to add the CUSTOMER table to the query.
5. Click the **Close** button to close the Show Table dialog box.
6. Rearrange and resize the query window objects in the Query1 query document window using standard Windows drag-and-drop techniques. Rearrange the window elements until they look as shown in Figure WA-3-9.
7. Note the elements of the Query1 window shown in Figure WA-3-9: Tables and their associated set of columns—called a *field list*—that are included in the query are shown in the upper pane, and the columns (fields) actually included in the query are shown in the lower pane. For each included column (field), you can set whether this column's data appear in

FIGURE WA-3-9

The QBE Query1 Query Window

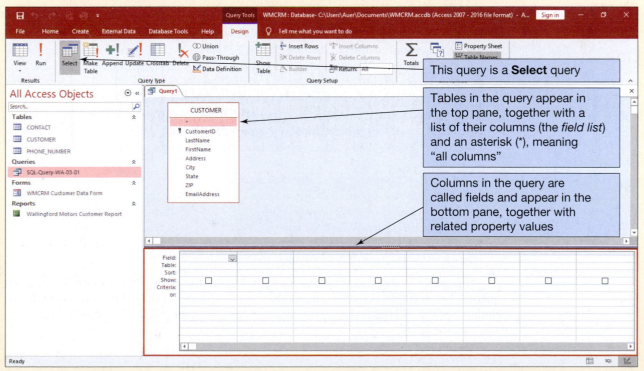

Access 2019, Windows 10, Microsoft Corporation.

(Continued)

FIGURE WA-3-10

Adding Columns to the QBE Query

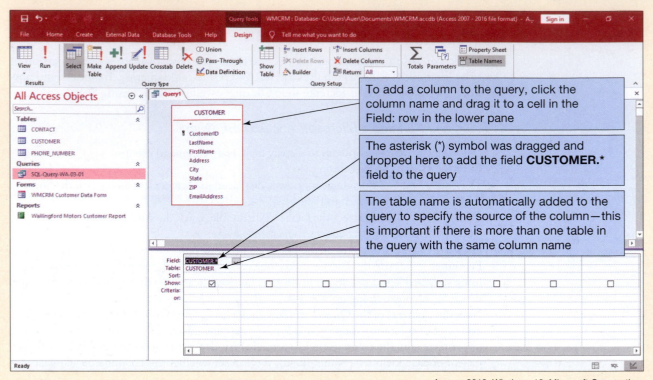

To add a column to the query, click the column name and drag it to a cell in the Field: row in the lower pane

The asterisk (*) symbol was dragged and dropped here to add the field **CUSTOMER.*** field to the query

The table name is automatically added to the query to specify the source of the column—this is important if there is more than one table in the query with the same column name

Access 2019, Windows 10, Microsoft Corporation.

the results, how the data are sorted, and the criteria for selecting which rows of data will be shown. Note that the first entry in the table's field list is the asterisk (*), which has its standard SQL meaning of "all columns in the table."

8. Include columns in the query by dragging them from the table's field list to a field column in the lower pane. Click and drag the * in CUSTOMER to the first field column, as shown in Figure WA-3-10. Note that the column is entered as **CUSTOMER**.* from the table CUSTOMER.

9. To save the QBE query, click the **Save** button on the Quick Access Toolbar to display the Save As dialog box. Type in the query name **QBE-Query-WA-03-01**, and then click the **OK** button. The query is saved, the window is renamed QBE-Query-WA-03-01, and a newly created QBE-Query-WA-03-01 query object appears in the Queries section of the Navigation Pane.

10. Click the **Run** button on the Query Design toolbar.

11. The query results appear, as shown in Figure WA-3-11. Note that these results are identical to the results shown in Figure WA-3-6.

12. Close the QBE-Query-WA-03-01 query.

13. If Access displays a dialog box asking whether you want to save changes to the layout of the query QBE-Query-WA-03-01, click the **Yes** button.

This query is about as simple as they get, but we can use QBE for more complicated queries. For example, consider a query that uses only some of the columns in the table, includes the SQL WHERE clause, and also sorts data using the SQL ORDER BY clause:

FIGURE WA-3-11

The QBE Query Results

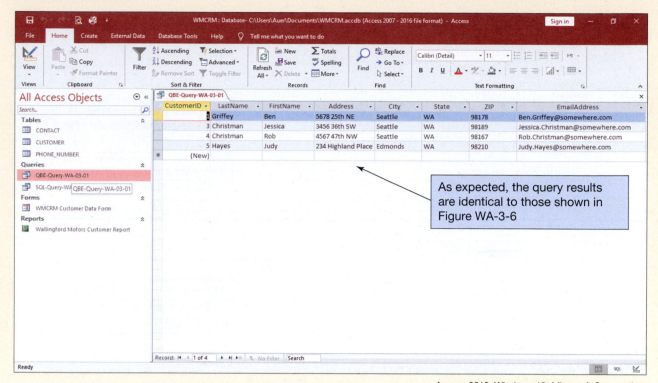

As expected, the query results are identical to those shown in Figure WA-3-6

Access 2019, Windows 10, Microsoft Corporation.

```
/* *** SQL Version of QBE-Query-WA-03-02 *** */
SELECT      CustomerID, LastName, FirstName
FROM        CUSTOMER
WHERE       CustomerID > 2
ORDER BY    LastName DESC;
```

This QBE query, named QBE-Query-WA-03-02, is shown in Figure WA-3-12. Note that now we've included the specific columns that we want used in the query instead of the asterisk, we've used the Sort property for LastName, and we've included row selection conditions in the Criteria property for CustomerID.

Creating and Running QBE-Query-WA-03-02

1. Using the previous instructions for QBE-Query-WA-03-01, create, run, and save QBE-Query-WA-03-02. The query results are shown in Figure WA-3-13.

Of course, we can use more than one table in a QBE query. Next, we'll create the QBE version of this SQL query:

```
/* *** SQL Version of QBE-Query-WA-03-03 *** */
SELECT      LastName, FirstName,
            ContactDate, ContactType, Remarks
FROM        CUSTOMER, CONTACT
WHERE       CUSTOMER.CustomerID = CONTACT.CustomerID
    AND     CUSTOMER.CustomerID = 3
ORDER BY    ContactDate;
```

(Continued)

FIGURE WA-3-12

The QBE-Query-WA-03-02 Query Window

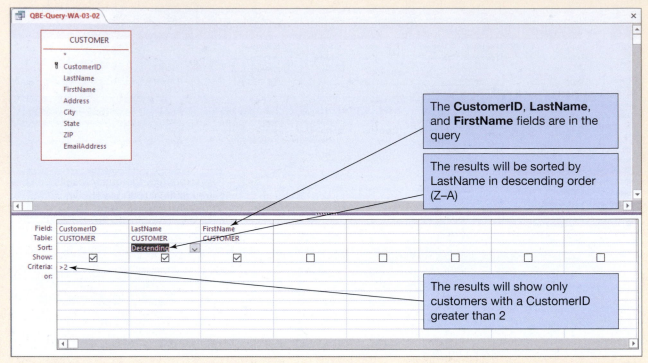

Access 2019, Windows 10, Microsoft Corporation.

FIGURE WA-3-13

The QBE-Query-WA-03-02 Query Results

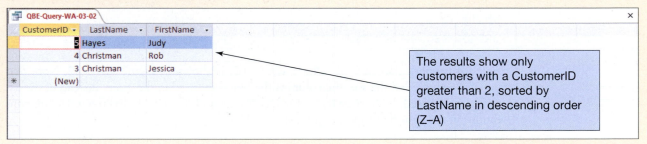

Access 2019, Windows 10, Microsoft Corporation.

Creating and Running a Microsoft Access QBE Query with Multiple Tables

1. Click the **Create** command tab.
2. Click the **Query Design** button. The Query1 tabbed document window is displayed in Design view, along with the Show Table dialog box.
3. Click **CUSTOMER** to select the CUSTOMER table. Click the **Add** button to add the CUSTOMER table to the query.
4. Click **CONTACT** to select the CONTACT table. Click the **Add** button to add the CONTACT table to the query.

5. Click the **Close** button to close the Show Table dialog box.
6. Rearrange and resize the query window objects in the Query1 query document window by using standard Windows drag-and-drop techniques. Rearrange the window elements until they look as shown in Figure WA-3-14. Note that the relationship between the two tables is already included in the diagram. This implements the SQL clause:

```
WHERE CUSTOMER.CustomerID = CONTACT.CustomerID
```

7. From the CUSTOMER table, click and drag the **CustomerID, LastName,** and **FirstName** column names to the first three field columns in the lower pane.
8. From the CONTACT table, click and drag the **ContactDate, ContactType,** and **Remarks** column names to the next three field columns in the lower pane.
9. In the field column for CustomerID, uncheck the **Show** check box so that the data from this column is not included in the results display.
10. In the field column for CustomerID, type the number **3** in the Criteria row.
11. In the field column for ContactDate, set the Sort setting to **Ascending**. The completed QBE query appears, as shown in Figure WA-3-15.
12. Click the **Run** button. The query results appear, as shown in Figure WA-3-16.
13. To save the query, click the **Save** button on the Quick Access Toolbar to display the Save As dialog box. Type in the query name **QBE-Query-WA-03-03**, and then click the **OK** button. The query is saved, the document window is renamed with the new query name, and the QBE-Query-WA-03-03 object is added to the Queries section of the Navigation Pane.
14. Close the QBE-Query-WA-03-03 window.

FIGURE WA-3-14

The Query Window with Two Tables

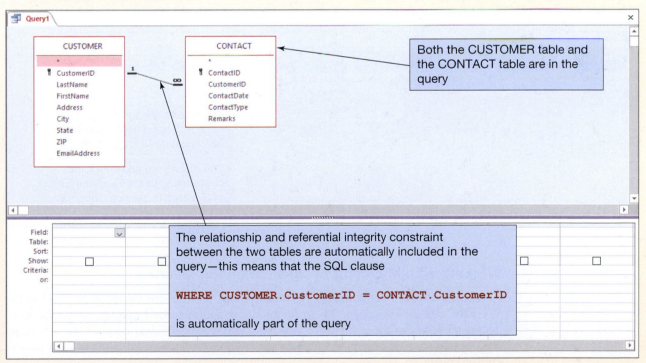

Access 2019, Windows 10, Microsoft Corporation.

(Continued)

FIGURE WA-3-15

The Completed Two-Table Query

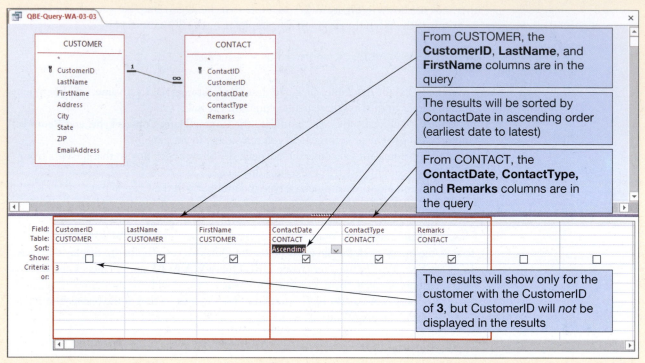

Access 2019, Windows 10, Microsoft Corporation.

FIGURE WA-3-16

The Two-Table Query Results

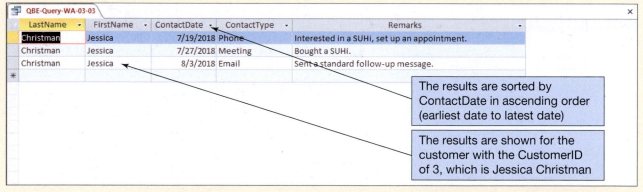

Access 2019, Windows 10, Microsoft Corporation.

Working with Microsoft Access Parameter Queries

Access allows us to construct queries that prompt the user for values to be used in the WHERE clause of the query. These are known as **parameterized queries**, where the word *parameter* refers to the column for which a value is needed. And because we can create reports that are based on queries, parameterized queries can be used as the basis of parameterized reports.

For an example of a parameterized query, we'll modify QBE-Query-WA-03-03 so that CustomerID is the parameter and the user is prompted for the CustomerID value when the query is run.

Creating and Running a Microsoft Access Parameterized Query

1. In the Navigation Pane, right-click the **QBE-Query-WA-03-03** query object to select it, open the shortcut menu, and then click the **Copy** button.
2. Click the **Home** command tab, and then click the **Paste** command to display the Paste As dialog box, as shown in Figure WA-3-17.
3. In the Query Name 'Copy of QBE-Query-WA-03-03' text box of the Paste As dialog box, edit the query name to read **QBE-Query-WA-03-04**.
4. Click the **OK** button to save the query.
5. Open the query by double-clicking on its name in the Navigator Pane, then click the **Design View** icon in the upper left to open the Design view of the query, which is now re-named QBE-Query-WA-03-04.
6. In the Criteria row of the CustomerID column, delete the number value (which is 3), and enter the text **[Enter the CustomerID Number:]** in its place. You will need to expand the CustomerID column width for all the text to be visible at the same time. The QBE-Query-WA-03-04 window now looks as shown in Figure WA-3-18.
7. Click the **Save** button on the Quick Access Toolbar to save the changes to the query design.
8. Click the **Run** button. The **Enter Parameter Value** dialog box appears, as shown in Figure WA-3-19. Note that the text we entered in the Criteria row now appears as a prompt in the dialog box.

FIGURE WA-3-17

The Paste As Dialog Box

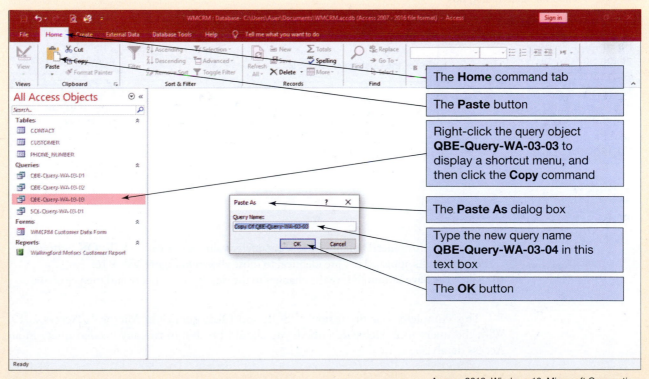

Access 2019, Windows 10, Microsoft Corporation.

(Continued)

FIGURE WA-3-18

The Completed Parameterized Query

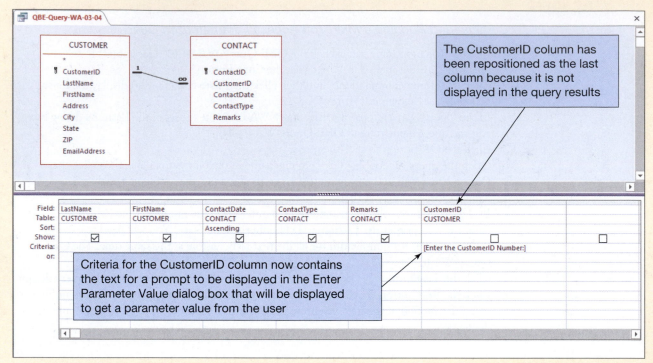

Access 2019, Windows 10, Microsoft Corporation.

FIGURE WA-3-19

The Enter Parameter Value Dialog Box

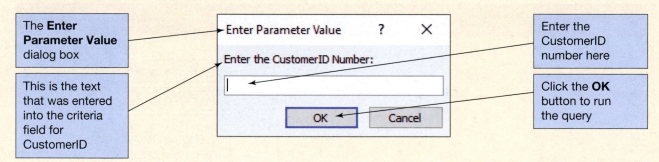

Access 2019, Windows 10, Microsoft Corporation.

9. Enter the CustomerID number **3** as a parameter value, and then click the **OK** button. The query results appear. They are identical to those shown in Figure WA-3-16.

10. Click the **Save** button to save the changes to the design of the query and then close the query.

This completes our discussion of SQL and QBE queries in Microsoft Access 2019. With the query tools we've described, you should be able to run any needed query in an Access database.

Creating Tables with Microsoft Access SQL

In previous sections of "Working with Microsoft Access," we created and populated Microsoft Access tables using Table Design view. Now we'll create and populate a table by using Microsoft Access SQL, as done in the SQL view of a query window. So far, the Wallingford Motors CRM database has been for use by only a single salesperson. Now we'll add a SALESPERSON table. Each salesperson at Wallingford Motors is identified by a nickname. The nickname may be the person's actual first name or a true nickname, but it must be unique. We can assume that one salesperson is assigned to each customer and that only that salesperson makes contact with the customer.

The full set of tables in the WMCRM database will now look like this:

SALESPERSON (<u>NickName</u>, LastName, FirstName, HireDate, WageRate, CommissionRate, OfficePhone, EmailAddress)

CUSTOMER (<u>CustomerID</u>, LastName, FirstName, Address, City, State, ZIP, EmailAddress, *NickName*)

PHONE_NUMBER (*CustomerID*, <u>PhoneNumber</u>, PhoneType)

CONTACT (<u>ContactID</u>, *CustomerID*, Date, Type, Remarks)

The referential integrity constraints are:

NickName in CUSTOMER must exist in NickName in SALESPERSON

CustomerID in CONTACT must exist in CustomerID in CUSTOMER

CustomerID in PHONE_NUMBER must exist in CustomerID in CUSTOMER

The database column characteristics for SALESPERSON are shown in Figure WA-3-20, and SALESPERSON data are shown in Figure WA-3-21.

FIGURE WA-3-20

Database Column Characteristics for the WMCRM SALESPERSON Table

Column Name	Type	Key	Required	Remarks
NickName	Short Text (35)	Primary Key	Yes	
LastName	Short Text (25)	No	Yes	
FirstName	Short Text (25)	No	Yes	
HireDate	Date/Time	No	Yes	Medium Date
WageRate	Number	No	Yes	Double, Currency, Default value = $12.50
CommissionRate	Number	No	Yes	Double, Percent, 3 Decimal places
OfficePhone	Short Text (12)	No	Yes	
EmailAddress	Short Text (100)	No	Yes	Unique

FIGURE WA-3-21

Data for the WMCRM SALESPERSON Table

Nick Name	Last Name	First Name	Hire Date	Wage Rate	Commission Rate	OfficePhone	EmailAddress
Tina	Smith	Tina	10-AUG-12	$ 15.50	12.500%	206-287-7010	Tina@WM.com
Big Bill	Jones	William	25-SEP-12	$ 15.50	12.500%	206-287-7020	BigBill@WM.com
Billy	Jones	Bill	17-MAY-13	$ 12.50	12.000%	206-287-7030	Billy@WM.com

(Continued)

Note that adding the SALESPERSON table will require alterations to the existing CUSTOMER table. We need a new column for the foreign key NickName, a referential integrity constraint between CUSTOMER and SALESPERSON, and new data for the column.

First, we'll build the SALESPERSON table. The correct SQL statement is:

```
/* *** SQL-CREATE-TABLE-WA-03-01 *** */
CREATE TABLE SALESPERSON(
  NickName         Char(35)          NOT NULL,
  LastName         Char(25)          NOT NULL,
  FirstName        Char(25)          NOT NULL,
  HireDate         Date              NOT NULL,
  WageRate         Numeric(5,2)      NOT NULL DEFAULT(12.50),
  CommissionRate   Numeric(5,3)      NOT NULL,
  OfficePhone      Char(12)          NOT NULL,
  EmailAddress     Varchar(100)      NOT NULL UNIQUE,
  CONSTRAINT       SALESPERSON_PK    PRIMARY KEY(NickName)
  );
```

This statement uses standard SQL data types, but this is not a problem because Access will correctly read them and translate them into Access data types. However, from the SQL discussion in this chapter, we know that Access does not support the numeric data type with the (m,n) syntax (where m = total number of digits and n = number of digits to the right of the decimal). Further, Access does not support the UNIQUE constraint or the DEFAULT keyword. Therefore, we have to create an SQL statement without these items and then use the Access GUI to fine-tune the table after it is created.

The SQL that will run in Access is:

```
/* *** SQL-CREATE-TABLE-WA-03-02 *** */
CREATE TABLE SALESPERSON(
  NickName         Char(35)          NOT NULL,
  LastName         Char(25)          NOT NULL,
  FirstName        Char(25)          NOT NULL,
  HireDate         Date              NOT NULL,
  WageRate         Numeric           NOT NULL,
  CommissionRate   Numeric           NOT NULL,
  OfficePhone      Char(12)          NOT NULL,
  EmailAddress     Varchar(100)      NOT NULL,
  CONSTRAINT       SALESPERSON_PK    PRIMARY KEY (NickName)
  );
```

Creating the SALESPERSON Table by Using Microsoft Access SQL

1. As described earlier in this chapter's section of "Working with Microsoft Access," open an Access query window in SQL view.
2. Type the SQL code into the query window. The query window now looks as shown in Figure WA-3-22.

FIGURE WA-3-22

The SQL CREATE TABLE SALESPERSON Statement

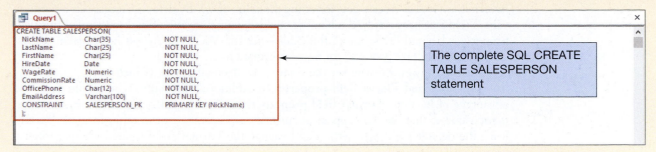

Access 2019, Windows 10, Microsoft Corporation.

FIGURE WA-3-23

The SALESPERSON Objects in the Navigation Pane

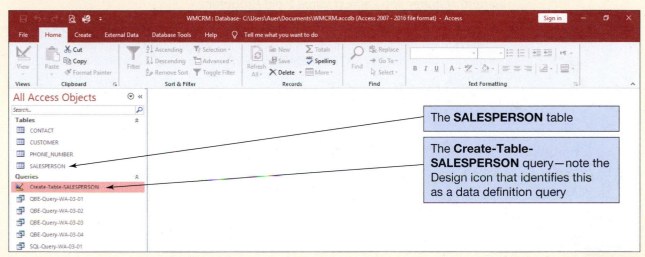

Access 2019, Windows 10, Microsoft Corporation.

3. Click the **Run** button. The statement runs, but because this statement creates a table, the only immediately visible results are that the SALESPERSON table object is added to the Tables section of the Navigation Pane.
4. Save the query as **Create-Table-SALESPERSON**.
5. Close the query window. The Create-Table-SALESPERSON query object now appears in the Queries section of the Navigation Pane, as shown in Figure WA-3-23.

Modifying Access Tables to Add Data Requirements Not Supported by Access SQL

To modify the SALESPERSON table to add the table requirements not supported by Access SQL, we use the Access table Design view.[6]

---

[6]Although we do not fully discuss the matter in this book, it's important to mention that Access SQL confounds the treatment of the SQL NOT NULL column constraint. When you use NOT NULL in defining a column, Access properly sets the column's Required field property to Yes. (We discussed how to do this manually in Chapter 1's section of "Working with Microsoft Access" when we created the CUSTOMER table.) However, Access adds a second field property, the **Allow Zero Length field property**, which it sets to Yes. To truly match NOT NULL, this value should be set to *No*. For a full discussion of setting the Allow Zero Length field property, see the Microsoft Access help system.

(Continued)

First, recall that Access SQL does not support the numeric (*m,n*) syntax, where *m* is the number of digits stored and *n* is the number of digits to the right of the decimal place. We can set the number of digits to some extent by setting the **Field Size field property** (which is as close as Access gets to setting the value of *m*). By default, Access sets a numeric value Field Size property to double. We could change this, but a full discussion of this field property is beyond the scope of this book—see the Microsoft Access help system discussion of the Field Size property for more information.

We can, however, easily set the number of decimal places (which is the value of *n*) using the **Decimal Places field property**. In addition, Microsoft Access does have the advantage of having a **Format field property** that allows us to apply formatting to a numeric value so that the data appear as currency, a percentage, or in other formats. We will leave the default Field Size setting and change the Format and Decimal Places property values.

Recall that Access SQL does not support the SQL DEFAULT keyword, so we will have to add any needed default values. We can do this using the **Default Value field property**.

Setting Number and Default Value Field Properties

1. To open the SALESPERSON table in Design view, right-click the **SALESPERSON** table object to select it and open the shortcut menu, and then click the **Design View** button in the shortcut menu. The SALESPERSON table appears in Design view, as shown in Figure WA-3-24.
2. Select the **WageRate** field. The WageRate field properties are displayed in the General tab, as shown in Figure WA-3-25.

FIGURE WA-3-24

The SALESPERSON Table in Design View

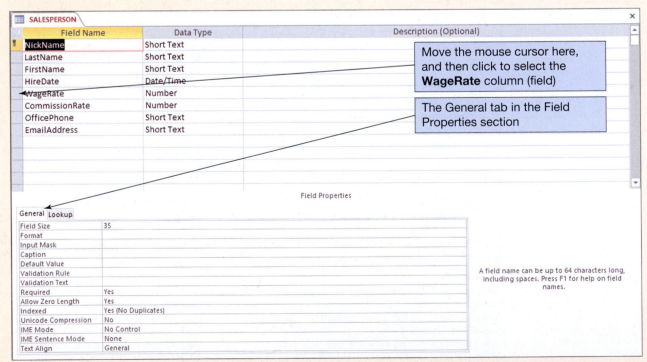

Access 2019, Windows 10, Microsoft Corporation.

FIGURE WA-3-25

The WageRate Field Properties

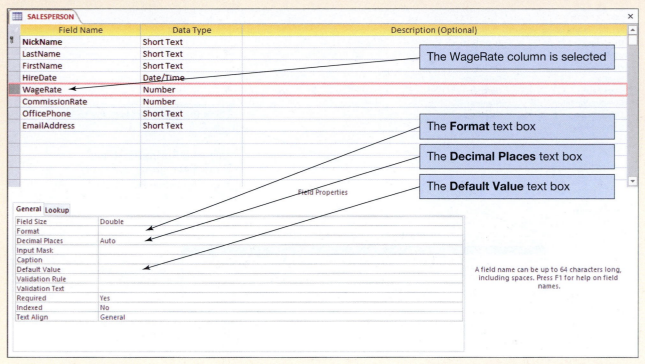

Access 2019, Windows 10, Microsoft Corporation.

3. Click the **Format** text field. A drop-down list arrow appears on the right end of the text field, as shown in Figure WA-3-26. Click the drop-down list arrow to display the list and select **Currency**.

■ **NOTE:** When you do this, a small icon appears to the left of the text field. This is the Property Update Options drop-down list. Simply ignore it, and it will disappear when you take the next action. Then it will reappear for that action! In general, ignore it and keep working.

4. Click the **Decimal Places** text field (which is currently set to Auto). Again, a drop-down list arrow appears. Use the drop-down list to select **2** decimal places.

5. Click the **Default Value** text box. The Expression Builder icon appears, as shown in Figure WA-3-27. We do not need to use the Expression Builder at this point. Type **12.50** into the Default Value text box. We have finished setting the field property values for WageRate. The final values are shown in Figure WA-3-28.

■ **NOTE:** Access actually stores this number as 12.5, which is the same value without the trailing zero. Don't be alarmed if you look at these property values again and notice the missing zero!

6. Click the **Save** button to save the completed changes to the SALESPERSON table.

7. Select the **CommissionRate** field. The CommissionRate field properties are displayed in the General tab.

8. Set the **Format** value to **Percent**.

9. Set the **Decimal Places** value to **3**.

10. Select the **HireDate** field. The HireDate field properties are displayed in the General tab.

11. Set the **Format** value to **Medium Date**.

12. Click the **Save** button to save the completed changes to the SALESPERSON table.

13. Leave the SALESPERSON table open in Design view for the next set of steps.

(Continued)

FIGURE WA-3-26

The Format Text Box

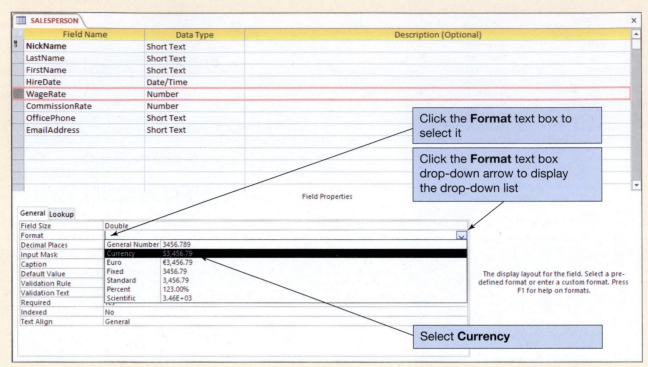

Access 2019, Windows 10, Microsoft Corporation.

FIGURE WA-3-27

The Default Value Text Box

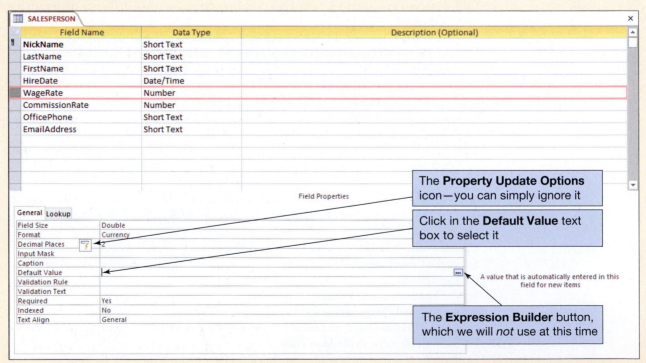

Access 2019, Windows 10, Microsoft Corporation.

FIGURE WA-3-28

The Completed WageRate Field Properties

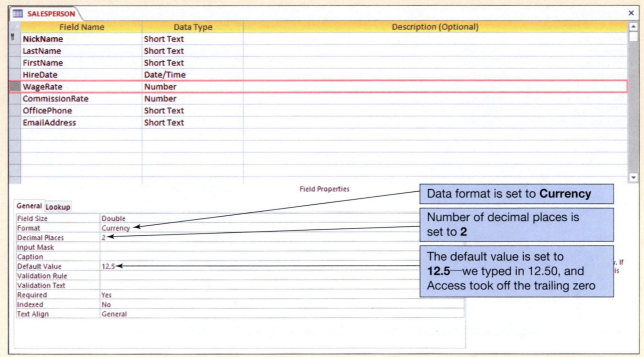

Access 2019, Windows 10, Microsoft Corporation.

The UNIQUE constraint is another SQL constraint that Access SQL does not support. To set a UNIQUE constraint in Access, we set the value of the **Indexed field property**. Access initially sets this value to No, which means that no index (a tool for making queries more efficient) is built for this column. The two other possible values of this property are **Yes (Duplicates OK)** and **Yes (No Duplicates)**. We enforce the UNIQUE constraint by setting the property value to **Yes (No Duplicates)**.

Setting Indexed Field Properties

1. The **SALESPERSON** table should already be open in Design view. If it isn't, open the table in Design view.
2. Select the **EmailAddress** field.
3. Click the **Indexed** text field. A drop-down list arrow button appears on the right end of the text field, as shown in Figure WA-3-29. Click the **Indexed** drop-down list arrow button to display the list and select **Yes (No Duplicates)**.
4. Click the **Save** button to save the completed changes to the SALESPERSON table.
5. Close the SALESPERSON table.

Finally, we'll implement the SQL CHECK constraint. When we created the CONTACT table, the only allowed data types for the Type column were Phone, Fax, Email, and Meeting. The correct SQL statement to add this constraint to the CONTACT table would be:

(Continued)

FIGURE WA-3-29

The EmailAddress Field Properties

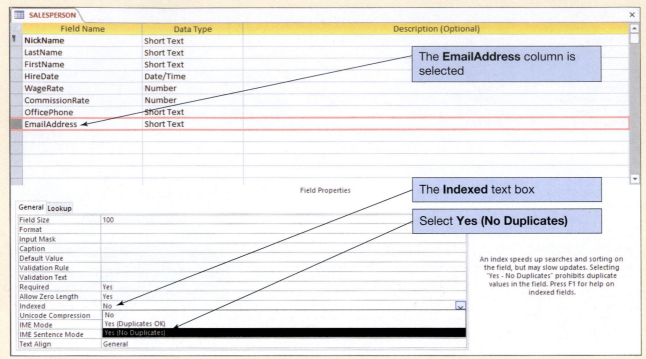

Access 2019, Windows 10, Microsoft Corporation.

```
/* *** SQL-ALTER-TABLE-WA-03-01 *** */
ALTER TABLE CONTACT
     ADD CONSTRAINT CONTACT_Check_ContactType
          CHECK (ContactType IN ('Phone', 'Fax', 'Email',
          'Meeting'));
```

To implement the CHECK constraint in Access, we set the value of the **Validation Rule field property** for the ContactType column.

Creating the CHECK Constraint for the CONTACT Table

1. Open the **CONTACT** table in Design view.
2. Select the **ContactType** column.
3. Click the Validation Rule text box and then type in the text **Phone or Fax or Email or Meeting**, as shown in Figure WA-3-30.
   - ■ **NOTE:** Do *not* enclose the allowed terms in quotation marks. Access will add quotation marks to each term when it saves the changes to the table design. If you add your own set of quotation marks, you'll end up with each word enclosed in two sets of quotes, and Access will not consider this a match to the existing data in the table when it runs the data integrity check discussed in step 4. Access will reformat this line to the expected syntax after it is entered.

FIGURE WA-3-30

Specifying a Validation Rule

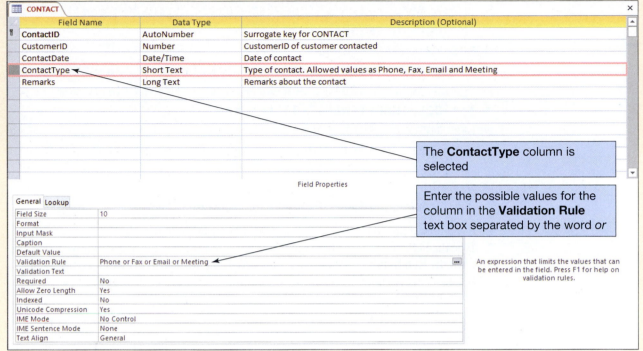

Access 2019, Windows 10, Microsoft Corporation.

FIGURE WA-3-31

The Data Integrity Warning Dialog Box

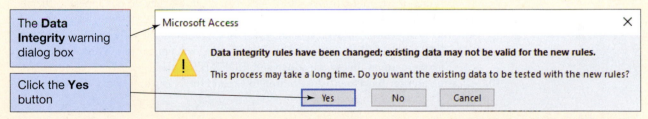

Access 2019, Windows 10, Microsoft Corporation.

4. Click the **Save** button on the Quick Access Toolbar to save the CONTACT table. As shown in Figure WA-3-31, Access displays a dialog box warning that existing data may not match the data integrity rule we have just established by setting a validation rule.
5. Click the **Yes** button on the dialog box.
6. Close the CONTACT table.

Inserting Data with Microsoft Access SQL

We can use Access SQL to enter the data shown in Figure WA-3-21 into the SALESPERSON table. The only problem here is that Access will not handle multiple SQL commands in one query, so each row of data must be input individually. The SQL commands to enter the data are:

(Continued)

```
/* *** SQL-INSERT-WA-03-01 *** */
INSERT INTO SALESPERSON
      VALUES('Tina', 'Smith', 'Tina', '10-AUG-12',
      '15.50', '.125', '206-287-7010', 'Tina@WM.com');
/* *** SQL-INSERT-WA-03-02 *** */
INSERT INTO SALESPERSON
      VALUES('Big Bill', 'Jones', 'William', '25-SEP-12',
      '15.50', '.125', '206-287-7020', 'BigBill@WM.com');
/* *** SQL-INSERT-WA-03-03 *** */
INSERT INTO SALESPERSON
      VALUES('Billy', 'Jones', 'Bill', '17-MAY-13',
      '12.50', '.120', '206-287-7030', 'Billy@WM.com');
```

Inserting Data into the SALESPERSON Table by Using Microsoft Access SQL

1. As described previously, open an Access query window in SQL view.
2. Type the SQL code for the first SQL INSERT statement into the query window.
3. Click the **Run** button. As shown in Figure WA-3-32, the query changes to Append Query, and a dialog box appears, asking you to confirm that you want to insert the data.
4. Click the **Yes** button in the dialog box. The data are inserted into the table.
5. Repeat steps 2, 3, and 4 for the rest of the SQL INSERT statements for the SALESPERSON data.
6. Close the Query1 window. A dialog box appears, asking if you want to save the query. Click the **No** button—there is no need to save this SQL statement.
7. Open the **SALESPERSON** table in Datasheet view.
8. Click the **Shutter Bar Open/Close** button to minimize the Navigation Pane and then arrange the columns so that all column names and data are displayed correctly.
9. The table looks as shown in Figure WA-3-33. Note that the rows are sorted alphabetically, in ascending order, on the primary key (NickName) value—they do not appear in the order in which they were input.
   - **NOTE:** This is *not* typical of an SQL DBMS. Normally, if you run a SELECT * FROM SALESPERSON query on the table, the data appear in the order in which they were input, unless you added an ORDER BY clause.
10. Click the **Shutter Bar Open/Close** button to expand the Navigation Pane.

FIGURE WA-3-32

Inserting Data into the SALESPERSON Table

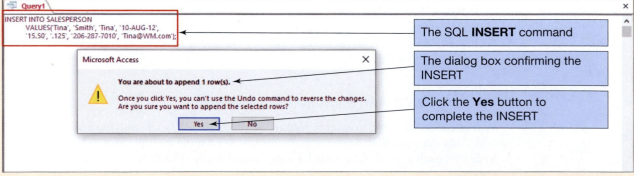

Access 2019, Windows 10, Microsoft Corporation.

FIGURE WA-3-33

The Data in the SALESPERSON Table

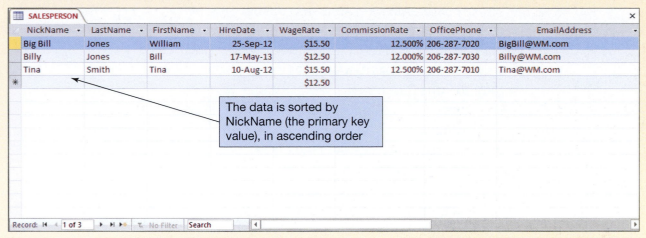

Access 2019, Windows 10, Microsoft Corporation.

11. Click the **Save** button on the Quick Access Toolbar to save the change to the table layout.
12. Close the SALESPERSON table.

At this point, the SALESPERSON table has been created and populated. At Wallingford Motors each customer is assigned to one and only one salesperson, so now we need to create the relationship between SALESPERSON and CUSTOMER. This will require a foreign key in CUSTOMER to provide the needed link to SALESPERSON.

The problem is that the column needed for the foreign key—NickName—does not exist in CUSTOMER. Therefore, before creating the foreign key constraint, we must modify the CUSTOMER table by adding the NickName column and the appropriate data values.

Figure WA-3-34 shows the column characteristics for the NickName column in the CUSTOMER table, and Figure WA-3-35 shows the data for the column.

As shown in Figure WA-3-34, NickName is constrained as NOT NULL. However, adding a populated NOT NULL column requires multiple steps. This topic is discussed in the online Extension B, "Advanced SQL." Here, we will simply walk through the needed steps. First, the column must be added as a NULL column. Next, the column values must be added. Finally, the column must be altered to NOT NULL. We could do this by using

FIGURE WA-3-34

Database Column Characteristics for the CUSTOMER Table NickName Column

Column Name	Short Text	Key	Required	Remarks
NickName	Short Text (35)	Foreign Key	Yes	Links to NickName in SALESPERSON

FIGURE WA-3-35

CUSTOMER Table NickName Data

CustomerID	LastName	FirstName	...	NickName
1	Griffey	Ben	...	Big Bill
3	Christman	Jessica	...	Billy
4	Christman	Rob	...	Tina
5	Hayes	Judy	...	Tina

(Continued)

Access's GUI interface, but because we are working with Access SQL in this section, we will do these steps in SQL. The needed SQL statements are:

```
/* *** SQL-ALTER-TABLE-WA-03-02 *** */
ALTER TABLE CUSTOMER
      ADD NickName Char(35) NULL;
/* *** SQL-UPDATE-WA-03-01 *** */
UPDATE CUSTOMER
      SET         NickName = 'Big Bill'
      WHERE       CustomerID = 1;
/* *** SQL-UPDATE-WA-03-02 *** */
UPDATE CUSTOMER
      SET         NickName = 'Billy'
      WHERE       CustomerID = 3;
/* *** SQL-UPDATE-WA-03-03 *** */
UPDATE CUSTOMER
      SET         NickName = 'Tina'
      WHERE       CustomerID = 4;
/* *** SQL-UPDATE-WA-03-04 *** */
UPDATE CUSTOMER
      SET         NickName = 'Tina'
      WHERE       CustomerID = 5;
/* *** SQL-ALTER-TABLE-WA-03-03 *** */
ALTER TABLE CUSTOMER
      ALTER COLUMN NickName Char(35) NOT NULL;
```

Creating and Populating the NickName Column in the CUSTOMER Table by Using Microsoft Access SQL

1. As described previously, open an Access query window in SQL view.
2. Type the SQL code for the first SQL ALTER TABLE statement into the query window.
3. Click the **Run** button.
   - **NOTE:**   The only indication that the command has run successfully is the fact that *no* error message is displayed.
4. Type the SQL code for the first SQL UPDATE statement into the query window.
5. Click the **Run** button. When the dialog box appears, asking you to confirm that you want to insert the data, click the **Yes** button in the dialog box. The data are inserted into the table.
6. Repeat steps 4 and 5 for the rest of the SQL UPDATE statements for the CUSTOMER data.
7. Type the SQL code for the second SQL ALTER TABLE statement into the query window.
8. Click the **Run** button.
   - **NOTE:**   Again, the only indication that the command has run successfully is the fact that *no* error message is displayed.
9. Close the Query1 window. A dialog box appears, asking if you want to save the query. Click the **No** button—there is no need to save this SQL statement.
10. Open the **CUSTOMER** table.

11. Click the **Shutter Bar Open/Close** button to minimize the Navigation Pane and then scroll to the right so that the added NickName column and the data in it are displayed. The table looks as shown in Figure WA-3-36.

12. Click the **Shutter Bar Open/Close** button to expand the Navigation Pane and then click the Design View button to switch the **CUSTOMER** table into Design view.

13. Click the **NickName** field name to select it.
    The table with the added NickName column looks as shown in Figure WA-3-37. Note that the data are required in the column—this is the Access equivalent of NOT NULL.

14. Close the CUSTOMER table.

FIGURE WA-3-36

The CUSTOMER Table with NickName Data

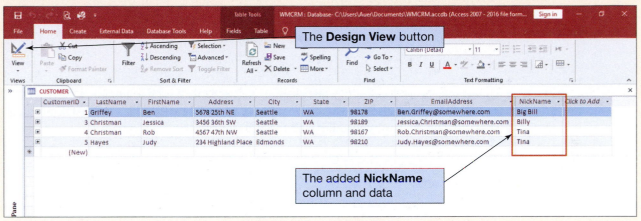

Access 2019, Windows 10, Microsoft Corporation.

FIGURE WA-3-37

The Altered CUSTOMER Table

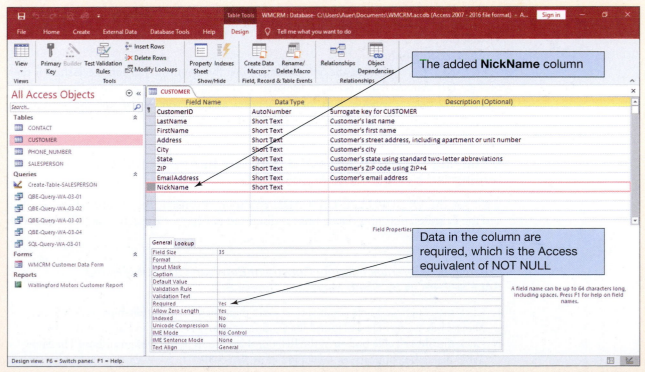

Access 2019, Windows 10, Microsoft Corporation.

(Continued)

Adding Referential Integrity Constraints by Using Microsoft Access SQL

Now that the NickName column has been added and populated in the CUSTOMER table, we can create the needed referential integrity constraint by adding a foreign key constraint between SALESPERSON and CUSTOMER. Because NickName is not a surrogate key, we will want any changed values of NickName in SALESPERSON to be updated in CUSTOMER. However, if a row is deleted from SALESPERSON, we do *not* want that deletion to cause the deletion of CUSTOMER data. Therefore, the needed constraint, written as an SQL ALTER TABLE statement, is:

```
/* *** SQL-ALTER-TABLE-WA-03-04 *** */
ALTER TABLE CUSTOMER
     ADD CONSTRAINT CUSTOMER_SP_FK FOREIGN KEY(NickName)
          REFERENCES SALESPERSON(NickName)
               ON UPDATE CASCADE;
```

Unfortunately, as discussed in this chapter, Access SQL does not support ON UPDATE and ON DELETE clauses. Therefore, we have to set ON UPDATE CASCADE manually after creating the basic constraint with the SQL statement:

```
/* *** SQL-ALTER-TABLE-WA-03-05 *** */
ALTER TABLE CUSTOMER
     ADD CONSTRAINT CUSTOMER_SP_FK FOREIGN KEY(NickName)
          REFERENCES SALESPERSON(NickName);
```

Creating the Referential Integrity Constraint Between CUSTOMER and SALESPERSON by Using Microsoft Access SQL

1. As described previously, open an Access query window in SQL view.
2. Type the SQL code for the SQL-ALTER-TABLE-WA-03-05 statement into the query window.
3. Click the **Run** button.
   - ■ **NOTE:** As before, the only indication that the command has run successfully is the fact that *no* error message is displayed.
4. Close the Query1 window. A dialog box appears, asking if you want to save the query. Click the **No** button; there is no need to save this SQL statement.

Modifying Microsoft Access Databases to Add Constraints Not Supported by Microsoft Access SQL

We'll set the ON UPDATE CASCADE constraint by using the Relationships window and the Edit Relationships dialog box, as discussed in Chapter 2's section of "Working with Microsoft Access."

Creating a Referential Integrity Constraint Between CUSTOMER and SALESPERSON by Using Microsoft Access SQL

1. Click the **Database Tools** command tab, and then click the **Relationships** button in the Show/Hide group. The Relationships window appears, as shown in Figure WA-3-38.
2. Click the **Show Table** button in the Relationships group of the Design ribbon. The Show Table dialog box appears, as shown in Figure WA-3-39.

FIGURE WA-3-38

The Relationships Window with the Current Relationship Diagram

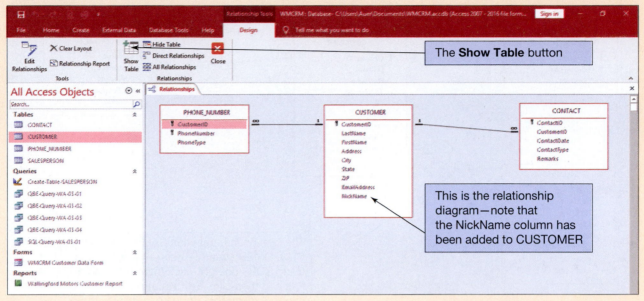

Access 2019, Windows 10, Microsoft Corporation.

FIGURE WA-3-39

Adding the SALESPERSON Table to the Relationship Diagram

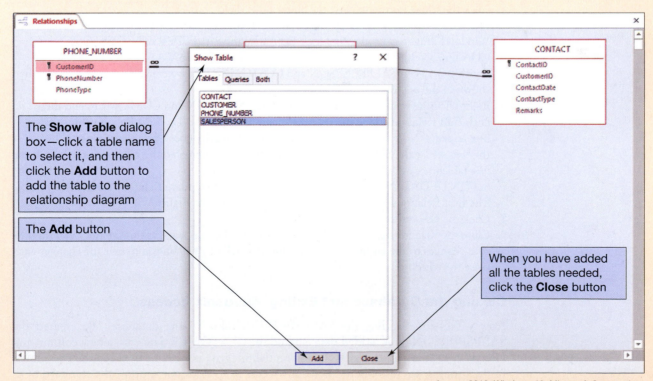

Access 2019, Windows 10, Microsoft Corporation.

(Continued)

FIGURE WA-3-40

The Updated Relationship Diagram

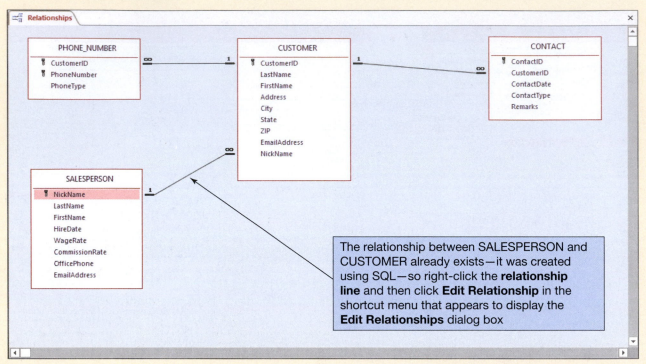

Access 2019, Windows 10, Microsoft Corporation.

3. In the Show Table dialog box, click **SALESPERSON** to select it, and then click the **Add** button to add SALESPERSON to the Relationships window.

4. Click the **Close** button to close the Show Table dialog box.

5. Rearrange and resize the table objects in the Relationships window by using standard Windows drag-and-drop techniques. Rearrange the SALESPERSON, CUSTOMER, and CONTACT table objects until they look as shown in Figure WA-3-40. Note that the relationship between SALESPERSON and CUSTOMER that we created using SQL is already shown in the diagram.

6. Right-click the **relationship line** between SALESPERSON and CUSTOMER, and then click **Edit Relationship** in the shortcut menu that appears. The **Edit Relationships** dialog box appears. Note that the **Enforce Referential Integrity** check box is already checked— this was set by the SQL ALTER TABLE statement that created the relationship between the two tables.

7. Set ON UPDATE CASCADE by clicking the **Cascade Update Related Fields** check box. The Edit Relationships dialog box now looks as shown in Figure WA-3-41.

8. Click the **OK** button.

9. Close the Relationships window. An Access dialog box appears, asking whether you want to save changes to the layout of "Relationships." Click the **Yes** button to save the changes and close the window.

Closing the Database and Exiting Microsoft Access

Now we're done adding the SALESPERSON table to the database. We created the SALESPERSON table, added data, altered the CUSTOMER data with a new column and foreign key values, and created the referential integrity constraint between the two tables. In the process, we saw where Microsoft Access SQL does not support the standard SQL

FIGURE WA-3-41

The Completed Edit Relationships Dialog Box

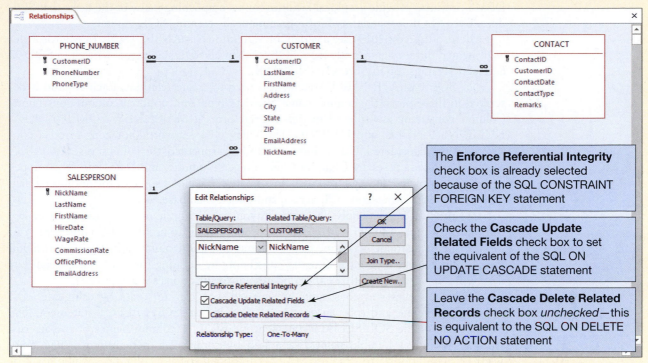

Access 2019, Windows 10, Microsoft Corporation.

language and learned how to use the Access GUI to compensate for the missing SQL language features.

That completes the work we'll do in this chapter's section of "Working with Microsoft Access." If you have taken a class in Microsoft Access, you probably did many of the tasks we covered in a different way. In Microsoft Access, SQL DDL is usually quite hidden, but in this section of "Working with Microsoft Access" we've shown you how to complete the tasks using SQL. As usual, we finish by closing the database and Access.

Closing the WMCRM Database and Exiting Microsoft Access

1. Close the WMCRM database and exit Access by clicking the **Close** button in the upper-right corner of the Microsoft Access window.

SUMMARY

Structured Query Language (SQL) is a data sublanguage that has constructs for defining and processing a database. SQL has several components, two of which are discussed in this chapter: a data definition language (DDL), which is used for creating database tables and other structures, and a data manipulation language (DML), which is used to query and modify database data. SQL can be embedded into scripting languages, such as VBScript, or programming languages, such as Java and C#. In addition, SQL statements can be processed from a command window. SQL was developed by IBM and has been endorsed as a national standard by the American National Standards Institute (ANSI) and as an international standard by the OSI. There have been several versions of SQL. Our discussion is based on SQL-92, but later versions exist that have added, in particular, support for Extensible Markup Language (XML) and JavaScript Object Notation (JSON). Modern DBMS products provide graphical facilities for accomplishing many of the tasks that SQL does. Use of SQL is mandatory for programmatically creating SQL statements.

Microsoft Access 2019 uses a variant of SQL known as ANSI-89 SQL, or Microsoft Jet SQL, which differs significantly from SQL-92. Not all SQL statements written in SQL-92 and later versions run in Access ANSI-89 SQL.

The SQL CREATE TABLE statement is used to create relations. Each column is described in three parts: the column name, the data type, and optional column constraints. Column constraints considered in this chapter are PRIMARY KEY, FOREIGN KEY, NULL, NOT NULL, and UNIQUE. The DEFAULT keyword (not considered a constraint) is also considered. If no column constraint is specified, the column is set to NULL.

Standard data types are Char, VarChar, Integer, Numeric, and DateTime. These types have been supplemented by DBMS vendors. Figure 3-5 shows some of the additional data types for MySQL, Microsoft SQL Server, and Oracle Database.

If a primary key has only one column, you can define it by using the primary key column constraint. Another way to define a primary key is to use the table constraint. You can use such constraints to define single-column and multicolumn primary keys, and you can also implement referential integrity constraints by defining foreign keys. Foreign key definitions can specify whether either updates and/or deletions should cascade.

After the tables and constraints are created, you can add data by using the SQL INSERT statement, and you can query data by using the SQL SELECT statement. The basic format of the SQL SELECT statement is SELECT (column names or the asterisk symbol [*]), FROM (table names, separated by commas if there is more than one), WHERE (conditions). You can use SELECT to obtain specific columns, specific rows, or both.

Conditions after WHERE require single quotes around values for Char and VarChar columns. However, single quotes are not used for Integer and Numeric columns. You can specify compound conditions with AND and OR. You can use sets of values with IN (match any in the set) and NOT IN (not match any in the set). You can use the wildcard symbols _ and % (? and * in Microsoft Access) with LIKE to specify a single unknown character or multiple unknown characters, respectively. You can use IS NULL to test for null values.

You can sort results by using the ORDER BY clause in the SQL SELECT statement. You can create groups by using the GROUP BY clause in the SQL SELECT statement, and you can limit groups by using the HAVING clause. If the WHERE and HAVING clauses both occur in an SQL SELECT statement, WHERE is applied before HAVING. There are five SQL built-in aggregate functions: COUNT, SUM, MAX, MIN, and AVG. SQL can also perform mathematical calculations. SQL built-in functions can be applied to groups or to an entire table.

You can query multiple tables by using either subqueries or joins. If all the result data come from a single table, then subqueries can be used. If results come from two or more tables, then joins must be used. The JOIN. . . ON syntax can be used for joins. Rows that do not match the join conditions do not appear in the results. Outer joins can be used to ensure that all rows from a table appear in the results.

You can modify data by using the SQL UPDATE. . . SET statement and delete data by using the SQL DELETE statement. The SQL UPDATE and SQL DELETE statements can easily cause disasters, so the commands must be used with great care.

You can remove tables (and their data) from a database by using the SQL DROP TABLE statement. You can remove constraints by using the SQL ALTER TABLE DROP CONSTRAINT command. You can modify tables and constraints by using the SQL ALTER TABLE statement. Finally, you can use the CHECK constraint to validate data values.

KEY TERMS

/* and */(SQL comment symbols)
≥ (greater than or equal to)
≤ (less than or equal to)
American National Standards
  Institute (ANSI)
ASC keyword
asterisk (*)
AVG
business rule
Cartesian product
CASCADE keyword
character strings
CHECK constraint
CONSTRAINT keyword
correlated subquery
COUNT
CROSS JOIN
data control language (DCL)
data definition language (DDL)
data manipulation language (DML)
data sublanguage
DEFAULT keyword
DESC keyword
DISTINCT keyword
explicit join
Extensible Markup Language
  (XML)
FOREIGN KEY constraint
graphical user interface (GUI)
implicit join
IN comparison operator
inner join
INNER keyword
International Organization for
  Standardization (ISO)
JavaScript Object Notation (JSON)
MAX
MIN
NO ACTION

NOT IN comparison operator
NOT logical operator
NOT NULL constraint
NULL
NULL constraint
ON DELETE phrase
ON UPDATE phrase
ORDER BY clause
percent sign (%) wildcard character
PRIMARY KEY constraint
Query by Example (QBE)
question mark (?)
recursive relationship
Safe Updates
set
set theory
SQL ALTER TABLE statement
SQL AND operator
SQL AS keyword
SQL asterisk (*) wildcard character
SQL BETWEEN comparison
  operator
SQL built-in aggregate functions
SQL comment
SQL comparison operators
SQL CREATE TABLE statement
SQL DELETE statement
SQL DROP TABLE statement
SQL equijoin
SQL expression
SQL FROM clause
SQL GROUP BY clause
SQL HAVING clause
SQL inner join
SQL INSERT statement
SQL IS keyword
SQL IS NOT NULL comparison
  operator
SQL IS NULL comparison operator

SQL JOIN keyword
SQL join operation
SQL JOIN ON syntax
SQL JOIN operator
SQL left outer join
SQL LEFT JOIN syntax
SQL LIKE comparison operator
SQL logical operators
SQL MERGE statement
SQL NOT operator
SQL NOT BETWEEN operator
SQL NOT LIKE comparison
  operator
SQL ON clause
SQL ON keyword
SQL OR operator
SQL outer join
SQL right outer join
SQL RIGHT JOIN syntax
SQL SELECT clause
SQL SELECT/FROM/WHERE
  framework
SQL set operators
SQL TRUNCATE TABLE
  statement
SQL UPDATE. . . SET statement
SQL view
SQL WHERE clause
SQL/Persistent stored modules
  (SQL/PSM)
SQL wildcard characters
Structured Query Language (SQL)
subquery
SUM
transaction control language (TCL)
underscore symbol (_) wildcard
  character
UNIQUE constraint

REVIEW QUESTIONS

3.1 What does *SQL* stand for?

3.2 What is a data sublanguage?

3.3 Explain the importance of SQL-92.

3.4 Why is it important to learn SQL?

3.5 Describe in your own words the purpose of the two business rules listed on page 141.

3.6   Why do some standard SQL-92 statements fail to run successfully in Microsoft Access?

Use the following tables for your answers to questions 3.7 through 3.48:

PET_OWNER (OwnerID, OwnerLastName, OwnerFirstName,
                        OwnerPhone, OwnerEmail)

PET (PetID, PetName, PetType, PetBreed, PetDOB, *OwnerID*)

Sample data for these tables are shown in Figures 3-26 and 3-27. For each SQL statement you write, show the results based on these data.

    If possible, run the statements you write for the questions that follow in an actual DBMS, as appropriate, to obtain results. Use data types that are consistent with the DBMS you are using. If you are not using an actual DBMS, consistently represent data types by using either the MySQL, Microsoft SQL Server, or Oracle Database data types shown in Figure 3-5.

3.7   Write an SQL CREATE TABLE statement to create the PET_OWNER table, with OwnerID as a surrogate key. Justify your choices of column properties. If you are using an actual DBMS, also insert the data using SQL.

3.8   Write an SQL CREATE TABLE statement to create the PET table *without* a referential integrity constraint on OwnerID in PET. Justify your choices of column properties. Why not make every column NOT NULL? If you are using an actual DBMS, also insert the data using SQL.

3.9   Create a referential integrity constraint on OwnerID in PET. Assume that deletions should not cascade.

3.10   Create a referential integrity constraint on OwnerID in PET. Assume that deletions should cascade.

The following table schema for the PET_2 table is an alternate version of the PET table—use it to answer review questions 3.11 and 3.12:

PET_2 (PetName, PetType, PetBreed, PetDOB, *OwnerID*)

FIGURE 3-26

PET_OWNER Data

OwnerID	OwnerLastName	OwnerFirstName	OwnerPhone	OwnerEmail
1	Downs	Marsha	555-537-8765	Marsha.Downs@somewhere.com
2	James	Richard	555-537-7654	Richard.James@somewhere.com
3	Frier	Liz	555-537-6543	Liz.Frier@somewhere.com
4	Trent	Miles		Miles.Trent@somewhere.com

FIGURE 3-27

PET Data

PetID	PetName	PetType	PetBreed	PetDOB	OwnerID
1	King	Dog	Std. Poodle	27-Feb-16	1
2	Teddy	Cat	Cashmere	01-Feb-17	2
3	Fido	Dog	Std. Poodle	17-Jul-15	1
4	AJ	Dog	Collie Mix	05-May-16	3
5	Cedro	Cat	Unknown	06-Jun-14	2
6	Wooley	Cat	Unknown		2
7	Buster	Dog	Border Collie	11-Dec-13	4

3.11 Write the required SQL statements to create the PET_2 table.

3.12 Is PET or PET_2 a better design? Explain your rationale.

3.13 Write the SQL statements necessary to remove the PET_OWNER table from the database. Assume that the referential integrity constraint is to be removed. *Do not run these commands in an actual database!*

3.14 Write the SQL statements necessary to remove the PET_OWNER table from the database. Assume that the PET table also needs to be removed. *Do not run these commands in an actual database!*

3.15 Write an SQL statement to display all columns of all rows of PET. Do not use the asterisk (*) notation.

3.16 Write an SQL statement to display all columns of all rows of PET. Use the asterisk (*) notation.

3.17 Write an SQL statement to display the breed and type of all pets.

3.18 Write an SQL statement to display the breed, type, and DOB of all pets having the type Dog.

3.19 Write an SQL statement to display the PetBreed column of PET.

3.20 Write an SQL statement to display the PetBreed column of PET. Do not show duplicates.

3.21 Write an SQL statement to display the breed, type, and DOB for all pets having the type Dog and the breed Std. Poodle.

3.22 Write an SQL statement to display the name, breed, and type for all pets that are not of type Cat, Dog, or Fish.

3.23 Write an SQL statement to display the pet ID, breed, and type for all pets having a four-character name starting with *K*. Note that the RTRIM function will be needed in the solution that uses a CHAR column, but not for one that uses a VARCHAR column.

3.24 Write an SQL statement to display the last name, first name, and email of all owners who have an email address ending with *somewhere.com*. Assume that email account names can be any number of characters. Note that the RTRIM function will be needed in the solution that uses a CHAR column, but not for one that uses a VARCHAR column.

3.25 Write an SQL statement to display the last name, first name, and email of any owner who has a NULL value for OwnerPhone.

3.26 Write an SQL statement to display the name and breed of all pets, sorted by PetName.

3.27 Write an SQL statement to display the name and breed of all pets, sorted by PetBreed in ascending order and by PetName in descending order within PetBreed.

3.28 Write an SQL statement to count the number of pets.

3.29 Write an SQL statement to count the number of distinct breeds.

The following table schema for the PET_3 table is another alternate version of the PET table:

PET_3 (PetID, PetName, PetType, PetBreed, PetDOB, PetWeight, *OwnerID*)

Data for PET_3 are shown in Figure 3-28. Except as specifically noted in the question itself, use the PET_3 table for your answers to all the remaining review questions.

3.30 Write the required SQL statements to create the PET_3 table. Assume that PetWeight is Numeric(4,1). If you are using an actual database, insert the data into the table using SQL.

3.31 Write an SQL statement to display the minimum, maximum, and average weight of dogs.

FIGURE 3-28

PET_3 Data

PetID	PetName	PetType	PetBreed	PetDOB	PetWeight	OwnerID
1	King	Dog	Std. Poodle	27-Feb-16	25.5	1
2	Teddy	Cat	Cashmere	01-Feb-17	10.5	2
3	Fido	Dog	Std. Poodle	17-Jul-15	28.5	1
4	AJ	Dog	Collie Mix	05-May-16	20.0	3
5	Cedro	Cat	Unknown	06-Jun-14	9.5	2
6	Wooley	Cat	Unknown		9.5	2
7	Buster	Dog	Border Collie	11-Dec-13	25.0	4

3.32 Write an SQL statement to group the data by PetBreed and display the average weight per breed.

3.33 Answer question 3.32, but consider only breeds for which two or more pets are included in the database.

3.34 Answer question 3.33, but do not consider any pet having the breed of Unknown.

3.35 Write an SQL statement to display the last name, first name, and email of any owners of cats. Use a subquery.

3.36 Write an SQL statement to display the last name, first name, and email of any owners of cats with a cat named Teddy. Use a subquery.

The following table schema for the BREED table shows a new table to be added to the pet database:

BREED (BreedName, MinWeight, MaxWeight, AverageLifeExpectancy)

Assume that PetBreed in PET_3 is a foreign key that matches the primary key BreedName in BREED and that we have the referential integrity constraint:

PetBreed in PET_3 must exist in BreedName in BREED

If needed, you may also assume that a similar referential integrity constraint exists between PET and BREED and between PET_2 and BREED. The BREED table data are shown in Figure 3-29.

3.37 Write SQL statements to (1) create the BREED table, (2) insert the data in Figure 3-29 into the BREED table, (3) alter the PET_3 table so that PetBreed is a foreign key referencing BreedName in BREED with cascading updates enabled, and (4) with the BREED table added to the pet database, write an SQL statement to display the last name, first name, and email of any owner of a pet that has an AverageLifeExpectancy value greater than 15. Use a subquery.

FIGURE 3-29

BREED Data

BreedName	MinWeight	MaxWeight	AverageLifeExpectancy
Border Collie	15.0	22.5	20
Cashmere	10.0	15.0	12
Collie Mix	17.5	25.0	18
Std. Poodle	22.5	30.0	18
Unknown			

FIGURE 3-30

Additional PET_OWNER Data

OwnerID	OwnerLastName	OwnerFirstName	OwnerPhone	OwnerEmail
5	Rogers	Jim	555-232-3456	Jim.Rogers@somewhere.com
6	Keenan	Mary	555-232-4567	Mary.Keenan@somewhere.com
7	Melnik	Nigel	555-232-5678	Nigel.Melnik@somewhere.com
8	Mayberry	Jenny	555-454-1243	
9	Roberts	Ken	555-454-2354	
10	Taylor	Sam	555-454-3465	

3.38 Answer question 3.35, but use a join using JOIN ON syntax. What are the consequences of using (or not using) the DISTINCT keyword in this version of the query?

3.39 Answer question 3.36, but use a join using JOIN ON syntax. What are the consequences of using (or not using) the DISTINCT keyword in this version of the query?

3.40 Answer part (4) of question 3.37, but use joins using JOIN ON syntax. What are the consequences of using (or not using) the DISTINCT keyword in this version of the query?

3.41 Write an SQL statement to display the OwnerLastName, OwnerFirstName, PetName, PetType, PetBreed, and AverageLifeExpectancy for pets with a known PetBreed.

3.42 Write SQL statements to add three new rows to the PET_OWNER table. Assume that OwnerID is a surrogate key and that the DBMS will provide a value for it. Use the first three lines of data provided in Figure 3-30.

3.43 Write SQL statements to add three new rows to the PET_OWNER table. Assume that OwnerID is a surrogate key and that the DBMS will provide a value for it. Assume, however, that you have only OwnerLastName, OwnerFirstName, and OwnerPhone and that therefore OwnerEmail is NULL. Use the last three lines of data provided in Figure 3-30.

3.44 Write an SQL statement to change the value of Std. Poodle in BreedName of BREED to Poodle, Std. When you ran this statement, what happened to the data values of PetBreed in the PET_3 table? Why did this occur?

3.45 Explain what will happen if you leave the WHERE clause off your answer to question 3.44.

3.46 Write an SQL statement to delete all rows of pets of type Anteater. What will happen if you forget to code the WHERE clause in this statement?

3.47 Write an SQL statement to add a PetWeight column like the one in PET_3 to the PET table, given that this column is NULL. Again, assume that PetWeight is Numeric(4,1).

3.48 Write SQL statements to insert data into the PetWeight column you created in question 3.47. Use the PetWeight data from the PET_3 table as shown in Figure 3-28.

EXERCISES

The following is a set of tables for the Art Course database shown in Figure 1-12. For the data for these tables, use the data shown in Figure 1-12.

CUSTOMER (<u>CustomerNumber</u>, CustomerLastName, CustomerFirstName, Phone)
COURSE (<u>CourseNumber</u>, Course, CourseDate, Fee)
ENROLLMENT (*<u>CustomerNumber</u>*, *<u>CourseNumber</u>*, AmountPaid)

where:

CustomerNumber in ENROLLMENT must exist in CustomerNumber in CUSTOMER
CourseNumber in ENROLLMENT must exist in CourseNumber in COURSE

CustomerNumber and CourseNumber are surrogate keys. Therefore, these numbers will never be modified, and there is no need for cascading updates. No customer data are ever deleted, so there is no need to cascade deletions. Courses can be deleted. If there are enrollment entries for a deleted class, they should also be deleted.

These tables, referential integrity constraints, and data are used as the basis for the SQL statements you will create in the exercises that follow. If possible, run these statements in an actual DBMS, as appropriate, to obtain results. Name your database ART_COURSE_ DATABASE. For each SQL statement you write, show the results based on these data. Use data types consistent with the DBMS you are using. If you are not using an actual DBMS, consistently represent data types using either the MySQL, Microsoft SQL Server, or Oracle Database data types shown in Figure 3-5.

3.49   Write and run the SQL statements necessary to create the tables and their referential integrity constraints.

3.50   Populate the tables with the data in Figure 1-12.

3.51   Write and run an SQL query to list all occurrences of Adv Pastels in the COURSE table. Include all associated data for each occurrence of the class.

3.52   Write and run an SQL query to list all students and courses they are registered for. Include, in this order, CustomerNumber, CustomerLastName, CustomerFirstName, Phone, CourseNumber, and AmountPaid.

3.53   Write and run an SQL query to list all students registered in Adv Pastels starting on October 1, 2019. Include, in this order, Course, CourseDate, Fee, CustomerLastName, CustomerFirstName, and Phone.

3.54   Write and run an SQL query to list all students registered in Adv Pastels starting on October 1, 2019. Include, in this order, Course, CourseDate, CustomerLastName, CustomerFirstName, Phone, Fee, and AmountPaid. Use a join using JOIN ON syntax. Can this query be run using one or more subqueries? If not, why not?

The following exercises are intended for use with a DBMS other than Microsoft Access. If you are using Microsoft Access, see the equivalent questions in the "Working with Microsoft Access" exercises that follow.

3.55   If you haven't done so, create the WP database, tables, and relationships described in this chapter, using the SQL DBMS of your choice. Be sure to populate the tables with the data shown in Figure 3-2.

3.56   Using the SQL DBMS of your choice, create and run queries to answer the questions in exercise WA.3.1.

3.57   Using the SQL DBMS of your choice, complete steps A through E in exercise WA.3.3, but *exclude step F*.

WORKING WITH MICROSOFT ACCESS

Key Terms

Allow Zero Length field property
Decimal Places field property
Default Value field property
Field Size field property
Format field property

Indexed field property
parameterized queries
Validation Rule field property
Yes (Duplicates OK)
Yes (No Duplicates)

Exercises

In the "Working with Microsoft Access" Exercises in Chapter 1 and Chapter 2, you created a database for Wedgewood Pacific (WP) of Seattle, Washington. In this set of exercises, you'll:

- Create and run queries against the database by using Access SQL.
- Create and run queries against the database by using Access QBE.
- Create tables and relationships by using Access SQL.
- Populate tables by using Access SQL.

WA.3.1 Using Access SQL, create and run queries to answer the questions that follow. Save each query using the query name format SQLQuery-WAE-3-1-## where the ## sign is replaced by the letter designator of the question. For example, the first query will be saved as SQLQuery-WAE-3-1-A.

- **A.** What projects are in the PROJECT table? Show all information for each project.
- **B.** What are the ProjectID, ProjectName, StartDate, and EndDate values of projects in the PROJECT table?
- **C.** What projects in the PROJECT table started before August 1, 2019? Show all the information for each project.
- **D.** What projects in the PROJECT table have not been completed? Show all the information for each project.
- **E.** Who are the employees assigned to each project? Show ProjectID, EmployeeNumber, LastName, FirstName, and OfficePhone.
- **F.** Who are the employees assigned to each project? Show ProjectID, ProjectName, and Department. Show EmployeeNumber, LastName, FirstName, and Office-Phone.
- **G.** Who are the employees assigned to each project? Show ProjectID, ProjectName, Department, and DepartmentPhone. Show EmployeeNumber, LastName, First-Name, and OfficePhone. Sort by ProjectID in ascending order.
- **H.** Who are the employees assigned to projects run by the Sales and Marketing department? Show ProjectID, ProjectName, Department, and DepartmentPhone. Show EmployeeNumber, LastName, FirstName, and OfficePhone. Sort by ProjectID in ascending order.
- **I.** How many projects are being run by the Sales and Marketing department? Be sure to assign an appropriate column name to the computed results.
- **J.** What is the total MaxHours of projects being run by the Sales and Marketing department? Be sure to assign an appropriate column name to the computed results.
- **K.** What is the average MaxHours of projects being run by the Sales and Marketing department? Be sure to assign an appropriate column name to the computed results.
- **L.** How many projects are being run by each department? Be sure to display each DepartmentName and to assign an appropriate column name to the computed results.

WA.3.2 Using Access QBE, create and run new queries to answer the questions in exercise WA.3.1. Save each query using the query name format QBEQuery-WAE-3-1-## where the ## sign is replaced by the letter designator of the question. For example, the first query will be saved as QBEQuery-WAE-3-1-A.

WA.3.3 WP has decided to keep track of computers used by the employees. To do this, two new tables will be added to the database. The schema for these tables, as related to the existing EMPLOYEE table, is (note that we are purposely excluding the recursive relationship in EMPLOYEE at this time):

(Continued)

EMPLOYEE (*EmployeeNumber*, FirstName, LastName, *Department*, Position, Supervisor, OfficePhone, EmailAddress)

COMPUTER (*SerialNumber*, Make, Model, ProcessorType, ProcessorSpeed, MainMemory, DiskSize)

COMPUTER_ASSIGNMENT (*SerialNumber*, *EmployeeNumber*, *DateAssigned*, DateReassigned)

The referential integrity constraints are:

Serial Number in COMPUTER_ASSIGNMENT must exist in SerialNumber in COMPUTER

EmployeeNumber in COMPUTER_ASSIGNMENT must exist in EmployeeNumber in EMPLOYEE

EmployeeNumber is a surrogate key and never changes. Employee records are never deleted from the database. SerialNumber is not a surrogate key because it is not generated by the database. However, a computer's SerialNumber never changes, and, therefore, there is no need to cascade updates. When a computer is at its end of life, the record in COMPUTER for that computer and all associated records in COMPUTER_ASSIGNMENT are deleted from the database.

A. Figure 3-31 shows the column characteristics for the WP COMPUTER table. Using the column characteristics, use Access SQL to create the COMPUTER table and its associated constraints in the WP.accdb database. Are there any table characteristics that cannot be created in SQL? If so, what are they? Use the Access GUI to finish setting table characteristics, if necessary.

B. The data for the COMPUTER table are in Figure 3-32. Use Access SQL to enter these data into your COMPUTER table.

C. Figure 3-33 shows the column characteristics for the WP COMPUTER_ASSIGNMENT table. Using the column characteristics, use Access SQL to create the COMPUTER_ASSIGNMENT table and the associated constraints in the WP.accdb database. Are there any table or relationship settings or characteristics that cannot be created in SQL? If so, what are they? Use the Access GUI to finish setting table characteristics and relationship settings, if necessary.

D. The data for the COMPUTER_ASSIGNMENT table are in Figure 3-34. Use Access SQL to enter these data into your COMPUTER_ASSIGNMENT table.

FIGURE 3-31

Database Column Characteristics for the WP COMPUTER Table

Column Name	Type	Key	Required	Remarks
SerialNumber	Number	Primary Key	Yes	Long Integer
Make	Short Text (12)	No	Yes	Must be "ASUS" or "Dell" or "HP" or "Other"
Model	Short Text (24)	No	Yes	
ProcessorType	Short Text (24)	No	No	
ProcessorSpeed	Number	No	Yes	Double [3,2]. Between 3.0 and 6.0
MainMemory	Short Text (15)	No	Yes	
DiskSize	Short Text (15)	No	Yes	

FIGURE 3-32

WP Database COMPUTER Table Data

Serial Number	Make	Model	ProcessorType	Processor Speed	MainMemory	DiskSize
9871234	HP	ProDesk 600 G3	Intel i5-7600	3.50	16.0 GBytes	1.0 TBytes
9871235	HP	ProDesk 600 G3	Intel i5-7600	3.50	16.0 GBytes	1.0 TBytes
9871236	HP	ProDesk 600 G3	Intel i5-7600	3.50	16.0 GBytes	1.0 TBytes
9871237	HP	ProDesk 600 G3	Intel i5-7600	3.50	16.0 GBytes	1.0 TBytes
9871238	HP	ProDesk 600 G3	Intel i5-7600	3.50	16.0 GBytes	1.0 TBytes
9871239	HP	ProDesk 600 G3	Intel i5-7600	3.50	16.0 GBytes	1.0 TBytes
9871240	HP	ProDesk 600 G3	Intel i5-7600	3.50	16.0 GBytes	1.0 TBytes
9871241	HP	ProDesk 600 G3	Intel i5-7600	3.50	16.0 GBytes	1.0 TBytes
9871242	HP	ProDesk 600 G3	Intel i5-7600	3.50	16.0 GBytes	1.0 TBytes
9871243	HP	ProDesk 600 G3	Intel i5-7600	3.50	16.0 GBytes	1.0 TBytes
6541001	Dell	OptiPlex 7060	Intel i7-8700	3.60	32.0 GBytes	2.0 TBytes
6541002	Dell	OptiPlex 7060	Intel i7-8700	3.60	32.0 GBytes	2.0 TBytes
6541003	Dell	OptiPlex 7060	Intel i7-8700	3.60	32.0 GBytes	2.0 TBytes
6541004	Dell	OptiPlex 7060	Intel i7-8700	3.60	32.0 GBytes	2.0 TBytes
6541005	Dell	OptiPlex 7060	Intel i7-8700	3.60	32.0 GBytes	2.0 TBytes
6541006	Dell	OptiPlex 7060	Intel i7-8700	3.60	32.0 GBytes	2.0 TBytes
6541007	Dell	OptiPlex 7060	Intel i7-8700	3.60	32.0 GBytes	2.0 TBytes
6541008	Dell	OptiPlex 7060	Intel i7-8700	3.60	32.0 GBytes	2.0 TBytes
6541009	Dell	OptiPlex 7060	Intel i7-8700	3.60	32.0 GBytes	2.0 TBytes
6541010	Dell	OptiPlex 7060	Intel i7-8700	3.60	32.0 GBytes	2.0 TBytes

FIGURE 3-33

Database Column Characteristics for the WP COMPUTER_ASSIGNMENT Table

Column Name	Type	Key	Required	Remarks
SerialNumber	Number	Primary Key, Foreign Key	Yes	Long Integer
EmployeeNumber	Number	Primary Key, Foreign Key	Yes	Long Integer
DateAssigned	Date/Time	Primary Key	Yes	Medium Date
DateReassigned	Date/Time	No	No	Medium Date

E. Who is currently using which computer at WP? Create an appropriate SQL query to answer this question. Show SerialNumber, Make, and Model. Show EmployeeID, LastName, FirstName, Department, and OfficePhone. Sort first by Department and then by employee LastName. Save this query using the query naming rules in exercise WA.3.1.

F. Who is currently using which computer at WP? Create an appropriate QBE query to answer this question. Show SerialNumber, Make, Model, ProcessorType, and ProcessorSpeed. Show the EmployeeID, LastName, FirstName, Department, and OfficePhone. Sort first by Department and then by employee LastName. Save this query using the query naming rules in exercise WA.3.2.

(Continued)

FIGURE 3-34

WP COMPUTER_
ASSIGNMENT Data

SerialNumber	EmployeeNumber	DateAssigned	DateReassigned
9871234	12	15-Sep-19	21-Oct-19
9871235	13	15-Sep-19	21-Oct-19
9871236	14	15-Sep-19	21-Oct-19
9871237	15	15-Sep-19	21-Oct-19
9871238	6	15-Sep-19	21-Oct-19
9871239	7	15-Sep-19	21-Oct-19
9871240	8	15-Sep-19	21-Oct-19
9871241	9	15-Sep-19	21-Oct-19
9871242	16	15-Sep-19	21-Oct-19
9871243	17	15-Sep-19	21-Oct-19
6541001	12	21-Oct-19	
6541002	13	21-Oct-19	
6541003	14	21-Oct-19	
6541004	15	21-Oct-19	
6541005	6	21-Oct-19	
6541006	7	21-Oct-19	
6541007	8	21-Oct-19	
6541008	9	21-Oct-19	
6541009	16	21-Oct-19	
6541010	17	21-Oct-19	
9871234	1	21-Oct-19	
9871235	2	21-Oct-19	
9S71236	3	21-Oct-19	
9871237	4	21-Oct-19	
9871238	5	21-Oct-19	
9871239	10	21-Oct-19	
9871240	11	21-Oct-19	
9871241	18	21-Oct-19	
9871242	19	21-Oct-19	
9871243	20	21-Oct-19	

CASE QUESTIONS

HEATHER SWEENEY DESIGNS

Heather Sweeney is an interior designer who specializes in home kitchen design. She offers a variety of seminars at home shows, kitchen and appliance stores, and other public locations. The seminars are free; she offers them as a way of building her customer base. She earns revenue by selling books and videos that instruct people on kitchen design. She also offers custom-design consulting services.

After someone attends a seminar, Heather wants to leave no stone unturned in attempting to sell that person one of her products or services. She would, therefore, like to develop a database to keep track of customers, the seminars they have attended, the contacts she has made with them, and the purchases they have made. She wants to use this database to continue to contact her customers and offer them products and services, including via a Web application that allows customers to create an account and purchase items online.

We use the task of designing a database for Heather Sweeney Designs (HSD) as an example for our discussion of developing first the HSD data model in Chapter 4 (pages 295–303) and then the HSD database design in Chapter 5 (pages 371–378). Although you will study the HSD database development in detail in these chapters, *you do not need to know that material to answer the following questions.* Here we will take that final database design for Heather Sweeney Designs (HSD) and actually implement it in a database using the SQL techniques that you learned in this chapter.

> ## BTW
>
> Some instructors and professors will follow the chapter order as we present it in this book, whereas others prefer to cover Chapter 4 and Chapter 5 before teaching the SQL techniques in this chapter. It is really a matter of personal preference (although you may hear some strong arguments in favor of one approach or the other), and these case questions are designed to be independent of the order in which you learn SQL, data modeling, and database design.

For reference, the SQL statements shown here are built from the HSD database design in Figure 5-26, the column specifications in Figure 5-25, and the referential integrity constraint specifications detailed in Figure 5-28.

Figure 3-35 shows the tables in the Heather Sweeney Designs database as they appear in the Microsoft Access 2019 Relationships view. This figure illustrates the tables in the HSD database and the relationships between them.

FIGURE 3-35

The Heather Sweeney Designs Database Tables in Microsoft Access 2019

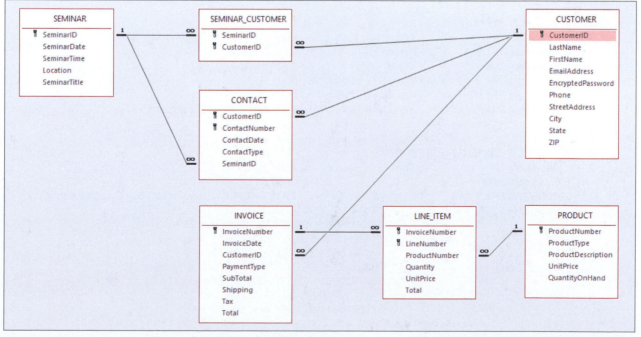

Access 2019, Windows 10, Microsoft Corporation.

The SQL statements to create the Heather Sweeney Designs (HSD) database are shown in Figure 3-36 in MySQL syntax. The SQL statements to populate the HSD database are shown in Figure 3-37, again in MySQL syntax.

Write SQL statements and answer questions for this database as follows:

A. Create a database named HSD in your DBMS.

B. Write an SQL script based on Figure 3-36 to create the tables and relationships for the HSD database. Save this script, and then execute the script to create the HSD tables.

C. Write an SQL script based on Figure 3-37 to insert the data for the HSD database. Save this script, and then execute the script to populate the HSD tables.

Note: For your answers to parts D through O, you should create an SQL script to save and store your SQL statements. You can use one script to contain all the necessary statements. You can also include your answer to part P, but be sure to put it in comment marks so that it is interpreted as a comment by the DBMS and cannot actually be run!

FIGURE 3-36

SQL Statements to Create the HSD Database

```sql
CREATE  TABLE CUSTOMER(
        CustomerID        Int          NOT NULL AUTO_INCREMENT,
        LastName          Char(25)     NOT NULL,
        FirstName         Char(25)     NOT NULL,
        EmailAddress      VarChar(100) NOT NULL,
        EncryptedPassword VarChar(50)  NULL,
        Phone             Char(12)     NOT NULL,
        StreetAddress     Char(35)     NULL,
        City              Char(35)     NULL DEFAULT 'Dallas',
        State             Char(2)      NULL DEFAULT 'TX',
        ZIP               Char(10)     NULL DEFAULT '75201',
        CONSTRAINT        CUSTOMER_PK    PRIMARY KEY(CustomerID),
        CONSTRAINT        CUSTOMER_EMAIL UNIQUE(EmailAddress)
        );

CREATE  TABLE SEMINAR(
        SeminarID         Int          NOT NULL AUTO_INCREMENT,
        SeminarDate       Date         NOT NULL,
        SeminarTime       Time         NOT NULL,
        Location          VarChar(100) NOT NULL,
        SeminarTitle      VarChar(100) NOT NULL,
        CONSTRAINT        SEMINAR_PK     PRIMARY KEY(SeminarID)
        );

CREATE  TABLE SEMINAR_CUSTOMER(
        SeminarID         Int          NOT NULL,
        CustomerID        Int          NOT NULL,
        CONSTRAINT        S_C_PK         PRIMARY KEY(SeminarID, CustomerID),
        CONSTRAINT        S_C_SEMINAR_FK FOREIGN KEY(SeminarID)
                            REFERENCES SEMINAR(SeminarID)
                                ON UPDATE NO ACTION
                                ON DELETE NO ACTION,
        CONSTRAINT        S_C_CUSTOMER_FK FOREIGN KEY(CustomerID)
                            REFERENCES CUSTOMER(CustomerID)
                                ON UPDATE NO ACTION
                                ON DELETE NO ACTION
        );
```

FIGURE 3-36 Continued

```
CREATE   TABLE CONTACT(
      CustomerID          Int              NOT NULL,
      ContactNumber       Int              NOT NULL,
      ContactDate         Date             NOT NULL,
      ContactType         VarChar(30)      NOT NULL,
      SeminarID           Int              NULL,
      CONSTRAINT          CONTACT_PK       PRIMARY KEY(CustomerID, ContactNumber),
      CONSTRAINT          CONTACT_ContactType
                              CHECK (ContactType IN ('Seminar',
                                     'WebAccountCreation', 'WebPurchase',
                                     'EmailAccountMessage', 'EmailSeminarMessage',
                                     'EmailPurchaseMessage',
                                     'EmailMessageExchange','FormLetterSeminar',
                                     'PhoneConversation')),
      CONSTRAINT          CONTACT_SEMINAR_FK FOREIGN KEY(SeminarID)
                              REFERENCES SEMINAR(SeminarID)
                                  ON UPDATE NO ACTION
                                  ON DELETE NO ACTION,
      CONSTRAINT          CONTACT_CUSTOMER_FK FOREIGN KEY(CustomerID)
                              REFERENCES CUSTOMER(CustomerID)
                                  ON UPDATE NO ACTION
                                  ON DELETE NO ACTION
      );


CREATE   TABLE PRODUCT(
      ProductNumber       Char(35)         NOT NULL,
      ProductType         Char(24)         NOT NULL,
      ProductDescription VarChar(100)      NOT NULL,
      UnitPrice           Numeric(9,2)     NOT NULL,
      QuantityOnHand      Int              NULL,
      CONSTRAINT          PRODUCT_PK       PRIMARY KEY(ProductNumber),
      CONSTRAINT          PRODUCT_ProductType
                              CHECK (ProductType IN ('Video',
                                     'Video Companion', 'Book'))
      );

CREATE   TABLE INVOICE(
      InvoiceNumber       Int              NOT NULL AUTO_INCREMENT,
      InvoiceDate         Date             NOT NULL,
      CustomerID          Int              NOT NULL,
      PaymentType         Char(25)         NOT NULL DEFAULT 'Cash',
      SubTotal            Numeric(9,2)     NULL,
      Shipping            Numeric(9,2)     NULL,
      Tax                 Numeric(9,2)     NULL,
      Total               Numeric(9,2)     NULL,
      CONSTRAINT          INVOICE_PK       PRIMARY KEY (InvoiceNumber),
      CONSTRAINT          INVOICE_PaymentType
                              CHECK (PaymentType IN ('VISA',
                                     'MasterCard', 'American Express',
                                     'PayPal', 'Check', 'Cash')),
      CONSTRAINT          INVOICE_CUSTOMER_FK FOREIGN KEY(CustomerID)
                              REFERENCES CUSTOMER(CustomerID)
                                  ON UPDATE NO ACTION
                                  ON DELETE NO ACTION
      );

ALTER TABLE INVOICE AUTO_INCREMENT = 35000;
```

(Continued)

FIGURE 3-36 Continued

```sql
CREATE  TABLE LINE_ITEM(
     InvoiceNumber        Int              NOT NULL,
     LineNumber           Int              NOT NULL,
     ProductNumber        Char(35)         NOT NULL,
     Quantity             Int              NOT NULL,
     UnitPrice            Numeric(9,2)     NULL,
     Total                Numeric(9,2)     NULL,
     CONSTRAINT           LINE_ITEM_PK     PRIMARY KEY (InvoiceNumber, LineNumber),
     CONSTRAINT           L_I_INVOICE_FK   FOREIGN KEY(InvoiceNumber)
                             REFERENCES INVOICE(InvoiceNumber)
                                ON UPDATE NO ACTION
                                ON DELETE CASCADE,
     CONSTRAINT           L_I_PRODUCT_FK   FOREIGN KEY(ProductNumber)
                             REFERENCES PRODUCT (ProductNumber)
                                ON UPDATE CASCADE
                                ON DELETE NO ACTION
     );
```

FIGURE 3-37

SQL Statements to Populate the HSD Database

```sql
/*****   CUSTOMER DATA    ******************************************************/
/* MySQL only: placing NULL for CustomoerID generates the next AUTO_INCREMENT value.*/

INSERT INTO CUSTOMER VALUES(
    NULL,'Jacobs', 'Nancy', 'Nancy.Jacobs@somewhere.com', 'nf46tG9E', '817-871-8123',
    '1440 West Palm Drive', 'Fort Worth', 'TX', '76110');
INSERT INTO CUSTOMER VALUES(
    NULL,'Jacobs', 'Chantel', 'Chantel.Jacobs@somewhere.com', 'b65TG03f', '817-871-8234',
    '1550 East Palm Drive', 'Fort Worth', 'TX', '76112');
INSERT INTO CUSTOMER VALUES(
    NULL,'Able', 'Ralph', 'Ralph.Able@somewhere.com', 'm56fGH08', '210-281-7987',
    '123 Elm Street', 'San Antonio', 'TX', '78214');
INSERT INTO CUSTOMER VALUES(
    NULL,'Baker', 'Susan', 'Susan.Baker@elsewhere.com', 'PC93fEk9', '210-281-7876',
    '456 Oak Street', 'San Antonio', 'TX', '78216');
INSERT INTO CUSTOMER VALUES(
    NULL,'Eagleton', 'Sam', 'Sam.Eagleton@elsewhere.com', 'bnvR44W8', '210-281-7765',
    '789 Pine Street', 'San Antonio', 'TX', '78218');
INSERT INTO CUSTOMER VALUES(
    NULL,'Foxtrot', 'Kathy', 'Kathy.Foxtrot@somewhere.com', 'aa8tY4GL', '972-233-6234',
    '11023 Elm Street', 'Dallas', 'TX', '75220');
INSERT INTO CUSTOMER VALUES(
    NULL,'George', 'Sally', 'Sally.George@somewhere.com', 'LK8G2tyF', '972-233-6345',
    '12034 San Jacinto', 'Dallas', 'TX', '75223');
INSERT INTO CUSTOMER VALUES(
    NULL,'Hullett', 'Shawn', 'Shawn.Hullett@elsewhere.com', 'bu78WW3t', '972-233-6456',
    '13045 Flora', 'Dallas', 'TX', '75224');
INSERT INTO CUSTOMER VALUES(
    NULL,'Pearson', 'Bobbi', 'Bobbi.Pearson@elsewhere.com', 'kq6N2O0p', '512-974-3344',
    '43 West 23rd Street', 'Austin', 'TX', '78710');
INSERT INTO CUSTOMER VALUES(
    NULL,'Ranger', 'Terry', 'Terry.Ranger@somewhere.com', 'bv3F9Qc4', '512-974-4455',
    '56 East 18th Street', 'Austin', 'TX', '78712');
INSERT INTO CUSTOMER VALUES(
    NULL,'Tyler', 'Jenny', 'Jenny.Tyler@somewhere.com', 'Yu4be77Z', '972-233-6567',
    '14056 South Ervay Street', 'Dallas', 'TX', '75225');
INSERT INTO CUSTOMER VALUES(
    NULL,'Wayne', 'Joan', 'Joan.Wayne@elsewhere.com', 'JW4TX6g', '817-871-8245',
    '1660 South Aspen Drive', 'Fort Worth', 'TX', '76115');
```

FIGURE 3-37 Continued

```
/*****    SEMINAR    *****************************************************/
/* MySQL only: placing NULL for SeminarID generates next AUTO_INCREMENT value.*/

INSERT INTO SEMINAR VALUES(
     NULL,'2018-10-12', '11:00', 'San Antonio Convention Center',
     'Kitchen on a Budget');
INSERT INTO SEMINAR VALUES(
     NULL,'2018-10-26', '16:00', 'Dallas Convention Center',
     'Kitchen on a Big D Budget');
INSERT INTO SEMINAR VALUES(
     NULL,'2018-11-02', '08:30', 'Austin Convention Center',
     'Kitchen on a Budget');
INSERT INTO SEMINAR VALUES(
     NULL,'2019-03-22', '11:00', 'Dallas Convention Center',
     'Kitchen on a Big D Budget');
INSERT INTO SEMINAR VALUES(
     NULL,'2019-03-23', '11:00', 'Dallas Convention Center',
     'Kitchen on a Big D Budget');
INSERT INTO SEMINAR VALUES(
     NULL,'2019-04-05', '08:30', 'Austin Convention Center',
     'Kitchen on a Budget');


/*****    SEMINAR_CUSTOMER DATA    ***********************************/

INSERT INTO SEMINAR_CUSTOMER VALUES(1, 1);
INSERT INTO SEMINAR_CUSTOMER VALUES(1, 2);
INSERT INTO SEMINAR_CUSTOMER VALUES(1, 3);
INSERT INTO SEMINAR_CUSTOMER VALUES(1, 4);
INSERT INTO SEMINAR_CUSTOMER VALUES(1, 5);
INSERT INTO SEMINAR_CUSTOMER VALUES(2, 6);
INSERT INTO SEMINAR_CUSTOMER VALUES(2, 7);
INSERT INTO SEMINAR_CUSTOMER VALUES(2, 8);
INSERT INTO SEMINAR_CUSTOMER VALUES(3, 9);
INSERT INTO SEMINAR_CUSTOMER VALUES(3, 10);
INSERT INTO SEMINAR_CUSTOMER VALUES(4, 6);
INSERT INTO SEMINAR_CUSTOMER VALUES(4, 7);
INSERT INTO SEMINAR_CUSTOMER VALUES(4, 11);
INSERT INTO SEMINAR_CUSTOMER VALUES(4, 12);


/*****    CONTACT DATA    *******************************************/

-- 'Nancy.Jacobs@somewhere.com'
INSERT INTO CONTACT VALUES(1, 1, '2018-10-12', 'Seminar', 1);
-- 'Chantel.Jacobs@somewhere.com'
INSERT INTO CONTACT VALUES(2, 1, '2018-10-12', 'Seminar', 1);
-- 'Ralph.Able@somewhere.com'
INSERT INTO CONTACT VALUES(3, 1, '2018-10-12', 'Seminar', 1);
-- 'Susan.Baker@elsewhere.com'
INSERT INTO CONTACT VALUES(4, 1, '2018-10-12', 'Seminar', 1);
-- 'Sam.Eagleton@elsewhere.com'
INSERT INTO CONTACT VALUES(5, 1, '2018-10-12', 'Seminar', 1);
```

(Continued)

FIGURE 3-37   Continued

```sql
-- 'Nancy.Jacobs@somewhere.com'
INSERT INTO CONTACT (CustomerID, ContactNumber, ContactDate,  ContactType)
    VALUES(1, 2, '2018-10-15', 'EmailSeminarMessage');
-- 'Chantel.Jacobs@somewhere.com'
INSERT INTO CONTACT (CustomerID, ContactNumber, ContactDate,  ContactType)
    VALUES(2, 2, '2018-10-15', 'EmailSeminarMessage');
-- 'Ralph.Able@somewhere.com'
INSERT INTO CONTACT (CustomerID, ContactNumber, ContactDate,  ContactType)
    VALUES(3, 2, '2018-10-15', 'EmailSeminarMessage');
-- 'Susan.Baker@elsewhere.com'
INSERT INTO CONTACT (CustomerID, ContactNumber, ContactDate,  ContactType)
    VALUES(4, 2, '2018-10-15', 'EmailSeminarMessage');
-- 'Sam.Eagleton@elsewhere.com'
INSERT INTO CONTACT (CustomerID, ContactNumber, ContactDate,  ContactType)
    VALUES(5, 2, '2018-10-15', 'EmailSeminarMessage');


-- 'Nancy.Jacobs@somewhere.com'
INSERT INTO CONTACT (CustomerID, ContactNumber, ContactDate,  ContactType)
    VALUES(1, 3, '2018-10-15', 'FormLetterSeminar');
-- 'Chantel.Jacobs@somewhere.com'
INSERT INTO CONTACT (CustomerID, ContactNumber, ContactDate,  ContactType)
    VALUES(2, 3, '2018-10-15', 'FormLetterSeminar');
-- 'Ralph.Able@somewhere.com'
INSERT INTO CONTACT (CustomerID, ContactNumber, ContactDate,  ContactType)
    VALUES(3, 3, '2018-10-15', 'FormLetterSeminar');
-- 'Susan.Baker@elsewhere.com'
INSERT INTO CONTACT (CustomerID, ContactNumber, ContactDate,  ContactType)
    VALUES(4, 3, '2018-10-15', 'FormLetterSeminar');
-- 'Sam.Eagleton@elsewhere.com'
INSERT INTO CONTACT (CustomerID, ContactNumber, ContactDate,  ContactType)
    VALUES(5, 3, '2018-10-15', 'FormLetterSeminar');


-- 'Kathy.Foxtrot@somewhere.com'
INSERT INTO CONTACT VALUES(6, 1, '2018-10-26', 'Seminar',2);
-- 'Sally.George@somewhere.com'
INSERT INTO CONTACT VALUES(7, 1, '2018-10-26', 'Seminar',2);
-- 'Shawn.Hullett@elsewhere.com'
INSERT INTO CONTACT VALUES(8, 1, '2018-10-26', 'Seminar',2);
-- 'Kathy.Foxtrot@somewhere.com'

INSERT INTO CONTACT (CustomerID, ContactNumber, ContactDate,  ContactType)
    VALUES(6, 2, '2018-10-30', 'EmailSeminarMessage');
-- 'Sally.George@somewhere.com'
INSERT INTO CONTACT (CustomerID, ContactNumber, ContactDate,  ContactType)
    VALUES(7, 2, '2018-10-30', 'EmailSeminarMessage');
-- 'Shawn.Hullett@elsewhere.com'
INSERT INTO CONTACT (CustomerID, ContactNumber, ContactDate,  ContactType)
    VALUES(8, 2, '2018-10-30', 'EmailSeminarMessage');
```

FIGURE 3-37   **Continued**

```
-- 'Kathy.Foxtrot@somewhere.com'
INSERT INTO CONTACT (CustomerID, ContactNumber, ContactDate,  ContactType)
    VALUES(6, 3, '2018-10-30', 'FormLetterSeminar');
-- 'Sally.George@somewhere.com'
INSERT INTO CONTACT (CustomerID, ContactNumber, ContactDate,  ContactType)
    VALUES(7, 3, '2018-10-30', 'FormLetterSeminar');
-- 'Shawn.Hullett@elsewhere.com'
INSERT INTO CONTACT (CustomerID, ContactNumber, ContactDate,  ContactType)
    VALUES(8, 3, '2018-10-30', 'FormLetterSeminar');


-- 'Bobbi.Pearson@elsewhere.com'
INSERT INTO CONTACT VALUES(9, 1, '2018-11-02', 'Seminar',3);
-- 'Terry.Ranger@somewhere.com'
INSERT INTO CONTACT VALUES(10, 1, '2018-11-02', 'Seminar',3);


-- 'Bobbi.Pearson@elsewhere.com'
INSERT INTO CONTACT (CustomerID, ContactNumber, ContactDate,  ContactType)
    VALUES(9, 2, '2018-11-06', 'EmailSeminarMessage');
-- 'Terry.Ranger@somewhere.com'
INSERT INTO CONTACT (CustomerID, ContactNumber, ContactDate,  ContactType)
    VALUES(10, 2, '2018-11-06', 'EmailSeminarMessage');
-- 'Bobbi.Pearson@elsewhere.com'
INSERT INTO CONTACT (CustomerID, ContactNumber, ContactDate,  ContactType)
    VALUES(9, 3, '2018-11-06', 'FormLetterSeminar');
-- 'Terry.Ranger@somewhere.com'
INSERT INTO CONTACT (CustomerID, ContactNumber, ContactDate,  ContactType)
    VALUES(10, 3, '2018-11-06', 'FormLetterSeminar');
-- 'Ralph.Able@somewhere.com'
INSERT INTO CONTACT (CustomerID, ContactNumber, ContactDate,  ContactType)
    VALUES(3, 4, '2019-02-20', 'WebAccountCreation');
-- 'Ralph.Able@somewhere.com'
INSERT INTO CONTACT (CustomerID, ContactNumber, ContactDate,  ContactType)
    VALUES(3, 5, '2019-02-20', 'EmailAccountMessage');
-- 'Kathy.Foxtrot@somewhere.com'
INSERT INTO CONTACT (CustomerID, ContactNumber, ContactDate,  ContactType)
    VALUES(6, 4, '2019-02-22', 'WebAccountCreation');
-- 'Kathy.Foxtrot@somewhere.com'
INSERT INTO CONTACT (CustomerID, ContactNumber, ContactDate,  ContactType)
    VALUES(6, 5, '2019-02-22', 'EmailAccountMessage');
-- 'Sally.George@somewhere.com'
INSERT INTO CONTACT (CustomerID, ContactNumber, ContactDate,  ContactType)
    VALUES(7, 4, '2019-02-25', 'WebAccountCreation');
-- 'Shawn.Hullett@elsewhere.com'
INSERT INTO CONTACT (CustomerID, ContactNumber, ContactDate,  ContactType)
    VALUES(8, 4, '2019-03-07', 'WebAccountCreation');
-- 'Shawn.Hullett@elsewhere.com'
INSERT INTO CONTACT (CustomerID, ContactNumber, ContactDate,  ContactType)
    VALUES(8, 5, '2019-03-07', 'EmailAccountMessage');
```

(Continued)

FIGURE 3-37 Continued

```
-- 'Kathy.Foxtrot@somewhere.com'
INSERT INTO CONTACT VALUES(6, 6, '2019-03-22', 'Seminar',4);
-- 'Sally.George@somewhere.com'
INSERT INTO CONTACT VALUES(7, 6, '2019-03-22', 'Seminar',4);
-- 'Jenny.Tyler@somewhere.com'
INSERT INTO CONTACT VALUES(11, 1, '2019-03-22', 'Seminar',4);
-- 'Joan.Wayne@elsewhere.com'
INSERT INTO CONTACT VALUES(12, 1, '2019-03-22', 'Seminar',4);


/*****    PRODUCT DATA    ***********************************************************/

INSERT INTO PRODUCT VALUES(
     'VK001', 'Video', 'Kitchen Remodeling Basics',14.95, 50);
INSERT INTO PRODUCT VALUES(
     'VK002', 'Video', 'Advanced Kitchen Remodeling', 14.95, 35);
INSERT INTO PRODUCT VALUES(
     'VK003', 'Video', 'Kitchen Remodeling Dallas Style', 19.95, 25);
INSERT INTO PRODUCT VALUES(
     'VK004', 'Video', 'Heather Sweeney Seminar Live in Dallas on 25-OCT-17',
     24.95, 20);
INSERT INTO PRODUCT VALUES(
     'VB001', 'Video Companion', 'Kitchen Remodeling Basics', 7.99, 50);
INSERT INTO PRODUCT VALUES(
     'VB002', 'Video Companion', 'Advanced Kitchen Remodeling I',7.99, 35);
INSERT INTO PRODUCT VALUES(
     'VB003', 'Video Companion', 'Kitchen Remodeling Dallas Style', 9.99, 25);
INSERT INTO PRODUCT VALUES(
     'BK001', 'Book', 'Kitchen Remodeling Basics For Everyone', 24.95, 75);
INSERT INTO PRODUCT VALUES(
     'BK002', 'Book', 'Advanced Kitchen Remodeling For Everyone', 24.95, 75);
INSERT INTO PRODUCT VALUES(
     'BK003', 'Book', 'Kitchen Remodeling Dallas Style For Everyone',
     24.95, 75);


/*****    INVOICE DATA    *********************************************************/
/* MySQL only: placing NULL for InvoiceNumber generates              */
/*    next AUTO_INCREMENT value.                                      */

/*****    Invoice 35000    *******************************************************/
-- 'Ralph.Able@somewhere.com'
INSERT INTO INVOICE VALUES(
   NULL, '2018-10-15', 3, 'VISA', 22.94, 5.95, 1.31, 30.20);
INSERT INTO LINE_ITEM VALUES(35000, 1, 'VK001', 1, 14.95, 14.95);
INSERT INTO LINE_ITEM VALUES(35000, 2, 'VB001', 1, 7.99, 7.99);

/*****    Invoice 35001    *******************************************************/
-- 'Susan.Baker@elsewhere.com'
INSERT INTO INVOICE VALUES(
   NULL, '2018-10-25', 4, 'MasterCard', 47.89, 5.95, 2.73, 56.57);
INSERT INTO LINE_ITEM VALUES(35001, 1, 'VK001', 1, 14.95, 14.95);
INSERT INTO LINE_ITEM VALUES(35001, 2, 'VB001', 1, 7.99, 7.99);
INSERT INTO LINE_ITEM VALUES(35001, 3, 'BK001', 1, 24.95, 24.95);
```

FIGURE 3-37   Continued

```
/*****    Invoice 35002    *****************************************/
-- 'Sally.George@somewhere.com'
INSERT INTO INVOICE VALUES(
    NULL, '2018-12-20', 7, 'VISA', 24.95, 5.95, 1.42, 32.32);
INSERT INTO LINE_ITEM VALUES(35002, 1, 'VK004', 1, 24.95, 24.95);


/*****    Invoice 35003    *****************************************/
-- 'Susan.Baker@elsewhere.com'
INSERT INTO INVOICE VALUES(
    NULL, '2019-03-25', 4, 'MasterCard', 64.85, 5.95, 3.70, 74.50);
INSERT INTO LINE_ITEM VALUES(35003, 1, 'VK002', 1, 14.95, 14.95);
INSERT INTO LINE_ITEM VALUES(35003, 2, 'BK002', 1, 24.95, 24.95);
INSERT INTO LINE_ITEM VALUES(35003, 3, 'VK004', 1, 24.95, 24.95);


/*****    Invoice 35004    *****************************************/
-- 'Kathy.Foxtrot@somewhere.com'
INSERT INTO INVOICE VALUES(
    NULL, '2019-03-27', 6, 'MasterCard', 94.79, 5.95, 5.40, 106.14);
INSERT INTO LINE_ITEM VALUES(35004, 1, 'VK002', 1, 14.95, 14.95);
INSERT INTO LINE_ITEM VALUES(35004, 2, 'BK002', 1, 24.95, 24.95);
INSERT INTO LINE_ITEM VALUES(35004, 3, 'VK003', 1, 19.95, 19.95);
INSERT INTO LINE_ITEM VALUES(35004, 4, 'VB003', 1, 9.99, 9.99);
INSERT INTO LINE_ITEM VALUES(35004, 5, 'VK004', 1, 24.95, 24.95);


/*****    Invoice 35005    *****************************************/
-- 'Sally.George@somewhere.com'
INSERT INTO INVOICE VALUES(
    NULL, '2019-03-27', 7, 'MasterCard', 94.80, 5.95, 5.40, 106.15);
INSERT INTO LINE_ITEM VALUES(35005, 1, 'BK001', 1, 24.95, 24.95);
INSERT INTO LINE_ITEM VALUES(35005, 2, 'BK002', 1, 24.95, 24.95);
INSERT INTO LINE_ITEM VALUES(35005, 3, 'VK003', 1, 19.95, 19.95);
INSERT INTO LINE_ITEM VALUES(35005, 4, 'VK004', 1, 24.95, 24.95);


/*****    Invoice 35006    *****************************************/
-- 'Bobbi.Pearson@elsewhere.com'
INSERT INTO INVOICE VALUES(
    NULL, '2019-03-31', 9, 'VISA', 47.89, 5.95, 2.73, 56.57);
INSERT INTO LINE_ITEM VALUES(35006, 1, 'BK001', 1, 24.95, 24.95);
INSERT INTO LINE_ITEM VALUES(35006, 2, 'VK001', 1, 14.95, 14.95);
INSERT INTO LINE_ITEM VALUES(35006, 3, 'VB001', 1, 7.99, 7.99);


/*****    Invoice 35007    *****************************************/
-- 'Jenny.Tyler@somewhere.com'
INSERT INTO INVOICE VALUES(
    NULL, '2019-04-03', 11, 'MasterCard', 109.78, 5.95, 6.26, 121.99);
INSERT INTO LINE_ITEM VALUES(35007, 1, 'VK003', 2, 19.95, 39.90);
INSERT INTO LINE_ITEM VALUES(35007, 2, 'VB003', 2, 9.99 , 19.98);
INSERT INTO LINE_ITEM VALUES(35007, 3, 'VK004', 2, 24.95, 49.90);
```

(Continued)

FIGURE 3-37 Continued

```
/*****    Invoice 35008    **************************************************/
-- 'Sam.Eagleton@elsewhere.com'
INSERT INTO INVOICE VALUES(
    NULL, '2019-04-08', 5, 'MasterCard', 47.89, 5.95, 2.73, 56.57);
INSERT INTO LINE_ITEM VALUES(35008, 1, 'BK001', 1, 24.95, 24.95);
INSERT INTO LINE_ITEM VALUES(35008, 2, 'VK001', 1, 14.95, 14.95);
INSERT INTO LINE_ITEM VALUES(35008, 3, 'VB001', 1, 7.99, 7.99);


/*****    Invoice 35009    **************************************************/
-- 'Nancy.Jacobs@somewhere.com'
INSERT INTO INVOICE VALUES(
    NULL, '2019-04-08', 1, 'VISA', 47.89, 5.95, 2.73, 56.57);
INSERT INTO LINE_ITEM VALUES(35009, 1, 'BK001', 1, 24.95, 24.95);
INSERT INTO LINE_ITEM VALUES(35009, 2, 'VK001', 1, 14.95, 14.95);
INSERT INTO LINE_ITEM VALUES(35009, 3, 'VB001', 1, 7.99, 7.99);


/*****    Invoice 35010    **************************************************/
-- 'Ralph.Able@somewhere.com'
INSERT INTO INVOICE VALUES(
    NULL, '2019-04-23', 3, 'VISA', 24.95, 5.95, 1.42, 32.32);
INSERT INTO LINE_ITEM VALUES(35010, 1, 'BK001', 1, 24.95, 24.95);


/*****    Invoice 35011    **************************************************/
-- 'Bobbi.Pearson@elsewhere.com'
INSERT INTO INVOICE VALUES(
    NULL, '2019-05-07', 9, 'VISA', 22.94, 5.95, 1.31, 30.20);
INSERT INTO LINE_ITEM VALUES(35011, 1, 'VK002', 1, 14.95, 14.95);
INSERT INTO LINE_ITEM VALUES(35011, 2, 'VB002', 1, 7.99, 7.99);


/*****    Invoice 35012    **************************************************/
-- 'Shawn.Hullett@elsewhere.com'
INSERT INTO INVOICE VALUES(
    NULL, '2019-05-21', 8, 'MasterCard', 54.89, 5.95, 3.13, 63.97);
INSERT INTO LINE_ITEM VALUES(35012, 1, 'VK003', 1, 19.95, 19.95);
INSERT INTO LINE_ITEM VALUES(35012, 2, 'VB003', 1, 9.99, 9.99);
INSERT INTO LINE_ITEM VALUES(35012, 3, 'VK004', 1, 24.95, 24.95);


/*****    Invoice 35013    **************************************************/
-- 'Ralph.Able@somewhere.com'
INSERT INTO INVOICE VALUES(
    NULL, '2019-06-05', 3, 'VISA', 47.89, 5.95, 2.73, 56.57);
INSERT INTO LINE_ITEM VALUES(35013, 1, 'VK002', 1, 14.95, 14.95);
INSERT INTO LINE_ITEM VALUES(35013, 2, 'VB002', 1, 7.99, 7.99);
INSERT INTO LINE_ITEM VALUES(35013, 3, 'BK002', 1, 24.95, 24.95);

/*****    Invoice 35014    **************************************************/
-- 'Jenny.Tyler@somewhere.com'
INSERT INTO INVOICE VALUES(
    NULL, '2019-06-05', 11, 'MasterCard', 45.88, 5.95, 2.62, 54.45);
INSERT INTO LINE_ITEM VALUES(35014, 1, 'VK002', 2, 14.95, 29.90);
INSERT INTO LINE_ITEM VALUES(35014, 2, 'VB002', 2, 7.99, 15.98);
```

FIGURE 3-37   Continued

```
/*****   Invoice 35015   ***********************************************/
-- 'Joan.Wayne@elsewhere.com'
INSERT INTO INVOICE VALUES(
    NULL, '2019-06-05', 12, 'MasterCard', 94.79, 5.95, 5.40, 106.14);
INSERT INTO LINE_ITEM VALUES(35015, 1, 'VK002', 1, 14.95, 14.95);
INSERT INTO LINE_ITEM VALUES(35015, 2, 'BK002', 1, 24.95, 24.95);
INSERT INTO LINE_ITEM VALUES(35015, 3, 'VK003', 1, 19.95, 19.95);
INSERT INTO LINE_ITEM VALUES(35015, 4, 'VB003', 1, 9.99, 9.99);
INSERT INTO LINE_ITEM VALUES(35015, 5, 'VK004', 1, 24.95, 24.95);


/*****   Invoice 35016   ***********************************************/
-- 'Ralph.Able@elsewhere.com'
INSERT INTO INVOICE VALUES(
    NULL, '2019-06-05', 3, 'VISA', 45.88, 5.95, 2.62, 54.45);
INSERT INTO LINE_ITEM VALUES(35016, 1, 'VK001', 1, 14.95, 14.95);
INSERT INTO LINE_ITEM VALUES(35016, 2, 'VB001', 1, 7.99, 7.99);
INSERT INTO LINE_ITEM VALUES(35016, 3, 'VK002', 1, 14.95, 14.95);
INSERT INTO LINE_ITEM VALUES(35016, 4, 'VB002', 1, 7.99, 7.99);


/**********************************************************************/
```

D. Write SQL statements to list all columns for all tables.

E. Write an SQL statement to list LastName, FirstName, and Phone for all customers who live in Dallas.

F. Write an SQL statement to list LastName, FirstName, and Phone for all customers who live in Dallas and have a LastName that begins with the letter *T*.

G. Write an SQL statement to list the InvoiceNumber for sales that include the *Heather Sweeney Seminar Live in Dallas on 25-OCT-17* video. Use a subquery.

H. Answer part G but use a join in JOIN ON syntax. What are the consequences of using (or not using) the DISTINCT keyword in this version of the query?

I. Write an SQL statement to list the FirstName, LastName, and Phone of customers (list each name only once) who have attended the *Kitchen on a Big D Budget* seminar.

J. Write an SQL statement to list the FirstName, LastName, Phone, ProductNumber, and ProductDescription for customers who have purchased a video product (list each combination of name and product only once). Sort the results by LastName in descending order, then by FirstName in descending order, and then by ProductNumber in descending order. (*Hint:* Video products have a ProductNumber that starts with *VK*.)

K. Write an SQL statement to show all Heather Sweeney Designs seminars and the customers who attended them. The output from this statement should include any seminars that do not have any customers shown as attending them. The SQL statement output should list SeminarID, SeminarDate, Location, SeminarTitle, CustomerID, LastName, and FirstName. Note that in Microsoft Access this requires multiple queries. (*Hint:* Use JOIN ON syntax.)

L. Write an SQL statement to show all customers and the products that they have purchased. The output from this statement should include any products that have not been purchased by any customer. The SQL statement output should list CustomerID, LastName, FirstName, InvoiceNumber, ProductNumber, ProductType, and ProductDescription. Note that in Microsoft Access this requires multiple queries. (*Hint:* Use JOIN ON syntax.)

M. Write an SQL statement to show the sum of Subtotal (this is the money earned by HSD on products sold exclusive of shipping costs and taxes) for INVOICE as SumOfSubTotal.

N. Write an SQL statement to show the average of Subtotal (this is the money earned by HSD on products sold exclusive of shipping costs and taxes) for INVOICE as AverageOfSubTotal.

O. Write an SQL statement to show both the sum and the average of Subtotal (this is the money earned by HSD on products sold exclusive of shipping costs and taxes) for INVOICE as SumOfSubTotal and AverageOfSubTotal, respectively.

P. Write an SQL statement to modify PRODUCT UnitPrice for ProductNumber VK004 to $34.95 instead of the current UnitPrice of $24.95.

Q. Write an SQL statement to undo the UnitPrice modification in part P.

R. *Do not run your answer to the following question in your actual database!* Write the fewest number of DELETE statements possible to remove all the data in your database but leave the table structures intact.

GARDEN GLORY PROJECT QUESTIONS

Assume that Garden Glory designs a database with the following tables:

OWNER (OwnerID, OwnerName, OwnerEmailAddress, OwnerType)

OWNED_PROPERTY (PropertyID, PropertyName, PropertyType, Street, City, State, Zip, *OwnerID*)

GG_SERVICE (ServiceID, ServiceDescription, CostPerHour);

EMPLOYEE (EmployeeID, LastName, FirstName, CellPhone, ExperienceLevel)

PROPERTY_SERVICE (PropertyServiceID, *PropertyID*, *ServiceID*, ServiceDate, *EmployeeID*, HoursWorked)

The referential integrity constraints are:

OwnerID in OWNED_PROPERTY must exist in OwnerID in OWNER

PropertyID in PROPERTY_SERVICE must exist in PropertyID in OWNED_PROPERTY

ServiceID in PROPERTY_SERVICE must exist in ServiceID in GG_SERVICE

EmployeeID in PROPERTY_SERVICE must exist in EmployeeID in EMPLOYEE

Assume that OwnerID in OWNER, PropertyID in PROPERTY, ServiceID in GG_SERVICE, EmployeeID in EMPLOYEE, and PropertyServiceID in PROPERTY_SERVICE are surrogate keys with values as follows:

OwnerID	Start at 1	Increment by 1
PropertyID	Start at 1	Increment by 1
ServiceID	Start at 1	Increment by 1
EmployeeID	Start at 1	Increment by 1
PropertyServiceID	Start at 1	Increment by 1

Sample data are shown in Figure 3-38, Figure 3-39, Figure 3-40, Figure 3-41, and Figure 3-42. OwnerType is either Individual or Corporation. PropertyType is one of Office, Apartments, or Private Residence. ExperienceLevel is one of Unknown, Junior, Senior, Master or SuperMaster. These tables, referential integrity constraints, and data are used

FIGURE 3-38

Sample Data for Garden Glory OWNER Table

OwnerID	OwnerName	OwnerEmailAddress	OwnerType
1	Mary Jones	Mary.Jones@somewhere.com	Individual
2	DT Enterprises	DTE@dte.com	Corporation
3	Sam Douglas	Sam.Douglas@somewhere.com	Individual
4	UNY Enterprises	UNYE@unye.com	Corporation
5	Doug Samuels	Doug.Samuels@somewhere.com	Individual

FIGURE 3-39

Sample Data for Garden Glory OWNED_PROPERTY Table

PropertyID	PropertyName	PropertyType	Street	City	State	ZIP	OwnerID
1	Eastlake Building	Office	123 Eastlake	Seattle	WA	98119	2
2	Elm St Apts	Apartments	4 East Elm	Lynwood	WA	98223	1
3	Jefferson Hill	Office	42 West 7th St	Bellevue	WA	98007	2
4	Lake View Apts	Apartments	1265 32nd Avenue	Redmond	WA	98052	3
5	Kodak Heights Apts	Apartments	65 32nd Avenue	Redmond	WA	98052	4
6	Jones House	Private Residence	1456 48th St	Bellevue	WA	98007	1
7	Douglas House	Private Residence	1567 51st St	Bellevue	WA	98007	3
8	Samuels House	Private Residence	567 151st St	Redmond	WA	98052	5

as the basis for the SQL statements you will create in the exercises that follow. If possible, run these statements in an actual DBMS, as appropriate, to obtain your results. Name your database GARDEN_GLORY.

Use data types consistent with the DBMS you are using. If you are not using an actual DBMS, consistently represent data types using either the MySQL, Microsoft SQL Server, or Oracle Database data types shown in Figure 3-5. For each SQL statement you write, show the results based on your data.

Write SQL statements and answer questions for this database as follows:

A. Write CREATE TABLE statements for each of these tables. Omit foreign keys.

B. Write foreign key constraints for the relationships in each of these tables. Make your own assumptions regarding cascading updates and deletions and justify those assumptions. (*Hint:* You can combine the SQL for your answers to parts A and B.)

C. Write SQL statements to insert the data into each of the five Garden Glory database tables. Assume that any surrogate key value will be supplied by the DBMS. Use the data in Figure 3-38, Figure 3-39, Figure 3-40, Figure 3-41, and Figure 3-42.

D. Write SQL statements to list all columns for all tables.

E. Write an SQL statement to list LastName, FirstName, and CellPhone for all employees having an experience level of Master.

F. Write an SQL statement to list LastName, FirstName, and CellPhone for all employees having an experience level of Master and FirstName that begins with the letter *J*.

FIGURE 3-40

Sample Data for Garden Glory EMPLOYEE Table

EmployeeID	LastName	FirstName	CellPhone	ExperienceLevel
1	Smith	Sam	206-254-1234	Master
2	Evanston	John	206-254-2345	Senior
3	Murray	Dale	206-254-3456	Junior
4	Murphy	Jerry	585-545-8765	Master
5	Fontaine	Joan	206-254-4567	Senior

FIGURE 3-41

Sample Data for Garden Glory GG_SERVICE Table

ServiceID	ServiceDescription	CostPerHour
1	Mow Lawn	25.00
2	Plant Annuals	25.00
3	Weed Garden	30.00
4	Trim Hedge	45.00
5	Prune Small Tree	60.00
6	Trim Medium Tree	100.00
7	Trim Large Tree	125.00

FIGURE 3-42

Sample Data for Garden Glory PROPERTY_SERVICE Table

PropertyServiceID	PropertyID	ServiceID	ServiceDate	EmployeeID	HoursWorked
1	1	2	2019-05-05	1	4.50
2	3	2	2019-05-08	3	4.50
3	2	1	2019-05-08	2	2.75
4	6	1	2019-05-10	5	2.50
5	5	4	2019-05-12	4	7.50
6	8	1	2019-05-15	4	2.75
7	4	4	2019-05-19	1	1.00
8	7	1	2019-05-21	2	2.50
9	6	3	2019-06-03	5	2.50
10	5	7	2019-06-08	4	10.50
11	8	3	2019-06-12	4	2.75
12	4	5	2019-06-15	1	5.00
13	7	3	2019-06-19	2	4.00

G. Write an SQL statement to list LastName, FirstName, and CellPhone of employees who have worked on a property in Seattle. Use a subquery.

H. Answer question G but use a join using JOIN ON syntax. What are the consequences of using (or not using) the DISTINCT keyword in this version of the query?

I. Write an SQL statement to list LastName, FirstName, and CellPhone of employees who have worked on a property owned by a corporation. Use a subquery.

J. Answer question I but use a join using JOIN ON syntax. What are the consequences of using (or not using) the DISTINCT keyword in this version of the query?

K. Write an SQL statement to show the LastName, FirstName, CellPhone, and sum of hours worked for each employee.

L. Write an SQL statement to show the sum of hours worked for each ExperienceLevel of EMPLOYEE. Sort the results by ExperienceLevel, in descending order.

M. Write an SQL statement to show the sum of HoursWorked for each type of OWNER but exclude services of employees who have ExperienceLevel of Junior.

N. Write an SQL statement to modify all EMPLOYEE rows with ExperienceLevel of Master to SuperMaster.

O. Write SQL statements to switch the values of ExperienceLevel so that all rows currently having the value Junior will have the value Senior and all rows currently having the value Senior will have the value Junior. (*Hint*: Use the value Unknown as a temporary third value.)

P. Given your assumptions about cascading deletions in your answer to part B, write the fewest number of DELETE statements possible to remove all the data in your database but leave the table structures intact. Do *not* run these statements if you are using an actual database!

JAMES RIVER JEWELRY PROJECT QUESTIONS

Assume that James River designs a database with the following tables:

CUSTOMER (<u>CustomerID</u>, LastName, FirstName, Phone, EmailAddress)
PURCHASE (<u>InvoiceNumber</u>, InvoiceDate, PreTaxAmount, *CustomerID*)
PURCHASE_ITEM (*<u>InvoiceNumber</u>*, <u>InvoiceLineNumber</u>, *ItemNumber*, RetailPrice)
ITEM (<u>ItemNumber</u>, ItemDescription, Cost, ArtistLastName, ArtistFirstName)

The referential integrity constraints are:

CustomerID in PURCHASE must exist in CustomerID in CUSTOMER
InvoiceNumber in PURCHASE_ITEM must exist in InvoiceNumber in PURCHASE
ItemNumber in PURCHASE_ITEM must exist in ItemNumber in ITEM

Assume that CustomerID of CUSTOMER, ItemNumber of ITEM, and InvoiceNumber of PURCHASE are all surrogate keys with values as follows:

CustomerID	Start at 1	Increment by 1
InvoiceNumber	Start at 1001	Increment by 1
ItemNumber	Start at 1	Increment by 1

FIGURE 3-43

Sample Data for JRJ CUSTOMER Table

CustomerID	LastName	FirstName	Phone	EmailAddress
1	Stanley	Elizabeth	555-236-7789	Elizabeth.Stanley@somewhere.com
2	Price	Fred	555-236-0091	Fred.Price@somewhere.com
3	Becky	Linda	555-236-0392	Linda.Becky@somewhere.com
4	Birch	Pamela	555-236-4493	Pamela.Birch@somewhere.com
5	Romez	Ricardo	555-236-3334	Ricardo.Romez@somewhere.com
6	Jackson	Samantha	555-236-1095	Samantha.Jackson@somewhere.com

FIGURE 3-44

Sample Data for JRJ ITEM Table

ItemNumber	ItemDescription	Cost	ArtistLastName	ArtistFirstName
1	Gold Bracelet	$ 120.00	Josephson	Mary
2	Gold Necklace	$ 160.00	Baker	Samantha
3	Bead Earrings	$ 50.00	Josephson	Mary
4	Gold Bracelet	$ 180.00	Baker	Samantha
5	Silver Necklace	$ 135.00	Baker	Sam
6	Bead Earrings	$ 25.00	Josephson	Mary
7	Bead Earrings	$ 22.50	Josephson	Mary
8	Gold Earrings	$ 50.00	Lintz	John
9	Gold Necklace	$ 160.00	Lintz	John
10	Bead Earrings	$ 20.00	Josephson	Mary
11	Bead Earrings	$ 35.00	Josephson	Mary
12	Bead Earrings	$ 45.00	Josephson	Mary
13	Gold Necklace	$ 225.00	Lintz	John
14	Silver Earrings	$ 55.00	Lintz	John
15	Gold Bracelet	$ 200.00	Lintz	John
16	Bead Earrings	$ 25.00	Josephson	Mary
17	Bead Earrings	$ 45.00	Josephson	Mary
18	Gold Bracelet	$ 210.00	Baker	Samantha
19	Silver Necklace	$ 165.00	Baker	Sam

Data for the James River Jewelry tables is shown in Figure 3-43, Figure 3-44, Figure 3-45, and Figure 3-46. These tables, referential integrity constraints, and data are used as the basis for the SQL statements you will create in the exercises that follow. If possible, run these statements in an actual DBMS, as appropriate, to obtain your results. Name your database JRJ.

Use data types consistent with the DBMS you are using. If you are not using an actual DBMS, consistently represent data types using either the MySQL, Microsoft SQL Server, or Oracle Database data types shown in Figure 3-5. For each SQL statement you write, show the results based on your data.

FIGURE 3-45

Sample Data for JRJ PURCHASE Table

InvoiceNumber	InvoiceDate	PreTaxAmount	CustomerID
1001	5/5/2019	$ 155.00	1
1002	5/7/2019	$ 203.00	2
1003	5/11/2019	$ 75.00	3
1004	5/15/2019	$ 67.00	4
1005	5/15/2019	$ 330.00	5
1006	5/16/2019	$ 25.00	1
1007	5/25/2019	$ 45.00	3
1008	6/6/2019	$ 445.00	1
1009	6/7/2019	$ 72.00	6

FIGURE 3-46

Sample Data for JRJ PURCHASE_ITEM Table

InvoiceNumber	InvoiceLineNumber	ItemNumber	RetailPrice
1001	1	1	$ 155.00
1002	1	2	$ 203.00
1003	1	3	$ 75.00
1004	1	6	$ 35.00
1004	2	7	$ 32.00
1005	1	4	$ 240.00
1005	2	8	$ 90.00
1006	1	10	$ 25.00
1007	1	11	$ 45.00
1008	1	5	$ 175.00
1008	2	9	$ 215.00
1008	3	12	$ 55.00
1009	1	14	$ 72.00

Write SQL statements and answer questions for this database as follows:

A. Write SQL CREATE TABLE statements for each of these tables. Omit foreign keys.

B. Write foreign key constraints for the relationships in each of these tables. Make your own assumptions regarding cascading deletions and justify those assumptions. (*Hint*: You can combine the SQL for your answers to parts A and B.)

C. Write SQL statements to insert the data shown in Figure 3-43, Figure 3-44, Figure 3-45, and Figure 3-46 into these tables. Assume that surrogate key column values will be supplied by the DBMS.

D. Write SQL statements to list all columns for all tables.

E. Write an SQL statement to list ItemNumber and ItemDescription for all items that cost more than $100.

F. Write an SQL statement to list ItemNumber and ItemDescription for all items that cost more than $100 and were produced by an artist with a name ending with the letters *son*.

G. Write an SQL statement to list LastName and FirstName of customers who have made at least one purchase with PreTaxAmount greater than $200. Use a subquery.

H. Answer part G but use a join using JOIN ON syntax. What are the consequences of using (or not using) the DISTINCT keyword in this version of the query?

I. Write an SQL statement to list LastName and FirstName of customers who have purchased an item that costs more than $50. Use a subquery.

J. Answer part I but use a join using JOIN ON syntax. What are the consequences of using (or not using) the DISTINCT keyword in this version of the query?

K. Write an SQL statement to list the LastName and FirstName of customers who have purchased an item that was created by an artist with a LastName that begins with the letter *J*. Use a subquery.

L. Answer part K but use a join using JOIN ON syntax. What are the consequences of using (or not using) the DISTINCT keyword in this version of the query?

M. Write an SQL statement to show the CustomerID, LastName, FirstName, and sum of PreTaxAmount for each customer. Use a join using JOIN ON syntax.

N. Write an SQL statement to show the sum of PreTaxAmount for each artist (Hint: The result will have only one line per each artist). Use a join using JOIN ON syntax, and sort the results by ArtistLastName and then ArtistFirstName in ascending order. Note that this should include the full PreTaxAmount for any purchase in which the artist had an item, even if other items in the purchase were created by other artists.

O. Write an SQL statement to show the sum of PreTaxAmount for each artist, as in Part N, but exclude any purchases with PreTaxAmount greater than $25. Use a join using JOIN ON syntax, and sort the results by ArtistLastName and then ArtistFirstName in descending order.

P. Write an SQL statement to show which customers bought which items, and include any items that have not been sold. Include CUSTOMER.LastName, CUSTOMER.FirstName, InvoiceNumber, InvoiceDate, ItemNumber, ItemDescription, ArtistLastName, and ArtistFirstName. Use a join using JOIN ON syntax, and sort the results by ArtistLastName and ArtistFirstName in ascending order. Note that in Microsoft Access this requires multiple queries.

Q. Write an SQL statement to modify all ITEM rows with an artist last name of Baxter to an artist first name of Rex.

R. Write SQL statements to switch the values of ArtistLastName so that all rows currently having the value Baker will have the value Baxter and all rows currently having the value Baxter will have the value Baker.

S. Given your assumptions about cascading deletions in your answer to part B, write the fewest number of DELETE statements possible to remove all the data in your database but leave the table structures intact. Do *not* run these statements if you are using an actual database!

THE QUEEN ANNE CURIOSITY SHOP PROJECT QUESTIONS

Assume that the Queen Anne Curiosity Shop designs a database with the following tables:

CUSTOMER (<u>CustomerID</u>, LastName, FirstName, Address, City, State, ZIP, Phone, EmailAddress)

EMPLOYEE (<u>EmployeeID</u>, LastName, FirstName, Phone, EmailAddress)

VENDOR (<u>VendorID</u>, CompanyName, ContactLastName, ContactFirstName, Address, City, State, ZIP, Phone, Fax, EmailAddress)

ITEM (<u>ItemID</u>, ItemDescription, PurchaseDate, ItemCost, ItemPrice, *VendorID*)

SALE (<u>SaleID</u>, *CustomerID*, *EmployeeID*, SaleDate, SubTotal, Tax, Total)

SALE_ITEM (<u>*SaleID*</u>, <u>SaleItemID</u>, *ItemID*, ItemPrice)

The referential integrity constraints are:

VendorID in ITEM must exist in VendorID in VENDOR

CustomerID in SALE must exist in CustomerID in CUSTOMER

EmployeeID in SALE must exist in EmployeeID in EMPLOYEE

SaleID in SALE_ITEM must exist in SaleID in SALE

ItemID in SALE_ITEM must exist in ItemID in ITEM

Assume that CustomerID of CUSTOMER, EmployeeID of EMPLOYEE, VendorID of VENDORE, ItemID of ITEM, and SaleID of SALE are all surrogate keys with values as follows:

CustomerID	Start at 1	Increment by 1
EmployeeID	Start at 1	Increment by 1
VendorID	Start at 1	Increment by 1
ItemID	Start at 1	Increment by 1
SaleID	Start at 1	Increment by 1

SaleItemID of SALE_ITEM is not a true surrogate key, but rather a counter that starts at 1 and increments by 1 for each SaleID in SALE. This number will require special handling in the database, needing to be either manually inserted or to have specific program logic written to insert the correct number. In this text we will simply insert the number manually.

A vendor may be an individual or a company. If the vendor is an individual, the CompanyName field is left blank, while the ContactLastName and ContactFirstName fields must have data values. If the vendor is a company, the company name is recorded in the CompanyName field, and the name of the primary contact at the company is recorded in the ContactLastName and ContactFirstName fields.

Sample data are shown in Figure 3-47, Figure 3-48, Figure 3-49, Figure 3-50, Figure 3-51, and Figure 3-52. These tables, referential integrity constraints, and data are used as the basis for the SQL statements you will create in the exercises that follow. If possible, run these statements in an actual DBMS, as appropriate, to obtain your results. Name your database QACS.

Use data types consistent with the DBMS you are using. If you are not using an actual DBMS, consistently represent data types using either the MySQL, Microsoft SQL Server, or Oracle Database data types shown in Figure 3-5. For each SQL statement you write, show the results based on your data.

Write SQL statements and answer questions for this database as follows:

A. Write SQL CREATE TABLE statements for each of these tables. Omit foreign keys.

B. Write foreign key constraints for the relationships in each of these tables. Make your own assumptions regarding cascading deletions and justify those assumptions. (*Hint:* You can combine the SQL for your answers to parts A and B.)

FIGURE 3-47

Sample Data for QACS Database CUSTOMER Table

CustomerID	LastName	FirstName	Address	City	State	ZIP	Phone	EmailAddress
1	Shire	Robert	6225 Evanston Ave N	Seattle	WA	98103	206-524-2433	Robert.Shire@somewhere.com
2	Goodyear	Katherine	7335 11th Ave NE	Seattle	WA	98105	206-524-3544	Katherine.Goodyear@somewhere.com
3	Bancroft	Chris	12605 NE 6th Street	Bellevue	WA	98005	425-635-9788	Chris.Bancroft@somewhere.com
4	Griffith	John	335 Aloha Street	Seattle	WA	98109	206-524-4655	John.Griffith@somewhere.com
5	Tiemey	Doris	14510 NE 4th Street	Bellevue	WA	98005	425-635-8677	Doris.Tiemey@somewhere.com
6	Anderson	Donna	1410 Hillcrest Parkway	Mt. Vemon	WA	98273	360-538-7566	Donna.Anderson@elsewhere.com
7	Svane	Jack	3211 42nd Street	Seattle	WA	98115	206-524-5766	Jack.Svane@somewhere.com
8	Walsh	Denesha	6712 24th Avenue NE	Redmond	WA	98053	425-635-7566	Denesha.Walsh@somewhere.com
9	Enquist	Craig	534 15th Street	Bellingham	WA	98225	360-538-6455	Craig.Enquist@elsewhere.com
10	Anderson	Rose	6823 17th Ave NE	Seattle	WA	98105	206-524-6877	Rose.Anderson@elsewhere.com

FIGURE 3-48

Sample Data for the QACS Database EMPLOYEE Table

EmployeeID	LastName	FirstName	Phone	EmailAddress
1	Stuart	Anne	206-527-0010	Anne.Stuart@QACS.com
2	Stuart	George	206-527-0011	George.Stuart@QACS.com
3	Stuart	Mary	206-527-0012	Mary.Stuart@QACS.com
4	Orange	William	206-527-0013	William.Orange@QACS.com
5	Griffith	John	206-527-0014	John.Griffith@QACS.com

C. Write SQL statements to insert the data into each of these tables. Assume that all surrogate key column values will be supplied by the DBMS. Use the data in Figure 3-47, Figure 3-48, Figure 3-49, Figure 3-50, Figure 3-51, and Figure 3-52.

D. Write SQL statements to list all columns for all tables.

E. Write an SQL statement to list ItemID and ItemDescription for all items that cost $1000 or more.

F. Write an SQL statement to list ItemID and ItemDescription for all items that cost $1000 or more and were purchased from a vendor whose CompanyName starts with the letters *New*.

G. Write an SQL statement to list LastName, FirstName, and Phone of the customer who made the purchase with SaleID 1. Use a subquery.

H. Answer part G but use a join using JOIN ON syntax. What are the consequences of using (or not using) the DISTINCT keyword in this version of the query?

I. Write an SQL statement to list LastName, FirstName, and Phone of the customers who made the purchases with SaleIDs 1, 2, and 3. Use a subquery.

J. Answer part I but use a join using JOIN ON syntax. What are the consequences of using (or not using) the DISTINCT keyword in this version of the query?

K. Write an SQL statement to list LastName, FirstName, and Phone of customers who have made at least one purchase with SubTotal greater than $500. Use a subquery.

L. Answer part K but use a join using JOIN ON syntax. What are the consequences of using (or not using) the DISTINCT keyword in this version of the query?

M. Write an SQL statement to list LastName, FirstName, and Phone of customers who have purchased an item that has an ItemPrice of $500 or more. Use a subquery.

N. Answer part M but use a join using JOIN ON syntax. What are the consequences of using (or not using) the DISTINCT keyword in this version of the query?

O. Write an SQL statement to list LastName, FirstName, and Phone of customers who have purchased an item that was supplied by a vendor with a CompanyName that begins with the letter *L*. Use a subquery.

P. Answer part O but use a join using JOIN ON syntax. What are the consequences of using (or not using) the DISTINCT keyword in this version of the query?

FIGURE 3-49

Sample Data for the QACS Database VENDOR Table

VendorID	CompanyName	ContactLastName	ContactFirstName	Address	City	State	ZIP	Phone	Fax	EmailAddress
1	Linens and Things	Huntington	Anne	1515 NW Market Street	Seattle	WA	98107	206-325-6755	206-329-9675	LAT@business.com
2	European Specialties	Tadema	Ken	6123 15th Avenue NW	Seattle	WA	98107	206-325-7866	206-329-9786	ES@business.com
3	Lamps and Lighting	Swanson	Sally	506 Prospect Street	Seattle	WA	98109	206-325-8977	206-329-9897	LAL@business.com
4	NULL	Lee	Andrew	1102 3rd Street	Kirkland	WA	98033	425-746-5433	NULL	Andrew.Lee@somewhere.com
5	NULL	Harrison	Denise	533 10th Avenue	Kirkland	WA	98033	425-746-4322	NULL	Denise.Harrison@somewhere.com
6	New York Brokerage	Smith	Mark	621 Roy Street	Seattle	WA	98109	206-325-9088	206-329-9908	NYB@business.com
7	NULL	Walsh	Denesha	6712 24th Avenue NE	Redmond	WA	98053	425-635-7566	NULL	Denesha.Walsh@somewhere.com
8	NULL	Bancroft	Chris	12605 NE 6th Street	Bellevue	WA	98005	425-635-9788	425-639-9978	Chris.Bancroft@somewhere.com
9	Specialty Antiques	Nelson	Fred	2512 Lucky Street	San Francisco	CA	94110	415-422-2121	415-423-5212	SA@business.com
10	General Antiques	Garner	Patty	2515 Lucky Street	San Francisco	CA	94110	415-422-3232	415-429-9323	GA@business.com

FIGURE 3-50

Sample Data for the QACS Database ITEM Table

ItemID	ItemDescription	PurchaseDate	ItemCost	ItemPrice	VendorID
1	Antique Desk	2018-11-07	$1,800.00	$3,000.00	2
2	Antique Desk Chair	2018-11-10	$300.00	$500.00	4
3	Dining Table Linens	2018-11-14	$600.00	$1,000.00	1
4	Candles	2018-11-14	$30.00	$50.00	1
5	Candles	2018-11-14	$27.00	$45.00	1
6	Desk Lamp	2018-11-14	$150.00	$250.00	3
7	Dining Table Linens	2018-11-14	$450.00	$750.00	1
8	Book Shelf	2018-11-21	$150.00	$250.00	5
9	Antique Chair	2018-11-21	$750.00	$1,250.00	6
10	Antique Chair	2018-11-21	$1,050.00	$1,750.00	6
11	Antique Candle Holders	2018-11-28	$210.00	$350.00	2
12	Antique Desk	2019-01-05	$1,920.00	$3,200.00	2
13	Antique Desk	2019-01-05	$2,100.00	$3,500.00	2
14	Antique Desk Chair	2019-01-06	$285.00	$475.00	9
15	Antique Desk Chair	2019-01-06	$339.00	$565.00	9
16	Desk Lamp	2019-01-06	$150.00	$250.00	10
17	Desk Lamp	2019-01-06	$150.00	$250.00	10
18	Desk Lamp	2019-01-06	$144.00	$240.00	3
19	Antique Dining Table	2019-01-10	$3,000.00	$5,000.00	7
20	Antique Sideboard	2019-01-11	$2,700.00	$4,500.00	8
21	Dining Table Chairs	2019-01-11	$5,100.00	$8,500.00	9
22	Dining Table Linens	2019-01-12	$450.00	$750.00	1
23	Dining Table Linens	2019-01-12	$480.00	$800.00	1
24	Candles	2019-01-17	$30.00	$50.00	1
25	Candles	2019-01-17	$36.00	$60.00	1

Q. Write an SQL statement to show the sum of SubTotal for each customer. List CustomerID, LastName, FirstName, Phone, and the calculated result. Name the sum of SubTotal as SumOfSubTotal and sort the results by CustomerID, in descending order.

R. Write an SQL statement to modify the vendor with CompanyName of *Linens and Things* to *Linens and Other Stuff*. Assume there is only one such vendor.

S. Write SQL statements to switch the values of vendor CompanyName so that all rows currently having the value *Linens and Things* will have the value *Lamps and Lighting* and all rows currently having the value *Lamps and Lighting* will have the value *Linens and Things*. If you have done part R in a DBMS, undo it before answering this question.

FIGURE 3-51

Sample Data for the QACS Database SALE Table

SaleID	CustomerID	EmployeeID	SaleDate	SubTotal	Tax	Total
1	1	1	2018-12-14	$3,500.00	$290.50	$3,790.50
2	2	1	2018-12-15	$1,000.00	$83.00	$1,083.00
3	3	1	2018-12-15	$50.00	$4.15	$54.15
4	4	3	2018-12-23	$45.00	$3.74	$48.74
5	1	5	2019-01-05	$250.00	$20.75	$270.75
6	5	5	2019-01-10	$750.00	$62.25	$812.25
7	6	4	2019-01-12	$250.00	$20.75	$270.75
8	2	1	2019-01-15	$3,000.00	$249.00	$3,249.00
9	5	5	2019-01-25	$350.00	$29.05	$379.05
10	7	1	2019-02-04	$14,250.00	$1,182.75	$15,432.75
11	8	5	2019-02-04	$250.00	$20.75	$270.75
12	5	4	2019-02-07	$50.00	$4.15	$54.15
13	9	2	2019-02-07	$4,500.00	$373.50	$4,873.50
14	10	3	2019-02-11	$3,675.00	$305.03	$3,980.03
15	2	2	2019-02-11	$800.00	$66.40	$866.40

FIGURE 3-52

Sample Data for the QACS Database SALE_ITEM Table

SaleID	SaleItemID	ItemID	ItemPrice
1	1	1	$3,000.00
1	2	2	$500.00
2	1	3	$1,000.00
3	1	4	$50.00
4	1	5	$45.00
5	1	6	$250.00
6	1	7	$750.00
7	1	8	$250.00
8	1	9	$1,250.00
8	2	10	$1,750.00
9	1	11	$350.00
10	1	19	$5,000.00
10	2	21	$8,500.00
10	3	22	$750.00
11	1	17	$250.00
12	1	24	$50.00
13	1	20	$4,500.00
14	1	12	$3,200.00
14	2	14	$475.00
15	1	23	$800.00

T. Given your assumptions about cascading deletions in your answer to part B, write the fewest number of DELETE statements possible to remove all the data in your database but leave the table structures intact. Do *not* run these statements if you are using an actual database!

U. Chapter 2 discussed multivalued dependencies and the associated multivalue, multicolumn problem and how to resolve it (pages 96–98). Does the VENDOR table have the multivalue, multicolumn problem? If so, use the discussion on pages 114–118 as the basis for solving it for the QACS database. Create a new table named PHONE_NUMBER, link it to the VENDOR table, populate the PHONE_NUMBER table, and finally alter the VENDOR table to remove any unneeded columns. *Hint:* Read the additional discussion of the SQL ALTER TABLE statement in online Extension B, "Advanced SQL."

PART 2 | Database Design

Part 1 introduced you to the fundamental concepts and techniques of relational database management. In Chapter 1, you learned that databases consist of related tables, and you learned the major components of a database system. Chapter 2 introduced you to the relational model, and you learned the basic ideas of functional dependencies and normalization. In Chapter 3, you learned how to use SQL statements to create and process a database.

All the material you have learned so far gives you a background for understanding the nature of database management and the required basic tools and techniques. However, you do not yet know how to apply all this technology to solve a business problem. Imagine, for example, that you walk into a small business—for example, a bookshop—and are asked to build a database to support a frequent buyer program. How would you proceed? So far, we have assumed that the database design already exists. How would you go about creating the design of the database? The next two chapters address this important topic. In Chapter 4, we begin with a discussion of systems analysis and design, and then provide an overview of the database design process. Finally, we describe data modeling, which is a technique for representing database requirements as a data model. In Chapter 5, you will learn how to transform a data model into a relational database design. After that database design is complete, it will be implemented in a DBMS using the SQL statements we previously discussed in Chapter 3. You will learn about managing and using the implemented database in Part 3.

Note the dual use of the term *database design*. We speak of database design as a process—the *database design process*—that results in a final product—the *database design*—that is the plan for actually building the database in a DBMS. The overall topic of Part 2 is database design as a process, and the topic of Chapter 5 is the database design as the final plan for the database.

4 Data Modeling and the Entity-Relationship Model

- Learn the basic steps of systems analysis and design
- Learn the basic stages of database development
- Understand the purpose and role of a data model
- Know the principal components of the E-R data model
- Understand how to interpret traditional E-R diagrams
- Understand how to interpret the Information Engineering (IE) model's Crow's Foot E-R diagrams
- Learn to construct E-R diagrams
- Know how to represent 1:1, 1: N, N:M, and binary relationships with the E-R model

- Understand two types of weak entities and know how to use them
- Understand nonidentifying and identifying relationships and know how to use them
- Know how to represent subtype entities with the E-R model
- Know how to represent recursive relationships with the E-R model
- Learn how to create an E-R diagram from source documents

The database development process, as we describe it here, is a subset of the systems development life cycle (SDLC) process used in systems analysis and design. It is important to understand and remember that database development is usually done as a part of an information system or application development process and that the database itself is only one component of the information system or application. Users use the entire information system or application—they do not just use the database by itself!

In this chapter, we will begin by defining information systems, and then look at the role of systems analysis and design in creating those systems. This discussion will include a review of the systems development life cycle (SDLC), and the role of the SDLC in creating information systems. From there, we will discuss specifically how databases are developed, and then focus on the main topics of this chapter: the data model, and how to create data models using the entity-relationship (E-R) diagrams.

SYSTEMS DEVELOPMENT AND ANALYSIS

In business, as in life, we often need to make a **decision**—what action should we take in our current situation? In order to make a decision, we need information upon which to base that decision. Let's define **data** as recorded facts and numbers. Based on this definition, we can now define[1] **information** as:

- Knowledge derived from data.
- Data presented in a meaningful context.
- Data processed by summing, ordering, averaging, grouping, comparing, or other similar operations.

Thus, before making a decision, we need to gather data and extract whatever information we can from that data.

What is an Information System?

If we define a **system** as a set of components that interact to achieve some purpose or goal, then an **information system** is a system that has the goal of producing information. While information systems do not necessarily have to use computers, our discussion will include computers (after all, this is a book about database systems that run on computers!). We can picture a **computer-based information system**, which we will hereinafter refer to as simply an *information system*, as having five components: computer hardware, software, data, procedures, and people. These components are illustrated in Figure 4-1.

Information systems must be *developed and used* to help businesses reach their goals and objectives, and their function is to support an organization's competitive strategy and help create a competitive advantage.

What is a Business Process?

A **business process** is a set of **activities** that transform **inputs** into **outputs**, as shown in Figure 4-2. For example, consider a simplified manufacturing process for a wheelbarrow. The parts needed to build the wheelbarrows (the *inputs* or **raw materials**) are put together (the assembly *activities*) to create the complete wheelbarrows (the *outputs* or **finished goods**). The input parts have been previously purchased and are stored in a **raw materials inventory**. These are the parts that are put into the manufacturing process, and after the wheelbarrows are built, they are stored in a **finished goods inventory**. Thus, the wheelbarrow manufacturing process can be illustrated as shown in Figure 4-3.

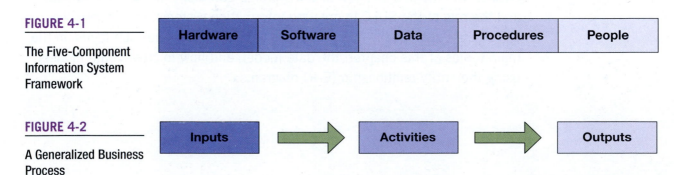

FIGURE 4-1

The Five-Component Information System Framework

| Hardware | Software | Data | Procedures | People |

FIGURE 4-2

A Generalized Business Process

Inputs → Activities → Outputs

---

[1]These definitions are from David M. Kroenke and Randall J Boyles's books: *Using MIS* (10th ed.) (Upper Saddle River, NJ: Pearson, 2018) and *Experiencing MIS* (8th ed.) (Upper Saddle River, NJ: Pearson, 2019). See these books for a full discussion of these definitions, as well as a discussion of a fourth definition, "a difference that makes a difference."

FIGURE 4-3

The Manufacturing Process

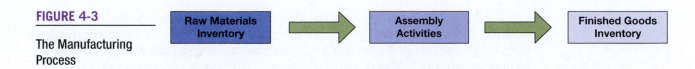

How Do Information Systems Support Business Processes?

The manufacturing process shown in Figure 4-3 does not necessarily include an information system—it may represent only the basic physical system of individual parts being put together by workers into wheelbarrows. However, we can introduce an information system to support this process by adding a computer application to track the raw materials inventory and finished goods inventory. As shown in Figure 4-4, the Inventory Control Application:

- Updates the raw materials inventory by subtracting the parts used in the assembly activities.
- Updates the finished goods inventory by adding each new wheelbarrow as it is completed.

Figure 4-4 illustrates that information systems exist to support business processes—they are *not* the business processes themselves.

A business process can be generalized as a conceptual **process** chain of **input →
process → output**. Information systems include such processes. For example, the inventory control application shown in Figure 4-4 will include these steps as:

- **Input data:** Using a computer on-screen form, a user will input data into the system, such as how many parts have been taken out of the raw materials inventory to build a wheelbarrow.
- **Process:** Another user may query the raw materials database to determine how many of each part remain in the raw materials inventory.
- **Output:** The answer to the query will be presented to the requesting user as a report detailing the current status of the parts in the raw materials inventory.

FIGURE 4-4

The Manufacturing Process with Supporting Information System

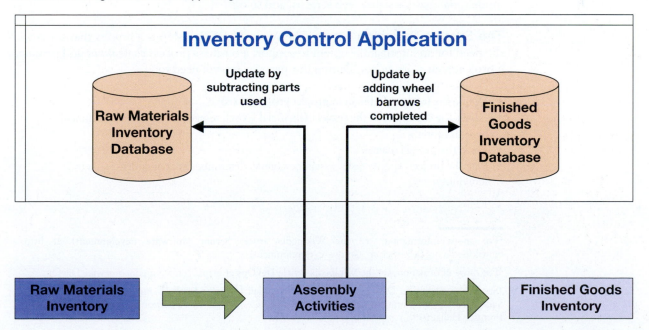

The output of this application may then become the input to another process. For example, if the number of wheelbarrow wheels in the raw materials inventory is determined to be too low on the basis of the report, this may start a parts order process to replenish the raw materials inventory of wheels.

Because the purpose of an information system is to support a business process, we have to understand the business process before we can design the information system. To do this, we study the process and document it using **business process modeling**. After documenting the process, we will generally understand something about what sort of information system is needed to support the process, and we can then use systems analysis and design methodology to create and maintain the needed information system.

What Is Systems Analysis and Design?

Systems analysis and design is the process of creating and maintaining information systems. The classic methodology used in systems analysis and design to develop information systems is called the **systems development life cycle (SDLC)**. While there are newer methodologies for creating information systems (including such methods as Scrum[2] and DevOps[3]), examining the SDLC provides a very clear picture of how systems analysis and design should work and what it should accomplish.

What Are the Steps in the SDLC?

There are different interpretations or conceptualizations of the SDLC, each of which uses a different number of steps. We will use the same set of five steps used by Kroenke:[4]

1. System definition
2. Requirements analysis
3. Component design
4. Implementation
5. System maintenance

These steps, together with the business process that determines the need for the information system to be created and the users of that system, are shown in Figure 4-5. Each step should result in one or more **deliverables**, such as documents, designs, prototypes, data models, database designs, Web screens, and so on.

The System Definition Step   The **system definition** step is a *process* that starts with the need for an information system to support a business process as its *input* and produces a **project plan** as its *output*. During this process, we will need to:

- Define the information system project goals and scope.
- Assess the feasibility of the project (financial [cost], temporal [schedule], technical, organizational).
- Form the project team.
- Plan the project (specify tasks, assign personnel, determine task dependencies, set schedules).

---

[2]For more information, see the Wikipedia article **Scrum (software development)** at https://en.wikipedia.org/wiki/Scrum_(software_development).

[3]For more information, see the Wikipedia article **DevOps** at https://en.wikipedia.org/wiki/DevOps.

[4]See the discussion in David M. Kroenke and Randall J. Boyle's books *Using MIS* (10th edition) (Upper Saddle River, NJ: Prentice Hall, 2018) and *Experiencing MIS* (8th edition) (Upper Saddle River, NJ: Prentice Hall, 2019).

FIGURE 4-5

The SDLC in Use

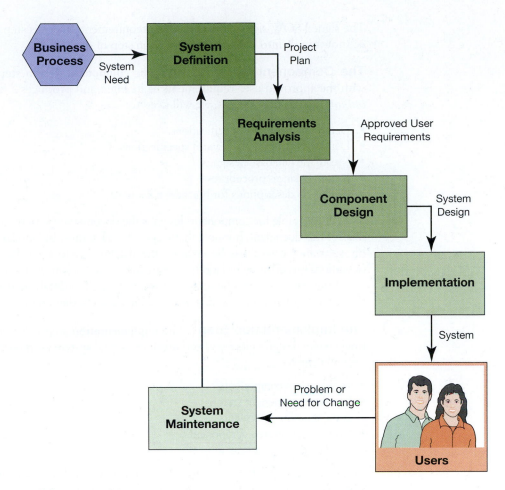

A deliverable for system definition is a project plan, which should include a **work-breakdown schedule (WBS)**.

The Requirements Analysis Step   The **requirements analysis** step is a *process* that starts with the project plan as its *input* and produces a set of **approved user requirements** as its *output*. During this process, we will need to:

- Conduct user interviews.
- Evaluate existing systems.
- Determine needed new forms/reports/queries.
- Identify needed new application features and functions.
- Consider security.
- Create the data model.
- Consider the five components of an information system—hardware, software, data, procedures, and people.

One important deliverable of this step is a **data model**. Data modeling is the subject of this chapter, and will be discussed in detail later in the chapter.

Another deliverable for requirements analysis is an approved set of user requirements as a **user requirements document (URD)**. The purpose of a URD is to formalize the project team's understanding of the users' requirements so that the users can review the document. Note that the data model for the database is presented as part of the URD. This allows the data model to be reviewed and approved by the users. Based on the review, the URD can be negotiated and revised until the document is approved by the users. At this point, the project team has an approved set of project requirements with which to work.

The deliverables may include an approved **statement of work (SOW)**. As with the URD, this document may be negotiated and revised until a final, signed SOW is produced.

The signed SOW signals the end of the requirements analysis step of the SDLC. The project now moves into the component design step of the SDLC.

The Component Design Step   The **component design** step is a *process* that starts with the approved user requirements as its *input* and produces a final **system design** as its *output*. During this process, we will need to:

- Determine hardware specifications.
- Determine program (software) specifications.
- Create the database design.
- Design business procedures.
- Create job descriptions for business personnel.

A deliverable for component design is the documented system design. There is no set format for this document, but note that it specifies what must be purchased (hardware and possibly software), what must be created (the database), and how the business must adjust its operations (procedures and job responsibilities) to actually implement that information system.

Note that one deliverable in the system design is a **database design**. Database design is the subject of Chapter 5, and is discussed in detail in that chapter.

The Implementation Step   The **implementation** step is a *process* that starts with the final system design as its *input* and produces a final **system** as its *output*. During this process, we will need to:

- Build system components.
- Conduct component tests.
- Integrate the components.
- Conduct integrated component tests.
- Convert to the new system.

The deliverable for the implementation step is the installed and functioning **information system** that was needed by the business process. In this step, we implement the elements of the final system design, as shown in Figure 4-6.

Note that one deliverable in implementation is a functioning **database**. Creating database structures and populating them with data is the subject of Chapter 3, and is discussed in detail in that chapter.

FIGURE 4-6

The SDLC Design and Implementation Steps for the Five Information System Components

	Hardware	Software	Data	Procedures	People
Component Design Step	Determine hardware specificiations	Select off-the-shelf software if available. Design custom programs if necessary	Design database and related application components	Design user and operational procedures	Develop job descriptions
Implementation Step	Obtain, install, and test hardware	License and install off-the-shelf software. Create custom programs if necessary. Test programs	Create database. Populate with data. Test database and data.	Document procedures. Create training programs. Review and test procedures	Train personnel. Hire new personnel if necessary.
Integrated Testing and Startup					

The System Maintenance Step   The **system maintenance** step is a *process* that starts with the implemented system as its *input* and produces an **updated system** or a **request for system modification** using the SDLC as its *output*. During this process, we will need to:

- Update the system with patches, service packs, and new software releases.
- Record and prioritize requests for system changes or enhancements.

The deliverables for system maintenance include an updated system and the start of a new SDLC cycle to enhance the information system. These are both common and typical events for any information system.

What are the Steps in the Database Development Process?

For our purposes, the **database development process** is a subset of the SDLC that consists of three major stages: requirements analysis, component design, and implementation. During the **requirements analysis stage** (also referred to as the requirements stage), system users are interviewed and sample forms, reports, queries, and descriptions of update activities are obtained. These system requirements are used to create a data model as part of the requirements analysis stage. A data model is a representation of the content, relationships, and constraints on the data needed to support the system requirements. Often, prototypes, or working demonstrations of selected portions of the future system, are created during the requirements phase. Such prototypes are used to obtain feedback from the system users.

During the **component design stage** (also referred to as the **system design stage** and the **design stage**), the data model is transformed into a database design. Such a design for a relational database consists of tables, relationships, and constraints. The design includes the table names and the names of all table columns. The design also includes the data types and properties of the columns as well as a description of primary and foreign keys. Data constraints consist of limits on data values (for example, part numbers are seven-digit numbers starting with the number 3), referential integrity constraints, and business rules. An example of a business rule for a manufacturing company is that every purchased part will have a quotation from at least two suppliers.

The last stage of database development is the **implementation stage**. During this stage, the database is constructed in the DBMS and populated with data; queries, forms, and reports are created; application programs are written; and all these are tested. Finally, during this stage users are trained, documentation is written, and the new system is put into use.

In this chapter, we will briefly discuss the requirements analysis stage and then focus on the data modeling component of requirements analysis. In Chapter 5, we will see how a data model is converted to a database design in the component design stage. The database itself would be built and populated with data in a DBMS during the implementation step of the SDLC, and this would be done using SQL as we previously described in Chapter 3.

REQUIREMENTS ANALYSIS

The first step in the database development process is user requirements analysis. Sources of user requirements are listed in Figure 4-7. The general practice is to identify the users of the new information system and to interview them. During the interviews, examples of existing forms, reports, queries, application programs and Web sites are obtained. In addition, the users are asked about the need for changes to any of these and also about the need for new forms, reports, queries, application programs, and Web sites.

Use cases are descriptions of the ways users will employ the features and functions of the new information system. A use case consists of a description of the roles users will play when utilizing the new system, together with descriptions of these activities' scenarios. Inputs provided to the system and outputs generated by the system are defined. Sometimes, dozens of such use cases are necessary. Use cases provide sources of requirements and also can be used to validate the data model, the database design, and the actual database implementation.

FIGURE 4-7

Sources of
Requirements for a
Database Application

> User interviews
> Forms
> Reports
> Queries
> Application programs
> Web sites
> Use cases
> Business rules

In addition to these requirements, you need to document characteristics of data items. For each data item in a form, report, query, application program, or Web site the team needs to determine its data type, properties, and limits on values.

Finally, during the process of establishing requirements, system developers need to document business rules that constrain actions on database activity. Generally, such rules arise from business policy and practice. For example, the following business rules could pertain to an academic database:

- Students must declare a major before enrolling in any class.
- Graduate classes can be taken by juniors or seniors with a grade point average of 3.70 or greater.
- No adviser may have more than 25 advisees.
- Students may declare one or two majors but no more.

THE ENTITY-RELATIONSHIP DATA MODEL

The system requirements described in the preceding section, although necessary and important as a first step, are not sufficient for designing a database. To be useful as the basis for a database design, these requirements must be transformed into a *data model*. When you write application programs, program logic must first be documented in flowcharts or object diagrams—when you create a database, data requirements must first be documented in a data model.

A number of different techniques can be used to create data models. By far the most popular is the **entity-relationship model**, first published by Peter Chen[5] in 1976. Chen's basic model has since been extended to create the **extended entity-relationship (E-R) model**. Today, when we say *E-R model*, we mean the extended E-R model, and we use it in this text.

Books on systems analysis and design often identify three design stages:

- Conceptual design (conceptual schema)
- Logical design (logical schema)
- Physical design (physical schema)

The *data model* we are discussing is equivalent to the *conceptual design* as defined in these books.

---

[5]Peter P. Chen, "The Entity-Relationship Model-Toward a Unified View of Data," *ACM Transactions on Database Systems* (March 1976): 9–36. For information on Peter Chen, see https://en.wikipedia.org/wiki/Peter_Chen, and for a copy of the article, see extras.springer.com/2002/978-3-642-59413-7/3/rom/pdf/Chen_hist.pdf.

Several versions of the E-R model are in use today. We begin with the traditional E-R model. Later in the chapter, after the basic principles of E-R models have been examined, we will look at and use another version of the E-R model.

The most important elements of the E-R model are entities, attributes, identifiers, and relationships. We now consider each of these in turn.

Entities

An **entity** is something that users want to track. Examples of entities are CUSTOMER John Doe, PURCHASE 12345, PRODUCT A4200, SALES_ORDER 1000, SALESPERSON John Smith, and SHIPMENT 123400. Entities of a given type are grouped into an **entity class**. Thus, the EMPLOYEE entity class is the collection of all EMPLOYEE entities. In this text, entity classes are shown in capital letters.

An **entity instance** of an entity class is the occurrence of a particular entity, such as CUSTOMER 12345. Understanding the differences between an entity class and an entity instance is important. An entity class is a collection of entities and provides the structure of the entities in that class. There are usually many instances of an entity in an entity class. For example, the class CUSTOMER has many instances—one for each customer represented in the database. The ITEM entity class and two of its instances are shown in Figure 4-8.

When developing a data model, the developers analyze the forms, reports, queries, application programs, Web pages, and other system requirements. Entities are usually the subject of one or more forms, reports, or Web pages, or they are a major section in one or more forms, reports, or Web pages. For example, a form named Product Data Entry Form indicates the likelihood of an entity class called PRODUCT. Similarly, a report named Customer Purchase Summary indicates that most likely the business has CUSTOMER and PURCHASE entities.

Attributes

Entities have **attributes**, which describe the entity's characteristics. Examples of attributes include EmployeeName, DateOfHire, and JobSkillCode. In this text, attributes are printed in a combination of uppercase and lowercase letters. The E-R model assumes that all instances of a given entity class have the same attributes. For example, in Figure 4-8 the ITEM entity has the attributes ItemNumber, Description, Cost, ListPrice, and QuantityOnHand.

FIGURE 4-8

The ITEM Entity and
Two Entity Instances

ITEM
ItemNumber
Description
Cost
ListPrice
QuantityOnHand

Entity Class

1100	2000
100 amp panel	Door handle set
$127.50	$39.38
$170.00	$52.50
14	0

Two Entity Instances

An attribute has a data type (character, numeric, date, currency, and the like) and properties that are determined from the requirements. Properties specify whether the attribute is required, whether it has a default value, whether its value has limits, and any other constraint.

Identifiers

Entity instances have **identifiers**, which are attributes that name, or identify, entity instances. For example, the ITEM entity in Figure 4-8 uses ItemNumber as an identifier. Similarly, EMPLOYEE instances could be identified by SocialSecurityNumber, by EmployeeNumber, or by EmployeeName. EMPLOYEE instances are not likely to be identified by attributes such as Salary or DateOfHire because these attributes normally are not used in a naming role as they are typically not unique. CUSTOMER instances could be identified by CustomerNumber or CustomerName, and SALES_ORDER instances could be identified by OrderNumber.

The identifier of an entity instance consists of one or more of the entity's attributes. Identifiers that consist of two or more attributes are called **composite identifiers**. Examples are (AreaCode, LocalNumber), (ProjectName, TaskName), and (FirstName, LastName, PhoneExtension).

An identifier may be either unique or nonunique. The value of a **unique identifier** identifies one, and only one, entity instance. In contrast, the value of a **nonunique identifier** identifies a set of instances. EmployeeNumber is normally a unique identifier, but EmployeeName is most likely a nonunique identifier (for example, more than one John Smith might be employed by the company). An entity class must have at least one unique identifier.

As shown in Figure 4-9, entities can be portrayed at three levels of detail in a data model. Sometimes an entity and all of its attributes are displayed. In such cases, the unique identifier of the entity is shown at the top of the entity and a horizontal line is drawn after the identifier, as shown in Figure 4-9(a). In a large data model, so much detail can make the data model diagrams unwieldy. In those cases, the entity diagram is abbreviated by showing just the identifier, as in Figure 4-9(b), or by showing just the name of the entity in a rectangle, as shown in Figure 4-9(c).

BTW

As you can tell from these definitions, identifiers are similar to keys in the relational model but with two important differences. First, an identifier is a logical concept: It is one or more attributes that users think of as indicating an occurrence (instance) of the entity. Such identifiers might or might not be represented as keys in the database design. Second, primary and candidate keys must be unique, whereas identifiers might or might not be unique.

FIGURE 4-9

Levels of Entity Attribute Display

ITEM

ItemNumber
Description
Cost
ListPrice
QuantityOnHand

(a) Entity with All Attributes

ITEM

ItemNumber

(b) Entity with Identifier Attribute Only

(c) Entity with No Attributes

FIGURE 4-10

Example Relationships

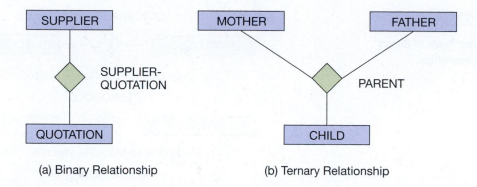

(a) Binary Relationship   (b) Ternary Relationship

Relationships

Entities can be associated with one another in **relationships**. The E-R model contains relationship classes and relationship instances. **Relationship classes** are associations among entity classes, and **relationship instances** are associations among entity instances. In the original specification of the E-R model, relationships could have attributes. In modern practice, that feature is not used, and only entities have attributes.

A relationship class can involve many entity classes. The number of entity classes in the relationship is known as the **degree** of the relationship. In Figure 4-10(a), the SUPPLIER-QUOTATION relationship is of degree two because it involves two entity classes: SUPPLIER and QUOTATION. The PARENT relationship in Figure 4-10(b) is of degree three because it involves three entity classes: MOTHER, FATHER, and CHILD. Relationships of degree two, which are the most common, are called **binary relationships**. Similarly, relationships of degree three are called **ternary relationships**.

> ### BTW
>
> You may be wondering what the difference is between an *entity* and a *table*. They may seem like different terms for the same thing. *The principal difference between an entity and a table is that you can express a relationship between entities without using foreign keys.* In the E-R model, you can specify a relationship just by drawing a line connecting two entities. Because you are doing *conceptual database design* and not logical or physical database design, you need not worry about primary and foreign keys, referential integrity constraints, and the like.
>
> This characteristic makes entities easier to work with than tables, especially early in a project when entities and relationships are fluid and uncertain. You can show relationships between entities before you even know what the identifiers are. For example, you can say that a DEPARTMENT relates to many EMPLOYEEs before you know any of the attributes of either EMPLOYEE or DEPARTMENT. This characteristic enables you to work from the general to the specific. When you are creating a data model, you first identify the entities, then you think about the relationships, and finally you determine the attributes.

Three Types of Binary Relationships   Figure 4-11 shows the three types of binary relationships:

- The one-to-one (1:1) relationship
- The one-to-many (1:N) relationship
- The many-to-many (N:M) relationship

FIGURE 4-11

Three Types of Binary
Relationships

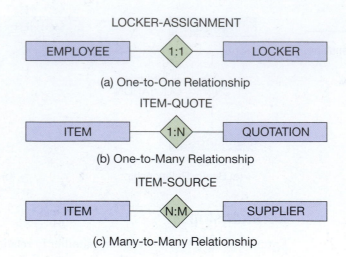

In a 1:1 relationship, a single entity instance of one type is related to a single entity instance of another type. In Figure 4-11(a), the LOCKER-ASSIGNMENT relationship associates a single EMPLOYEE with a single LOCKER. According to this diagram, no employee has more than one locker assigned, and no locker is assigned to more than one employee.

Figure 4-11(b) shows a 1:N binary relationship. In this relationship, which is called the ITEM-QUOTE relationship, a single instance of ITEM relates to many instances of QUOTATION. According to this sketch, an item has many quotations, but a quotation has only one item.

Think of the diamond as representing the relationship. The position of the 1 is nearest the line connecting ITEM, and the position of the N is nearest the line connecting QUOTATION. Thus, one ITEM can have many QUOTATIONS. Notice that if the 1 and the N were reversed and the relationship were written N:1, then one QUOTATION would have many ITEMS.

When discussing 1:N relationships, the terms *parent* and *child* are sometimes used. The **parent entity** is the entity on the one side of the relationship and the **child entity** is the entity on the many side of the relationship. Thus, in the 1:N relationship between ITEM and QUOTATION, ITEM is the parent and QUOTATION is the child.

Figure 4-11(c) shows an N:M binary relationship. This relationship is named ITEM-SOURCE, and it relates instances of ITEM to instances of SUPPLIER. In this case, an item can be supplied by many suppliers, and a supplier can supply many items.

Maximum Cardinality   The three types of binary relationships are named and classified by their **cardinality**, which is a word that means *count*. In each of the relationships in Figure 4-11, the numbers inside the relationship diamond show the *maximum* number of entity instances that can occur on each side of the relationship. These numbers are called the relationship's **maximum cardinality**, which is the maximum number of entity instances that can participate in a relationship instance.

The ITEM-QUOTE relationship in Figure 4-11(b), for example, is said to have a maximum cardinality of 1:N. However, the cardinalities are not restricted to the values shown here. It is possible, for example, for the maximum cardinality to be other than 1 and N. The relationship between BASKETBALL-TEAM and PLAYER, for example, could be 1:5, indicating that a basketball team has at most five players.

Minimum Cardinality   Relationships also have a **minimum cardinality**, which is the minimum number of entity instances that *must* participate in a relationship instance. Minimum cardinality can be shown in several different ways. One way, illustrated in Figure 4-12, is to place a *hash mark* across the relationship line to indicate that every instance of the other

FIGURE 4-12

A Relationship with
Minimum Cardinalities

ITEM-SOURCE

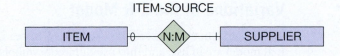

entity in the relationship must be related to at least one of these entities, and to place an *oval* across the relationship line to indicate that an instance of the other entity in the relationship need not be related to any of these entities.

Accordingly, Figure 4-12 shows that an ITEM must have a relationship with at least one SUPPLIER but that a SUPPLIER is not required to have a relationship with an ITEM. The complete relationship restrictions are that an ITEM has a minimum cardinality of zero and a maximum cardinality of many—a SUPPLIER can supply *many* items, but does *not* have to supply any. A SUPPLIER has a minimum cardinality of one and a maximum cardinality of many—an ITEM may be available from *many* suppliers, and *must* be associated with at least one supplier.

If the minimum cardinality is zero, the entity's participation in the relationship is **optional**. If the minimum cardinality is one, the entity's participation in the relationship is **mandatory**. It is mandatory for ITEM to have a SUPPLIER, but optional for a SUPPLIER to be the source of an ITEM.

BTW

Interpreting minimum cardinalities in diagrams such as Figure 4-12 is often one of the most difficult parts of E-R models. Becoming confused about which entity is optional and which is required (mandatory) is very easy to do. An easy way to clarify this situation is to imagine that you are standing in the diamond, on the relationship line, and looking toward one of the entities. If you see an oval in that direction, then that entity is optional (has a minimum cardinality of zero). If you see a hash mark, then that entity is required (has a minimum cardinality of one). Thus, in Figure 4-12, if you stand on the diamond and look toward SUPPLIER, you see a hash mark. This means that SUPPLIER is required in the relationship (every ITEM *must* have a SUPPLIER).

ENTITY-RELATIONSHIP DIAGRAMS

The sketches in Figure 4-11 and Figure 4-12 are called **entity-relationship (E-R) diagrams**. Such diagrams are standardized but only loosely. According to this standard, entity classes are shown using rectangles, relationships are shown using diamonds, the maximum cardinality of the relationship is shown inside the diamond, and the minimum cardinality is shown by the oval or hash marks next to the entity. The name of the entity is shown inside the rectangle, and the name of the relationship is shown near the diamond. You will see examples of such E-R diagrams, and it is important for you to be able to interpret them.

BTW

Relationships like those in Figures 4-11 and 4-12 are sometimes called **HAS-A relationships**. This term is used because each entity instance has a relationship to a second entity instance. An employee has a badge, and a badge has an employee. If the maximum cardinality is greater than one, then each entity has a set of other entities. An employee has a set of skills, for example, and a skill has a set of employees who have that skill.

Variations of the E-R Model

This original notation is seldom used today. Instead, a number of different versions of the E-R model are in use, and they use different symbols.

At least three different versions of the E-R model are currently in use. One of them, called **Information Engineering (IE)**, was developed by James Martin in 1990. This model uses "crow's feet" to show the many side of a relationship, and it is sometimes called the **IE Crow's Foot model**. It is easy to understand, and we will use it in this text.

Other significant variations include the IDEF1X version and the Unified Modeling Language (UML) version of the E-R model.[6] In 1993, the National Institute of Standards and Technology announced that the **Integrated Definition 1, Extended (IDEF1X)**[7] version of the E-R model would be a national standard. This standard incorporates the basic ideas of the E-R model but uses different graphical symbols that, unfortunately, make it difficult to understand and use. Still, it is a national standard used in government work, and therefore it may be important to you. To add further complication, an object-oriented development methodology called the **Unified Modeling Language (UML)** adopted the E-R model but introduced its own symbols while putting an object-oriented programming spin on it. UML has begun to be widely used among object-oriented programming (OOP) practitioners, and you may encounter UML notation in systems development courses.

In addition to differences due to different versions of the E-R model, differences also arise due to software products. For example, two products that both implement the IE Crow's Foot model may do so in different ways. Thus, when creating a data model diagram, you need to know not just the version of the E-R model you are using but also the idiosyncrasies of the data modeling product you use.

The IE Crow's Foot E-R Model

Figure 4-13 shows the same N:M optional-to-mandatory relationship in two different models. Figure 4-13(a) shows the original E-R model version. Figure 4-13(b) shows the IE Crow's Foot model using common IE Crow's Foot symbols. Notice that the line representing the relationship is drawn as a dashed line. (The reason for this is explained later in this chapter.) Notice the **crow's foot symbol** used to show the many side of the relationship. The IE Crow's Foot model uses the notation shown in Figure 4-14 to indicate relationship cardinality.

FIGURE 4-13

Two Versions of a 1:N O-M Relationship

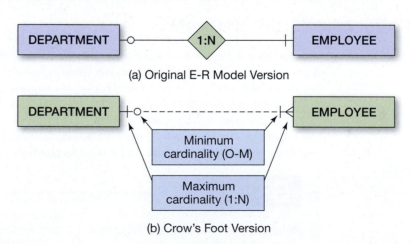

(a) Original E-R Model Version

(b) Crow's Foot Version

---

[6]For more information on these models, see David M. Kroenke, David J. Auer, Scott L. Vandenberg, and Robert C. Yoder, *Database Processing: Fundamentals, Design, and Implementation*, 15th ed. (Upper Saddle River, NJ: Pearson, 2019), Appendix C (E-R Diagrams and the IDEF1X and UML Standards).

[7]National Institute of Standards and Technology, *Integrated Definition for Information Modeling (IDEF1X)*. Federal Information Processing Standards Publication 184, 1993.

FIGURE 4-14

Crow's Foot Notation

Symbol	Meaning	Numeric Meaning
———++—	Mandatory—One	Exactly one
———+⋖	Mandatory—Many	One or more
———○+	Optional—One	Zero or one
———○⋖	Optional—Many	Zero or more

In the IE Crow's Foot model, the symbol closest to the entity shows the maximum cardinality, and the other symbol shows the minimum cardinality. A hash mark indicates one (for maximum cardinality) or mandatory (for minimum cardinality), a circle indicates optional (for minimum cardinality), and the crow's foot indicates many (for maximum cardinality). Thus, the diagram in Figure 4-13(b) shows that a DEPARTMENT has one or more EMPLOYEEs (the symbol shows many and mandatory), and an EMPLOYEE belongs to zero or one DEPARTMENT (the symbol shows one and optional).

A 1:1 relationship would be drawn in a similar manner in IE Crow's Foot notation, but the ends of the line connecting the entities would both be similar to the connection shown for the one side of the 1:N relationship in Figure 4-13(b).

Figure 4-15 shows the same N:M optional-to-mandatory relationship in two different models. According to the original E-R model diagram shown in Figure 4-15(a), an EMPLOYEE must have a SKILL and may have several. At the same time, although a particular SKILL may or may not be held by any EMPLOYEE, a SKILL may also be held by several EMPLOYEES. The IE Crow's Foot version in Figure 4-15(b) shows the N:M cardinalities using the notation in Figure 4-14. The crow's foot symbols again indicate the maximum cardinalities for the relationship.

Throughout the rest of this text, we use the IE Crow's Foot model for E-R diagrams. There is no completely standard set of symbols for the IE Crow's Foot notation, but we use the symbols and notation described in this chapter. You can obtain various modeling products that will produce IE Crow's Foot models, and they are easily understood and related to the original E-R model. However, those products may use the oval, hash mark, crow's foot, and other symbols in slightly different ways.

FIGURE 4-15

Two Versions of a N:M
O-M Relationship

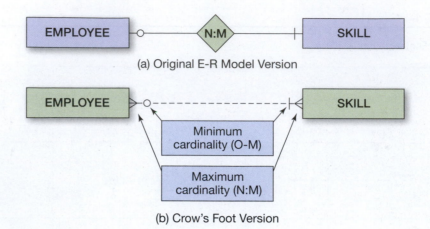

(a) Original E-R Model Version

(b) Crow's Foot Version

BTW

You can try a number of modeling products, each with its own idiosyncrasies. First, ERwin, Inc. produces erwin Data Modeler, a commercial data modeling product (available in several editions) that handles both data modeling and database design tasks. You can use ERwin to produce either IE Crow's Foot or IDEF1X diagrams. Second, you can also try ER-Assistant, which is free and downloadable from Software Informer. Third, Microsoft Visio Professional 2019 is also a possibility. A trial version is available from the Microsoft Web site. For more information on working with Microsoft Visio 2019, see this chapter's section of "Working with Microsoft Access," which includes a discussion of creating data models in Microsoft Visio 2019. Finally, Oracle is continuing development of the MySQL Workbench, which is both the GUI utility for the MySQL database and a database design tool. The MySQL Workbench is downloadable at the MySQL developer Web site (http://dev.mysql.com). (*Note:* If you are using a Windows operating system, you should install the MySQL Workbench using the MySQL Installer for Windows available at the MySQL developer Web site at http://dev.mysql.com). Although MySQL Workbench is better for database designs than data models, it is a very useful tool, and the database designs it produces can be used with any DBMS, not just MySQL. For more information on working with the MySQL Workbench, see online Extension A, "Working with MySQL." These are just a few of the many data modeling products available.

Weak Entities

The E-R model defines a special type of entity called a weak entity. A **weak entity** is an entity that cannot exist in a database unless another type of entity also exists in that database. An entity that is *not* weak is called a **strong entity**.

ID-Dependent Entities

The E-R model includes a special type of weak entity called an **ID-dependent entity**. With this type of entity, the identifier of the entity includes the identifier of another entity. Consider the entities BUILDING and APARTMENT, shown in Figure 4-16(a).

FIGURE 4-16

Example ID-Dependent Entities

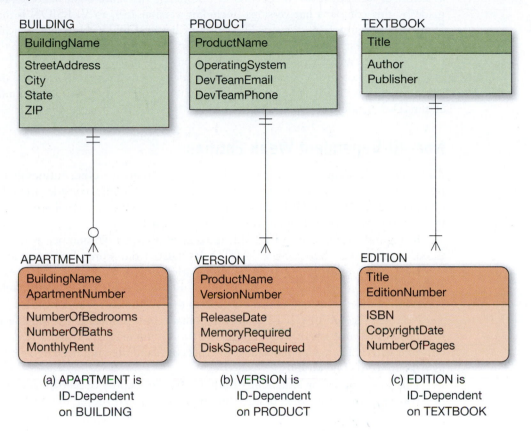

(a) APARTMENT is
ID-Dependent
on BUILDING

(b) VERSION is
ID-Dependent
on PRODUCT

(c) EDITION is
ID-Dependent
on TEXTBOOK

As you would expect, the identifier of BUILDING is a single attribute, in this case BuildingName. The identifier of APARTMENT, however, is *not* the single attribute ApartmentNumber but rather the composite identifier (BuildingName, ApartmentNumber). This happens because logically and physically an APARTMENT simply cannot exist unless a BUILDING exists for that APARTMENT to be part of. Whenever this type of situation occurs, an ID-dependent entity exists. In this case, APARTMENT is ID-dependent on BUILDING. The identifier of an ID-dependent entity is always a composite that includes the identifier of the entity that the ID-dependent entity depends on for its existence.

As shown in Figure 4-16, in our E-R models we use an entity with rounded corners to represent the ID-dependent entity. We also use a solid line to represent the relationship between the ID-dependent entity and its parent. This type of a relationship is called an **identifying relationship**. A relationship drawn with a dashed line (refer to Figure 4-13) is used between strong entities (or between a weak entity and a strong entity that it does not depend on) and is called a **nonidentifying relationship** because the relationship is not used to identify an ID-dependent entity.

ID-dependent entities are common. Another example is shown in Figure 4-16(b), where the entity VERSION is ID-dependent on the entity PRODUCT. Here PRODUCT is a software product, and VERSION is a release of that software product. The identifier of PRODUCT is ProductName, and the identifier of VERSION is (ProductName, VersionNumber). A third example is shown in Figure 4-16(c), where EDITION is ID-dependent on TEXTBOOK. The identifier of TEXTBOOK is Title, and the identifier of EDITION is (Title, EditionNumber). In each of these cases, the ID-dependent entity cannot exist unless the parent (the entity on which it depends) also exists. Thus, the minimum cardinality from the ID-dependent entity to the parent is always one.

However, whether the parent is required to have an ID-dependent entity depends on business requirements. In Figure 4-16(a), the database can contain any BUILDING, such as a store or warehouse, so APARTMENT is optional. In Figure 4-16(b), every PRODUCT made by this company has versions (including version 1.0), so VERSION is mandatory. Similarly, in Figure 4-16(c), every TEXTBOOK has an EDITION number (including the first edition), which makes EDITION mandatory. Those restrictions arise from the nature of each business and its applications and not from any logical requirement.

Finally, notice that you cannot add an ID-dependent entity instance until the parent entity instance is created, and when you delete the parent entity instance you must delete all the ID-dependent entity instances as well.

Non–ID-Dependent Weak Entities

All ID-dependent entities are weak entities. However, there are other entities that are weak but not ID-dependent. To understand this kind of weak entity, consider the relationship between the AUTO_MODEL and VEHICLE entity classes in the database of a car manufacturer, such as Ford or Honda, as shown in Figure 4-17.

In Figure 4-17(a), each VEHICLE is assigned a sequential number as it is manufactured. So, for the "Super SUV" AUTO_MODEL from Ford, for example, the first VEHICLE manufactured gets a ManufacturingSeqNumber of 1, the next gets a ManufacturingSeqNumber of 2, and so on. This is clearly an ID-dependent relationship because ManufacturingSeqNumber is based on the Manufacturer and Model.

Now let us assign VEHICLE an identifier that is independent of the Manufacturer and Model. We will use a VIN (vehicle identification number), as shown in Figure 4-17(b). Now the VEHICLE has a unique identifier of its own and does not need to be identified by its relation to AUTO_MODEL.

This is an interesting situation. VEHICLE has an identity of its own and therefore is not ID-dependent (note the dashed line in Figure 4-17(b)), yet the VEHICLE is an

FIGURE 4-17

Weak Entity Examples

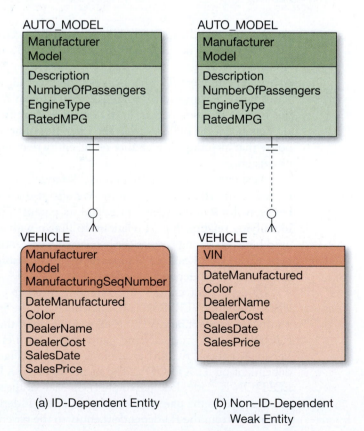

(a) ID-Dependent Entity   (b) Non–ID-Dependent
                                       Weak Entity

AUTO_MODEL, and if that particular AUTO_MODEL did not exist, the VEHICLE itself would never have existed. Therefore, VEHICLE is now a *weak but non–ID-dependent entity.* In our E-R diagrams, while we will continue to use rounded corners to indicate ID-dependent weak entities, we will now use square corners on non-ID-independent weak entities. Note that both types of weak entities are shown as tan colored to flag that, whether ID-dependent or not, they are weak entities.

Consider *your* car—let us say it is a Ford Mustang just for the sake of this discussion. Your individual Mustang is a VEHICLE, and it exists as a physical object and is identified by the VIN that is required for each licensed automobile. It is *not* ID-dependent on AUTO_MODEL, which in this case is Ford Mustang, for its identity. However, if the Ford Mustang had never been created as an AUTO_MODEL—a logical concept that was first designed on paper—your car would never have been built because *no* Ford Mustangs would ever have been built! Therefore, your physical individual VEHICLE would not exist without a logical AUTO_MODEL of Ford Mustang, and in a data model (which *is* what we're talking about) a VEHICLE cannot exist without a related AUTO_MODEL. This makes VEHICLE a weak but non–ID-dependent entity.

Unfortunately, an ambiguity is hidden in the definition of *weak entity*, and this ambiguity is interpreted differently by different database designers (as well as different textbook authors). The ambiguity is that, in a strict sense, if a weak entity is defined as any entity whose presence in the database depends on another entity, then any entity that participates in a relationship having a minimum cardinality of one to a second entity is a weak entity. Thus, in an academic database, if a STUDENT must have an ADVISER, then STUDENT is a weak entity because a STUDENT entity cannot be stored without an ADVISER.

This interpretation seems too broad to some people. A STUDENT is not physically dependent on an ADVISER (unlike an APARTMENT to a BUILDING), and a STUDENT is not logically dependent on an ADVISER (despite how it might appear to either the student or the adviser). Therefore, STUDENT should be considered a strong entity.

To avoid such situations, some people interpret the definition of weak entity more narrowly. They say that to be a weak entity an entity must logically depend on another entity. According to this definition, APARTMENT is a weak entity, but STUDENT is not. An APARTMENT cannot exist without a BUILDING in which it is located. However, a STUDENT can logically exist without an ADVISER, even if a business rule requires it.

To illustrate this interpretation, consider the examples shown in Figure 4-18. Suppose that a data model includes the relationship between an ORDER and a SALESPERSON shown in Figure 4-18(a). Although you might state that an ORDER must have a SALESPERSON, it does not necessarily require one for its existence. (The ORDER could be a cash sale in which the salesperson is not recorded.) Hence, the minimum cardinality of one arises from a business rule, not from logical necessity. Thus, ORDER requires a SALESPERSON but is not existence-dependent on it. Therefore, ORDER is a strong entity.

Now, consider ASSIGNMENT in Figure 4-18(b), which is ID-dependent on PROJECT, and the identifier of ASSIGNMENT contains the identifier of PROJECT. Here, not only does ASSIGNMENT have a minimum cardinality of one and not only is ASSIGNMENT existence-dependent on PROJECT, but ASSIGNMENT is also ID-dependent on PROJECT because its identifier requires the key of the parent entity. Thus, ASSIGNMENT is a weak entity that is ID-dependent.

Finally, consider the relationship of PATIENT and PRESCRIPTION in Figure 4-18(c). Here a PRESCRIPTION cannot logically exist without a PATIENT. Hence, not only is the minimum cardinality one, but the PRESCRIPTION is also existence-dependent on PATIENT. Thus, PRESCRIPTION is a weak entity, but is not ID-dependent because it has its own unique identifier.

In this text, we define a weak entity as an entity that logically depends on another entity. Hence, not all entities that have a minimum cardinality of one in relation to another entity are weak. Only those that are logically dependent are weak. This definition implies that all ID-dependent entities are weak. In addition, every weak entity has a minimum

FIGURE 4-18

Examples of Required
Entities

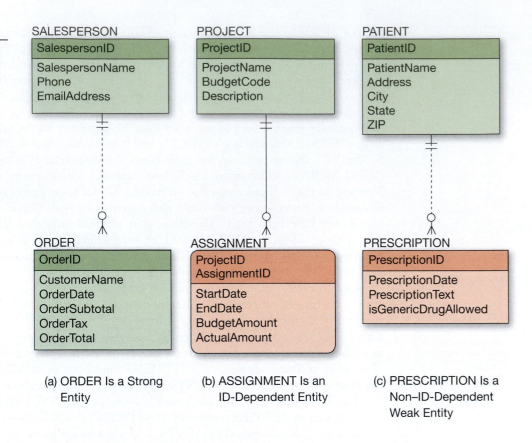

(a) ORDER Is a Strong
Entity

(b) ASSIGNMENT Is an
ID-Dependent Entity

(c) PRESCRIPTION Is a
Non–ID-Dependent
Weak Entity

cardinality of one on the entity on which it depends, but every entity that has a minimum cardinality of one is not necessarily weak.

As illustrated in Figure 4-17 and Figure 4-18, in our E-R models we again use an entity with square corners to represent the non–ID-dependent weak entity, and we also use a dashed line to represent the nonidentifying relationship between the non–ID-dependent entity and its parent.

Associative Entities

Let's take another look at the Wedgewood Pacific (WP) database that we used in our discussion of SQL in Chapter 3. At WP, employees are assigned to projects. If all we are interested in knowing is (1) which employees are assigned to a single project and (2) which projects a single employee has been assigned to, we have a simple N:M relationship between EMPLOYEE and PROJECT. This is illustrated in Figure 4-19(a).

However, WP also wants to record the number of hours each employee works on each project in an attribute named HoursWorked. Where should we put this attribute? If we add it to EMPLOYEE, it will total the number of hours that employee has worked on all assigned projects, not the number of hours worked per project. Similarly, if we add it to PROJECT, it will record the total number of hours worked on that project by all assigned employees. Neither of these solutions will record the data that WP needs.

One way of thinking about this situation is that HoursWorked is an attribute of the assignment relationship between EMPLOYEE and PROJECT. But we can't put an attribute in a relationship (note the original E-R model allowed for this, but the current version of the E-R model does not). So what can we do?

The answer is to create a new entity between EMPLOYEE and PROJECT named ASSIGNMENT to record both (1) the actual assignments of employees to projects and (2) the hours each employee works on each project in the HoursWorked attribute. This type of entity is called an **associative entity** (or **association entity**) and is used whenever a pure

FIGURE 4-19

The Associative Entity

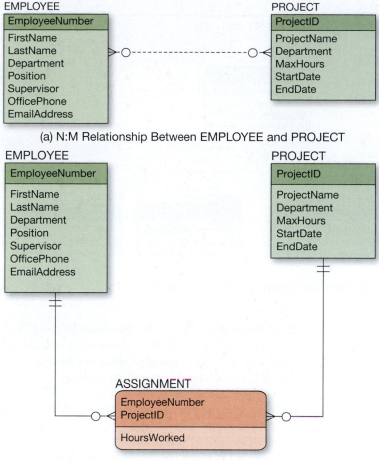

(a) N:M Relationship Between EMPLOYEE and PROJECT

(b) EMPLOYEE and PROJECT 1:N Relationships with the Associative Entity ASSIGNMENT

N:M relationship cannot properly hold attributes that are describing aspects of the relationship between two entities. This is illustrated in Figure 4-19(b), and if you look back at Figure 3-1, you will see that the WP database has always had such a structure.

Subtype Entities

The extended E-R model introduced the concept of subtypes. A **subtype entity** is a special case of another entity called the **supertype entity**. Students, for example, may be classified as undergraduate or graduate students. In this case, STUDENT is the supertype, and UNDERGRADUATE and GRADUATE are subtypes. Figure 4-20 shows these subtypes for a student database. Note that the identifier of the supertype is also the identifier of the subtypes.

Alternatively, a student could be classified as a freshman, sophomore, junior, or senior. In that case, STUDENT would be the supertype, and FRESHMAN, SOPHOMORE, JUNIOR, and SENIOR would be the subtypes.

As illustrated in Figure 4-20, in our E-R models we use a circle with a line under it as a subtype symbol to indicate a supertype/subtype relationship. Think of this as a symbol for an optional (the circle) 1:1 (the line) relationship. In addition, we use a solid line to represent an ID-dependent subtype entity because each subtype is ID-dependent on the supertype. Also note that none of the line end symbols shown in Figure 4-14 are used on the connecting lines.

In some cases, an attribute of the supertype indicates which of the subtypes is appropriate for a given instance. An attribute that determines which subtype is appropriate is called a **discriminator**. In Figure 4-20(a), the attribute isGradStudent (which has only the

FIGURE 4-20

Example Subtype Entities

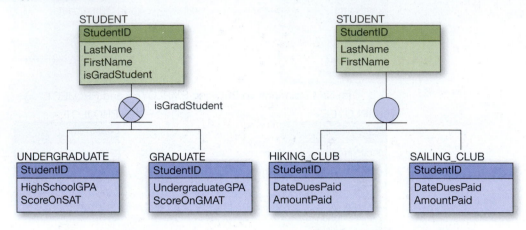

(a) Exclusive Subtypes with Discriminator   (b) Inclusive Subtypes

values Yes and No) is the discriminator. In our E-R diagrams, the discriminator is shown next to the subtype symbol, as illustrated in Figure 4-20(a). Not all supertypes have a discriminator. Where a supertype does not have a discriminator, application code must be written to determine the appropriate subtype.

Subtypes can be exclusive or inclusive. With **exclusive subtypes**, a supertype instance is related to at most one subtype. With **inclusive subtypes**, a supertype instance can relate to one or more subtypes. In Figure 4-20(a), the X in the circle means that the UNDERGRADUATE and GRADUATE subtypes are exclusive. Thus, a STUDENT can be either an UNDERGRADUATE or a GRADUATE, but not both.

Figure 4-20(b) shows that a STUDENT can join either the HIKING_CLUB or the SAILING_CLUB or both or neither. These subtypes are inclusive (note that there is no X in the circle). Because a supertype may relate to more than one subtype, inclusive subtypes do not have a discriminator.

Some models include another dimension of subtypes, called the *total* or *partial* distinction: For example, in Figure 4-20(b), can there be students who are in *neither* club? If so, the subtype/supertype relationship is **partial**; if not, it is **total**. To indicate a total requirement, we would put a hash mark on the relationship line just below the supertype entity to indicate that the supertype, and thus at least one of the subtypes, is mandatory in the relationship.

Subtypes are used in a data model, among other reasons, to avoid inappropriate NULL values. Undergraduate students take the SAT exam and report that score, whereas graduate students take the GMAT and report their score on that exam. Thus, the SAT score would be NULL in all STUDENT entities for graduates, whereas the GMAT score would be NULL for all undergraduates. Such NULL values can be avoided by creating subtypes.

The relationships that connect supertypes and subtypes are called **IS-A relationships** because a subtype *is* the same entity as the supertype. Because this is so, the identifier of a supertype and all its subtypes must be the same; they all represent different aspects of the same entity. Contrast this with HAS-A relationships, in which an entity has a relationship to another entity but the identifiers of the two entities are different.

FIGURE 4-21

Example Recursive
Relationship

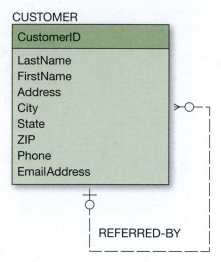

Recursive Relationships

It is possible for an entity to have a relationship to itself. Figure 4-21 shows a CUSTOMER entity in which one customer can refer many other customers to the business. This is called a **recursive relationship** (and because it has only one entity, it is also known as a **unary relationship**). As with binary relationships, recursive relationships can be 1:1, 1:N (shown in Figure 4-21), and N:M. We discuss each of these three types further in Chapter 5.

DEVELOPING AN EXAMPLE E-R DIAGRAM

The best way to gain proficiency with data modeling is to do it. In this section, we examine a set of documents used by a small business and create a data model from those documents. After you have read this section, you should practice creating data models with one or more of the projects at the end of the chapter.

Heather Sweeney Designs

Heather Sweeney is an interior designer who specializes in home kitchen design. She offers a variety of seminars at home shows, kitchen and appliance stores, and other public locations. The seminars are free; she offers them as a way of building her customer base. She earns revenue by selling books and videos that instruct people on kitchen design. She also offers custom-design consulting services.

After someone attends a seminar, Heather wants to leave no stone unturned in attempting to sell that person one of her products or services. She would therefore like to develop a database to keep track of customers, the seminars they have attended, the contacts she has made with them, and the purchases they have made. She wants to use this database to continue to contact her customers and offer them products and services.

The Seminar Customer List

Figure 4-22 shows the seminar customer list form that Heather or her assistant fills out at seminars. This form includes basic data about the seminar as well as the name, phone, and email address of each seminar attendee. If we examine this list in terms of a data model, you see two potential entities: SEMINAR and CUSTOMER. From the form in Figure 4-22, we can conclude that a SEMINAR relates to many CUSTOMERs, and we can make the initial E-R diagram shown in Figure 4-23(a).

FIGURE 4-22

Example Seminar
Customer List

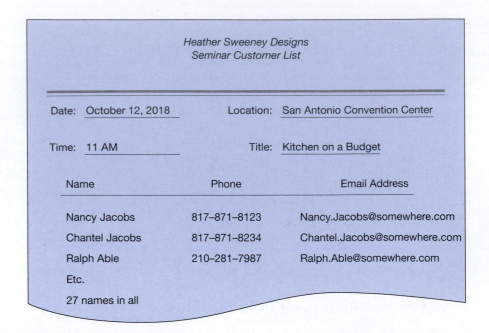

Heather Sweeney Designs
Seminar Customer List

Date: October 12, 2018   Location: San Antonio Convention Center

Time: 11 AM   Title: Kitchen on a Budget

Name	Phone	Email Address
Nancy Jacobs	817–871–8123	Nancy.Jacobs@somewhere.com
Chantel Jacobs	817–871–8234	Chantel.Jacobs@somewhere.com
Ralph Able	210–281–7987	Ralph.Able@somewhere.com
Etc.		

27 names in all

FIGURE 4-23

Initial E-R Diagram
for Heather Sweeney
Designs

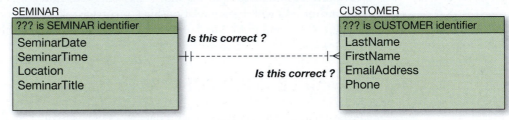

(a) First Version of the SEMINAR and CUSTOMER E-R Diagram

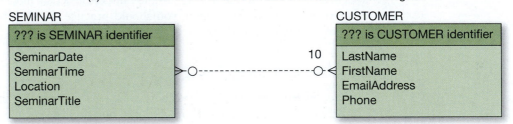

(b) Second Version of the SEMINAR and CUSTOMER E-R Diagram

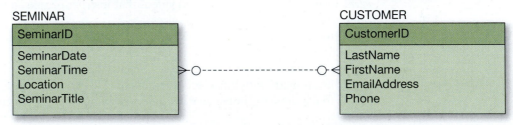

(c) Third Version of the SEMINAR and CUSTOMER E-R Diagram

However, from this single document we *cannot* determine a number of other facts. For example, we are not sure about cardinalities. Currently, we show a 1:N relationship, with both entities required in the relationship, but we are not certain about this. Neither do we know what to use for the identifier of each entity.

Having missing facts is typical during the data modeling process. We examine documents and conduct user interviews, and then we create a data model with the data we have. We also note where data are missing and supply those data later as we learn more. Thus, there is no need to stop data modeling when something is unknown; we just note that it is unknown and keep going, with the goal of supplying missing information at some later point.

Suppose we talk with Heather and determine that customers can attend as many seminars as they would like, but she would like to be able to record customers even if they have not been to a seminar. ("Frankly, I'll take a customer wherever I can find one!" was her actual response.) Also, she never offers a seminar to fewer than 10 attendees. Given this information, you can fill out more of the E-R diagram, as shown in Figure 4-23(b).

Before continuing, consider the minimum cardinality of the relationship from SEMINAR to CUSTOMER in Figure 4-23(b). The notation says that a seminar must have at least 10 customers, which is what we were told. However, this means that we cannot add a new SEMINAR to the database unless it already has 10 customers. This is incorrect. When Heather first schedules a seminar, it probably has no customers at all, but she would still like to record it in the database. Therefore, even though she has a business policy of requiring at least 10 customers at a seminar, we cannot place this limit as a constraint in the data model.

In Figure 4-23(b), neither of the entities has an identifier. For SEMINAR, the composites (SeminarDate, SeminarTime, Location) and (SeminarDate, SeminarTime, SeminarTitle) are probably unique, and either could be the identifier. However, identifiers will become table keys during database design, and these will be large character keys. A surrogate key is probably a better idea here, so we should create an equivalent unique identifier (SeminarID) for this entity. For CUSTOMER, looking at the data and thinking about the nature of email addresses, we can reasonably suppose that EmailAddress can be the identifier of CUSTOMER. However, some couples share an email address, and it may not be completely unique. Therefore, we will use CustomerID as our unique identifier. All these decisions are shown for the E-R diagram in Figure 4-23(c).

The Customer Form Letter

Heather records every customer contact she makes. She considers customer attendance at a seminar as one type of customer contact, and Figure 4-24 shows a form letter that Heather Sweeney Designs uses as another type of customer contact and as a follow-up to seminar attendance.

Heather also sends messages like this via email. In fact, she sends both a written letter and an email message as a follow-up with every seminar attendee. We should therefore represent this form letter with an entity called CONTACT, which could be a letter, an email, or some other form of customer contact. Heather uses several different form letters and emails, and she refers to each one by a specific name (form letter seminar, email seminar message, email purchase message, and so on). For now, we will represent the attributes of CONTACT as ContactNumber (the first, second, and so on, contact for a specific customer); ContactDate; and ContactType, where ContactType can be Seminar, FormLetterSeminar, EmailSeminarMessage, EmailPurchaseMessage, or some other type.

Reading the form letter, we see that it refers to both a seminar and a customer. Therefore, we can add it to the E-R diagram with relationships to both of those entities, as shown in Figure 4-25.

As shown in the design in Figure 4-25(a), a seminar can result in many contacts and a customer may receive many contacts, so the maximum cardinality of these relationships is N. However, neither a customer nor a seminar need generate a contact, so the minimum cardinality of these relationships is zero.

Working from CONTACT back to SEMINAR and CUSTOMER, we can determine that the contact is for a single CUSTOMER and refers to a single SEMINAR, so the maximum cardinality in that direction is one. Also, some of the messages to customers refer to

FIGURE 4-24

Heather Sweeney
Designs Customer
Form Letter

Heather Sweeney Designs
122450 Rockaway Road
Dallas, Texas 75227
972-233-6165

Ms. Nancy Jacobs
1440 West Palm Drive
Fort Worth, Texas 76110

Dear Ms. Jacobs:

Thank you for attending my seminar "Kitchen on a Budget" at the San Antonio Convention Center. I hope that you found the seminar topic interesting and helpful for your design projects.

As a seminar attendee, you are entitled to a 15 percent discount on all of my video and book products. I am enclosing a product catalog and I would also like to invite you to visit our Web site at www.Sweeney.com.

Also, as I mentioned at the seminar, I do provide customized design services to help you create that just-perfect kitchen. In fact, I have a number of clients in the Fort Worth area. Just give me a call at my personal phone number of 555-122-4873 if you'd like to schedule an appointment.

Thanks again and I look forward to hearing from you!

Best regards,

Heather Sweeney

seminars and some do not, so the minimum cardinality back to SEMINAR is zero. However, a contact must have a customer, so the minimum cardinality of that relationship is one. These cardinalities are shown in Figure 4-25(a).

Now, however, consider the identifier of CONTACT, which is shown as unknown in Figure 4-25(a). What could be the identifier? None of the attributes by itself suffices because many contacts will have the same values for ContactNumber, ContactDate, or ContactType. Reflect on this for a minute, and you will begin to realize that some attribute of CUSTOMER has to be part of CONTACT. That realization is a signal that something is wrong. In a data model, the same attribute should not logically need to be part of two different entities.

Could it be that CONTACT is a weak entity? Can a CONTACT logically exist without a SEMINAR? Yes, because not all CONTACTs refer to a SEMINAR. Can a CONTACT logically exist without a CUSTOMER? The answer to that question has to be no. Who would we be contacting without a CUSTOMER? Aha! That is it: CONTACT is a weak entity, depending on CUSTOMER. In fact, it is an ID-dependent entity because the identifier of CONTACT includes the identifier of CUSTOMER.

Figure 4-25(b) shows the data model with CONTACT as an ID-dependent entity on CUSTOMER. After further interviews with Heather, we determine that she often contacts a customer more than once on the same day (both the form letter and email message

FIGURE 4-25

Heather Sweeney Designs Data Model with CONTACT

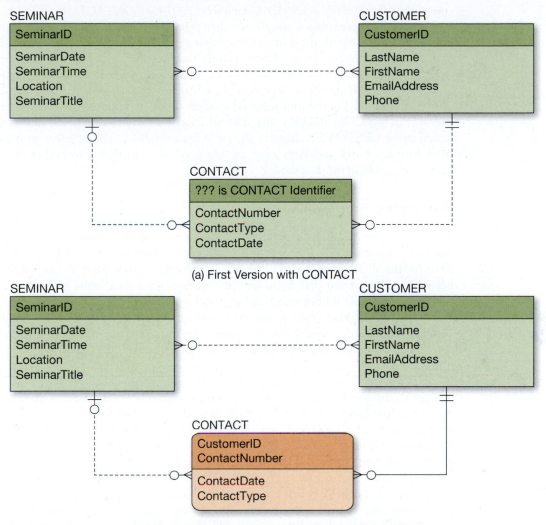

(a) First Version with CONTACT

(b) Second Version with CONTACT as a Weak Entity

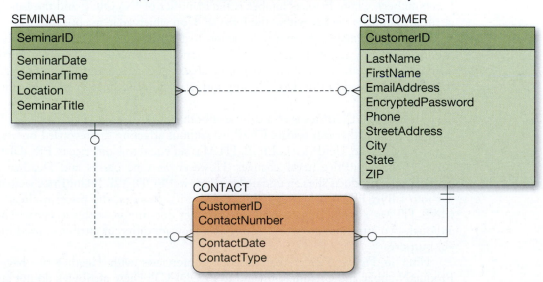

(c) Third Version with Modified CUSTOMER

thanking the customer for seminar attendance are always sent on the same day), so (CustomerID, Date) cannot be the identifier of CONTACT. We will choose to use the ContactNumber attribute, which is a simple sequence number, as the second part of the composite identifier (CustomerID, ContactNumber) for CONTACT.

This E-R diagram has a couple of other problems, because Heather has some other data requirements. First, the contact letter has the customer's address, but the CUSTOMER entity has no address attributes. Consequently, they need to be added. Second, Heather allows customers to create a login account on her Web site so that they can purchase items online securely. She uses the customers' EmailAddress as their login name, and has them create a password. For security, we need to allow for encryption of this password and storage of it in the CUSTOMER entity. The additional attributes for these requirements are added to the CUSTOMER entity, as shown in Figure 4-25(c). This adjustment is typical; as more forms, reports, and Web pages are obtained, new attributes and other changes will need to be made to the data model.

The Sales Invoice

The sales invoice that Heather uses to sell books and videos is shown in Figure 4-26. The sales invoice itself needs to be an entity, and because the sales invoice has customer data it has a relationship back to CUSTOMER. (Note that we do not duplicate the customer data because we can obtain data items via the relationship; if data items are missing, we add them to CUSTOMER.) Because Heather runs her computer with minimal security, she decided that she did not want to record credit card numbers in her computer database. Instead, she records only the PaymentType value in the database and files the credit card receipts in a (locked) physical file with a notation that relates them back to an invoice number.

Figure 4-27 shows the completion of the Heather Sweeney Designs data model. Figure 4-27(a) shows a first attempt at the data model with INVOICE. This diagram is missing data about the line items on the order. Because there are multiple line items, the line item data cannot be stored in INVOICE. Instead, an ID-dependent entity, LINE_ITEM, must be defined. The need for an ID-dependent entity is typical for documents that contain a group of repeating data. If the repeating group is not logically independent, then it must be made into an ID-dependent weak entity. Figure 4-27(b) shows the adjusted design.

Because LINE_ITEM belongs to an identifying relationship from INVOICE, it needs an attribute that can be used to identify a particular LINE_ITEM within an INVOICE. The identifier we will use for LINE_ITEM will be the composite (InvoiceNumber, LineNumber), where InvoiceNumber is the identifier of INVOICE and the LineNumber attribute identifies the line within the INVOICE on which an item appears.

We need to make one more correction to this data model. Heather sells standard products—that is, her books and videos have standardized names and prices. She does not want the person who fills out an order to be able to use nonstandard names or prices. We therefore need to add a PRODUCT entity and relate it to LINE_ITEM, as shown in Figure 4-27(c).

Observe that UnitPrice is an attribute of both PRODUCT and LINE_ITEM. This was done so that Heather can update UnitPrice without affecting the recorded orders. At the time a sale is made, UnitPrice in LINE_ITEM is set equal to UnitPrice in PRODUCT. The LINE_ITEM UnitPrice never changes. However, as time passes and Heather changes prices for her products she can update UnitPrice in PRODUCT. If UnitPrice were not copied into LINE_ITEM, when the PRODUCT price changes, the price in already stored LINE_ITEMs would change as well, and Heather does not want this to occur. Therefore, although two attributes are named UnitPrice, they are different attributes used for different purposes.

Note in Figure 4-27(c) that based on interviews with Heather we have added ProductNumber and QuantityOnHand to PRODUCT. These attributes do not appear in any of the documents, but they are known by Heather and are important to her.

FIGURE 4-26

Heather Sweeney Designs Sales Invoice

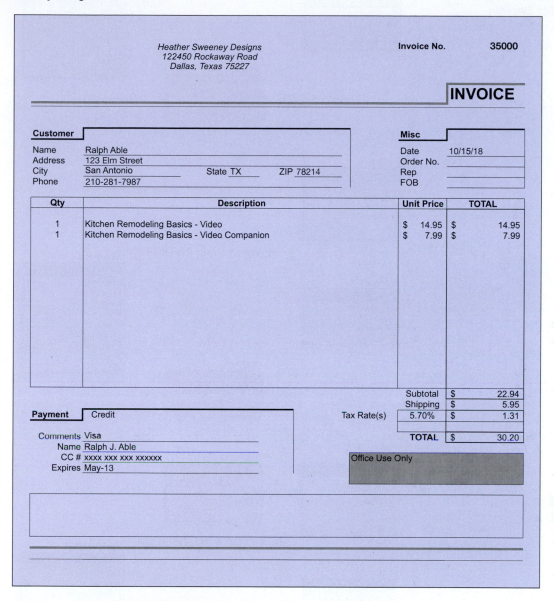

Attribute Specifications

The data model in Figure 4-27(c) shows entities, attributes, and entity relationships, but it does not document details about attributes. These details are normally dealt with as column specifications during the creation of the database design from the data model as described in Chapter 5. However, during the requirements analysis, you may learn of some desired or required attribute specifications (such as default values). These should be documented for use in creating the database design column specifications.

Business Rules

When creating a data model, we need to be on the lookout for business rules that constrain data values and the processing of the database. We encountered such a business rule with regard to CONTACT, when Heather Sweeney stated that multiple contacts, for example, more than one email message, may be made with one customer on the same day.

FIGURE 4-27

The Final Data Model
for Heather Sweeney
Designs

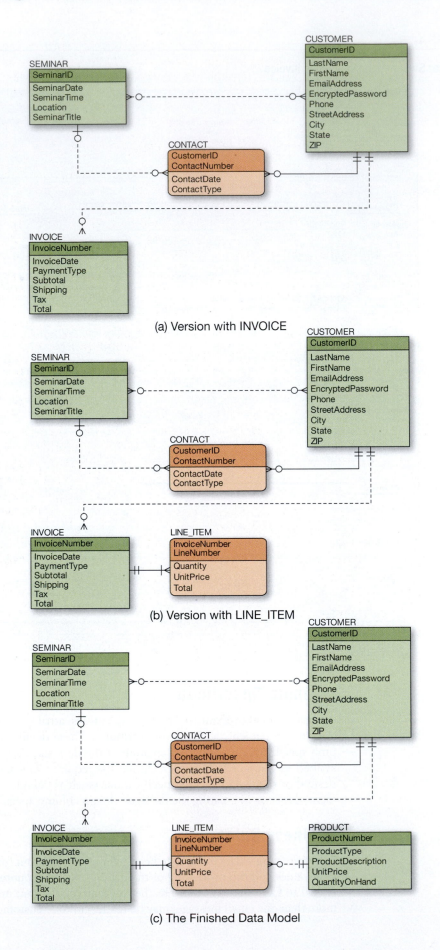

(a) Version with INVOICE

(b) Version with LINE_ITEM

(c) The Finished Data Model

In more complicated data models, many such business rules would exist. Some of these rules can be implemented in the DBMS using built-in constraints, triggers, or stored procedures (see Chapter 6 and online Extension B, "Advanced SQL"), but many of these rules are too specific or too complicated to be enforced by the DBMS. Rather, application programs or other forms of procedural logic need to be developed to enforce such rules.

Validating the Data Model

After a data model has been completed, it needs to be validated. The most common way to do this is to show it to the users and obtain their feedback. However, a large, complicated data model is off-putting to many users, so often the data model needs to be broken into sections and validated piece by piece or expressed in some other terms that are more understandable.

As mentioned earlier in this chapter, prototypes are sometimes constructed for users to review. Prototypes are easier for users to understand and evaluate than data models. We can develop prototypes that show the consequences of data model design decisions without requiring the users to learn E-R modeling. For example, showing a form or Web page with room for only one customer is a way of indicating that the maximum cardinality of a relationship is one. If the users respond to such a form with the question "But where do I put the second customer?" you know that the maximum cardinality is greater than one.

Creating mock-ups of forms and reports is relatively easy using Microsoft Access wizards. We can even develop such mock-ups in situations where Microsoft Access is not going to be used as the operational DBMS because they are still useful for demonstrating the consequences of data modeling decisions.

Finally, a data model needs to be evaluated against all use cases. For each use case, we need to verify that all the data and relationships necessary to support the use case are present and accurately represented in the data model.

Data model validation is exceedingly important. Correcting errors at this stage is far easier and less expensive than it is after the database has been designed and implemented. Changing the cardinality in a data model is a simple adjustment to a document, but changing the cardinality later might require the construction of new tables, new relationships, new queries, new forms, new reports, new applications, new Web pages, and so forth. So every minute spent validating a data model will pay great dividends down the line.

WORKING WITH MICROSOFT ACCESS

Section 4

Data Modeling with Microsoft Visio and Prototyping Using Microsoft Access

In this chapter, we discussed how to create a data model, and mentioned that Microsoft Visio could be used to create diagrams of data models. Here, we will use Microsoft Visio 2019. In this section of "Working with Microsoft Access," we will use Visio to create a data model of the Wedgeword Pacific (WP) database we used in Chapter 3.

In this chapter, we also talked about building a **prototype database** for users to review as a model-validation technique. Prototypes are easier for users to understand and evaluate than data models. In addition, they can be used to show the consequences of data-model design decisions. Because creating mock-ups of forms and reports by using Microsoft Access wizards is relatively easy to do, mock-ups are often developed even in situations in which Microsoft Access is not going to be used as the operational DBMS. The mock-ups

(*Continued*)

can be used as a prototyping tool to demonstrate the consequences of data modeling decisions. In this section, you will use Microsoft Access as a prototyping tool.

To illustrate prototyping, we will continue to use the WMCRM database. At this point, we have created and populated the CONTACT, CUSTOMER, PHONE_NUMBER, and SALESPERSON tables. In the preceding sections of "Working with Microsoft Access," you also learned how to create forms, reports, and queries. And if you studied online Extension B's section of "Working with Microsoft Access" together with Chapter 3, you have learned how to create and use view-equivalent queries.

Creating a Data Model in Microsoft Visio 2019

To illustrate creating a data model in Microsoft Visio 2019, we will use the Wedgewood Pacific (WP) database that we used for our work with SQL in Chapter 3. We will use the WP database because this database contains an associative entity, which we will use to illustrate M:N relationships and relationships that require an associative entity.

How Do I Start Micrsoft Visio 2019?

To start Microsoft Visio 2019 running in Microsoft Windows 10, click the Windows Start button, and then scroll down the application menu to the Visio icon and then click the icon. We suggest that when you find the Visio icon, you right-click the icon to bring up a shortcut menu and use the **More | Pin to taskbar** command to place the Visio icon on the Taskbar for easier access. The Microsoft Visio 2019 splash screen is displayed, followed by the Microsoft Visio 2019 window with the backstage view displayed, as shown in Figure WA-4-1.

FIGURE WA-4-1

The Microsoft Visio 2019 Backstage View

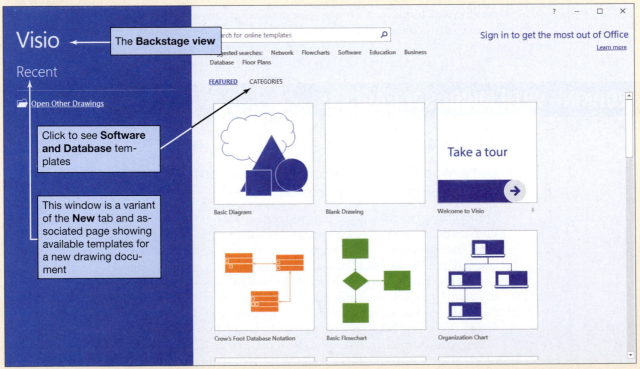

Visio 2019, Windows 10, Microsoft Corporation.

Microsoft Visio 2019 uses the Microsoft Office Fluent user interface found in most (but not all) Microsoft Office 2007, Office 2010, Office 2013, Office 2016, and Office 2019 products. Here we note that Microsoft Visio 2019 opens with a variant of the New command tab and associated page of the Backstage view displayed (the Backstage view is displayed when the File command tab is selected).

How Do I Create a Database Model Diagram in Microsoft Visio 2019?

To open a template for data models, click the **Categories** tab, and scroll to the **Software and Database** templates, as shown in Figure WA-4-2. Click the Software and Database templates icon to display the templates in this category, as shown in Figure WA-4-3. These templates include the template we want to use—the Crow's Foot Database Notation template. Click the template to select it. The **Crow's Foot Database Notation** is the one that Microsoft Visio 2019 uses for data models with the IE Crow's Foot notation as used in Chapter 4. Note that the name *Database Notation* is somewhat misleading, as we are creating data models using E-R diagrams as we understand them from our discussion in Chapter 4. Nonetheless, this is the template we want, and we will have to sort things out as we go along. Also note that there are templates available for use with IDEF1X notation and for use with UML notation. We briefly mentioned both the IDEF1X and UML notations in Chapter 4, but we are using IE Crow's Foot notation as our standard in this book. Again, we will just have to sort things out as we go along. Click the **Create** button to create a new Database Model Diagram document, as displayed in Figure WA-4-4.

As shown in Figure WA-4-4, a new, blank diagram document, named Drawing1, is created and the appropriate Shapes stencils (a **stencil** is Microsoft Visio 2019's term for a

FIGURE WA-4-2

The Software and Database Template Category

(Continued)

FIGURE WA-4-3

The Crow's Foot Database Notation Template

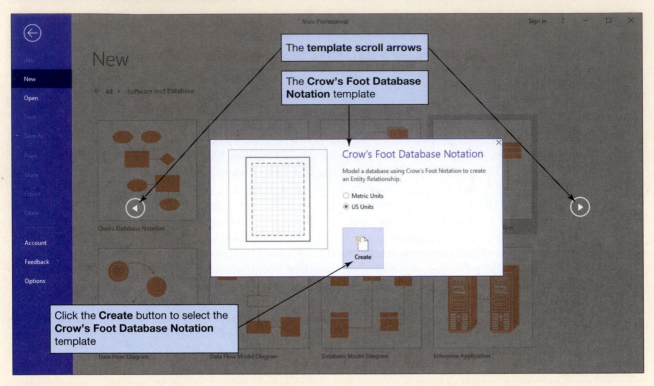

FIGURE WA-4-4

The Microsoft Visio 2019 Data Model Diagram

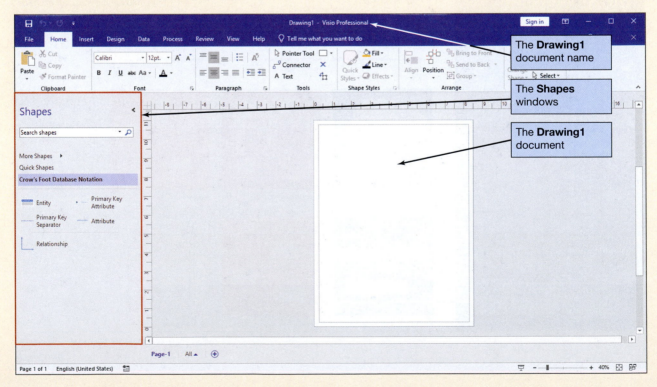

FIGURE WA-4-5

The Shapes Window

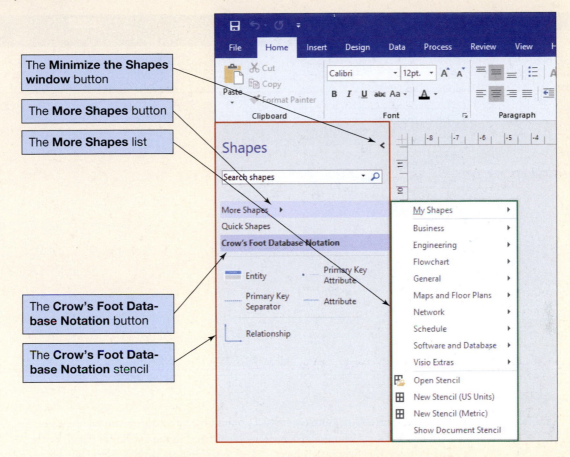

- The **Minimize the Shapes window** button
- The **More Shapes** button
- The **More Shapes** list
- The **Crow's Foot Database Notation** button
- The **Crow's Foot Database Notation** stencil

group of template objects) are displayed in the Shapes window. Figure WA-4-5 shows more detail of the Shapes window, including:

- The **Minimize the Shapes window button** — As the name says, use this to minimize the Shapes window.
- The **More Shapes button** — Use this to display the **More Shapes list**, as shown in Figure WA-4, if you need to add additional shape templates to the drawing.
- The **Crow's Foot Database Notation button** — Use this to display the Entity Relationship (US units) shapes pane.
- The **Crow's Foot Database Notation stencil** — The set of shape objects in the Entity Relations (US units) stencil.

Figure WA-4-6 shows the same screen but illustrates what happens when we click on one of the command tabs. Here, we have clicked on the Home tab, and the associated ribbon with the Home tab command groups is displayed. This is how we access commands on the ribbon, but note that when we do this we may cover up some of the drawing we are working on.

The Crow's Foot Database Notation stencil contains all the template objects we will use to build our data models. As shown in Figure WA-4-7, it contains:

- The **Entity object** — Use this object to create entities for data models in the Microsoft Visio database model diagram.
- The **Relationship object** — Use this object to create relationships between entities in data models (it is actually what Microsoft usually refers to as a dynamic connector).

(Continued)

FIGURE WA-4-6

The Home Command Tab Ribbon

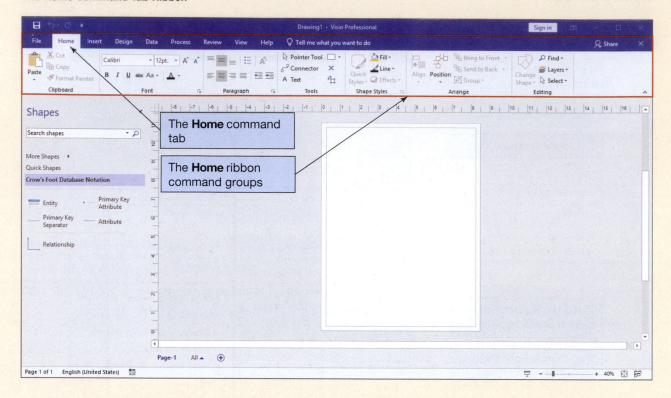

• The **Primary Key Attribute object** — Use this object to add additional identifier attributes (as, for example, in composite identifiers) to the entities in data models.
• The **Primary Key Separator object** — Use this object to insert a visible line between identifier attributes and other attributes in the entities in data models.
• The **Attribute object** — Use this object to add additional attributes to entities in data models.

FIGURE WA-4-7

The Crow's Foot Database Notation (US units) Stencil Objects

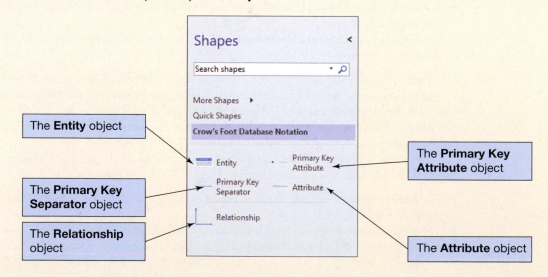

FIGURE WA-4-8

The Microsoft Visio 2019 Database Model Diagram with Minimized Shapes Window

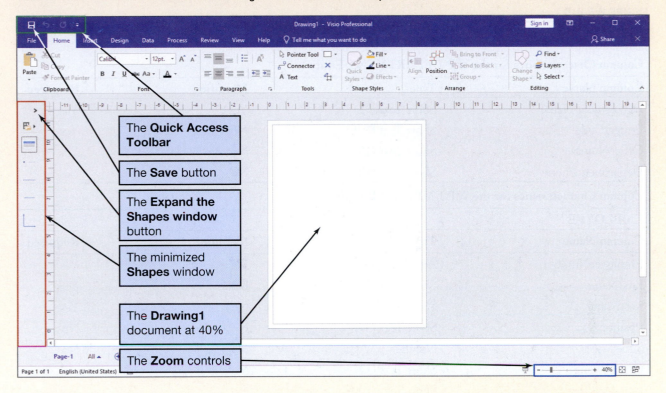

Figure WA-4-8 shows the Microsoft Visio 2019 window with:

- The **Shapes** windows minimized — Note that all of the Crow's Foot Database Notation (US units) stencil objects are still visible.
- The **Expand the Shapes window** button — Use this to restore the Shapes window to its full size.
- The **Quick Access Toolbar** —The Quick Access Toolbar with buttons are displayed on it.
- The **Zoom** controls — Use these to control the displayed size of the drawing, now shown at 51%.

By configuring the Microsoft Visio 2019 window in this manner, we have a much more efficient working area.

How Do I Name and Save a Database Model Diagram in Microsoft Visio 2019?

We will illustrate creating data models and database designs in Microsoft Visio 2019 by creating an E-R diagram for the Wedgewood Pacific (WP) database that we created in Microsoft Access as part of the Working with Microsoft Access Exercises in Chapters 1 and 2

(Continued)

and in MySQL 8.0 in Chapter 3.[8] The column characteristics for each of the WP tables are shown in Figure WA-4-9.

FIGURE WA-4-9

The WP Database Entity Column Characteristics

Column Characteristics for the WP DEPARTMENT Entity

Column Name	Type	Identifier	Required
Department Name	Short Text (35)	Yes	Yes
BudgetCode	Short Text (30)	No	Yes
OfficeNumber	Short Text (15)	No	Yes
DepartmentPhone	Short Text (12)	No	Yes

Column Characteristics for the WP EMPLOYEE Entity

EMPLOYEE

Column Name	Type	Identifier	Required
EmployeeNumber	AutoNumber	Yes	Yes
FirstName	Short Text (25)	No	Yes
LastName	Short Text (25)	No	Yes
Position	Short Text (35)	No	No
Supervisor	Number	No	No
OfficePhone	Short Text (12)	No	No
EmailAddress	Short Text (100)	No	Yes

Column Characteristics for the WP PROJECT Entity

Column Name	Type	Identifier	Required
ProjectID	Number	Yes	Yes
ProjectName	Short Text (50)	No	Yes
MaxHours	Number	No	Yes
StartDate	Date/Time	No	No
EndDate	Date/Time	No	No

Column Characteristics for the WP ASSIGNMENT Entity

Column Name	Type	Identifier	Required
ProjectID	Number	Yes	Yes
EmployeeNumber	Number	Yes	Yes
HoursWorked	Number	No	No

---

[8]Of course, it could be argued that we really should have created the database design first and then implemented that design. In many database courses, the data modeling and database design topics (which we cover in Chapters 4 and 5) are taught before using SQL to create the databases (which we cover in Chapter 3). In this case, the database design will precede the actual implementation of the database in the DBMS. We prefer to introduce SQL queries earlier. There are two reasons for this. First, users who are never involved in creating databases still often use SQL or QBE for querying databases (usually data warehouses or data marts as discussed in Chapter 7) to gather information. Second, we like to get our students involved with DBMSs, databases, and SQL as early in the course as possible. Either approach works, and your professor will choose the one that he or she likes best.

To save a Microsoft Visio 2019 database model diagram drawing, click the Save button in the Quick Access Toolbar. The first time we save the drawing, Microsoft Visio 2019 opens a **Save As** backstage view. This is a standard Microsoft Office 2019 feature. Click the **Browse** button to open the **Save As** dialog box, and save the drawing as **WP-Data-Model**.

As we discuss in this chapter and Chapter 5, one of the main differences between a data model and a database design is how N:M relationships are handled. In a data model, N:M relationships exist as N:M non-identifying relationships between two strong entities. In a database design, N:M relationships are broken into two 1:N identifying relationships between three ID-dependent entities. So, we will build the entities we need and then consider exactly how Microsoft Visio 2019 handles data models.

Also as we discuss in this chapter and Chapter 5, the diagrams we are creating are entity-relationship models, and we are using the IE Crow's Foot notation as our standard. We will also see how well Microsoft Visio 2019 supports IE Crow's Foot notation.

How Do I Create Entities in a Database Model Diagram in Microsoft Visio 2019?

Now that we have a blank document available to use as an E-R diagram work area, we can build the E-R diagram itself. We start by adding an entity to the E-R diagram. We will add the DEPARTMENT entity. By looking at the column characteristics of the DEPARTMENT table in Figure WA-4-9, we can see the columns that are used in the DEPARTMENT table.

Creating an Entity in the Microsoft Visio E-R Diagram:

1. Using the Zoom controls shown in Figure 4-8, set the document size to 100%.
2. In the Shapes window, click-and-hold the **Entity** object shown in Figure WA-4-7.
3. Move the cursor over the blank E-R diagram area, and then release the left mouse button. A new entity object named Entity Name is created on the E-R diagram, as shown in Figure WA-4-10.
4. Each line of text in the entity is a formatted text box. To edit the text in a text box, just double-click the text.
5. Double-click Entity Name to select it, and type in the entity name **DEPARTMENT**.
6. Right-click the text to display the shortcut menu as shown in Figure WA-4-11.
7. Format the table name DEPARTMENT as centered, 12pt, bold, black text with the default fill color. The final entity name appears as shown in Figure WA-4-12.

Now that we have named the DEPARTMENT entity, we have to deal with the fact that data models and the entities in them do not have primary keys—they have identifiers. There is no symbol, such as PK for primary key, for an identifier. Therefore, we have to make a choice—either use the PK text boxes for identifiers or not use these boxes at all.

For the sake of simplicity, we will use the PK boxes for our identifiers. This simply cuts down on the work we have to do to create the data models. But as we gain more skill using Visio 2019, we opt for more work and a cleaner and more consistent data model approach.

Creating the DEPARTMENT Entity Identifier (PK) Attribute in the Visio E-R Diagram:

1. In the DEPARTMENT entity object, double-click the **PK attribute name** text box.
2. Edit the text to read **DepartmentName**.
3. Format the text as left aligned, normal, black text with default fill color.

(Continued)

FIGURE WA-4-10

The Entity Name Entity Object

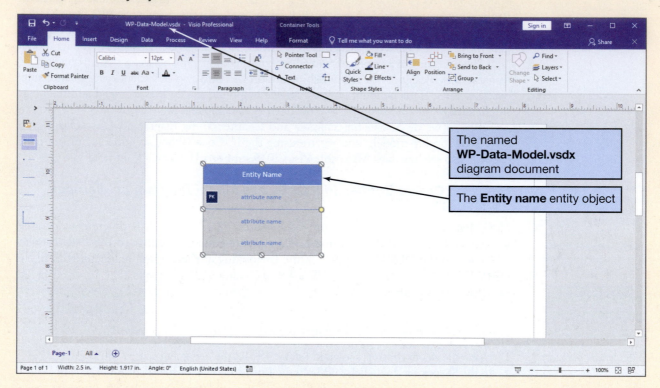

FIGURE WA-4-11

Naming and Formatting the Entity

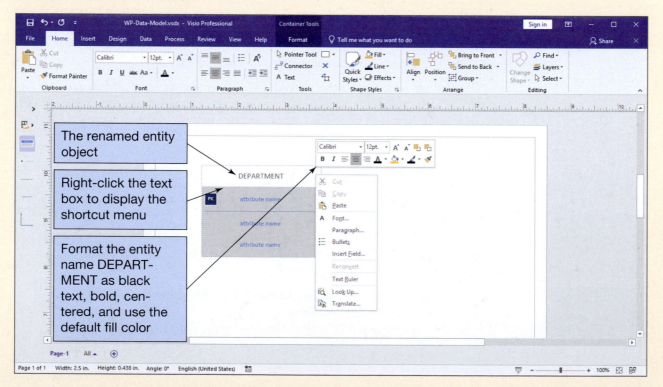

4. The DEPARTMENT entity object now appears as shown in Figure WA-4-13.
5. Naming the other attributes is done the same way. And if we need more attributes (which we will for the DepartmentPhone attribute), we just drag a new attribute object and attach it to the bottom of the entity object. The final DEPARTMENT entry is shown in Figure WA-4-14.

FIGURE WA-4-12

The Named and Formatted DEPARTMENT Entity

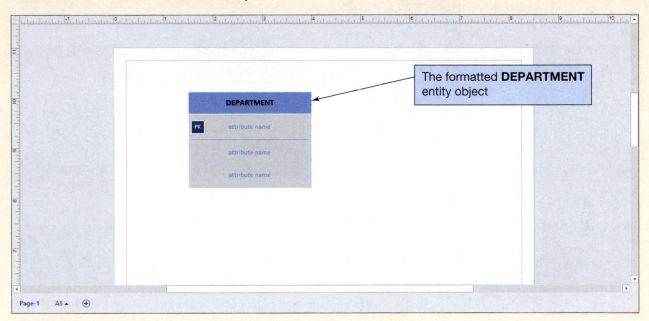

FIGURE WA-4-13

Naming the Primary Key Attribute

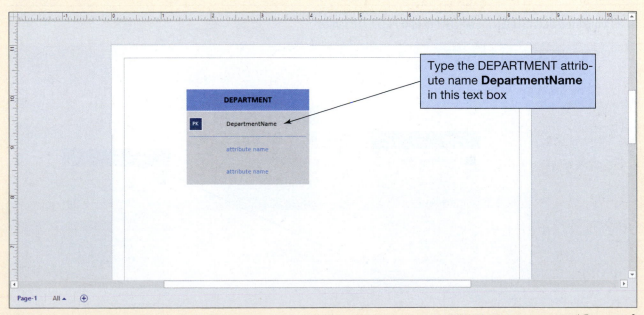

(Continued)

FIGURE WA-4-14

The Complete DEPARTMENT Entity

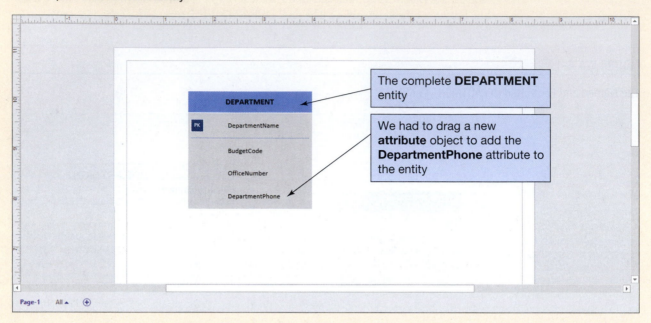

Now we will build the EMPLOYEE and PROJECT tables, but we will wait to build the ASSIGNMENT table until we discuss how to create relationships. The process is similar to the process we used to build the DEPARTMENT table, and the results are shown in Figure WA-4-15. Note that the table objects have been resized and rearranged, and the page itself is in landscape orientation instead of portrait orientation (to set this use the **File | Print** command and change the **Orientation** setting). Also note that the an attribute for Department does not appear in either the EMPLOYEE or PROJECT entities. This is because foreign keys do *not* appear in data models—they are added when data models are converted to database designs, which we will do in Chapter 5.

FIGURE WA-4-15

The Completed DEPARTMENT, EMPLOYEE, and PROJECT Tables

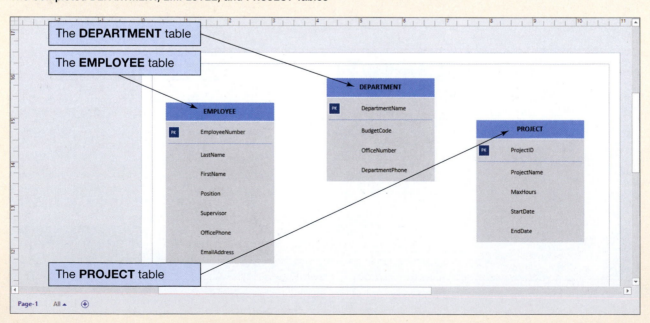

How Do I Create Relationships Between Entities in a Data Model Diagram in Microsoft Visio 2019?

Now that we have created the entities, we need to connect them with relationships. To do this we use the **Relationship connector object**. This is really a renamed form of the standard Microsoft Visio 2019 **Dynamic connector**—used between two entities, this is just a line with formattable line endings.

The type of relationship displayed and other relationship parameters are controlled by the connector properties. That is how we know if we have, for example, a **1:1 non-identifying relationship**, a **1:N non-identifying relationship**, or a **1:N identifying relationship**.

> ## BTW
>
> Microsoft Visio 2019 uses the term *non-identifying relationship*, whereas in the chapter text we use the term *nonidentifying relationship*. We have seen the term *non identifying relationship* used in other contexts. All three terms mean exactly the same thing, and which one is used is a matter of style. Since Microsoft Visio 2019 uses *non-identifying*, we will also use that term in this section of "Working with Microsoft Access" for consistency with the Microsoft Visio 2019 screen shots while remaining well aware that we have used *nonidentifying* in the chapter text itself.

It is also how we handle N:M relationships. In a data model, N:M relationships exist as N:M non-identifying relationships between two strong entities. In a database design, as we will see in Chapter 5, N:M relationships are broken into two 1:N identifying relationships between three ID-dependent entities.

Now we will build a data model and a database design to consider exactly how Microsoft Visio 2019 handles these diagrams.

How Do I Create Data Models Using Relationships in Microsoft Visio 2019?

At this point, we need to create two 1:N non-identifying relationships, one between DEPARTMENT and EMPLOYEE and one between DEPARTMENT and PROJECT. We will start with the relationship between DEPARTMENT and EMPLOYEE.

Creating a 1:N Nonidentifying Relationship Between Two Tables:

1. Click-and-hold the **Relationship** object.
2. Drag the object into the E-R diagram, and move it toward the center of the EMPLOYEE table. When the EMPLOYEE table is outlined in green, the connector is attached to the table object—release the mouse button. The E-R diagram now appears similar to Figure WA-4-16.
3. Locate the dynamic connector object in the E-R diagram, and drag the free end of it toward the center of the DEPARTMENT table. When the DEPARTMENT table is outlined in green, the connector is attached to the table object—release the mouse button. The E-R diagram now appears as shown in Figure WA-4-17.
4. The term *Dynamic Connector* means that if we move any of the objects to which the connector is attached, then the connector will automatically adjust its size and position to match. In Figure WA-4-18, we have moved the DEPARTMENT table toward the center of the E-R diagram, and the connector has adjusted itself as needed.
5. We can format the line properties of the relationship. Click the relationship object to select it, and then right-click to display the shortcut menu as shown in Figure WA-4-19.

(Continued)

FIGURE WA-4-16

The Dynamic Connector Attached to the EMPLOYEE Table

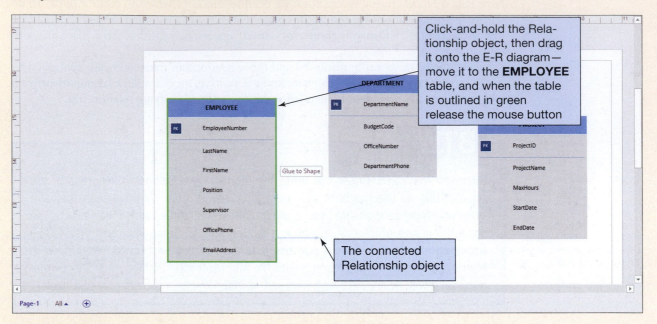

Click-and-hold the Relationship object, then drag it onto the E-R diagram—move it to the **EMPLOYEE** table, and when the table is outlined in green release the mouse button

The connected Relationship object

FIGURE WA-4-17

The Relationship Object Attached to Both the EMPLOYEE and DEPARTMENT Tables

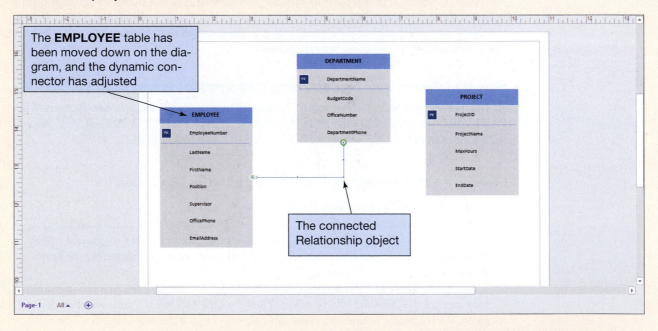

The **EMPLOYEE** table has been moved down on the diagram, and the dynamic connector has adjusted

The connected Relationship object

6. In the shortcut menu, click the Set Begin Symbol command to display the Set Begin Symbol menu. In the **Set Begin Symbol** menu, note that Zero or more is set. The **Begin Symbol** needs to be set to **1 or more**. To understand what Crow's Foot symbol this corresponds to, look at Figure 4-14 in the chapter text. "Zero or more" corresponds to the optional-many Crow's Foot symbol, and "One or more" corresponds to the mandatory-many symbol.

7. This is the correct setting for this line end, but note that we can easily adjust it to any of the four Crow's Foot symbols as needed.

FIGURE WA-4-18

The Dynamic Connector Adjusts as DEPARTMENT Table is Moved

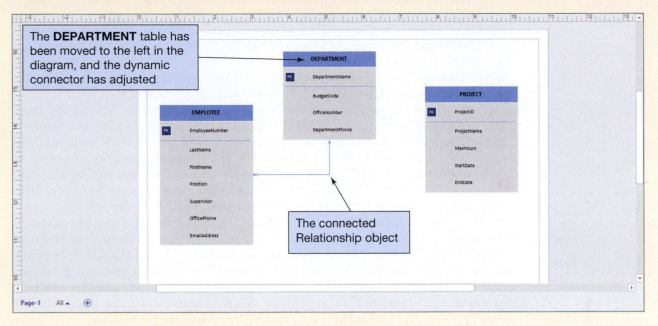

The **DEPARTMENT** table has been moved to the left in the diagram, and the dynamic connector has adjusted

The connected Relationship object

FIGURE WA-4-19

The Shortcut Menu

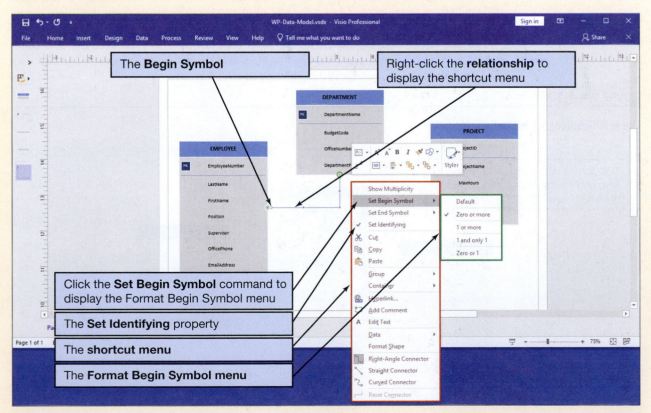

The **Begin Symbol**

Right-click the **relationship** to display the shortcut menu

Click the **Set Begin Symbol** command to display the Format Begin Symbol menu

The **Set Identifying** property

The **shortcut menu**

The **Format Begin Symbol menu**

(Continued)

8. Since this is a non-identifying relationship, the line should be a dashed line. In the shortcut menu, click the **Set Identifying** property to remove the check mark and make this a non-identifying relationship.
9. The other end of the line is correct.
10. Click the **Save** button on the Quick Access Toolbar to save the work on the data model.

This allows us to format the relationship lines between the entities using the appropriate symbols for the style of E-R diagram we are creating. We can use these to create IE Crow's Foot data models. At this point, you need to simply experiment with how to format the connector lines in Microsoft Visio 2019. For example, the size of the Crow's Foot line end symbols can be changed using the Format Shape command on the shortcut menu. The relationship between DEPARTMENT and PROJECT is also a 1:N non-identifying relationship and can be created exactly the same way. The recursive 1:N non-identifying relationship within EMPLOYEE can be created in a similar manner. You should create those relationships now and save the data model work again. Note that creating the recursive relationship within EMPLOYEE may require some dexterity with the mouse! *Hint*: Try attaching the line end symbol to an attribute rather than to the entire entity.

Using Microsoft Visio 2019 relationships, we can, in fact, model N:M relationships. At this point, based on the WP database in Figure WA-4-9, we still need to build the ASSIGNMENT table and its relationships with EMPLOYEE and PROJECT. However, for our WP data model, let's assume that we simply want an N:M relationship between EMPLOYEE and PROJECT. That is, employees will work on projects, and projects must have employees to work on them, and that we will not record hours worked. Figure WA-4-20 shows the N:M relationship, using the same dynamic connector construction.

The important question for a *data model* design tool is whether or not we can model an N:M non-identifying relationship between two entities. As discussed in this chapter and Chapter 5, an N:M relationship only exists in a data model (as a non-identifying relationship between two strong enties). In a database design, the N:M relationship becomes two 1:N ID-dependent identifying relationships linking the two original tables through a new, third table called an intersection table (which is similar to an associative entity in a data model E-R diagram). Note that both line ends in an N:M relationship must be mandatory-many.

At this point, you should create the N:M relationship and then save the WP-Data-Model.vsdx file. We will leave adding the ASSIGNMENT associative entity to the data model for the Exercises at the end of this appendix.

FIGURE WA-4-20

The N:M Relationship in the Data Model

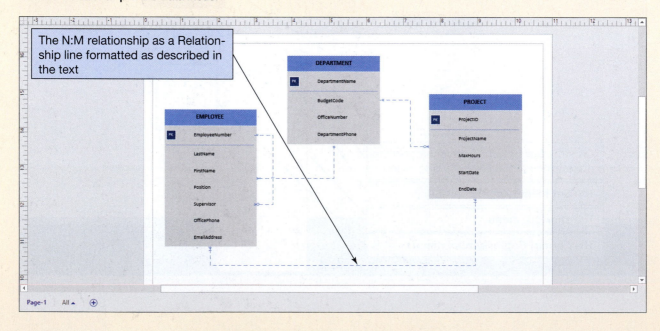

FIGURE WA-4-21

The Final WP Data Model

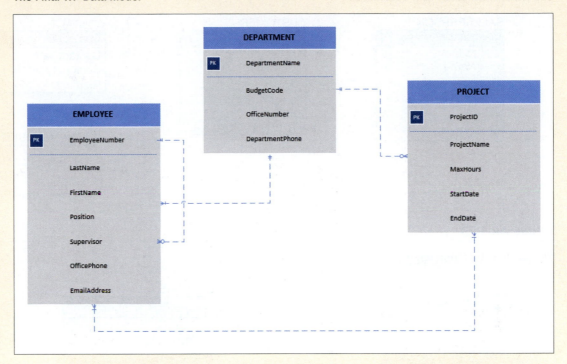

In this model, the non-identifying relationships are correct (all three entities are strong entities), but what about the minimum cardinalities?

Does a DEPARTMENT have to have at least one employee? This is actually a business rule question, but we will assume that the answer for WP is yes, and that WP does not allow departments without employees to exist. This means we will need to change the EMPLOYEE end of the EMPLOYEE-to-DEPARTMENT relationship to "one or more."

Does an EMPLOYEE have to be assigned to a department? Again, this is a business rule question, but the fact that EMPLOYEE.Department is NOT NULL with a DEFAULT value of Human Resources is a good indication that the answer for WP is yes, and that WP does not allow employees unassigned to departments to exist, so the diagram is correct for that minimum cardinality.

We will also assume that every project has to have at least one employee assigned to it and that every employee has to work on at least one project. Therefore, the minimum cardinalities for the N:M relationship both need to be changed. Note that if optional minimum cardinalites are allowed, we just need to change which line end we use! The final WP data model to this point, with the corrected line ends, is shown in Figure WA-4-21. Save the WP-Data-Model.vsdx file a final time, and then click **File | Close** to close the drawing.

Prototyping a Database in Microsoft Access 2019

Now let's turn to using Microsoft Access 2019 as a prototyping tool. We will start by considering what the WMCRM database looks like from a data modeling point of view. Figure WA-4-22 shows the WMCRM database as an IE Crow's Foot E-R model.

This model is based on the business rule that each CUSTOMER works with one and only one SALESPERSON. Therefore, we have a 1:N relationship between SALESPERSON and CUSTOMER, which shows that each SALESPERSON can work with many CUSTOMERs but each CUSTOMER is attended to by only one SALESPERSON. Further, because there is no doubt about which SALESPERSON is involved in each CONTACT with a CUSTOMER, the connection to CONTACT is a 1:N relationship from CUSTOMER.

(Continued)

FIGURE WA-4-22

The WMCRM Database as a Data Model

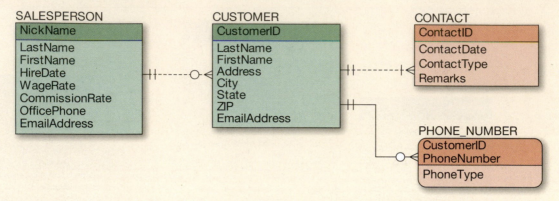

FIGURE WA-4-23

The Modified WMCRM Data Model

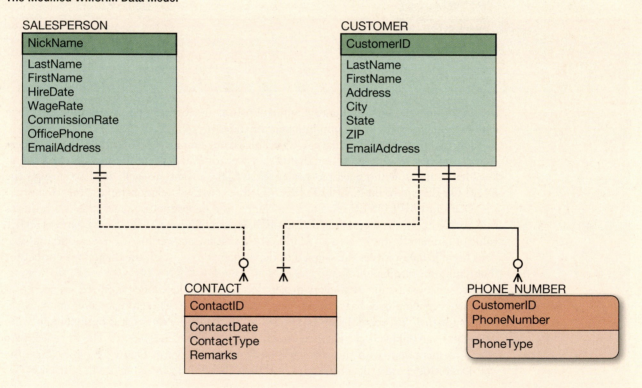

But all this would change if the business rule were that any CUSTOMER could work with more than one SALESPERSON. This would allow any SALESPERSON to contact the CUSTOMER as needed rather than relying on just one SALESPERSON to be available whenever needed for work with a particular CUSTOMER. Each CONTACT would now need to be linked to the CUSTOMER contacted and the SALEPERSON making the CONTACT. This results in a data model like the one shown in Figure WA-4-23.

Here we have a 1:N relationship between SALESPERSON and CONTACT instead of between SALESPERSON and CUSTOMER, while the 1:N relationship between CUSTOMER and CONTACT remains the same. CONTACTs for one CUSTOMER can now be linked to various SALESPERSONs.

Imagine that you have been hired as a consultant to create the WMCRM database. You now have two alternative data models that you need to show to managers at Wallingford Motors so that they can make a decision about which model to use. But they do not understand E-R data modeling.

How can you illustrate the differences between the two data models? One way is to generate some mock-up prototype forms and reports in Microsoft Access. Some users can more easily understand forms and reports than they can understand your abstract E-R model.

Creating a Prototype Form for the Original Data Model

We will start by creating a sample form in the current version of the WMCRM database, which we are treating here as a prototype we created to illustrate the first data model. (This includes populating the database with sample data.) The database structure for this database is shown in the Relationships window in Figure WA-4-24.

Using a Form That Includes Multiple Tables

In Chapter 1's section of "Working with Microsoft Access," we created a data entry form for a single table using the CUSTOMER table. Now we will create a Microsoft Access form that will let us work with the combined data from multiple tables.

Creating a Form for Multiple Tables

1. Click the **Create** command tab.
2. Click the **Form Wizard** button in the Forms command group, as shown in Figure WA-4-25. The Form Wizard appears, as shown in Figure WA-4-26.

FIGURE WA-4-24

The Original WMCRM Database

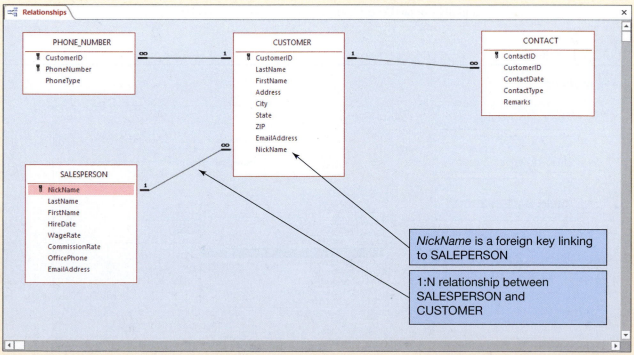

Access 2019, Windows 10, Microsoft Corporation.

(Continued)

FIGURE WA-4-25

The Form Wizard Button

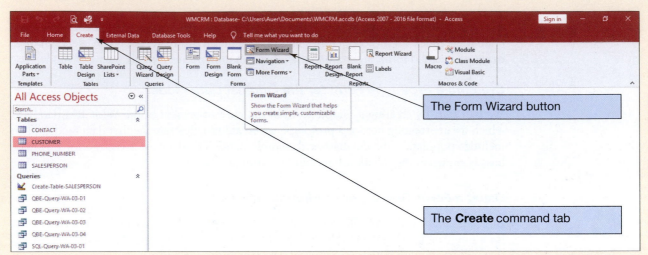

Access 2019, Windows 10, Microsoft Corporation.

3. Select the **SALESPERSON** table in the Tables/Queries drop-down list. Individually select and add the **NickName, LastName, FirstName, OfficePhone**, and **EmailAddress** columns to the Selected Fields list by using the **right-facing single-chevron** button, as shown in Figure WA-4-27. Do *not* click the **Next** button yet.

4. Select the **CUSTOMER** table in the Tables/Queries drop-down list. Individually select and add the **LastName, FirstName, Address, City, State, ZIP**, and **EmailAddress** columns to the Selected Fields list by using the **right-facing single-chevron** button. Do *not* click the **Next** button yet.

5. Select the **CONTACT** table in the Tables/Queries drop-down list. Individually select and add the **ContactDate, ContactType**, and **Remarks** columns to the Selected Fields list by

FIGURE WA-4-26

The Form Wizard

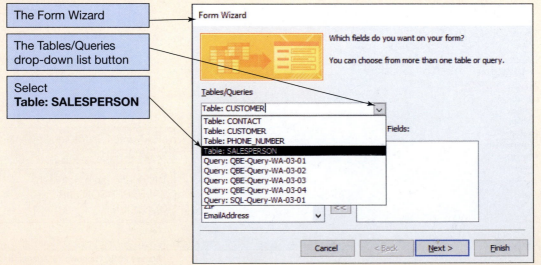

Access 2019, Windows 10, Microsoft Corporation.

FIGURE WA-4-27

Selecting Form Fields

The **Selected Fields** list

The **right-facing single –chevron** button–use this button to add one field at a time to the Selected Fields list

The **Available Fields** list

The **right-facing double–chevron** button–use this button to add all the available fields to the Selected Fields list

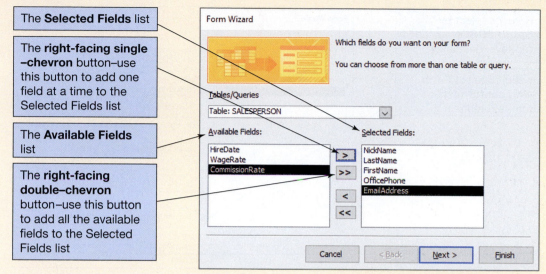

Access 2019, Windows 10, Microsoft Corporation.

using the **right-facing single-chevron** button. Do *not* click the **Next** button yet. The Form Wizard now appears as shown in Figure WA-4-28. Do *not* click the **Next** button yet.

6. Now click the **Next** button.
   - **NOTE:** You have just created a set of columns from three tables that you want to appear on one form.
7. When asked "How do you want to view your data?" use the default **by SALESPERSON** selection because we want to see all contacts for each salesperson. Also use the selected **Forms with subform(s)** option to treat the CUSTOMER and CONTACT data as subforms within the SALESPERSON form. The Form Wizard now appears as shown in Figure WA-4-29.

FIGURE WA-4-28

The Complete Selected Fields List

The complete **Selected Fields** list–this list now includes fields (columns) from three different tables

The **Next** button

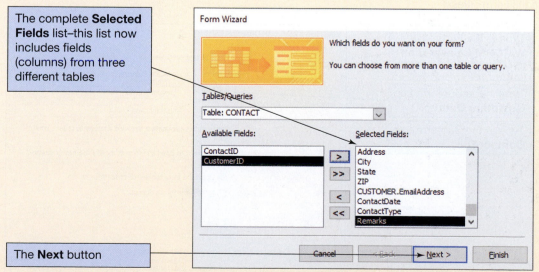

Access 2019, Windows 10, Microsoft Corporation.

(Continued)

FIGURE WA-4-29

Specifying How to View the Data

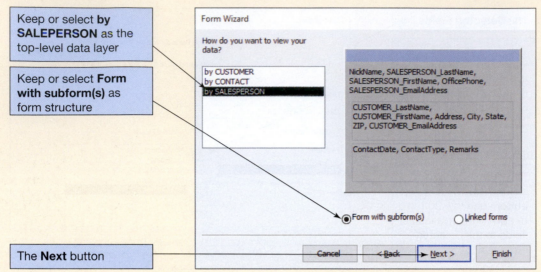

Keep or select **by SALEPERSON** as the top-level data layer

Keep or select **Form with subform(s)** as form structure

The **Next** button

Access 2019, Windows 10, Microsoft Corporation.

8. Click the **Next** button.
9. When asked "What layout would you like for each subform?" click the **Next** button to use the default Datasheet layouts.
10. When asked "What titles do you want for your forms?" type the form title **WMCRM Salesperson Contacts Form** into the Form: text box, the subform title **Customer Data** into the first Subform: text box, and the form title **Contact Data** into the second Subform: text box. The Form Wizard now appears as shown in Figure WA-4-30.
11. Click the **Finish** button. The completed form appears as shown in Figure WA-4-31.
12. Unfortunately, the form is not that well designed. To make modifications to the form, click the **Layout View** button in the View drop-down list to switch to Layout view. Figure WA-4-32 shows modifications to the layout of the WMCRM Salesperson Contacts form. You can select various elements of the form, and rearrange them as needed.

FIGURE WA-4-30

Specifying the Form Titles

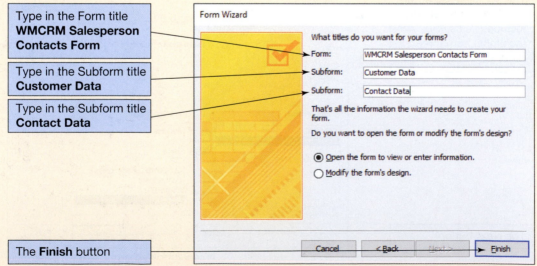

Type in the Form title **WMCRM Salesperson Contacts Form**

Type in the Subform title **Customer Data**

Type in the Subform title **Contact Data**

The **Finish** button

Access 2019, Windows 10, Microsoft Corporation.

FIGURE WA-4-31

The Generated Form for Salesperson Contacts Data

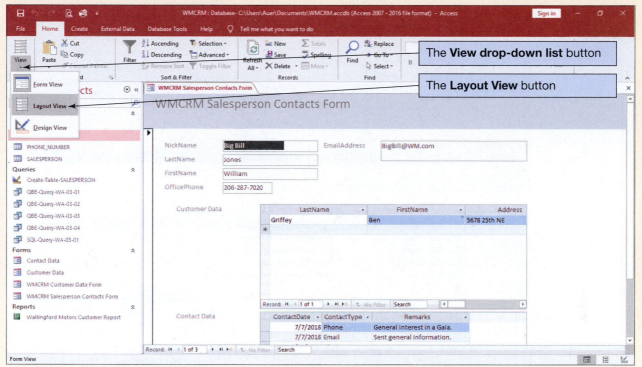

Access 2019, Windows 10, Microsoft Corporation.

FIGURE WA-4-32

Modifying the WMCRM Salesperson Contacts Form

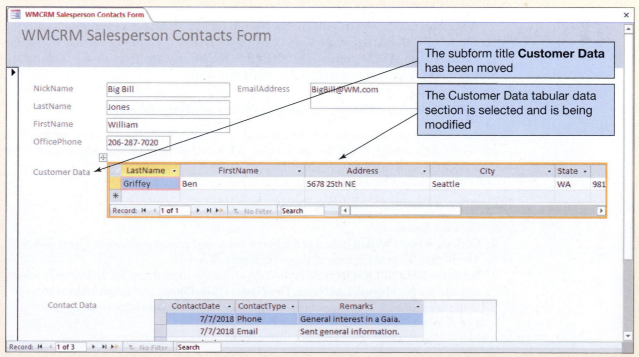

Access 2019, Windows 10, Microsoft Corporation.

(Continued)

FIGURE WA-4-33

The Final WMCRM Salesperson Contacts Form

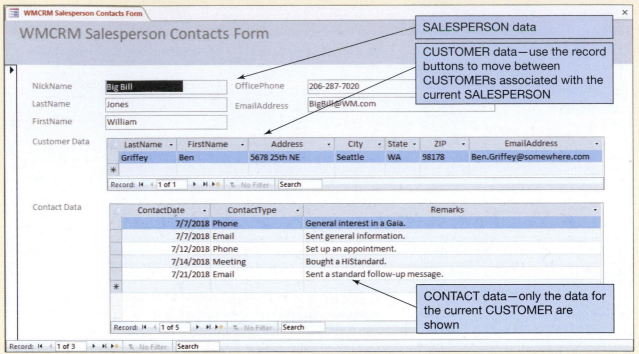

Access 2019, Windows 10, Microsoft Corporation.

13. Figure WA-4-33 shows the final modified WMCRM Salesperson Contacts form. After you have the form looking approximately like this, click the **Save** button to save the changes.
14. Close the form window.

This form has three distinct sections: The top section shows SALESPERSON data, the middle section shows selectable CUSTOMER data, and the bottom section shows the CONTACT data for the current CUSTOMER. Explaining this form to the Wallingford Motors management and users should be fairly easy to do.

Creating a Report That Includes Data from Multiple Tables

In this section, we will create a report that includes data from two or more tables. This Microsoft Access report will let us use the combined data from the SALESPERSON, CUSTOMER, and CONTACT tables.

Creating a Report for Multiple Tables

1. Click the **Create** tab.
2. Click the **Report Wizard** button in the Forms command group, as shown in Figure WA-4-34. The Report Wizard appears, as shown in Figure WA-4-35.
3. Select the **SALESPERSON** table in the Tables/Queries drop-down list. Individually select and add the **NickName, LastName, FirstName, OfficePhone**, and **EmailAddress** columns to the Selected Fields list by using the **right-facing single-chevron** button, as shown in Figure WA-4-36. Do *not* click the **Next** button yet.

FIGURE WA-4-34

The Report Wizard Button

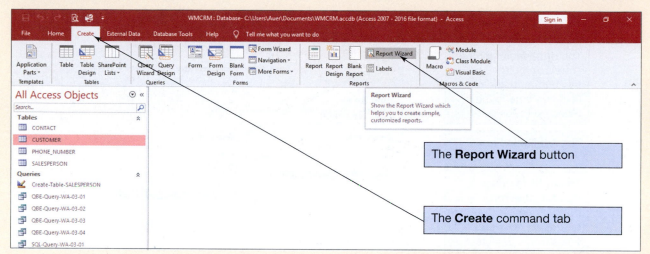

Access 2019, Windows 10, Microsoft Corporation.

4. Select the **CUSTOMER** table in the Tables/Queries drop-down list. Individually select and add the **LastName, FirstName**, and **EmailAddress** columns to the Selected Fields list by using the **right-facing single-chevron** button. Do *not* click the **Next** button yet.

5. Select the **CONTACT** table in the Tables/Queries drop-down list. Individually select and add the **ContactDate, ContactType**, and **Remarks** columns to the Selected Fields list by using the **right-facing single-chevron** button. Do *not* click the **Next** button yet. The Form Wizard now appears as shown in Figure WA-4-37.

FIGURE WA-4-35

The Report Wizard

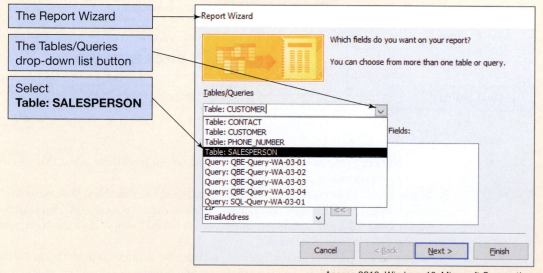

Access 2019, Windows 10, Microsoft Corporation.

(Continued)

FIGURE WA-4-36

Selecting Report Fields

The **Selected Fields** list

The **right-facing single –chevron** button–use this button to add one field at a time to the Selected Fields list

The **Available Fields** list

The **right-facing double–chevron** button–use this button to add all the available fields to the Selected Fields list

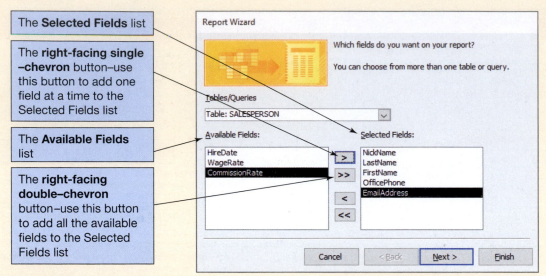

Access 2019, Windows 10, Microsoft Corporation.

FIGURE WA-4-37

The Complete Report Selected Fields List

The complete **Selected Fields** list–this list now includes fields (columns) from three different tables

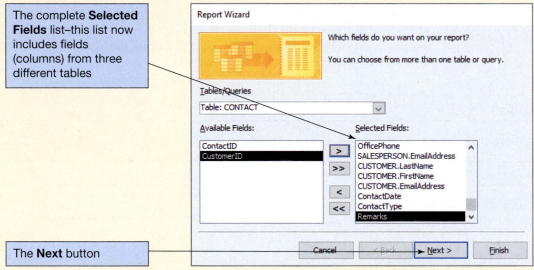

The **Next** button

Access 2019, Windows 10, Microsoft Corporation.

6. Now click the **Next** button.
   - **NOTE:** You have just created a set of columns from three tables that you want to appear on one report.
7. When asked "How do you want to view your data?" click the **Next** button to use the default **by SALESPERSON** selection (to see all customer contacts for each salesperson).
8. When asked "Do you want to add any grouping levels?" simply click the **Next** button to use the default column structure.
9. We are now asked "What sort order do you want for detail records?" This is the sort order for the CONTACT data. The most useful sorting order is by date, in ascending order. Click the **sort field 1** drop-down list arrow and select **ContactDate**. Leave the sort order button set to **Ascending** as shown in Figure WA-4-38. Click the **Next** button.

FIGURE WA-4-38

The Report Sort Order

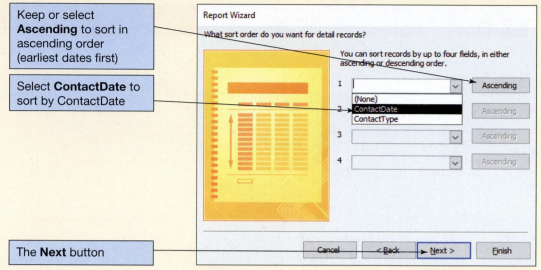

Keep or select **Ascending** to sort in ascending order (earliest dates first)

Select **ContactDate** to sort by ContactDate

The **Next** button

Access 2019, Windows 10, Microsoft Corporation.

10. We are now asked "How would you like to lay out your report?" Use the default setting of stepped layout, but click the **Landscape** orientation radio button to change the report orientation to landscape, and then click the **Next** button.

11. When asked "What title do you want for your report?" edit the report title to read **WMCRM Salesperson Contacts Report**. Leave the **Preview the report** radio button selected, as shown in Figure WA-4-39.

12. Click the **Finish** button. The completed report is displayed in Print Preview mode. Click the **Shutter Bar Open/Close** button to minimize the Navigation Pane. The completed report is shown in Figure WA-4-40.

Unfortunately the report is not that well designed. To correct the report, we use the Microsoft Access Banded Report Editor.

FIGURE WA-4-39

Specifying the Report Title

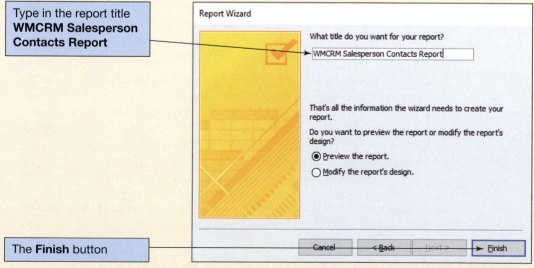

Type in the report title **WMCRM Salesperson Contacts Report**

The **Finish** button

Access 2019, Windows 10, Microsoft Corporation.

(Continued)

FIGURE WA-4-40

The Generated Report for Salesperson Contact Data

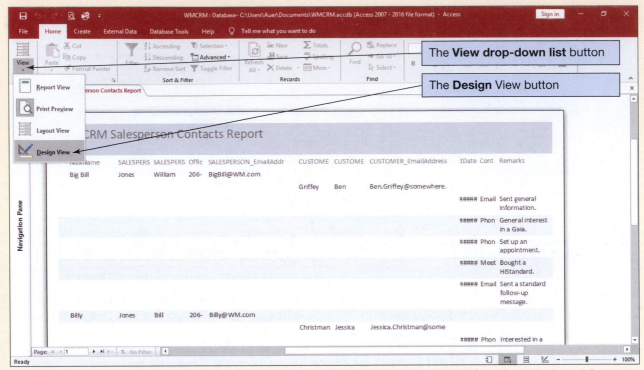

Access 2019, Windows 10, Microsoft Corporation.

Using the Microsoft Access Banded Form and Report Editors

Microsoft Access uses a **banded form editor** and a **banded report editor**, where each element of the form or report is displayed in its own band (for example, Header, Detail, or Footer), which makes rearranging very easy to do. Although we will illustrate using the report editor here, the form editor works exactly the same way.

You can resize form and report sections as necessary, and you can resize the entire form or report itself. You change the size and position of areas. You can move or resize the labels and text boxes that display the data by using standard Windows drag-and-drop actions. You can edit label text, and you can add additional labels or other text.

Using the Microsoft Access Banded Report Editor

1. Click the **Design View** button in the View drop-down list, shown in Figure WA-4-40, to put the report into Design view, as shown in Figure WA-4-41.
2. The report in Figure WA-4-42 has extensively rearranged labels and data text boxes in the Customer and Contact sections of the form. This is the final version of the report. Use the banded report editor to make your report look something like this.
3. Save the changes to the report.
4. Click the **Shutter Bar Open/Close** button to expand the Navigation Pane.
5. Click the document window's **Close** button to close the report window.
6. To close the WMCRM database and exit Microsoft Access, click the **Close** button in the upper-right corner of the Microsoft Access Window.

FIGURE WA-4-41

The Microsoft Access Banded Report Editor

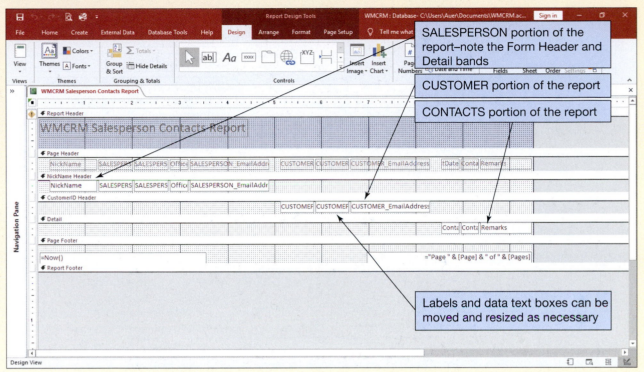

Access 2019, Windows 10, Microsoft Corporation.

Creating a Prototype Form for the Modified Data Model

Before we can create the equivalent WMCRM Salesperson Contacts Form for the second data model, we must prototype the resulting database in Microsoft Access. Fortunately, we do not need to create a new database from scratch—we can simply make a copy of the existing Microsoft Access database. One of the nice features of Microsoft Access is that each database is stored in one *.accdb file. For example, recall from Chapter 1's section of "Working with Microsoft Access" that the original database was named WMCRM.accdb and stored in the Documents library. We can make renamed copies of this file as the basis for prototyping other data models.

Copying the WMCRM.accdb Database

1. Select **Start | Documents** to open the My Documents library.
2. Right-click the **WMCRM.accdb** file object to display the shortcut menu, and then click **Copy**.
3. Right-click anywhere in the empty area of the Documents library window to display the shortcut menu, and then click **Paste**. A file object named **WMCRM - Copy.accdb** appears in the Documents library window.
4. Right-click the **WMCRM - Copy.accdb** file object to display the shortcut menu, and then click **Rename**.
5. Edit the file name to read **WMCRM-WA04-v02.accdb**, and then press the **Enter** key.

(Continued)

FIGURE WA-4-42

The Final WMCRM Salesperson Contacts Report

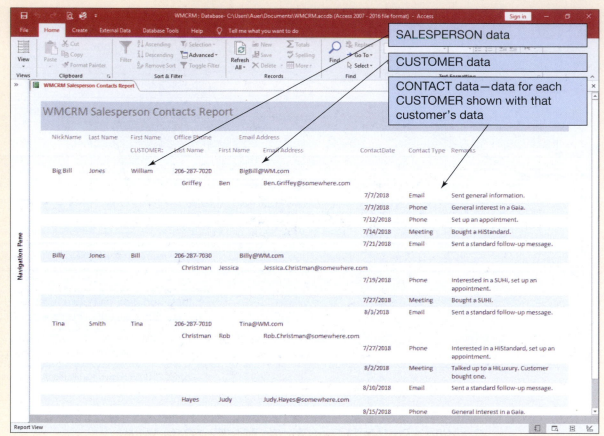

Access 2019, Windows 10, Microsoft Corporation.

Now, we need to modify this database file. The goal is the set of database relationships shown in Figure WA-4-43.

The modifications are straightforward, and we have done most of the steps in previous sections. We need to:

- Remove the relationship between SALESPERSON and CUSTOMER (this is new).
- Delete the NickName field in CUSTOMER.
- Add the NickName field to CONTACT as NULL.
- Populate the NickName field in CONTACT.
- Modify the NickName field in CONTACT to NOT NULL.
- Create the relationship between SALESPERSON and CONTACT.

The only new steps are deleting a relationship and deleting a field from a table.

Deleting the SALESPERSON-to-CUSTOMER Relationship

1. Start Microsoft Access 2019.
2. The Backstage view Recent page is displayed. Click the **Open Other Files** button. The Backstage view Open page is displayed. Click the **Browse** button. The Open dialog box appears. Browse to the **WMCRM-WA04-v02.accdb** file, click the file name to highlight it, and then click the **Open** button.
3. The **Security Warning** bar appears with the database. Click the Security Warning bar's **Enable Content** button.

FIGURE WA-4-43

The Modified WMCRM Database

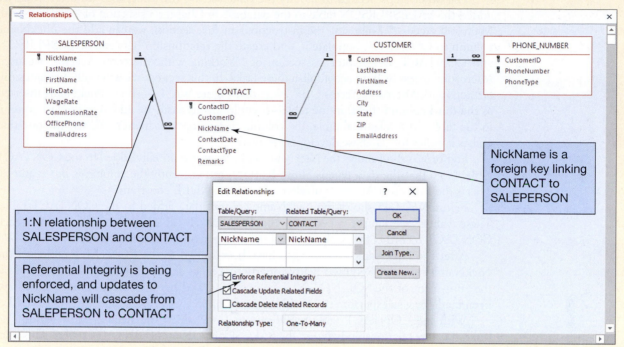

Access 2019, Windows 10, Microsoft Corporation.

4. Click the **Database Tools** command tab.
5. Click the **Relationships** button in the Relationships command group. The Relationships tabbed document window appears. Note that along with the Relationships window, a contextual tab named Relationship Tools is displayed and that this tab adds a new command tab named Design to the set of command tabs displayed.
6. Right-click the **relationship line** between SALESPERSON and CUSTOMER to display the shortcut menu, and then click **Delete**.
7. A dialog box appears with the message "Are you sure you want to permanently delete the selected relationship from your database?" Click the **Yes** button.
8. Click the Relationships window's **Close** button to close the window.
9. If a dialog box appears with the message "Do you want to save the changes to the layout of 'Relationships'?" click the **Yes** button.

With the SALESPERSON-to-CUSTOMER relationship now deleted, we can proceed to delete the NickName field from the CUSTOMER table.

Deleting a Column (Field) from a Microsoft Access Table

1. Open the **CUSTOMER** table in Design view.
2. Select the **NickName** column (field).
3. Right-click anywhere in the selected row to display the shortcut menu. Click **Delete Rows**.
   - **NOTE:** A Delete Rows button is also included in the Tools group on the Design command tab of the Table Tools contextual command tab. You can use this button instead of the shortcut menu if you want to.
4. A dialog box appears with the message "Do you want to permanently delete the selected field(s) and all the data in the field(s)?" To permanently delete the column, click the **Yes** button.

(Continued)

5. Click the **Save** button on the Quick Access Toolbar to save the changes to the table design.
6. Close the **CUSTOMER** table.

The other steps needed to modify the database are the same ones we used when we added the SALESPERSON table to the database in Chapter 3's section of "Working with Microsoft Access." Following the instructions in that section, we can add the NickName column to CONTACT, populate it, and create the relationship between SALESPERSON and CONTACT. In Chapter 3's section of "Working with Microsoft Access," we used Microsoft Access SQL to accomplish these tasks. In this section, we will walk through similar steps with Microsoft Access QBE. Note that Figure WA-4-44 shows NickName inserted as the third column (field) in the table—it could just as easily be added as the last column in the table. In a relational table, the column order does not matter: We use the one that makes it easier for database developers to read!

Figure WA-4-44 shows the NickName column as it is initially added to the CONTACT table. Note that the data type is Short Text(35), but currently the column is *not* required. This is the Microsoft Access equivalent of the SQL NULL constraint.

Figure WA-4-45 shows the NickName column data added to the CONTACT table. These values are simply typed into the CONTACT table in Data View. Now, each CONTACT record contains the name of the salesperson making the contact.

After the NickName column data have been added to the CONTACT table, set the NickName column's Required field property to Yes, as shown in Figure WA-4-46. This is the equivalent of the SQL NOT NULL constraint, and because every contact must have been made by a salesperson, the NickName column in CONTACT must be NOT NULL.

With the CONTACT table modifications done, open the Relationships window to build the new relationship between the SALESPERSON and CONTACT tables. This relationship is shown in Figure WA-4-43, with the Edit Relationships dialog box showing that

FIGURE WA-4-44

The NickName Column in CONTACT

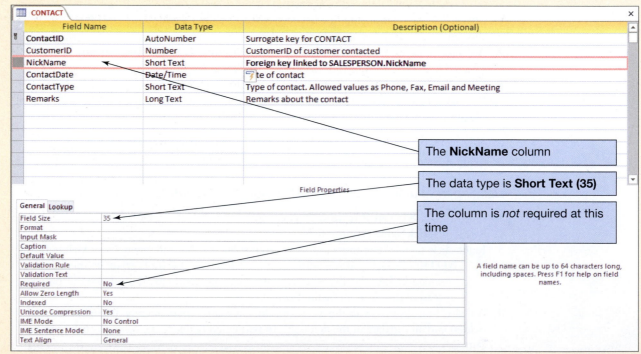

Access 2019, Windows 10, Microsoft Corporation.

FIGURE WA-4-45

The NickName Data in CONTACT

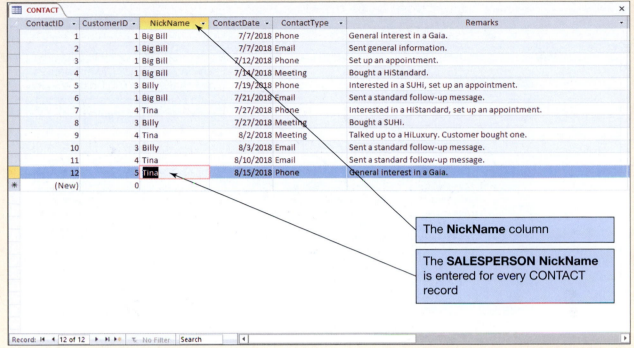

ContactID ▼	CustomerID ▼	NickName ▼	ContactDate ▼	ContactType ▼	Remarks ▼
1	1	Big Bill	7/7/2018	Phone	General interest in a Gaia.
2	1	Big Bill	7/7/2018	Email	Sent general information.
3	1	Big Bill	7/12/2018	Phone	Set up an appointment.
4	1	Big Bill	7/14/2018	Meeting	Bought a HiStandard.
5	3	Billy	7/19/2018	Phone	Interested in a SUHi, set up an appointment.
6	1	Big Bill	7/21/2018	Email	Sent a standard follow-up message.
7	4	Tina	7/27/2018	Phone	Interested in a HiStandard, set up an appointment.
8	3	Billy	7/27/2018	Meeting	Bought a SUHi.
9	4	Tina	8/2/2018	Meeting	Talked up to a HiLuxury. Customer bought one.
10	3	Billy	8/3/2018	Email	Sent a standard follow-up message.
11	4	Tina	8/10/2018	Email	Sent a standard follow-up message.
12	5	Tina	8/15/2018	Phone	General interest in a Gaia.
* (New)	0				

The **NickName** column

The **SALESPERSON NickName** is entered for every CONTACT record

Record: ◄ ◄ 12 of 12 ► ►► ►* No Filter   Search

FIGURE WA-4-46

The Required NickName Column in CONTACT

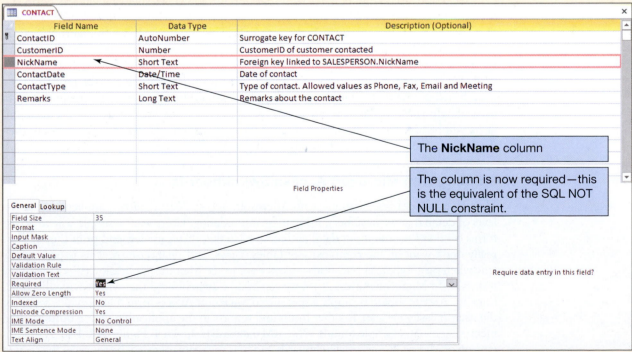

Field Name	Data Type	Description (Optional)
ContactID	AutoNumber	Surrogate key for CONTACT
CustomerID	Number	CustomerID of customer contacted
NickName	Short Text	Foreign key linked to SALESPERSON.NickName
ContactDate	Date/Time	Date of contact
ContactType	Short Text	Type of contact. Allowed values as Phone, Fax, Email and Meeting
Remarks	Long Text	Remarks about the contact

The **NickName** column

The column is now required—this is the equivalent of the SQL NOT NULL constraint.

Field Properties

General | Lookup

Field Size	35
Format	
Input Mask	
Caption	
Default Value	
Validation Rule	
Validation Text	
Required	Yes
Allow Zero Length	Yes
Indexed	No
Unicode Compression	Yes
IME Mode	No Control
IME Sentence Mode	None
Text Align	General

Require data entry in this field?

(Continued)

FIGURE WA-4-47

The WMCRM Salesperson Contacts Form for the Modified Database

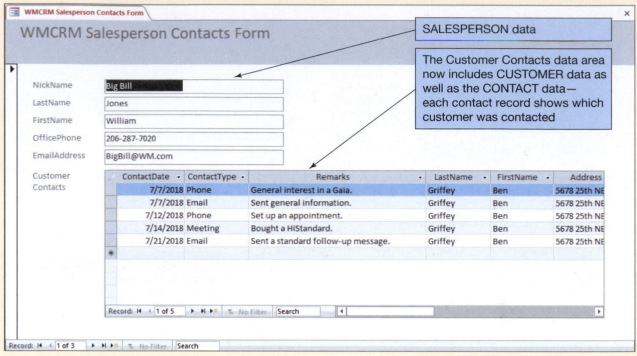

Access 2019, Windows 10, Microsoft Corporation.

referential integrity is being enforced for the relationship, and Cascade Update Related Fields is also checked. Close the Relationships window.

With these modifications done, now create another version of the WMCRM Salesperson Contacts Form. To do this, first delete the existing WMCRM Salesperson Contacts Form and the associated Customer Data and Contact Data forms in WMCRM-WA04-02.accdb, and then use the Form Wizard to create the new form. This version is shown in Figure WA-4-47.

This form has two distinct sections: The top section shows SALESPERSON data, and the bottom section shows that the data for each CUSTOMER are combined with the CONTACT data for each customer contact. This form is distinctively different from the form based on the first data model, but, again, it should be fairly easy to explain this form to Wallingford Motors' management and users. Based on the two forms, management and users will be able to decide how they want the data presented, and this decision will then determine which data model should be used.

Working with Microsoft Access Switchboards

Most users would find working with Microsoft Access 2019 database applications at the level of detail that we have been using to be intimidating. Users want a simple way to access forms (so that they can input data) and reports (so that they can view and print them). They really don't want all the complexity of tables, views, and relationships. This is particularly true when prototyping applications—users want to see what the application can do, not how it does it! In Microsoft Access 2019, we can build a **switchboard** that will provide this functionality. A switchboard is simply a specialized Microsoft Access form that provides a way for the user to easily navigate to other forms and reports in the application with a button-based menu system. An example for our WMCRM database is shown in Figure WA-4-48. A full discussion of Microsoft Access switchboards and how to create them can be found in the section of "Working with Microsoft Access" in the online extension "Advanced BI and Big Data."

FIGURE WA-4-48

A Microsoft Access 2019 Switchboard

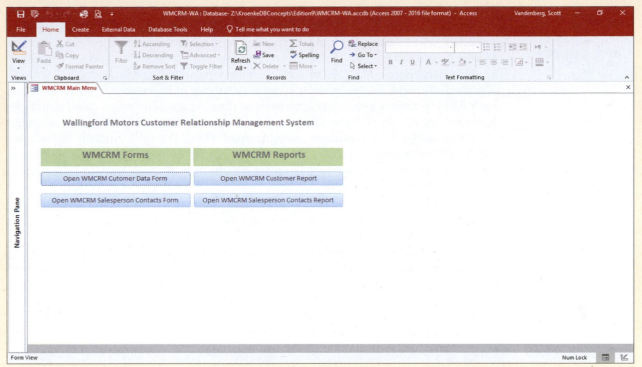

Access 2019, Windows 10, Microsoft Corporation.

Closing the Database and Exiting Microsoft Access

This completes the work we will do in this chapter's "Working with Microsoft Access." As usual, we finish by closing the database and Microsoft Access.

Closing the WMCRM-WA04-v02 Database

1. To close the WMCRM-WA04-v02 database and exit Microsoft Access, click the **Close** button in the upper-right corner of the Microsoft Access window.

SUMMARY

We make decisions based on information, and information is extracted from data. A computer-based information system is a system that uses computers to product information from data. A business process is a set of activities that transform inputs (such as raw materials) into outputs (such as finished goods). Information systems support business processes, and that is their reason for existence.

Systems analysis and design is the process of creating and maintaining information systems. The systems development life cycle (SDLC) is the classic method used to develop information systems. The SDLC consists of five steps: system definition, requirements analysis, component design, implementation, and system maintenance.

The process of developing a database system occurs in the context of the system development life cycle (SDLC), and consists of three stages: requirements analysis, component design, and implementation. During the requirements analysis stage, you interview users, document systems requirements, and construct a data model. Oftentimes, you will create prototypes of selected portions of the future system. During the component design stage, you transform the data model into a relational database design. During the implementation stage, you construct the database; fill it with data; and create queries, forms, reports, application programs, and Web pages.

In addition to creating a data model, you must also determine data-item data types, properties, and limits on data values. You also need to document business rules that constrain database activity.

The entity-relationship (E-R) model is the most popular tool used to develop a data model. With the E-R model, entities, which are identifiable things of importance to the users, are defined. All the entities of a given type form an entity class. A particular entity is called an instance. Attributes describe the characteristics of entities, and one or more attributes identify an entity.

Relationships are associations among entities. The E-R model explicitly defines relationships. Each relationship has a name, and there are relationship classes as well as relationship instances. According to the original specification of the E-R model, relationships may have attributes; however, this is not common in contemporary data models.

The degree of a relationship is the number of entities participating in the relationship. Most relationships are binary. The three types of binary relationships are 1:1, 1:N, and N:M. A recursive relationship occurs when an entity has a relationship to itself.

In traditional E-R diagrams, entities are shown in rectangles and relationships are shown in diamonds. The maximum cardinality of a relationship is shown inside the diamond. The minimum cardinality is indicated by a hash mark or an oval.

A weak entity is one whose existence depends on another entity; an entity that is not weak is called a strong entity. In this text, we further define a weak entity as an entity that logically depends on another entity. An entity can have a minimum cardinality of one in a relationship with another entity and not necessarily be a weak entity. ID-dependent entities must include the identifier of the entity on which the ID-dependent entity depends as part of the identifier of the ID-dependent entity.

When a data model has one or more attributes that seem to be associated with a relationship between two entities rather than with either of the entities themselves, an associative entity (also called an association entity) must be added to the data model. Each of the original entities will have a 1:N relationship with the associative entity, which will have a composite primary key consisting of the two primary keys of the original entities. The associative entity will be ID-dependent on both of the original entities.

The extended E-R model introduced the concept of subtypes. A subtype entity is a special case of another entity known as its supertype. In some cases, an attribute of the supertype, called a discriminator, indicates which of the subtypes is appropriate for a given instance. Subtypes can be exclusive (the supertype relates to at most one subtype) or inclusive (the supertype can relate to one or more subtypes). The identifier of the subtype is the identifier of the supertype.

This text's E-R diagrams use the Information Engineering Crow's Foot E-R model. You should be familiar with diagrams of that style, but you should also realize that when creating a database design no fundamental difference exists between the traditional style and this style. When creating a data model, documenting business rules that constrain database activity is important.

After E-R models are completed, they must be evaluated. You can show the data model, or portions of the data model, directly to the users for evaluation. This requires the users to learn how to interpret an E-R diagram. Sometimes, instead of showing users a data model, you may create prototypes that demonstrate the consequences of the data model. Such prototypes are easier for users to understand.

KEY TERMS

activities	attribute	cardinality
approved user requirements	binary relationship	child entity
association entity	business process	component design
associative entity	business process modeling	component design stage

composite identifier
computer-based information
  system
crow's foot symbol
data
data model
database
database design
database development process
decision
degree
deliverables
design stage
discriminator
entity
entity class
entity instance
entity-relationship (E-R) diagram
entity-relationship model
exclusive subtype
extended entity-relationship (E-R)
  model
finished goods
finished goods inventory
HAS-A relationship
ID-dependent entity
identifier

identifying relationship
IE Crow's Foot model
implementation
implementation stage
inclusive subtype
information
Information Engineering (IE)
information system
input → process → output
inputs
Integrated Definition 1, Extended
  (IDEF1X)
IS-A relationship
mandatory
maximum cardinality
minimum cardinality
nonidentifying relationship
nonunique identifier
optional
outputs
parent entity
partial
process
project plan
raw materials
raw materials inventory
recursive relationship

relationship
relationship class
relationship instance
request for system modification
requirements analysis
requirements analysis stage
statement of work (SOW)
strong entity
subtype entity
supertype entity
system
system definition
system design
system design stage
system maintenance
systems analysis and design
systems development life cycle (SDLC)
ternary relationship
total
unary relationship
Unified Modeling Language (UML)
unique identifier
updated system
use case
user requirements document (URD)
work breakdown schedule (WBS)
weak entity

REVIEW QUESTIONS

4.1 What is a *decision*?

4.2 What is *data*?

4.3 What is *information*?

4.4 What is a *system*? What is an *information system*?

4.5 What is a *computer-based information system*? Describe the five components of a computer-based information system.

4.6 What is a *business process*?

4.7 How do information systems support business processes?

4.8 Describe how information systems include processes.

4.9 What is *systems analysis and design*?

4.10 Describe the *systems development life cycle (SDLC)* model.

4.11 What is a *user requirements document (URD)*? What purpose does it serve?

4.12 Name the three stages in the process of developing database systems. Summarize the tasks in each.

4.13 What is a *data model*, and what is its purpose?

4.14 What is a *prototype*, and what is its purpose?

4.15 What is a *use case*, and what is its purpose?

4.16 Give an example of a data constraint.

4.17 Give an example of a business rule that would need to be documented in a database development project.

4.18 Define the term *entity*, and give an example other than those used in this book.

4.19 Explain the difference between an entity class and an entity instance.

4.20 Define the term *attribute*, and give examples for the entity you described in question 4.18.

4.21 Define the term *identifier*, and indicate which attribute(s) defined in your answer to question 4.20 identifies the entity.

4.22 Define the term *composite identifier*, and give an example other than those used in this book.

4.23 Define the term *relationship*, and give an example other than those used in this text.

4.24 Explain the difference between a relationship class and a relationship instance.

4.25 Define the term *degree of relationship*. Give an example, other than one used in this text, of a relationship greater than degree two.

4.26 List and give an example of the three types of binary relationships other than the ones used in this book. Draw both a traditional E-R diagram and an IE Crow's Foot E-R diagram for each.

4.27 Define the terms *maximum cardinality* and *minimum cardinality*.

4.28 Draw an IE Crow's Foot E-R diagram for the entities DEPARTMENT and EMPLOYEE and the 1:N relationship between them. Assume that a DEPARTMENT does not need to have an EMPLOYEE but that every EMPLOYEE is assigned to a DEPARTMENT. Include appropriate identifiers and attributes for each entity.

4.29 Define the term *ID-dependent entity*, and give an example other than one used in this text. Draw an IE Crow's Foot E-R diagram for your example.

4.30 Define the term *weak entity*, and give an example of a non-ID-dependent weak entity other than one used in this text. Draw an IE Crow's Foot E-R diagram for your example.

4.31 Explain the ambiguity in the definition of the term *weak entity*. Explain how this book interprets this term.

4.32 Define the term *associative entity*, and give an example other than one used in this text. Your example should start with a N:M relationship between two strong entities and then be modified by an additional data requirement. Draw IE Crow's Foot E-R diagrams for both your N:M relationship and for the relationships among the three entities that include the associative entity.

4.33 Define the terms *supertype*, *subtype*, and *discriminator*.

4.34 What is an exclusive subtype relationship? Give an example other than one shown in this book. Draw an IE Crow's Foot E-R diagram for your example.

4.35 What is an inclusive subtype relationship? Give an example other than one shown in this chapter. Draw an IE Crow's Foot E-R diagram for your example.

4.36 Give an example of a recursive relationship other than the one shown in this chapter. Draw an IE Crow's Foot E-R diagram for your example.

4.37 Give an example of a business rule for your work for question 4.28.

4.38 Describe why evaluating a data model is important.

4.39 Summarize one technique for evaluating a data model and explain how that technique could be used to evaluate the data model in Figure 4-27(c).

EXERCISES

4.40 Suppose that Heather Sweeney wants to include records of her consulting services in her database. Extend the data model in Figure 4-27(c) to include CONSULTING_PROJECT and DAILY_PROJECT_HOURS entities. CONSULTING_PROJECT contains data about a particular project for one of Heather's customers, and DAILY_PROJECT_HOURS contains data about the hours spent and a description of the work accomplished on a particular day for a particular project. Use strong and/or weak entities, as appropriate. Specify minimum and maximum cardinalities. Use the IE Crow's Foot E-R model for your E-R diagram.

4.41   Extend your work for exercise 4.40 to include supplies that Heather uses on a project. Assume that she wants to track the description, price, and amount used of each supply. Supplies are used on multiple days of a project. Use the IE Crow's Foot E-R model for your E-R diagrams.

4.42   Using recursive relationships, as appropriate, develop a data model of the boxcars on a railway train. Use the IE Crow's Foot E-R model for your E-R diagrams.

4.43   Develop a data model of a genealogical diagram. Model only biological parents; do not model stepparents. Use the IE Crow's Foot E-R model for your E-R diagrams.

4.44   Develop a data model of a genealogical diagram. Model all parents, including stepparents. Use the IE Crow's Foot E-R model for your E-R diagrams.

WORKING WITH MICROSOFT ACCESS

Key Terms

1:1 non-identifying relationship	Entity object
1:N identifying relationship	Microsoft Visio 2019
1:N non-identifying relationship	Primary Key Attribute object
Attribute object	Primary Key Separator object
backstage view	prototype database
banded form editor	Relationship connector object
banded report editor	stencil
Crow's Foot database notation template	switchboard
dynamic connector	

Review Questions

WA.4.1   What is Microsoft Visio 2019?

WA.4.2   What is the Backstage view?

WA.4.3   How do you create a new database model diagram drawing in Microsoft Visio 2019?

WA.4.4   Describe the Shapes window and the objects in the Shapes window.

WA.4.5   What shapes are included in the **Crow's Foot Database Notation** stencil, and what is the purpose of each shape?

WA.4.6   How do you create entities in a data model diagram?

WA.4.7   When should you use the Relationship connector object?

WA.4.8   How do you format a Relationship object so that it displays IE Crow's Foot E-R notation?

WA.4.9   How do you connect a Relationship object to two tables? What significance is there to which end of the Relationship is attached to which table?

WA.4.10   How are Relationship connector cardinalities set? What is the correspondence between the cardinality terms used in the dynamic connector and the IE Crow's Foot E-R notation shown in Figure 4-14?

Exercises

This chapter's section of "Working with Microsoft Access" describes how to create data models using Microsoft Visio 2019, and how to create prototype databases and sample forms and reports in Microsoft Access 2019. In the following set of exercises, you will:

- Create data models.
- Create prototype forms.
- Create prototype reports.

WA.4.11   If you haven't already done so, work through the steps described in this section of "Working with Microsoft Access" to create the data model and database design for the WP database. Create a copy of the WP-Data-Model.vsdx file, and name it WP-Data-Model-with-ASSIGNMENT.vsdx. Modify the data model to include the ASSIGNMENT associative entity as shown in the column characteristics in Figure WA-4-9.

WA.4.12   A data model for the Heather Sweeney Designs HSD database is shown in Figure 4-27(c). In Microsoft Visio 2019, create a file named HSD-Data-Model.vsdx, and use it to recreate the data model shown in Figure 4-27(c).

WA.4.13   The data model for the Wallingford Motors Customer Relationship WMCRM database is shown in Figure WA-4-22. In Microsoft Visio 2019, create a file named WMCRM-Data-Model.vsdx, and use it to recreate the data model shown in Figure WA-4-22.

WA.4.14   Using the WMCRM-WA04-02.accdb database, recreate the WMCRM Salesperson Contacts Report so that it is based on the rearranged set of relationships. *Hint*: To do this, you must first delete the existing version of the report.

WA.4.15   You have built an extensive database for Wedgewood Pacific (WP.accdb). You will now use it to build some prototype forms and reports so that the users at WP can evaluate the proposed database. In this case, there is no need to restructure the database.

A.   Create a form that allows users to view and edit employee data. The form should show information about the employee, the department that he or she works for, and which projects the employee is assigned to.

B.   Create a report that displays the employee information shown on the form you created in part A. The report should show this information for all users, sorted alphabetically in ascending order by LastName.

C.   Create a form that allows users to view and edit project data. The form should show information about the project and the department that is responsible for the project, and it should list all employees who are assigned to work on that project.

D.   Create a report that displays the project information shown on the form you created in part C. The report should show this information for all projects, sorted in ascending order by ProjectID.

CASE QUESTIONS

HIGHLINE UNIVERSITY MENTOR PROGRAM

Highline University is a four-year undergraduate school located in the Puget Sound region of Washington State.[9] Highline University, like many colleges and universities in the Pacific Northwest, is accredited by the Northwest Commission on Colleges and Universities (NWCCU—see **www.nwccu.org**). Like all the colleges and universities accredited by the

---

[9]Highline University is a *fictional* university and should not be confused with Highline Community College located in Des Moines, Washington. Any resemblance between Highline University and Highline Community College is unintentional and purely coincidental.

NWCCU, Highline University must be reaccredited at approximately five-year intervals. Additionally, the NWCCU requires annual status-update reports. Highline University is made up of five colleges: the College of Business, the College of Social Sciences and Humanities, the College of Performing Arts, the College of Sciences and Technology, and the College of Environmental Sciences. Jan Smathers is the president of Highline University, and Dennis Endersby is the provost (a provost is a vice president of academics; the deans of the colleges report to the provost).

In this set of case questions, we will consider an information system for Highline University that will be used by Highline University's Mentor Program. The Highline University Mentor Program recruits business professionals as mentors for Highline University students. The mentors are unpaid volunteers who work together with the students' advisers to ensure that the students in the mentoring program learn needed and relevant management skills. In this case study, you will develop a data model for the Mentor Program Information System.

A. Draw an E-R data model for the Highline University Mentor Program Information System (MPIS). Use the IE Crow's Foot E-R model for your E-R diagrams. Justify the decisions you make regarding minimum and maximum cardinalities.

Your model should track students, advisers, and mentors. Additionally, Highline University needs to track alumni because the program administrators view alumni as potential mentors.

1. Create separate entities for students, alumni, faculty advisers, and mentors.

   - At Highline University, all students are required to live on campus and are assigned Highline University ID numbers and email accounts in the format *FirstName. LastName@students.hu.edu.* The student entity should track student last name, student first name, student University ID number, student email address, dorm name, dorm room number, and dorm phone number.
   - At Highline University, all faculty advisers have on-campus offices and are assigned Highline University ID numbers and email accounts in the format *FirstName. LastName@hu.edu.* The faculty entity should track faculty last name, faculty first name, faculty University ID number, faculty email address, department, office building name, office building room number, and office phone number.
   - Highline University alumni live off campus and were previously assigned Highline University ID numbers. Alumni have private email accounts in the format *FirstName. LastName@somewhere.com.* The alumni entity should track alumnus last name, alumnus first name, alumnus former-student number, email address, home address, home city, home state, home ZIP code, and phone number.
   - Highline University mentors work for companies and use their company address, phone, and email address for contact information. They do not have Highline University ID numbers as mentors. Email addresses are in the format *FirstName. LastName@companyname.com.* The mentor entity should track mentor last name, mentor first name, mentor email address, company name, company address, company city, company state, company ZIP code, and company phone number.

2. Create relationships between entities based on the following facts:

   - Each student is assigned one and only one faculty adviser and must have an adviser. One faculty member may advise several students, but faculty members are not required to advise students. Only the fact of this assignment is to be recorded in the data model—not possible related data (such as the date the adviser was assigned to the student).
   - Each student may be assigned one and only one mentor, but students are not required to have a mentor. One mentor may mentor several students, and a person may be listed as a mentor before he or she is actually assigned students to mentor. Only the fact of this assignment is to be recorded in the data model—not possible related data (such as the date the mentor was assigned to the student).
   - Each mentor is assigned to work and coordinate with one and only one faculty member, and each mentor must work with a faculty member. One faculty member may

work with several mentors, but faculty members are not required to work with mentors. Only the fact of this assignment is to be recorded in the data model—not possible related data (such as the date the faculty member was assigned to the mentor).

- Each mentor may be an alumnus, but mentors are not required to be alumni. Alumni cannot, of course, be required to become mentors.

B. Revise the E-R data model you created in part A to create a new E-R data model based on the fact that students, faculty, alumni, and mentors are all a PERSON. Use the IE Crow's Foot E-R model for your E-R diagrams. Justify the decisions you make regarding minimum and maximum cardinalities. Note that while the following business rules need to be implemented in your design, the E-R model notation may not be able to express them, in which case you will need to add text notes to your diagram indicating which rules will be enforced in SQL structures or application code (alternatively, write a memo to accompany your E-R diagram that contains these notes). The relevant business rules are:

- A person may be a current student, an alumnus, or both because Highline University does have alumni return for further study.
- A person may be a faculty member or a mentor, but not both.
- A person may be a faculty member and an alumnus.
- A person may be a mentor and an alumnus.
- A current student cannot be a mentor.
- Each mentor may be an alumnus, but mentors are not required to be alumni. Alumni cannot, of course, be required to become mentors.

C. Extend and modify the E-R data model you created in part B to allow more data to be recorded in the MPIS system. Use the IE Crow's Foot E-R model for your E-R diagrams. Justify the decisions you make regarding minimum and maximum cardinalities. The MPIS needs to record:

- The date a student enrolled at Highline University, the date the student graduated, and the degree the student received
- The date an adviser was assigned to a student and the date the assignment ended
- The date an adviser was assigned to work with a mentor and the date the assignment ended
- The date a mentor was assigned to a student and the date the assignment ended

D. Write a short discussion of the difference between the three data models you have created. How does data model B differ from data model A, and how does data model C differ from data model B? What additional features of the E-R data model were introduced when you created data models B and C?

WRITER'S PATROL

Consider the Writer's Patrol traffic citation shown in Figure 4-28. The rounded corners on this form provide visual hints about the boundaries of the entities represented.

A. Draw an E-R data model based on the traffic citation form. Use five entities, create identifiers (watch out for any composite identifiers that may be needed, and you can use surrogate identifiers if appropriate), and use the data items on the form to specify attributes for the entities. Use the IE Crow's Foot E-R model for your E-R diagram.

B. Specify relationships among the entities. Name the relationships, and specify the relationship types and cardinalities. Justify the decisions you make regarding minimum and maximum cardinalities, indicating which cardinalities can be inferred from the data on the form and which need to be checked out with the system users.

FIGURE 4-28

Writer's Patrol Traffic
Citation

WRITER'S PATROL CORRECTION NOTICE

NAME   Kroenke   , David   M
       LAST   FIRST
ADDRESS   5053   88   Ave   SE

CITY Mercer Island   STATE Wa   ZIP CODE 98040

DRIVERS LICENSE   STATE [M]   BIRTH DATE   HGT   WGT EYES
   00000   Wa [F]   2/27 46   6   165 BI

VEHICLES LICENSE   STATE   COLOR   YEAR   MAKE   TYPE
   AAA000   Wa   90   Saab   900

VIN

REGISTERED

OWNER

ADDRESS

VIOLATION DATE   DIST   DETACH
MO 11 DAY 7   YEAR 2018 TIME HOUR: 935   2   17

LOCATION
17 MILES E   OF   Enumckum   ON SR410

VIOLATIONS
     Writing text while driving

OFFICERS   PERSONNEL
SIGNATURE S Scott   NUMBER   850

[X] This is a warning, no further action is required.

[ ] You are released to take this vehicle to a place of repair.
     Continued operation on the roadway is not authorized.

[ ] CORRECT VIOLATION(S) IMMEDIATELY. Return this signed card
     for proof of compliance within 15/30 days. (if this box checked)

X DRIVERS
   SIGNATURE

GARDEN GLORY PROJECT QUESTIONS

Garden Glory wants to expand its database applications beyond the recording of property services. The company still wants to maintain data on owners, properties, employees, services, and the service work done at the properties, but it wants to include other data as well. Specifically, Garden Glory wants to track equipment, how it is used during services, and equipment repairs. In addition, employees need to be trained before they use certain equipment, and management wants to be able to determine who has obtained training on which equipment.

With regard to properties, Garden Glory has determined that most of the properties it services are too large and complex to be described in one record. The company wants the database to allow for many subproperty descriptions of a property. Thus, a particular property might have subproperty descriptions such as Front Garden, Back Garden, Second-Level Courtyard, and so on. For better accounting to the customers, services are to be related to the subproperties rather than to the overall property.

A. Draw an E-R data model for the Garden Glory database schema shown in Chapter 3's "Garden Glory Project Questions." Use the IE Crow's Foot E-R model for your E-R diagrams. Justify the decisions you make regarding minimum and maximum cardinalities.

B. Extend and modify the E-R data model to meet Garden Glory's new requirements. Use the IE Crow's Foot E-R model for your E-R diagrams. Create appropriate identifiers and attributes for each entity. Justify the decisions you make regarding minimum and maximum cardinalities.

C. Describe how you would go about validating the model in part B.

JAMES RIVER JEWELRY PROJECT QUESTIONS

James River Jewelry wants to expand its database applications beyond the recording of purchases and purchase awards. (See the description of the award program in the James River Jewelry Project Questions for Chapter 1.) The company still wants to maintain data on customers, purchases, and awards, but it wants to include other data as well. Specifically, James River Jewelry wants to record artists and styles and keep track of which customers are interested in which artists and styles.

James River Jewelry sells most of its jewelry on consignment, so the company does not pay the artist of a piece of jewelry until it is sold. Typically, the company pays artists 60 percent of the sales price, but the terms are negotiated separately for each item. For some items, the artists earn a larger percentage and for others they earn less. Artists and James River Jewelry personnel agree on the initial sales price at the time the item is brought to the shop. When an item has been in the shop for some time, James River Jewelry may reduce the price; sometimes it renegotiates the sales percentage.

A. Draw an E-R data model for the James River Jewelry database schema shown in the James River Jewelry Project Questions for Chapter 3. Use the IE Crow's Foot E-R model for your E-R diagrams. Justify the decisions you make regarding minimum and maximum cardinalities.

B. Extend and modify the E-R data model to show James River Jewelry's award program. Use the IE Crow's Foot E-R model for your E-R diagrams. Create appropriate identifiers and attributes for each entity. Justify the decisions you make regarding minimum and maximum cardinalities.

C. Extend and modify the E-R data model in part B to meet James River Jewelry's new requirements. Use the IE Crow's Foot E-R model for your E-R diagrams. Create appropriate identifiers and attributes for each entity. Justify the decisions you make regarding minimum and maximum cardinalities.

D. Describe how you would go about validating the data model in part C.

THE QUEEN ANNE CURIOSITY SHOP PROJECT QUESTIONS

The Queen Anne Curiosity Shop wants to expand its database applications beyond the current recording of sales. The company still wants to maintain data on customers, employees, vendors, sales, and items, but it wants to (a) modify the way it handles inventory and (b) simplify the storage of customer and employee data.

Currently, each item is considered unique, which means the item must be sold as a whole, and multiple units of the item in stock must be treated as separate items in the ITEM table. The Queen Anne Curiosity Shop management wants the database modified to include an inventory system that will allow multiple units of an item to be stored under one ItemID. The system should allow for a quantity on hand, a quantity on order, and an order due date. If the identical item is stocked by multiple vendors, the item should be orderable from any of these vendors. The SALE_ITEM table should then include Quantity and ExtendedPrice columns to allow for sales of multiple units of an item.

The Queen Anne Curiosity Shop management has noticed that some of the fields in CUSTOMER and EMPLOYEE store similar data. Under the current system, when an employee buys something at the store, his or her data has to be reentered into the CUSTOMER table. The managers would like to have the CUSTOMER and EMPLOYEE tables redesigned using subtypes.

A. Draw an E-R data model for the Queen Anne Curiosity Shop database schema shown in Chapter 3's "The Queen Anne Curiosity Shop Project Questions." Use the IE Crow's Foot E-R model for your E-R diagrams. Justify the decisions you make regarding minimum and maximum cardinalities.

B. Extend and modify the E-R data model by adding *only* the Queen Anne Curiosity Shop's inventory system requirements. Use the IE Crow's Foot E-R model for your E-R diagrams. Create appropriate identifiers and attributes for each entity. Justify the decisions you make regarding minimum and maximum cardinalities.

C. Extend and modify the E-R data model by adding *only* the Queen Anne Curiosity Shop's need for more efficient storage of CUSTOMER and EMPLOYEE data. Use the IE Crow's Foot E-R model for your E-R diagrams. Create appropriate identifiers and attributes for each entity. Justify the decisions you make regarding minimum and maximum cardinalities.

D. Combine the E-R data models from parts B and C to meet all the new requirements for The Queen Anne Curiosity Shop, making additional modifications, as needed. Use the IE Crow's Foot E-R model for your E-R diagrams.

E. Describe how you would go about validating your data model in part D.

- Learn how to transform E-R data models into relational designs
- Practice applying the normalization process
- Understand the need for denormalization
- Learn how to represent weak entities with the relational model

- Know how to represent 1:1, 1:N, and N:M binary relationships
- Know how to represent 1:1, 1:N, and N:M recursive relationships
- Learn SQL statements for creating joins over binary and recursive relationships

n Chapter 4, we defined the database development process as consisting of three major stages: requirements analysis, component design, and implementation. We then discussed the requirements analysis stage and how to create a **data model** in entity-relationship (E-R) notation. This chapter describes a process for converting an E-R data model into a relational *database design*. We begin by explaining how data model entities are expressed as relations (or tables) in a relational database design. We then apply the normalization process that you learned in Chapter 2. Next, we show how to represent relationships using foreign keys, including how to use these techniques for representing recursive relationships. Finally, we apply all these techniques to design a database for the data model of Heather Sweeney Designs that we developed in Chapter 4.

Database design occurs in the **component design** step of the **systems development life cycle (SDLC)** as discussed in Chapter 4.

THE PURPOSE OF A DATABASE DESIGN

A **database design** is a set of database specifications that can actually be implemented as a database in a DBMS. The *data model* we discussed in Chapter 4 is a *generalized, non-DBMS-specific* design. A database design, on the other hand, is a *DBMS-specific* design intended to be implemented in a DBMS product such as Microsoft SQL Server 2017 or MySQL 8.0. Because each DBMS product has its own way of doing things, even if based on the same relational database model and the same SQL standards, each database design must be created for a particular DBMS product. The same data model will result in slightly different database designs, depending on the intended DBMS product.

Books on systems analysis and design often identify three design stages:

- Conceptual design (conceptual schema)
- Logical design (logical schema)
- Physical design (physical schema)

The *database design* we are discussing is basically equivalent to *logical design*, which is defined in these books as the conceptual design as modified to be implemented in a specific DBMS product. The *physical design* deals with aspects of the database encountered when it is actually implemented in the DBMS, such as physical record and file structure and organization, indexing, and query optimization. However, our discussion of database design *will* include data type specifications, which is often considered a physical design issue in systems analysis and design.

TRANSFORMING A DATA MODEL INTO A DATABASE DESIGN

The steps for transforming a data model into a database design are shown in Figure 5-1. First, we create a table for each entity in the data model, including creating a primary key and specifying column properties. Then we make sure that each of the tables is properly normalized. Finally, we create the relationships between the tables.[1]

As you learned in Chapter 2, the technically correct term for the representation of an entity in a relational model is **relation**. However, the use of the synonym **table** is common, and we use it in this chapter. Just remember that the two terms mean the same thing when used to discuss databases.

---

[1]The transformation is actually a bit more complex than this when you consider the need to enforce minimum cardinalities. Although the referential integrity constraints (with ON UPDATE and ON DELETE) handle some parts of this, application logic is required to handle other parts, and that is beyond the scope of this book. See David M. Kroenke, David J. Auer, Scott L. Vandenberg, and Robert C. Yoder, *Database Processing: Fundamentals, Design, and Implementation*, 15th ed. (Upper Saddle River, NJ: Pearson, 2019), Chapter 6.

FIGURE 5-1

The Steps for
Transforming a Data
Model into a Database
Design

1. Create a table for each entity:

   – Specify primary key (consider surrogate keys as appropriate)

   – Specify properties for each column:

      • Data type

      • Null status

      • Default value (if any)

      • Specify data constraints (if any)

   – Verify normalization

2. Create relationships by placing foreign keys:

   – Strong entity relationships (1:1, 1:N, N:M)

   – ID-dependent and non–ID-dependent weak entity relationships

   – Subtypes

   – Recursive (1:1, 1:N, N:M)

REPRESENTING ENTITIES WITH THE RELATIONAL MODEL

The representation of entities using the relational model is direct and straightforward. First, you define a table for each entity and give that table the same name as the entity. You make the primary key of the relation the identifier of the entity. Then you create a column in the relation for each attribute in the entity. Finally, you apply the normalization process described in Chapter 2 to remove any modification anomalies. To understand this process, we will consider three examples.

Representing the ITEM Entity

Consider the ITEM entity shown in Figure 5-2(a), which contains the attributes ItemNumber, Description, Cost, ListPrice, and QuantityOnHand. To represent this entity with a table, we define a table named ITEM and place the attributes in it as columns in the relation. ItemNumber is the identifier of the entity and becomes the primary key of the table. The result is shown in Figure 5-2(b), where a key symbol identifies the primary key. The ITEM table can also be written as:

ITEM (<u>ItemNumber</u>, Description, Cost, ListPrice, QuantityOnHand)

Note that in this notation the primary key of the table is underlined.

Surrogate Keys   The ideal primary key is short, numeric, and nonchanging. Item-Number meets these criteria. However, if the primary key does not meet these criteria, a DBMS-generated **surrogate key** should be used. Surrogate key values are numeric, are

FIGURE 5-2

The ITEM Entity
and Table

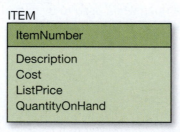

(a) The ITEM Entity

(b) The ITEM Table

unique within a table, and never change. These keys are assigned when a row is created and removed when the row is deleted—the numbers are never reused. Surrogate keys would be ideal primary keys except for a couple of considerations.

First, the numbers generated have no intrinsic meaning. For example, if surrogate key values are used as the values of ItemNumber in the ITEM table, you cannot interpret them in a meaningful way. Second, although the surrogate key values may not be duplicated within a table, they may not be unique between two databases. Consider two databases, each of which has an ITEM table with the surrogate ID of ItemNumber. If the data from these databases are ever shared, this may present a problem. Nonetheless, surrogate keys are very useful and are commonly used as ID numbers in tables.

Column Properties

Note that each attribute in the ITEM entity has become a column in the ITEM table. You need to specify certain **column properties** for each column, as mentioned in the discussion of attributes at the end of Chapter 4. These include data types, null status, default values, and any constraints on the values.

Data Types   Each DBMS supports certain **data types**. (Data types for MySQL 8.0 SQL Server 2017, and Oracle Database XE were discussed in Chapter 3, and data types for Microsoft Access 2019 were discussed in Chapter 1.) For each column, you indicate exactly what type of data will be stored in that column. Data types are usually set when the table is actually created in the database, as discussed in Chapter 3.

NULL Status   Next, you need to decide which column must have data values entered when a new row is created in the table. If a column *must* have a data value entered, then this column will be designated NOT NULL. If the value can be left empty, then the column will be designated NULL. The **NULL status**—NULL or NOT NULL—of the column is usually set when the table is actually created in the database, as discussed in Chapter 3.

You have to be careful here: If you specify columns as NOT NULL when you do not know the data value at the time the row is being created, you will not be able to create the row. For this reason, some columns that may appear to you as needing to be NOT NULL must actually be specified as NULL. This data will be entered, but not at the exact moment the row is created in the table.

For the ITEM table, you set only ListPrice as NULL. This is a number that may not have been determined by management at the time data on an ITEM are entered into the database. All other columns should have known values at the time a row is created and are NOT NULL.

Default Values   A **default value** is a value that the DBMS automatically supplies when a new row is created. The default value may be a static value (one that remains the same) or one calculated by application logic. In this book, we deal with only static values. Default values are usually set when the table is actually created in the database, as discussed in Chapter 3. In the ITEM table, you should specify a default of 0 for QuantityOnHand. This will indicate that the ITEM is out of stock until this value is updated.

Data Constraints   The data values in some columns may be subject to restrictions on the values that can exist in those columns. Such limitations are called **data constraints**. An example we have already seen is the referential integrity constraint, which states that the only values allowed in a foreign key column are values already existing in the corresponding primary key column in the related table. Data constraints are usually set when the table is actually created in the database, as discussed in Chapter 3. In the ITEM table, one needed data constraint is (ListPrice > Cost), which ensures that you do not inadvertently sell an ITEM for less than you paid for it.

Verifying Normalization

Finally, you need to verify that the ITEM table is properly normalized because the table resulting from converting an entity sometimes has modification problems. Therefore, the next step is to apply the normalization process from Chapter 2, and we strongly suggest that at this point you review the normalization definitions and processes discussed in that chapter so that you are familiar with them before proceeding with our discussion of normalization.

In the case of ITEM, the only candidate key is the primary key, which is ItemNumber, and no other functional dependencies exist. Therefore, the ITEM table is normalized to **Boyce-Codd Normal Form (BCNF)**. The final ITEM table, with column types, surrogate key indicator, and NULL/NOT NULL constraints indicated, is shown in Figure 5-3. Generally, we do not show this much detail in the illustrations of tables in this chapter, but note that these types of details are available in commercial database design programs and can usually be displayed as needed.

Representing the CUSTOMER Entity

To understand an entity that gives rise to modification problems, consider the CUSTOMER entity in Figure 5-4(a). If you transform the entity as just described, you obtain the table shown in Figure 5-4(b):

CUSTOMER (CustomerNumber, CustomerName, StreetAddress, City, State, ZIP, ContactName, Phone)

CustomerNumber is the key of the relation, and you can assume that you have done all the necessary work on column definition.

According to the normalization process (see pages 89–91), you need to check for functional dependencies besides those involving the primary key. At least one exists:[2]

ZIP → (City, State)

FIGURE 5-3

The Final ITEM Table

ITEM

🔑 ItemNumber: int IDENTITY(10000,1)

Description: varchar(100) NOT NULL
Cost: numeric(9,2) NOT NULL
ListPrice: numeric(9,2) NULL
QuantityOnHand: int NOT NULL

FIGURE 5-4

The CUSTOMER Entity and Table

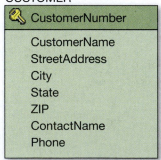

CUSTOMER

CustomerNumber

CustomerName
StreetAddress
City
State
ZIP
ContactName
Phone

CUSTOMER

🔑 CustomerNumber

CustomerName
StreetAddress
City
State
ZIP
ContactName
Phone

(a) The CUSTOMER Entity   (b) The CUSTOMER Table

[2]While the example of ZIP determining City and State is a commonly used and very understandable example, a five-digit ZIP code (as commonly used instead of a nine-digit number) does not, in fact, determine City and State! There are cases of one ZIP code determining more than one city and state. For example, both Sparta, Illinois, and Eden, Illinois, have the ZIP code 62286.

The only candidate key in CUSTOMER is CustomerNumber. ZIP is *not* a candidate key for this relation; therefore, this relation is not normalized. Furthermore, another possible functional dependency involves Phone. Is Phone the phone number of the CUSTOMER, or is it the phone number of the contact? If PhoneNumber is the phone number of the CUSTOMER, then:

CustomerNumber → Phone

and no additional normalization problem exists. However, if the PhoneNumber is that of the contact, then:

ContactName → Phone

and because ContactName is not a candidate key, there are modification problems here as well.

   You can determine whose phone number it is by asking the users. Assume that you do that, and the users say that it is indeed the phone number of the contact. Thus:

ContactName → Phone

Given these facts, you can proceed to normalize the CUSTOMER table. According to the normalization process, you pull the attributes of the functional dependencies out of the tables while leaving a copy of their determinants in the original relation as foreign keys. The result is the three relations shown in Figure 5-5:

CUSTOMER (<u>CustomerNumber</u>, CustomerName, StreetAddress, *ZIP, ContactName*)
ZIP (<u>ZIP</u>, City, State)
CONTACT (<u>ContactName</u>, Phone)

with the referential integrity constraints:

ZIP in CUSTOMER must exist in ZIP in ZIP
ContactName in CUSTOMER must exist in ContactName in CONTACT

These three relations are now normalized, and you can continue with the design process. However, let us first consider another perspective on normalization.

FIGURE 5-5

The Normalized CUSTOMER and Associated Tables

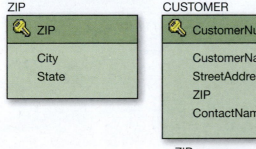

Denormalization

It is possible to take normalization too far. Most practitioners would consider the construction of a separate ZIP table to be going too far. People are accustomed to writing their city, state, and ZIP as a group, and breaking City and State away from ZIP will make the design difficult to use. It will also mean that the DBMS has to read two separate tables just to get the customer's address. Therefore, even though it results in normalization problems, a better overall design would result by leaving ZIP, City, and State in the CUSTOMER relation. This is an example of **denormalization**.

What are the consequences of this decision to denormalize? Consider the three basic operations: insert, update, and delete. If you leave ZIP, City, and State in CUSTOMER, then you will not be able to insert data for a new ZIP code until a customer has that ZIP code. However, you will never want to do that. You only care about ZIP code data when one of the customers has that ZIP code. Therefore, leaving the ZIP data in CUSTOMER does not pose problems when inserting.

What about modifications? If a city changes its ZIP code, then you might have to change multiple rows in CUSTOMER. How frequently do cities change their ZIP codes, though? Because the answer is almost never, updates in the denormalized relation are not a problem. Finally, what about deletes? If only one customer has the ZIP data (80210, Denver, Colorado), then if you delete that customer you will lose the fact that 80210 is in Denver. This does not really matter because when another customer with this ZIP code is inserted, that customer also will provide the city and state.

Therefore, denormalizing CUSTOMER by leaving the attributes ZIP, City, and State in the relation will make the design easier to use and not cause modification problems. The denormalized design is better, and it is shown in Figure 5-6:

CUSTOMER (<u>CustomerNumber</u>, CustomerName, StreetAddress, City, State, ZIP, *ContactName*)

CONTACT (<u>ContactName</u>, Phone)

with the referential integrity constraints:

ContactName in CUSTOMER must exist in ContactName in CONTACT

The need for denormalization can also arise for reasons such as security and performance. If the cost of modification problems is low (as for ZIP codes) and if other factors cause denormalized relations to be preferred, then denormalizing is a good idea.

FIGURE 5-6

The Denormalized CUSTOMER and Associated CONTACT Tables

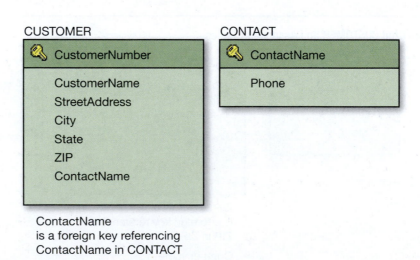

CUSTOMER

🔑 CustomerNumber
CustomerName
StreetAddress
City
State
ZIP
ContactName

CONTACT

🔑 ContactName
Phone

ContactName
is a foreign key referencing
ContactName in CONTACT

A Relational Design for the SALES_COMMISSION Entity

To summarize the discussion so far, when representing an entity with the relational model the first step is to construct a table that has all the entity's attributes as columns. The identifier of the entity (usually) becomes the primary key of the table, and we define the column constraints. Then the table is normalized. A reason might exist for leaving parts of a table denormalized.

By proceeding in this way, we always consider the normalized design. If we make a decision to denormalize, we then do so from a position of knowledge and not from ignorance.

To reinforce these ideas, let us consider a third example: the SALES_COMMISSION entity in Figure 5-7(a). First, you create a relation that has all the attributes as columns, as shown in Figure 5-7(b):

SALES_COMMISSION (SalespersonNumber, SalespersonLastName, SalespersonFirstName, Phone, <u>CheckNumber</u>, CheckDate, CommissionPeriod, TotalCommissionSales, CommissionAmount, BudgetCategory)

As shown, the primary key of the table is CheckNumber, the identifier of the entity. The attributes of the relation have three additional functional dependencies:

SalespersonNumber →
   (SalespersonLastName, SalespersonFirstName, Phone, BudgetCategory)

CheckNumber → CheckDate

(SalespersonNumber, CommissionPeriod) →
   (TotalCommissionSales, CommissionAmount, CheckNumber, CheckDate)

According to the normalization process, you extract the attributes of these functional dependencies from the original table and make the determinants the primary keys of the new tables. You also leave a copy of the determinants in the original table as foreign keys. The only complication in this case is that the name of the original table actually makes more sense when used for one of the new tables that has been created! The original table, given the primary key CheckNumber, should actually be called COMMISSION_CHECK, and it has been renamed as such in the normalization results shown in Figure 5-8:

SALESPERSON (<u>SalespersonNumber</u>, SalespersonLastName, SalespersonFirstName, Phone, BudgetCategory)

SALES_COMMISSION (*<u>SalespersonNumber</u>*, <u>CommissionPeriod</u>, TotalCommissionSales, CommissionAmount, *CheckNumber*)

COMMISSION_CHECK (<u>CheckNumber</u>, CheckDate)

FIGURE 5-7

The SALES_COMMISSION Entity and Table

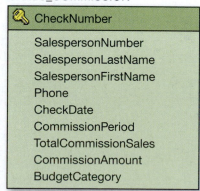

	SALES_COMMISSION
CheckNumber	
SalespersonNumber	
SalespersonLastName	
SalespersonFirstName	
Phone	
CheckDate	
CommissionPeriod	
TotalCommissionSales	
CommissionAmount	
BudgetCategory	

(a) The SALES_COMMISSION Entity   (b) The SALE_COMMISSION Table

FIGURE 5-8

The Normalized SALES_COMMISSION and Associated Tables

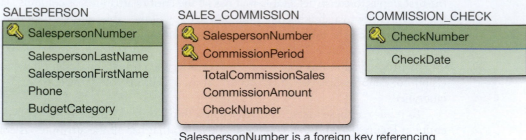

SalespersonNumber is a foreign key referencing
SalespersonNumber in SALESPERSON

SALES_COMMISSION is ID-dependent on SALESPERSON

CheckNumber is a foreign key referencing CheckNumber
in COMMISSION_CHECK

with the referential integrity constraints:

SalespersonNumber in SALES_COMMISSION must exist in SalespersonNumber
  in SALESPERSON
CheckNumber in SALES_COMMISSION must exist in CheckNumber in
  COMMISSION_CHECK

Now consider denormalization. Is there any reason not to create these new relations? Is the design better if you leave them in the COMMISSION_CHECK relation (the renamed SALES_COMMISSION relation)? In this case, there is no reason to denormalize, so you leave the normalized relations alone.

Representing Weak Entities

The process described so far works for all entity types, but weak entities sometimes require special treatment. Recall that a weak entity logically depends on another entity. In Figure 5-8, SALES_COMMISSION is an ID-dependent weak entity that depends on SALESPERSON for its existence. In this model, there cannot be a SALES_COMMISSION without a SALESPERSON. Also note that in Figure 5-8 we consider COMMISSION_CHECK to be a strong entity because after the check is written it has a separate, physical existence of its own, just like a SALESPERSON (an alternate conceptualization would require an additional CHECKING_ACCOUNT entity as the strong entity with CHECK as an ID-dependent weak entity, in which case the composite primary key of CHECK would be used as the foreign key in SALES_COMMISSION).

If a weak entity is not ID-dependent, it can be represented as a table, using the techniques just described. The dependency needs to be recorded in the relational design so that no application will create a weak entity without its proper parent (the entity on which the weak entity depends). Finally, a business rule will need to be implemented so that when the parent is deleted the weak entity is also deleted. These rules are part of the relational design and, in this case, take the form of an ON DELETE CASCADE constraint on the weak, non–ID-dependent table.

The situation is slightly different if a weak entity is also ID-dependent. This is the case in the dependence of SALES_COMMISSION on SALESPERSON because each SALES_COMMISSION is identified by the SALESPERSON who made the sale. When creating a table for an ID-dependent entity, we must ensure that the identifier of the parent and the identifier of the ID-dependent weak entity itself appear in the table. For example, consider what

FIGURE 5-9

Relational Representation of a Weak Entity

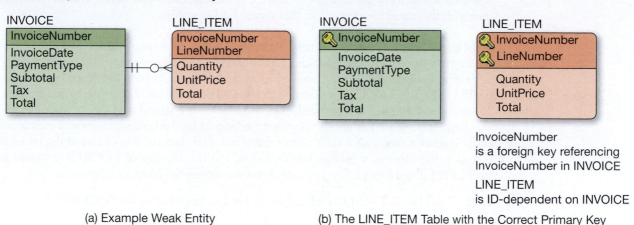

(a) Example Weak Entity   (b) The LINE_ITEM Table with the Correct Primary Key

would happen if you established the table for SALES_COMMISSION without including the key of SALESPERSON. What would be the key of this table? It would be just CommissionPeriod, but because SALES_COMMISSION is ID-dependent, this is not a complete key. In fact, without the needed reference to SALESPERSON included, CommissionPeriod by itself cannot be the primary key because this table would likely have duplicate rows, or, even worse, many of the salespeople could have the same commission period key value. (This would happen if two occurrences of a specific CommissionPeriod had the same TotalCommissionSales in the same BudgetCategory, which could happen because this table records data for more than one SALESPERSON.) Thus, for an ID-dependent weak entity it is necessary to add the primary key of the parent entity to the weak entity's table, and this added attribute becomes part of that table's key. In Figure 5-8, note that SALES_COMMISSION has the correct composite primary key (SalespersonNumber, CommissionPeriod).

As another example, consider Figure 5-9(a), where LINE_ITEM is an ID-dependent weak entity. It is weak because its logical existence depends on INVOICE, and it is ID-dependent because its identifier contains the identifier of INVOICE. Again, consider what would happen if you established a relation for LINE_ITEM without including the key of INVOICE. What would be the key of this relation? It would be just LineNumber, but because LINE_ITEM is ID-dependent it cannot be a complete key. Without the needed reference to ITEM included, LINE_ITEM, like SALESPERSON_SALES in the previous example, would likely have duplicate rows, or, even worse, many line items would have the line number 1. (This would happen if two invoices had the same quantity of the same item on the same line.) Figure 5-9(b) shows LINE_ITEM with the correct composite primary key (InvoiceNumber, LineNumber). Note that the tables in Figure 5-9(b) are intentionally shown without a relationship—we discuss adding relationships in the next section.

REPRESENTING RELATIONSHIPS

So far, you have learned how to create a relational design for the entities in an E-R model. However, to convert a data model to a relational design we must also represent the relationships by placing foreign keys into tables.

The techniques used to represent E-R relationships depend on the maximum cardinality of the relationships. As you saw in Chapter 4, three relationship possibilities exist: one-to-one (1:1), one-to-many (1:N), and many-to-many (M:N). A fourth possibility, many-to-one (N:1), is represented in the same way as 1:N, so we need not consider it as a separate case. The following sections discuss foreign key placement in various types of relationships.

Relationships Between Strong Entities

The easiest relationships to work with are relationships between strong entities. We will start with these and then consider other types of relationships.

Representing 1:1 Strong Entity Relationships   The simplest form of a binary relationship is a 1:1 relationship, in which an entity of one type is related to at most one entity of another type. In Figure 5-10(a), the same 1:1 relationship that was used in Figure 4-11(a) between EMPLOYEE and LOCKER is shown in IE Crow's Foot notation. According to this diagram, an employee is assigned at most one locker, and a locker is assigned to at most one employee.

Representing a 1:1 relationship with the relational model is straightforward. First, each entity is represented with a table as just described, and then the key of one of the tables is placed in the other as a foreign key. In Figure 5-10(b), the key of LOCKER is stored in EMPLOYEE as a foreign key, and you create the referential integrity constraint:

LockerNumber in EMPLOYEE must exist in LockerNumber in LOCKER

In Figure 5-10(c), the key of EMPLOYEE is stored in LOCKER as a foreign key, and you create the referential integrity constraint:

EmployeeNumber in LOCKER must exist in EmployeeNumber in EMPLOYEE

In general, for a 1:1 relationship the key of either table can be placed as a foreign key in the other table. To verify that this is so, consider both cases in Figure 5-10.

Suppose that for the design in Figure 5-10(b) you have an employee and want the locker assigned to that employee. To get the employee data, you use EmployeeNumber to obtain the employee's row in EMPLOYEE. From this row, you obtain the LockerNumber of the locker assigned to that employee. You then use that number to look up the locker data in LOCKER.

Now consider the other direction. Assume that you have a locker and want to know which employee is assigned to that locker. Using the design in Figure 5-10(c), you access the

FIGURE 5-10

1:1 Strong Entity Relationships

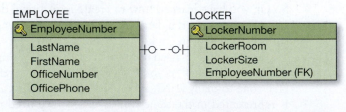

(a) Example 1:1 Strong Entity Relationship

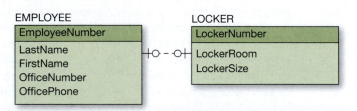

(b) Placing the Primary Key of LOCKER into EMPLOYEE

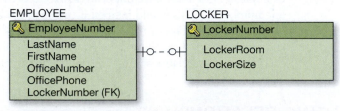

(c) Placing the Primary Key of EMPLOYEE into LOCKER

LOCKER table and look up the row that has the given LockerNumber. The EmployeeNumber of the employee who has been assigned that locker appears in that row. You now use that EmployeeNumber in the EMPLOYEE table to obtain the data about that employee.

In this situation, we are using the term *look up* to mean "to find a row given a value of one of its columns." Another way to view this is in terms of joins. For the relations in Figure 5-10(b), you can form the following join:

```
/* *** EXAMPLE CODE-DO NOT RUN *** */
/* *** SQL-QUERY-CH05-01 *** */
SELECT    *
FROM      EMPLOYEE JOIN LOCKER
    ON    EMPLOYEE.LockerNumber=LOCKER.LockerNumber;
```

Because the relationship is 1:1, the result of this join will have a single row for a given combination of employee and locker. The row will have all columns from both tables.

For the relations in Figure 5-10(c), you can join the two tables on EmployeeNumber as follows:

```
/* *** EXAMPLE CODE - DO NOT RUN *** */
/* *** SQL-QUERY-CH05-02 *** */
SELECT    *
FROM      EMPLOYEE JOIN LOCKER
    ON    EMPLOYEE.EmployeeNumber=LOCKER.EmployeeNumber;
```

Again, one row will be found for each combination of employee and locker. In both of these joins, neither unassigned employees nor unassigned lockers will appear.

Although the two designs in Figure 5-10(b) and Figure 5-10(c) are equivalent in concept, they may differ in performance. For instance, if a query in one direction is more common than a query in the other, we might prefer one design to the other. Also, depending on underlying structures, if an index (a metadata structure that makes searches for specific data faster) for EmployeeNumber is in both tables but no index on LockerNumber is in either table, then the first design is better. In addition, considering the join operation, if one table is much larger than the other, then one of these joins might be faster to perform than the other.

However, if one of the entities has mandatory participation, the choice is obvious. Consider the example of a 1:1 strong entity relationship is the relationship between the CUSTOMER and CONTACT tables shown in Figure 5-6. For each CUSTOMER, there is one and only one CONTACT, and, based on our normalization process, we have used the primary key of CONTACT as the foreign key in CUSTOMER. The resulting relationship is shown in Figure 5-11.

FIGURE 5-11

1:1 Strong Entity Relationship Between CUSTOMER and CONTACT

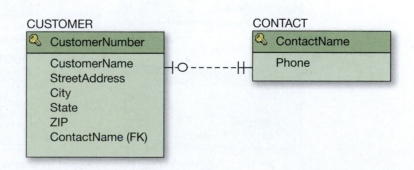

To actually implement a 1:1 relationship in a database, we must constrain the values of the designated foreign key as UNIQUE. This can be done in the SQL CREATE TABLE statement that is to build the table containing the foreign key, or it can be done by altering the table structure after the table is created using the SQL ALTER TABLE statement. Consider the EMPLOYEE-to-LOCKER relationships. If, for example, we decide that to place the foreign key EmployeeNumber in the LOCKER table to create the relationship, we will need to constrain EmployeeNumber in LOCKER as UNIQUE. To do this we will use the SQL statement:

```
/* *** EXAMPLE CODE - DO NOT RUN *** */
/* *** SQL-CONSTRAINT-CH05-01 *** */
CONSTRAINT   UniqueEmployeeNumber   UNIQUE(EmployeeNumber)
```

as a line of SQL code either in the original CREATE TABLE LOCKER command or in the following ALTER TABLE LOCKER command (which assumes that any data already in LOCKER will not violate the UNIQUE constraint),

```
/* *** EXAMPLE CODE - DO NOT RUN *** */
/* *** SQL-ALTER-TABLE-CH05-01 *** */
ALTER TABLE LOCKER
     ADD CONSTRAINT UniqueEmployeeNumber
          UNIQUE (EmployeeNumber);
```

Representing 1:N Strong Entity Relationships   The second type of binary relationship, known as 1:N, is a relationship in which an entity of one type can be related to many entities of another type. In Figure 5-12(a), the 1:N relationship that was used in Figure 4-11(b) between ITEM and QUOTATION is shown in IE Crow's Foot notation. According to this diagram, we have received from zero to several quotations for each item in the database.

The terms **parent** and **child** are sometimes applied to relations in 1:N relationships. The parent relation is on the one side of the relationship, and the child relation is on the many side. In Figure 5-12(a), ITEM is the parent entity and QUOTATION is the child entity.

Representing 1:N relationships is simple and straightforward. First, each entity is represented by a table, as described, and then the key of the table representing the *parent entity* is placed in the table representing the *child entity* as a foreign key. Thus, to represent the relationship in Figure 5-12(a) you place the primary key of ITEM, which is ItemNumber,

FIGURE 5-12

1:N Strong Entity
Relationships

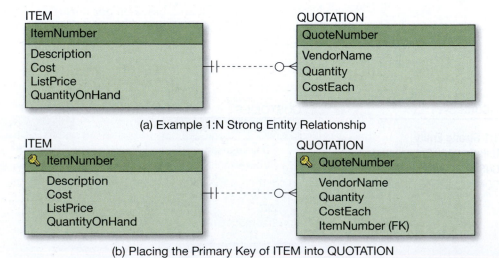

(a) Example 1:N Strong Entity Relationship

(b) Placing the Primary Key of ITEM into QUOTATION

into the QUOTATION table, as shown in Figure 5-12(b), and you create the referential integrity constraint:

ItemNumber in QUOTATION must exist in ItemNumber in ITEM

Notice that with ItemNumber stored as a foreign key in QUOTATION, you can process the relationship in both directions. Given a QuoteNumber, you can look up the appropriate row in QUOTATION and get the ItemNumber of the item from the row data. To obtain the rest of the ITEM data, you use the ItemNumber obtained from QUOTATION to look up the appropriate row in ITEM. To determine all the quotes associated with a particular item, you look up all rows in QUOTATION that have the item's ItemNumber as a value for ItemNumber. Quotation data are then taken from those rows.

In terms of joins, you can obtain the item and quote data in one table with the following:

```
/* *** EXAMPLE CODE - DO NOT RUN *** */
/* *** SQL-QUERY-CH05-03 *** */
SELECT     *
FROM       ITEM JOIN QUOTATION
    ON     ITEM.ItemNumber = QUOTATION.ItemNumber;
```

Contrast this 1:N relationship design strategy with that for 1:1 relationships. In both cases, we store the key of one relation as a foreign key in the second relation. In a 1:1 relationship, we can place the key of either relation in the other. In a 1:N relationship, however, the key of the parent relation *must* be placed in the child relation.

To understand this better, notice what would happen if you tried to put the key of the child into the parent relation (that is, put QuoteNumber in ITEM). Because attributes in a relation can have only a single value, each ITEM record has room for only one QuoteNumber. Consequently, such a structure cannot be used to represent the many side of the 1:N relationship. Hence, to represent a 1:N relationship we must always place the key of the parent relation in the child relation.

To actually implement a 1:N relationship in a database, we only need to add the foreign key column to the table holding the foreign key. Because this column will normally be unconstrained in terms of how many times a value can occur, a 1:N relationship is established by default. In fact, this is the reason that we must use a UNIQUE column constraint to create a 1:1 relationship, as discussed early in this chapter. We will illustrate this point in this chapter's section of "Working with Microsoft Access."

Representing N:M Strong Entity Relationships   The third and final type of binary relationship is N:M, in which an entity of one type corresponds to many entities of the second type and an entity of the second type corresponds to many entities of the first type.

Figure 5-13(a) shows an E-R diagram of the N:M relationship between students and classes. A STUDENT entity can correspond to many CLASS entities, and a CLASS entity can correspond to many STUDENT entities. Notice that both participants in the relationship are optional: A student does not need to be enrolled in a class, and a class is not required to have any students. Figure 5-13(b) gives sample data.

N:M relationships cannot be represented directly by relations in the same way that 1:1 and 1:N relationships are represented. To understand why this is so, try using the same strategy as for 1:1 and 1:N relationships—placing the key of one relation as a foreign key into the other relation. First, define a relation for each of the entities; call them STUDENT and CLASS. Then try to put the primary key of STUDENT, which is SID, into CLASS. Because multiple values are not allowed in the cells of a relation, you have room for only one StudentNumber, so you have no place to record the StudentNumber of the second and subsequent students.

FIGURE 5-13

N:M Strong Entity
Relationships

(a) Example N:M Strong Entity Relationship

(b) Sample Data for the STUDENT-to-CLASS Relationship

A similar problem occurs if you try to put the primary key of CLASS, which is ClassNumber, into STUDENT. You can readily store the identifier of the first class in which a student is enrolled, but you have no place to store the identifier of additional classes.

Figure 5-14 shows another (but incorrect) strategy. In this case, a row is stored in the CLASS relation for each STUDENT enrolled in one class, so you have two records for Class 10 and two for Class 30. The problem with this scheme is that it duplicates the class data and creates modification anomalies. Many rows will need to be changed if, for example, the schedule for Class 10 is modified. Also, consider the insertion and deletion anomalies: How can you schedule a new class until a student has enrolled? In addition, what will happen if Student 300 drops out of Class 40? This strategy is unworkable.

The solution to this problem is to create a third table, called an **intersection table**[3], that represents the relationship itself. The intersection table is a *child* table that is

FIGURE 5-14

Incorrect
Representation of an
N:M Relationship

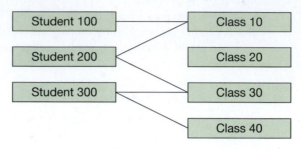

STUDENT

CLASS

---

[3]Although we use the term *intersection table* in this book, this table structure is known by many other names. In fact, Wikipedia currently lists 15 alternate names, including *intersection table, junction table, bridge table*, and *association table*. We reserve the term *association table* for an *association relationship* (as explained later in this chapter), but your instructor may prefer one of the other terms for this table structure. For more information, see the Wikipedia article **Junction table** at **https://en.wikipedia.org/wiki/Associative_entity.**

FIGURE 5-15

Representing an N:M Strong Entity Relationship

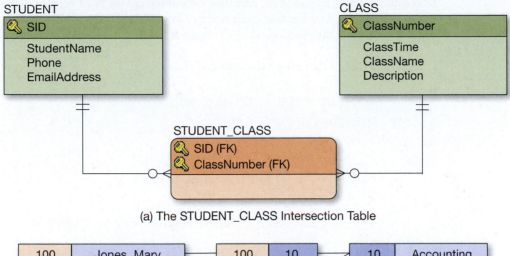

(a) The STUDENT_CLASS Intersection Table

100	Jones, Mary
200	Parker, Fred
300	Wu, Jason

100	10
200	10
200	30
300	30
300	40

10	Accounting
20	Finance
30	Marketing
40	Database

(b) Sample Data for the STUDENT-to-CLASS Relationship

connected to two *parent* tables by *two* 1:N relationships that replace the *single* N:M relationship in the data model. Thus, we define a table named STUDENT_CLASS, as shown in Figure 5-15(a):

STUDENT (SID, StudentName, Phone, EmailAddress)

CLASS (ClassNumber, ClassTime, ClassName, Description)

STUDENT_CLASS (*SID*, *ClassNumber*)

with the referential integrity constraints:

SID in STUDENT_CLASS must exist in SID in STUDENT
   ClassNumber in STUDENT_CLASS must exist in ClassNumber in CLASS

Some instances of this relation are shown in Figure 5-15(b). Such relations are called *intersection tables* because each row documents the intersection of a particular student with a particular class. Notice in Figure 5-15(b) that the intersection relation has one row for each line between STUDENT and CLASS, as in Figure 5-13(b).

In Figure 5-15(a), notice that the relationship from STUDENT to STUDENT_CLASS is 1:N and the relationship from CLASS to STUDENT_CLASS is also 1:N. In essence, we have decomposed the M:N relationship into two 1:N relationships. The key of STUDENT_CLASS is (SID, ClassNumber), which is the combination of the primary keys of both of its parents. The key for an intersection table is *always* the combination of parent keys. Note that the parent relations are *both* required because a parent must now exist for each key value in the intersection relation.

Finally, notice that STUDENT_CLASS is an ID-dependent weak entity, which is ID-dependent on both STUDENT and CLASS. To create a database design for an N:M *strong entity* relationship, we have had to introduce an ID-dependent *weak entity*! (We will have more to say about relationships with weak entities in the next section.)

To summarize the preceding discussion, to actually implement an N:M relationship in a database we must create a new intersection table, to which we add foreign key columns linking to the two tables in the N:M relationship. These foreign key columns will be the corresponding primary keys of the two tables, and together they will form a composite primary key in the intersection table. The relationship between each table and the intersection table will be a 1:N relationship, and thus we implement an N:M relation by creating two 1:N relationships. And because each primary key in the original tables appears as in the primary key of the intersection table, the intersection table is ID-dependent on both original tables.

You can obtain data about students and classes by using the following SQL statement:

```
/* *** EXAMPLE CODE - DO NOT RUN *** */
/* *** SQL-Query-CH05-04 *** */
SELECT    *
FROM      STUDENT JOIN STUDENT_CLASS
    ON    STUDENT.SID = STUDENT_CLASS.SID
          JOIN CLASS
             ON STUDENT_CLASS.ClassNumber = CLASS.ClassNumber;
```

The result of this SQL statement is a table with all columns for a student and the classes the student takes. The student data will be repeated in the table for as many classes as the student takes, and the class data will be repeated in the relation for as many students as are taking the class.

Relationships Using Weak Entities

Because weak entities exist, they are bound to end up as tables in relationships! We have just seen one place where this occurs: in the case of the STUDENT and CLASS entities in Figure 5-15, a new ID-dependent entity is created and becomes the table that represents an N:M relationship. Note that the intersection table that is formed in this case has only the columns that make up its composite primary key. In the STUDENT_CLASS table, this key is (SID, ClassNumber).

Now that you know that an N:M relationship in a data model is transformed into two 1:N relationships in a database design, let us revisit the topic of data modeling and database design software products discussed in Chapter 4. Some products, such as erwin Data Modeler, can create true data models with correctly drawn N:M relationships. These products are also capable of correctly transforming the data models into database designs with intersection tables. Oracle's MySQL Workbench (even though it displays an N:M relationship as an option) cannot correctly draw a data model N:M relationship. Instead, it immediately creates a database design with an intersection table and two 1:N relationships. Nonetheless, creating database designs in MySQL Workbench can be helpful in modeling, designing, and building a database. For example, Figure 5-16 shows the database design for the Wedgewood Pacific database used in Chapter 3 (including the recursive relationship for EMPLOYEE) in MySQL Workbench, and Figure 5-17 shows just the resulting database design. Note that MySQL Workbench uses the same symbols for line ends and line types (solid or dashed) as are used in Chapter 4 and the current chapter. See online Extension A, "Working with MySQL," for more information on using MySQL Workbench.

FIGURE 5-16

A Database Design in MySQL Workbench

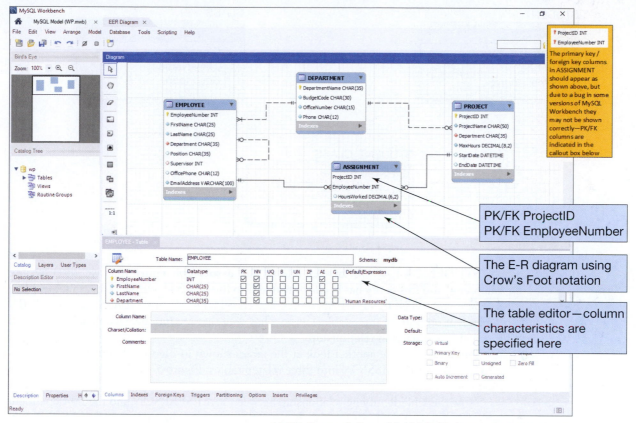

MySQL Community Server 8.0, MySQL Workbench, Oracle Corporation.

FIGURE 5-17

The WP Database Design in Crow's Foot Notation

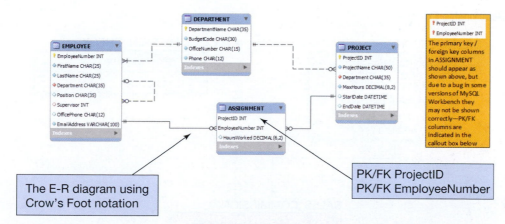

MySQL Community Server 8.0, MySQL Workbench, Oracle Corporation.

Another ID-dependent weak entity occurs when we take an intersection table and add entity attributes (table columns) beyond those in the composite primary key. For example, Figure 5-18 shows the table and relationship structure of Figure 5-15(a) but with one new attribute (column)—Grade—added to STUDENT_CLASS.

FIGURE 5-18

The Association Relationship

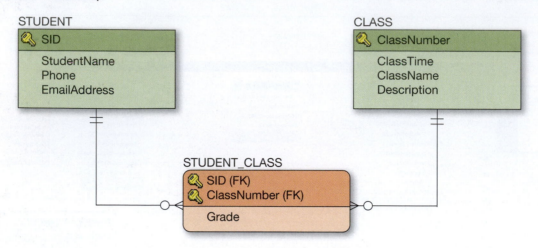

STUDENT_CLASS is an example of the **associative entity** that we discussed in Chapter 4, and this entity has been converted into the new STUDENT_CLASS table. Note that although STUDENT_CLASS still connects STUDENT and CLASS (and is still ID-dependent on both of these tables), it now has data that are uniquely its own. This pattern is called an **association relationship**.

Finally, let us take another look at the tables shown in Figure 5-8, where you normalized SALES_COMMISSION into three related tables. Figure 5-19 shows these tables with their correct relationships.

Note the 1:N identifying relationship between SALESPERSON and the ID-dependent table SALES_COMMISSION, which correctly uses the primary key of SALESPERSON as part of the composite primary key of SALES_COMMISSION. Also note the 1:1 relationship between SALES_COMMISSION and COMMISSION_CHECK. Because

FIGURE 5-19

Mixed Entity Relationship Example

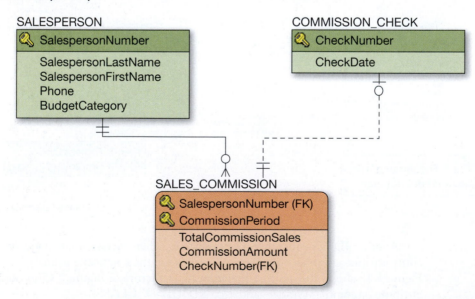

COMMISSION_CHECK is a strong entity and has its own unique primary key, this is a nonidentifying relationship. This set of tables and relationships illustrates a **mixed entity pattern**.[4]

Relationships with Subtypes

Because the identifier of a subtype entity is the identifier of the associated supertype entity, creating relationships between the STUDENT table and its subtypes is simple. The identifier of the subtype becomes the primary key of the subtype *and* the foreign key linking the subtype to the supertype. Figure 5-20(a) shows the E-R model in Figure 4-20(a), and Figure 5-20(b) shows the equivalent database design.

Representing Recursive Relationships

A recursive relationship is a relationship among entities of the same class. Recursive relationships are not fundamentally different from other relationships and can be represented using the same techniques. As with nonrecursive relationships, three types of recursive relationships are possible: 1:1, 1:N, and N:M. Figure 5-21 shows an example of each of these three types.

Let us start by considering the 1:1 recursive SPONSORED_BY relationship in Figure 5-21(a). As with a regular 1:1 relationship, one person can sponsor another person, and each person is sponsored by no more than one person. Figure 5-22(a) shows sample data for this relationship.

To represent 1:1 recursive relationships, we take an approach nearly identical to that for regular 1:1 relationships; that is, we can place the key of the person being sponsored in the row of the sponsor, or we can place the key of the sponsor in the row of the person being sponsored. Figure 5-22(b) shows the first alternative, and Figure 5-22(c) shows the second. Both work.

FIGURE 5-20

Representing Subtypes

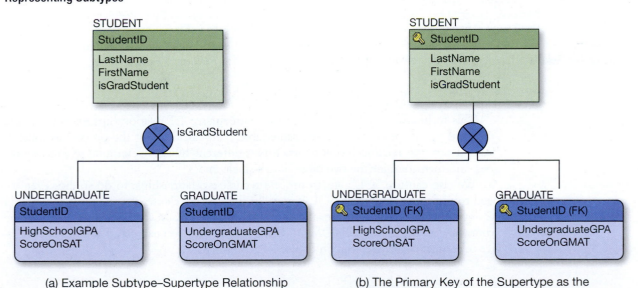

(a) Example Subtype–Supertype Relationship

(b) The Primary Key of the Supertype as the Primary Key and Foreign Key of the Subtype

---

[4]For more information on mixed entity patterns, see David M. Kroenke, David J. Auer, Scott L. Vandenberg, and Robert C. Yoder, *Database Processing: Fundamentals, Design, and Implementation*, 15th ed. (Upper Saddle River, NJ: Pearson, 2019): 238–241, 288–289.

FIGURE 5-21

Example Recursive Relationships

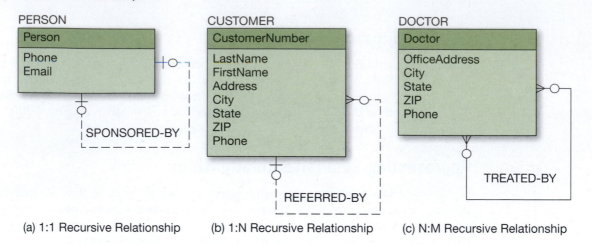

(a) 1:1 Recursive Relationship   (b) 1:N Recursive Relationship   (c) N:M Recursive Relationship

FIGURE 5-22

Example 1:1 Recursive Relationship

Person

Person
Jones
Smith
Parks
Myrtle
Pines

PERSON1 Relation

Person	PersonSponsored	Other Attributes
Jones	Smith	. . .
Smith	Parks	. . .
Parks	null	. . .
Myrtle	Pines	. . .
Pines	null	. . .

Referential integrity constraint:
PersonSponsored in PERSON1
must exist in Person in PERSON1

PERSON2 Relation

Person	PersonSponsoredBy	Other Attributes
Jones	null	. . .
Smith	Jones	. . .
Parks	Smith	. . .
Myrtle	null	. . .
Pines	Myrtle	. . .

Referential integrity constraint:
PersonSponsoredBy in PERSON2
must exist in Person in PERSON2

(a) Sample Data for a 1:1   (b) First Alternative for Representing a   (c) Second Alternative for Representing a
    Recursive Relationship   1:1 Recursive Relationship   1:1 Recursive Relationship

This technique is identical to that for nonrecursive 1:1 relationships except that the child and parent rows reside in the same table. You can think of the process as follows: Pretend that the relationship is between two different tables. Determine where the key goes, and then combine the two tables into a single one.

We also can use SQL joins to process recursive relationships; to do so, however, we need to introduce additional SQL syntax. In the FROM clause, it is possible to assign a synonym for a table name. For example, the expression FROM CUSTOMER A assigns the synonym A to the table CUSTOMER. Using this syntax, you can create a join on a recursive relationship for the design in Figure 5-22(b) as follows:

```
/* *** EXAMPLE CODE - DO NOT RUN *** */
/* *** SQL-Query-CH05-05 *** */
SELECT     *
FROM       PERSON1 A JOIN PERSON1 B
    ON     A.Person = B.PersonSponsored;
```

The result is a table with one row for each person that has all the columns of the person and also of the person that he or she sponsors.

Similarly, to create a join of the recursive relationship shown in Figure 5-22(c), you would use:

```
/* *** EXAMPLE CODE - DO NOT RUN *** */
/* *** SQL-Query-CH05-06 *** */
SELECT    *
FROM      PERSON2 A JOIN PERSON2 B
   ON     A.Person = B.PersonSponsoredBy;
```

The result is a table with a row for each person that has all the columns of the person and also of the sponsoring person.

Now consider the 1:N recursive relationship REFERRED-BY in Figure 5-21(b). This is a 1:N relationship, as shown in the sample data in Figure 5-23(a).

When these data are placed in a table, one row represents the referrer, and the other rows represent those who have been referred. The referrer row takes the role of the parent, and the referred rows take the role of the child. As with all 1:N relationships, you place the key of the parent in the child. In Figure 5-21(b), you place the CustomerNumber of the referrer in all the rows for people who have been referred.

You can join the 1:N recursive relationship with:

```
/* *** EXAMPLE CODE - DO NOT RUN *** */
/* *** SQL-Query-CH05-07 *** */
SELECT    *
FROM      CUSTOMER A JOIN CUSTOMER B
   ON     A.CustomerNumber = B.ReferredBy;
```

The result is a row for each customer that is joined to the data for the customer who referred the person. To show data for customers that did not have any referrals from other customers, we would use an OUTER JOIN as described in Chapter 3.

FIGURE 5-23

Example 1:N Recursive Relationship

Customer Number	Referred These Customers
100	200, 400
300	500
400	600, 700

CUSTOMER Relation

CustomerNumber	CustomerData	ReferredBy
100	. . .	null
200	. . .	100
300	. . .	null
400	. . .	100
500	. . .	300
600	. . .	400
700	. . .	400

Referential integrity constraint:
ReferredBy in CUSTOMER must exist in
CustomerNumber in CUSTOMER

(a) Sample Data for a 1:N Recursive Relationship

(b) Representing a 1:N Recursive Relationship Within a Table

Finally, let us consider N:M recursive relationships. The TREATED-BY relationship in Figure 5-21(c) represents a situation in which doctors give treatments to each other. Sample data are shown in Figure 5-24(a).

As with other N:M relationships, you must create an intersection table that shows pairs of related rows. The name of the doctor in the first column is the one who provided the treatment, and the name of the doctor in the second column is the one who received the treatment. This structure is shown in Figure 5-24(b). You can join the N:M relationship with:

```
/* *** EXAMPLE CODE - DO NOT RUN *** */
/* *** SQL-Query-CH05-08 *** */
SELECT     *
FROM       DOCTOR A JOIN TREATMENT-INTERSECTION, DOCTOR B
    ON     A.Name = TREATMENT-INTERSECTION.Physician
           JOIN DOCTOR B
              ON TREATMENT-INTERSECTION.Patient = B.Name;
```

The result of this is a table that has rows of doctor (as treatment provider) joined to doctor (as patient). The doctor data will be repeated once for every patient (as treatment receiver) treated and once for every time a doctor (as treatment provider) gave a treatment.

Recursive relationships are thus represented in the same way as are other relationships; however, the rows of the tables can take two different roles. Some are parent rows, and others are child rows. If a key is supposed to be a parent key and the row has no parent, its value is NULL. If a key is supposed to be a child key and the row has no child, its value is NULL. For more on recursive relationships, see the online extension "Advanced SQL."

FIGURE 5-24

Example N:M Recursive Relationship

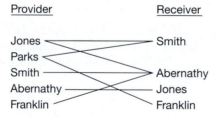

Provider	Receiver
Jones	Smith
Parks	
Smith	Abernathy
Abernathy	Jones
Franklin	Franklin

DOCTOR Relation

Name	Other Attributes
Jones	. . .
Parks	. . .
Smith	. . .
Abernathy	. . .
O'Leary	. . .
Franklin	. . .

TREATMENT-INTERSECTION Relation

Physician	Patient
Jones	Smith
Parks	Smith
Smith	Abernathy
Abernathy	Jones
Parks	Franklin
Franklin	Abernathy
Jones	Abernathy

Referential integrity constraints:
   Physician in TREATMENT-INTERSECTION
   must exist in Name in DOCTOR

   Patient in TREATMENT-INTERSECTION
   must exist in Name in DOCTOR

(a) Sample Data for an N:M Recursive Relationship

(b) Representing an N:M Recursive Relationship Using Tables

DATABASE DESIGN AT HEATHER SWEENEY DESIGNS

Figure 5-25 shows the final E-R diagram for Heather Sweeney Designs, the database example discussed in Chapter 4. To transform this E-R diagram into a relational design, we follow the process described in the preceding sections. First, represent each entity with a relation of its own, and specify a primary key for each relation:

SEMINAR (<u>SeminarID</u>, SeminarDate, SeminarTime, Location, SeminarTitle)

CUSTOMER (<u>CustomerID</u>, LastName, FirstName, EmailAddress, EncryptedPassword, Phone, StreetAddress, City, State, ZIP)

CONTACT (*<u>CustomerID</u>*, <u>ContactNumber</u>, ContactDate, ContactType)

PRODUCT (<u>ProductNumber</u>, ProductType, ProductDescription, UnitPrice, QuantityOnHand)

INVOICE (<u>InvoiceNumber</u>, InvoiceDate, PaymentType, SubTotal, Shipping, Tax, Total)

LINE_ITEM (*<u>InvoiceNumber</u>*, <u>LineNumber</u>, Quantity, UnitPrice, Total)

Weak Entities

This model has two weak entities, and they are both ID-dependent. CONTACT is a weak entity, and its identifier depends, in part, on the identifier of CUSTOMER. Thus, we have placed the key of CUSTOMER, which is CustomerID, into CONTACT. Similarly, LINE_ITEM is a weak entity, and its identifier depends on the identifier of INVOICE.

FIGURE 5-25

The Final Data Model for Heather Sweeney Designs

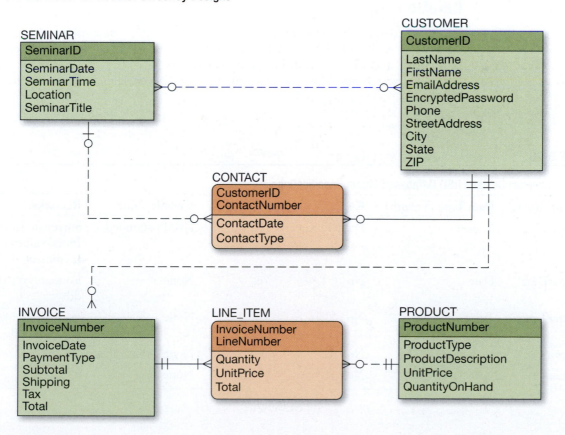

Consequently, we have placed the key of INVOICE in LINE_ITEM. Note that in the preceding schema. text both CONTACT.CustomerID and LINE_ITEM. InvoiceNumber are underlined and italicized because they are part of a primary key and also a foreign key. These are the only two foreign keys already in the schema.

Verifying Normalization

Next, apply the normalization process to each of these tables. Do any of them have a functional dependency that does not involve the primary key? From what we know so far, the only such functional dependency to consider moving to a separate table is:

ZIP → (City, State)

However, for the reasons explained earlier, we choose not to place ZIP in its own table.

One possible functional dependency concerns locations, dates, times, or titles. If, for example, Heather offers seminars only at certain times in some locations or if she only gives certain seminar titles in some locations, then a functional dependency would exist with Location as its determinant. It would be important for the design team to check this out, but for now assume that no such dependency exists.

Specifying Column Properties

The data model in Figure 5-25 shows entities, attributes, and entity relationships, but it does not document details about attributes. We do this as part of creating the database design columns. Figure 5-26 documents the data type, null status, default values, data constraints, and other properties of the columns in each table *before the addition of foreign keys other than those already in the data model because of ID-dependent entities.*

Relationships

Now, considering the relationships in this diagram, 1:N relationships exist between SEMINAR and CONTACT, between CUSTOMER and INVOICE, and between PRODUCT and LINE_ITEM. For each of these, we place the key of the parent in the child as a foreign key. Thus, we place the key of SEMINAR in CONTACT, the key of

FIGURE 5-26

Heather Sweeney Designs HSD Database Column Specifications

Column Name	Data Type (Length)	Key	Required	Default Value	Remarks
SeminarID	Integer	Primary Key	Yes	DBMS supplied	Surrogate Key: Initial value=1 Increment=1
SeminarDate	Date	No	Yes	None	Format: yyyy-mm-dd
SeminarTime	Time	No	Yes	None	Format: 00:00:00.000
Location	VarChar (100)	No	Yes	None	
SeminarTitle	VarChar (100)	No	Yes	None	

(a) SEMINAR

FIGURE 5-26 Continued

Column Name	Data Type (Length)	Key	Required	Default Value	Remarks
CustomerID	Integer	Primary Key	Yes		DBMS Supplied Surrogate Key: Initial Value=1 Increment=1
LastName	Char (25)	No	Yes	None	
FirstName	Char (25)	No	Yes	None	
EmailAddress	VarChar (100)	Primary Key	Yes	None	
EncryptedPassword	VarChar(50)	No	No	None	
Phone	Char (12)	No	Yes	None	Format: ###-###-####
StreetAddress	Char (35)	No	No	None	
City	Char (35)	No	No	Dallas	
State	Char (2)	No	No	TX	Format: AA
ZIP	Char (10)	No	No	75201	Format: #####-####

(b) CUSTOMER

Column Name	Data Type (Length)	Key	Required	Default Value	Remarks
CustomerID	Integer	Primary Key, Foreign Key	Yes	None	REF: CUSTOMER
ContactNumber	Integer	Primary Key	Yes	None	
ContactDate	Date	No	Yes	None	Format: yyyy-mm-dd
ContactType	Char (15)	No	Yes	None	

(c) CONTACT

Column Name	Data Type (Length)	Key	Required	Default Value	Remarks
InvoiceNumber	Integer	Primary Key	Yes	DBMS supplied	Surrogate Key: Initial value=35000 Increment=1
InvoiceDate	Date	No	Yes	None	Format: yyyy-mm-dd
PaymentType	Char (25)	No	Yes	Cash	
Subtotal	Numeric (9,2)	No	No	None	
Shipping	Numeric (9,2)	No	No	None	
Tax	Numeric (9,2)	No	No	None	
Total	Numeric (9,2)	No	No	None	

(d) INVOICE

FIGURE 5-26   Continued

Column Name	Data Type (Length)	Key	Required	Default Value	Remarks
InvoiceNumber	Integer	Primary Key, Foreign Key	Yes	None	REF: INVOICE
LineNumber	Integer	Primary Key	Yes	None	This is not quite a Surrogate Key—for *each* InvoiceNumber: Increment=1 Application logic will be needed to supply the correct value
Quantity	Integer	No	No	None	
UnitPrice	Numeric (9,2)	No	No	None	
Total	Numeric (9,2)	No	No	None	

(e) LINE_ITEM

Column Name	Data Type (Length)	Key	Required	Default Value	Remarks
ProductNumber	Char (35)	Primary Key	Yes	None	
ProductType	Char (24)	No	Yes	None	
ProductDescription	VarChar (100)	No	Yes	None	
UnitPrice	Numeric (9, 2)	No	Yes	None	
QuantityOnHand	Integer	No	Yes	0	

(f) PRODUCT

CUSTOMER in INVOICE, and the key of PRODUCT in LINE_ITEM. The relations are now as follows:

SEMINAR (SeminarID, SeminarDate, SeminarTime, Location, SeminarTitle)

CUSTOMER (CustomerID, LastName, FirstName, EmailAddress, EncryptedPassword, Phone, StreetAddress, City, State, ZIP)

CONTACT (*CustomerID*, ContactNumber, ContactDate, ContactType, *SeminarID*)

PRODUCT (ProductNumber, ProductType, ProductDescription, UnitPrice, QuantityOnHand)

INVOICE (InvoiceNumber, InvoiceDate, *CustomerID*, PaymentType, SubTotal, Shipping, Tax, Total)

LINE_ITEM (*InvoiceNumber*, LineNumber, *ProductNumber*, Quantity, UnitPrice, Total)

Finally, one N:M relationship exists between SEMINAR and CUSTOMER. To represent it, we create an intersection table, which we name SEMINAR_CUSTOMER. As with all intersection tables, its columns are the keys of the two tables involved in the N:M relationship. The final set of tables is:

SEMINAR (SeminarID, SeminarDate, SeminarTime, Location, SeminarTitle)

CUSTOMER (CustomerID, LastName, FirstName, EmailAddress, EncryptedPassword, Phone, StreetAddress, City, State, ZIP)

SEMINAR_CUSTOMER (*SeminarID*, *CustomerID*)

CONTACT (*CustomerID*, ContactDate, ContactDate, ContactType, *SeminarID*)

PRODUCT (ProductNumber, ProductType, ProductDescription, UnitPrice, QuantityOnHand)

INVOICE (InvoiceNumber, InvoiceDate, *CustomerID*, PaymentType, SubTotal, Shipping, Tax, Total)

LINE_ITEM (*InvoiceNumber*, LineNumber, *ProductNumber*, Quantity, UnitPrice, Total)

The set of referential integrity constraints will be discussed in the next section.

Now, to express the minimum cardinalities of children back to their parents, we need to decide whether foreign keys are required. In Figure 5-25, we see that an INVOICE is required to have a CUSTOMER and that LINE_ITEM is required to have a PRODUCT. Thus, we will make INVOICE.CustomerID and LINE_ITEM.ProductNumber required. CONTACT.SeminarID will not be required because a contact is not required to refer to a seminar. The final design is shown in the database design diagram in Figure 5-27, and the revised table column specification for those tables affected by the addition of foreign keys is shown in Figure 5-28.

FIGURE 5-27

Database Design for Heather Sweeney Designs

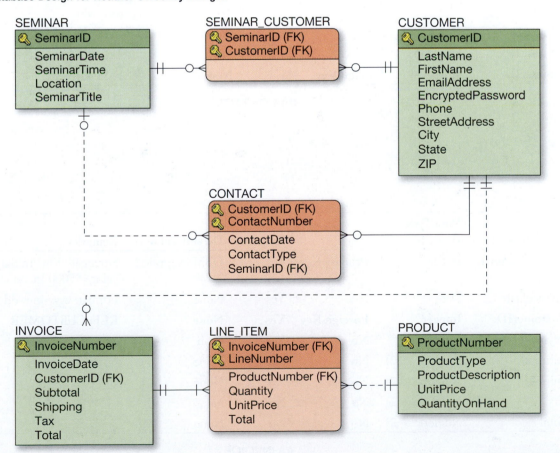

FIGURE 5-28

Modified Column Specifications for HSD Tables with Added Foreign Keys

Column Name	Data Type (Length)	Key	Required	Default Value	Remarks
SeminarID	Integer	Primary Key, Foreign Key	Yes	None	
CustomerID	Integer	Primary Key, Foreign Key	Yes	None	

(a) SEMINAR_CUSTOMER

Column Name	Data Type (Length)	Key	Required	Default Value	Remarks
CustomerID	Integer	Primary Key, Foreign Key	Yes	None	REF: CUSTOMER
ContactNumber	Integer	Primary Key	Yes	None	This is not quite a Surrogate Key—for *each* ContactNumber: Start=1 Increment=1 Application logic will be needed to supply the correct value
ContactDate	Date	No	Yes	None	Format: yyyy-mm-dd
ContactType	Char (15)	No	Yes	None	
SeminarID	Integer	Foreign Key	No	None	REF: SEMINAR

(b) CONTACT

Column Name	Data Type (Length)	Key	Required	Default Value	Remarks
InvoiceNumber	Integer	Primary Key	Yes	DBMS supplied	Surrogate Key: Initial value=35000 Increment=1
InvoiceDate	Date	No	Yes	None	Format: yyyy-mm-dd
CustomerID	Integer	Foreign Key	Yes	None	REF: CUSTOMER
PaymentType	Char (25)	No	Yes	Cash	
Subtotal	Numeric (9,2)	No	No	None	
Shipping	Numeric (9,2)	No	No	None	
Tax	Numeric (9,2)	No	No	None	
Total	Numeric (9,2)	No	No	None	

(c) INVOICE

FIGURE 5-28 Continued

Column Name	Data Type (Length)	Key	Required	Default Value	Remarks
InvoiceNumber	Integer	Primary Key, Foreign Key	Yes	None	REF: INVOICE
LineNumber	Integer	Primary Key	Yes	None	This is not quite a Surrogate Key—for *each* InvoiceNumber: Start=1 Increment=1 Application logic will be needed to supply the correct value
ProductNumber	**Char (35)**	**Foreign Key**	**Yes**	**None**	**REF: PRODUCT**
Quantity	Integer	No	No	None	
UnitPrice	Numeric (9,2)	No	No	None	
Total	Numeric (9,2)	No	No	None	

(d) LINE_ITEM

Enforcing Referential Integrity

Figure 5-29 summarizes the relationship enforcement for Heather Sweeney Designs. SeminarID is a surrogate key, so no cascading update behavior will be necessary for any of the relationships that it carries. Similarly, CustomerID in CUSTOMER and InvoiceNumber

FIGURE 5-29

Referential Integrity Constraint Enforcement for Heather Sweeney Designs

Relationship		Referential Integrity Constraint	Cascading Behavior	
Parent	Child		On Update	On Delete
SEMINAR	SEMINAR_CUSTOMER	SeminarID in SEMINAR_CUSTOMER must exist in SeminarID in SEMINAR	No	No
CUSTOMER	SEMINAR_CUSTOMER	CustomerID in SEMINAR_CUSTOMER must exist in CustomerID in CUSTOMER	No	No
SEMINAR	CONTACT	SeminarID in CONTACT must exist in SeminarID in SEMINAR	No	No
CUSTOMER	CONTACT	CustomerID in CONTACT must exist in CustomerID in CUSTOMER	No	No
CUSTOMER	INVOICE	CustomerID in INVOICE must exist in CustomerID in CUSTOMER	No	No
INVOICE	LINE_ITEM	InvoiceNumber in LINE_ITEM must exist in InvoiceNumber in INVOICE	No	Yes
PRODUCT	LINE_ITEM	ProductNumber in LINE_ITEM must exist in ProductNumber in PRODUCT	Yes	No

in INVOICE are unchanging values, so these relationships do not need cascading updates. However, updates of ProductNumber do need to cascade through their relationships.

With regard to cascading deletions, rows in the intersection table require a SEMINAR and a CUSTOMER parent. Therefore, when a user attempts to cancel a seminar or to remove a customer record, the deletion must either cascade or be prohibited. We must discuss this issue with Heather and her employees and determine whether users should be able to remove seminars that have customers enrolled or to remove customers who have enrolled in a seminar. We decide that neither seminars nor customers are *ever* deleted from the database (Heather *never* cancels a seminar, even if no customers show up, and once Heather has a customer record she *never* lets go of it!). Hence, as shown in Figure 5-29, neither of these relationships has cascading deletions.

Figure 5-29 shows other decisions reached in the example. Because of the need to keep historic information about seminar attendance and contacts, we cannot delete a customer record. Doing so would distort seminar attendance data and data about contacts such as email messages and regular mail letters, which need to be accounted for. Foreign key constraints thus prohibit deleting the primary key record in CUSTOMER.

As shown in Figure 5-29, the deletion of an INVOICE will cause the deletion of related LINE_ITEMs. Finally, an attempt to delete a PRODUCT that is related to one or more LINE_ITEMs will fail; cascading the deletion here would cause LINE_ITEMs to disappear out of ORDERs, a situation that cannot be allowed.

The database design for the Heather Sweeney Designs database is now complete enough to create tables, columns, relationships, and referential integrity constraints using a DBMS. Before going on, we would need to document any additional business rules to be enforced by application programs or other DBMS techniques. After this, the database can be created, using the SQL statements discussed in Chapter 3. The full set of the SQL statements needed to create and populate the database in MySQL are located in the Chapter 3 Heather Sweeney Designs Case Questions on pages 244–257. These SQL statements will need to be slightly modified for use with SQL Server 2017 or Oracle Database XE.

WORKING WITH MICROSOFT ACCESS

Section 5

Database Designs in Microsoft Visio and Relationships in Microsoft Access

At this point, we have created and populated the CONTACT, CUSTOMER, and SALESPERSON tables in the Wallingford Motors CRM database. You learned how to create forms, reports, and queries in the preceding sections of "Working with Microsoft Access." If you have worked through Chapter 3's section of "Working with Microsoft Access," you know how to create and use view equivalent queries.

All the tables you have used so far have had 1:N relationships. But how are 1:1 and N:M relationships managed in Microsoft Access? In this section, you will:

- Understand 1:1 relationships in Microsoft Access.
- Understand N:M relationships in Microsoft Access.

But first, let's consider whether or not to create database designs in Microsoft Visio 2019.

Should I Create Database Designs in Microsoft Visio 2019?

In the section of "Working with Microsoft Access" in Chapter 4, we discussed how to create data models in Microsoft Visio 2019. This chapter discussed how to create a database design from a data model. This raises the question, should I use Visio to create database designs?

There are actually two questions here: (1) *can* I use Visio to create database designs, and (2) *should* I use Visio to create database designs?.

Technically, we can create database designs in Visio 2019. Based on the discussion in this chapter, to create a database design we must:

- Create a table from the data model entity, and designate primary keys
- Designate or add foreign keys
- Create Intersection tables to replace M:N relationships
- Optionally, indicate column characteristics such as NOT NULL

All of this can be done in Visio 2019. We are already using Visio's primary key icon to indicate the data model identifiers. Using Visio's shortcut menus we can also designate foreign keys with the foreign key icons. Intersection tables are just another table to be added to the model, and this can be easily done. We can also use the shortcut menu **Set Required** setting to indicate NOT NULL columns (which appear in bold type in the table structures). Figure WA-5-1 shows the data model for the WP database after the ASSIGNMENT associative entity has been added in as described in Exercise WA.4.11 (note the line ends

FIGURE WA-5-1

The WP Data Model in Visio 2019

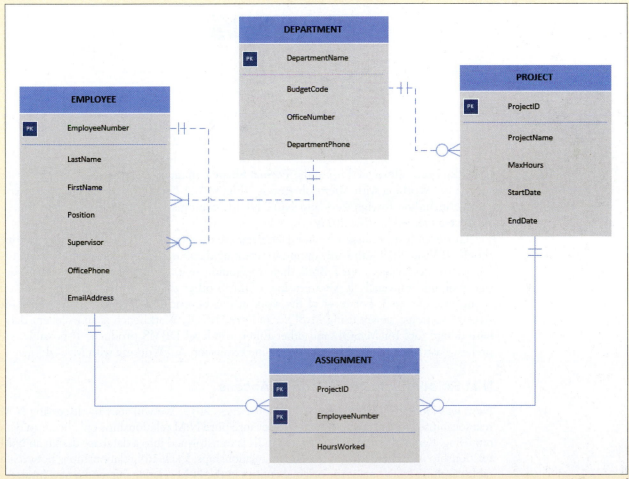

(*Continued*)

The WP Database Design in Visio 2019

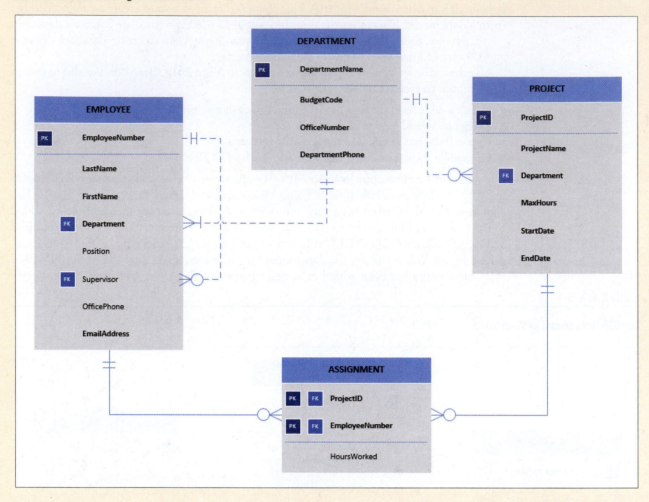

have also been reformated using the **Format Shape** command as suggested in Chapter 4's section of "Working with Microsoft Access." Figure WA-5-2 shows the resulting database design (including foreign keys and NOT NULL columns [indicated by the bold font]). Both were created in Visio 2019.

However, just because we can create database designs in Visio 2019 doesn't mean we should. If Visio 2019 is the only option for creating database designs, especially if we're using Microsoft Access as our DBMS, then we should use it. If there is a better database design tool, and especially if we are using a DBMS other than Microsoft Access, then we should use that tool. For most of the work in this beyond the "Working with Microsoft Access" sections, we are using MySQL, and the MySQL Workbench is an excellent database design tool for MySQL and other Enterprise-level DBMS products. If possible, we prefer to use MySQL Workbench (see online Extension A, "Working with MySQL").

N:M Relationships in Microsoft Access

Now, let's look at relationships in Microsoft Access 2019. We will start by discussing N:M relationships. This is actually a nonissue because pure N:M relationships only occur in data modeling. Remember that when a data model is transformed into a database design an N:M relationship is broken down into two 1:N relationships. Each 1:N relationship is between a table resulting from one of the original entities in the N:M relationship and a new intersection table. If this does not make sense to you, then review the chapter section "Representing

FIGURE WA-5-3

The WMCRM Database Design with VEHICLE

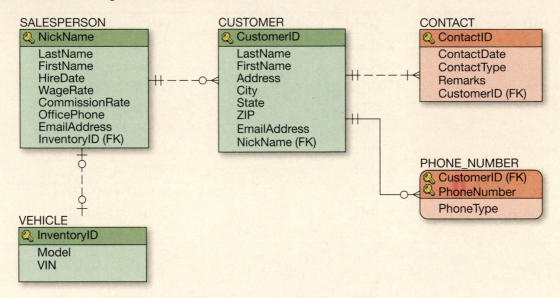

N:M Strong Entity Relationships" and see Figure 5-13 and Figure 5-15 for an illustration of how N:M relationships are converted to two 1:N relationships.

Because databases are built in DBMSs, such as Microsoft Access, from the database design, Microsoft Access only deals with the resulting 1:N relationships. As far as Microsoft Access is concerned, there are no N:M relationships!

1:1 Relationships in Microsoft Access

Unlike N:M relationships, 1:1 relationships definitely exist in Microsoft Access. At this point the WMCRM database does not contain a 1:1 relationship, and here we will add one. We will let each SALESPERSON use one and only one car from the Wallingford Motors inventory as a demo vehicle. The database design with this addition is shown in Figure WA-5-3.

Note that both SALESPERSON and VEHICLE are optional in this relationship. First, a VEHICLE does not have to be assigned to a SALESPERSON, which makes sense because there will be a lot of cars in inventory and only a few SALESPERSONs. Second, a SALESPERSON does not have to take a demo car and may choose not to. (Yeah, right!) Also note that we have chosen to put the foreign key in SALESPERSON. In this case, there is an advantage to putting the foreign key in one table or the other because if we put it in VEHICLE, the foreign key column (which would have been NickName) would be NULL for every car except the few used as demo vehicles. Finally, note that we are using this table just to illustrate a 1:1 relationship—a functional VEHICLE table would have a lot more columns.

The column characteristics for the VEHICLE table are shown in Figure WA-5-4, and the data for the table are shown in Figure WA-5-5.

FIGURE WA-5-4

Database Column Characteristics for the WMCRM VEHICLE Table

Column Name	Type	Key	Required	Remarks
InventoryID	AutoNumber	Primary Key	Yes	Surrogate Key
Model	Short Text (25)	No	Yes	
VIN	Short Text (35)	No	Yes	

(Continued)

Wallingford Motors VEHICLE Data

InventoryID	Model	VIN
[AutoNumber]	HiStandard	G19HS123400001
[AutoNumber]	HiStandard	G19HS123400002
[AutoNumber]	HiStandard	G19HS123400003
[AutoNumber]	HiLuxury	G19HL234500001
[AutoNumber]	HiLuxury	G19HL234500002
[AutoNumber]	HiLuxury	G19HL234500003
[AutoNumber]	SUHi	G19HU345600001
[AutoNumber]	SUHi	G19HU345600002
[AutoNumber]	SUHi	G19HU345600003
[AutoNumber]	HiElectra	G19HE456700001

Let us open the WMCRM.accdb database and add the VEHICLE table to it.

Opening the WMCRM.accdb Database

1. Start Microsoft Access.
2. If necessary, click the **File** command tab, and then click the **WMCRM.accdb** file name in the quick access list of recently opened databases to open the database.

We already know how to create a table and populate it with data, so we will go ahead and add the VEHICLE table and its data to the WMCRM.accdb database. Next, we need to modify SALESPERSON by adding the InventoryID column and populating it with data. The column characteristics for the new InventoryID column in the SALESPERSON table are shown in Figure WA-5-6, and the data for the column are shown in Figure WA-5-7. (Tina and Big Bill are driving the HiLuxury model, whereas Billy opted for a SUHi.)

There is nothing here that you do not know how to do—you altered the CUSTOMER table in a similar way in Chapter 3's section of "Working with Microsoft Access"—so you

Database Column Characteristics for the InventoryID Column in the WMCRM SALESPERSON Table

Column Name	Type	Key	Required	Remarks
InventoryID	Long Integer	Foreign Key	No	

SALESPERSON InventoryID Data

NickName	LastName	FirstName	...	InventoryID
Tina	Smith	Tina	...	4
Big Bill	Jones	William	...	5
Billy	Jones	Bill	...	7

FIGURE WA-5-8

The Relationships
Window with the
Current Relationship
Diagram

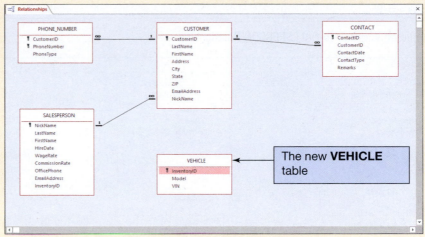

Access 2019, Windows 10, Microsoft Corporation.

can go ahead and add the InventoryID column and its data to the SALESPERSON table. This is an easier table alteration to make than the one we made to CUSTOMER because the InventoryID column in SALESPERSON is NULL, so you do not have to set it to NOT NULL after entering the data.

Now, we are ready to establish the relationship between the two tables.

Creating the Relationship Between SALESPERSON and VEHICLE

1. If you have any tables open, close them, and the click the **Database Tools** command tab.
2. Click the **Shutter Bar Open/Close** button to minimize the Navigation Pane.
3. Click the **Relationships** button in the Relationships group. The Relationships tabbed document window appears.
   - ■ **NOTE: Warning!** The next steps lead to a peculiarity of Microsoft Access, not the final outcome that we want. Remember that we want a 1:1 relationship. See whether you can figure out what is happening as we go along.
4. Click the **Show Table** button in the Relationships group of the Design ribbon.
5. In the Show Table dialog box, click **VEHICLE** to select it, and then click the **Add** button to add VEHICLE to the Relationships window.
6. In the Show Table dialog box, click the **Close** button to close the dialog box.
7. Rearrange and resize the table objects in the Relationships window by using standard Windows drag-and-drop techniques. Rearrange the SALESPERSON, CUSTOMER, PHONE_NUMBER, CONTACT, and VEHICLE table objects until they look as shown in Figure WA-5-8.
   - ■ **NOTE:** Remember that we create a relationship between two tables in the Relationships window by dragging a *primary key* column and dropping it on top of the *corresponding foreign key* column.
8. Click and hold the column name **InventoryID** in the VEHICLE table object, drag it over the column name **InventoryID** in the **SALESPERSON** table, and then release the mouse button. The Edit Relationships dialog box appears.
9. Click the **Enforce Referential Integrity** check box.
10. Click the **Create** button to create the relationship between VEHICLE and SALESPERSON.
11. Right-click the **relationship line** between VEHICLE and SALESPERSON, and then click **Edit Relationship** in the shortcut menu that appears. The **Edit Relationships** dialog box appears. The relationship between the tables now appears in the Relationships window, as shown in Figure WA-5-9.

But now we have a serious problem: The relationship that was created is a 1:N relationship, not the 1:1 relationship that we wanted. It seems like there should be a way to fix the

(Continued)

FIGURE WA-5-9

The Completed VEHICLE-to-SALESPERSON Relationship

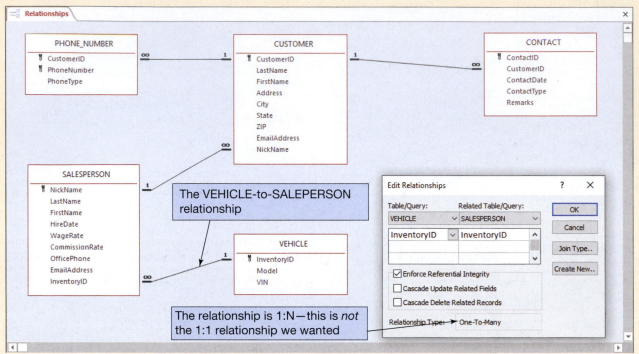

Access 2019, Windows 10, Microsoft Corporation.

relationship somewhere on the Edit Relationships dialog box. Unfortunately, there is not. Go ahead and try everything you can think of, but it will not work. This is the peculiarity of Microsoft Access that was mentioned earlier.

So what is the trick to creating a 1:1 relationship in Microsoft Access? As discussed in this chapter, the trick is to create a UNIQUE constraint on the foreign key column. To do this in Microsoft Access, we set the **Indexed field property** of the foreign key column (InventoryID in SALESPERSON in this case) to **Yes (No Duplicates)**, as shown in Figure WA-5-10. As long as the same value can occur more than once in the foreign key column, Microsoft Access will create a 1:N relationship instead of the desired 1:1 relationship.

To create the 1:1 relationship, we need to delete the existing relationship, modify the InventoryID property in SALESPERSON, and create a new relationship between the tables. First, we will delete the existing 1:N relationship.

Deleting the Incorrect Relationship Between SALESPERSON and VEHICLE

1. Click the **OK** button on the Edit Relationships dialog box.
2. Right-click the **relationship line** between VEHICLE and SALESPERSON to display the shortcut menu, and then click **Delete**.
3. A dialog box appears asking whether you are sure you want to permanently delete the selected relationship from your database. Click the **Yes** button.
4. Close the Relationships window.
5. A dialog box appears asking whether you want to save the changes to the layout of Relationships. Click the **Yes** button.
6. Click the **Shutter Bar Open/Close** button to expand the Navigation Pane.

Next, we will modify the SALESPERSON table.

FIGURE WA-5-10

Setting the Indexed Property Value in the SALESPERSON Table

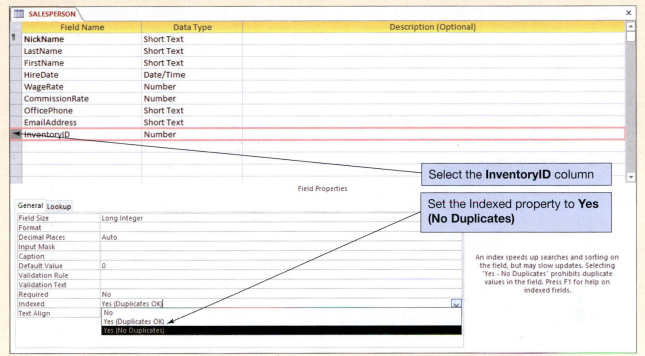

Access 2019, Windows 10, Microsoft Corporation.

Setting the Indexed Property of the InventoryID Column in SALESPERSON

1. Open the **SALESPERSON** table in Design view.
2. Select the **InventoryID** field. The InventoryID field properties are displayed in the General tab.
3. Click the **Indexed** text field. A drop-down list arrow appears on the right end of the text field. Click the drop-down list arrow to display the list and select **Yes (No Duplicates)**. The result appears as shown in Figure WA-5-10. Note that because the InventoryID column Required field is set to *No*, a row of SALESPERSON is *not* required to have a VEHICLE assigned to it.
4. Click the **Save** button to save the completed changes to the SALESPERSON table.
5. Close the SALESPERSON table.

Finally, we create the 1:1 relationship that we want between the SALESPERSON and VEHICLE tables.

Creating the Correct 1:1 Relationship Between SALESPERSON and VEHICLE

1. Click the **Database Tools** command tab.
2. Click the **Shutter Bar Open/Close** button to minimize the Navigation Pane.
3. Click the **Relationships** button in the Relationships group. The Relationships tabbed document window appears.
4. Click and hold the column name **InventoryID** in the **VEHICLE** table object, drag it over the column name **InventoryID** in the **SALESPERSON** table, and then release the mouse button. The Edit Relationships dialog box appears.

(Continued)

FIGURE WA-5-11

The Correct 1:1 VEHICLE-to-SALESPERSON Relationship

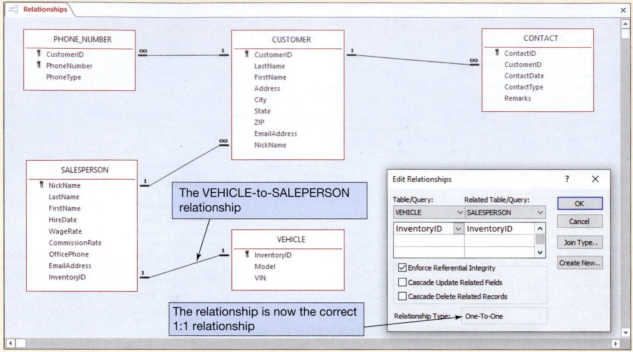

Access 2019, Windows 10, Microsoft Corporation.

5. Click the **Enforce Referential Integrity** check box.
6. Click the **Create** button to create the relationship between VEHICLE and SALESPERSON.
7. To verify that you now have the correct 1:1 relationship, right-click the **relationship line** between SALESPERSON and VEHICLE, and then click **Edit Relationship** in the shortcut menu that appears. The **Edit Relationships** dialog box appears.
8. Note that the correct one-to-one relationship between the tables now appears in the Relationships window, as shown in Figure WA-5-11.
9. Click the **Cancel** button on the Edit Relationships dialog box.
10. Close the Relationships window.
11. If a dialog box appears asking whether you want to save the changes to the layout of Relationships window, click the **Yes** button.
12. Click the **Shutter Bar Open/Close** button to expand the Navigation Pane.

We have successfully created the 1:1 relationship that we wanted. We just had to learn the Microsoft Access way of doing it.

Closing the Database and Exiting Microsoft Access

That completes the work we will do in this chapter's section of "Working with Microsoft Access." As usual, we finish by closing the database and Microsoft Access.

Closing the WMCRM Database and Exiting Microsoft Access

1. To close the WMCRM database and exit Microsoft Access, click the Microsoft Access **Close** button in the upper-right corner of the Microsoft Access window.

SUMMARY

To transform an E-R data model into a relational database design, you create a table for each entity. The attributes of the entity become the columns of the table, and the identifier of the entity becomes the primary key of the table. For each column, you must define data types, null status, any default values, and any data constraints. You then apply the normalization process to each table and create additional tables, if necessary. In some cases, you need to denormalize a table. When you do, the table could have insertion, update, and deletion modification problems.

Denormalization makes sense if the benefit of not normalizing outweighs the possible problems that could be caused by such modifications.

Weak entities are represented by a table. ID-dependent entities must include the key columns of the tables on which they depend as well as of the identifiers of the entities themselves. Non–ID-dependent weak entities must have their existence dependence recorded as business rules, and will still have a foreign key linking them to another table.

Supertypes and subtypes are each represented by separate tables. The identifier of the supertype entity becomes the primary key of the supertype table, and the identifiers of the subtype entities become the primary keys of the subtype tables. The primary key of each subtype is also the same primary key that is used for the supertype, and the primary key of each subtype serves as a foreign key that links the subtype back to the supertype.

The E-R model has three types of binary relationships: 1:1, 1:N, and N:M. To represent a 1:1 relationship, you place the key of one table into the other table. To implement the 1:1 relationship, the specified foreign key must be constrained as UNIQUE. To represent a 1:N relationship, you place the key of the parent table in the child table. Finally, to represent an M:N relationship, you create an intersection table that contains the keys of the other two tables.

Recursive relationships are relationships in which the participants in the relationship arise from the same entity class. The three types of recursive relationships are 1:1, 1:N, and N:M. These types of relationships are represented in the same way as are their equivalent nonrecursive relationships. For 1:1 and 1:N relationships, you add a foreign key to the relation that represents the entity. For an N:M recursion, you create an intersection table that represents the M:N relationship.

KEY TERMS

associative entity	data model	NULL status
association relationship	data type	parent
Boyce-Codd Normal Form (BCNF)	database design	relation
child	default value	surrogate key
column properties	denormalization	systems development life cycle
component design	intersection table	(SDLC)
data constraints	mixed entity pattern	table

REVIEW QUESTIONS

5.1 Explain how entities are transformed into tables.

5.2 Explain how attributes are transformed into columns. What column properties do you take into account when making the transformations?

5.3   Why is it necessary to apply the normalization process to the tables created according to your answer to question 5.1?

5.4   What is denormalization?

5.5   When is denormalization justified?

5.6   Explain the problems that denormalized tables may have for insert, update, and delete actions.

5.7   Explain how the representation of weak entities differs from the representation of strong entities.

5.8   Explain how supertype and subtype entities are transformed into tables.

5.9   List the three types of binary relationships, and give an example of each. Do not use the examples given in this text.

5.10   Define the term *foreign key,* and give an example.

5.11   Show two different ways to represent the 1:1 relationship in your answer to question 5.9. Use IE Crow's Foot E-R diagrams.

5.12   For your answers to question 5.11, describe a method for obtaining data about one of the entities, given the key of the other. Describe a method for obtaining data about the second entity, given the key of the first. Describe methods for both of your alternatives in question 5.11.

5.13   Code SQL statements to create a join that has all data about both tables from your work for question 5.11.

5.14   Define the terms *parent* and *child* as they apply to tables in a database design, and give an example of each.

5.15   Show how to represent the 1:N relationship in your answer to question 5.9. Use an IE Crow's Foot E-R diagram.

5.16   For your answer to question 5.15, describe a method for obtaining data for all the children, given the key of the parent. Describe a method for obtaining data for the parent, given a key of the child.

5.17   For your answer to question 5.15, code an SQL statement that creates a table that has all data from both tables.

5.18   For a 1:N relationship, explain why you must place the key of the parent table in the child table rather than place the key of the child table in the parent table.

5.19   Give examples of binary 1:N relationships, other than those in this text, for (a) an optional-to-optional relationship, (b) an optional-to-mandatory relationship, (c) a mandatory-to-optional relationship, and (d) a mandatory-to-mandatory relationship. Illustrate your answer by using IE Crow's Foot E-R diagrams.

5.20   Show how to represent the N:M relationship in your answer to question 5.9. Use an IE Crow's Foot E-R diagram.

5.21   Explain the meaning of the term *intersection table.*

5.22   Explain how the terms *parent table* and *child table* relate to the tables in your answer to question 5.20.

5.23   For your answers to questions 5.20, 5.21, and 5.22, describe a method for obtaining the children for one of the entities in the original data model, given the primary key of the table based on the second entity. Also, describe a method for obtaining the children for the second entity, given the primary key of the table based on the first entity.

5.24   For your answer to question 5.20, code an SQL statement that creates a relation that has all data from all tables.

5.25   Why is it not possible to represent N:M relationships with the same strategy used to represent 1:N relationships?

5.26 What is an *associative entity* (also called an *association entity*)? What is an *association relationship*? Give an example of an association relationship other than one shown in this text. Illustrate your answer using an IE Crow's Foot E-R diagram.

5.27 Give an example of a 1:N relationship with an ID-dependent weak entity, other than one shown in this text. Illustrate your answer using an IE Crow's Foot E-R diagram.

5.28 Give an example of a supertype–subtype relationship, other than one shown in this text. Illustrate your answer using an IE Crow's Foot E-R diagram.

5.29 Define the three types of recursive binary relationships, and give an example of each, other than the ones shown in this text.

5.30 Show how to represent the 1:1 recursive relationship in your answer to question 5.29. How does this differ from the representation of 1:1 nonrecursive relationships?

5.31 Code an SQL statement that creates a table with all columns from the parent and child tables in your answer to question 5.30.

5.32 Show how to represent a 1:N recursive relationship in your answer to question 5.29. How does this differ from the representation of 1:N nonrecursive relationships?

5.33 Code an SQL statement that creates a table with all columns from the parent and child tables in your answer to question 5.32.

5.34 Show how to represent the M:N recursive relationship in your answer to question 5.29. How does this differ from the representation of M:N nonrecursive relationships?

5.35 Code an SQL statement that creates a table with all columns from the parent and child tables in your answer to question 5.34. Code an SQL statement using a left outer join that creates a table with all columns from the parent and child tables. Explain the difference between these two SQL statements.

EXERCISES

5.36 Consider the following table, which holds data about employee project assignments:

ASSIGNMENT (<u>EmployeeNumber</u>, <u>ProjectNumber</u>, ProjectName, HoursWorked)

Assume that ProjectNumber determines ProjectName, and explain why this relation is not normalized. Demonstrate an insertion anomaly, a modification anomaly, and a deletion anomaly. Apply the normalization process to this relation. State the referential integrity constraint.

5.37 Consider the following relation that holds data about employee assignments:

ASSIGNMENT (<u>EmployeeNumber</u>, ProjectNumber, ProjectName, HoursWorked)

Assume that ProjectNumber determines ProjectName, and explain why this relation is not normalized. Demonstrate an insertion anomaly, a modification anomaly, and a deletion anomaly. Apply the normalization process to this relation. State the referential integrity constraint.

5.38   Explain the difference between the two ASSIGNMENT tables in exercises 5.36 and 5.37. Under what circumstances is the table in exercise 5.36 more correct? Under what circumstances is the table in exercise 5.37 more correct?

5.39   Create a relational database design for the data model you developed for exercise 4.41.

5.40   Create a relational database design for the data model you developed for exercise 4.42.

5.41   Create a relational database design for the data model you developed for exercise 4.43.

5.42   Create a relational database design for the data model you developed for exercise 4.44.

WORKING WITH MICROSOFT ACCESS

Key Terms

Indexed field property

Exercises

WA.5.1   Using an IE Crow's Foot E-R diagram, draw a database design for the Wedgewood Pacific (WP) database completed at the end of Chapter 3's section of "Working with Microsoft Access."

WA.5.2   This chapter's section of "Working with Microsoft Access" describes how to create 1:1 relationships in Microsoft Access. In particular, we added the business rule that each salesperson at Wallingford Motors can have one and only one vehicle as a demo car. Suppose that the rule has been changed so that each salesperson can have one or more cars as demo vehicles.

    A.   Using an IE Crow's Foot E-R diagram, redraw the database design in Figure WA-5-1 to show the new relationship between VEHICLE and SALESPERSON. Which table(s) is (are) the parent(s) in the relationship? Which table(s) is (are) the child(ren)? In which table(s) do you place a foreign key?

    B.   Start with the Wallingford Motors database that you have created so far (WMCRM.accdb) as it exists after working through all the steps in this chapter's section of "Working with Microsoft Access." (If you have not completed those actions, do so now.) Copy the WMCRM.accdb database and rename the copy WMCRM-WA-05-v02.accdb. Modify the WMCRM-WA-05-v02.accdb database to implement the new relationship between VEHICLE and SALESPERSON. (*Note:* Copying a Microsoft Access database is discussed in Chapter 4's section of "Working with Microsoft Access.")

WA.5.3   This chapter's section of "Working with Microsoft Access" describes how to create 1:1 relationships in Microsoft Access. In particular, we added the business rule that each salesperson at Wallingford Motors can have one and only one vehicle as a demo car. Suppose that the rule has been changed so that (1) each salesperson can have one or more cars as demo vehicles and (2) each demo vehicle can be shared by two or more salespersons.

    A.   Using an IE Crow's Foot E-R diagram, redraw the database design in Figure WA-5-1 to show the new relationship between VEHICLE and SALESPERSON. Which table(s) is (are) the parent(s) in the relationship? Which table(s) is (are) the child(ren)? In which table(s) do you place a foreign key?

B. Start with the Wallingford Motors database that you have created so far (WM-CRM.accdb) as it exists after working through all the steps in this chapter's section of "Working with Microsoft Access." (If you have not completed those actions, do so now.) Copy the WMCRM.accdb database and rename the copy WMCRM-WA-05-v03.accdb. Modify the WMCRM-WA-05-v03.accdb database to implement the new relationship between VEHICLE and SALESPERSON. (*Note:* Copying a Microsoft Access database is discussed in Chapter 4's section of "Working with Microsoft Access.")

CASE QUESTIONS

SAN JUAN SAILBOAT CHARTERS

San Juan Sailboat Charters (SJSBC) is an agency that leases (charters) sailboats. SJSBC does not own the boats. Instead, SJSBC leases boats on behalf of boat owners who want to earn income from their boats when they are not using them, and SJSBC charges the owners a fee for this service. SJSBC specializes in boats that can be used for multiday or weekly charters. The smallest sailboat available is 28 feet in length and the largest is 51 feet in length.

Each sailboat is fully equipped at the time it is leased. Most of the equipment is provided at the time of the charter. Most of the equipment is provided by the owners, but some is provided by SJSBC. The owner-provided equipment includes equipment that is attached to the boat, such as radios, compasses, depth indicators and other instrumentation, stoves, and refrigerators. Other owner-provided equipment, such as sails, lines, anchors, dinghies, life preservers, and equipment in the cabin (dishes, silverware, cooking utensils, bedding, and so on), is not physically attached to the boat. SJSBC provides consumable supplies, such as charts, navigation books, tide and current tables, soap, dish towels, toilet paper, and similar items. The consumable supplies are treated as equipment by SJSBC for tracking and accounting purposes.

Keeping track of equipment is an important part of SJSBC's responsibilities. Much of the equipment is expensive, and those items not physically attached to the boat can be easily damaged, lost, or stolen. SJSBC holds the customer responsible for all the boat's equipment during the period of the charter.

SJSBC likes to keep accurate records of its customers and charters, and customers are required to keep a log during each charter. Some itineraries and weather conditions are more dangerous than others, and the data from these logs provide information about the customer experience. This information is useful for marketing purposes as well as for evaluating a customer's ability to handle a particular boat and itinerary.

Sailboats need maintenance. Note that two definitions of *boat* are (1) "break out another thousand" and (2) "a hole in the water into which one pours money." SJSBC is required by its contracts with the boat owners to keep accurate records of all maintenance activities and costs.

A data model of a proposed database to support an information system for SJSBC is shown in Figure 5-30. Note that because the OWNER entity allows for owners to be companies as well as individuals, SJSBC can be included as an equipment owner (note that the cardinalities in the diagram allow SJSBC to own equipment while *not* owning any boats). Also note that this model relates EQUIPMENT to CHARTER rather than BOAT even when the equipment is physically attached to the boat. This is only one possible way to handle EQUIPMENT, but it is satisfactory to the managers of SJSBC.

A. Convert this data model to a database design. Specify tables, primary keys, and foreign keys. Using Figure 5-26 and Figure 5-28 as guides, specify column properties.

B. Describe how you have represented weak entities, if any exist.

C. Describe how you have represented supertype and subtype entities, if any exist.

D. Create a visual representation of your database design as an IE Crow's Foot E-R diagram similar to the one in Figure 5-27.

E. Document referential integrity constraint enforcement, using Figure 5-29 as a guide.

FIGURE 5-30

Data Model for San Juan Sailboat Charters

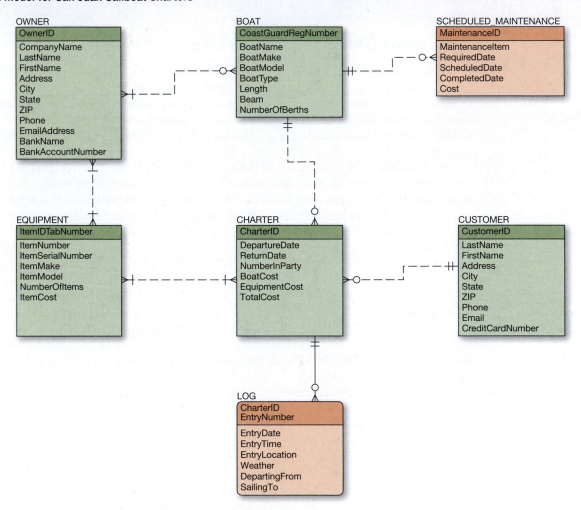

WRITER'S PATROL

Answer the Writer's Patrol Case Questions in Chapter 4 if you have not already done so. Design a database for your data model from Chapter 4. Your design should include a specification of tables and (using Figure 5-26 and Figure 5-28 as guides) column properties as well as primary, candidate, and foreign keys. Create a visual representation of your database design as an IE Crow's Foot E-R diagram similar to the one in Figure 5-27. Document your referential integrity constraint enforcement in the format shown in Figure5-29.

GARDEN GLORY PROJECT QUESTIONS

Convert the data model you constructed for Garden Glory in part B at the end of Chapter 4 (or an equivalent data model that your instructor provides for you to use) into a relational database design for Garden Glory. Document your database design as follows.

A. Specify tables, primary keys, and foreign keys. Using Figure 5-26 and Figure 5-28 as guides, specify column properties.

B. Describe how you have represented weak entities, if any exist.

C. Describe how you have represented supertype and subtype entities, if any exist.

D. Create a visual representation of your database design as an IE Crow's Foot E-R diagram similar to the one in Figure 5-27.

E. Document referential integrity constraint enforcement, using Figure 5-29 as a guide.

F. Document any business rules that you think might be important.

G. Describe how you would validate that your design is a good representation of the data model on which it is based.

JAMES RIVER JEWELRY PROJECT QUESTIONS

Convert the data model you constructed for James River Jewelry in part C of the James River Jewelry Project Questions at the end of Chapter 4 (or an equivalent data model that your instructor provides for you to use) into a relational database design for James River Jewelry. Document your database design as follows.

A. Specify tables, primary keys, and foreign keys. Using Figure 5-26 and Figure 5-28 as guides, specify column properties.

B. Describe how you have represented weak entities, if any exist.

C. Describe how you have represented supertype and subtype entities, if any exist.

D. Create an IE Crow's Foot E-R diagram similar to the one in Figure 5-27.

E. Document referential integrity constraint enforcement, using Figure 5-29 as a guide.

F. Document any business rules that you think might be important.

G. Describe how you would validate that your design is a good representation of the data model on which it is based.

THE QUEEN ANNE CURIOSITY SHOP PROJECT QUESTIONS

Convert the data model you constructed for the Queen Anne Curiosity Shop in part D at the end of Chapter 4 (or an equivalent data model that your instructor provides for you to use) into a relational database design for the Queen Anne Curiosity Shop. Document your database design as follows.

A. Specify tables, primary keys, and foreign keys. Using Figure 5-26 and Figure 5-28 as guides, specify column properties.

B. Describe how you have represented weak entities, if any exist.

C. Describe how you have represented supertype and subtype entities, if any exist.

D. Create a visual representation of your database design as an IE Crow's Foot E-R diagram similar to the one in Figure 5-27.

E. Document referential integrity constraint enforcement, using Figure 5-29 as a guide.

F. Document any business rules that you think might be important.

G. Describe how you would validate that your design is a good representation of the data model on which it is based.

Database Management

So far, you have been introduced to the fundamental concepts and techniques of relational database management and database design. In Chapter 1, you learned about databases and the major components of a database system. Chapter 2 introduced you to the relational model, functional dependencies, and normalization. In Chapter 3, you learned how to use SQL statements to create and process a database. Chapter 4 gave you an overview of the database design process and a detailed introduction to data modeling. In Chapter 5, you learned how to transform a data model into a relational database design. Now that you know how to design, create, and query databases, it is time to learn how to manage databases and use them to solve business problems.

In Chapter 6, you will learn about database management and some of the problems that occur when a database is processed concurrently by more than one user. You will also learn about database security, and how to control user and application developer use of databases. In Chapter 7, you will learn how databases support data warehouses and modern business intelligence (BI) systems and about Big Data, the NoSQL movement, and cloud computing. After completing these chapters, you will have surveyed all the basics of database technology.

CHAPTER OBJECTIVES

- Understand the need for and importance of database administration
- Know basic administrative and managerial DBA functions
- Understand the need for concurrency control, security, and backup and recovery
- Learn about typical problems that can occur when multiple users process a database concurrently
- Understand the use of locking and the problem of deadlock
- Learn the difference between optimistic and pessimistic locking

- Know the meaning of ACID transaction
- Learn the four 1992 ANSI standard isolation levels
- Learn different ways of processing a database using cursors
- Understand the need for security and specific tasks for improving database security
- Know the difference between recovery via reprocessing and recovery via rollback/rollforward
- Understand the nature of the tasks required for recovery using rollback/rollforward

This chapter describes the major tasks of an important business function called *database administration.* This function involves managing a database to maximize its value to an organization. Usually, database administration involves balancing the conflicting goals of protecting the database and maximizing its availability and benefit to users. Both the terms *data administration* and *database administration* are used in the industry. In some cases, the terms are considered to be synonymous; in other cases, they have different meanings. Most commonly, the term **data administration** refers to a function that applies to an entire organization; it is a management-oriented function that concerns corporate data privacy and security issues. The term **database administration** refers to a more technical function that is specific to a particular database, including the applications that process that database. This chapter addresses database administration.

Databases vary considerably in size and scope, from single-user personal databases to large interorganizational databases, such as airline reservation systems. All databases have a need for database administration, although the tasks to be accomplished vary in complexity. When using a personal database, for example, individuals follow simple procedures for backing up their data, and they keep minimal records for documentation. In this case, the person who uses the database also performs the DBA functions, even though he or she is probably unaware of it.

For multiuser database applications, database administration becomes both more important and more difficult. Consequently, it generally has formal recognition. For some applications, one or two people are given this function on a part-time basis. For large Internet or intranet databases, database administration responsibilities are often too time-consuming and too varied to be handled even by a single full-time person. Supporting a database with dozens or hundreds of users requires considerable time as well as both technical knowledge and diplomatic skill, and it is usually handled by an office of database administration. The manager of the office is often known as the **database administrator**. In this case, **DBA** refers to either the office or the manager.

The overall responsibility of a DBA is to facilitate the development and use of a database. Usually, this means balancing the conflicting goals of protecting the database and maximizing its availability and benefit to users. The DBA is responsible for the development, operation, and maintenance of the database and its applications. The DBMS software must be kept up to date with the latest fixes. The DBA also monitors database and application performance and adjusts configuration parameters, the physical placement of the data, and the use of indices.

In this chapter, we examine three important database administration functions: concurrency control, security, and backup and recovery. Then we discuss the need for configuration change management. But before you learn about any of this, we will create the Heather Sweeney Designs database discussed in the previous chapters; you'll use it as an example database for the discussion in this chapter and in Chapter 7.

THE HEATHER SWEENEY DESIGNS DATABASE

The SQL statements to create the Heather Sweeney Designs (HSD) database are shown in Figure 3-37. These SQL statements are in MySQL 8.0 syntax. The SQL statements are built from the HSD database design in Figure 5-27, and the column constraints follow the attribute specifications in Figure 5-26 and Figure 5-28 and the referential integrity constraint specifications outlined in Figure 5-29.

The SQL statements to populate the HSD database are shown in Figure 3-38. The completed HSD database is shown in the MySQL Workbench in Figure 6-1.

THE NEED FOR CONTROL, SECURITY, AND RELIABILITY

Databases come in a variety of sizes and scopes, from single-user databases to huge, interorganizational databases, such as inventory management systems. As shown in Figure 6-2, databases also vary in the way they are processed.

It is possible for every one of the application elements in Figure 6-2 to be operating at the same time. Queries, forms, and reports can be generated while Web pages (using Active Server Pages [ASP] and Java Server Pages [JSP], PHP, or other options) access the database, possibly invoking stored procedures. Traditional application programs running in Visual Basic, C#, Java, and other programming languages can be processing transactions on the database. All this activity can cause pieces of programming code stored in the DBMS—which are known as **SQL/Persistent Stored Modules (SQL/PSM)**, and which include **user-defined functions**, **triggers**, and **stored procedures**, and which are discussed in the online Extension B "Advanced SQL," to be invoked. While all this is occurring,

FIGURE 6-1

The HSD Database in MySQL Workbench

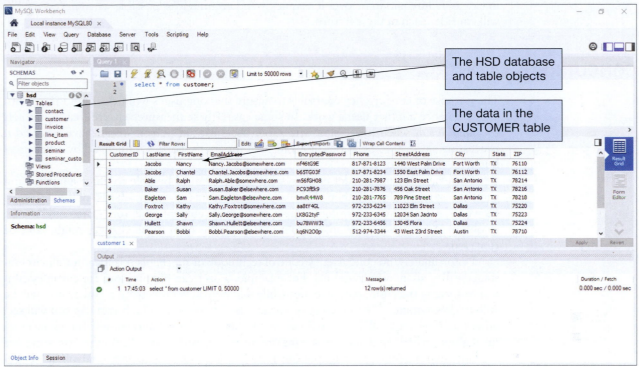

Oracle MySQL Community Server 8.0, Oracle Corporation.

FIGURE 6-2

The Database
Processing
Environment

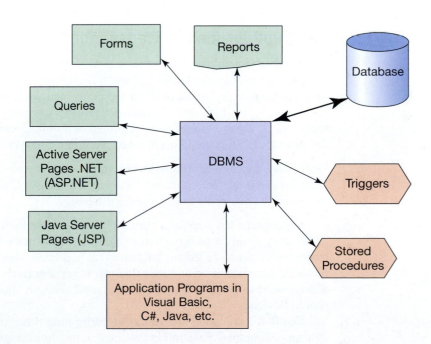

constraints, such as those on referential integrity, must be enforced. Finally, hundreds, or even thousands, of people might be using the system, and they might want to process the database 24 hours a day, 7 days a week.

Three database administration functions are necessary to bring order to this potential chaos. First, the actions of concurrent users must be controlled to ensure that results are consistent with what is expected. Second, security measures must be in place and enforced so that only authorized users can take authorized actions at appropriate times. Finally, backup and recovery techniques and procedures must be operating to protect the database in case of failure and to recover it as quickly and accurately as possible when necessary. We will consider each of these in turn.

CONCURRENCY CONTROL

The purpose of concurrency control is to ensure that one user's work does not inappropriately influence another user's work. In some cases, these measures ensure that a user gets the same result when processing with other users as that person would have received if processing alone. In other cases, it means that the user's work is influenced by other users but in an anticipated way.

For example, in an order-entry system, a user should be able to enter an order and get the same result, whether there are no other users or hundreds of other users. However, a user who is printing a report of the most current inventory status might want to obtain in-process data changes from other users, even if those changes might later be canceled.

Unfortunately, no concurrency control technique or mechanism is ideal for all circumstances; they all involve trade-offs. For example, a user can obtain strict concurrency control by locking the entire database, but while that person is processing no other user will be able to do anything. This is robust protection, but it comes at a high cost. As you will see, other measures are available that are more difficult to program and enforce but allow more **throughput**, which is defined as the maximum rate of processing. Still other measures are available that maximize throughput but for a low level of concurrency control. When designing multiuser database applications, developers need to choose among these trade-offs.

The Need for Atomic Transactions

In most database applications, users submit work in the form of **transactions**, also known as **logical units of work (LUWs)**. A transaction (or LUW) is a series of actions to be taken on a database such that all of them are performed successfully or none of them are performed at all, in which case the database remains unchanged. Such a transaction is sometimes called *atomic* because it is performed as a unit. Consider the following sequence of database actions that could occur when recording a new order:

1. Change the customer record, increasing the value of Amount Owed.
2. Change the salesperson record, increasing the value of Commission Due.
3. Insert the new-order record into the database.

Suppose the last step fails, perhaps because of insufficient file space. Imagine the confusion that would ensue if the first two changes were made but the third one was not. The customer would be billed for an order that was never received, and a salesperson would receive a commission on an order that was never sent to the customer. Clearly, these three actions need to be taken as a unit: Either all of them should be done or none of them should be done.

Figure 6-3 compares the results of performing these activities as a series of independent steps [Figure 6-3(a)] and as an atomic transaction [Figure 6-3(b)].

Notice that when the steps are carried out atomically and one fails, no changes are made in the database. Also note that the application program must issue the commands equivalent to the *Start Transaction* (marks the beginning of the transaction), *Commit Transaction* (saves the new data to the database and ends the transaction), and *Rollback Transaction* (undoes any data changes and ends the transaction) commands shown in Figure 6-3(b) to mark the boundaries of the transaction logic. The particular

FIGURE 6-3

Comparison of the
Results of Applying
Serial Actions Versus
a Multiple-Step
Transaction

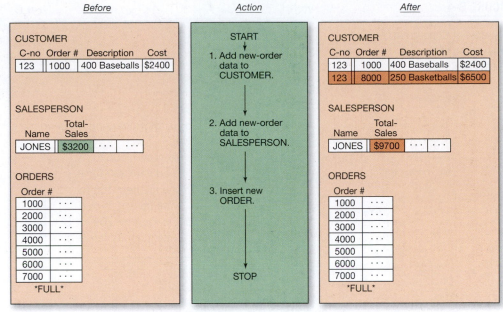

(a) Two of Three Activities Successfully Completed, Resulting in Database Anomalies

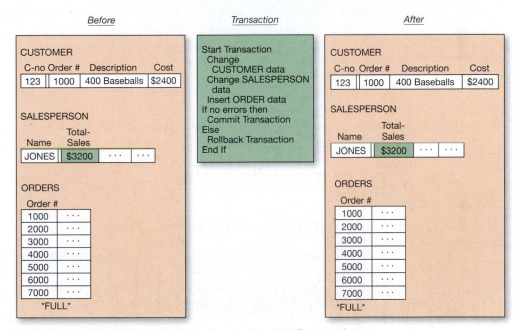

(b) No Change Made Because Entire Transaction Not Successful

syntax of these commands varies from one DBMS product to another. In SQL, this set of commands is known as *SQL Transaction Control Language (TCL)*, and we will discuss it later in this chapter.

Concurrent Transaction Processing

When two transactions are being processed against a database at the same time, they are termed **concurrent transactions**. Although it might appear to the users that concurrent transactions are being processed simultaneously, this is not necessarily true because modern multi-core central processing units (CPUs) of the machine processing the database can execute only a few instructions at a time. Usually transactions are interleaved, which means

User A

1. Read Item 100.
2. Change Item 100.
3. Write Item 100.

User B

1. Read Item 200.
2. Change Item 200.
3. Write Item 200.

One possible order of processing at database server

1. Read Item 100 for A.
2. Read Item 200 for B.
3. Change Item 100 for A.
4. Write Item 100 for A.
5. Change Item 200 for B.
6. Write Item 200 for B.

the operating system switches CPU services among tasks so that only a portion of each of them is carried out in a given interval. This switching among tasks is done so quickly that two people seated at browsers side by side, processing against the same database, might believe that their two transactions are completed simultaneously. However, in reality the two transactions are interleaved.

Figure 6-4 shows two concurrent transactions. User A's transaction reads Item 100, changes it, and rewrites it in the database. User B's transaction takes the same actions but on Item 200. The CPU processes User A's transaction until the CPU must wait for a read or write operation to complete or for some other action to finish. The operating system then shifts control to User B. The CPU processes User B's transaction until a similar interruption in the transaction processing occurs, at which point the operating system passes control back to User A. Again, to the users, the processing appears to be simultaneous, but in reality it is interleaved, or concurrent.

The Lost Update Problem

The concurrent processing illustrated in Figure 6-4 poses no problems because the users are processing different data. Now suppose both users want to process Item 100. For example, User A wants to order 5 units of Item 100, and User B wants to order 3 units of Item 100. Figure 6-5 illustrates this problem.

User A reads Item 100's record (from the database on disk), which is transferred into a user work area (in memory). According to the record, 10 items are in inventory. Then User B reads Item 100's record, and it goes into another user work area. Again, according to the record, 10 items are in inventory. Now, User A takes 5 of them, decrements the count of items in its user work area to 5, and rewrites the record for Item 100. Then User B takes 3, decrements the count in its user work area to 7, and rewrites the record for Item 100. The database now shows, incorrectly, that 7 units of Item 100 remain in inventory. To review, the inventory started at 10, then User A took 5, User B took 3, and the database wound up showing that 7 were left in inventory. Clearly, this is a problem.

Both users obtained data that were correct at the time they obtained the data. However, when User B read the record, User A already had a copy that it was about to update. This situation is called the **lost update problem** or the **concurrent update problem**. Another similar problem is called the **inconsistent read problem**. In this situation, User A reads data that have been processed by only a portion of a transaction from User B. As a result, User A reads incorrect data.

FIGURE 6-5

Example of the Lost
Update Problem

User A

1. Read Item 100
   (assume item count is 10).
2. Reduce count of items by 5.
3. Write Item 100.

User B

1. Read Item 100
   (assume item count is 10).
2. Reduce count of items by 3.
3. Write Item 100.

Order of processing at database server

1. Read Item 100 (for A).
2. Read Item 100 (for B).
3. Set item count to 5 (for A).
4. Write Item 100 for A.
5. Set item count to 7 (for B).
6. Write Item 100 for B.

Note: The change and write in steps 3 and 4 are lost.

Resource Locking

One remedy for the inconsistencies caused by concurrent processing is to prevent multiple applications from obtaining copies of the same rows or tables when those rows or tables are about to be changed. This remedy, called **resource locking**, prevents concurrent processing problems by disallowing sharing by locking data that are retrieved for update. Figure 6-6 shows the order of processing using lock commands.

Because of the lock, User B's transaction must wait until User A is finished with the Item 100 data. Using this strategy, User B can read Item 100's record only after User A has completed the modification. In this case, the final item count stored in the database is 2, which is what it should be. (It started with 10, then A took 5 and B took 3, leaving 2.)

FIGURE 6-6

Example of Concurrent
Processing with
Explicit Locks

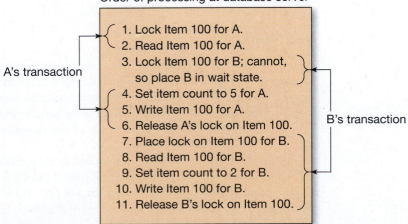

User A

1. Lock Item 100.
2. Read Item 100.
3. Reduce count by 5.
4. Write Item 100.

User B

1. Lock Item 100.
2. Read Item 100.
3. Reduce count by 3.
4. Write Item 100.

Order of processing at database server

A's transaction

1. Lock Item 100 for A.
2. Read Item 100 for A.
3. Lock Item 100 for B; cannot,
   so place B in wait state.
4. Set item count to 5 for A.
5. Write Item 100 for A.
6. Release A's lock on Item 100.
7. Place lock on Item 100 for B.
8. Read Item 100 for B.
9. Set item count to 2 for B.
10. Write Item 100 for B.
11. Release B's lock on Item 100.

B's transaction

Locks can be placed automatically by the DBMS or by a command issued to the DBMS from the application program or by running a query. Locks placed by the DBMS are called **implicit locks**; those placed by command are called **explicit locks**.

In the preceding example, the locks were applied to rows of data; however, not all locks are applied at this level. Some DBMS products lock at the page level (group of rows stored together physically in secondary memory), some at the table level, and some at the database level. The size of a lock is referred to as the **lock granularity**. Locks with large granularity (table and database levels) are easy for the DBMS to administer but frequently cause conflicts. Locks with small granularity (page, row, or field) are difficult to administer, because the DBMS has many more details to keep track of and check, but conflicts are less common.

Locks also vary by type. An **exclusive lock** locks an item from access of any type. No other transaction can read or change the data. A **shared lock** locks an item from being changed but not from being read; that is, other transactions can read the item as long as they do not attempt to alter it.

Serializable Transactions

When two or more transactions are processed concurrently, the results in the database should be logically consistent with the results that would have been achieved had the transactions been processed in an arbitrary serial fashion. **Serial** means that the currently executing transaction runs to completion before any other transaction, or part of a transaction, is executed: there is no interleaving or concurrency. This differs from **parallel**, which means that two or more actions can be done at once, or concurrent, which is when actions from different transactions are interleaved. A scheme for processing concurrent transactions in such a way that the database results are consistent with a serial execution way is said to be **serializable**.

Serializability can be achieved through a number of different means. One way is to process the transaction by using **two-phase locking**. With this strategy, transactions are allowed to obtain locks as necessary, but once the first lock is released, no new locks can be obtained. Transactions thus have a growing phase in which the locks are obtained and a shrinking phase in which the locks are released.

A special case of two-phase locking, called **strict two-phase locking**, is used with a number of DBMS products. With it, locks are obtained throughout the transaction, but no lock is released until the COMMIT or ROLLBACK command is issued. This strategy is more restrictive than two-phase locking requires, but it is easier to implement.

Consider an order-entry transaction that involves processing data in the CUSTOMER, SALESPERSON, and ORDER tables. To make sure the database will suffer no anomalies due to concurrency, the order-entry transaction issues locks on CUSTOMER, SALESPERSON, and ORDER as needed; makes all the database changes; and then releases all its locks.

Deadlock

Although locking solves one problem, it causes another. Consider what might happen when two users each want to order two items from inventory. Suppose User A wants to order some paper, and, if she can get the paper, she also wants to order some pencils. In addition, suppose that User B wants to order some pencils, and, if he can get the pencils, he also wants to order some paper. An example of the possible order of processing is shown in Figure 6-7.

In this figure, Users A and B are locked in a condition known as **deadlock**, sometimes called the **deadly embrace**. Each is waiting for a resource that the other person has locked. Two common ways of solving this problem are preventing the deadlock from occurring and allowing the deadlock to occur and then breaking it.

FIGURE 6-7

Example of Deadlock

User A

1. Lock paper.
2. Take paper.
3. Lock pencils.

User B

1. Lock pencils.
2. Take pencils.
3. Lock paper.

Order of processing at database server

1. Lock paper for User A.
2. Lock pencils for User B.
3. Process A's request; write paper record.
4. Process B's request; write pencil record.
5. Put A in wait state for pencils.
6. Put B in wait state for paper.
                ** Locked **

Deadlock can be prevented in several ways. One way is to allow users to issue only one lock request at a time; in essence, users must lock all the resources they want at once. For example, if User A in Figure 6-7 had locked both the paper and the pencil records at the beginning, the deadlock would not have occurred. A second way to prevent deadlock is to require all application programs to lock resources in the same order.

Almost every DBMS has algorithms for detecting deadlock. When deadlock occurs, the normal solution is to roll back one of the transactions to remove its changes from the database.

Optimistic Versus Pessimistic Locking

Locks can be invoked in two basic styles. With **optimistic locking**, the assumption is made that no conflict will occur. Data are read, the transaction is processed, updates are issued, and then a check is made to see whether conflict occurred. If there was no conflict, the transaction finishes. If there was conflict, the transaction is repeated until it processes with no conflict. With **pessimistic locking**, the assumption is made that conflict will occur. Locks are issued, the transaction is processed, and then the locks are freed.

Figure 6-8 and Figure 6-9 show examples of both styles of locking for a transaction that is reducing the quantity of the pencil row in the PRODUCT table by 5. Figure 6-8 shows optimistic locking. First, the data are read and the current value of Quantity of pencils is saved in the variable OldQuantity. The transaction is then processed, and, if no errors have occurred, a lock is obtained on PRODUCT. The lock might be only for the pencil row, or it might be at a larger level of granularity. In any case, an SQL statement is issued to update the pencil row with a WHERE condition that the current value of Quantity equals OldQuantity. If no other transaction (or set of transactions) has changed the Quantity of the pencil row, then this UPDATE will be successful. If another transaction (or set of transactions) has changed the Quantity of the pencil row, the UPDATE will fail, and the transaction will need to be repeated.

Figure 6-9 shows the logic for the same transaction using pessimistic locking. In this case, a lock is obtained on PRODUCT (at some level of granularity) before any work is begun. Then values are read, the transaction is processed, the UPDATE occurs, and PRODUCT is unlocked.

The advantage of optimistic locking is that the lock is obtained only after the transaction has been processed. Thus, the lock is held for less time than with pessimistic locking. If the transaction is complicated or if the client is slow (due to transmission delays or to the

FIGURE 6-8

Example of Optimistic Locking

```
SELECT    PRODUCT.Name, PRODUCT.Quantity
FROM      PRODUCT
WHERE     PRODUCT.Name = 'Pencil'

OldQuantity = PRODUCT.Quantity

Set NewQuantity = PRODUCT.Quantity – 5

{process transaction – take exception action if NewQuantity < 0, etc.}

{If no errors have occurred:}

LOCK PRODUCT {at some level of granularity}

UPDATE    PRODUCT
SET       PRODUCT.Quantity = NewQuantity
WHERE     PRODUCT.Name = 'Pencil'
     AND  PRODUCT.Quantity = OldQuantity

UNLOCK  PRODUCT

{check to see if update was successful;
if not, repeat transaction}
```

FIGURE 6-9

Example of Pessimistic Locking

```
LOCK      PRODUCT {at some level of granularity}

SELECT    PRODUCT.Name, PRODUCT.Quantity
FROM      PRODUCT
WHERE     PRODUCT.Name = 'Pencil'

Set NewQuantity = PRODUCT.Quantity – 5

{process transaction – take exception action if NewQuantity < 0, etc.}

{If no errors have occurred:}

UPDATE    PRODUCT
SET       PRODUCT.Quantity = NewQuantity
WHERE     PRODUCT.Name = 'Pencil'

UNLOCK    PRODUCT

{no need to check if update was successful}
```

user doing other work, getting a cup of coffee, or shutting down without exiting the application), the lock will be held for considerably less time. This advantage is especially important if the lock granularity is large (for example, the entire PRODUCT table).

The disadvantage of optimistic locking is that if a lot of activity occurs on the pencil row, the transaction might have to be repeated many times. Thus, transactions that involve a lot of activity on a given row (purchasing a popular stock, for example) are poorly suited for optimistic locking. Optimistic locking is often confused with **optimistic concurrency control**, in part because some optimistic concurrency control schemes are implemented without any locking at all, unlike the scheme proposed in this chapter. The details of these mechanisms are beyond the scope of this book.

FIGURE 6-10

Example of Marking
Transaction Boundaries

```
START TRANSACTION:

SELECT      PRODUCT.Name, PRODUCT.Quantity
FROM        PRODUCT
WHERE       PRODUCT.Name = 'Pencil'

Set NewQuantity = PRODUCT.Quantity – 5

{process part of transaction – take exception action if NewQuantity < 0, etc.}

UPDATE      PRODUCT
SET         PRODUCT.Quantity = NewQuantity
WHERE       PRODUCT.Name = 'Pencil'

IF transaction has completed normally        THEN

       COMMIT

ELSE

       ROLLBACK

END IF

Continue processing other actions not part of this transaction . . .
```

SQL TRANSACTION CONTROL LANGUAGE AND DECLARING LOCK CHARACTERISTICS

Concurrency control is a complicated subject; some of the decisions about lock types and strategy have to be made on the basis of trial and error. For this and other reasons, database application programs generally do not explicitly issue locks, as shown in Figure 6-8 and Figure 6-9. Instead, the programs mark transaction boundaries using **SQL Transaction Control Language (TCL)**, and then declare the type of locking behavior they want the DBMS to use. In this way, the DBMS can place and remove locks and even change the level and type of locks dynamically.

Figure 6-10 shows the pencil transaction with transaction boundaries marked with the MySQL commands for controlling transactions, which are slightly different than the ISO SQL standard TCL commands listed here:

- The **SQL BEGIN TRANSACTION statement**,
- The **SQL COMMIT TRANSACTION statement**,
- The **SQL ROLLBACK TRANSACTION statement**.

The SQL BEGIN TRANSACTION statement explicitly marks the start of a new transaction, whereas the SQL COMMIT TRANSACTION statement makes any database changes made by the transaction permanent and marks the end of the transaction. If there is a need to undo the changes made during the transaction due to an error in the process, the SQL ROLLBACK TRANSACTION statement is used to undo all transaction changes and return the database to the state it was in before the transaction was attempted. Thus, the SQL ROLLBACK TRANSACTION statement also marks the end of the transaction but with a very different outcome.

These boundaries are the essential information that the DBMS needs to enforce the different locking strategies. If the developer now declares via a system parameter that he or she wants optimistic locking, the DBMS will implicitly set locks for that locking style. If, however, the developer declares pessimistic locking, the DBMS will set the locks differently.

> **BTW**
>
> You may be wondering when transactions begin and end when you run SQL queries directly against the database from a GUI utility program such as MySQL Workbench. In this case, transaction boundaries are set automatically by the DBMS. Each DBMS does this in a slightly different way, and each system also allows the user to explicitly commit or rollback the current transaction (query). By default, each SQL statement in MySQL Workbench is a transaction, so MySQL commits after each SQL statement that does not return an error. This can be overridden by using START TRANSACTION and COMMIT or ROLLBACK commands explicitly. For more detail, see the documentation for MySQL Workbench (or whatever DBMS/GUI you are using).

Consistent Transactions

Sometimes the acronym *ACID* is applied to transactions. An **ACID transaction** is one that is *atomic, consistent, isolated*, and *durable. Atomic* and *durable* are easy to define. As mentioned earlier in this chapter, an **atomic** transaction is one in which all the database actions occur or none of them do. A **durable** transaction is one in which all committed changes are permanent. The DBMS will not remove such changes, even in the case of failure. If the transaction is durable, the DBMS will provide facilities to recover (redo) the changes of all committed actions when necessary.

The terms *consistent* and *isolated* are not as definitive as the terms *atomic* and *durable*. Consider the following SQL UPDATE command:

```
/* *** EXAMPLE CODE - DO NOT RUN *** */
/* *** SQL-UPDATE-CH06-01 *** */
UPDATE     CUSTOMER
  SET      AreaCode = '425'
  WHERE    ZIPCode = '98050';
```

Suppose the CUSTOMER table has 500,000 rows, and 500 of them have a ZIPCode value equal to 98050. It will take some time for the DBMS to find all 500 rows. During that time, will other transactions be allowed to update the AreaCode or ZIPCode fields of CUSTOMER? If the SQL statement is **consistent**, such updates will be disallowed. The update will apply to the set of rows as they existed at the time the SQL statement started. Such consistency is called **statement-level consistency**.

Now consider a MySQL transaction that contains two SQL UPDATE statements:

```
/* *** EXAMPLE CODE - DO NOT RUN *** */
/* *** SQL-TRANSACTION-CH06-01 *** */
START TRANSACTION;
/* *** SQL-UPDATE-CH06-01 *** */
UPDATE     CUSTOMER
  SET      AreaCode = '425'
  WHERE    ZIPCode = '98050';
. . .
{other transaction work}
. . .
```

```
/* *** SQL-UPDATE-CH06-02 *** */
UPDATE    CUSTOMER
  SET     Discount = 0.05
  WHERE   AreaCode = '425';
...
{other transaction work}
...
COMMIT;
```

In this context, what does *consistent* mean? Statement-level consistency means that each statement independently processes consistent rows, but changes from other users to those rows might be allowed during the interval between the two SQL statements. **Transaction-level consistency** means that all rows affected by either of the SQL statements are protected from changes during the entire transaction.

However, for some implementations of transaction-level consistency, a transaction will not see its own changes. In this example, the second SQL statement might not see rows changed by the first SQL statement.

Thus, when you hear the term *consistent,* look further to determine which type of consistency is intended. Be aware as well of the potential trap of transaction-level consistency. The situation is even more complicated for the term *isolated*, which we consider next.

Transaction Isolation Level

The term *isolated* has several different meanings. To understand those meanings, we need first to define several terms that describe various problems that can occur when we read data from a database, which are summarized in Figure 6-11.

- A **dirty read** occurs when one transaction reads a changed record that has not been committed to the database. This can occur, for example, if one transaction reads a row changed by a second transaction and the second transaction later cancels its changes.
- A **nonrepeatable read** occurs when a transaction rereads data it has previously read and finds modifications or deletions caused by another transaction.
- **A phantom read occurs when a transaction rereads data and finds new rows that were inserted by a different transaction after the prior read.**

To deal with these potential data read problems, the SQL standard defines four **transaction isolation levels** or **isolation levels** that specify which of the concurrency control problems are allowed to occur. These isolation levels are summarized in Figure 6-12.

FIGURE 6-11

Summary of Data Read Problems

Data Read Problem Type	Definition
Dirty Read	The transaction reads a row that has been changed, but the change has *not* been committed. If the change is rolled back, the transaction has incorrect data.
Nonrepeatable Read	The transaction rereads data that has been changed, and finds changes due to committed transactions.
Phantom Read	The transaction rereads data and finds new rows inserted by a committed transaction.

FIGURE 6-12

Summary of Isolation Levels

Problem Type		Isolation Level			
		Read Uncommitted	**Read Committed**	**Repeatable Read**	**Serializable**
Problem Type	**Dirty Read**	Possible	Not possible	Not possible	Not possible
	Nonrepeatable Read	Possible	Possible	Not possible	Not possible
	Phantom Read	Possible	Possible	Possible	Not possible

The goal of having four isolation levels is to allow the application programmer, DBA, or sophisticated end user to declare the type of isolation level desired and then to have the DBMS manage locks to achieve that level of isolation. The transaction isolation levels shown in Figure 6-12 can be defined as:

- The **read uncommitted isolation level** allows dirty reads, nonrepeatable reads, and phantom reads to occur.
- The **read committed isolation level** allows nonrepeatable reads and phantom reads but disallows dirty reads.
- The **repeatable read isolation level** allows phantom reads but disallows both dirty reads and nonrepeatable reads.
- The **serializable isolation level** does not allow any of these three data read problems to occur.

Generally, the more restrictive the isolation level, the less throughput, although much depends on the workload and how the application programs were written. Moreover, not all DBMS products support all these levels. Products also vary in the way they are supported and in the burden they place on the application programmer or DBA.

CURSOR TYPES

A cursor is a pointer into a set of rows that are the result set from an SQL SELECT statement, and cursors are usually defined using SELECT statements in program code. For example, the following MySQL statement defines a cursor named TransCursor that operates over the set of rows indicated by this SELECT statement:

```
/* *** EXAMPLE CODE - DO NOT RUN *** */
/* *** SQL-DECLARE-CURSOR-CH06-01 *** */
DECLARE CURSOR TransCursor FOR
    SELECT      *
    FROM        [TRANSACTION]
    WHERE       PurchasePrice > 10000;
```

After an application program opens a cursor, it can place the cursor somewhere in the result set. Most commonly, the cursor is placed on the first or last row, but other possibilities exist. Each row from the result set is retrieved using the MySQL FETCH SQL command. There is an ISO standard for defining cursors, and most DBMSs have their own extensions for declaring and processing cursors.

FIGURE 6-13

Summary of Cursor
Types

Cursor Type	Description	Comments
Static	Application sees the data as they were at the time the cursor was opened.	Changes made by this cursor are visible. Changes from other sources are not visible. Backward and forward scrolling are allowed.
Keyset	When the cursor is opened, a primary key value is saved for each row in the recordset. When the application accesses a row, the key is used to fetch the current values for the row.	Updates from any source are visible. Inserts from sources outside this cursor are not visible (there is no key for them in the keyset). Inserts from this cursor appear at the bottom of the recordset. Deletions from any source are visible. Changes in row order are not visible. If the isolation level is dirty read, then committed updates and deletions are visible; otherwise, only committed updates and deletions are visible.
Dynamic	Changes of any type and from any source are visible.	All inserts, updates, deletions, and changes in recordset order are visible. If the isolation level is dirty read, then uncommitted changes are visible. Otherwise, only committed changes are visible.

A transaction can open several cursors—either sequentially or simultaneously. In addition, two or more cursors may be open on the same table either directly on the table or through an SQL view on that table. Because cursors require considerable memory, having many cursors open at the same time (for example, for a thousand concurrent transactions) consumes considerable memory. One way to reduce cursor burden is to define reduced-capability cursors and use them when a full-capability cursor is not needed.

Figure 6-13 lists three cursor types supported by Microsoft SQL Server. In SQL Server, cursors may be either forward-only cursors or scrollable cursors. With a **forward-only cursor**, the application can only move forward through the records, and changes made by other cursors in this transaction and other transactions will be visible only if they occur to the rows ahead of the cursor. With a **scrollable cursor**, the application can scroll forward and backward through the records.

There are three types of SQL Server cursors, each of which can be implemented as either a forward-only or scrollable cursor. A **static cursor** takes a snapshot of a relation and processes that snapshot. Changes made using this cursor are visible; changes from other sources are not visible. MySQL just supports static, forward-only cursors.

A **dynamic cursor** is a fully featured cursor. All inserts, updates, deletions, and changes in row order are visible to a dynamic cursor. Unless the isolation level of the transaction is read uncommitted, only committed changes are visible.

Keyset cursors combine some features of static cursors with some features of dynamic cursors. When the cursor is opened, a primary key value is saved for each row. When the application positions the cursor on a row, the DBMS uses the key value to read the current value of the row. Inserts of new rows by other cursors (in this transaction or in other transactions) are not visible. If the application issues an update on a row that has been deleted by a different cursor, the DBMS creates a new row with the old key value and places the updated values in the new row (assuming that all required fields are present). As with dynamic cursors, unless the isolation level of the transaction is read uncommitted, only committed updates and deletions are visible to the cursor.

The amount of overhead and processing required to support a cursor is different for each type. In general, the cost goes up as you move down the cursor types shown in Figure 6-13. To improve DBMS performance, therefore, an application developer should create cursors that are just powerful enough to do the job. Understanding how a particular DBMS implements cursors and whether cursors are located on the server or on the client are also very important. In some cases, placing a dynamic cursor on the client might be better than having a static cursor on the server. No general rule can be stated because performance depends on the implementation used by the DBMS product and the application requirements.

> ## BTW
>
> A word of caution: If you do *not* specify the isolation level of a transaction or do not specify the type of cursors you open, the DBMS will use a default level and type. These defaults may be perfect for your application, but they also may be terrible. Thus, even though you can ignore these issues, you cannot avoid their consequences. You must learn the capabilities of your DBMS product.

DATABASE SECURITY

The goal of database security is to ensure that only authorized users can perform authorized activities at authorized times. This goal is usually broken into two parts: **authentication**, which makes sure the user has the basic right to use the system in the first place, and **authorization**, which assigns the authenticated user specific rights or **permissions** to do specific activities on the system. As shown in Figure 6-14, user authentication is achieved by requiring the user to log in to the system with a password (or other means of positive identification, such as a biometric scan of a fingerprint), whereas user authorization is achieved by granting DBMS-specific permissions.

Note that authentication (when the user logs in to the system) by itself is not sufficient for use of the database—unless the user has been granted permissions, he or she cannot access the database or take any actions that use it.

Permissions can be managed using **SQL Data Control Language (DCL)** statements:

- The **SQL GRANT statement** is used to assign permissions to users and groups so that the users or groups can perform various operations on the data in the database.
- The **SQL REVOKE statement** is used to take existing permissions away from users and groups.

FIGURE 6-14

Database Security Authentication and Authorization

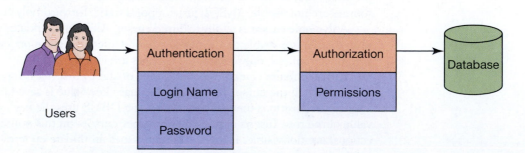

```
/* *** EXAMPLE CODE - DO NOT RUN *** */
/* *** SQL-GRANT-CH06-01 *** */
GRANT SELECT, INSERT, UPDATE ON EMPLOYEE TO Admin1;
```

The preceding SQL GRANT statement gives the Admin1 user the ability to execute SELECT, INSERT, and UPDATE commands on the EMPLOYEE table. Although these statements can be used in SQL scripts and with SQL command line utilities, we will find it much easier to use the GUI DBMS administration utilities provided for use with each of the major DBMS products to manage user permissions. The MySQL Workbench program serves this purpose.

The goal of database security is difficult to achieve, and to make any progress at all the database development team must determine (1) which users should be able to use the database (authentication) and (2) the processing rights and responsibilities of each user. These security requirements can then be enforced using the security features of the DBMS as well as additions to those features that are written into the application programs.

User Accounts

Consider, for example, the database security needs of Heather Sweeney Designs. There must be some means of controlling which employees can have access to the database. There is: You can create a **user account** for each employee. Figure 6-15 shows the creation of the user login HsdUser in MySQL.

This step creates the initial HsdUser account in the DBMS. The password being assigned is HSD-User+password. Note that in the Windows environment there are sometimes two choices for controlling authentication: We can use the Windows operating system to control authentication, or we can create a DBMS internal user account with its

FIGURE 6-15

Creating the MySQL User Login

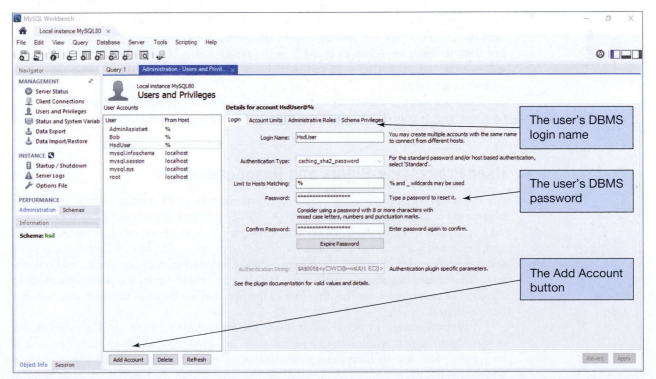

Oracle MySQL Community Server 8.0, Oracle Corporation.

FIGURE 6-16

Using the Workbench to Grant Privileges to a Database Schema

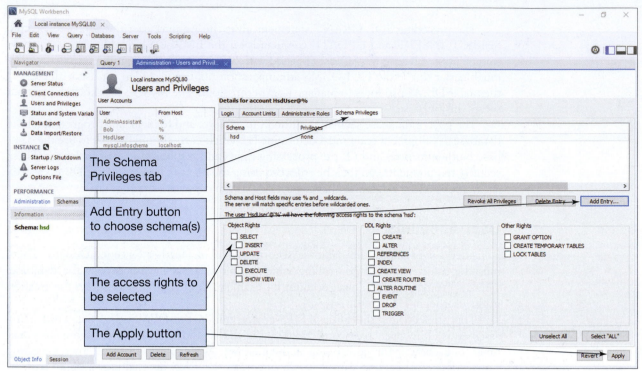

Oracle MySQL Community Server 8.0, Oracle Corporation.

own login name and password. For MySQL, only the second option of internal MySQL user accounts can be used except for the MySQL Enterprise Edition. After creating the user account, we can associate it with all schemas or specific ones. Figure 6-16 shows how the user login HSD-User is connected to a specific database schema named "hsd" because MySQL only allows lowercase schema names. We will use HSD in the text for readability purposes, though. We can specify various privileges using this feature of the Workbench, but the privileges would apply to ALL of the tables within the HSD schema. Instead, we will use the SQL GRANT commands in the next section for finer control on the access rights to each table.

User accounts and passwords need to be managed carefully. The exact terminology, features, and functions of DBMS account and password security depend on the DBMS product used.

User Processing Rights and Responsibilities

All major DBMS products provide security tools that limit certain actions on certain objects to certain users. A general model of DBMS security is shown in Figure 6-17.

According to Figure 6-17, a user can be assigned to zero or one or more roles (groups), and a role can have zero or one or more users. Users, roles, and objects (used in a generic sense) have many permissions. Each permission is assigned to one user or role and one object. After a user is authenticated by the DBMS, the DBMS limits the person's actions to the defined permissions for that user and to the permissions for roles to which that user has been assigned.

A very important principle of database security administration (and of network administration) is that administrative permissions are given to user *groups* (also known as user *roles*) and *not* to individual users unless necessary. There may be some cases in which specific users need to be assigned permissions within the database, but we want to

FIGURE 6-17

A Model of DBMS
Security

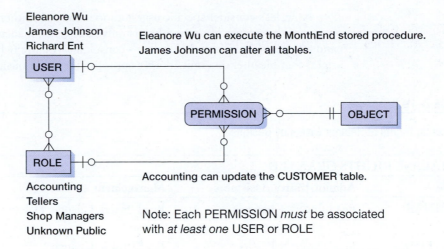

Eleanore Wu
James Johnson
Richard Ent

Eleanore Wu can execute the MonthEnd stored procedure.
James Johnson can alter all tables.

Accounting can update the CUSTOMER table.

Accounting
Tellers
Shop Managers
Unknown Public

Note: Each PERMISSION *must* be associated
with *at least one* USER or ROLE

avoid this whenever possible. Note that because groups or roles are used, having a means for assigning users to groups or roles is necessary. When an administrator logs in to the server that manages the HSD database, some means must be available to determine which role(s) he or she belongs to. The specifics for assigning roles vary among database systems.

MySQL supports global "Administrative Roles" that specify privileges that apply to all database schemas in the server. Thus, we can easily create accounts that can perform all tasks, or limit administrative functions to monitor the server, back up any database that the server manages, or create new users and assign privileges to them. More than one Administrative Role can be assigned to a user. Figure 6-18 shows the Administrative Roles that can be assigned to a MySQL user.

FIGURE 6-18

MySQL Administrative Roles

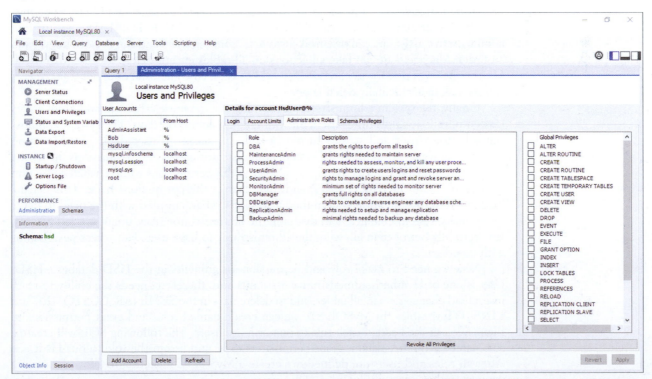

Oracle MySQL Community Server 8.0, Oracle Corporation.

Now, let's consider specific user authorization at Heather Sweeney Designs. The company has three types of users: administrative assistants, management (Heather and others), and a system administrator (Heather's consultant). Figure 6-19 summarizes the processing rights that Heather determined were appropriate for her business.

FIGURE 6-19

Processing Rights at Heather Sweeney Designs

DATABASE RIGHTS GRANTED

Table	Administrative Assistants	Management	System Administrator
SEMINAR	Read, Insert, Change	Read, Insert, Change, Delete	Grant Rights, Modify Structure
CUSTOMER	Read, Insert, Change	Read, Insert, Change	Grant Rights, Modify Structure
SEMINAR_CUSTOMER	Read, Insert, Change, Delete	Read, Insert, Change, Delete	Grant Rights, Modify Structure
CONTACT	Read, Insert, Change	Read, Insert, Change, Delete	Grant Rights, Modify Structure
INVOICE	Read, Insert, Change	Read, Insert, Change, Delete	Grant Rights, Modify Structure
LINE_ITEM	Read, Insert, Change, Delete	Read, Insert, Change, Delete	Grant Rights, Modify Structure
PRODUCT	Read, Insert, Change	Read, Insert, Change, Delete	Grant Rights, Modify Structure

Administrative assistants can read, insert, and change data in all tables. However, they can delete data only from SEMINAR_CUSTOMER and LINE_ITEM. This means that administrative assistants can disenroll customers from seminars and can remove items from an order. Management can take all actions on all tables except delete CUSTOMER data. Heather believes that for as hard as she works to get a customer, she does not want to ever run the risk of accidentally deleting one.

Finally, the system administrator can modify the database structure and grant rights (assign permissions) to other users but can take no action on data. The system administrator is not a user and so should not be allowed access to user data. This limitation might seem weak. After all, if the system administrator can assign permissions, he or she can get around the security system by changing the permissions to take whatever action is desired, make the data changes, and then change the permissions back. This is true, but it would leave an audit trail in the DBMS logs. That, coupled with the need to make the security system changes, will dissuade the administrator from unauthorized activity. It is certainly better than allowing the administrator to have user data access permissions with no effort.

Now we need to make role and permission assignments in the HSD database. HSD-User is one of Heather's administrative assistants and, therefore, needs the ability to read, insert, and change data in all tables, and to delete data in the SEMINAR_CUSTOMER and LINE_ITEM tables. In MySQL 8.0, we can create named roles and grant permissions to them. We can then assign each role to one or more users. The following SQL will create a role named AdminAssistant, grant permissions to it, and assign the role to our HsdUser. After all roles and users are defined, we create a MySQL Connection to allow the user to connect to the server and login.

```
/* *** EXAMPLE CODE - DO NOT RUN *** */
/* *** SQL-GRANT-CH06-02 *** */
CREATE ROLE 'AdminAssistant';
GRANT SELECT, INSERT, UPDATE ON hsd.SEMINAR TO
  'AdminAssistant';
GRANT SELECT, INSERT, UPDATE ON hsd.CUSTOMER TO
  'AdminAssistant';
GRANT SELECT, INSERT, UPDATE, DELETE ON hsd.SEMINAR_
  CUSTOMER TO 'AdminAssistant';
GRANT SELECT, INSERT, UPDATE ON hsd.CONTACT TO
  'AdminAssistant';
GRANT SELECT, INSERT, UPDATE ON hsd.INVOICE TO
  'AdminAssistant';
GRANT SELECT, INSERT, UPDATE, DELETE ON hsd.LINE_ITEM TO
  'AdminAssistant';
GRANT SELECT, INSERT, UPDATE ON hsd.PRODUCT TO
  'AdminAssistant';
GRANT 'AdminAssistant' TO 'HsdUser';
SET DEFAULT ROLE 'AdminAssistant' to 'HsdUser';
```

Figure 6-20 shows the creation of the MySQL Connector named HsdConnection so that user HsdUser can connect to the server from the Workbench and log in with the assigned privileges.

FIGURE 6-20

Creating a New Connection for HsdUser

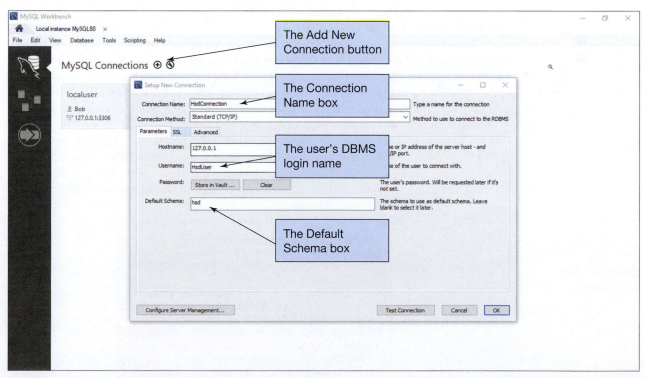

Oracle MySQL Community Server 8.0, Oracle Corporation.

In this discussion, we have used the phrase *processing rights and responsibilities.* As this phrase implies, responsibilities go with processing rights. If, for example, the system administrator deletes CUSTOMER data, it is that person's responsibility to ensure that those deletions do not adversely affect the company's operation, accounting, and so forth.

Processing responsibilities cannot be enforced by the DBMS or the database applications. Responsibilities are, instead, encoded in manual procedures and explained to users during systems training. These are topics for a systems development book, and we do not consider them further here except to reiterate that responsibilities go with rights. Such responsibilities must be documented and enforced.

The DBA has the task of managing processing rights and responsibilities, which change over time. As the database is used and as changes are made to the applications and to the DBMS's structure, the need for new or different rights and responsibilities will arise. The DBA is a focal point for the discussion of such changes and for their implementation.

After processing rights have been defined, they can be implemented at many levels: operating system, network directory service, Web server, DBMS, and application. The next two sections consider the DBMS and application aspects. The other aspects are beyond the scope of this book.

DBMS-Level Security

Security guidelines for a DBMS are shown in Figure 6-21. First, the DBMS should be run behind a firewall. In most cases, no communication with the DBMS or database applications should be allowed to be initiated from outside the organization's network. For example, the company's Web site should be hosted on a separate, dedicated Web server. The Web server will have to communicate through the firewall, and the DBMS server should be protected behind it.

Second, service packs and fixes for the operating system and the DBMS must be applied as soon as possible. In spring 2003, the slammer worm exploited a security hole in SQL Server, bringing major organizational database applications to their knees. Microsoft had published a patch that eliminated the hole prior to the release of the slammer worm, so any organization that had applied that patch was not affected by the worm. In some organizations, the DBA applies the service packs; in others a system administrator applies service packs in coordination with the DBA.

A third protection is for the DBA to limit the capabilities of the DBMS to only those features and functions that the applications need. For example, Oracle Database can support many different communications protocols. To improve security, any Oracle-supported protocol that is not used should be removed or disabled. Similarly, every DBMS ships with hundreds of system-stored procedures. Any procedure that is not used should be removed from operational databases.

Another important security measure is to protect the computer that runs the DBMS. No users should be allowed to work on the DBMS computer, and that computer should reside in a separate facility behind locked doors. Visits to the room housing the DBMS should be logged with date and time. Further, because people can log in to DBMS servers

FIGURE 6-21

DBMS Security
Guidelines

- Run the DBMS behind a firewall
- Apply the latest operating system and DBMS service packs and fixes
- Limit DBMS functionality to needed features
- Protect the computer that runs the DBMS
- Manage accounts and passwords
- Encryption of sensitive data transmitted across the network
- Encryption of sensitive data stored in databases

via remote-control software (such as Microsoft Remote Desktop Connection in the Windows environment), who has (and who can grant) remote access must be controlled.

A user can enter a name and password; in some applications, the name and password are entered on behalf of the user. The security systems used by SQL Server, Oracle Database, and MySQL are variations of the model shown in Figure 6-17. The terminology used might vary, but the essence of their security systems is the same.

Application-Level Security

Although most DBMS products provide substantial database security capabilities, they are generic by their very nature. If an application requires specific security measures—such as disallowing users to view a row of a table or a join of a table that has an employee name other than the user's own—the DBMS facilities will not be adequate. In these cases, the security system must be augmented by features in the associated application programming.

For example, application security in Internet applications is often provided on the Web server computer. When application security is executed on this server, sensitive security data do not need to be transmitted over the network. To understand this better, suppose an application is written such that when users click a particular button on a browser page the following query is sent to the Web server and then to the DBMS:

```
/* *** EXAMPLE CODE - DO NOT RUN *** */
/* *** SQL-QUERY-CH06-01 *** */
SELECT      *
FROM        EMPLOYEE;
```

This statement returns all EMPLOYEE rows. If the application security allows employees to access only their own data, then a Web server could add the following WHERE clause to this query:

```
/* *** EXAMPLE CODE - DO NOT RUN *** */
/* *** SQL-QUERY-CH06-02 *** */
SELECT      *
FROM        EMPLOYEE
WHERE       EMPLOYEE.Name = '<%SESSION("EmployeeName")%>';
```

An expression like this causes the Web server to fill in the employee's name for the WHERE clause. For a user signed on under the name Benjamin Franklin, the following statement results from this expression:

```
/* *** EXAMPLE CODE - DO NOT RUN *** */
/* *** SQL-QUERY-CH06-03 *** */
SELECT      *
FROM        EMPLOYEE
WHERE       EMPLOYEE.Name = 'Benjamin Franklin';
```

Because the name is inserted by a program on the Web server, the browser user does not know it is occurring and cannot interfere with it. Such security processing can be done as shown here on a Web server, and it can also be done within the application programs themselves or written as code stored within the DBMS to be executed by the DBMS at the appropriate times. The DBA and application programmer must do this carefully; otherwise, database security can be compromised by techniques such as SQL injection attacks.

You can also store additional data in a security database that is accessed by the Web server as well as by stored DBMS code. That security database could contain, for example, the identities of users paired with additional values of WHERE clauses. For example, suppose the users in the personnel department can access more than just their own data. The predicates for appropriate WHERE clauses could be stored in the security database, read by the application program, and appended to SQL SELECT statements, as necessary.

Many other possibilities exist for extending DBMS security with application processing. In general, you should use the DBMS security features first. Only if they are inadequate for the requirements should you add to them with application code. The closer the security enforcement is to the data, the lower the chance for infiltration. Also, using the DBMS security features is faster, less expensive, and likely to produce higher-quality results than if you develop your own.

DATABASE BACKUP AND RECOVERY

Computer systems fail. Hardware breaks. Programs have bugs. Procedures written by humans contain errors. People make mistakes. All these failures can and do occur in database applications. Because a database is shared by many people and because it often is a key element of an organization's operations, recovering it as soon as possible is important.

Several problems must be addressed. First, from a business standpoint, business functions must continue. For example, customer orders, financial transactions, and packing lists must be completed manually. Later, when the database application is operational again, the new data can be entered. Second, computer operations personnel must restore the system to a usable state as quickly as possible and as close as possible to what it was when the system crashed. Third, users must know what to do when the system becomes available again. Some work might need to be re-entered, and users must know how far back they need to go.

When failures occur, simply fixing the problem and resuming processing is impossible. Even if no data are lost during a failure (which assumes that all types of memory are nonvolatile—an unrealistic assumption), the timing and scheduling of computer processing are too complex to be accurately recreated. Enormous amounts of overhead data and processing would be required for the operating system to be able to restart processing precisely where it was interrupted. Turning back the clock and putting all the electrons in the same configuration they were in at the time of the failure is simply not possible. However, two other approaches are possible: **recovery via reprocessing** and **recovery via rollback/rollforward**.

Recovery via Reprocessing

Because processing cannot be resumed at a precise point, the next-best alternative is to go back to a known point and reprocess the workload from there. The simplest form of this type of recovery involves periodically making a copy of the database (called a *database save* or *backup*) and keeping a record of all transactions processed since the save. Then, when failure occurs, the operations staff can restore the database from the save and reprocess all the transactions.

Unfortunately, this simple strategy normally is not feasible. First, reprocessing transactions takes the same amount of time as processing them in the first place. If the computer is heavily scheduled, the system might never catch up. Second, when transactions are processed concurrently, events are asynchronous. Slight variations in human activity, such as a user reading an email message before responding to an application prompt, could change the order of the execution of concurrent transactions. Therefore, whereas Customer A got the last seat on a flight during the original processing, Customer B might get the last seat during reprocessing. For these reasons, reprocessing is normally not a viable form of recovery from failure in multiuser systems.

Recovery via Rollback and Rollforward

A second approach to database recovery involves periodically making a copy of the database (the database save or backup) and keeping a log of the changes made by transactions against the database since the save. Then, when a failure occurs, one of two methods (or a combination of both) can be used. With the first method, called **rollforward**, the database is restored using the saved data and all valid transactions since the save are reapplied. Note that we are not reprocessing the transactions because the application programs are not involved in the rollforward. Instead, the processed changes, as recorded in the log, are reapplied. At this point, any transactions in process at the time of the failure are restarted.

With the second method, **rollback**, we correct mistakes caused by erroneous or partially processed transactions by undoing the changes they made in the database. Then the valid transactions that were in process at the time of the failure are restarted. Note that the rollback method doesn't actually use the database save (backup), but all DBMSs create backups because they are useful in recovering from a failed hard drive (versus a system crash, which we emphasize here).

As stated, both of these methods require that a **log** of the transaction results be kept. This log contains records of the data changes in chronological order. Note that transactions must be written to the log before they are applied to the database. That way, if the system crashes between the time a transaction is logged and the time it is applied, at worst, there is a record of an unapplied transaction. If transactions were applied before being logged, it would be possible (and undesirable) to change the database without having a record of the change. If this happens, an unwary user might re-enter an already completed transaction.

In the event of a failure, we use the log to undo and redo transactions, as shown in Figure 6-22. To undo a transaction as shown in Figure 6-22(a), the log must contain a copy of every database record before it was changed. Such records are called **before-images**. A transaction is undone by applying before-images of all of its changes to the database.

To redo a transaction as shown in Figure 6-22(b), the log must contain a copy of every database record (or page) after it was changed. These records are called **after-images**. A transaction is redone by applying after-images of all of its changes to the database. Possible data items of a transaction log are shown in Figure 6-23.

For this example transaction log, each transaction has a unique name for identification purposes. Furthermore, all images for a given transaction are linked together with pointers. One pointer points to the previous change made by this transaction (the reverse pointer),

FIGURE 6-22

Undo and Redo Transactions

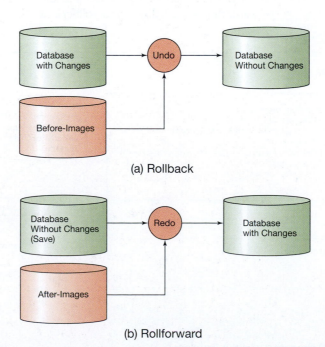

(a) Rollback

(b) Rollforward

FIGURE 6-23

Transaction Log
Example

Relative Record Number	Transaction ID	Reverse Pointer	Forward Pointer	Time	Type of Operation	Object	Before-Image	After-Image
1	OT1	0	2	11:42	START			
2	OT1	1	4	11:43	MODIFY	CUST 100	(old value)	(new value)
3	OT2	0	8	11:46	START			
4	OT1	2	5	11:47	MODIFY	SP AA	(old value)	(new value)
5	OT1	4	7	11:47	INSERT	ORDER 11		(value)
6	CT1	0	9	11:48	START			
7	OT1	5	0	11:49	COMMIT			
8	OT2	3	0	11:50	COMMIT			
9	CT1	6	10	11:51	MODIFY	SP BB	(old value)	(new value)
10	CT1	9	0	11:51	COMMIT			

and the other points to the next change made by this transaction (the forward pointer). A zero in the pointer field means that this is the end of the list. The DBMS recovery subsystem uses these pointers to locate all records for a particular transaction. Figure 6-23 shows an example of the linking of log records.

Other data items in the log are:

- The time of the action (timestamp)
- The type of operation (START marks the beginning of a transaction, and COMMIT terminates a transaction, releasing all locks that were in place)
- The object acted upon, such as record type and identifier
- The before-image and after-image, as applicable

Given a log with before-images and after-images, the undo and redo actions are straightforward. Figure 6-24 shows how rollback recovery for a system crash is accomplished.

FIGURE 6-24

Recovery Example

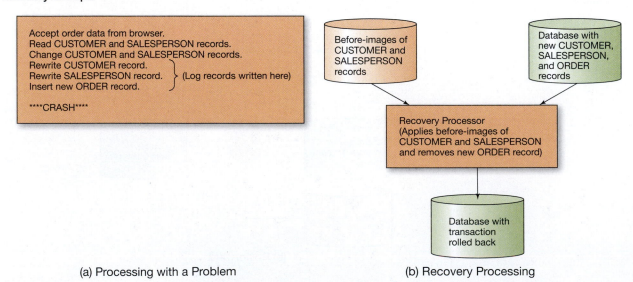

(a) Processing with a Problem   (b) Recovery Processing

To undo the (uncommitted) transaction in Figure 6-24(a), the recovery processor simply replaces each changed record with its before-image, as shown in Figure 6-24(b). When all before-images have been restored, the transaction is undone. To redo a transaction, the recovery processor starts with the version of the database at the time the transaction started and applies all after-images. This action assumes that an earlier version of the database is available from a backup.

Most modern DBMSs actually use a combination of rollback and rollforward recovery, rather than just one of them. In addition, unless a catastrophic disk failure has occurred, most systems will start from the database as it exists on disk when the system comes back up from its failure; this tends to avoid a lot of unnecessary rollforward actions. A common general approach is to start with the existing (potentially inconsistent) database state as recovery begins, then undo (rollback) any transactions that were uncommitted at the time of the failure, then redo (rollforward) any transactions that committed after the most recent time when the database was known to be consistent. The rollback step is necessary because some database updates may have been recorded to disk even for transactions that have not yet committed. The rollforward step is necessary because most systems will record a database change to the log before recording it in the actual database, so some of those logged updates may not have made it to the database at the time of the failure.

How do we know when a database on disk was most recently consistent? Certainly a backup copy of the database will be consistent, but restoring a database to its most recent save and reapplying all transactions might require considerable processing. To reduce the delay, DBMS products usually use checkpoints. A **checkpoint** is a point of synchronization between the database and the transaction log. To perform a checkpoint, the DBMS temporarily refuses new requests, finishes processing outstanding requests, and writes its buffers to disk. The DBMS then waits until the operating system notifies it that all outstanding write requests to the database and to the log have been completed successfully. At this point, the log and the database are synchronized. A checkpoint record is then written to

FIGURE 6-25

Backing Up the HSD Database

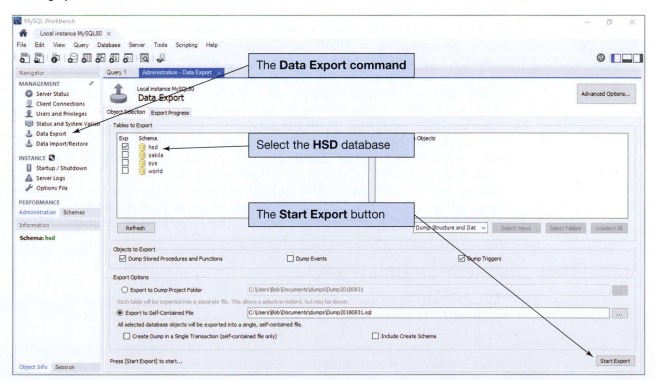

Oracle MySQL Community Server 8.0, Oracle Corporation.

the log. Later, the database can be recovered from the checkpoint, and only after-images for transactions that started after the checkpoint need to be applied.

Checkpoints are inexpensive operations, and making three or four (or more) per hour is feasible. This way, no more than 15 or 20 minutes of processing needs to be recovered. Most DBMS products perform automatic checkpoints, making human intervention unnecessary.

You will need to learn more about backup and recovery if you work in database administration using products such as SQL Server, Oracle Database, or MySQL. For now, you just need to understand the basic ideas and to realize that the DBA is responsible for ensuring that adequate backup and recovery plans have been developed and that database saves (backups), checkpoints, and logs are generated as required. You should also understand that many DBMS GUI utilities allow the DBA to easily make database backups as needed, even without a backup plan and backup schedule. Figure 6-25 shows the MySQL Workbench being used to make a simple recovery model full database backup of the HSD database.

PHYSICAL DATABASE DESIGN AND OPTIMIZATION

Another important consideration for DBAs involves the efficient performance of the DBMS. One basic concept here is that of the **index**, a secondary structure that can speed up access to data for certain types of queries. As an example, if queries such as SQL-QUERY-CH06-03 are common, then an index on the EMPLOYEE.Name field could speed up such queries by one or more orders of magnitude. An index is one component of what is called **physical database design**. Other aspects of physical database design include DBA decisions about database usage of primary memory and the sizes of blocks of data that are read into main memory from secondary memory: The DBA must have a good understanding of the relative sizes and speeds of primary and secondary memory to create the best physical database design. A DBA may also be able to influence the amount of replication of data: common data storage techniques such as **disk mirroring** (maintaining two copies of the data so a disk failure need not result in unavailable data) and various forms of **redundant array of independent disks (RAID)** storage, which take advantage of using multiple disks to store a single database, using combinations of duplication of data and spreading data among several disks.

In addition to physical database design issues, which mostly involve a static picture of the database, the DBA must pay careful attention to the performance of specific queries as the database evolves. Every DBMS has a component called a **query optimizer**, which will evaluate several potential ways to execute a query, and will execute the one with the lowest expected execution time. The optimizer will look at things such as different ways of joining several tables (for example, should we join tables A and B, then join the result to C, or should we join B and C first, then join the result to A?) and which algorithm to use to compute a join (there are several), whether to use an existing index to speed up a query, and so on. This all happens automatically, but the DBA can greatly influence the choices available to the optimizer. As a database changes over time, the DBA might decide to create a new index, delete an existing index, alter the amount of memory used by the DBMS, help the query optimizer by providing it with some hints, and so on. The details of physical database design and query processing/optimization are beyond the scope of this book, but it is important to know that these issues can be crucial for the DBA of a large database.

ADDITIONAL DBA RESPONSIBILITIES

Concurrency control, security, and reliability are the three major concerns of database administration. However, other administrative and managerial DBA functions are also important.

For one, a DBA needs to ensure that a system exists to gather and record user-reported errors and other problems. A procedure needs to be devised to prioritize those errors and problems and to ensure that they are corrected accordingly. In this regard, the DBA works with the development team not only to resolve these problems but also to evaluate features and functions of new releases of the DBMS.

As the database is used and as new requirements develop and are implemented, requests for changes to the structure of the database will occur. Changes to an operational database need to be made with great care and thoughtful planning. Because databases are shared resources, a change to the structure of a database to implement features desired by one user or group can be detrimental to the needs of other users or groups.

Therefore, a DBA needs to create and manage a process for controlling the database configuration. Such a process includes procedures for recording change requests, conducting user and developer reviews of such requests, and creating projects and tasks for implementing changes that are approved. All these activities need to be conducted with a community-wide view.

Managing databases in the cloud has its own challenges. In that case we are using computers, data storage, and network equipment owned by another organization, so the DBA must learn to use the cloud provider's Web portal, and understand network security enough to restrict access from some ranges of Internet Protocol (IP) addresses if necessary. Every organization should have a **Service Level Agreement** (SLA) with the cloud provider that covers backups, application response time, and error reporting.

Finally, a DBA is responsible for ensuring that appropriate documentation is maintained about database structure, concurrency control, security, backup and recovery, applications use, and a myriad of other details that concern the management and use of the database. Some vendors provide tools for recording such documentation. At a minimum, a DBMS will have its own metadata that it uses to process the database. Some products augment these metadata with facilities for storing and reporting application metadata, as well as operational procedures.

A DBA has significant responsibilities in the management and administration of a database. These responsibilities vary with the database type and size, the number of users, and the complexity of the applications. However, the responsibilities are important for all databases. You should know about the need for DBA services and consider the material in this chapter even for small, personal databases.

WORKING WITH MICROSOFT ACCESS

Section 6

Database Administration in Microsoft Access

At this point, we have created and populated the CONTACT, CUSTOMER, SALESPERSON, PHONE_NUMBER, and VEHICLE tables in the Wallingford Motors' CRM database. We have learned how to create forms, reports, and queries in the preceding sections of "Working with Microsoft Access" and how to create and use view-equivalent queries in online extension B, "Advanced SQL." We have also studied how 1:1. 1:N, and N:M relationships are created and managed in Microsoft Access 2019.

This chapter deals with database administration topics, and in this section of "Working with Microsoft Access" we will look at database security in Microsoft Access. As a personal DBMS, Access lacks many of the administrative options available in enterprise DBMSs, so we will focus on what is available. In this section, you will:

- Understand database security in Microsoft Access 2019.

(Continued)

Database Security in Microsoft Access

Until Microsoft Access 2007, Microsoft Access had a user-level security system that allowed a DBA to grant specific database permissions to individual users or groups of users on a basis similar to that discussed in this chapter. Starting with Microsoft Access 2007, however, a very different security model has been implemented. This model is based on whether the entire database itself is trustworthy, and it seems like Microsoft is saying that Microsoft Access really is for personal (or small workgroup) databases and that if you need user-level security you should be using SQL Server (especially because the SQL Server Express edition is a free download). At the same time, Microsoft Access 2019 (and the earlier Microsoft Access 2007, 2010, 2013, and 2019) will still work with the earlier user-level security system for Microsoft Access databases in the Microsoft Access 2003 (and earlier) *.mdb file format. In this section of "Working with Microsoft Access," we focus on the current Microsoft Access 2019 security system.

To do the work in this section of "Working with Microsoft Access," we *must* be able to see the file extension for each database file that we are working on—Microsoft actually uses several different file extensions in Microsoft Access 2019. By default, Windows File Manager and therefore Microsoft Access 2019 do not display the file extensions of known file types. Up until now, this really hasn't mattered to us, but now we need to be able to distinguish between different Microsoft Access 2019 file types.

To make the file extensions visible, we need to:

- Open Windows **File Explorer**.
- Click the **View** tab, click the **Options** button, and then select **Change folder and search options**.
- In the Folder Options dialog box, click the **View** tab.
- In the Advanced Settings, uncheck the **Hide extensions for known file types** check box.
- While we are here, we will also take this opportunity to uncheck the **Use Sharing Wizard (Recommended)** check box! We do *not* recommend using that Wizard!
- Click the **Apply** button, and then click the **OK** button.

Now we need to make a copy of our WMCRM.accdb database file. This is necessary because we have already enabled all security features of that database. In earlier sections of "Working with Microsoft Access," we learned how to make copies of Microsoft Access 2019 databases—we simply make a copy of the **WMCRM.accdb** database file in the Documents folder in the Documents library and rename this new file **WMCRM-WA06-v01.accdb**.

Types of Database Security in Microsoft Access 2019

You can secure Microsoft Access 2019 files in three basic ways:

- By creating trusted locations for Microsoft Access database storage
- By password encrypting and decrypting Microsoft Access databases
- By deploying secure databases using compilation or digital signatures

Let us look at each of these in turn.

Trusted Locations

Up until now, whenever we have opened a Microsoft Access database for the first time during our work in "Working with Microsoft Access," the **Security Warning message bar** appears, as shown in Figure AW-6-1 where we have just opened the WMCRM-WA06-v01.accdb database for the first time.

Thus far, we have always clicked the **Enable Content** button to enable the disabled content. Note that we only need to do this once for each database—the first time we open the database after it has been created. We have done this so we can use Microsoft Access features that are otherwise disabled and unavailable to us, including:

FIGURE WA-6-1

The Security Warning Message Bar

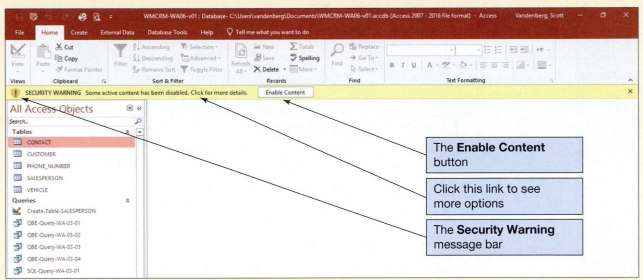

The **Enable Content** button

Click this link to see more options

The **Security Warning** message bar

Access 2019, Windows 10, Microsoft Corporation.

- Microsoft Access database queries (either SQL or QBE) that add, update, or delete data
- Data definition language (DDL) (either SQL or QBE) actions that create or alter database objects, such as tables
- SQL commands being sent from a Microsoft Access application to a database server, such as Microsoft SQL Server, that supports the Open Database Connectivity (ODBC) standard
- ActiveX controls

We obviously need the first two features if we are going to build Microsoft Access 2019 databases. The third feature is important if we are using a Microsoft Access 2019 database as an application front end (containing the application forms, queries, and reports) for data stored in an SQL Server database. Finally, **ActiveX controls** are software code written to Microsoft's **ActiveX specification**, and they are often used as Web browser plug-ins. The risk here is that Microsoft Access 2019 databases can be targeted by code written in ActiveX-compliant programming languages that can manipulate the databases just as Microsoft Access itself would.

Although we can simply click the **Enable Content** button to activate these features, note that Microsoft Access 2019 also provides other options for dealing with this security problem. If we click the link labeled *Some active content has been disabled. Click for more details* shown in Figure WA-6-1, we are switched to the Info page in the Backstage view and specifically to the Security Warning section of that page, as shown in Figure WA-6-2.

Clicking the **Enable Content** button displays two options, as shown in Figure WA-6-3—*Enable All Content* and *Advanced Options*. Clicking the **Enable All Content** button produces the same results as clicking the Enable Content button on the Security Warning toolbar, and all features of the database will always be available to us. Clicking the **Advanced Options** button displays the Microsoft Office Security Options dialog box, as shown in Figure WA-6-4.

The Microsoft Office Security Options dialog box provides the final two options. The first option is to allow Microsoft Access to continue to disable the possible security risks. Thus the *Help protect me from unknown content (recommended)* radio button is selected as the default. This option is the same as simply closing the Security Warning toolbar when it is first displayed. The second option is to enable the content in the database for *only* this

(Continued)

FIGURE WA-6-2

The Security Warning Section of the File | Info Page

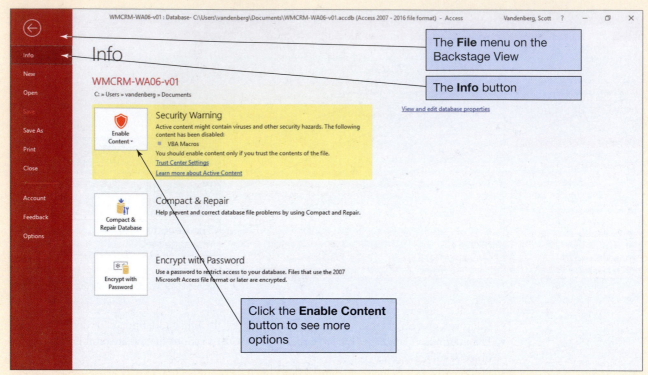

Access 2019, Windows 10, Microsoft Corporation.

FIGURE WA-6-3

The Enable Content Options

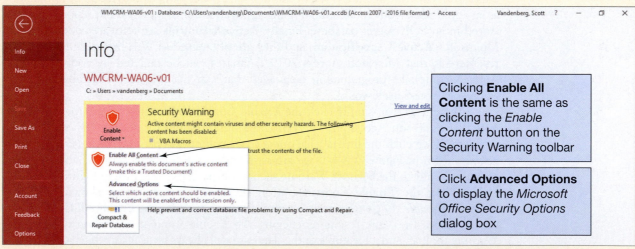

Access 2019, Windows 10, Microsoft Corporation.

use ("session") of the database by checking the *Enable content for this session* radio button. This is the first new choice we have really been given, and we will open the database using this option. Note that this means that the Security Warning message bar will be displayed again the next time this database file is opened!

However, we (nearly) always need these Microsoft Access features enabled. Is there a way to permanently enable them so that we do not have to deal with the Security Warning bar every time we open a new Microsoft Access database? Yes, there is.

FIGURE WA-6-4

The Microsoft Office Security Options Dialog Box

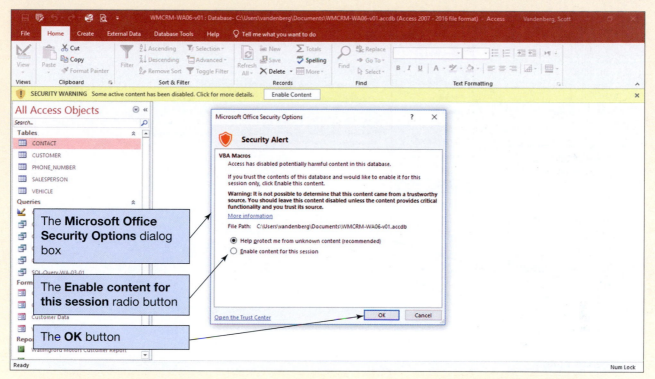

The Microsoft Office Security Options dialog box

The Enable content for this session radio button

The OK button

The word Microsoft uses to describe our situation is *trust*: Do we *trust the content* of our database? If so, we can create a **trusted location** in which to store our trusted databases. And databases we use from the trusted location are opened *without* the security warning but *with* all features enabled.

Creating a Trusted Location

1. Start Microsoft Access 2019.
2. Double-click the **WMCRM-WA06-v01.accdb** file in the Recent list, and then click the **Enable Content** button. If you are asked whether you want to make this database a trusted document, click the **No** button.
3. Click the **File** command tab to display the Backstage view.
4. Click the **Options** command on the Backstage view. The Access Options dialog box appears.
5. Click the **Trust Center** button to display the Trust Center page, as shown in Figure WA-6-5.
6. Click the **Trust Center Settings** button to display the Trust Center dialog box, as shown in Figure WA-6-6. Note that the *Message Bar Settings for all Office Applications* page is currently displayed and that the setting that enables the display of the Security Options message bar is currently selected.
7. Click the **Trusted Locations** button to display the Trusted Locations page, as shown in Figure WA-6-7. Note that the only currently trusted location is the folder that stores the Microsoft Access wizard databases. Also note that we have the ability to disable all trusted locations if we choose to do so.

(Continued)

FIGURE WA-6-5

The Access Options Trust Center Page

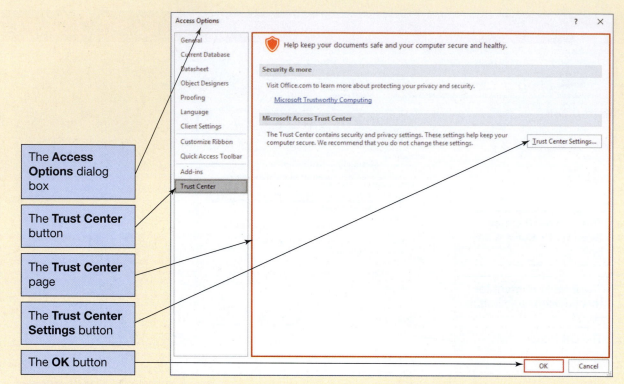

The **Access Options** dialog box

The **Trust Center** button

The **Trust Center** page

The **Trust Center Settings** button

The **OK** button

Access 2019, Windows 10, Microsoft Corporation.

FIGURE WA-6-6

The Trust Center Dialog Box

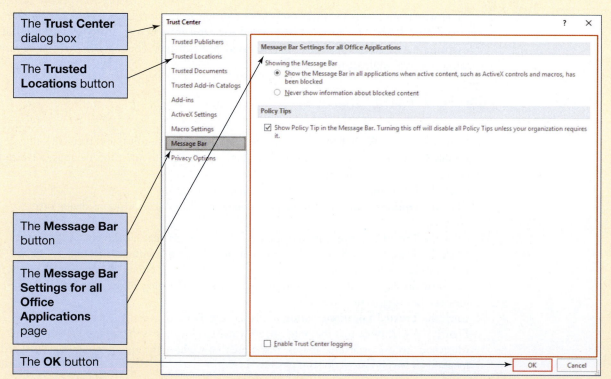

The **Trust Center** dialog box

The **Trusted Locations** button

The **Message Bar** button

The **Message Bar Settings for all Office Applications** page

The **OK** button

Access 2019, Windows 10, Microsoft Corporation.

FIGURE WA-6-7

The Trusted Locations Page

The **Trusted Locations** button

The **Trusted Locations** page

Currently the only trusted location is where Access wizards are stored

The **Add new location** button

We can disable all trusted locations if necessary

The **OK** button

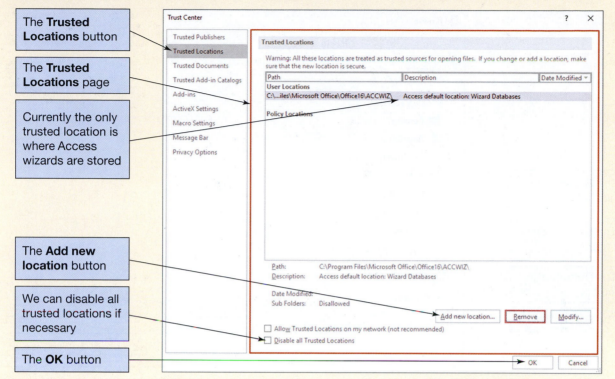

Access 2019, Windows 10, Microsoft Corporation.

FIGURE WA-6-8

The Microsoft Office Trusted Location Dialog Box

The **Microsoft Office Trusted Location** dialog box

The **Browse** button

We can enable trust of all subfolders of the trusted location

The **OK** button

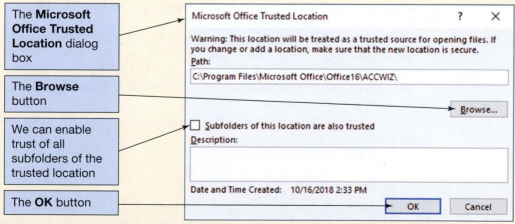

Access 2019, Windows 10, Microsoft Corporation.

8. Click the **Add new location** button to display the Microsoft Office Trusted Location dialog box, as shown in Figure WA-6-8.
9. Click the **Browse** button. The Browse dialog box appears, as shown in Figure WA-6-9. Note that your browse window may open by default to a different location than shown in Figure WA-6-9.

(Continued)

FIGURE WA-6-9

The Browse Dialog Box

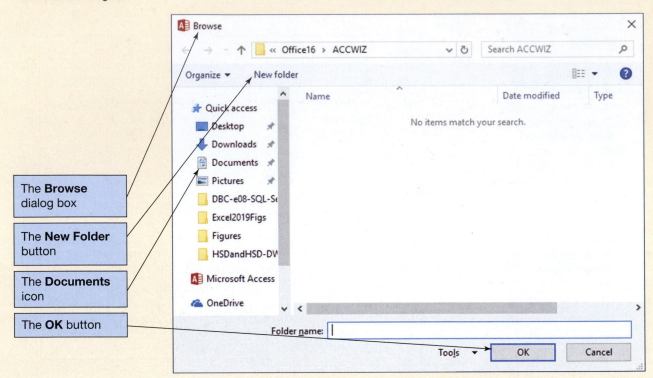

Access 2019, Windows 10, Microsoft Corporation.

10. Click the **Documents** icon to select the Documents library.
11. Click the **New Folder** button to create a new folder named New Folder in edit mode.
12. Rename the new folder as **My-Trusted-Location**. When you have finished typing in the folder name *My-Trusted-Location*, press the **Enter** key. The My-Trusted-Location folder now appears, as shown in Figure WA-6-10.
13. Click the **OK** button on the Browse dialog box. The Microsoft Office Trusted Location dialog box appears, with the new trusted location in the Path text box.
14. Click the **OK** button on the Microsoft Office Trusted Location dialog box. The Trust Center dialog box appears, with the new path added to the User Locations section of the Trusted Locations list.
15. Click the **OK** button on the Trust Center dialog box to return to the Trust Center page of the Access Options dialog box.
16. Click the **OK** button on the Trust Center page of the Access Options dialog box to close it.
17. Close Microsoft Access.

Earlier in this section of "Working with Microsoft Access" we created a copy of the WMCRM.accdb database file as the new file WMCRM-WA06-v01.accdb. We used this file in our discussion of the Security Warning message bar and its associated options. At this point, we will still see the Security Warning message bar whenever we open the WMCRM-WA06-v01.accdb database file in its current location in the Documents library.

Now we make a copy of the **WMCRM-WA06-v01.accdb** file in the Document library and rename it as **WMCRM-WA06-v02.accdb**. After making the WMCRM-WA06-v02.accdb file, we move it to the My-Trusted-Location folder. Now we can try opening the WMCRM-WA06-v02.accdb file from a Microsoft Access 2019 trusted location.

FIGURE WA-6-10

The My-Trusted-Location Folder

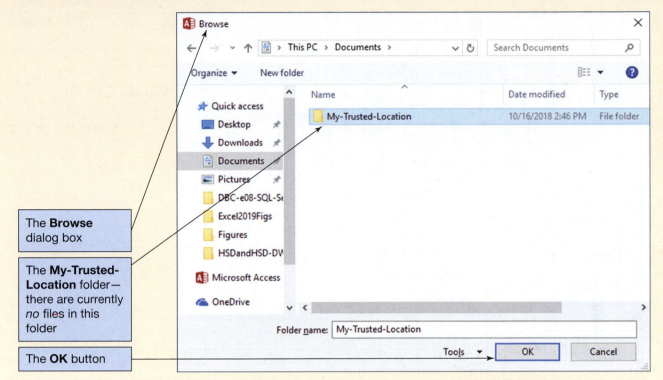

The **Browse** dialog box

The **My-Trusted-Location** folder— there are currently *no* files in this folder

The **OK** button

Access 2019, Windows 10, Microsoft Corporation.

Opening a Microsoft Access Database from a Trusted Location

1. Start Microsoft Access.
2. Click the **Open Other Files** command in the Recent list.
3. Click the **Browse** command tab to display the Microsoft Access Open dialog box.
4. Browse to the **WMCRM-WA06-v02.accdb** file in the My-Trusted-Location folder, as shown in Figure WA-6-11.
5. Click the file name to highlight it, and then click the **Open** button.
6. The Microsoft Access 2019 application window appears, with the WMCRM-WA06-v02 database open in it. Note that the Security Warning bar does *not* appear when the database is opened.
7. Close Microsoft Access 2019 and the WMCRM-WA06-v02 database.

Database Encryption with Passwords

Next, let us look at database encryption. In this case, Microsoft Access will encrypt the database, which will convert it into a secure, unreadable file format. To be able to use the encrypted database, a Microsoft Access user must enter a password to prove that he or she has the right to use the database. After the password is entered, Microsoft Access will decrypt the database and allow the user to work with it.

Each password should be a **strong password**—a password that includes lowercase letters, uppercase letters, numbers, and special characters (symbols) and that is at least 15 characters in length. Be sure to remember or record your password in a safe place—lost or forgotten passwords cannot be recovered!

For this example, we want to use a new copy of the **WMCRM.accdb** database file so that our encryption actions apply only to that file. Specifically, make a copy of

(Continued)

FIGURE WA-6-11

The WMCRM-WA06-v02 File in the Open Dialog Box

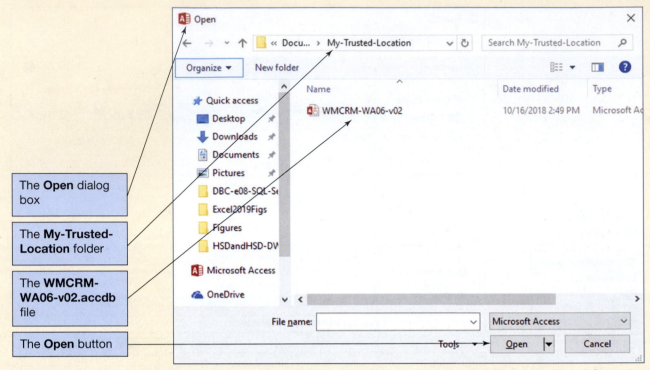

The **Open** dialog box

The **My-Trusted-Location** folder

The **WMCRM-WA06-v02.accdb** file

The **Open** button

Access 2019, Windows 10, Microsoft Corporation.

WMCRM-WA06-v02.accdb in the My-Trusted-Location folder and name this new file **WMCRM-WA06-v03.accdb**.

To encrypt a Microsoft Access database file, the file must be opened in **Exclusive mode**. This gives us exclusive use of the database and prevents any other users who have rights to use the database from opening it or using it. We start by opening WMCRM-WA06-v03.accdb for our exclusive use.

Opening a Microsoft Access Database in Exclusive Mode

1. Start Microsoft Access 2019.
2. Click the **Open Other Files** command in the Recent list.
3. Click the **Browse** command tab to display the Microsoft Access Open dialog box.
4. Browse to the **WMCRM-WA06-v03.accdb** file in the My-Trusted-Location folder. Click the file object *once* to select it, but *not* twice, which would open the file in Microsoft Access.
5. Click the **Open** button drop-down list arrow, as shown in Figure WA-6-12. The Open button drop-down list appears.
6. Click the **Open Exclusive** button in the Open button drop-down list to open the WMCRM-WA06-v03 database in Microsoft Access 2019.
   - ■ **NOTE:** The Security Warning bar does *not* appear when the database is opened because you are opening it from a trusted location.
   - ■ **NOTE:** The Open button mode options shown in Figure WA-6-12 are always available when you open a Microsoft Access database. Normally, you use just Open mode because you want complete read and write permission in the database. Open Read-Only mode prevents the user from making changes to the database. Exclusive mode, as you have seen, stops other users from using the database while you are using it. Exclusive Read-Only mode, as the name implies, combines Exclusive and Read-Only modes.

Now that the database is open in Exclusive mode, we can encrypt the database and set the database password.

FIGURE WA-6-12

The Open Exclusive Button

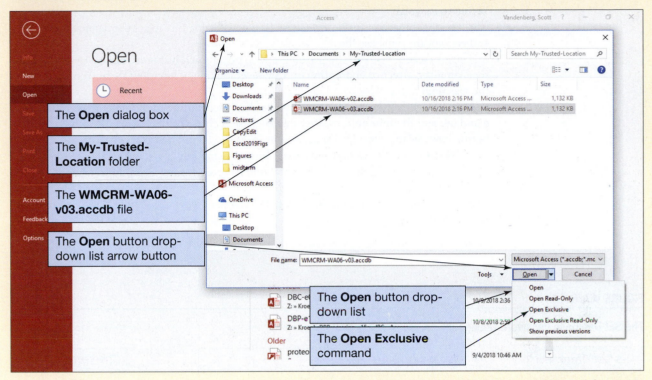

The **Open** dialog box

The **My-Trusted-Location** folder

The **WMCRM-WA06-v03.accdb** file

The **Open** button drop-down list arrow button

The **Open** button drop-down list

The **Open Exclusive** command

Access 2019, Windows 10, Microsoft Corporation.

Encrypting a Microsoft Access Database

1. Click the **File** command tab to display the Backstage view.
2. The Info page should be displayed. If it is not, click the **Info** button to display the Info page, as shown in Figure WA-6-13.
3. In the Encrypt with Password section of the Info page, click the **Encrypt with Password** button. The **Set Database Password** dialog box appears, as shown in Figure WA-6-14.

FIGURE WA-6-13

The File | Info Page

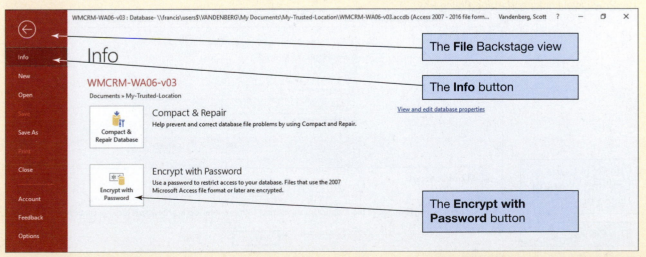

The **File** Backstage view

The **Info** button

The **Encrypt with Password** button

Access 2019, Windows 10, Microsoft Corporation.

(Continued)

4. In the **Password** text box of the Set Database Password dialog box, type in the password **WA06+password**.
5. In the **Verify** text box of the Set Database Password dialog box, again type in the password **WA06+password**.
6. Click the **OK** button of the Set Database Password dialog box to set the database password and encrypt the database file.
7. Microsoft Access displays the warning dialog box shown in Figure WA-6-15 regarding the effect of encrypting on row-level locking. Click the **OK** button to clear the warning.
8. You can check that the encryption action has been accomplished by clicking the **File** command tab and the **Info** button. After the database is encrypted, the Encrypt with Password button changes to a Decrypt Database button, as shown in Figure WA-6-16.
   ▪ **NOTE:** As the Decrypt Database button name implies, if we wanted to change the database file back to its original unencrypted form we can do so using that button.
9. Click the **Close** button to close the WMCRM-WA06-v03 database while leaving Microsoft Access 2019 open.

   Now we can open the newly encrypted WMCRM-WA06-v03.accdb database file.

FIGURE WA-6-14

The Set Database Password Dialog Box

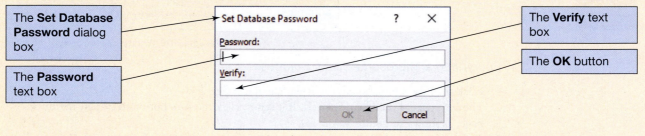

The **Set Database Password** dialog box

The **Password** text box

The **Verify** text box

The **OK** button

Access 2019, Windows 10, Microsoft Corporation.

FIGURE WA-6-15

The Row Level Locking Warning Dialog Box

The **Row Level Locking Warning** dialog box

The **OK** button

Access 2019, Windows 10, Microsoft Corporation.

FIGURE WA-6-16

The Decrypt Database Button

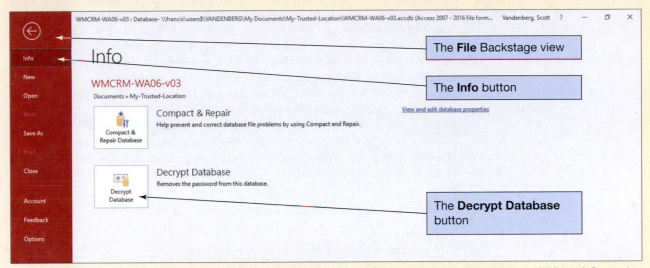

Access 2019, Windows 10, Microsoft Corporation.

Opening an Encrypted Microsoft Access Database

1. Microsoft Access should still be open. If it is not, start Microsoft Access.
2. Click the **File** command tab to display the Backstage view, and then click the **Open** command.
3. Double-click the **WMCRM-WA06-v03.accdb** file name in the quick access list of recent databases. As shown in Figure WA-6-17, the **Password Required** dialog box appears.
4. In the **Enter database password** text box, type in the password **WA06+password**, and then click the **OK** button. The Microsoft Access 2019 application window appears, with the WMCRM-WA06-v03 database open in it.
   - ■ **NOTE:** The Security Warning bar does *not* appear when the database is opened because you are opening it from a trusted location.
5. Close the WMCRM-WA06-v03 database and exit Microsoft Access 2019.

Deploying Secure Databases

Microsoft has included some tools in Microsoft Access 2019 to help us distribute secured copies of Microsoft Access databases to users. One approach is to remove insecure source code from an Access database using compilation. The other approach allows recipients of a deployed database to ensure the database came from the proper source. Let us look at how to use each of these techniques in turn.

FIGURE WA-6-17

The Password Required Dialog Box

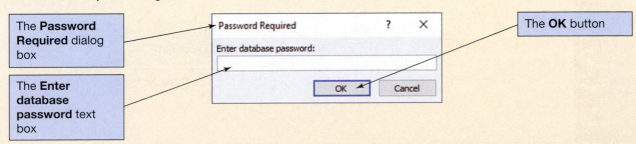

Access 2019, Windows 10, Microsoft Corporation.

(Continued)

Compiling Microsoft Visual Basic for Applications (VBA) Code

Microsoft **Visual Basic for Applications (VBA)** is included in Microsoft Access. VBA is a version of the Microsoft Visual Basic programming language that is intended to help users add specific programmed actions to Microsoft Access applications. How to use VBA is beyond the scope of this section of "Working with Microsoft Access," but we need to know how to secure VBA code if it is included in a Microsoft Access database.

Microsoft Access 2019 includes a **Make ACCDE command** to compile and hide VBA code so that although the VBA programming still functions correctly, the user can no longer see or modify the VBA code. When we use this tool, Microsoft Access creates a version of the database file with an ***.accde file extension**.

In the next set of steps, we will use another copy of the **WMCRM.accdb** database file so that our actions apply only to that file. Specifically, make a copy of **WMCRM-WA06-v02.accdb** in the My-Trusted-Location folder and name this new file **WMCRM-WA06-v04.accdb**. We start by opening the WMCRM-WA06-v04.accdb database file.

Creating a Microsoft Access *.accde Database

1. Open Microsoft Access.
2. Click the **Open Other Files** command in the Recent list.
3. Click the **Browse** command tab to display the Microsoft Access Open dialog box.
4. Browse to the **WMCRM-WA06-v04.accdb** file in the My-Trusted-Location folder. Double-click the file object to open it.
   - **NOTE:** The Security Warning bar does *not* appear when the database is opened because you are opening it from a trusted location.
5. Click the **File** command tab to display the Backstage view.
6. Click the **Save As** button to display the Save As page, as shown in Figure WA-6-18.

FIGURE WA-6-18

The File | Save As Page – Make ACCDE Command

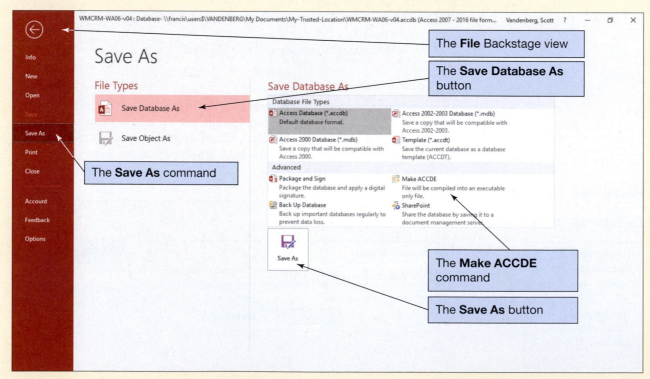

FIGURE WA-6-19

The Save As Dialog Box

The **Save As** dialog box

The **My-Trusted-Location** folder

The file extension is **accde**

The **Save** button

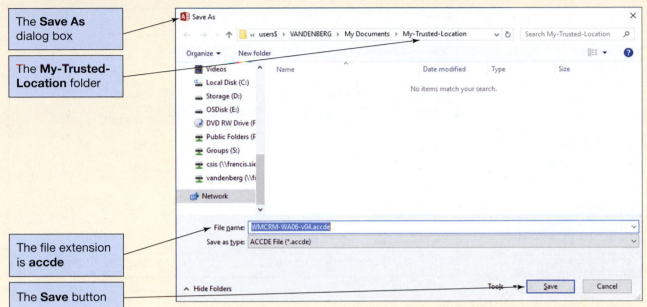

Access 2019, Windows 10, Microsoft Corporation.

7. Click the **Make ACCDE** button in the Advanced group in the Save Database As section, and then click the **Save As** button. The Save As dialog box appears, as shown in Figure WA-6-19.
8. Click the **Save** button in the Save As dialog box. The WMCRM-WA06-v04.accde file is created.
   - NOTE: The displayed database name does *not* change. The only sign that this action has been completed is that the WMCRM-WA06-v04.accde object will now be displayed in the list of Microsoft Access files in the Open dialog box (and other file system tools, such as Windows Explorer) and the file icon contains a lock.
9. Close the WMCRM-WA06-v04 database and exit Microsoft Access.

   To see the new database, we open it as we would any other Microsoft Access database.

*Opening a Microsoft Access *.accde Database*

1. Start Microsoft Access.
2. Click the **Open Other Files** command in the Recent list.
3. Click the **Browse** command to display the Microsoft Access Open dialog box.
4. Browse to the **WMCRM-WA06-v04.accde** file in the My-Trusted-Location folder, as shown in Figure WA-6-20.
5. Click the **Open** button. The Microsoft Access 2019 application window appears, with the WMCRM-WA06-v04.accde database open in it.
   - NOTE: The Security Warning bar does *not* appear when the database is opened because you are opening it from a trusted location.
   - NOTE: Although any previously existing VBA modules have been compiled and all editable source code for them has been removed, the functionality of this code is still in the database. Further note that VBA itself is still functional in the database—it has *not* been disabled.
6. Close the WMCRM-WA06-v04 database and exit Microsoft Access.

(Continued)

FIGURE WA-6-20

The WMCRM-WA06-v04.accde File

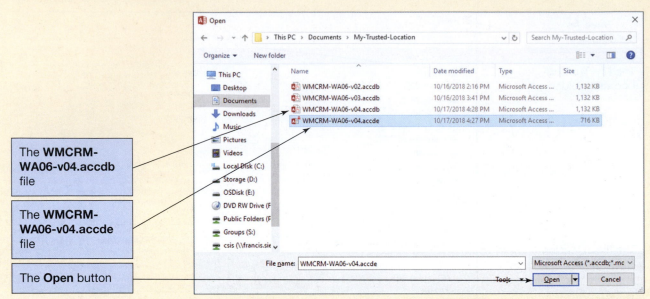

The **WMCRM-WA06-v04.accdb** file

The **WMCRM-WA06-v04.accde** file

The **Open** button

Access 2019, Windows 10, Microsoft Corporation.

Creating a Signed Package in Microsoft Access

A **digital signature scheme** is a type of **public-key cryptography** (also known as **asymmetric cryptography**), which uses two encryption keys (a **private key** and a **public key**) to encode documents and files to protect them. Although fascinating and important topics in their own right, cryptography in general and public-key cryptography in particular are beyond the scope of this section of "Working with Microsoft Access."[1] For our purposes, a **digital signature** is a means of guaranteeing another user of a database that the database is, indeed, from us and that it is safe to use.

To use a digital signature, of course, we must have one, so the first thing we have to do is to create one. This is not done in Microsoft Access but rather with the **SELFCERT.exe utility** provided with Microsoft Office 2019. For the 32-bit version of Microsoft Office 2019, the file is located in the *c:/Program Files (x86)/Microsoft Office/root/Office16* folder. For the 64-bit version of Microsoft Office 2019, the file is located in the *c:/Program Files/ Microsoft Office/root/Office16* folder.

Creating a Digital Signature

1. Open Microsoft File Explorer, and locate **SELFCERT.exe**. Double-click the SELFCERT. exe icon to open the Create Digital Certificate dialog box, as shown in Figure WA-6-21.
2. In the **Your certificate's name** text box, type the text **Digital-Certificate-WA06-01,** and then click the **OK** button. The certificate is created, and the SelfCert Success dialog box appears, as shown in Figure WA-6-22.
3. Click the **OK** button in the SelfCert Success dialog box.

Now that we have a digital certificate, we can use it to package and sign our database.

---

[1]For more information, see the following Wikipedia articles: **Public-Key Cryptography, Digital Signature**, and **Public Key Certificate**.

FIGURE WA-6-21

The Create Digital
Certificate Dialog Box

The **Create Digital Certificate** dialog box

The **Your certificate's name** text box

The **OK** button

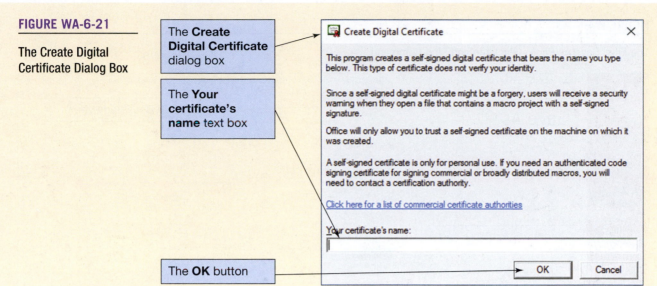

Access 2019, Windows 10, Microsoft Corporation.

FIGURE WA-6-22

The SelfCert Success
Dialog Box

The **SelfCert Success** dialog box

The **OK** button

The digital certificate name we provided

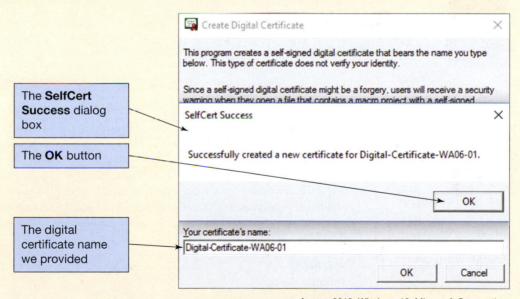

Access 2019, Windows 10, Microsoft Corporation.

Creating a Microsoft Access Signed Package

1. Start Microsoft Access.
2. Open the **WMCRM-WA06-v04.accde** database file from the Recent list.
   - **NOTE:** The Security Warning bar does *not* appear when the database is opened because you are opening it from a trusted location.
3. Click the **File** command tab to display the Backstage view.
4. Click the **Save As** command to display the Save As page, as shown in Figure WA-6-23.

(Continued)

FIGURE WA-6-23

The File | Save As Page – Package and Sign Command

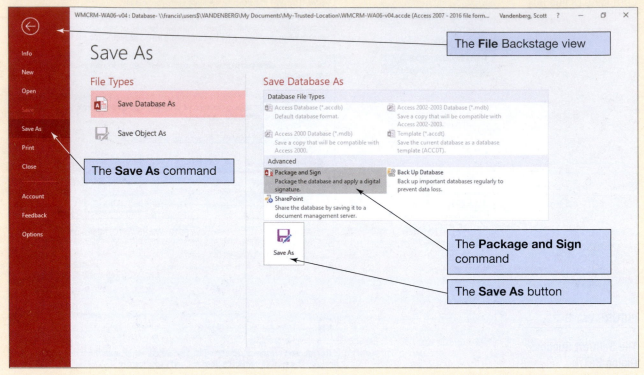

Access 2019, Windows 10, Microsoft Corporation.

5. Click the **Package and Sign** button to select the Package and Sign option, and then click the **Save As** button. The Windows Security Confirm Certificate dialog box appears, as shown in Figure WA-6-24. If you have other certificates, you will get a "Select a Certificate" dialog box instead, in which case you may need to click a "More choices" link in order to select the proper certificate to use.

6. Select the certificate you want to use. However, to verify this, click the **Click here to view certificate properties** link. The Certificate Details dialog box appears, as shown in Figure WA-6-25, and our certificate name is clearly visible in the dialog box.

FIGURE WA-6-24

The Windows Security Dialog Box

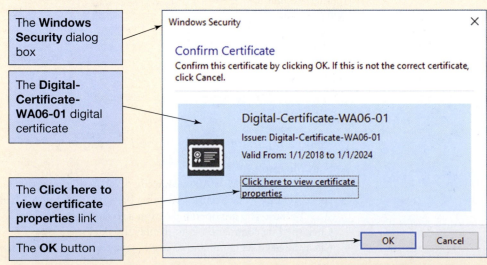

Access 2019, Windows 10, Microsoft Corporation.

FIGURE WA-6-25

The Certificate Details
Dialog Box

The **Certificate Details** dialog box

The **Digital-Certificate-WA06-01** digital certificate name is displayed here

The **OK** button

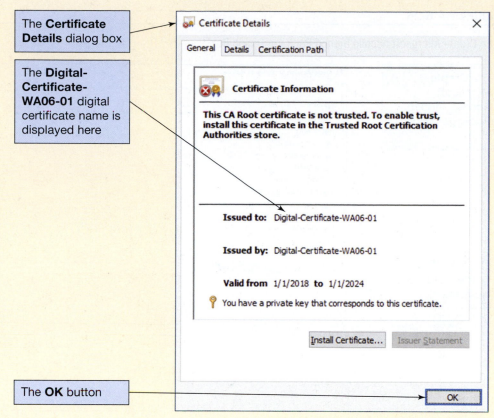

Access 2019, Windows 10, Microsoft Corporation.

7. Click the **OK** button in the Certificate Details dialog box to close the dialog box.
8. Click the **OK** button in the Microsoft Security Confirm Certificate dialog box to close the dialog box. The Create Microsoft Access Signed Package dialog box appears, as shown in Figure WA-6-26.
9. Click the **Create** button to create the signed package as the file **WMCRM-WA06-v04.accdc**. Note the use of the *.accdc file extension.
10. Close the **WMCRM-WA06-v04** database and Microsoft Access 2019.

We now have a signed package, which uses the ***.accdc file extension**, ready to distribute to other users. To simulate this, in the My Documents folder of the Documents library, create a new folder named **My-Distributed-Databases,** and then copy the WMCRM-WA06-v04.accdc file into it. Now we can open the signed package from this location.

Opening a Microsoft Access *.accdc Database

1. Start Microsoft Access.
2. Browse to the **WMCRM-WA06-v04.accdc** file in the My-Distributed-Databases folder, as shown in Figure WA-6-27. Note that you must change file type to see any of the *.accdc files.
3. Click the **WMCRM-WA06-v04.accdc** file to select it, and then click the **Open** button. The Microsoft Access Security Notice dialog box appears, as shown in Figure WA-6-28.
4. Click the **Open** button. The **Extract Database To** dialog box appears. This dialog box is essentially the same as a Save As dialog box, so browse to the My-Distributed-Databases folder, and then click the **OK** button.

(Continued)

FIGURE WA-6-26

The Create Microsoft Access Signed Package Dialog Box

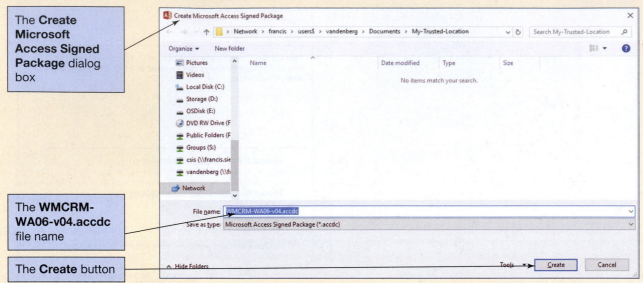

The **Create Microsoft Access Signed Package** dialog box

The **WMCRM-WA06-v04.accdc** file name

The **Create** button

Access 2019, Windows 10, Microsoft Corporation.

FIGURE WA-6-27

The WMCRM-WA06-v04.accdc File

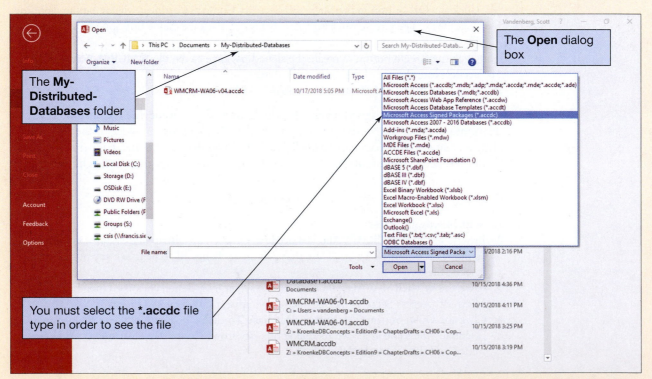

The **Open** dialog box

The **My-Distributed-Databases** folder

You must select the ***.accdc** file type in order to see the file

Access 2019, Windows 10, Microsoft Corporation.

FIGURE WA-6-28

The Microsoft Access Security Notice Dialog Box

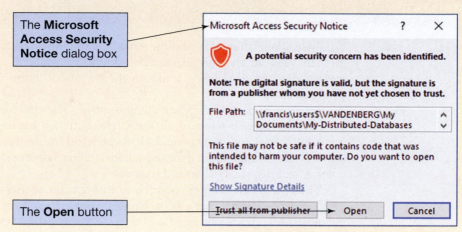

The **Microsoft Access Security Notice** dialog box

The **Open** button

Access 2019, Windows 10, Microsoft Corporation.

5. Another **Microsoft Access Security Notice** dialog box similar to the one shown in Figure WA-6-28 may appear. If it does, then click the **Open** button.
6. The **WMCRM-WA06-v04.accde** database is opened in Microsoft Access.
   - **NOTE:** The Security Warning bar does *not* appear when the database is opened because you have chosen to trust the source of the database as documented in the digital certificate rather than open it from a trusted location.
7. Close the WMCRM-WA06-v04 database and Microsoft Access 2019.

Using Windows Explorer, look at the contents of the This PC\Documents\My-Distributed-Databases folder. Notice that the WMCRM-WA06-v04.accde file has been extracted from the WMCRM-WA06-v04.accdc package and is now available for use. This is the database file that the user will open when he or she uses the database. Also note that when users open the database, they will see the Microsoft Access Security Notice dialog box just discussed.

This completes our discussion of how Microsoft Access 2019 handles database security for Microsoft Access 2019 *.accdb files. Note that Microsoft Access 2019 can also open and work with older Microsoft Access 2003 *.mdb database files, which have a built-in user-level database security system that is very different from the Microsoft Access 2019 database security we have discussed. If you need to work with one of these older *.mdb files, consult the Microsoft Access documentation.

SUMMARY

Database administration is a business function that involves managing a database to maximize its value to an organization. The conflicting goals of protecting the database and maximizing its availability and benefit to users must be balanced using good administration.

All databases need database administration. The database administration for small, personal databases is informal; database administration for large, multiuser databases can involve an office and many people. DBA can stand for *database administration* or *database administrator*. Three basic database administration functions are necessary: concurrency control, security, and backup and recovery.

The goal of concurrency control is to ensure that one user's work does not inappropriately influence another user's work. No single concurrency control technique is ideal for all circumstances. Trade-offs need to be made between the level of protection and data throughput.

A transaction, or logical unit of work, is a series of actions taken against a database that occur as an atomic unit; either all of them occur or none of them do. The activity of concurrent transactions is interleaved on the database server. In some cases, updates can be lost if concurrent transactions are not controlled. Another concurrency problem concerns inconsistent reads.

A dirty read occurs when one transaction reads a changed record that has not been committed to the database. A nonrepeatable read occurs when one transaction rereads data it has previously read and finds modifications or deletions caused by another transaction. A phantom read occurs when a transaction rereads data and finds new rows that were inserted by a different transaction.

To avoid concurrency problems, database elements are locked. Implicit locks are placed by the DBMS; explicit locks are issued by the application program. The size of a locked resource is called lock granularity. An exclusive lock prohibits other users from reading or updating the locked resource; a shared lock allows other users to read the locked resource but not to update it.

Two transactions that run concurrently and generate results that are consistent with the results that would have occurred if the transactions had run separately are referred to as serializable transactions. Two-phase locking, in which locks are acquired in a growing phase and released in a shrinking phase, is one scheme for serializability. A special case of two-phase locking, called strict two-phase locking, is to acquire locks throughout the transaction but not to free any lock until the transaction is finished.

Deadlock, or the deadly embrace, occurs when two transactions are each waiting on a resource that the other transaction holds. Deadlock can be prevented by requiring transactions to acquire all locks at the same time. When deadlock occurs, the only way to cure it is to abort one of the transactions and back out of partially completed work.

Optimistic locking assumes that no transaction conflict will occur and then deals with the consequences if it does. Pessimistic locking assumes that conflict will occur and so prevents it ahead of time with locks. In general, optimistic locking is preferred for the Internet and for many intranet applications.

Most application programs do not explicitly declare locks. Instead, they mark transaction boundaries with SQL transaction control statements—such as BEGIN, COMMIT, and ROLLBACK statements—and declare the concurrent behavior they want. The DBMS then places locks for the application that will result in the desired behavior. An ACID transaction is one that is atomic, consistent, isolated, and durable. Durable means that database changes are permanent. Consistency can refer to either statement-level or transaction-level consistency. With transaction-level consistency, a transaction may not see its own changes.

The three types of data read problems that can occur are dirty read, nonrepeatable read, and phantom read. These problems are summarized in Figure 6-11. The 1992 SQL standard defines four transaction isolation levels: read uncommitted, read committed, repeatable read, and serializable. The characteristics of each are summarized in Figure 6-12.

A cursor is a pointer into a set of records. Four cursor types are prevalent: forward only, static, keyset, and dynamic. Developers should select isolation levels and cursor types that are appropriate for their application workload and for the DBMS product in use.

The goal of database security is to ensure that only authorized users can perform authorized activities at authorized times. To develop effective database security, the processing rights and responsibilities of all users must be determined.

DBMS products provide security facilities. Most involve the declaration of users, groups, objects to be protected, and permissions or privileges on those objects. Almost all DBMS products use some form of user name and password security. DBMS security can be augmented by application security.

In the event of system failure, the database must be restored to a usable state as soon as possible. Transactions in process at the time of the failure must be reapplied or restarted. Although in some cases recovery can be done by reprocessing, the use of logs and before-images and after-images with rollback and rollforward is almost always preferred. Checkpoints can be made to reduce the amount of work that needs to be done after a failure.

In addition to concurrency control, security, and backup and recovery, a DBA needs to ensure that a system exists to gather and record errors and problems. The DBA works with the development team to resolve such problems on a prioritized basis and also to evaluate features and functions of new releases of the DBMS. In addition, the DBA needs to create and manage a process for controlling the database configuration so that changes to the database structure are made with a community-wide view. Efficient performance of a database is crucial, and the DBA needs to make physical design decisions and be aware of query optimization techniques to obtain the best performance from the database. Finally, the DBA is responsible for ensuring that appropriate documentation is maintained about database structure, concurrency control, security, backup and recovery, and other details that concern the management and use of the database.

KEY TERMS

ACID transaction
after-image
atomic
authentication
authorization
before-image
checkpoint
concurrent transaction
concurrent update problem
consistent
data administration
database administration
database administrator
DBA
deadlock
deadly embrace
dirty read
disk mirroring
durable
dynamic cursor
exclusive lock

explicit lock
forward-only cursor
implicit lock
inconsistent read problem
index
isolation level
keyset cursor
lock granularity
log
logical unit of work (LUW)
lost update problem
nonrepeatable read
optimistic concurrency control
optimistic locking
parallel
permissions
pessimistic locking
phantom read
physical database design
query optimizer
read committed isolation level

read uncommitted isolation level
recovery via reprocessing
recovery via rollback/rollforward
redundant array of independent
  disks (RAID)
repeatable read isolation level
resource locking
rollback
rollforward
scrollable cursor
serial
serializable
serializable isolation level
service level agreement (SLA)
shared lock
SQL BEGIN TRANSACTION
  statement
SQL COMMIT TRANSACTION
  statement
SQL Data Control Language (DCL)
SQL GRANT statement

SQL/Persistent Stored Modules (SQL/PSM)
SQL REVOKE statement
SQL ROLLBACK TRANSACTION statement
SQL Transaction Control Language (TCL)

statement-level consistency
static cursor
stored procedure
strict two-phase locking
throughput
transaction
transaction isolation level

transaction-level consistency
trigger
two-phase locking
user account
user-defined function

REVIEW QUESTIONS

6.1   What is the purpose of database administration?

6.2   Explain how database administration tasks vary with the size and complexity of the database.

6.3   What are two interpretations of the abbreviation *DBA*?

6.4   What is the purpose of concurrency control? What is *throughput*, and how is concurrency control related to throughput?

6.5   What is the goal of a database security system?

6.6   Explain the meaning of the word *inappropriately* in the phrase "one user's work does not inappropriately influence another user's work."

6.7   Explain the major trade-off that exists in concurrency control.

6.8   Describe what an atomic transaction is, and explain why atomicity is important.

6.9   Explain the difference between concurrent transactions and simultaneous transactions. How many CPUs are required for simultaneous transactions?

6.10   Give an example, other than the one in this text, of the lost update problem.

6.11   Define the terms *dirty read, nonrepeatable read*, and *phantom read.*

6.12   Explain the difference between an explicit lock and an implicit lock.

6.13   What is lock granularity?

6.14   Explain the difference between an exclusive lock and a shared lock.

6.15   Explain two-phase locking.

6.16   How does releasing all locks at the end of a transaction relate to two-phase locking?

6.17   What is deadlock? How can it be avoided? How can it be resolved when it occurs?

6.18   Explain the difference between optimistic and pessimistic locking.

6.19   Explain the benefits of marking transaction boundaries, declaring lock characteristics, and letting a DBMS place locks.

6.20   Explain the use of the SQL transaction control language (TCL) statements BEGIN TRANSACTION, COMMIT TRANSACTION, and ROLLBACK TRANSACTION.

6.21   Explain the meaning of the expression *ACID transaction.*

6.22   Describe statement-level consistency.

6.23   Describe transaction-level consistency. What disadvantage can exist with it?

6.24   What is the purpose of transaction isolation levels?

6.25   Explain what read uncommitted isolation level is. Give an example of its use.

6.26   Explain what read committed isolation level is. Give an example of its use.

6.27   Explain what repeatable read isolation level is. Give an example of its use.

6.28   Explain what serializable isolation level is. Give an example of its use.

6.29   Explain the term *cursor.*

6.30 Explain why a transaction may have many cursors. Also, how is it possible that a transaction may have more than one cursor on a given table?

6.31 What is the advantage of using different types of cursors?

6.32 Explain forward-only cursors. Give an example of their use.

6.33 Explain static cursors. Give an example of their use.

6.34 Explain keyset cursors. Give an example of their use.

6.35 Explain dynamic cursors. Give an example of their use.

6.36 What happens if you do not declare transaction isolation level and cursor type to a DBMS? Is not declaring the isolation level and cursor type good or bad?

6.37 Explain the necessity of defining processing rights and responsibilities. How are such responsibilities enforced? What is SQL data control language (DCL), and what SQL statements are used in DCL?

6.38 Explain the relationships of users, groups, permission, and objects for a generic database security system.

6.39 Describe the advantages and disadvantages of DBMS-provided security.

6.40 Describe the advantages and disadvantages of application-provided security.

6.41 Explain how a database could be recovered via reprocessing. Why is this generally not feasible?

6.42 Define the terms *rollback* and *rollforward.*

6.43 Why is it important to write to a log before changing the database values?

6.44 Describe the rollback process. Under what conditions should rollback be used?

6.45 Describe the rollforward process. Under what conditions should rollforward be used?

6.46 What is the advantage of making frequent checkpoints of a database?

6.47 Summarize a DBA's responsibilities for managing database user problems.

6.48 Summarize a DBA's responsibilities for configuration control.

6.49 Summarize a DBA's responsibilities for documentation.

6.50 Summarize a DBA's responsibilities for database system performance.

EXERCISES

6.51 If you have access to MySQL 8.0, search its help system to answer the following questions.

A. How does MySQL use read locks and write locks?

B. What, if any, levels of transaction isolation are available in MySQL?

C. What types of cursors, if any, does MySQL use?

D. How does the security model for MySQL differ from that shown in Figure 6-17?

E. Summarize the backup capabilities of MySQL.

F. Summarize the recovery capabilities of MySQL.

WORKING WITH MICROSOFT ACCESS

Key Terms

*.accdc file extension	Make ACCDE command
*.accde file extension	private key
ActiveX controls	public key
ActiveX specification	public-key cryptography
asymmetric cryptography	Security Warning message bar
digital signature	strong password
digital signature scheme	trusted location
Exclusive mode	Visual Basic for Applications (VBA)

Exercises

WA.6.1   Use the Wedgewood Pacific (WP) database developed in previous sections of "Working with Microsoft Access" to answer the following questions.

A.   Analyze the data in the WP database tables (particularly DEPARTMENT and EMPLOYEE), and create a database security plan, using Figure 6-17 as an example.

B.   If you have not already created a My-Trusted-Location folder, follow the steps in this chapter's section of "Working with Microsoft Access" to do so now.

C.   Make a copy of the WP.accdb file in the My-Trusted-Location folder, and name it *WP-WA06-v01.accdb*. Open the WP-WA06-v01.accdb database to confirm that it opens without displaying the Security Warning bar, and then close the database.

D.   Make a copy of the WP.accdb file in the My-Trusted-Location folder, and name it *WP-WA06-v02.accdb*. Encrypt the WP-WA06-v02.accdb database with the password *WA06EX+password*. Close the WP-WA06-v02.accdb database, and then reopen it to confirm that it opens properly using the password. Close the WP-WA06-v02.accdb database.

E.   If you have not already created the Digital-Certificate-WA06-001 digital certificate, follow the steps in this chapter's section of "Working with Microsoft Access" to do so now.

F.   Make a copy of the WP.accdb file in the My-Trusted-Location folder, and name it *WP-WA06-v03.accdb*. Create an ACCDE version of the WP-WA06-v03.accdb database. Create a signed package using the WP-WA06-v03.accde database and the Digital-Certificate-WA06-001 digital certificate.

G.   If you have not already created a My-Distributed-Databases folder, follow the steps in this chapter's section of "Working with Microsoft Access" to do so now.

H.   Make a copy of the WP-WA06-v03.accdc file in the My-Distributed-Databases folder. Extract the WP-WA06-v03.accde file into the folder, and then open it to confirm that the database opens properly. Close the database.

MARCIA'S DRY CLEANING

Ms. Marcia Wilson owns and operates Marcia's Dry Cleaning, which is an upscale dry cleaner in a well-to-do suburban neighborhood. Marcia makes her business stand out from the competition by providing superior customer service. She wants to keep track of each of her customers and their orders. Ultimately, she wants to notify them that their clothes are ready via email.

Assume that Marcia has hired you as a database consultant to develop an operational database having the following four tables:

CUSTOMER (<u>CustomerID</u>, FirstName, LastName, Phone, EmailAddress)

INVOICE (<u>InvoiceNumber</u>, *CustomerID*, DateIn, DateOut, Subtotal, Tax, TotalAmount)

INVOICE_ITEM (<u>*InvoiceNumber*</u>, <u>ItemNumber</u>, *ServiceID*, Quantity, UnitPrice, ExtendedPrice)

SERVICE (<u>ServiceID</u>, ServiceDescription, UnitPrice)

A. Assume that Marcia's has the following personnel: two owners, a shift manager, a part-time seamstress, and two salesclerks. Prepare a two- to three-page memo that addresses the following points:

   1. The need for database administration.
   2. Your recommendation as to who should serve as database administrator. Assume that Marcia's is not sufficiently large to need or afford a full-time database administrator.
   3. Using the main topics in this chapter as a guide, describe the nature of database administration activities at Marcia's. As an aggressive consultant, keep in mind that you can recommend yourself for performing some of the DBA functions.

B. For the employees described in part A, define users, groups, and permissions on data in these four tables. Use the security scheme shown in Figure 6-17 as an example. Create a table like that in Figure 6-19. Don't forget to include yourself.

C. Suppose that you are writing a part of an application to create new records in SERVICE for new services that Marcia's will perform. Suppose that you know that while your procedure is running, another part of the same application that records new or modifies existing customer orders and order line items can also be running. Additionally, suppose that a third part of the application that records new customer data also can be running.

   1. Give an example of a dirty read, a nonrepeatable read, and a phantom read among this group of applications.
   2. What concurrency control measures are appropriate for the part of the application that you are creating?
   3. What concurrency control measures are appropriate for the two other parts of the application?

GARDEN GLORY PROJECT QUESTIONS

The following Garden Glory database design is used in Chapter 3:

OWNER (<u>OwnerID</u>, OwnerName, OwnerEmailAddress, OwnerType)
OWNED_PROPERTY (<u>PropertyID</u>, PropertyName, Street, City, State, ZIP, OwnerID)
GG_SERVICE (<u>ServiceID</u>, ServiceDescription, CostPerHour)
EMPLOYEE (<u>EmployeeID</u>, LastName, FirstName, CellPhone, ExperienceLevel)
PROPERTY_SERVICE (<u>PropertyServiceID</u>, *PropertyID*, *ServiceID*, ServiceDate,
    EmployeeID, HoursWorked)

The referential integrity constraints are:

OwnerID in OWNED_PROPERTY must exist in OwnerID in OWNER

PropertyID in PROPERTY_SERVICE must exist in PropertyID in OWNED_
    PROPERTY

ServiceID in PROPERTY_SERVICE must exist in ServiceID in GG_SERVICE

EmployeeID in PROPERTY_SERVICE must exist in EmployeeID in EMPLOYEE

Garden Glory has modified the EMPLOYEE table by adding a TotalHoursWorked
column:

EMPLOYEE (<u>EmployeeID</u>, LastName, FirstName, CellPhone, ExperienceLevel,
    TotalHoursWorked)

The office personnel at Garden Glory use a database application to record services
and related data changes in this database. For a new service, the service-recording application reads a row from the OWNED_PROPERTY table to get the PropertyID. It then
creates a new row in GG_SERVICE and updates TotalHoursWorked in EMPLOYEE by
adding the HoursWorked value in the new PROPERTY_SERVICE record to TotalHours
Worked. This operation is referred to as a Service Update Transaction.

In some cases, the employee record does not exist before the service is recorded. In
such a case, a new EMPLOYEE row is created, and then the service is recorded. This is
called a Service Update for New Employee Transaction.

A. Explain why it is important for the changes made by the Service Update Transaction to
be atomic.

B. Describe a scenario in which an update of TotalHoursWorked could be lost during a
Service Update Transaction.

C. Assume that many Service Update Transactions and many Service Update for
New Employee Transactions are processed concurrently. Describe a scenario for a
nonrepeatable read and a scenario for a phantom read.

D. Explain how locking could be used to prevent the lost update in your answer to part B.

E. Is it possible for deadlock to occur between two Service Update Transactions? Why
or why not? Is it possible for deadlock to occur between a Service Update Transaction
and a Service Update for New Employee Transaction? Why or why not?

F. Do you think optimistic or pessimistic locking would be better for the Service Update
Transactions?

G. Suppose Garden Glory identifies three groups of users: managers, administrative personnel, and system administrators. Suppose further that the only job of administrative personnel is to make Service Update Transactions. Managers can make Service Update Transactions and Service Updates for New Employee Transactions. System administrators have unrestricted access to the tables. Describe processing rights that you think would be appropriate for this situation. Use Figure 6-19 as an example. What problems might this security system have?

H. Garden Glory has developed the following procedure for backup and recovery. The company backs up the database from the server to a second computer on its network each night. Once a month, it copies the database to a CD and stores it at a manager's house. It keeps paper records of all services provided for an entire year. If it ever loses its database, it plans to restore it from a backup and reprocess all service requests. Do you think this backup and recovery program is sufficient for Garden Glory? What problems might occur? What alternatives exist? Describe any changes you think the company should make to this system.

JAMES RIVER JEWELRY PROJECT QUESTIONS

The James River Jewelry database design that was used in the James River Jewelry Project Questions for Chapter 3 was:

CUSTOMER (CustomerID, LastName, FirstName, Phone, EmailAddress)
PURCHASE (InvoiceNumber, InvoiceDate, PreTaxAmount, *CustomerID*)
PURCHASE_ITEM (*InvoiceNumber*, InvoiceLineNumber, *ItemNumber*, RetailPrice)
ITEM (ItemNumber, ItemDescription, Cost, ArtistLastName, ArtistFirstName)

The referential integrity constraints are:

CustomerID in PURCHASE must exist in CustomerID in CUSTOMER
InvoiceNumber in PURCHASE_ITEM must exist in InvoiceNumber in PURCHASE
ItemNumber in PURCHASE_ITEM must exist in ItemNumber in ITEM

James River Jewelry has modified the database by adding two tables—OWNER and JEWELRY_ITEM—as shown in the following:

OWNER (OwnerID, LastName, FirstName, Phone, EmailAddress, AmountOwed)
JEWELRY_ITEM (*ItemNumber*, DateReceived, DateSold, NegotiatedSalesPrice, ActualSalesPrice, CommissionPercentage, *OwnerID*)

where

OwnerID in JEWELRY_ITEM must exist in OwnerID in OWNER
ItemNumber in JEWELRY_ITEM must exist in ItemNumber in ITEM

The tables are used to record data and maintain owner data about jewelry accepted on consignment. JEWELRY_ITEM (which is a subtype of ITEM—note the referential integrity constraint) is used to record the negotiated sales price, the commission percentage, and the actual sales price for each item of consigned jewelry.

Assume that office personnel at James River Jewelry use a database application to record consignment data. When an item is received on consignment, owner data are stored in OWNER if the owner is new; otherwise existing owner data are used. New ITEM and JEWELRY_ITEM rows are created. In ITEM, ItemNumber and Description are recorded, Cost is set to $0.00, and if there is an artist associated with the piece, ArtistLastName and ArtistFirstName are entered if known. For JEWELRY_ITEM, data are stored for all columns except DateSold and ActualSalesPrice. James River Jewelry personnel refer to these actions as an Acceptance Transaction. Later, if the jewelry item does not sell, the NegotiatedSalesPrice and CommissionPercentage values may be reduced. This is called a Price Adjustment Transaction. Finally, when an item sells, the DateSold and Actual-SalesPrice fields for the item are given values, and the AmountOwed value in OWNER is updated by increasing AmountOwed by the owner's percentage of the ActualSalesPrice value. This third transaction is called a Sales Transaction.

A. Explain why it is important for the changes made by each of these transactions to be atomic.

B. Describe a scenario in which an update of AmountOwed could be lost.

C. Describe a scenario for a nonrepeatable read and a scenario for a phantom read.

D. Explain how locking could be used to prevent the lost update in your answer to part B.

E. Is it possible for deadlock to occur between two Acceptance Transactions? Why or why not? Is it possible for deadlock to occur between two Sales Transactions? Why or why not? Is it possible for deadlock to occur between an Acceptance Transaction and a Sales Transaction? Why or why not?

F. For each of these three types of transaction, describe whether you think optimistic or pessimistic locking would be better. Explain the reasons for your answer.

G. Suppose James River Jewelry identifies three groups of users: managers, administrative personnel, and system administrators. Suppose further that managers and administrative personnel can perform Acceptance Transactions and Sales Transactions, but only managers can perform Price Adjustment Transactions. Describe processing rights that you think would be appropriate for this situation. Use Figure 6-19 as an example.

H. James River Jewelry has developed the following procedure for backup and recovery. The company backs up the database from the server to a second computer on its network each night. Once a month, it copies the database to a CD and stores it at a manager's house. It keeps paper records of all purchase and sales transactions for an entire year. If it ever loses its database, it plans to restore it from a backup and unrecorded transactions. Do you think this backup and recovery program is sufficient for James River Jewelry? What problems might occur? What alternatives exist? Describe any changes you think the company should make to this system.

THE QUEEN ANNE CURIOSITY SHOP PROJECT QUESTIONS

The Queen Anne Curiosity Shop database design used in Chapter 3 was:

CUSTOMER (<u>CustomerID</u>, LastName, FirstName, Address, City, State, ZIP, Phone, EmailAddress)

EMPLOYEE (<u>EmployeeID</u>, LastName, FirstName, Phone, EmailAddress)

VENDOR (<u>VendorID</u>, CompanyName, ContactLastName, ContactFirstName, Address, City, State, ZIP, Phone, Fax, EmailAddress)

ITEM (<u>ItemID</u>, ItemDescription, PurchaseDate, ItemCost, ItemPrice, *VendorID*)

SALE (<u>SaleID</u>, *CustomerID*, *EmployeeID*, SaleDate, SubTotal, Tax, Total)

SALE_ITEM (<u>*SaleID*</u>, <u>SaleItemID</u>, *ItemID*, ItemPrice)

The referential integrity constraints are:

VendorID in ITEM must exist in VendorID in VENDOR
CustomerID in SALE must exist in CustomerID in CUSTOMER
EmployeeID in SALE must exist in EmployeeID in EMPLOYEE
SaleID in SALE_ITEM must exist in SaleID in SALE
ItemID in SALE_ITEM must exist in ItemID in ITEM

The Queen Anne Curiosity Shop has modified the ITEM and SALE_ITEM tables as follows:

ITEM (<u>ItemID</u>, ItemDescription, UnitCost, UnitPrice, QuantityOnHand, *VendorID*)
SALE_ITEM (<u>*SaleID*</u>, <u>SaleItemID</u>, *ItemID*, Quantity, ItemPrice, Extended Price)

These changes allow the sales system to handle nonunique items that can be bought and sold in quantity. When new items from vendors arrive at the Queen Anne Curiosity Shop, the office personnel unpack the items, put them in the stockroom, and run an Item Quantity Received Transaction that adds the quantity received to QuantityOnHand. At the same time, another transaction, called an Item Price Adjustment Transaction is run, if necessary, to adjust UnitCost and UnitPrice. Sales may occur at any time, and when a sale occurs the Sale Transaction is run. Every time a SALE_ITEM line is entered, the input Quantity is subtracted from QuantityOnHand in ITEM, and the ItemPrice is set to the UnitPrice.

A. Explain why it is important for the changes made by each of these transactions to be atomic.

B. Describe a scenario in which an update of QuantityOnHand could be lost.

C. Describe a scenario for a nonrepeatable read and a scenario for a phantom read.

D. Explain how locking could be used to prevent the lost update in your answer to part B.

E. Is it possible for deadlock to occur between two Sale Transactions? Why or why not? Is it possible for deadlock to occur between a Sale Transaction and an Item Quantity Received Transaction? Why or why not?

F. For each of the three types of transaction, describe whether you think optimistic or pessimistic locking would be better. Explain the reasons for your answer.

G. Suppose that the Queen Anne Curiosity Shop identifies four groups of users: sales personnel, managers, administrative personnel, and system administrators. Suppose further that managers and administrative personnel can perform Item Quantity Received Transactions, but only managers can perform Item Price Adjustment Transactions. Describe processing rights that you think would be appropriate for this situation. Use Figure 6-19 as an example.

H. The Queen Anne Curiosity Shop has developed the following procedure for backup and recovery. The company backs up the entire database from the server to tape every Saturday night. The tapes are taken to a safety deposit box at a local bank on the following Thursday. Printed paper records of all sales are kept for five years. If the database is ever lost, the plan is to restore the database from the last full backup and reprocess all the sales records. Do you think this backup and recovery program is sufficient for the Queen Anne Curiosity Shop? What problems might occur? What alternatives exist? Describe any changes you think the company should make to this system.

This chapter introduces topics that build on the fundamentals you have learned in the first six chapters of this book. Now that we have designed and built a database, we are ready to put it to work. This chapter looks at the problems associated with the rapidly expanding amount of data that is being stored and used in enterprise information systems and some of the technology that is being used to address those problems. These problems are generally included in the need to deal with **Big Data**, which is the current term for the enormous datasets generated by applications such as search tools (for example, Google and Bing); Web 2.0 social networks (for example, Facebook, LinkedIn, and Twitter); scientific and sensor-based data (for example, the Large Hadron Collider and DNA-derived genomics data); and large volumes of historical transactional data (such as that generated by banks and large retailers).

Just how big is Big Data? Figure 7-1 defines some commonly used terms for data storage capacity. Note that computer storage is calculated based on binary numbers (base 2), not the usual decimal (base 10) numbers with which we are more familiar. Therefore, a kilobyte is 1,024 bytes instead of the 1,000 bytes we would otherwise expect.

If we consider the desktop and notebook computers generally in use as this book is being updated (summer 2018), a quick check online of available computers shows hard drives with a capacity of 5 TB available for laptops, whereas some desktops are available with up to 12 TB or more. That is just for one computer. Facebook stores hundreds of billions of photos in its database, with about 350 million photos uploaded each day.[1] If a typical

---

[1]https://www.omnicoreagency.com/facebook-statistics/ (accessed August 2018).

FIGURE 7-1

Storage Capacity
Terms

Name	Symbol	Approximate Value for Reference	Actual Value
Byte			8 bits [Store one character]
Kilobyte	KB	About 10^3	$2^{10} = 1,024$ bytes
Megabyte	MB	About 10^6	$2^{20} = 1,024$ KB
Gigabyte	GB	About 10^9	$2^{30} = 1,024$ MB
Terabyte	TB	About 10^{12}	$2^{40} = 1,024$ GB
Petabyte	PB	About 10^{15}	$2^{50} = 1,024$ TB
Exabyte	EB	About 10^{18}	$2^{60} = 1,024$ PB
Zettabyte	ZB	About 10^{21}	$2^{70} = 1,024$ EB
Yottabyte	YB	About 10^{24}	$2^{80} = 1,024$ ZB

digital photo is about 2 MB in size, the images from one year alone require more than 230 PB of storage!

As another measure of Big Data, Amazon.com reported that on its most recent "Prime Day" (actually 1.5 days, over July 16 and 17, 2018), orders for more than 100 million products were placed. This is an average of 770 product orders per second.[2] Amazon.com also reported that for the 2017 holiday season, it processed more than a billion product orders just for its small business and entrepreneur sellers (versus products purchased directly from Amazon).[3] This volume of both primary business transactions (item sales) and supporting transactions (shipping, tracking, and financial transactions) truly requires Amazon.com to handle Big Data. As another example, the Large Hadron Collider generates about 30 petabytes of data annually for physicists to analyze.[4] The Internet of Things (IOT, see Chapter 1) continues to grow, with 200 billion devices providing information projected by 2020.[5] If each such device produces one byte of information each hour (and many will do much more than this), that becomes nearly 2 PB of data generated every week by the IOT.

The need to deal with larger and larger datasets has grown over time. We will look at some of the components of this growth. We will start with the need for business analysts to have large datasets (such as data warehouses or simply large production databases) available for analysis by business intelligence (BI) applications and briefly look at BI systems, particularly online analytical processing (OLAP), and the data warehouse structures that were designed for their use. Although these new and often very visible applications and methods

---

[2]https://www.amazon.com/Prime-Day/b?ie=UTF8&node=13887280011 (accessed August 2018).

[3]https://www.businesswire.com/news/home/20171226005146/en/ (accessed August 2018).

[4]http://home.cern/about/computing (accessed August 2018).

[5]https://www.intel.com/content/www/us/en/internet-of-things/infographics/guide-to-iot.html (accessed August 2018).

are highlighting the problems of dealing with large datasets, many of the other techniques being brought to bear on Big Data (such as cloud storage and data models more complex than the relational model) have origins in earlier, more traditional avenues of database development such as distributed databases and object-relational databases. We will thus look at distributed databases (precursors of cloud databases), object-relational systems (which include complex data types like those used in many NoSQL systems), and finally the evolving NoSQL systems that have been developed in large part to manage Big Data. Because the development of NoSQL and the cloud are so closely related, we will also briefly describe cloud computing and the related virtualization technology that enables cloud computing. Many NoSQL systems are deployed in the cloud, and many cloud-based databases are NoSQL systems; thus, a typical NoSQL database existing in the cloud brings together earlier ideas from object-relational and distributed database systems while at the same time providing an affordable platform for business intelligence (BI) activities to be pursued on large datasets. For a more detailed presentation of BI (including specific techniques such as recency, frequency, monetary (RFM) analysis; market basket analysis; and decision trees); see online extension C "Advanced Business Intelligence and Big Data." This extension also contains more thorough descriptions of the varieties of NoSQL systems, focusing on cloud and document database systems, including extended coverage of XML and JSON modeling concepts and specific cloud and NoSQL systems.

In this chapter, we will continue to use the Heather Sweeney Designs database that we modeled in Chapter 4, designed in Chapter 5, and created in Chapter 6. The name of the database is HSD, and a MySQL Workbench database diagram for the HSD database is shown in Figure 7-2.

FIGURE 7-2

The HSD Database Diagram

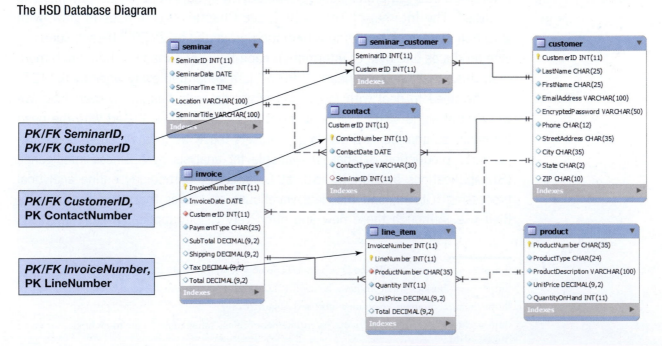

BUSINESS INTELLIGENCE SYSTEMS

Business intelligence (BI) systems are information systems that assist managers and other professionals in the analysis of current and past activities and in the prediction of future events. Unlike transaction processing systems, they do not support routine operational activities, such as the recording and processing of orders. Instead, BI systems are used to support management assessment, analysis, planning, control, and, ultimately, decision making.

THE RELATIONSHIP BETWEEN OPERATIONAL AND BI SYSTEMS

Figure 7-3 summarizes the relationship between operational and business intelligence systems. **Operational systems**—such as sales, purchasing, and inventory-control systems—support primary business activities. They use a DBMS to retrieve, modify, and store data in the operational database. They are also known as **transactional systems** or **online transaction processing (OLTP) systems** because they record the ongoing stream of business transactions.

Instead of supporting the primary business activities, BI systems support management's analysis and decision-making activities. BI systems obtain data from three possible sources. First, they read and process data existing in the operational database—they use the operational DBMS to obtain such data, but they do not insert, modify, or delete operational data. Second, BI systems process data that are extracted from operational databases. In this situation, they manage the extracted database using a BI DBMS, which may be different from the operational DBMS. Finally, BI systems read and process data purchased from data vendors.

We will look at BI systems in more detail in online extension C, but for now we will summarize the basic elements of a BI system.

FIGURE 7-3

The Relationship Between Operational and BI Applications

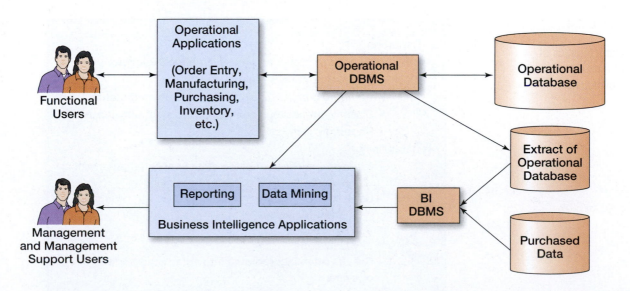

REPORTING SYSTEMS AND DATA MINING APPLICATIONS

BI systems fall into two broad categories: reporting systems and data mining applications. **Reporting systems** sort, filter, group, and make elementary calculations on operational data. **Data mining applications**, in contrast, perform sophisticated analyses on data, analyses that usually involve complex statistical and mathematical processing. The characteristics of BI applications are summarized in Figure 7-4.

Reporting Systems

Reporting systems filter, sort, group, and make simple calculations. All reporting analyses can be performed using standard SQL, although extensions to SQL, such as those used for **online analytical processing (OLAP)**, are sometimes used to ease the task of report production. Another kind of reporting, called RFM analysis, is described in online extension C.

Reporting systems summarize the current status of business activities and compare that status with past or predicted future activities. Reports must be delivered to the proper users on a timely basis in the appropriate format to maximize the value of the information presented. For example, reports may be delivered on paper, via a Web browser, or in some other format.

Data Mining Applications

Data mining applications use sophisticated statistical and mathematical techniques to perform what-if analyses, to make predictions, and to facilitate decision making. For example, data mining techniques can analyze past cell phone usage and predict which customers are likely to switch to a competing phone company. Data mining can also be used to analyze past loan behavior to determine which customers are most (or least) likely to default on a loan.

Report delivery is not as important for data mining systems as it is for reporting systems. First, most data mining applications have only a few users, and those users have sophisticated computer skills. Second, the results of a data mining analysis are usually incorporated into some other report, analysis, or information system. In the case of cell phone usage, the characteristics of customers who are in danger of switching to another company,

FIGURE 7-4

Characteristics of Business Intelligence Applications

- Reporting
    - Filter, sort, group, and make simple calculations
    - Summarize current status
    - Compare current status to past or predicted status
    - Classify entities (customers, products, employees, etc.)
    - Report delivery crucial
- Data Mining
    - Often employ sophisticated statistical and mathematical techniques
    - Used for:
        - What-if analyses
        - Predictions
        - Decisions
    - Results often incorporated into some other report or system

called "customer churn," may be given to the sales department for action. Or the parameters of an equation for determining the likelihood of a loan default may be incorporated into a loan approval application. Two common forms of data mining—market basket analysis and decision trees—are described in online extension C.

DATA WAREHOUSES AND DATA MARTS

As shown in Figure 7-3, some BI applications read and process operational data directly from the operational database. Although this is possible for simple reporting systems and small databases, such direct reading of operational data is not feasible for more complex applications or larger databases. Operational data are difficult to use for several reasons:

- Querying data for BI applications can place a substantial burden on the DBMS and unacceptably impair the performance of operational applications.
- The creation and maintenance of BI systems require application programs, facilities, and expertise that are not normally available from operations departments.
- Operational data may have accuracy or consistency problems and often change rapidly, limiting their usefulness for BI applications.

Therefore, larger organizations usually process a separate database constructed from an extract of the operational database. Some organizations will go even farther and create a **data lake**, which is a repository that includes all data relevant to a business, some of it relational and some not (for example, files of any type, photos, documents, and so on). This information can come from databases, Web sites, and other applications. Typically, it is used by more sophisticated users for purposes of advanced analytics, machine learning, data mining, and so on, and not for standard BI tasks. Amazon.com's AWS service, discussed later in this chapter, provides data lake capabilities in the cloud.

The Components of a Data Warehouse

A **data warehouse** is a database system that has data, programs, and personnel that specialize in the preparation of data for BI processing. Figure 7-5 shows the components of the basic data warehouse architecture. Data are read from operational databases by the **extract, transform, and load (ETL) system**. The ETL system then cleans and prepares the data for BI processing. This can be a complex process.

FIGURE 7-5

Components of a Data Warehouse

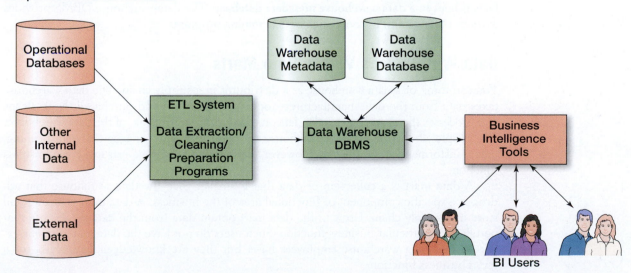

First, operational data often cannot be directly loaded into BI applications. Some of the problems of using operational data for BI processing include:

- "Dirty data" (for example, problematic data such as value of "G" for customer gender, a value of "213" for customer age, a value of "999-999-9999" for a U.S. phone number, or a part color of "gren")
- Missing values
- Inconsistent data (for example, data that have changed, such as a customer's phone number or address)
- Nonintegrated data (for example, data from two or more sources, possibly using different codes or formats, that need to be combined for BI use)
- Incorrect format (for example, data with either too many digits or not enough digits, such as time measured in either seconds or hours when they are needed in minutes for BI use)
- Too much data (for example, an excess of columns [attributes], rows [records], or both)

Second, data may need to be changed or transformed for use in a data warehouse. For example, the operational systems may store data about countries using standard two-letter country codes, such as US (United States) and CA (Canada). However, applications using the data warehouse may need to use the country names in full. Thus, the data transformation {**CountryCode** → **CountryName**} will be needed before the data can be loaded into the data warehouse.

When the data are prepared for use, the ETL system loads the data into the data warehouse database. The extracted data are stored in a data warehouse database using a data warehouse DBMS, which may be from a different vendor than the organization's operational DBMS. For example, an organization might use Oracle Database for its operational processing but use SQL Server for its data warehouse.

Problematic operational data that have been cleaned in the ETL system can also be used to update the operational system to fix the original data problems.

Metadata concerning the data's source, format, assumptions, constraints, and other facts is kept in a **data warehouse metadata database**. The data warehouse DBMS provides extracts of its data to BI tools, such as data mining programs.

Data Warehouses Versus Data Marts

You can think of a data warehouse as a distributor in a supply chain. The data warehouse takes data from the data manufacturers (operational systems and purchased data), cleans and processes them, and locates the data on the shelves, so to speak, of the data warehouse. The people who work in a data warehouse are experts at data management, data cleaning, data transformation, and the like. However, they are not usually experts in a given business function.

A **data mart** is a collection of data that is smaller than the data warehouse that addresses a specific component or functional area of the business. A data mart is like a retail store in a supply chain. Users in the data mart obtain data from the data warehouse that pertain to a particular business function. Such users do not have the data management expertise that data warehouse employees have, but they are knowledgeable analysts for a given business function.

FIGURE 7-6

Data Warehouses and Data Marts

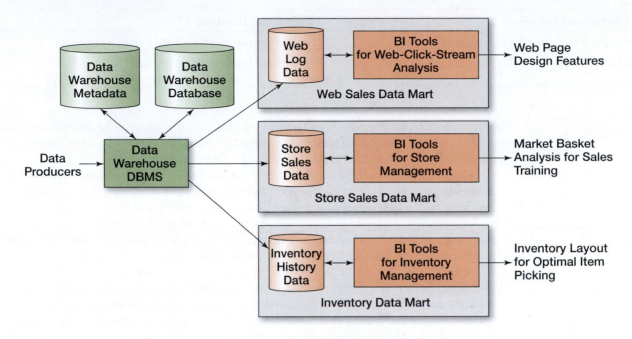

Figure 7-6 illustrates these relationships. The data warehouse takes data from the data producers and distributes the data to three data marts. One data mart analyzes **click-stream data** for the purpose of designing Web pages. A second data mart analyzes store sales data and determines which products tend to be purchased together for the purpose of training sales staff. A third data mart analyzes customer order data for the purpose of reducing labor costs when picking up items at the warehouse. Companies such as Amazon.com go to great lengths to organize their warehouses to reduce picking times and expenses.

When the data mart structure is combined with the data warehouse architecture as shown in Figure 7-6, the combined system is known as an **enterprise data warehouse (EDW) architecture**. In this configuration, the data warehouse maintains all enterprise BI data and acts as the authoritative source for data extracts provided to the data marts. The data marts receive all their data from the data warehouse—they do not add or maintain any additional data.

Of course, creating, staffing, and operating data warehouses and data marts is expensive, and only large organizations with deep pockets can afford to operate a system such as an EDW. Smaller organizations operate subsets of such systems. For example, they may have just a single data mart for analyzing marketing and promotion data.

Dimensional Databases

The databases in a data warehouse or data mart are built to a different type of database design than the normalized relational databases used for operational systems. The data warehouse databases are built in a design called a **dimensional database** that is designed for efficient analysis and efficient queries of the type useful for BI applications (as opposed to operational queries). A dimensional database is used to store historical data rather than just the current data stored in an operational database. Figure 7-7 compares operational databases and dimensional databases.

A **dimension** within a dimensional database is a column or set of columns that describes some aspect of the enterprise (for example, a location or a customer). Typically in a

FIGURE 7-7

Characteristics of Operational and Dimensional Databases

Operational Database	Dimensional Database
Used for structured transaction data processing	Used for unstructured analytical data processing
Current data are used	Current and historical data are used
Data are inserted, updated, and deleted by users	Data are loaded and updated systematically, not by users

data warehouse, a dimension is modeled as a table based on one or more columns from an operational database. An address field, for example, could be expanded into a location dimension table with separate street, city, and state columns.

Because dimensional databases are used for analysis of historical data, they must be designed to handle data that change over time. To track such changes, a dimensional database must have a **date dimension** or **time dimension** as well. For example, a customer may have moved from one residence to another in the same city or to a completely different city and state. This address column (or dimension) example is called a **slowly changing dimension** because changes to such data are infrequent.

The Star Schema   Rather than using the normalized database designs used in operational databases, a dimensional database uses a star schema. A **star schema**, so named because, as shown in Figure 7-8, it visually resembles a star, has a **fact table** at the center of the star and **dimension tables** radiating out from the center. The fact table is always fully normalized, but dimension tables may be non-normalized.

> **BTW**
>
> There is a more complex version of the star schema called the *snowflake schema*. In the snowflake schema, each dimension table is normalized, which may create additional tables attached to the dimension tables.

A star schema for a dimensional database named HSD-DW for BI use by Heather Sweeney Designs is shown in Figure 7-9. The SQL statements needed to create the tables in the HSD-DW database are shown in Figure 7-10, and the data in the HSD-DW database are shown in Figure 7-11. Compare this model to the HSD database diagram shown in Figure 7-2, and note how data in the HSD database have been used in the HSD-DW schema. Some of the details from the LINE_ITEM table are aggregated into the fact table of the dimensional database.

FIGURE 7-8

A Star Schema

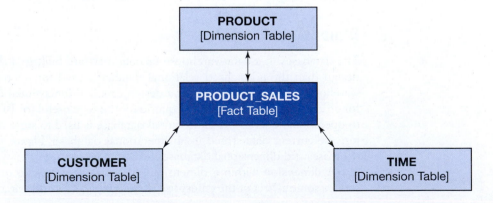

FIGURE 7-9

The HSD-DW Star Schema

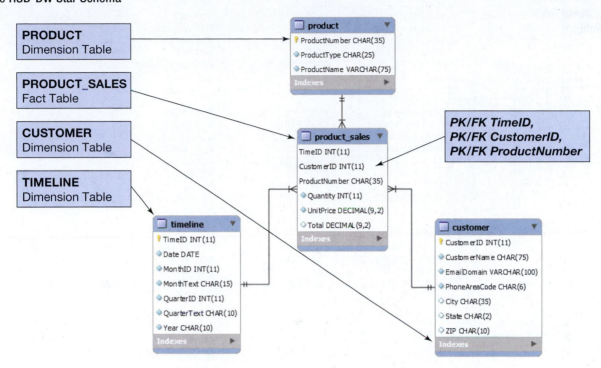

Oracle MySQL Community Server 8.0, Oracle Corporation.

Note that in the HSD-DW database the CUSTOMER table uses the same surrogate primary key (CustomerID) as does the operational database, which has an integer value. Also note that we have concatenated LastName and FirstName into a single CustomerName column and are using only the customer's area code prefix, not the entire phone number. Finally, note that we do not use individual EmailAddress values in the HSD-DW database, only values of EmailDomain, which is not unique. This is a simple way of aggregating data.

A fact table is used to store **measures** of business activity, which are quantitative or factual data about the entity represented by the fact table. For example, in the HSD-DW database, the fact table is PRODUCT_SALES:

PRODUCT_SALES (*TimeID*, *CustomerID*, *ProductNumber*, Quantity, UnitPrice, Total)

This table contains the following measures:

- Quantity is quantitative data that record how many of the item were sold.
- UnitPrice is quantitative data that record the dollar price of each item sold.
- Total (= Quantity * UnitPrice) is quantitative data that record the total dollar value of the sale of this item.

The measures in the PRODUCT_SALES table are for *units of product per customer per day*. We do not use individual sale data (which would be based on InvoiceNumber) but rather data summed for each customer for each day. For example, if you compare the HSD

FIGURE 7-10

The HSD-DW
SQL Create Table
Statements

```
CREATE TABLE TIMELINE(
    TimeID              Int                 NOT NULL,
    Date                Date                NOT NULL,
    MonthID             Int                 NOT NULL,
    MonthText           Char(15)            NOT NULL,
    QuarterID           Int                 NOT NULL,
    QuarterText         Char(10)            NOT NULL,
    Year                Char(10)            NOT NULL,
    CONSTRAINT          TIMELINE_PK         PRIMARY KEY(TimeID)
    );

CREATE TABLE CUSTOMER(
    CustomerID          Int                 NOT NULL,
    CustomerName        Char(75)            NOT NULL,
    EmailDomain         VarChar(100)        NOT NULL,
    PhoneAreaCode       Char(6)             NOT NULL,
    City                Char(35)            NULL,
    State               Char(2)             NULL,
    ZIP                 Char(10)            NULL,
    CONSTRAINT          CUSTOMER_PK         PRIMARY KEY(CustomerID)
    );

CREATE TABLE PRODUCT(
    ProductNumber       Char(35)            NOT NULL,
    ProductType         Char(25)            NOT NULL,
    ProductName         VarChar(75)         NOT NULL,
    CONSTRAINT          PRODUCT_PK          PRIMARY KEY(ProductNumber)
    );

CREATE TABLE PRODUCT_SALES(
    TimeID              Int                 NOT NULL,
    CustomerID          Int                 NOT NULL,
    ProductNumber       Char(35)            NOT NULL,
    Quantity            Int                 NOT NULL,
    UnitPrice           Numeric(9,2)        NOT NULL,
    Total               Numeric(9,2)        NULL,
    CONSTRAINT          PRODUCT_SALES_PK
                            PRIMARY KEY (TimeID, CustomerID, ProductNumber),
    CONSTRAINT          PS_TIMELINE_FK FOREIGN KEY(TimeID)
                            REFERENCES TIMELINE(TimeID)
                                ON UPDATE NO ACTION
                                ON DELETE NO ACTION,
    CONSTRAINT          PS_CUSTOMER_FK FOREIGN KEY(CustomerID)
                            REFERENCES CUSTOMER(CustomerID)
                                ON UPDATE NO ACTION
                                ON DELETE NO ACTION,
    CONSTRAINT          PS_PRODUCT_FK FOREIGN KEY(ProductNumber)
                            REFERENCES PRODUCT(ProductNumber)
                                ON UPDATE NO ACTION
                                ON DELETE NO ACTION

    );
```

database INVOICE data in Figure 3-38 for Ralph Able (CustomerID = 3) for 6/5/19, you will see that Ralph made two purchases on that date (InvoiceNumber 35013 and InvoiceNumber 35016). In the HSD-DW database, however, these two purchases are summed into the PRODUCT_SALES data for Ralph for 6/5/19 (TimeID = 43261).

The TimeID values are the sequential *serial values* used in Microsoft Excel to represent dates. Starting with 01-JAN-1900 as date value 1, the date value is increased by 1 for each calendar day. Thus, 05-JUN-2019 = 43261. For more information, search "Date formats" in the Microsoft Excel help system.

FIGURE 7-11

The HSD-DW Table Data

TimeID	Date	MonthID	MonthText	QuarterID	QuarterText	Year
43388	2018-10-15	10	October	3	Qtr3	2018
43398	2018-10-25	10	October	3	Qtr3	2018
43454	2018-12-20	12	December	3	Qtr3	2018
43549	2019-03-25	3	March	1	Qtr1	2019
43551	2019-03-27	3	March	1	Qtr1	2019
43555	2019-03-31	3	March	1	Qtr1	2019
43558	2019-04-03	4	April	2	Qtr2	2019
43563	2019-04-08	4	April	2	Qtr2	2019
43578	2019-04-23	4	April	2	Qtr2	2019
43592	2019-05-07	5	May	2	Qtr2	2019
43606	2019-05-21	5	May	2	Qtr2	2019
43621	2019-06-05	6	June	2	Qtr2	2019

Oracle MySQL Community Server 8.0, Oracle Corporation.

(a) TIMELINE Dimension Table

CustomerID	CustomerName	EmailDomain	PhoneAreaCode	City	State	ZIP
1	Jacobs, Nancy	somewhere.com	817	Fort Worth	TX	76110
2	Jacobs, Chantel	somewhere.com	817	Fort Worth	TX	76112
3	Able, Ralph	somewhere.com	210	San Antonio	TX	78214
4	Baker, Susan	elsewhere.com	210	San Antonio	TX	78216
5	Eagleton, Sam	elsewhere.com	210	San Antonio	TX	78218
6	Foxtrot, Kathy	somewhere.com	972	Dallas	TX	75220
7	George, Sally	somewhere.com	972	Dallas	TX	75223
8	Hullett, Shawn	somewhere.com	972	Dallas	TX	75224
9	Pearson, Bobbi	elsewhere.com	512	Austin	TX	78710
10	Ranger, Terry	somewhere.com	512	Austin	TX	78712
11	Tyler, Jenny	somewhere.com	972	Dallas	TX	75225
12	Wayne, Joan	elsewhere.com	817	Fort Worth	TX	76115

Oracle MySQL Community Server 8.0, Oracle Corporation.

(b) CUSTOMER Dimension Table

ProductNumber	ProductType	ProductName
BK001	Book	Kitchen Remodeling Basics For Everyone
BK002	Book	Advanced Kitchen Remodeling For Everyone
BK003	Book	Kitchen Remodeling Dallas Style For Everyone
VB001	Video Companion	Kitchen Remodeling Basics Video Companion
VB002	Video Companion	Advanced Kitchen Remodeling Video Companion
VB003	Video Companion	Kitchen Remodeling Dallas Style Video Companion
VK001	Video	Kitchen Remodeling Basics
VK002	Video	Advanced Kitchen Remodeling
VK003	Video	Kitchen Remodeling Dallas Style
VK004	Video	Heather Sweeney Seminar Live in Dallas on 25-OCT-17

Oracle MySQL Community Server 8.0, Oracle Corporation.

(c) PRODUCT Dimension Table

TimeID	CustomerID	ProductNumber	Quantity	UnitPrice	Total
43388	3	VB001	1	7.99	7.99
43388	3	VK001	1	14.95	14.95
43398	4	BK001	1	24.95	24.95
43398	4	VB001	1	7.99	7.99
43398	4	VK001	1	14.95	14.95
43454	7	VK004	1	24.95	24.95
43549	4	BK002	1	24.95	24.95
43549	4	VK002	1	14.95	14.95
43549	4	VK004	1	24.95	24.95
43551	6	BK002	1	24.95	24.95
43551	6	VB003	1	9.99	9.99
43551	6	VK002	1	14.95	14.95
43551	6	VK003	1	19.95	19.95
43551	6	VK004	1	24.95	24.95
43551	7	BK001	1	24.95	24.95
43551	7	BK002	1	24.95	24.95
43551	7	VK003	1	19.95	19.95
43551	7	VK004	1	24.95	24.95
43555	9	BK001	1	24.95	24.95
43555	9	VB001	1	7.99	7.99
43555	9	VK001	1	14.95	14.95
43558	11	VB003	2	9.99	19.98
43558	11	VK003	2	19.95	39.90
43558	11	VK004	2	24.95	49.90
43563	1	BK001	1	24.95	24.95
43563	1	VB001	1	7.99	7.99
43563	1	VK001	1	14.95	14.95
43563	5	BK001	1	24.95	24.95
43563	5	VB001	1	7.99	7.99
43563	5	VK001	1	14.95	14.95
43578	3	BK001	1	24.95	24.95
43592	9	VB002	1	7.99	7.99
43592	9	VK002	1	14.95	14.95
43606	8	VB003	1	9.99	9.99
43606	8	VK003	1	19.95	19.95
43606	8	VK004	1	24.95	24.95
43621	3	BK002	1	24.95	24.95
43621	3	VB001	1	7.99	7.99
43621	3	VB002	2	7.99	15.98
43621	3	VK001	1	14.95	14.95
43621	3	VK002	2	14.95	29.90
43621	11	VB002	2	7.99	15.98
43621	11	VK002	2	14.95	29.90
43621	12	BK002	1	24.95	24.95
43621	12	VB003	1	9.99	9.99
43621	12	VK002	1	14.95	14.95
43621	12	VK003	1	19.95	19.95
43621	12	VK004	1	24.95	24.95

Oracle MySQL Community Server 8.0, Oracle Corporation.

(d) PRODUCT_SALES Fact Table

A dimension table is used to record values of attributes that describe the fact measures in the fact table, and these attributes are used in queries to select and group the measures in the fact table. Thus, CUSTOMER records data about the customers referenced by CustomerID in the SALES table, TIMELINE provides data that can be used to interpret the SALES event in time (which month? which quarter?), and so on. A query to summarize product units sold by Customer (CustomerName) and Product (ProductName) would be:

```
/* *** SQL-QUERY-CH07-01 *** */
SELECT    C.CustomerID, C.CustomerName,
          P.ProductNumber, P.ProductName,
          SUM(PS.Quantity) AS TotalQuantity
```

```
FROM      CUSTOMER C, PRODUCT_SALES PS, PRODUCT P
WHERE     C.CustomerID = PS.CustomerID
  AND     P.ProductNumber = PS.ProductNumber
GROUP BY  C.CustomerID, C.CustomerName,
          P.ProductNumber, P.ProductName
ORDER BY  C.CustomerID, P.ProductNumber;
```

The results of this query are shown in Figure 7-12.

FIGURE 7-12

The HSD-DW Query Results: Summarize Product Units Sold by Customer and Product

CustomerID	CustomerName	ProductNumber	ProductName	TotalQuantity
1	Jacobs, Nancy	BK001	Kitchen Remodeling Basics For Everyone	1
1	Jacobs, Nancy	VB001	Kitchen Remodeling Basics Video Companion	1
1	Jacobs, Nancy	VK001	Kitchen Remodeling Basics	1
3	Able, Ralph	BK001	Kitchen Remodeling Basics For Everyone	1
3	Able, Ralph	BK002	Advanced Kitchen Remodeling For Everyone	1
3	Able, Ralph	VB001	Kitchen Remodeling Basics Video Companion	2
3	Able, Ralph	VB002	Advanced Kitchen Remodeling Video Companion	2
3	Able, Ralph	VK001	Kitchen Remodeling Basics	2
3	Able, Ralph	VK002	Advanced Kitchen Remodeling	2
4	Baker, Susan	BK001	Kitchen Remodeling Basics For Everyone	1
4	Baker, Susan	BK002	Advanced Kitchen Remodeling For Everyone	1
4	Baker, Susan	VB001	Kitchen Remodeling Basics Video Companion	1
4	Baker, Susan	VK001	Kitchen Remodeling Basics	1
4	Baker, Susan	VK002	Advanced Kitchen Remodeling	1
4	Baker, Susan	VK004	Heather Sweeney Seminar Live in Dallas on 25-OCT-17	1
5	Eagleton, Sam	BK001	Kitchen Remodeling Basics For Everyone	1
5	Eagleton, Sam	VB001	Kitchen Remodeling Basics Video Companion	1
5	Eagleton, Sam	VK001	Kitchen Remodeling Basics	1
6	Foxtrot, Kathy	BK002	Advanced Kitchen Remodeling For Everyone	1
6	Foxtrot, Kathy	VB003	Kitchen Remodeling Dallas Style Video Companion	1
6	Foxtrot, Kathy	VK002	Advanced Kitchen Remodeling	1
6	Foxtrot, Kathy	VK003	Kitchen Remodeling Dallas Style	1
6	Foxtrot, Kathy	VK004	Heather Sweeney Seminar Live in Dallas on 25-OCT-17	1
7	George, Sally	BK001	Kitchen Remodeling Basics For Everyone	1
7	George, Sally	BK002	Advanced Kitchen Remodeling For Everyone	1
7	George, Sally	VK003	Kitchen Remodeling Dallas Style	1
7	George, Sally	VK004	Heather Sweeney Seminar Live in Dallas on 25-OCT-17	2
8	Hullett, Shawn	VB003	Kitchen Remodeling Dallas Style Video Companion	1
8	Hullett, Shawn	VK003	Kitchen Remodeling Dallas Style	1
8	Hullett, Shawn	VK004	Heather Sweeney Seminar Live in Dallas on 25-OCT-17	1
9	Pearson, Bobbi	BK001	Kitchen Remodeling Basics For Everyone	1
9	Pearson, Bobbi	VB001	Kitchen Remodeling Basics Video Companion	1
9	Pearson, Bobbi	VB002	Advanced Kitchen Remodeling Video Companion	1
9	Pearson, Bobbi	VK001	Kitchen Remodeling Basics	1
9	Pearson, Bobbi	VK002	Advanced Kitchen Remodeling	1
11	Tyler, Jenny	VB002	Advanced Kitchen Remodeling Video Companion	2
11	Tyler, Jenny	VB003	Kitchen Remodeling Dallas Style Video Companion	2
11	Tyler, Jenny	VK002	Advanced Kitchen Remodeling	2
11	Tyler, Jenny	VK003	Kitchen Remodeling Dallas Style	2
11	Tyler, Jenny	VK004	Heather Sweeney Seminar Live in Dallas on 25-OCT-17	2
12	Wayne, Joan	BK002	Advanced Kitchen Remodeling For Everyone	1
12	Wayne, Joan	VB003	Kitchen Remodeling Dallas Style Video Companion	1
12	Wayne, Joan	VK002	Advanced Kitchen Remodeling	1
12	Wayne, Joan	VK003	Kitchen Remodeling Dallas Style	1
12	Wayne, Joan	VK004	Heather Sweeney Seminar Live in Dallas on 25-OCT-17	1

Oracle MySQL Community Server 8.0, Oracle Corporation.

In Chapter 5, we discussed how an N:M relationship is created in a database as two 1:N relationships by use of an intersection table. We also discussed how additional attributes can be added to the intersection table in an association relationship. Similarly, the fact table is an intersection table for the relationships between the dimension tables with additional measures also stored in it. And, as with all intersection tables, the key of the fact table is a composite key made up of all the foreign keys to the dimension tables.

Illustrating the Dimensional Model   When you think of the word *dimension*, you might think of "two-dimensional" or "three-dimensional." The dimensional models can be illustrated by using a two-dimensional matrix and a three-dimensional cube. Figure 7-13 shows the SQL query results from Figure 7-12 displayed as a two-dimensional matrix of Product (using ProductNumber) and Customer (using CustomerID), with each cell showing the number of units of each product purchased by each customer. Note how Product-Number and CustomerID define the two dimensions of the matrix: CustomerID labels the *x*-axis and ProductNumber labels the *y*-axis of the chart.

Figure 7-14 shows a three-dimensional cube with the same ProductNumber and CustomerID dimensions but now with the added Time dimension on the *z*-axis. Now, instead of occupying a two-dimensional box, the total quantity of a product purchased by a customer on a specific day occupies a small three-dimensional cube, and all these small cubes are combined to form a large cube.

As human beings, we can visualize two-dimensional matrices and three-dimensional cubes. Although we cannot picture models with four, five, and more dimensions, BI systems and dimensional databases routinely handle such models.

FIGURE 7-13

The Two-Dimensional ProductNumber-CustomerID Matrix

> Each cell shows the total quantity of each product that has been purchased by each customer

ProductNumber	CustomerID											
	1	2	3	4	5	6	7	8	9	10	11	12
BK001	1		1	1			1		1			
BK002			1	1		1	1					1
VB001	1		2	1	1				1			
VB002			2						1		2	
VB003						1		1			2	1
VK001	1		2	1	1				1			
VK002			2	1		1			1		2	1
VK003						1	1	1			2	1
VK004				1		1	2	1			2	1

FIGURE 7-14

The Three-Dimensional Time-ProductNumber-CustomerID Cube

> Each cell will show the total quantity of each product that has been purchased by each customer on a specific date

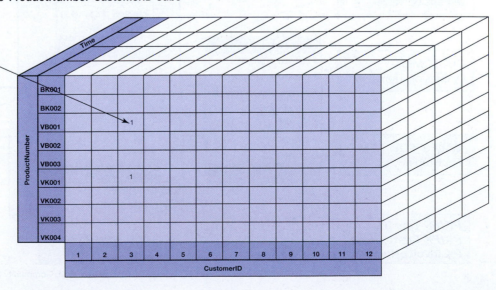

Multiple Fact Tables and Conformed Dimensions   Data warehouse systems build dimensional models, as needed, to analyze BI questions, and the HSD-DW star schema in Figure 7-9 would be just one schema in a set of schemas. Figure 7-15 shows an extended HSD-DW schema.

In Figure 7-15, a second fact table named SALES_FOR_RFM has been added:

SALES_FOR_RFM (*TimeID*, *CustomerID*, InvoiceNumber, PreTaxTotalSale)

Why would we add a fact table named SALES_FOR_RFM? This table would be used to collect and process data for a **RFM analysis**, which analyzes and ranks customers according to their purchasing patterns. It is a simple customer classification technique that considers how *recently* (R) a customer ordered, how *frequently* (F) a customer orders, and *how much money* (M) the customer spends per order. RFM analysis is a commonly used BI report, and it is discussed in detail in online extension C.

This table shows that fact table primary keys do not need to be composed solely of foreign keys that link to dimension tables. In SALES_FOR_RFM, the primary key includes the InvoiceNumber attribute. This attribute is necessary because the composite key (TimeID, CustomerID) will not be unique and cannot be the primary key (a customer can place multiple orders on the same day). Note that SALES_FOR_RFM links to the same

FIGURE 7-15

The HSD-DW Star Schema Extended for RFM Analysis

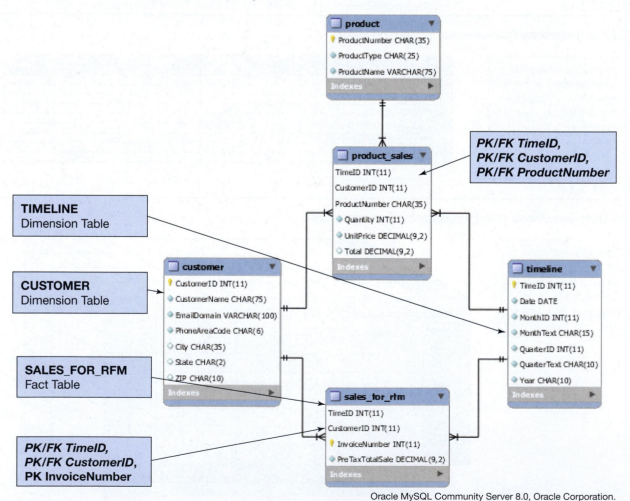

Oracle MySQL Community Server 8.0, Oracle Corporation.

CUSTOMER and TIMELINE dimension tables as PRODUCT_SALES. This is done to maintain consistency within the data warehouse. When a dimension table links to two or more fact tables, it is called a **conformed dimension**.

OLAP

For an example of a BI report, we will look at OLAP, which provides the ability to sum, count, average, and perform other simple arithmetic operations on groups of data. OLAP systems produce **OLAP reports**. An OLAP report is also called an **OLAP cube**. This is a reference to the dimensional data model, and some OLAP products show OLAP displays using three axes, like a geometric cube. The remarkable characteristic of an OLAP report is that it is dynamic: The format of an OLAP report can be changed by the viewer, hence the term *online* in the name *online analytical processing*.

OLAP uses the dimensional database model discussed earlier in this chapter, so it is not surprising to learn that an OLAP report has measures and dimensions. Recall that a *measure* is a dimensional model *fact*—the data item of interest that is to be summed or averaged or otherwise processed in the OLAP report. For example, sales data (in dollars) is a measure that may be summed to produce Total Sales or averaged to produce Average Sales. The term measure is used because you are dealing with quantities that have been or can be measured and recorded. A dimension, as you have already learned, is an attribute or a characteristic of a measure. Purchase date (TimeID), customer location (City), and sales region (ZIP or State) are all examples of dimensions, because they describe when and where the sales occurred. In the HSD-DW database you saw how the time dimension is important.

In this section, we will generate an OLAP report by using an SQL query from the HSD-DW database and a Microsoft Excel **PivotTable**.

We use MySQL and Microsoft Excel to illustrate this discussion of OLAP reports and PivotTables. For other DBMS products, such as SQL Server or Oracle Database, you can use the DataPilot feature of the Calc spreadsheet application in the LibreOffice or Apache OpenOffice product suites.

Now we use Microsoft Excel to

Either:

- Place the data into a Microsoft Excel worksheet:
  - ➤ Copy the SQL query results into a Microsoft Excel worksheet.
  - ➤ Add column names to the results.
  - ➤ Format the query results as a Microsoft Excel table (optional).
  - ➤ Select the Microsoft Excel range containing the results with column names.

Or:

- Connect to a DBMS data source.

Then:

- Click the PivotTable button in the Tables group of the Insert ribbon.
- Specify that the PivotTable should be in a new worksheet.
- Select the column variables (Column Labels), row variables (Row Labels), and the measure to be displayed (Values). See the section "Working with Access" for more details.

To use the first approach, we can write an SQL query and then copy the data into a Microsoft Excel worksheet. In this example, we create a query that will tell us how many of each specific product was purchased by each customer during each quarter. The SQL query, as used in MySQL, is:

```
/* *** SQL-QUERY-CH07-02 *** */
SELECT    C.CustomerID, CustomerName, C.City,
          P.ProductNumber, P.ProductName,
          T.Year, T.QuarterText,
          SUM(PS.Quantity) AS TotalQuantity
FROM      CUSTOMER C, PRODUCT_SALES PS, PRODUCT P, TIMELINE T
WHERE     C.CustomerID = PS.CustomerID
  AND     P.ProductNumber = PS.ProductNumber
  AND     T.TimeID = PS.TimeID
GROUP BY  C.CustomerID, C.CustomerName, C.City,
          P.ProductNumber, P.ProductName,
          T.QuarterText, T.Year
ORDER BY  C.CustomerName, T.Year, T.QuarterText;
```

However, if we want to use the second approach (connect Microsoft Excel to a DBMS data source), we must first create a view based on the preceding query. (Views, which are essentially named queries stored in the database, are discussed in more detail in online extension B, "Advanced SQL.") This is because MySQL (and other SQL-based DBMS products, such as Oracle Database and SQL Server) can store views but not queries. The SQL query to create the HSDDWProductSalesView, as used in MySQL, is:

```
/* *** SQL-CREATE-VIEW-CH07-01 *** */
CREATE VIEW HSDDWProductSalesView AS
   SELECT    C.CustomerID, C.CustomerName, C.City,
             P.ProductNumber, P.ProductName,
             T.Year, T.QuarterText,
             SUM(PS.Quantity) AS TotalQuantity
   FROM      CUSTOMER C, PRODUCT_SALES PS, PRODUCT P, TIMELINE T
   WHERE     C.CustomerID = PS.CustomerID
     AND     P.ProductNumber = PS.ProductNumber
     AND     T.TimeID = PS.TimeID
   GROUP BY  C.CustomerID, C.CustomerName, C.City,
             P.ProductNumber, P.ProductName,
             T.QuarterText, T.Year;
```

Figure 7-16 shows the results of SQL-QUERY-CH07-02 (which can also be obtained by using the HSDDWProductSalesView).

Figure 7-17 shows the OLAP report as a Microsoft Excel PivotTable. Here the measure is quantity sold, and the dimensions are ProductNumber and City. This report shows how quantity varies by product and city. For example, four copies of VB003 (Kitchen Remodeling Dallas Style Video Companion) were sold in Dallas, but none were sold in Austin.

FIGURE 7-16

The HSD-DW Query for OLAP Results: Time-Product-Customer Cube

CustomerID	CustomerName	City	ProductNumber	ProductName	Year	QuarterText	TotalQuantity
3	Able, Ralph	San Antonio	VK001	Kitchen Remodeling Basics	2018	Qtr3	1
3	Able, Ralph	San Antonio	VB001	Kitchen Remodeling Basics Video Companion	2018	Qtr3	1
3	Able, Ralph	San Antonio	VB001	Kitchen Remodeling Basics Video Companion	2019	Qtr2	1
3	Able, Ralph	San Antonio	BK002	Advanced Kitchen Remodeling For Everyone	2019	Qtr2	1
3	Able, Ralph	San Antonio	VK002	Advanced Kitchen Remodeling	2019	Qtr2	2
3	Able, Ralph	San Antonio	VB002	Advanced Kitchen Remodeling Video Companion	2019	Qtr2	2
3	Able, Ralph	San Antonio	BK001	Kitchen Remodeling Basics For Everyone	2019	Qtr2	1
3	Able, Ralph	San Antonio	VK001	Kitchen Remodeling Basics	2019	Qtr2	1
4	Baker, Susan	San Antonio	BK001	Kitchen Remodeling Basics For Everyone	2018	Qtr3	1
4	Baker, Susan	San Antonio	VK001	Kitchen Remodeling Basics	2018	Qtr3	1
4	Baker, Susan	San Antonio	VB001	Kitchen Remodeling Basics Video Companion	2018	Qtr3	1
4	Baker, Susan	San Antonio	BK002	Advanced Kitchen Remodeling For Everyone	2019	Qtr1	1
4	Baker, Susan	San Antonio	VK002	Advanced Kitchen Remodeling	2019	Qtr1	1
4	Baker, Susan	San Antonio	VK004	Heather Sweeney Seminar Live in Dallas on 25-OCT-17	2019	Qtr1	1
5	Eagleton, Sam	San Antonio	VB001	Kitchen Remodeling Basics Video Companion	2019	Qtr2	1
5	Eagleton, Sam	San Antonio	BK001	Kitchen Remodeling Basics For Everyone	2019	Qtr2	1
5	Eagleton, Sam	San Antonio	VK001	Kitchen Remodeling Basics	2019	Qtr2	1
6	Foxtrot, Kathy	Dallas	BK002	Advanced Kitchen Remodeling For Everyone	2019	Qtr1	1
6	Foxtrot, Kathy	Dallas	VK002	Advanced Kitchen Remodeling	2019	Qtr1	1
6	Foxtrot, Kathy	Dallas	VK004	Heather Sweeney Seminar Live in Dallas on 25-OCT-17	2019	Qtr1	1
6	Foxtrot, Kathy	Dallas	VB003	Kitchen Remodeling Dallas Style Video Companion	2019	Qtr1	1
6	Foxtrot, Kathy	Dallas	VK003	Kitchen Remodeling Dallas Style	2019	Qtr1	1
7	George, Sally	Dallas	VK004	Heather Sweeney Seminar Live in Dallas on 25-OCT-17	2018	Qtr3	1
7	George, Sally	Dallas	BK002	Advanced Kitchen Remodeling For Everyone	2019	Qtr1	1
7	George, Sally	Dallas	BK001	Kitchen Remodeling Basics For Everyone	2019	Qtr1	1
7	George, Sally	Dallas	VK004	Heather Sweeney Seminar Live in Dallas on 25-OCT-17	2019	Qtr1	1
7	George, Sally	Dallas	VK003	Kitchen Remodeling Dallas Style	2019	Qtr1	1
8	Hullett, Shawn	Dallas	VB003	Kitchen Remodeling Dallas Style Video Companion	2019	Qtr2	1
8	Hullett, Shawn	Dallas	VK004	Heather Sweeney Seminar Live in Dallas on 25-OCT-17	2019	Qtr2	1
8	Hullett, Shawn	Dallas	VK003	Kitchen Remodeling Dallas Style	2019	Qtr2	1
1	Jacobs, Nancy	Fort Worth	VB001	Kitchen Remodeling Basics Video Companion	2019	Qtr2	1
1	Jacobs, Nancy	Fort Worth	BK001	Kitchen Remodeling Basics For Everyone	2019	Qtr2	1
1	Jacobs, Nancy	Fort Worth	VK001	Kitchen Remodeling Basics	2019	Qtr2	1
9	Pearson, Bobbi	Austin	BK001	Kitchen Remodeling Basics For Everyone	2019	Qtr1	1
9	Pearson, Bobbi	Austin	VK001	Kitchen Remodeling Basics	2019	Qtr1	1
9	Pearson, Bobbi	Austin	VB001	Kitchen Remodeling Basics Video Companion	2019	Qtr1	1
9	Pearson, Bobbi	Austin	VK002	Advanced Kitchen Remodeling	2019	Qtr2	1
9	Pearson, Bobbi	Austin	VB002	Advanced Kitchen Remodeling Video Companion	2019	Qtr2	1
11	Tyler, Jenny	Dallas	VK003	Kitchen Remodeling Dallas Style	2019	Qtr2	2
11	Tyler, Jenny	Dallas	VK002	Advanced Kitchen Remodeling	2019	Qtr2	2
11	Tyler, Jenny	Dallas	VB002	Advanced Kitchen Remodeling Video Companion	2019	Qtr2	2
11	Tyler, Jenny	Dallas	VB003	Kitchen Remodeling Dallas Style Video Companion	2019	Qtr2	2
11	Tyler, Jenny	Dallas	VK004	Heather Sweeney Seminar Live in Dallas on 25-OCT-17	2019	Qtr2	2
12	Wayne, Joan	Fort Worth	VB003	Kitchen Remodeling Dallas Style Video Companion	2019	Qtr2	1
12	Wayne, Joan	Fort Worth	VK004	Heather Sweeney Seminar Live in Dallas on 25-OCT-17	2019	Qtr2	1
12	Wayne, Joan	Fort Worth	VK003	Kitchen Remodeling Dallas Style	2019	Qtr2	1
12	Wayne, Joan	Fort Worth	BK002	Advanced Kitchen Remodeling For Everyone	2019	Qtr2	1
12	Wayne, Joan	Fort Worth	VK002	Advanced Kitchen Remodeling	2019	Qtr2	1

Oracle MySQL Community Server 8.0, Oracle Corporation.

We generated the OLAP report in Figure 7-17 by using a simple SQL query and Microsoft Excel, but many DBMS and BI products include more powerful and sophisticated tools. For example, SQL Server includes SQL Server Analysis Services,[6] and

---

[6]Although OLAP reports *can* be done without SQL Server Analysis Services, Analysis Services adds a lot of functionality. SQL Server Analysis Services is a standard part of the SQL Server Developer edition.

FIGURE 7-17

The HSD-DW OLAP ProductNumber by City Report

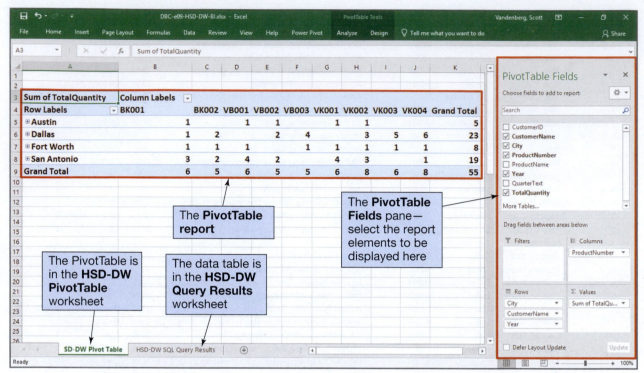

Excel 2019, Windows 10, Microsoft Corporation.

third-party tools are available for doing the same thing with MySQL. It is possible to display OLAP cubes in many ways in addition to Microsoft Excel. Some third-party vendors provide more sophisticated graphical displays, and OLAP reports can be delivered just like any of the other reports described for report management systems.

The distinguishing characteristic of an OLAP report is that the user can alter the format of the report. Figure 7-18 shows an alteration in which the user added two additional dimensions, customer and year, to the horizontal display. Quantity sold is now broken out by customer within each city and, in one case, by year within a customer.

FIGURE 7-18

The HSD-DW OLAP ProductNumber by City Report: CustomerName and Year Dimensions Added

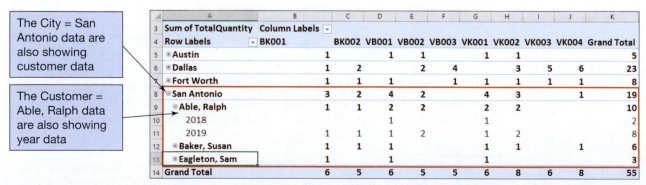

Excel 2019, Windows 10, Microsoft Corporation.

FIGURE 7-19

The HSD-DW OLAP City by ProductNumber, CustomerName, and Year Report

	A	B	C	D	E	F
3	Sum of TotalQuantity	Column Labels				
4	Row Labels	Austin	Dallas	Fort Worth	San Antonio	Grand Total
5	⊞ BK001		1	1	1	3	6
6	⊞ BK002		2	1	2	5
7	⊟ VB001	1		1	4	6
8	⊟ Able, Ralph				2	2
9	2018				1	1
10	2019				1	1
11	⊞ Baker, Susan				1	1
12	⊞ Eagleton, Sam				1	1
13	⊞ Jacobs, Nancy			1		1
14	⊞ Pearson, Bobbi	1				1
15	⊞ VB002	1	2		2	5
16	⊞ VB003		4	1		5
17	⊞ VK001	1		1	4	6
18	⊞ VK002	1	3	1	3	8
19	⊞ VK003		5	1		6
20	⊞ VK004		6	1	1	8
21	Grand Total	5	23	8	19	55

Callouts:
- The city variable is on the column designator
- The ProductID variable is on the primary row designator
- The ProductID = VB001 data are also showing **Customer** data
- The Customer = Able, Ralph data are also showing Year data

Excel 2019, Windows 10, Microsoft Corporation.

With an OLAP report, it is possible to **drill down** into the data; that is, to further divide the data into more detail. In Figure 7-18, for example, the user has drilled down into the San Antonio data to display all customer data for that city and to display yearly sales data for Ralph Able.

In an OLAP report, it is also possible to change the order of the dimensions. Figure 7-19 shows city quantities as vertical data and ProductID quantities as horizontal data. This OLAP report shows quantity sold by city, by product, by customer, and by year.

Both displays are valid and useful, depending on the user's perspective. A product manager might like to see product families first (ProductID) and then location data (city). A sales manager might like to see location data first and then product data. OLAP reports provide both perspectives, and the user can switch between them while viewing a report.

DISTRIBUTED DATABASE PROCESSING

One of the first solutions to increase the amount of data that could be stored and processed by a DBMS was to simply spread the data among several database servers instead of just one. A group of associated servers is known as a **server cluster**,[7] and the database shared between them is called a distributed database. A **distributed database** is a database that is stored and processed on more than one computer. Depending on the type of database and the processing that is allowed, distributed databases can present significant problems as well as significant opportunities. Let us consider the types of distributed databases.

---

[7]For more information on computer clusters, see the Wikipedia article **Computer cluster**, https://en.wikipedia.org/wiki/Computer_cluster.

Types of Distributed Databases

A database can be distributed by **partitioning**, which means breaking the database into pieces and storing the pieces on multiple computers; by **replication**, which means storing copies of the database on multiple computers; or by a combination of replication and partitioning. Figure 7-20 illustrates these alternatives.

Figure 7-20(a) shows a nondistributed database with four pieces labeled W, X, Y, and Z and two applications labeled AP_1 and AP_2. In Figure 7-20(b), the database has been partitioned but not replicated. Portions W and X are stored and processed on Computer 1, and portions Y and Z are stored and processed on Computer 2. Figure 7-20(c) shows a database that has been replicated but not partitioned. The entire database is stored and processed on Computers 1 and 2. Finally, Figure 7-20(d) shows a database that is partitioned and replicated. Portion Y of the database is stored and processed on Computers 1 and 2.

The portions to be partitioned or replicated can be defined in many different ways. A database that has five tables (for example, CUSTOMER, SALESPERSON, INVOICE, LINE_ITEM, and PART) could be partitioned by assigning CUSTOMER to portion W, SALESPERSON to portion X, INVOICE and LINE_ITEM to portion Y, and PART to portion Z. Alternatively, different rows of each of these five tables could be assigned to different computers, or different columns of each of these tables could be assigned to different computers.

Databases are distributed for two major reasons: performance and control. Having a database on multiple computers can improve throughput, either because multiple computers

FIGURE 7-20

Types of Distributed Databases

Single Processing Computer

(a) Nonpartitioned, Nonreplicated
    Alternative

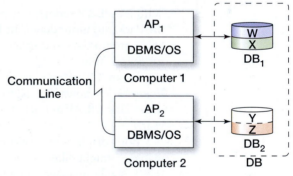

(b) Partitioned, Nonreplicated Alternative

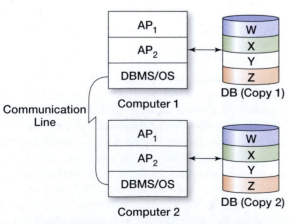

(c) Nonpartitioned, Replicated Alternative

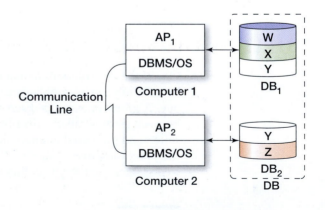

(d) Partitioned, Replicated Alternative

are sharing the workload or because communications delays can be reduced by placing the computers closer to their users. Distributing the database can improve control by segregating different portions of the database to different computers, each of which can have its own set of authorized users and permissions.

Challenges of Distributed Databases

Significant challenges must be overcome when distributing a database, and those challenges depend on the type of distributed database and the activity that is allowed. In the case of a fully replicated database, if only one computer is allowed to make updates on one of the copies, then the challenges are not too great. All update activity occurs on that single computer, and copies of that database are periodically sent to the replication sites. The challenge is to ensure that only a logically consistent copy of the database is distributed (no partial or uncommitted transactions, for example) and to ensure that the sites understand that they are processing data that might not be current because changes could have been made to the updated database after the local copy was made.

If multiple computers can make updates to a replicated database, then difficult problems arise. Specifically, if two computers are allowed to process the same row at the same time, they can cause three types of error: They can make inconsistent changes, one computer can delete a row that another computer is updating, or the two computers can make changes that violate uniqueness constraints (for example, two computers inserting data into a table with the same primary key).

To prevent these problems, some type of record locking is required (locking is discussed in Chapter 6). Because multiple computers are involved, standard record locking does not work. Instead, a far more complicated locking scheme, called **distributed two-phase locking**, must be used. The specifics of the scheme are beyond the scope of this discussion; for now, just know that implementing this algorithm is difficult and expensive. If multiple computers can process multiple replicas of a distributed database, then significant problems must be solved.

If the database is partitioned but not replicated (Figure 7-20(b)), then problems will occur if any transaction updates data that span two or more distributed partitions. For example, suppose the CUSTOMER and SALESPERSON tables are placed on a partition on one computer and that INVOICE, LINE_ITEM, and PART tables are placed on a second computer. Further suppose that when recording a sale, all five tables are updated in an atomic transaction. In this case, a transaction must be started on both computers, and it can be allowed to commit on one computer only if it can be allowed to commit on both computers. In this case, distributed two-phase locking also must be used.

If the data are partitioned in such a way that no transaction requires data from both partitions, then regular locking will work. However, in this case the databases are actually two separate databases, and some would argue that they should not be considered a distributed database.

If the data are partitioned in such a way that no transaction updates data from both partitions but that one or more transactions read data from one partition and update data on a second partition, then problems might or might not result with regular locking. If dirty reads are possible, then some form of distributed locking is required; otherwise, regular locking should work.

If a database is partitioned and at least one of those partitions is replicated, then the locking requirements are a combination of those just described. If the replicated portion is updated, if transactions span the partitions, or if dirty reads are possible, then distributed two-phase locking is required; otherwise, regular locking might suffice.

Distributed processing is complicated and can create substantial problems. Except in the case of replicated, read-only databases, only experienced teams with a substantial budget and significant time to invest should attempt distributed databases. Such databases also require data communications expertise. Distributed databases are not for the faint of heart.

OBJECT-RELATIONAL DATABASES

Object-oriented programming (OOP) is a methodology for designing and writing computer programs. Today, most new program development is done using OOP techniques. Java, Python, C++, C#, and Visual Basic.NET are object-oriented programming languages.

Objects are data structures that have both **methods**, which are programs that perform some task with the object, and **properties**, which are data items particular to an object. Objects are organized into classes, and all objects of a given class have the same methods, but each has its own set of data item values. When using an OOP language, the properties of the object are created and stored in main memory. Permanently storing the values of properties of an object in secondary memory (usually disk) is called **object persistence**. Many different techniques have been used for object persistence. One of them is to use some variation of database technology.

Although relational databases can be used for object persistence, using this method requires substantial work on the part of the programmer. The problem is that, in general, object data structures are more complicated than a row of a table. Typically, several, or even many, rows of several different tables are required to store object data. This means the OOP programmer must design a mini-database just to store objects. Usually, many objects are involved in an information system, so many different mini-databases need to be designed and processed. This method is so undesirable that it is seldom used.

In the early 1990s, several vendors developed special-purpose DBMS products for storing object data. These products, which were called **object-oriented DBMSs (OODBMSs)**, never achieved widespread commercial success. The problem was that by the time they were introduced, billions of bytes of data were already stored in relational DBMS format, and very few organizations wanted to convert their data to OODBMS format to be able to use an OODBMS. Consequently, such products failed to capture a large share of the relational data market, but some of these OODBMSs are still available and occupy a niche market for DBMSs (ObjectDB, Objectivity, ObjectStore—notice the pattern—Versant, and so on).

However, the need for object persistence did not disappear. The current SQL standard defines many object-based features (classes, methods, and so on). Some vendors, most notably Oracle, added many of these features and functions to their relational DBMS products to create **object-relational databases**. PostgreSQL is another popular object-relational database management system. These features and functions are basically add-ons to a relational DBMS that facilitate object persistence. With these features, object data can be stored more readily than with a purely relational database. However, an object-relational database can still process relational data at the same time.[8]

Although OODBMSs have not achieved commercial success, OOP is here to stay, and modern programming languages are object-based. This is important because these are the programming languages that are being used to create the latest technologies that are dealing with Big Data. This is also useful when embedding queries in a programming language: A more straightforward mapping of concepts is possible when the type systems of the programming language and the DBMS match. This reduces what is often called the "impedance mismatch" between the ways the object and relational paradigms manage data structuring and processing. In addition, many of the complex data structuring concepts developed for object-oriented and object-relational systems are used heavily in NoSQL databases and the languages that support them, so both object-oriented and object-relational databases have played an important role in the development of DBMS technology.

---

[8]To learn more about object-relational databases, see the Wikipedia article **Object-relational database**, https://en.wikipedia.org/wiki/Object-relational_database.

VIRTUALIZATION

Virtualization is using hardware and software to simulate another hardware resource. For example, we can provide the illusion of additional, virtual memory by storing small chunks of memory called pages on disk drives and moving them back and forth between the real (physical) memory and disk. The CPU chip and the operating system assist in providing this resource to application programs that run as if they had their own copy of the full set of memory that the CPU architecture provides.

A major development in computing occurred when systems administrators realized that the hardware resources (CPU, memory, input/output from/to disk storage) were often underutilized on most servers in a data center. This realization led to the idea of combining several servers into one larger server. Managing multiple server environments (including the operating system, libraries, and applications) would be cheaper and easier to do if they were consolidated into a larger server with a higher utilization. This can also conserve data center space, electricity, air conditioning, hardware maintenance, and software licensing costs.

But how can this be done? The answer is to have one physical computer host one or more virtual computers, more commonly known as **virtual machines**. To do this, the actual computer hardware, now called the **host machine**, runs a special program known as a **virtual machine manager** or **hypervisor**. The hypervisor creates and manages the virtual machines and controls the interaction between each virtual machine and the physical hardware. For example, if a virtual machine has been allocated two gigabytes of main memory for its use, the hypervisor is responsible for making sure the actual physical memory is allocated and available to the virtual machine. The virtual machines are unaware that they are sharing a physical computer with other virtual machines. The systems administrator can interact with the hypervisor to start new virtual machine instances, shut them down, or adjust virtual machine configurations.

There are two basic ways to implement hypervisors. The first is the "bare metal" or type 1 hypervisors, as shown in Figure 7-21(a). These are loaded into memory or "booted"

FIGURE 7-21

Type 1 and Type 2 Hypervisors versus Containers

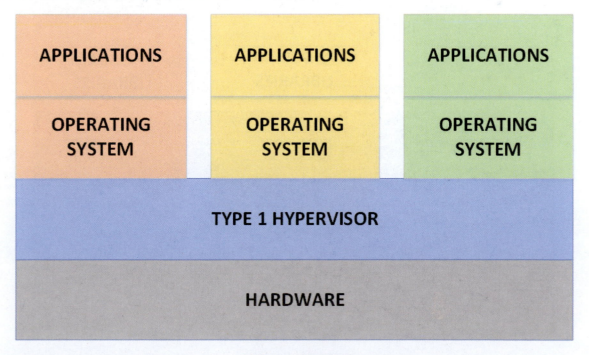

(a) Type 1 Hypervisor

FIGURE 7-21   Continued

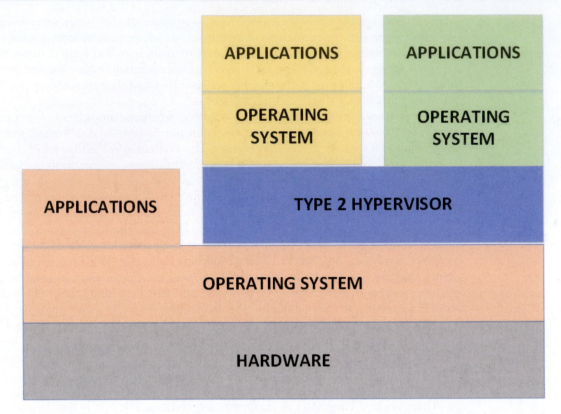

(b) Type 2 Hypervisor

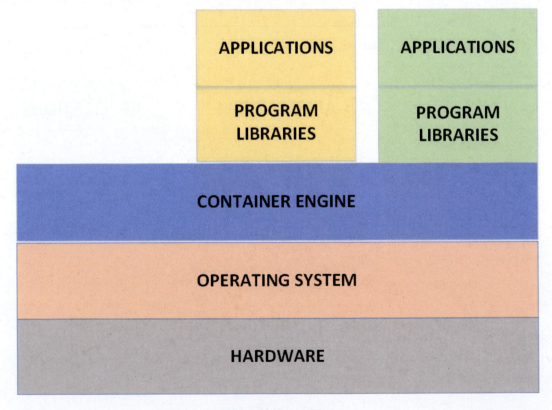

(c) Container Architecture

before any other programs. Thus, the hypervisor has direct control over the hardware and provides the illusion to virtual machines that they are running on the physical hardware. Type 1 hypervisors are typically used in large data centers. Type 2 or "hosted" hypervisors, as shown in Figure 7-21(b), are typically used by students and other computer users to run multiple operating systems as regular applications on their desktop or laptop computer. If you own a Mac, you know that Microsoft Access is not available on Apple's Mac OS. However, you can use a type 2 hypervisor to load Windows as another application on your Mac and use the Windows version of Office on your Mac. Another common scenario is to be able to boot Linux as an application on a Windows machine. Both type 1 and type 2 hypervisors can run different operating systems as "guest" operating systems in virtual machines.

Type 1 hypervisor products include VMware's vSphere and ESXi, the open source KVM and Xen hypervisors, Red Hat's Enterprise Virtualization, and Microsoft's Hyper-V. Type 2 hypervisors include VMware's Fusion and Workstation, Oracle's VirtualBox, and Parallels' Desktop for Mac. Some type 2 products are designed to run on a PC, others run on Macs.

Another form of virtualization, known as **containerization**, shown in Figure 7-21(c), is becoming more popular and is used to support the rapid and seamless deployment of new software releases. Rather than simulating an entire machine, containerization simulates separate operating system environments—the program libraries, filesystems, and configuration files—needed to run applications. This approach to virtualization is sometimes called "operating system–level virtualization."

A "Container Engine" manages the execution of several container instances. Note that the Container Engine itself runs on a single copy of an operating system. Container instances managed by the same engine share some of the resources of the underlying operating system. Thus, all container instances must use the same underlying operating system. Containers were originally developed for Unix systems but are now available on Windows as well. Applications are isolated from each other by separate filesystems and library versions that the application depends on. Thus, applications that use different versions of software libraries can run on the same host.

A major advantage of container instances is that they are smaller than virtual machine instances, allowing them to be moved from place to place and started up very quickly. Perhaps containers are not quite as reliable as virtual machines in providing execution independence for separate applications, but operating systems are very stable nowadays and the ease of deploying new containers makes up for this disadvantage in many cases. Although not shown here, running containers in a virtual machine is possible. This is known as "hybrid containerization," where the Container Engine runs on top of an operating system that in turn runs on a hypervisor.

Containerization vendors include Docker, Rancher Labs, Iron, Cloud66, OpenShift, and Kubernetes.

CLOUD COMPUTING

For many years, systems administrators and database administrators knew exactly where their servers (physical or virtual) were located—in a dedicated, secure machine room on the company premises. With the advent of the Internet, companies started offering hosting services on servers (physical or virtual) that were located away from their customers' premises. The term **cloud computing** is somewhat of a misnomer. Although networks are sometimes diagrammed using cloud icons, the important thing to remember is that cloud services are ultimately provided by large data centers. It is possible to reconfigure cloud-based data center resources (servers, storage, and network capacity) dynamically by software control or commands from administrators. This allows customers to expand or contract the data center capacity they lease to meet their current needs. That is why Amazon's cloud services is called EC2—Elastic Compute Cloud.

Advanced virtualization technologies are key to providing cloud services. For example, disk storage is external to servers for maximum flexibility, reliability, and speed. **Storage area networks (SANs)** have dedicated network paths from servers to disk arrays, where several physical disks are combined together to act as a single, larger disk. These **redundant array of independent disks (RAID)** systems can be configured for maximum access speed or for reliability to keep operating even if some disks fail. Other sophisticated virtualization features include server and storage migration. Server migration allows running virtual machines to move from one physical server host to another. Storage migration allows active files to be moved from one set of disks to another, and possibly to other file servers, all without noticeable delays or downtime.

There are three basic ways to lease cloud services. The simplest is **software as a service (SaaS)**, where access to specific software applications is provided. An example of this type of service is Salesforce.com. Its **customer relationship management (CRM)** application is hosted on Salesforce's servers and accessed by customers remotely. The software and user data are also maintained by Salesforce.com. Companies wanting to develop their own software and deploy it over the Web can choose **platform as a service (PaaS)**, where operating systems, software development tools, and system program libraries are provided for customers to add their applications to. Lastly, some companies may want to lease only the physical hardware such as servers, disk storage, and network devices and manage their own software environment completely using **infrastructure as a service (IaaS)**. There is no doubt that we will see more and more use of cloud computing.

Hosting services in the cloud has become an established and lucrative business. Hosting companies range from Web site hosting companies such as eNom, HostMonster, and Aabaco Small Business to companies that offer complete business support packages such as Microsoft Office 365 and Google Business Solutions to companies that provide various components such as complete virtual servers, file storage, DBMS services, and much more.

In this last category, significant players include Microsoft with **Microsoft Azure** (http://azure.microsoft.com/en-us/) and Amazon.com with **Amazon Web Services (AWS)** (http://aws.amazon.com/). Of course, there are others, but these two provide a good starting point. Microsoft Azure, like any Microsoft product, is Microsoft-centric and not currently as expansive in its product offerings as AWS. Azure has both relational and nonrelational DBMS services, along with Hadoop cluster processing capabilities, as described in the next sections. Online extension C has an example of using Azure to establish and use a cloud-based database. Of particular interest in AWS are the **EC2 service**, which provides complete virtual servers, the **DynamoDB** database service, which provides a NoSQL data store (discussed later in this chapter); and the **Relational DBMS Service (RDS)**, which provides online instances of Microsoft SQL Server, Oracle Database, and MySQL database services. AWS can also provide Hadoop servers for Big Data analysis. Free trial accounts are available on both Azure and AWS, providing an excellent way to continue learning about cloud computing.

BIG DATA AND THE NOT ONLY SQL MOVEMENT

We have used the relational database model and SQL throughout this book. However, another school of thought has led to what was originally known as the **NoSQL** movement but now is usually referred as the **Not only SQL** movement.[9] It has been noted that most, but not all, DBMSs associated with the NoSQL movement are nonrelational DBMSs.

A NoSQL DBMS is often a distributed, replicated database, as described earlier in this chapter, and used where this type of DBMS is needed to support large datasets. NoSQL databases also often use cloud or virtualization technology and some of the post-relational data structuring concepts from object-relational systems.

---

[9]For a good overview, see the Wikipedia article **NoSQL**, https://en.wikipedia.org/wiki/NoSQL.

Design Decisions and the CAP Theorem

As with relational database management systems, there are many important trade-offs to consider when choosing a DBMS and when implementing the database within that DBMS. Many concepts and design decisions present in relational databases, and described in Chapters 1–6 of this book, have counterparts in NoSQL databases. For example, Chapter 6 briefly discusses some performance issues important in relational databases, such as indexing, query optimization, and physical placement of data in secondary storage. The details of these issues are beyond the scope of this book, but you should be aware that such decisions made by a DBA can greatly affect the performance of the DBMS in NoSQL systems as well as in relational systems. Readers interested in more details of how these design choices can be made in a document database are encouraged to read online Appendix L of *Database Processing*,[10] which describes some of these issues in the context of ArangoDB and document databases and includes enough detail to install and use ArangoDB effectively for a document database (see www.pearsonhighered.com/kroenke).

In the relational setting, you might need to decide whether to use Microsoft Access or MySQL. And after you have made that decision, you might have to decide whether to denormalize a relation, as described in Chapter 5. Similar decisions need to be made when choosing a NoSQL DBMS and using it to implement a specific database. Because most NoSQL databases used to store Big Data will be distributed databases, many of these fundamental tradeoffs and concepts are encapsulated in the CAP theorem. The **CAP theorem** originated in 2000, when Eric Brewer made a proposal in his keynote presentation at the Symposium on Principles of Distributed Computing (PODC). The proposal was formally proved as a theorem by Seth Gilbert and Nancy Lynch. It is now known as the CAP theorem. There is currently an ongoing discussion of the CAP theorem, and Brewer himself has been involved in this discussion.

Basically, the CAP theorem defines three properties of distributed database systems:

1. Consistency
2. Availability
3. Partition tolerance

Consistency means that all the database replicas see the same data at any given point in time. **Availability** means that every request received by a server will result in a response, as long as the network is available. **Partition tolerance** means that the distributed database can continue to operate even when the cluster is partitioned by network failures into two or more disconnected sections (partitions).

The CAP theorem, illustrated in Figure 7-22, basically states that all three of these properties cannot be guaranteed at the same time—at least one of the properties will be at least somewhat compromised, as there may be several levels of these properties.

For example, allowing partition tolerance will degrade consistency if each partition independently allows updates, resulting in different values for the same data item in other replica sets. Alternatively, we could choose to lose availability by only allowing reads or by shutting down the entire system in the event of a partition. The CAP theorem thus provides us with a framework for thinking about some of the important concepts and tradeoffs in NoSQL DBMSs: Each such DBMS has its own levels of support for the three properties listed in the CAP theorem, and we can use that as a guide to choosing an appropriate NoSQL DBMS. In addition, some NoSQL DBMSs allow the DBA to make choices about the levels of support for these concepts, and the CAP theorem can help a DBA with these choices as well. Online extension C describes some of these issues in the context of ArangoDB, a multimodel NoSQL DBMS.

---

[10]David M. Kroenke, David J. Auer, Scott L. Vandenberg, and Robert C. Yoder, *Database Processing: Fundamentals, Design, and Implementation*, 15th ed. (Upper Saddle River, NJ: Pearson/Prentice Hall, 2019).

FIGURE 7-22

The CAP Theorem—You Can't Have All Three at the Same Time!

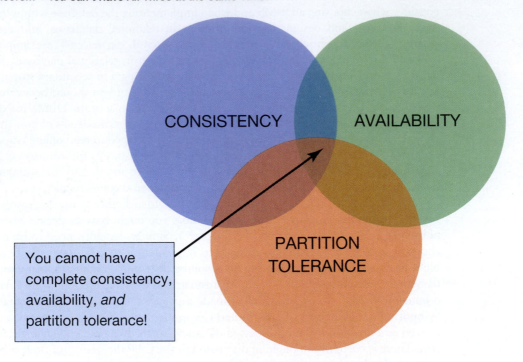

The CAP theorem also gives us the basis for a comparison of relational DBMSs to non-relational "NoSQL" DBMSs. Relational DBMSs can be said to favor consistency (see Chapter 6) and availability (because they are often running on a single, non-partitioned database system), whereas nonrelational DBMS systems must be designed according to whether they want to emphasize consistency or availability in their design (because they are by definition designed for clustered, distributed, and, therefore, potentially partitioned systems).

Categories of NoSQL Database Management Systems

Several classification systems have been proposed for grouping and classifying NoSQL databases.[11] For our purposes, we will adopt and use a set of four categories of NoSQL databases that is based on the structure of the data stored in the database:[12]

- **Key-value database**—Examples are Dynamo, MemcacheDB, and Redis
- **Document database**—Examples are Couchbase, ArangoDB, and MongoDB
- **Column family database**—Examples are Vertica, Apache Cassandra, and HBase
- **Graph database**—Examples are Neo4j, AllegroGraph, and Titan

It should be noted that many NoSQL DBMSs have features from more than one category, and some NoSQL DBMSs are **multimodel**: ArangoDB, for example, supports document,

---

[11]Wikipedia article **NoSQL** (accessed August, 2018), https://en.wikipedia.org/wiki/NoSQL.

[12]This set of categories corresponds to the four major (non-hybrid) categories used in the Wikipedia article **NoSQL** (https://en.wikipedia.org/wiki/NoSQL) as Wikipedia's taxonomy of NoSQL databases and is also used in Ian Robinson, Jim Webber, and Emil Eifrem's *Graph Databases* (Sebastopol, CA: O'Reilly Media, 2013).

key-value, and graph data. NoSQL databases are used by widely recognized Web applications—both Facebook and Twitter, for example, use the Apache Software Foundation's Cassandra database. In this chapter, we discuss document databases and JavaScript Object Notation (JSON) using some examples, as such systems are widely in use and an example will illustrate some important conceptual similarities and differences among relational and NoSQL databases. We discuss all four types in more detail in online extension C, which gives a more detailed description of cloud and NoSQL databases and a more complete presentation of how data can be structured and shared using JSON and XML, all with the goal of furthering business intelligence (BI).

Document Databases and JSON Document databases store data according to a document-oriented format, the two most popular of which are XML (Extensible Markup Language) and **JavaScript Object Notation (JSON)**. Both XML and JSON are described in more detail in online extension C. Two document DBMS examples are Couchbase Server and ArangoDB, which use JSON storage. MongoDB is another popular document database; it uses BSON (Binary JSON) storage, which is a binary-encoded version of JSON documents, with a few additional data types available.

JSON is a data model in which there is no notion of any schema external to the data. A **document** ("object" in JSON terminology) consists of a set of (field: value) pairs. Values can be simple values (strings or numbers) or other objects. Values can also be arrays of values or objects. In a document database, documents (for example, JSON objects) are usually stored within a set (in most document DBMSs, including ArangoDB, this is called a **collection**).

Here are some sample data that might appear in a document database containing student information. Each document, like a relational record, would be stored in a collection of similar "Student" documents. The curly braces indicate a document—a set of (field: value) pairs—and the square brackets indicate an array. The syntax is standard JSON syntax:

```
{
id: "student1",
lastName: "Smith",
firstName: "John",
dormAddress: "123 Gates Hall",
majors: ["History", "Computer Science"]
}
{
id: "student2",
firstName: "Mary",
minor: "English",
majors: ["Math"],
GPA: 3.2,
favoritePet:
    {
        name: "Tiger",
        species: "cat"
    }
}
```

This example illustrates a number of important conceptual differences between relational and document data. The number, order, types, and (in some systems) names of columns are less restricted in a document database. In addition, columns can be multivalued, such as the preceding majors column. Notice that the second student has some columns the first does not (for example, GPA), and vice versa. Column values can also be documents, as in the "favoritePet" column of the second student. As you can see, document databases may be a good choice when your data have some structure, but that structure may be complex or inconsistent among the various documents.

As with other styles of NoSQL databases, some interaction with the database is done either from within a program written in a programming language like Java or Python or via a command-line environment. Typical commands available in a document database (using a generic syntax) include:

- **insert (doc, collection):** Put document "doc" into the collection
- **update (collection, doc_specifier, update_action):** Within the collection, update all documents matching the "doc_specifier" (for example all students with last name 'Smith'). The "update_action" can alter the values of multiple fields within each document.
- **delete (collection, doc_specifier):** Removes all documents from collection that match the "doc_specifier"
- **find (collection, doc_specifier):** Retrieves all documents in a collection matching the "doc_specifier"

In addition, most document databases provide some level of built-in support for map-reduce (discussed later in this chapter) and other aggregation tasks.

Increasingly, however, support for queries is being provided at a larger scale in document databases. Some of these languages have many similarities to SQL (for example, ArangoDB's **AQL (ArangoDB Query Language)**), while others may look entirely different (such as MongoDB's query language, whose queries are actually written in a JSON-like format). These document database query languages support queries based on the internal structure of the document. For example, the following query, based on a document version of the Art Course database described in Chapter 1, retrieves the course title, course date, and last names of enrolled students for all courses with a fee more than $400:

```
/* *** AQL-QUERY-CH07-01 *** */
FOR C in Courses
    FILTER C.Fee>400
    RETURN {CourseName: C.Course,
            CourseDate: C.CourseDate,
            StudentLastNames: C.Enrollments[*].
            CustomerLastName}
```

The "*" syntax instructs ArangoDB to find the CustomerLastName field of every enrollment stored within the course; each enrollment is a customer document. The SQL equivalent of this query on the relational Art Course database from Chapter 1 is:

```
/* *** SQL-QUERY-CH07-03 *** */
SELECT    COURSE.Course, COURSE.CourseDate, CUSTOMER.
          CustomerLastName
FROM      CUSTOMER, COURSE, ENROLLMENT
WHERE     COURSE.CourseNumber = ENROLLMENT.CourseNumber
  AND     ENROLLMENT.CustomerNumber = CUSTOMER.
          CustomerNumber
  AND     COURSE.Fee>400;
```

FIGURE 7-23

An ArangoDB AQL Query and JSON Results

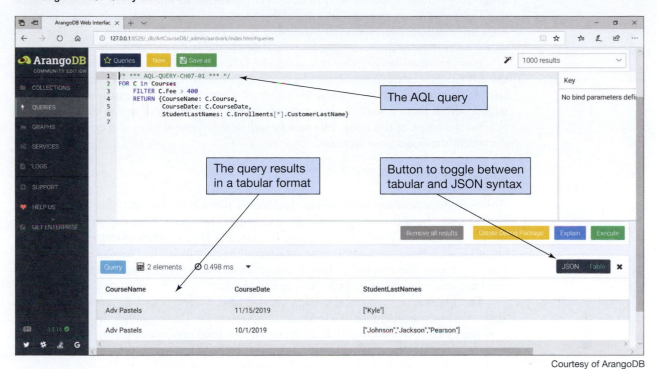

Courtesy of ArangoDB

Figure 7-23 shows AQL-QUERY-CH07-01 as executed in ArangoDB, along with the results of that query. Note that the results are displayed in a somewhat tabular format, with the list of student last names stored within each course. Here are the results of the query in JSON format:

```
[
  {
    "CourseName": "Adv Pastels",
    "CourseDate": "10/1/2019",
    "StudentLastNames": [
      "Johnson",
      "Jackson",
      "Pearson"
    ]
  },
  {
    "CourseName": "Adv Pastels",
    "CourseDate": "11/15/2019",
    "StudentLastNames": [
      "Kyle"
    ]
  }
]
```

This is definitely not relational: It violates first normal form! The structure of the result is based in part on the structure of the data stored in the database and in part on the syntax in the AQL "return" clause used to construct the result. In this example, the DBA made the decision to store courses as the main objects in the database, with each course containing a list of enrollments, and each enrollment being an entire student document. The query and the structure of the result give you some idea of the structure of the JSON data.

It is important to note that this is not the only way a DBA could choose to structure the Art Course data in a document database. A more customer-centric design would have customers as the main documents, with perhaps a list of courses taken by each customer stored within that customer's document. A detailed discussion of such design choices is beyond the scope of this book, but understanding that these choices and concepts exist in document databases are important.

MapReduce

Although document and other storage techniques provide the means to store data in a Big Data system, the data themselves can be analyzed in many ways. One important way of doing this is using the **MapReduce** process. Because Big Data involves extremely large datasets, it is difficult for one computer to process all the data by itself. Therefore, a set of clustered computers is employed using a distributed processing system based on the distributed database concepts discussed previously in this chapter.

The MapReduce process is used to break a large analytical task into smaller tasks, assign (map) each smaller task to a separate computer in the cluster, gather the results of each of those tasks, and combine (reduce) them into the final product of the original task. The term *Map* refers to the work done on each individual computer, and the term *Reduce* refers to the combining of the individual results into the final result.

A commonly used example of the MapReduce process is counting how many times each word is used in a document. This is illustrated in Figure 7-24, where we can see how the original document is broken into sections, and then each section is passed to a separate computer in the cluster for processing by the Map process. The output from each of the Map processes is then passed to one computer, which uses the Reduce process to combine the results from each Map process into the final output, which is the list of the words in the document and how many times each word appears in the document. Most NoSQL database systems support MapReduce and other, similar processes.

Hadoop

Another Apache Software Foundation project that is becoming a fundamental Big Data development platform is the **Hadoop Distributed File System (HDFS)**, which provides standard file services to clustered servers so that their file systems can function as one distributed, replicated file system that can support large-scale MapReduce processing. Hadoop originated as part of Cassandra, but the Hadoop project has spun off a nonrelational data store of its own called HBase and a query language named Pig. The Hadoop project also includes Hive, a data warehouse infrastructure that supports data aggregation (summarization), data analysis, and a query language similar to SQL called HiveQL.

Further, all the major DBMS players are supporting Hadoop. Microsoft has deployed a Microsoft Hadoop distribution called HDInsight as part of its Azure cloud service[13] and has teamed up with HP, Dell, and others to offer the Microsoft Analytics Platform System (formerly known as SQL Server Parallel Data Warehouse).[14] Oracle has developed the Oracle Big Data Appliance that uses Hadoop.[15] A search of the Web on the term "MySQL Hadoop" quickly reveals that a lot is being done by the MySQL team as well.

---

[13]https://azure.microsoft.com/en-us/services/hdinsight

[14]http://www.microsoft.com/en-us/sql-server/analytics-platform-system

[15]https://www.oracle.com/engineered-systems/big-data-appliance/index.html

FIGURE 7-24

MapReduce

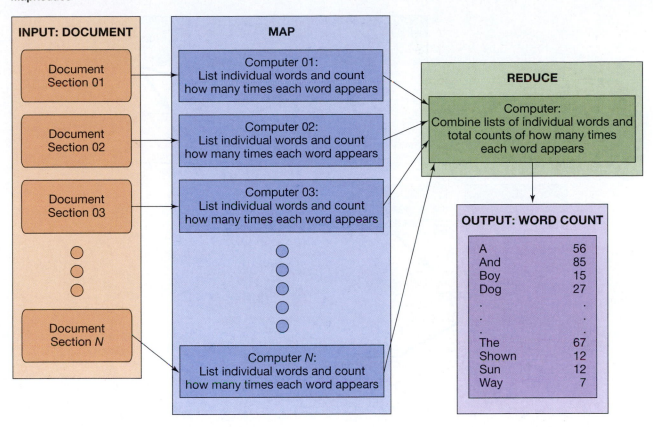

New developments in the Big Data world recognize that some forms of analysis may not easily fit the MapReduce processing model. Sometimes many chained MapReduce steps are needed to obtain the required result. Each MapReduce step requires reading and writing to the filesystem, slowing things down. Recent Hadoop releases support **Apache Tez**, a programming framework that supports a more generalized processing model than MapReduce. Tez processing can be modeled by a Directed Acyclic Graph (a process-flow model that does not have loops in it). Figure 7-25 gives an example. A graph data structure is created to direct Tez processing. The data is read from HDFS at the start of the process (at the top of the diagram), and written back to HDFS at the end of the process (at the bottom of the diagram). The intermediate steps are performed in memory. Tez is replacing MapReduce in Hadoop's Hive and Pig products.

There are also new products that use the Tez processing model, such as **Apache Spark**, a "unified analytics engine for large-scale data processing"[16] that allows programmers to quickly write data analysis applications in several languages: SQL, Python, Scala, Java, and R—a powerful statistical and graphing language. Many machine learning functions are available in Spark's MLlib library. Spark can connect to several types of data sources including Hive, HBase, Cassandra, HDFS, and cloud provider data stores including Amazon's EMR filesystem and Microsoft's Azure Storage.

For more information on Big Data and the various types of NoSQL databases, see online extension C. The usefulness and importance of these Big Data products to

---

[16]https://spark.apache.org

FIGURE 7-25

Example of Apache Tez Directed Acyclic Graph

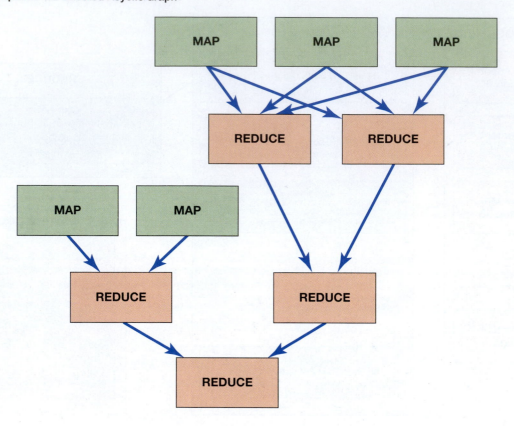

organizations such as Facebook demonstrate that we can look forward to the development of not only improvements to relational DBMSs but also to a very different approach to data storage and information processing. Big Data and products associated with Big Data are rapidly changing and evolving, and you should expect many developments in this area in the near future.

BTW

The Not only SQL world is an exciting one, but you should be aware that if you want to participate in it you will need to sharpen your OOP programming skills. Although we can develop and manage databases in Microsoft Access and Oracle MySQL using management and application development tools that are very user-friendly (Microsoft Access itself, MySQL Workbench), application development in the NoSQL world is currently done primarily in programming languages.

This, of course, may change, and we look forward to seeing the future developments in the Not only SQL realm. For now, you'll need to sign up for that programming course!

WORKING WITH MICROSOFT ACCESS

Section 7

Business Intelligence Systems Using Microsoft Access

In this section, we explore how to produce an OLAP report by using the Microsoft Excel 2019 PivotTable feature. We will build an OLAP report in Microsoft Excel 2019 based on data in a Microsoft Access 2019 database. We will start by creating an OLAP report for the WMCRM database, as we left it from the Working with Access section from Chapter 5.

Creating a View Query for an OLAP Report

To create an OLAP report, we need to create a new view. In Microsoft Access, a view is simply a saved query. We will start by displaying a list of customer contacts. The list will contain a combination of data from the CONTACT and CUSTOMER tables. Figure WA-7-1 shows the details of the initial viewCustomerContacts query, and Figure WA-7-2 shows the results of running that query.

We will then modify the query by concatenating the customer's first and last names into a single customer name, and we need to add a quantitative measure so that we can easily analyze the number of contacts made by the Wallingford Motors sales staff. We will save the modified query as viewCustomerContactsCount.

Creating the viewCustomerContacts and viewCustomerContactsCount Queries

1. Start Microsoft Access 2019 and open the copy of the **WMCRM.accdb** database file that you created in the Chapter 5 **Working with Access**.
2. Click the **Create** tab at the top, then **Query Design**. Add the **Customer** and **Contact** tables.
3. Add the fields from the tables as shown in Figure WA-7-1.

FIGURE WA-7-1

The viewCustomerContacts Query

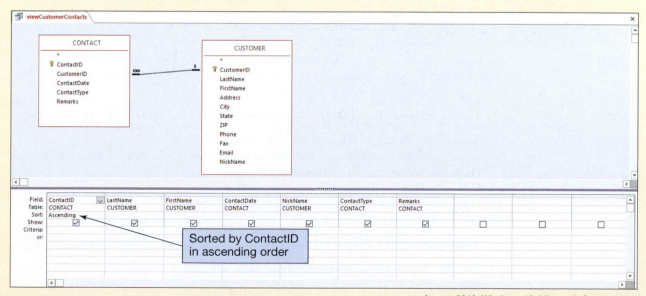

(Continued)

FIGURE WA-7-2

viewCustomerContacts Query Results

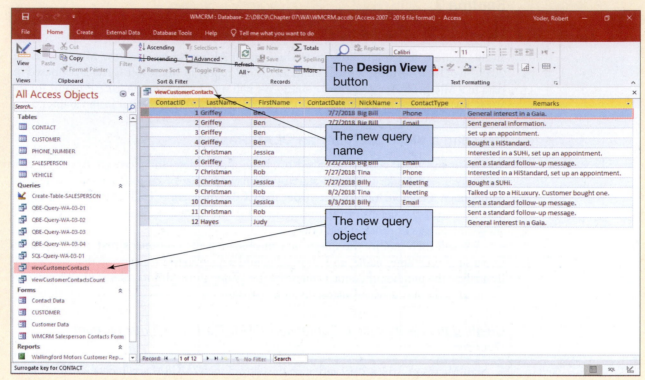

Access 2019, Windows 10, Microsoft Corporation.

4. Click the **Design** tab again and run the query. The results should match Figure WA-7-2. This result is useful, but lacks quantitative measures needed for BI analysis. Save your query as **viewCustomerContacts**.

5. We will now convert the query into something more quantitative. Click the **Design View** button in the Views group of the Home ribbon to switch the query to Design view.

6. Click the **Totals** button in the Show/Hide group of the Query Tools Design ribbon to display the **Total** row in the fields pane.

7. Right-click the **LastName** field name in the LastName column to display the shortcut menu, as shown in Figure WA-7-3.

8. Click the **Build** button in the shortcut menu to display the Expression Builder.

9. Create an expression that concatenates LastName and FirstName data into a combined attribute named CustomerName as:

CustomerName:[CUSTOMER]![LastName]&", "&[CUSTOMER]![FirstName]

Figure WA-7-4 shows the completed expression.

10. Create the expression in Expression Builder as shown in Figure WA-7-4, and then click the **OK** button in the Expression Builder.

11. Delete the **FirstName** column from the query design.

12. Delete the **Remarks** column from the query design.

13. Add a column named **ContactCount** to the query, as shown in Figure WA-7-5.

ContactCount: [CONTACT]![ContactType] then set the TOTAL field to COUNT.

14. Save the query as **viewCustomerContactsCount** (File | Save As) and then run it. The query results are shown in Figure WA-7-6.

15. Close the WMCRM database and Microsoft Access.

FIGURE WA-7-3

The Shortcut Menu

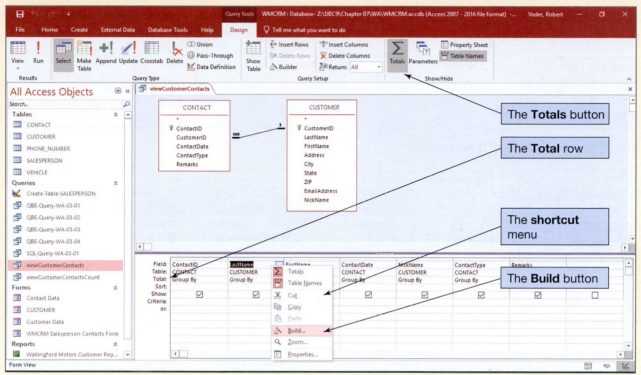

Access 2019, Windows 10, Microsoft Corporation.

FIGURE WA-7-4

The Completed Expression in the Expression Builder

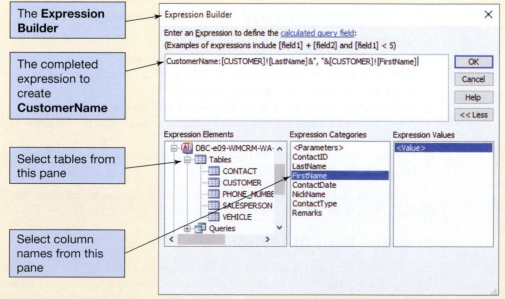

Access 2019, Windows 10, Microsoft Corporation.

(Continued)

FIGURE WA-7-5

The ContactCount Column

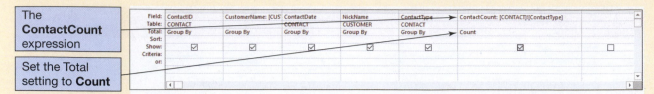

Access 2019, Windows 10, Microsoft Corporation.

FIGURE WA-7-6

viewCustomerContactsCount Query Results

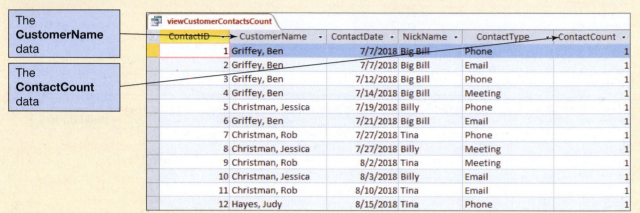

Access 2019, Windows 10, Microsoft Corporation.

Creating a Microsoft Excel Worksheet for an OLAP Report

Because the OLAP report will be in a Microsoft Excel 2019 workbook, we need to create a new workbook to hold the OLAP report. Continue to use your Wallingford Motors folder as the storage location, and now we will create a Microsoft Excel 2019 workbook named WM-DW-BI.xlsx in that folder.

Creating the Microsoft Excel 2019 WM-DW-BI Workbook

1. Start Windows Explorer.
2. Browse to the folder containing your WMCRM database.
3. Right-click anywhere in the right-hand folder and file pane to open the shortcut menu.
4. In the shortcut menu, click the **New** command.
5. In the list of new objects, click the **Microsoft Excel Worksheet** command.
   A new Microsoft Excel 2019 workbook object is created, with the file name highlighted in Edit mode.
6. Edit the file name to read **WM-DW-BI**, and then press the **Enter** key. It will automatically be given a file extension of xlsx.

   Now you can open the WM-DW-BI workbook by double-clicking the WM-DW-BI filename. The **WM-DW-BI** workbook is displayed, as shown in Figure WA-7-7.

Creating a Basic OLAP Report

We can now create an OLAP report in the Microsoft Excel 2019 WM-DW-BI workbook. Fortunately, Microsoft has made it possible to link directly to Microsoft Access 2019 to obtain the data needed for the report. We will connect the Microsoft Excel workbook to the Microsoft Access database and create the basic, blank OLAP report PivotTable.

FIGURE WA-7-7

The WM-DW-BI Workbook

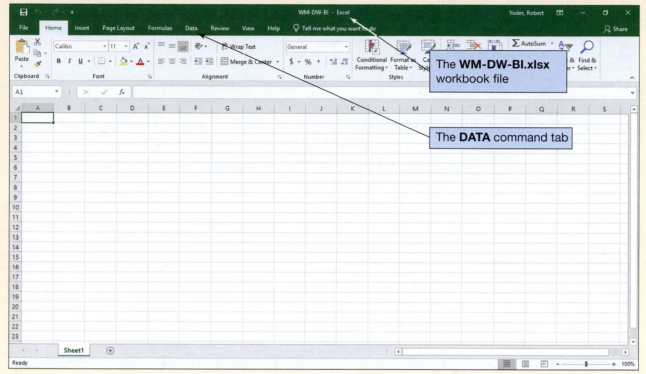

Excel 2019, Windows 10, Microsoft Corporation.

Microsoft Excel 2019 uses the same Microsoft Office fluent user interface that you have learned to use in Microsoft Access 2019. Because you should already be familiar with the Microsoft Office fluent user interface, we do not discuss the Microsoft Excel variant of this interface.

Creating the Basic OLAP Report PivotTable

1. In the WM-DW-BI workbook, click the **Data** command tab to display the Data command groups, as shown in Figure WA-7-8.
2. Click the **Get Data** button in the **Get & Transform Data** group of the Data ribbon. A sub-menu appears. Select **From Database**, then **From Microsoft Access database,** as shown in Figure WA-7-8.
3. In the Import Data dialog box, which functions just like an Open dialog box, browse to your working folder containing your WMCRM database. Select the Microsoft Access **WMCRM.accdb** database file, and then click the **Import** button.

   As shown in Figure WA-7-9, the Navigator dialog box appears.
4. In the Navigator dialog box, select the new **viewCustomerContactsCount** query, and then (carefully) click the down-arrow next to the **Load** button to get a sub-menu. Select the "Load To. . ." option.

   As shown in Figure WA-7-10, the Import Data dialog box appears.

(Continued)

FIGURE WA-7-8

The Excel Data Command Tab

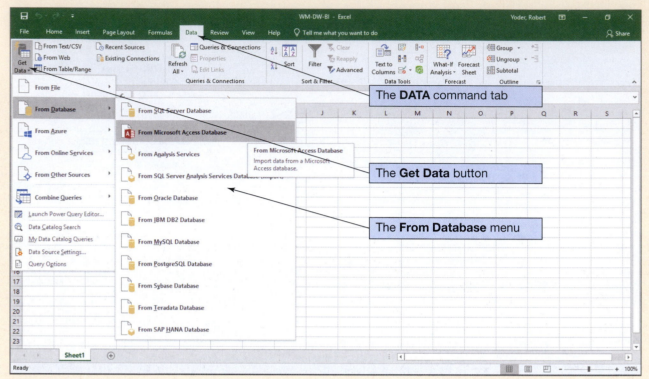

Excel 2019, Windows 10, Microsoft Corporation.

FIGURE WA-7-9

The Select Table Dialog Box

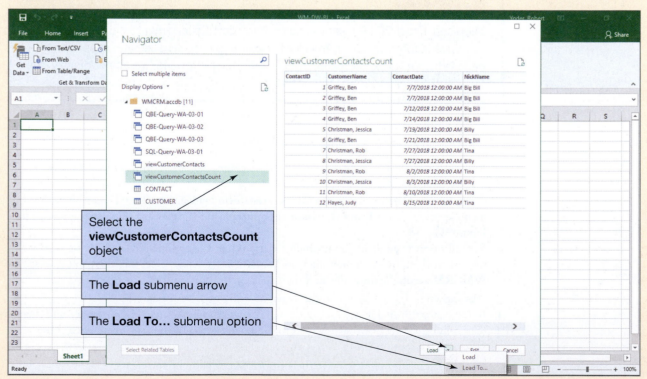

Excel 2019, Windows 10, Microsoft Corporation.

FIGURE WA-7-10

The Import Data Dialog Box

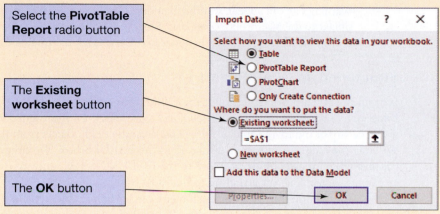

Excel 2019, Windows 10, Microsoft Corporation.

FIGURE WA-7-11

The Basic PivotTable Report Structure

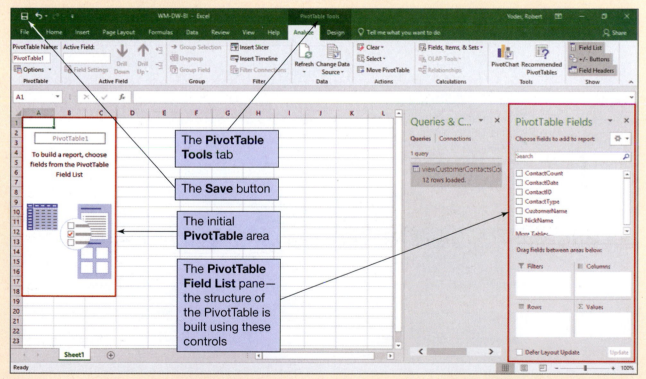

Excel 2019, Windows 10, Microsoft Corporation.

5. In the Import Data dialog box, select the **PivotTable Report** and **Existing worksheet** options, then click the **OK** button.

As shown in Figure WA-7-11, the basic PivotTable report structure is displayed in the Microsoft Excel worksheet. Go ahead and close the Queries & Connections (middle) pane.

(Continued)

6. Click the **Save** button on Microsoft Excel Quick Access Toolbar to save your work to this point.

■ **NOTE:** From now on, when you open the WM-DW-BI workbook, a Security Warning bar will appear, warning that data connections have been disabled. This is similar to the Microsoft Access 2019 Security Warning bar you have already learned to use, and essentially the same action is necessary: Click the **Enable Content** button.

Structuring an OLAP Report

We can now create the structure of the OLAP report. We do this by using the Microsoft Excel PivotTable Field List pane, shown in Figure WA-7-11 and Figure WA-7-12. To build the structure of the PivotTable, we drag and drop the field objects from the field object list. We drag the measures we want displayed to the VALUES box. We drag the dimension attributes we want as column structure to the COLUMNS box, and we drag the dimension attributes we want as row structure to the ROWS box.

For the Wallingford Motors Customer Contact PivotTable, we will use ContactCount as the measure, so it needs to go in the Values box. The column structure will have customer attributes, in this case only CustomerName. Finally, the row structure will have contact attributes—NickName (for SalesPerson) first, followed by ContactType and then Contact Date.

FIGURE WA-7-12

The PivotTable Field List Pane

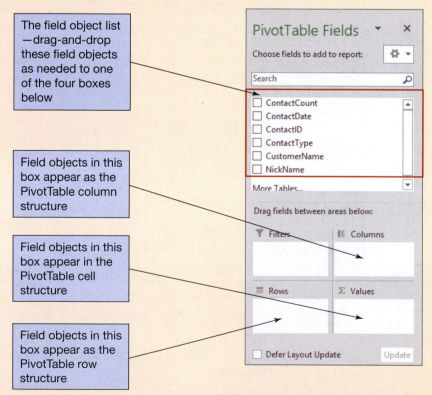

Excel 2019, Windows 10, Microsoft Corporation.

Creating the OLAP Report's PivotTable Structure

1. Click and hold the **CustomerName** field object, drag it to the COLUMNS box, and drop it there. As shown in Figure WA-7-13, the CustomerName labels and a GrandTotal label are added to the worksheet columns, the CustomerName field object in the field objects list is checked and displayed in bold, and the field object CustomerName is listed in the COLUMNS box.
2. Click and hold the **ContactCount** field object, drag it to the VALUES box, and drop it there. As shown in Figure WA-7-14, the sum of the ContactCount values is added to the worksheet, the ContactCount field object in the field objects list is checked and displayed in bold, and the field object Sum of ContactCount is listed in the VALUES box.
3. Click and hold the **NickName** field object, drag it to the ROWS box, and drop it there. As shown in Figure WA-7-15, the sum of the NickName row labels is added to the worksheet, the NickName field object in the field objects list is checked and displayed in bold, and the field object NickName is listed in the ROWS Labels box. In addition, the values in the report are starting to show up.
4. Click and hold the **ContactType** field object, drag it to the ROWS box, and drop it there, *below* NickName. As shown in Figure WA-7-16, the sum of the NickName row labels is divided into contact type, the ContactType field object in the field objects list is checked and displayed in bold, and the field object ContactType is listed in the ROWS box. In addition, the values in the report are now distributed according to salesperson (NickName) and type of contact (ContactType) within each salesperson.

FIGURE WA-7-13

The CustomerName Column Labels

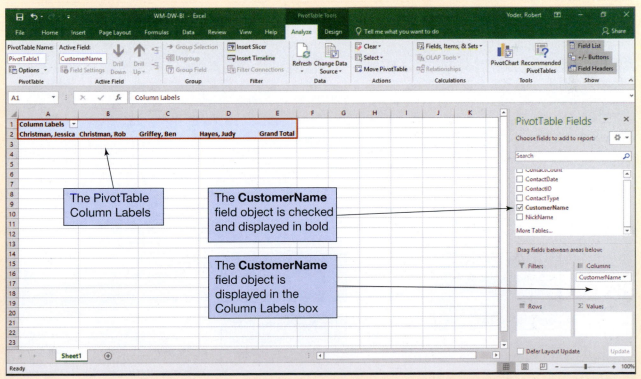

Excel 2019, Windows 10, Microsoft Corporation.

(Continued)

FIGURE WA-7-14

The CustomerCount Values

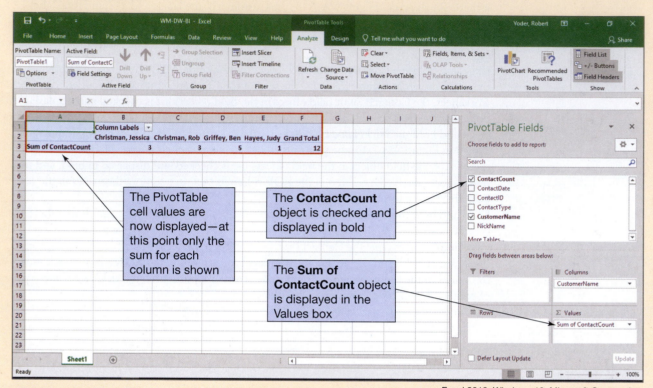

FIGURE WA-7-15

The NickName Row Labels

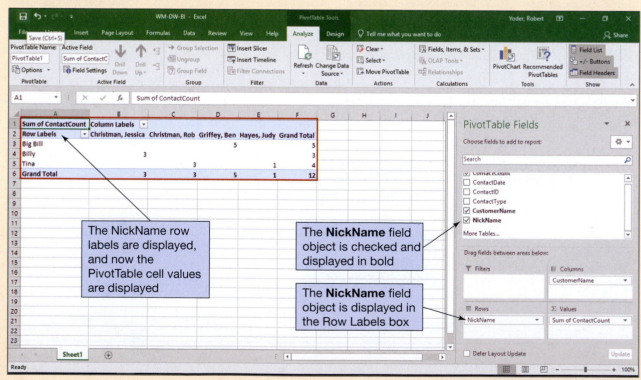

FIGURE WA-7-16

The ContactType Row Labels

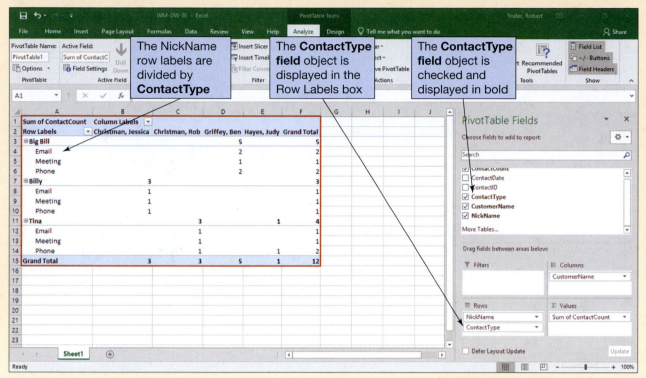

Excel 2019, Windows 10, Microsoft Corporation.

5. Click and hold the **ContactDate** field object, drag it to the ROWS box, and drop it there, *below* ContactType. For Excel 2016 and 2019, the ContactDate is part of Months, and Months will appear as well. The order of fields in the ROWS box should be: NickName, ContactType, Months, ContactDate. You can adjust the order by clicking on the down-arrow next to each field name and moving up or down as needed. As shown in Figure WA-7-17, the sum of the NickName row labels is divided into contact type and month (date), the ContactDate field in the field objects list is checked and displayed in bold, and the field ContactDate is listed in the ROWS box below "Months." In addition, the values in the report are now distributed according to salesperson (NickName), type of contact (ContactType), Months (if using Excel 2016 or 2019), and date of contact (ContactDate). We expanded the July month field for Big Bill in the figure to show date details.

6. Click the **Save** button on the Microsoft Excel Quick Access Toolbar to save your work to this point.

Modifying an OLAP Report

We have finished building our OLAP report. We can modify it as needed by moving the field objects in the PivotTable Field List pane. We can also format the OLAP report to make it look the way we want it to.

Modifying the OLAP Report PivotTable Structure

1. Click the **ContactType** field object in the ROWS box. A menu will appear. Select **Move to End**. The ROWS order is now NickName, Months, ContactDate, ContactType. As shown in Figure WA-7-18, the order of the row labels in the OLAP report changes, and the data move, too.

(Continued)

FIGURE WA-7-17

The ContactDate Row Labels

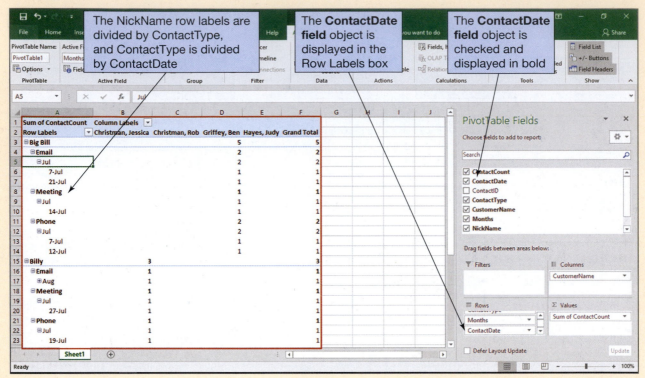

Excel 2019, Windows 10, Microsoft Corporation.

FIGURE WA-7-18

The Rearranged Row Labels

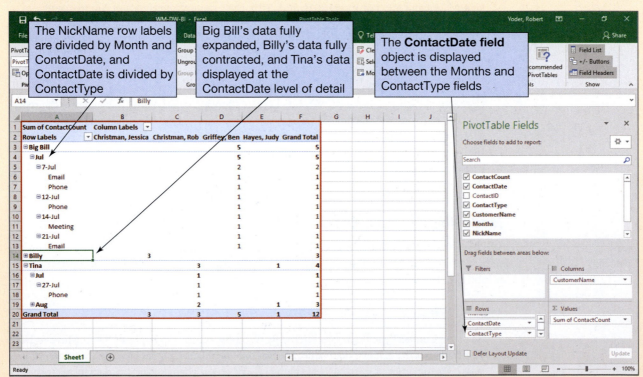

Excel 2019, Windows 10, Microsoft Corporation.

2. As shown in Figure WA-7-18, you can contract and expand various portions of the OLAP report by clicking on the + and − symbols to the left of the row labels. In that figure, the data for Big Bill are shown fully expanded, while Billy's data are completely contracted. The data for Tina are shown at the Date level of detail but without Type detail.

Formatting the OLAP Report

1. Click the PivotTable Tools **Design** command tab to display the Design command groups, as shown in Figure WA-7-19.
2. Click the **Banded Columns** check box in the PivotTable Style Options command group.
3. Click the **PivotTable Styles Gallery** drop-down arrow button to display the PivotTable Styles Gallery, as shown in Figure WA-7-20.
4. Select the PivotTable style shown in Figure WA-7-20 to format the OLAP report.

FIGURE WA-7-19

The Excel PivotTable Tools Design Command Tab

Excel 2019, Windows 10, Microsoft Corporation.

FIGURE WA-7-20

The Excel PivotTable Styles Gallery

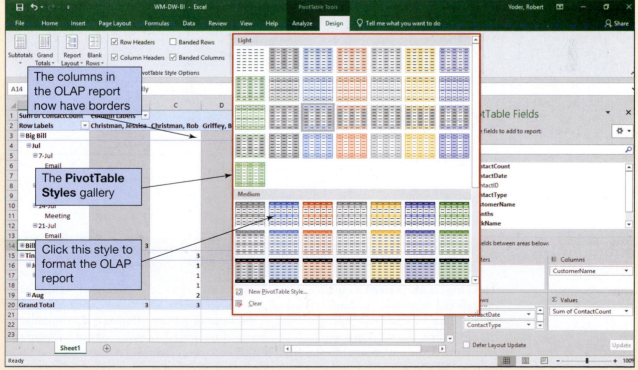

Excel 2019, Windows 10, Microsoft Corporation.

(Continued)

5. If desired, adjust the column widths of columns B, C, D, E, and F.
   The final, formatted PivotTable OLAP report is shown in Figure WA-7-21.
6. Click the **Save** button on the Microsoft Excel Quick Access Toolbar.
7. Close the WM-DW-BI workbook.
8. Close Microsoft Excel.

In Closing

Our work is done. In "Working with Access," you have learned the essentials of working with Microsoft Access (and just a bit about working with Microsoft Excel). You have not learned everything there is to know, but now you can create and populate Microsoft Access databases; build and use Microsoft Access queries (including view-equivalent queries), forms, and reports; secure a Microsoft Access database; and create a PivotTable OLAP report. You now have a solid foundation to build on, which was, after all, the overall goal of "Working with Access."

FIGURE WA-7-21

The Final PivotTable OLAP Report

Big Bill's data fully expanded, Billy's data fully contracted, and Tina's data displayed at the Date level of detail

	A	B	C	D	E	F
1	Sum of ContactCount	Column Labels				
2	Row Labels	Christman, Jessica	Christman, Rob	Griffey, Ben	Hayes, Judy	Grand Total
3	⊟ Big Bill			5		5
4	⊟ Jul			5		5
5	⊟ 7-Jul			2		2
6	Email			1		1
7	Phone			1		1
8	⊟ 12-Jul			1		1
9	Phone			1		1
10	⊟ 14-Jul			1		1
11	Meeting			1		1
12	⊟ 21-Jul			1		1
13	Email			1		1
14	⊞ Billy	3				3
15	⊟ Tina		3		1	4
16	⊟ Jul		1			1
17	⊞ 27-Jul		1			1
18	⊟ Aug		2		1	3
19	⊞ 2-Aug		1			1
20	⊞ 10-Aug		1			1
21	⊞ 15-Aug				1	1
22	Grand Total	3	3	5	1	12

Excel 2019, Windows 10, Microsoft Corporation.

SUMMARY

This chapter introduced a number of concepts that go beyond the "standard" setting of an operational relational database housed on a single computer. Databases can support more than routine, operational SQL querying, in the form of BI reporting and data mining. At the same time, the sheer volume and complexity of modern data management have led to a resurrection and expansion of ideas from distributed computing and object databases, now used in DBMS processing in the form of cloud+virtualization and NoSQL databases.

Business intelligence (BI) systems assist managers and other professionals in the analysis of current and past activities and in the prediction of future events. BI applications are of two major types: reporting applications and data mining applications. Reporting applications make elementary calculations on data; data mining applications use sophisticated mathematical and statistical techniques.

BI applications obtain data from three sources: operational databases, extracts of operational databases, and purchased data. A BI system sometimes has its own DBMS, which may or not be the operational DBMS. Characteristics of reporting and data mining applications are listed in Figure 7-4.

Direct reading of operational databases is not feasible for any but the smallest and simplest BI applications and databases for several reasons. Querying operational data can unacceptably slow the performance of operational systems; operational data have problems that limit their usefulness for BI applications; and BI system creation and maintenance require programs, facilities, and expertise that are normally not available for an operational database.

Because of the problems with operational data, many organizations have chosen to create and staff data warehouses and data marts. Extract, transform, and load (ETL) systems are used to extract data from operational systems; transform the data and load them into data warehouses; and maintain metadata that describe the source, format, assumptions, and constraints of the data. A data mart is a collection of data that is smaller than that held in a data warehouse and addresses a particular component or functional area of the business.

Operational databases and dimensional (data warehouse) databases have different characteristics, as shown in Figure 7-7. Dimensional databases use a star schema and must deal with slowly changing dimensions, so a time dimension is important. Fact tables hold measures of interest, and dimension tables hold attribute values used in queries. The star schema can be extended with additional fact tables, dimension tables, and conformed dimensions.

The purpose of a reporting system is to create meaningful information from disparate data sources and to deliver that information to the proper users on a timely basis. Reports are produced by sorting, filtering, grouping, and making simple calculations on the data. RFM analysis is a typical reporting application. An RFM report can be produced using SQL statements.

Online analytical processing (OLAP) reporting applications enable users to dynamically restructure reports utilizing measures and dimensions. A measure is a data item of interest. A dimension is a characteristic of a measure. An OLAP report, or OLAP cube, is an arrangement of measures and dimensions. With OLAP, users can drill down and exchange the order of dimensions.

A distributed database is a database that is stored and processed on more than one computer. Variations of distributed databases include replicated and partitioned databases. A replicated database is one in which multiple copies of some or all of the database are stored on different computers. A partitioned database is one in which different pieces of the database are stored on different computers. A distributed database can include both replication and partitioning.

Distributed databases pose processing challenges. If a database is updated on a single computer, then the challenge is simply to ensure that the copies of the database are logically consistent when they are distributed. However, if updates are to be made on more than one computer, the challenges become significant. If the database is partitioned and not replicated, then challenges occur if transactions span data on more than one computer. If the database is replicated and if updates occur to the replicated portions, then a special locking algorithm called distributed two-phase locking is required. Implementing this algorithm can be difficult and expensive. Many Big Data databases and NoSQL databases, both of which are used to support BI, are distributed.

Objects consist of methods and properties or data values. All objects of a given class have the same methods, but they can have different property values. Object persistence is the process of storing object property values on disk. Relational databases are difficult to use for object persistence. Some specialized products called object-oriented DBMSs were developed in the 1990s but never received large-scale commercial acceptance. Oracle and others, following the SQL standard, have extended the capabilities of their relational DBMS products to provide support for object persistence. Such databases are referred to as object-relational databases. Some of these data structuring techniques are found in NoSQL databases.

The physical setting for much NoSQL and Big Data work is often in the cloud and/or on virtual machines, which allows us to consolidate several logical servers into one larger physical one and to provide tremendous flexibility in dynamically provisioning servers, storage, and network resources. A special program called a hypervisor provides the virtual environment and manages the virtual machines. Containers are another form of virtualization that allows applications to share the same operating system, but also have different libraries and filesystems. Cloud computing allows remote computers to host data, software, or both, taking advantage of the Internet to provide availability and scalability. Thus, portions of data centers can be leased by customers who are charged only for the resources they use.

The NoSQL movement (now often read as "Not only SQL") is built on the need to meet the Big Data storage needs of companies such as Amazon.com, Google, and Facebook. These systems typically make use of cloud technology (derived in part from earlier work on distributed databases) and complex structuring techniques (derived in part from earlier work on object databases). The tools used to do this are nonrelational DBMSs, sometimes referred to as semi-structured storage or NoSQL DBMSs. Such systems have their own design decisions that a DBA needs to make, much as in a relational DBMS. Some of these important choices are captured in the CAP theorem, which states that no DBMS can provide partition tolerance, availability, and consistency at the same time.

An early NoSQL DBMS was Cassandra, and more recent popular examples are MongoDB and ArangoDB, each supporting a document DBMS. Document DBMS products most often use JSON (or sometimes XML) to structure the data, which allows documents (analogous to records) to contain simple values, other documents, or arrays of values or documents. Other varieties of NoSQL DBMS include key-value, column store, and graph DBMSs, all of which are described in more detail in online extension C. Data processing of the very large datasets found in Big Data is often done by the MapReduce process, which breaks a data processing task into many parallel tasks performed by many computers in the cluster and then combines these partial results to produce a final result. An emerging product that is supported by Microsoft and Oracle Corporation is the Hadoop Distributed File System (HDFS), with its spinoffs HBase, a nonrelational storage component, and Pig, a query language. Newer versions of Hadoop use Apache Tez, an improvement over the original MapReduce model that allows processing to be defined in a more general manner and avoids writing to files by using in-memory processing whenever possible.

KEY TERMS

Amazon Web Services (AWS)
Apache Spark
Apache Tez
AQL (ArangoDB Query Language)
availability
Big Data
business intelligence (BI) system
CAP theorem
click-stream data
cloud computing
collection
column family database
conformed dimension
consistency
containerization

customer relationship management (CRM)
data lake
data mart
data mining application
data warehouse
data warehouse metadata database
date dimension
dimension
dimension table
dimensional database
distributed database
distributed two-phase locking
document
document database
drill down

DynamoDB
EC2 service
enterprise data warehouse (EDW) architecture
extract, transform, and load (ETL) system
fact table
graph database
Hadoop Distributed File System (HDFS)
host machine
hypervisor
infrastructure as a service (IaaS)
JavaScript Object Notation (JSON)
key-value database
MapReduce

measure
method
Microsoft Azure
multimodel
NoSQL
Not only SQL
object
object-oriented DBMS (OODBMS)
object-oriented programming
  (OOP)
object persistence
object-relational database
OLAP cube

OLAP report
online analytical processing (OLAP)
online transaction processing
  (OLTP) system
operational system
partition tolerance
partitioning
PivotTable
platform as a service (PaaS)
property
redundant array of independent
  disks (RAID)
Relational DBMS Service (RDS)

replication
reporting system
RFM analysis
server cluster
slowly changing dimension
software as a service (SaaS)
star schema
storage area network (SAN)
time dimension
transactional system
virtual machine
virtual machine manager
virtualization

REVIEW QUESTIONS

7.1 What are BI systems?

7.2 How do BI systems differ from transaction processing systems?

7.3 Name and describe the two main categories of BI systems.

7.4 What are the three sources of data for BI systems?

7.5 Summarize the problems with operational databases that limit their usefulness for BI applications.

7.6 What is an ETL system, and what functions does it perform?

7.7 What problems in operational data create the need to clean data before loading the data into a data warehouse?

7.8 What does it mean to transform data? Give an example other than the ones used in this book.

7.9 Why are data warehouses necessary?

7.10 Give examples of data warehouse metadata.

7.11 Explain the difference between a data warehouse and a data mart. Give an example other than the ones used in this book.

7.12 What is the enterprise data warehouse (EDW) architecture?

7.13 Describe the differences between operational databases and dimensional databases.

7.14 What is a star schema?

7.15 What is a fact table? What types of data are stored in fact tables?

7.16 In relation to fact tables, what is a *measure*?

7.17 What is a dimension table? What types of data are stored in dimension tables?

7.18 What is a slowly changing dimension?

7.19 Why is the time dimension important in a dimensional model?

7.20 What is a conformed dimension?

7.21 What does OLAP stand for?

7.22 What is the distinguishing characteristic of OLAP reports?

7.23 Define *measure, dimension*, and *cube* in the context of OLAP reports.

7.24 Give an example, other than ones in this text, of a measure, two dimensions related to your measure, and a cube.

7.25 What is drill down?

7.26 Explain two ways that the OLAP report in Figure 7-19 differs from that in Figure 7-18.

7.27   Define *distributed database*.

7.28   Explain one way to partition a database that has three tables: T1, T2, and T3.

7.29   Explain one way to replicate a database that has three tables: T1, T2, and T3.

7.30   Explain what must be done when fully replicating a database but allowing only one computer to process updates.

7.31   If more than one computer can update a replicated database, what three problems can occur?

7.32   What solution is used to prevent the problems in question 7.31?

7.33   Explain what problems can occur in a distributed database that is partitioned but not replicated.

7.34   What organizations should consider using a distributed database?

7.35   Explain the meaning of the term *object persistence*.

7.36   In general terms, explain why relational databases are difficult to use for object persistence.

7.37   What does *OODBMS* stand for, and what is the purpose of an OODBMS?

7.38   According to this chapter, why were OODBMSs not successful?

7.39   What is an object-relational database?

7.40   What is Big Data?

7.41   What is the relationship between 1 MB of storage and 1 EB of storage?

7.42   What is the NoSQL movement?

7.43   What is the CAP theorem? How has it stood up over time?

7.44   What are the main features of data in a document database? Include an example of JSON data unrelated to any databases in this book, with at least one example each of arrays and documents within other documents.

7.45   What are the basic operations and utilities provided by a document DBMS?

7.46   Explain MapReduce processing.

7.47   What is Hadoop, and what is the history of the development of Hadoop to its current state? What are HBase and Pig?

7.48   Why is the new Tez processing model an improvement over MapReduce?

7.49   What is virtualization?

7.50   What is a hypervisor, and what is the difference between a type 1 hypervisor and a type 2 hypervisor?

7.51   What is containerization? How is it different from hypervisor-based virtualization?

7.52   What is cloud computing? What major technology enables cloud computing?

7.53   What are the differences between SaaS, PaaS, and IaaS?

EXERCISES

7.54   Based on the discussion of the Heather Sweeney Designs operational database (HSD) and dimensional database (HSD-DW) in the text, answer the following questions.

   A.   Using the SQL statements shown in Figure 7-10, create the HSD-DW database in a DBMS.

   B.   What transformations of data were made before HSD-DW was loaded with data? List all the transformations, showing the original format of the HSD data and how they appear in the HSD-DW database.

C. Write the complete set of SQL statements necessary to load the transformed data into the HSD-DW database.

D. Populate the HSD-DW database, using the SQL statements you wrote to answer part C.

E. Figure 7-26 shows the SQL code to create the SALES_FOR_RFM fact table shown in Figure 7-15. Using those statements, add the SALES_FOR_RFM table to your HSD-DW database.

F. What transformations of data are necessary to load the SALES_FOR_RFM table? List any needed transformations, showing the original format of the HSD data and how they appear in the HSD-DW database.

G. What data will be used to load the SALES_FOR_RFM fact table? Write the complete set of SQL statements necessary to load this data.

H. Populate the SALES_FOR_RFM fact table, using the SQL statements you wrote to answer part G.

I. Write an SQL query similar to SQL-Query-CH07-01 that uses the total dollar amount of each day's product sales as the measure (instead of the number of products sold each day).

J. Write the SQL view equivalent of the SQL query you wrote to answer part I.

K. Create the SQL view you wrote to answer part J in your HSD-DW database.

L. Create a Microsoft Excel 2019 workbook named HSD-DW-BI-Exercises.xlsx.

M. Using either the results of your SQL query from part K (copy the results of the query into a worksheet in the HSD-DW-BI.xlsx workbook and then format this range as a worksheet table) or your SQL view from part K (create a Microsoft Excel data connection to the view), create an OLAP report similar to the OLAP report shown in Figure 7-17. (*Hint:* If you need help with the needed Microsoft Excel actions, search in the Microsoft Excel help system for more information.)

FIGURE 7-26

The HSD-DW SALES_FOR_RFM SQL Create Table Statement

```
CREATE TABLE SALES_FOR_RFM(
    TimeID              Int                 NOT NULL,
    CustomerID          Int                 NOT NULL,
    InvoiceNumber       Int                 NOT NULL,
    PreTaxTotalSale     Numeric(9,2)        NOT NULL,
    CONSTRAINT          SALES_FOR_RFM_PK
                        PRIMARY KEY (TimeID, CustomerID, InvoiceNumber),
    CONSTRAINT          SRFM_TIMELINE_FK FOREIGN KEY(TimeID)
                        REFERENCES TIMELINE(TimeID)
                            ON UPDATE NO ACTION
                            ON DELETE NO ACTION,
    CONSTRAINT          SRFM_CUSTOMER_FK FOREIGN KEY(CustomerID)
                        REFERENCES CUSTOMER(CustomerID)
                            ON UPDATE NO ACTION
                            ON DELETE NO ACTION
);
```

N. Heather Sweeney is interested in the effects of payment type on sales in dollars.

1. Modify the design of the HSD-DW dimensional database to include a PAYMENT_TYPE dimension table.

2. Modify the HSD-DW database to include the PAYMENT_TYPE dimension table.

3. What data will be used to load the PAYMENT_TYPE dimension table? What data will be used to load foreign key data into the PRODUCT_SALES fact table? Write the complete set of SQL statements necessary to load these data.

4. Populate the PAYMENT_TYPE and PRODUCT_SALES tables, using the SQL statements you wrote to answer part 3.

5. Create the SQL queries or SQL views needed to incorporate the PaymentType attribute.

6. Create a Microsoft Excel 2019 OLAP report to show the effect of payment type on product sales in dollars.

WORKING WITH MICROSOFT ACCESS

Exercises

AW.7.1   Using the discussion of dimensional models and OLAP reports in the text and the specific discussion of OLAP reports based on a Microsoft Access 2019 database in this chapter's section of "Working with Access" as your reference, complete exercise 7.54 (excluding part N) for Heather Sweeney Designs. Create your HSD-DW database in Microsoft Access 2019 and your OLAP report in Microsoft Excel 2019.

CASE QUESTIONS

MARCIA'S DRY CLEANING

Ms. Marcia Wilson owns and operates Marcia's Dry Cleaning, which is an upscale dry cleaner in a well-to-do suburban neighborhood. Marcia makes her business stand out from the competition by providing superior customer service. She wants to keep track of each of her customers and their orders. Ultimately, she wants to notify them via email that their clothes are ready.

Assume that Marcia has hired you as a database consultant to develop an operational database named MDC that has the following four tables:

CUSTOMER (<u>CustomerID</u>, FirstName, LastName, Phone, EmailAddress)

INVOICE (<u>InvoiceNumber</u>, *CustomerID*, DateIn, DateOut, Subtotal, Tax, TotalAmount)

INVOICE_ITEM (*InvoiceNumber*, <u>ItemNumber</u>, *ServiceID*, Quantity, UnitPrice, ExtendedPrice)

SERVICE (<u>ServiceID</u>, ServiceDescription, UnitPrice)

The Database Concepts Web site is at **www.pearsonhighered.com/kroenke**. You may use either Access or MySQL for this question. If you are using Access, use the pre-built MDC database from our Web site. If you are using MySQL, use the scripts to create and populate the MDC tables from our Web site. Sample data for the CUSTOMER table are shown in Figure 7-27, for the SERVICE table in Figure 7-28, for the INVOICE table in Figure 7-29, and for the INVOICE_ITEM table in Figure 7-30.

A. If using Microsoft Access, download the database provided at the book's Web site, referenced earlier. If using MySQL, create a database named MDC and use the MDC SQL scripts to create and populate the database tables. Create a user named MDC-User with the password MDC-User+password. Assign this user all privileges for the MDC database.

B. Using your existing MDC database as a starting point, design a data warehouse star schema for a dimensional database named MDC-DW. The fact table measure will be ExtendedPrice.

C. Create the MDC-DW database in your DBMS product.

FIGURE 7-27

Sample Data for the MDC CUSTOMER Table

CustomerID	FirstName	LastName	Phone	EmailAddress
100	Nikki	Kaccaton	723-543-1233	Nikki.Kaccaton@somewhere.com
105	Brenda	Catnazaro	723-543-2344	Brenda.Catnazaro@somewhere.com
110	Bruce	LeCat	723-543-3455	Bruce.LeCat@somewhere.com
115	Betsy	Miller	723-654-3211	Betsy.Miller@somewhere.com
120	George	Miller	723-654-4322	George.Miller@somewhere.com
125	Kathy	Miller	723-514-9877	Kathy.Miller@somewhere.com
130	Betsy	Miller	723-514-8766	Betsy.Miller@elsewhere.com

FIGURE 7-28

Sample Data for the MDC SERVICE Table

ServiceID	ServiceDescription	UnitPrice
10	Men's Shirt	$1.50
11	Dress Shirt	$2.50
15	Women's Shirt	$1.50
16	Blouse	$3.50
20	Slacks – Men's	$5.00
25	Slacks – Women's	$6.00
30	Skirt	$5.00
31	Dress Skirt	$6.00
40	Suit – Men's	$9.00
45	Suit – Women's	$8.50
50	Tuxedo	$10.00
60	Formal Gown	$10.00

FIGURE 7-29

Sample Data for the MDC INVOICE Table

InvoiceNumber	CustomerID	DateIn	DateOut	SubTotal	Tax	TotalAmount
2019001	100	04-Oct-19	06-Oct-19	$158.50	$12.52	$171.02
2019002	105	04-Oct-19	06-Oct-19	$25.00	$1.98	$26.98
2019003	100	06-Oct-19	08-Oct-19	$49.00	$3.87	$52.87
2019004	115	06-Oct-19	08-Oct-19	$17.50	$1.38	$18.88
2019005	125	07-Oct-19	11-Oct-19	$12.00	$0.95	$12.95
2019006	110	11-Oct-19	13-Oct-19	$152.50	$12.05	$164.55
2019007	110	11-Oct-19	13-Oct-19	$7.00	$0.55	$7.55
2019008	130	12-Oct-19	14-Oct-19	$140.50	$11.10	$151.60
2019009	120	12-Oct-19	14-Oct-19	$27.00	$2.13	$29.13

D. What transformations of data will need to be made before the MDC-DW database can be loaded with data? List all the transformations, showing the original format of the MDC data and how it appears in the MDC-DW database.

E. Write the complete set of SQL statements necessary to load the transformed data into the MDC-DW database.

F. Populate the MDC-DW database, using the SQL statements you wrote to answer part E.

G. Write an SQL query similar to SQL-QUERY-CH07-01 (in the Dimensional Databases section of this chapter) that uses ExtendedPrice as the measure.

H. Write the SQL view equivalent of the SQL query you wrote to answer part G.

I. Create the SQL view you wrote to answer part H in your MDC-DW database.

J. Create a Microsoft Excel 2019 workbook named MDC-DW-BI-Exercises.xlsx.

K. Using either the results of your SQL query from part G (copy the results of the query into a worksheet in the MDC-DW-BI.xlsx workbook and then format this range as a worksheet table) or your SQL view from part I (create a Microsoft Excel data connection to the view), create an OLAP report similar to the OLAP report shown in Figure 7-17. (*Hint:* If you need help with the needed Microsoft Excel actions, search in the Microsoft Excel help system for more information.)

GARDEN GLORY PROJECT QUESTIONS

If you have not already implemented the Garden Glory database shown in Chapter 3 in a DBMS product, create and populate the Garden Glory database now in the DBMS of your choice (or as assigned by your instructor).

A. You need about 20 PROPERTY_SERVICE records in the database. Write the needed SQL statements for any needed additional PROPERTY_SERVICE records and insert the data into your database.

B. Design a data warehouse star schema for a dimensional database named GG-DW. The fact table measure will be HoursWorked.

FIGURE 7-30

Sample Data for the MDC INVOICE_ITEM Table

InvoiceNumber	ItemNumber	ServiceID	Quantity	UnitPrice	ExtendedPrice
2019001	1	16	2	$3.50	$7.00
2019001	2	11	5	$2.50	$12.50
2019001	3	50	2	$10.00	$20.00
2019001	4	20	10	$5.00	$50.00
2019001	5	25	10	$6.00	$60.00
2019001	6	40	1	$9.00	$9.00
2019002	1	11	10	$2.50	$25.00
2019003	1	20	5	$5.00	$25.00
2019003	2	25	4	$6.00	$24.00
2019004	1	11	7	$2.50	$17.50
2019005	1	16	2	$3.50	$7.00
2019005	2	11	2	$2.50	$5.00
2019006	1	16	5	$3.50	$17.50
2019006	2	11	10	$2.50	$25.00
2019006	3	20	10	$5.00	$50.00
2019006	4	25	10	$6.00	$60.00
2019007	1	16	2	$3.50	$7.00
2019008	1	16	3	$3.50	$10.50
2019008	2	11	12	$2.50	$30.00
2019008	3	20	8	$5.00	$40.00
2019008	4	25	10	$6.00	$60.00
2019009	1	40	3	$9.00	$27.00

C. Create the GG-DW database in a DBMS product.

D. What transformations of data will need to be made before the GG-DW database can be loaded with data? List all the transformations, showing the original format of the Garden Glory data and how it appears in the GG-DW database.

E. Write the complete set of SQL statements necessary to load the transformed data into the GG-DW database.

F. Populate the GG-DW database, using the SQL statements you wrote to answer part A.

G. Write an SQL query similar to SQL-QUERY-CH07-01 (in the Dimensional Databases section of this chapter) that uses the hours worked per day as the measure.

H. Write the SQL view equivalent of the SQL query you wrote to answer part G.

I. Create the SQL view you wrote to answer part H in your GG-DW database.

J. Create a Microsoft Excel 2019 workbook named GG-DW-BI-Exercises.xlsx.

K. Using either the results of your SQL query from part G (copy the results of the query into a worksheet in the GG-DW-BI.xlsx workbook and then format this range as a worksheet table) or your SQL view from part I (create a Microsoft Excel data connection to the view), create an OLAP report similar to the OLAP report shown in Figure 7-17. (*Hint:* If you need help with the needed Microsoft Excel actions, search in the Microsoft Excel help system for more information.)

JAMES RIVER JEWELRY PROJECT QUESTIONS

If you have not already implemented the James River Jewelry database shown in the James River Jewelry Project Questions for Chapter 3 in a DBMS product, create and populate the James River Jewelry database now in the DBMS of your choice (or as assigned by your instructor). Note that this assignment uses SQL views, which are discussed in online extension B.

A. Design a data warehouse star schema for a dimensional database named JRJ-DW. The fact table measure will be RetailPrice.

B. Create the JRJ-DW database in a DBMS product.

C. What transformations of data will need to be made before the JRJ-DW database can be loaded with data? List all the transformations, showing the original format of the James River Jewelry database data and how it appears in the JRJ-DW database.

D. Write the complete set of SQL statements necessary to load the transformed data into the JRJ-DW database.

E. Populate the JRJ-DW database, using the SQL statements you wrote to answer part D.

F. Write an SQL query similar to SQL-QUERY-CH07-01 (in the Dimensional Databases section of this chapter) that uses retail price as the measure.

G. Write the SQL view equivalent of the SQL query you wrote to answer part F.

H. Create the SQL view you wrote to answer part G in your JRJ-DW database.

I. Create a Microsoft Excel 2019 workbook named JRJ-DW-BI-Exercises.xlsx.

J. Using either the results of your SQL query from part F (copy the results of the query into a worksheet in the JRJ-DW-BI-Exercises.xlsx workbook and then format this range as a worksheet table) or your SQL view from part H (create a Microsoft Excel data connection to the view), create an OLAP report similar to the OLAP report shown in Figure 7-17. (Hint: If you need help with the needed Microsoft Excel actions, search in the Microsoft Excel help system for more information.)

THE QUEEN ANNE CURIOSITY SHOP PROJECT QUESTIONS

If you have not already implemented the Queen Anne Curiosity Shop database shown in Chapter 3 in a DBMS product, create and populate the QACS database now in the DBMS of your choice (or as assigned by your instructor).

A. Using your existing QACS database as a starting point, design a data warehouse star schema for a dimensional database named QACS-DW. The fact table measure will be ItemPrice.

B. Create the QACS-DW database in a DBMS product.

C. What transformations of data will need to be made before the QACS-DW database can be loaded with data? List all the transformations, showing the original format of the QACS data and how it appears in the QACS-DW database.

D. Write the complete set of SQL statements necessary to load the transformed data into the QACS-DW database.

E. Populate the QACS-DW database, using the SQL statements you wrote to answer part D.

F. Write an SQL query similar to SQL-QUERY-CH07-01 (in the Dimensional Databases section of this chapter) that uses retail price as the measure.

G. Write the SQL view equivalent of the SQL query you wrote to answer part F.

H. Create the SQL view you wrote to answer part G in your QACS-DW database.

I. Create a Microsoft Excel 2019 workbook named QACS-DW-BI-Exercises.xlsx.

J. Using either the results of your SQL query from part F (copy the results of the query into a worksheet in the QACS-DW-BI.xlsx workbook and then format this range as a worksheet table) or your SQL view from part H (create a Microsoft Excel data connection to the view), create an OLAP report similar to the OLAP report shown in Figure 7-17. (*Hint:* If you need help with the needed Microsoft Excel actions, search in the Microsoft Excel help system for more information.)

Online Extensions

Complete versions of these extensions are available on the textbook's Web site:
www.pearsonhighered.com/kroenke

Extension A
Working with MySQL

Extension B
Advanced SQL

Extension C
Advanced Business Intelligence and Big Data

Glossary

Although this section defines many of the key terms in the book, it is not meant to be exhaustive. Terms related to a specific DBMS product, for example, should be referenced in the chapter or online extension dedicated to that product. These references can be found in the index. Similarly, SQL concepts are included, but details of SQL commands and syntax should be referenced in the chapters that discuss those details, and Microsoft Access 2019 terms should be referenced in the sections of "Working with Microsoft Access."

ACID transaction: A transaction that is *atomic, consistent, isolated,* and *durable*. An atomic transaction is one in which a set of database changes are committed as a unit; either all of them are completed or none of them are. A consistent transaction is one in which all actions are taken against rows in the same logical state. An isolated transaction is one that is protected from changes by other users. A durable transaction is one that, once committed to a database, is permanent regardless of subsequent failure. There are different levels of consistency and isolation. *See* **transaction-level consistency** and **statement-level consistency**. *See also* **transaction isolation level**.

After-image: A record of a database entity (normally a row or a page) after a change. Used in recovery to perform rollforward.

Alternate key: In entity-relationship models, a synonym for candidate key.

Amazon Web Services (AWS): A cloud computing environment provided by Amazon.com.

American National Standards Institute (ANSI): The American standards organization that creates and publishes the SQL standards.

Android operating system: An operating system (OS) developed by Google and widely used on tablets and smartphones.

Anomaly: In normalization, an undesirable consequence of a data modification. With an insertion anomaly, facts about two or more different themes must be added to a single row of a relation. With a deletion anomaly, facts about two or more themes are lost when a single row is deleted.

App: A short term for *application*; normally applied to applications running on tablets and smartphones.

Apple II: A pioneering PC introduced in 1977 by Apple Inc.

Apple iPad: A pioneering tablet computer introduced in 2010 by Apple Inc.

ArangoDB: A multimodel NoSQL DBMS, supporting the document, graph, and key-value data models.

ArangoDB query language (AQL): A language allowing querying of data in the ArangoDB NoSQL DBMS.

ARPANET: A network forerunner of the Internet that was created by the Advanced Research Projects Agency at the Department of Defense in 1969.

Association relationship: In database design, a table pattern where an intersection table contains additional attributes beyond the attributes that make up the composite primary key.

Associative entity: Also called an association entity, this is an entity that represents the combination of at least two other objects and that contains data about that combination. It is often used in contracting and assignment data models.

Asterisk (*): A wildcard character used in Microsoft Access queries to represent one or more unspecified characters. *See* **SQL percent sign (%) wildcard character**.

Atomic transaction: A group of logically related database operations that are performed as a unit. Either all the operations are performed or none of them are.

Attribute: (1) A value that represents a characteristic of an entity. (2) A column of a relation.

Authentication: The credentials, usually a user name and password, used to allow a user to log into a computer, server, network, or application.

Authorization: A set of processing permissions that describes which users or user groups can take particular actions against particular portions of the database.

Availability: In a distributed database, data are available if a request for the data results in a response from some server.

Before-image: A record of a database entity (normally a row or a page) before a change. Used in recovery to perform rollback.

Big Data: The current term for the enormous datasets created by Web applications, Web 2.0 social networks, scientific applications, and transaction data.

Binary relationship: A relationship between exactly two entities or tables.

Boyce-Codd Normal Form (BCNF): A relation in third normal form in which every determinant is a candidate key.

Business intelligence (BI) systems: Information systems that assist managers and other professionals in analyzing current and past activities and in predicting future events. Two major categories of BI systems are reporting systems and data mining systems.

Business rule: A statement of a policy in a business that restricts the ways in which data can be inserted, updated, or deleted in the database.

Candidate key: An attribute or a group of attributes that identifies a unique row in a relation. One of the candidate keys is chosen to be the primary key.

CAP theorem: In distributed databases, it is not possible to achieve all three goals of consistency, availability, and partition tolerance simultaneously. *See also* **consistency, availability, partition tolerance**.

Cardinality: In a binary relationship, the maximum or minimum number of elements allowed on each side of the relationship. The maximum cardinality can be 1:1, 1:N, N:1, or N:M. The minimum cardinality can be optional/optional, optional/mandatory, mandatory/optional, or mandatory/mandatory.

Cascading deletion: A property of a relationship that indicates that when a parent row is deleted, related child rows should be deleted as well.

Cascading update: A referential integrity action specifying that when the key of a parent row is updated, the foreign keys of matching child rows should be updated as well.

Cell phone: A term for a *mobile phone*, which is a device that connects to the telephone system via radio signals. *See also* **mobile phone**.

Checkpoint: The point of synchronization between a database and a transaction log. At the checkpoint, all buffers are written to external storage. (This is the standard definition of *checkpoint*, but DBMS vendors sometimes use this term in other ways.)

Child: A row, record, or node on the many side of a one-to-many relationship. *See also* **parent**.

Child entity: An entity on the many side of a one-to-many relationship.

Click-stream data: Data about a customer's clicking behavior on a Web page; such data are often analyzed by e-commerce companies.

Client: In client-server architecture, the software that resides on the user's computer, tablet, or smartphone. *See also* **client-server architecture**.

Client (applications): *See* **Client**.

Client-server architecture: A computer application architecture that divides the application into two parts: the *client*, which resides on the users' device, and the *server*, which resides on a centralized server computer. The server responds to requests from clients.

Cloud computing: The use of networks, such as the Internet, to deliver services to users, where users are unconcerned about exactly where the servers delivering the services are located. Thus, the servers are said to be "in the cloud." Cloud services are typically provided by large data centers owned by cloud providers.

Collection: In a document database, a set of documents, typically with similar structure.

Column: A logical group of bytes in a row of a relation or a table. The meaning of a column is the same for every row of the relation, and represents an attribute of a relation.

Column family: A form of semistructured NoSQL database in which the basic unit of data is the column. Rows consist of sets of column (name, value) pairs and rows need not contain the same columns. A column family in a column family DBMS is loosely analogous to a relational table; each row in a column family must have a key. Also sometimes called a column database, column-oriented database, or column store.

Commit: A command issued to a DBMS to make database modifications permanent. After the command has been processed, the changes are written to the database and to a log in such a way that they will survive system crashes and other failures. A commit is usually used at the end of an atomic transaction. Contrast this with **rollback**.

Component design: *See* **Component design stage**.

Component design stage: The third step in the systems development life cycle (SDLC) model. The system is designed based on specific hardware and software. The database design is created in this step, based on the data model created during the requirements analysis stage. *See also* **systems development life cycle (SDLC)**.

Composite identifier: An identifier of an entity that consists of two or more attributes.

Composite key: A key of a relation that consists of two or more columns.

Computed value: A column of a table that is computed from other column values. Values are not stored but are computed when they are to be displayed.

Concurrency: A condition in which two or more transactions are processed against the database at the same time. In a single CPU system, the changes are interleaved; in a multi-CPU system, the transactions may be processed simultaneously, and the changes on the database server are interleaved.

Concurrent transactions: Two or more transactions that are being processed at the same time. *See also* **concurrency**.

Concurrent update problem: An error condition in which one user's data changes are overwritten by another user's data changes. Also called *lost update problem*.

Confidence: In market basket analysis, the probability of a customer's buying one product, given that the customer has purchased another specific product.

Conformed dimension: In a dimensional database design, a dimension table that has relationships to two or more fact tables.

Consistency: (1) Two or more concurrent transactions are consistent if the result of their being processed is the same as it would have been had they been processed in some sequential order. (2) In a distributed database, all copies of a data item have the same value at the same time.

Consistent: In an ACID transaction, either statement-level or transaction-level consistency. *See* **ACID transaction, consistency, statement-level consistency**, and **transaction-level consistency**.

Containerization: A form of virtualization in which only certain components of the operating system and programming environment (e.g., file system, code libraries) are provided, rather than an entire virtual machine. Multiple containers can run on the same virtual or physical machine without interference.

COUNT: In SQL, an aggregate function that counts the number of rows in a query result. *See* **SQL built-in aggregate function**.

Crow's foot symbol: A symbol in the IE Crow's Foot E-R model that indicates a many side of the relationship. It visually resembles a bird's foot, thus the name *crow's foot*.

CRUD: An acronym for create, read, update, and delete. It is used to describe the four actions done to data by a DBMS.

Cursor: An indicator of the current position in a query result file for a query that is embedded in a program.

Customer relationship management (CRM): An application designed for sales and marketing personnel to help manage their relationships and contacts with customers.

Data: The values stored in database tables.

Data administration: An enterprise-wide function that concerns the effective use and control of an organization's data assets. A person can perform it, but more often it is performed by a group. Specific functions include setting data standards and policies and providing a forum for conflict resolution. *See also* **database administration** and **DBA**.

Data constraint: A limitation on a data value. *See also* **domain integrity constraint**.

Data control language (DCL): A language used to describe the permissions granted in a database. SQL DCL is that portion of SQL that is used to grant and revoke database permissions.

Data definition language (DDL): A language used to describe the structure of a database.

Data manipulation language (DML): A language used to describe the processing of a database.

Data lake: an organization-wide online repository containing all data relevant to a business. Some of this data may be in a database and some may not.

Data mart: A facility similar to a data warehouse but with a restricted domain. Often, the data are restricted to particular types, business functions, or business units.

Data mining application: The use of statistical and mathematical techniques to find patterns in database data.

Data model: (1) A model of users' data requirements, usually expressed in terms of the entity-relationship model. It is sometimes called a users' data model. (2) A language for describing the structure and processing of a database.

Data sublanguage: A language for defining and processing a database intended to be embedded in programs written in another language—in most cases, a procedural language such as PHP, C#, or Visual Basic. A data sublanguage is an incomplete programming language because it contains only constructs for data definition and processing.

Data type: The representation category of the data in a column. For example, Char, Varchar, Integer, and so on.

Data warehouse: A store of enterprise data that is designed to facilitate management decision making. A data warehouse includes not only data but also metadata, tools, procedures, analysis programs, training, personnel information, and other resources that make access to the data easier and more relevant to decision makers.

Data warehouse metadata database: The database used to store the data warehouse metadata.

Database: A self-describing collection of related records or, for relational databases, of related tables.

Database administration (DBA): A function that concerns the effective use and control of a particular database and its related applications.

Database administrator (DBA): A person or group responsible for establishing policies and procedures to control and protect a database. They work within guidelines set by data administration to control the database structure, manage data changes, and maintain DBMS programs.

Database application: An application that uses a database to store the data needed by the application.

Database backup: A copy of database files that can be used to restore a database to some previous, consistent state.

Database design: The process in which a general data model is translated into entities, relationships, and constraints for a specific DBMS.

Database development process: A subset of the systems development life cycle (SDLC) that specifically designs and implements the database. *See also* **systems development life cycle (SDLC).**

Database integrity: The result of implementing domain integrity, entity integrity, and referential integrity in a database.

Database management system (DBMS): A set of programs used to define, administer, and process a database and its applications.

Database schema: A complete logical view of a database.

Database system: An information system composed of users, database applications, a database management system (DBMS), and a database.

Date dimension: In a dimensional database, a dimension that stores date (and possibly time) values. *See also* **dimensional database.**

DBA: An acronym for both database administrator and database administration. *See also* **database administrator, database administration.**

Deadlock: A condition that can occur during concurrent processing in which each of two (or more) transactions is waiting to access data that the other transaction has locked. It also is called the *deadly embrace.*

Deadly embrace: *See* **deadlock.**

Decision support system (DSS): One or more applications designed to help managers make decisions.

Default value: A value assigned to an attribute if there is no other value assigned to it when a new row is created in a table.

Degree: In the entity-relationship model, the number of entities participating in a relationship.

Deletion anomaly: In a relation, the situation in which the removal of one row of a table deletes facts about two or more themes.

Denormalization: The process of intentionally designing a relation that is not normalized. Denormalization is done to improve performance or security.

Determinant: One or more attributes that functionally determine another attribute or attributes. In the functional dependency (A, B) → (D, C), the attributes (A, B) are the determinant.

Device: Any equipment, such as a personal computer, that is connected to the Internet.

Dimension: In a dimensional database, a column or set of columns describing an aspect of an enterprise. *See* **Dimension table.**

Dimension table: In a star schema dimensional database, the tables that connect to the central fact table. Dimension tables hold attributes (dimensions) used in the organizing queries in analyses such as those of OLAP cubes.

Dimensional database: A database design that is used for data warehouses and is designed for efficient queries and analysis. It contains a central fact table connected to one or more dimension tables.

Dirty read: A read of data that have been changed but not yet committed to a database. Such changes may later be rolled back and removed from the database.

Discriminator: In the entity-relationship model, an attribute of a supertype entity that determines which subtype pertains to the supertype.

Disk mirroring: Maintaining two copies of the data so a single disk failure does not result in unavailable data.

Distributed database: A database that is stored and processed on two or more computers.

Distributed two-phase locking: A sophisticated form of record locking that must be used when database transactions are processed on two or more machines.

Document: A nonrelational database structure based on data stored as documents. The structure is commonly based on Extensible Markup Language (XML) or JavaScript Object Notation (JSON).

Domain: (1) The set of all possible values an attribute can have. (2) A description of the format (data type, length) and the semantics (meaning) of an attribute.

Domain integrity constraint: Also called a *domain constraint*, a data constraint that limits data values to a particular set of values.

Domain/key normal form (DK/NF): A relation in which all constraints are logical consequences of domains and keys. In this text, this definition has been simplified to a relation in which the determinants of all functional dependencies are candidate keys.

Drill down: User-directed disaggregation of data used to break higher-level totals into components.

Durable: In an ACID transaction, the database changes are permanent. *See* **ACID transaction.**

Dynamic cursor: A fully featured cursor. All inserts, updates, deletions, and changes in row order are visible to a dynamic cursor.

DynamoDB: A nonrelational unstructured data store developed by Amazon.com.

EC2 service: The Amazon Web Service's Elastic Compute Cloud service, which provides virtual servers to customers. *See also* **virtualization.**

Enterprise-class database system: A DBMS product capable of supporting the operating requirements of large organizations.

Enterprise data warehouse (EDW) architecture: A data warehouse architecture that links specialized data marts to a central data warehouse for data consistency and efficient operations.

Entity: Something of importance to a user that needs to be represented in a database. In the entity-relationship model, entities are restricted to things that can be represented by a single table. *See also* **strong entity** and **weak entity**.

Entity class: A design for a collection of entities of the same type. Typically a table or relation describes an entity class, for example an EMPLOYEE entity class. *Compare with* Entity instance.

Entity instance: A particular occurrence of an entity; for example, Employee 100 (an EMPLOYEE) and Accounting Department (a DEPARTMENT).

Entity integrity constraint: The constraint that the primary key column or columns must have unique values so that each row can be uniquely identified.

Entity-relationship diagram (E-R diagram): A graphic used to represent entities and their relationships. Entities are normally shown in squares or rectangles, and relationships are shown by lines connecting entities. This text uses the IE (Information Engineering) Crow's Foot model. Other popular data modeling standards standards include the Integrated Definition 1, Extended (IDEF1FX) model, and UML (Unified Modeling Language).

Entity-relationship model (E-R model): The constructs and conventions used to create a model of users' data. The things in the users' world are represented by entities, and the associations among those things are represented by relationships. The results are usually documented in an entity-relationship diagram. *See also* **data model**.

Ethernet networking technology: A commonly used network standard.

Exclusive lock: A lock on a data resource that no other transaction can read or update.

Exclusive subtype: A subtype in which a supertype instance is related to at most one subtype in a set of possible subtypes.

Explicit lock: A lock requested by a command from an application program.

Export: A function of a DBMS that writes a file of data in bulk. The file is intended to be read by another DBMS or program.

Extended entity-relationship (E-R) model: A set of constructs and conventions, including supertypes and subtypes, used to create data models. The things in the users' world are represented by entities, and the associations among those things are represented by relationships. The results are usually documented in an entity-relationship (E-R) diagram.

Extensible Markup Language (XML): A markup language whose tags can be extended by document designers.

Extract, transform, and load (ETL) system: The portion of a data warehouse that converts operational data to data warehouse data.

Fact table: The central table in a dimensional database. Its attributes are called measures. *See also* **measure**.

Field: (1) A logical group of bytes in a record used with file processing. (2) In the context of the relational model, a synonym for *attribute*.

Fifth normal form (5NF): A normal form necessary to eliminate an anomaly where a table can be split apart but not correctly joined back together. Also known as Project-Join Normal Form (PJ/NF).

First normal form (1NF): Any table that fits the definition of a relation.

Foreign key: An attribute or set of attributes that is a key of one or more relations other than the one in which it appears.

Foreign key constraint: A data constraint between two tables requiring that before a data value can be inserted into a foreign key column, that data value must already exist in the associated primary key column.

Form: A structured on-screen presentation of selected data from a database. Forms are used for both data input and data reading. A form is part of a database application. Compare this with a report.

Forward-only cursor: A type of cursor that can only move through the data in one direction. *See also* **cursor**.

Fourth normal form (4NF): A relation in BCNF in which every multivalued dependency is a functional dependency.

Functional dependency: A relationship between attributes in which one attribute or group of attributes determines the value of another. The expressions $X \rightarrow Y$, "X determines Y," and "Y is functionally dependent on X" mean that given a value of X, we can determine a specific value of Y.

Graph [NoSQL database category]: A nonrelational database structure based on graph theory. The structure is based on nodes, properties, and edges.

Graphical user interface (GUI): A user interface in which the user interacts with the application using icons and other visual cues instead of text-based commands.

Hadoop: *See* **Hadoop Distributed File System (HDFS)**.

Hadoop Distributed File System (HDFS): An open source file distribution system that provides standard file services to clustered servers so that their file systems can function as one distributed file system.

HAS-A relationship: A relationship between two entities or objects that are of different logical types; for example, EMPLOYEE HAS-A(n) AUTO. Contrast this with an IS-A relationship.

Host machine: (1) In networking, any computer or device connected to the Internet. (2) In virtualization, the physical machine that emulates one or more other computer systems.

Hypervisor: The software that creates, controls, and communicates with virtual machines.

IBM Personal Computer (IBM PC): A pioneering personal computer developed in 1981 by the IBM corporation.

ID column: A column used as a primary key that usually has surrogate key values.

ID-dependent entity: An entity that cannot logically exist without the existence of another entity. APPOINTMENT, for example, cannot exist without CLIENT to make the appointment. To be an ID-dependent entity, the identifier of the entity must contain the identifier of the entity on which it depends. Such entities are a subset of a weak entity. *See also* **strong entity** and **weak entity**.

Identifier: In an entity, a group of one or more attributes that determine entity instances. *See also* **nonunique identifier** and **unique identifier**.

Identifying relationship: A relationship that is used when the child entity is ID-dependent upon the parent entity.

IDENTITY ({Identity seed}, {Identity increment}): For Microsoft SQL Server 2017, the attribute specification that is used to create a surrogate key.

IE Crow's Foot model: Formally known as the Information Engineering (IE) Crow's Foot model, it is a system of symbology used to construct E-R diagrams in data modeling and database design.

Implementation stage: In the systems development life cycle (SDLC), the stage where hardware is acquired, software is installed, and the designed information system actually made functional for users. *See also* **systems development life cycle (SDLC)**.

Implicit lock: A lock that is placed automatically by a DBMS.

Inclusive subtype: In data modeling and database design, a subtype that allows a supertype entity to be associated with more than one subtype.

Inconsistent backup: A backup file that contains uncommitted changes.

Inconsistent read problem: An anomaly that occurs in concurrent processing in which transactions execute a series of reads that are inconsistent with one another. This problem can be prevented by using two-phase locking and other strategies.

Index: A secondary data structure, typically stored on disk, created by the DBA to improve access and sorting performance on certain queries.

Information: (1) Knowledge derived from data, (2) data presented in a meaningful context, or (3) data processed by summing, ordering, averaging, grouping, comparing, or other similar operations.

Information Engineering (IE) model: An E-R model developed by James Martin.

Infrastructure as a service (IaaS): The provision of virtual machines to users by a cloud computing service provider such as Amazon Web Services or Microsoft Azure.

Inner join: *See* **join operation**.

Insertion anomaly: In a relation, a condition that exists when, to add a complete row to a table, one must add facts about two or more logically different themes.

Instance: A specific occurrence of an object of interest.

Integrated Definition 1, Extended (IDEF1X): A version of the entity-relationship model, adopted as a national standard but difficult to understand and use. Most organizations use a simpler E-R version like the crow's foot model.

International Organization for Standardization (ISO): The international standards organization that works on SQL standards, among others.

Internet: The network that connects the entire Earth, and the basis for much of modern computing.

Intersection table: A table (also called a relation) used to represent a many-to-many relationship. It contains the keys of the relations in the relationship. When used to represent entities having a many-to-many relationship, it may have nonkey data if the relationship contains data. If it has nonkey data, the join table becomes an **Associative entity**.

iPhone: A smartphone built by Apple Inc.

IS-A relationship: A relationship between a supertype and a subtype. For example, EMPLOYEE and ENGINEER have an IS-A relationship.

Isolation level: *See* **transaction isolation level**.

JavaScript: A proprietary scripting language originally created by Netscape but now owned by Oracle Corporation. The Microsoft version is called JScript; the standard version is called ECMA-262. These are easily learned interpreted languages that are used for both Web server and Web client application processing. Sometimes written as *Java Script*.

JavaScript Object Notation (JSON): a data structuring format based on (1) documents consisting of name/value pairs and (2) arrays. Values can be simple data values, documents, or arrays.

Join operation: A relational algebra operation on two relations, A and B, that produces a third relation, C. A row of A is concatenated with a row of B to form a new row in C if the rows in A and B meet restrictions concerning their values. For example, A1 is an attribute in A, and B1 is an attribute in B. The join of A with B in which (A1 = B1) will result in a relation, C, having the concatenation of rows in A and B in which the value of A1 is equal to the value of B1. In theory, restrictions other than equality are allowed—a join could be made in which A1 < B1. However, such non-equal joins are not used in practice. Also known as inner join. *See also* **natural join**.

JSON: *see* **JavaScript Object Notation**.

Key: (1) A group of one or more attributes that identifies a unique row in a relation. Because relations cannot have duplicate rows, every relation must have at least one key that is the composite of all the attributes in the relation. A key is sometimes called a logical key. (2) With some relational DBMS products, an index on a column used to improve access and sorting speed. In this case, it is sometimes called a physical key. *See also* **nonunique key** and **unique key**.

Key-value [NoSQL database category]: A nonrelational database structure based on data values identified by key values.

Keyset cursor: An SQL cursor that combines some of the features of static cursors with some of the features of dynamic cursors. *See also* **cursor**.

List: A set of values, usually written in a vertical column, of some entity. The set may or may not be sorted in some ordering.

Local Area Networks (LANs): A computer network that operates with computers in a definable small area, such as a business or university.

Lock: To allocate a database resource to a particular transaction in a concurrent-processing system. The size at which the resource can be locked is known as the lock granularity. *See also* **exclusive lock** and **shared lock**.

Lock granularity: The size of the object accessed with a lock.

Log: A file that contains a record of database changes. The log contains before-images and after-images.

Logical unit of work (LUW): An equivalent term for transaction. *See* **transaction**.

Lost update problem: Same as concurrent update problem.

Mandatory: In a relationship, when the minimum number of entity instances that *must* participate in a relationship is one, then participation in the relationship is said to be *mandatory*. *See also* **minimum cardinality, optional**.

MapReduce: A **big data** processing technique that breaks a data analysis into many parallel processes (the Map function) and then combines the results of these processes into one final result (the Reduce function).

MAX: In SQL, an aggregate function that determines the largest value in a set of numbers. *See* **SQL built-in aggregate function**.

Maximum cardinality: (1) The maximum number of values that an attribute can have within a semantic object. (2) In a relationship between tables, the maximum number of rows to which a row of one table can relate in the other table.

Measure: In OLAP, a data value that is summed, averaged, or processed in some simple arithmetic manner.

Metadata: Data concerning the structure of data in a database used to describe tables, columns, constraints, indexes, and so forth. Metadata is also stored in a **data warehouse** to describe its contents.

Method: A program attached to an object in object-oriented programming or in an object-oriented or object-relational database.

Microsoft Azure: Microsoft's cloud computing infrastructure provided by several data centers managed by Microsoft. The original name was Windows Azure.

Microsoft SQL Server 2017: The current release of Microsoft's SQL Server product. It is available in several editions, including the freely downloadable Developer edition and Express edition.

Microsoft SQL Server 2017 Management Studio: The GUI utility that is used with Microsoft SQL Server 2017.

MIN: In SQL, an aggregate function that determines the smallest value in a set of numbers. *See* **SQL built-in aggregate function**.

Minimum cardinality: (1) In a binary relationship in the entity-relationship model, the minimum number of entities required on each side of a relationship. (2) In a binary relationship in the relational model, the minimum number of rows required on each side of a relationship. Common values of minimum cardinality for both definitions are optional to optional (O-O), mandatory to optional (M-O), optional to mandatory (O-M), and mandatory to mandatory (M-M).

Mixed entity pattern: A portion of an E-R diagram in which a weak entity participates in both identifying and non-identifying relationships.

Mobile phone: A handheld device that connects to the telephone system via radio signals. *See also* **cell phone**.

Modification action: An action that changes the value of a data item.

Modification problem: A situation that exists when the storing of one row in a table records facts about two themes or the deletion of a row removes facts about two themes, or when a data change must be made in multiple rows for consistency.

Multimodel: A NoSQL DBMS that provides more than one of the four standard NoSQL data models for data storage and processing.

Multivalued dependency: A condition in a relation with three or more attributes in which independent attributes appear to have relationships they do not have. Formally, in a relation R (A, B, C), having key (A, B, C) where A is matched with multiple values of B (or of C or of both), B does not determine C, and C does not determine B. An example is the relation EMPLOYEE (EmpNumber, EmpSkill, DependentName), where an employee can have multiple values of EmpSkill and DependentName. EmpSkill and DependentName do not have any relationship, but they do appear to in the relation.

MySQL 8.0 Community Server: The current freely downloadable version of Oracle's MySQL database product.

MySQL 8.0 Workbench: The GUI utility used with MySQL 8.0.

N:M: An abbreviation for a many-to-many relationship between the rows of two tables.

Natural join: A join of a relation A having attribute A1 with relation B having attribute B1, where A1 = B1. The joined relation, C, contains either column A1 or B1 but not both.

Nonidentifying relationship: In data modeling, a relationship between two entities such that one is *not* ID-dependent on the other. *See* **identifying relationship**.

Nonrelational database: A database constructed on a methodology other the relational database methodology.

Nonrepeatable read: A situation that occurs when a transaction reads data it has previously read and finds modifications or deletions caused by a committed transaction.

Nonunique identifier: An identifier that determines a group of entity instances. *See also* **unique identifier**.

Nonunique key: A key that potentially identifies more than one row.

Normal form: A rule or set of rules governing the allowed structure of relations. The rules apply to attributes, functional dependencies, multivalued dependencies, domains, and constraints. The most important normal forms are 1NF, 2NF, 3NF, BCNF, 4NF, 5NF, and DK/NF.

Normalization: (1) The process of constructing one or more relations such that in every relation the determinant of every functional dependency is a candidate key (BCNF). (2) The process of removing multivalued dependencies (4NF). (3) In general, the process of evaluating a relation to determine whether it is in a specified normal form and of converting it to relations in that specified normal form, if necessary.

NoSQL: *See* **Not only SQL**.

Not only SQL: Actually referring to the creation and use of nonrelational DBMS products instead of just not using the SQL language, this movement was originally mislabeled as the NoSQL movement. Such systems may or may not use SQL-like query languages for data retrieval. It is now recognized that both relational and nonrelational DBMS products are needed in management information systems and that they must interact with each other. Thus, the term *not only SQL*.

Null value: An attribute value that has never been supplied. Such values are ambiguous and can mean the value is unknown, the value is not appropriate, or the value is known to be blank.

Object: In object-oriented programming, as well as both object-oriented and object-relational databases, an abstraction that is defined by its properties and methods. *See also* **object-oriented programming (OOP)**.

Object persistence: Permanently storing the property values of an object in a database.

Object-oriented DBMS (OODBMS): A type of DBMS that provides object persistence. OODBMSs have not received commercial acceptance.

Object-oriented programming (OOP): A programming methodology that defines objects and the interactions between them to create application programs.

Object-relational database: A database created by a DBMS that provides a relational model interface as well as structures for object persistence. Oracle Database is the leading object-relational DBMS.

OLAP cube: In OLAP, a set of measures and dimensions arranged, normally, in the format of a three-dimensional table, where each dimension corresponds to a set of attribute values such as Time, ProductNumber, and CustomerID.

OLAP report: The output of an OLAP analysis in tabular format. For example, this can be a Microsoft Excel PivotTable. *See* **OLAP cube**.

1:1: An abbreviation for a one-to-one relationship between the rows of two tables.

1:N: An abbreviation for a one-to-many relationship between the rows of two tables.

Online analytical processing (OLAP): A technique for analyzing data values, called measures, against characteristics associated with those data values, called dimensions.

Online transaction processing (OLTP) system: An operational database system available for, and dedicated to, transaction processing.

Operational system: A database system in use for the daily operations of the enterprise, typically an OLTP system. *See* **online transaction processing (OLTP) system**.

Optimistic concurrency control: A concurrency control that assumes no conflict will occur, processes a transaction, and then checks to determine whether conflict did occur. If so, the transaction is aborted. If not, the updates are processed. *See also* **optimistic locking**.

Optimistic locking: A form of optimistic concurrency control in which, if no conflicts occurred, the data objects are locked, updated, and unlocked. *See also* **optimistic concurrency control**.

Optional: In a relationship, when the minimum number of entity instances that *must* participate in a relationship is zero, then participation in the relationship is said to be *optional*. *See also* **mandatory, minimum cardinality**.

Oracle Database Express Edition (Oracle Database XE): The express edition of Oracle Database, Oracle's relational database product. It is a free, entry-level version that is easier to install and administer, but it is lacking some advanced features.

Oracle SQL Developer: The GUI utility for Oracle Database and Oracle Database XE.

Outer join: A join in which all the rows of a table appear in the resulting relation, regardless of whether they have a match in the join condition. In a left outer join, all the rows in the left-hand relation appear; in a right outer join, all the rows in the right-hand relation appear.

Parent: A row, record, or node on the *one* side of a one-to-many relationship. *See also* **child**.

Parent entity: An entity on the *one* side of a one-to-many relationship. *See also* **child entity**.

Parent mandatory and child mandatory (M-M): A relationship where the minimum cardinality of the parent is 1 and the minimum cardinality of the child is 1.

Parent mandatory and child optional (M-O): A relationship where the minimum cardinality of the parent is 1 and the minimum cardinality of the child is 0.

Parent optional and child mandatory (O-M): A relationship where the minimum cardinality of the parent is 0 and the minimum cardinality of the child is 1.

Parent optional and child optional (O-O): A relationship where the minimum cardinality of the parent is 0 and the minimum cardinality of the child is 0.

Partition tolerance: In distributed databases, a DBMS that can continue operating even when the network containing the database servers has been separated by failures into two or more completely separate, but still functioning, sections (partitions).

Partitioning: For distributed databases, separating a database into parts, which will normally be stored on separate DBMS servers.

Permissions: The various forms of interaction a user is allowed to have with data in a database. These permissions, or privileges, are typically granted to a user by either a DBA or the data's creator to allow other users to see or modify the data.

Personal computer (PC): Also known as a *micro-computer*, a small computer intended for use by one person as his or her own computer.

Personal database system: A DBMS product intended for use by an individual or small workgroup. Such products typically include application development tools such as form and report generators in addition to the DBMS. For example, Microsoft Access 2019.

Pessimistic locking: A locking strategy that prevents conflict by placing locks before processing database read and write requests. *See also* **deadlock** and **optimistic locking**.

Phantom read: A situation that occurs when a transaction reads data it has previously read and then finds new rows that were inserted by a committed transaction.

Physical database design: An area of DBA responsibility that involves issues such as indexes, placement of data in secondary memory, usage of primary memory, data replication and distribution, and so on.

PivotTable: A Microsoft Excel data summarization tool that can be used to produce OLAP reports. *See also* **OLAP**.

Platform as a service (PaaS): A type of cloud computing service that supports the creating of applications in the cloud without requiring the customer to rent and support a complete virtual server. The operating system and software development tools are typically provided for clients.

Point of Sale (POS) system: A database application used in retail stores to record customer purchase data and to control inventory.

Primary key: A candidate key selected to be the key of a relation.

Processing rights and responsibilities: Organizational policies regarding which groups can take which actions on specified data items or other collections of data.

Properties: Same as attributes.

Query by Example (QBE): A style of query interface, first developed by IBM but now used by other vendors, that enables users to express queries by providing examples of the results they seek. Microsoft Access provides this functionality.

Query optimizer: A component of a DBMS that evaluates alternative strategies for executing a query and chooses an efficient strategy.

Question mark (?) wildcard character: A character used in Microsoft Access 2019 queries to represent a single unspecified character. *See* **SQL underscore (_) wildcard character**.

Read committed isolation: A level of transaction isolation that prohibits dirty reads but allows nonrepeatable reads and phantom reads.

Read uncommitted isolation: A level of transaction isolation that allows dirty reads, nonrepeatable reads, and phantom reads to occur.

Record: (1) A group of fields pertaining to the same entity; used in file-processing systems. (2) In the relational model, a synonym for row and tuple. *See also* **row**.

Recovery via reprocessing: Recovering a database by restoring the last full backup, and then recreating each transaction since the backup.

Recovery via rollback/rollforward: Recovering a database by restoring the last full backup, and then using data stored in a transaction log to modify the database as needed by either adding transactions (roll forward) or removing erroneous transactions (rollback).

Recursive relationship: A relationship among entities, objects, or rows of the same type. For example, if CUSTOMERs refer other CUSTOMERs, the relationship is recursive.

Redundant array of independent disks (RAID): A group of techniques for placing data onto several physical disks that act as one logical disk to gain reliability or access speed.

Referential integrity constraint: A relationship constraint on foreign key values. A referential integrity constraint specifies that the values of a foreign key must be a subset of the values of the primary key to which it refers.

Related tables: Tables in a relational database that are connected by a foreign key column and a referential integrity constraint.

Relation: A two-dimensional array that contains single-value entries and no duplicate rows. The meaning of the columns is the same in every row. The order of the rows and columns is immaterial.

Relational database: A database that consists of relations. In practice, relational databases contain relations with duplicate rows. Most DBMS products include a feature that removes duplicate rows when necessary and appropriate. Such removal is not done as a matter of course because it can be time-consuming and expensive.

Relational DBMS Service (RDS): A part of Amazon's AWS that provides a relational database service in the cloud.

Relational model: A data model in which data are stored in relations and relationships between rows are represented by data values.

Relational schema: A set of relations with referential integrity constraints.

Relationship: An association between two entities, objects, or rows of relations.

Relationship cardinality constraint: A constraint on the number of rows that can participate in a relationship. Minimum cardinality constraints determine the number of rows that must participate; maximum cardinality constraints specify the largest number of rows that can participate. *See also* **maximum cardinality, minimum cardinality**

Relationship class: An association between entity classes.

Relationship instance: (1) An association between entity instances, (2) a specific relationship between two tables in a database.

Repeatable reads isolation: A level of transaction isolation that disallows dirty reads and nonrepeatable reads. Phantom reads can occur.

Replication: In distributed databases, the act of maintaining multiple copies of the same data (relation or partition) on more than one computer.

Report: A formatted set of information created to meet a user's need.

Reporting systems: Business intelligence (BI) systems that process data by filtering, sorting, and making simple calculations. OLAP is a type of reporting system.

Requirements analysis stage: The stage in the system development life cycle where the data model is created. *See also* **systems development life cycle (SDLC)**.

Resource locking: *See* **lock**.

RFM analysis: A type of reporting system in which customers are classified according to how recently (R), how frequently (F), and how much money (M) they spend on their orders.

Rollback: A process that involves recovering a database in which before-images are applied to the database to return to an earlier checkpoint or other point at which the database is logically consistent.

Rollforward: A process that involves recovering a database by applying after-images to a saved copy of the database to bring it to a checkpoint or other point at which the database is logically consistent.

Row: A group of columns in a table. All the columns in a row pertain to the same entity. Also known as tuple or record.

Schema-valid document: An XML document that conforms to XML Schema.

Scrollable cursor: A cursor type that enables forward and backward movement through a recordset. Three scrollable cursor types discussed in this text are snapshot, keyset, and dynamic.

Second normal form (2NF): A relation in first normal form in which all non-key attributes are dependent on all the attributes of a key.

Self-describing: In a database, the characteristic of including data about the database in the database itself. Thus, the data that define a table are included in a database along with the data that are contained in that table. These descriptive data are called *metadata*. *See also* **metadata, relation, table**.

Serializable isolation level: A level of transaction isolation that disallows dirty reads, nonrepeatable reads, and phantom reads.

Server: A robust computer operated by information systems staff and used to run the server portion of client-server application such as Web pages and email. Servers are thus said to provide services to users. *See also* **service, client-server architecture**.

Server cluster: A group of servers that communicate and coordinate with each other.

Service: The provision of some utility to users. For example, a Web server provides the Web service, which is providing Web pages to users. *See also* **server**.

Shared lock: A lock against a data resource in which no transaction can update the data but many transactions can concurrently read those data.

Slowly changing dimension: In a dimensional database, a data column with values that change occasionally but irregularly over time; for example, a customer's address or phone number.

Smartphone: A cell phone that is capable of running user client applications (apps) in a client-server environment. *See also* **cell phone, client-server architecture**.

Software as a service (SaaS): An arrangement whereby a customer pays for access to specific software (e.g., a relational or NoSQL database management system, or a Customer Relationship Management application) in the cloud.

SQL: *See* **Structured Query Language (SQL)**.

SQL AND logical operator: The SQL logical operator used to combine conditions in an SQL WHERE clause.

SQL built-in aggregate function: In SQL, any of the functions COUNT, SUM, AVG, MAX, or MIN.

SQL CREATE TABLE statement: The SQL command used to create a database table.

SQL CREATE VIEW statement: The SQL command used to create a database view.

SQL FROM clause: The part of an SQL SELECT statement that specifies conditions used to determine which tables are used in a query.

SQL GROUP BY clause: The part of an SQL SELECT statement that specifies conditions for grouping rows when determining the query results.

SQL HAVING clause: The part of an SQL SELECT statement that specifies conditions used to determine which rows appear in the results based on the values of aggregate functions.

SQL OR logical operator: The SQL logical operator used to specify alternate conditions in an SQL WHERE clause.

SQL ORDER BY clause: The part of an SQL SELECT statement that specifies how the query results should be sorted when they are displayed.

SQL percent sign (%) wildcard character: The standard SQL wildcard character used to specify zero or more characters. Microsoft Access uses an asterisk (*) character instead of the percent sign character.

SQL SELECT clause: The part of an SQL SELECT statement that specifies which columns are displayed in the query results.

SQL SELECT/FROM/WHERE framework: The basic structure of an SQL query. This framework includes which fields to display, the tables the attributes come from, and the conditions under which rows are included in the result. *See* **SQL SELECT clause, SQL FROM clause, SQL WHERE clause, SQL ORDER BY clause, SQL GROUP BY clause, SQL HAVING clause, SQL AND operator**, and **SQL OR operator**.

SQL SELECT * statement: A variant of an SQL SELECT query that returns all columns for all tables in the query.

SQL SELECT...FOR XML statement: A variant of an SQL SELECT query that returns the query results in XML format.

SQL underscore (_) wildcard character: The standard SQL wildcard character used to specify a *single* character. Microsoft Access uses a question mark (?) character instead of the underscore character.

SQL view: A relation that is constructed from a single SQL SELECT statement. The term *view* in most DBMS products, including Microsoft Access, Microsoft SQL Server, Oracle Database, and MySQL, means SQL view.

SQL WHERE clause: The part of an SQL SELECT statement that specifies conditions used to determine which rows are in the query results.

SQL/Persistent stored modules (SQL/PSM): SQL statements that extend SQL by adding procedural programming capabilities, such as variables and flow-of-control statements, and thus provide some programmability within the SQL framework. SQL/PSM is used to create user-defined functions, stored procedures, and triggers. *See also* **trigger, stored procedure, user-defined function**.

Star schema: In a dimensional database and as used in an OLAP database, the structure of a central fact table linked to dimension tables.

Statement-level consistency: A situation in which all rows affected by a single SQL statement are protected from changes made by other users during the execution of the statement. *See also* **transaction-level consistency**.

Static cursor: A cursor that takes a snapshot of a relation and processes that snapshot.

Storage area network (SAN): A dedicated network connecting server computers to external storage devices.

Stored procedure: A collection of SQL statements stored as a file that can be invoked by a single command. Usually, DBMS products provide a language for creating stored procedures that augments SQL with programming language constructs. Oracle provides PL/SQL for this purpose, and SQL Server provides Transact-SQL (T-SQL). MySQL supports SQL/Persistent Stored Modules (SQL/PSM), an implementation of an SQL standard. With some products, stored procedures can be written in a standard language such as Java. Stored procedures are often stored within the database.

Strict two-phase locking: A version of two-phase locking in which all locks, once obtained, are held until the end of the transaction. *See also* **two-phase locking**.

Strong entity: In the entity-relationship model, any entity whose existence in the database does not depend on the existence of any other entity. *See also* **ID-dependent entity** and **weak entity**.

Structured Query Language (SQL): A language for defining the structure and processing of a relational database. It can be used as a stand-alone query language, or it can be embedded in application programs. SQL was developed by IBM and is accepted as a national standard by the American National Standards Institute.

Subquery: A SELECT statement that appears in the WHERE, FROM, or HAVING clause of an SQL statement. The results from the subquery are used by the calling query. Subqueries can be nested within each other.

Subtype entity: In generalization (IS-A) hierarchies, an entity or object that is a subspecies or subcategory of a higher-level type, called a supertype. For example, ENGINEER is a subtype of EMPLOYEE.

SUM: In SQL, an aggregate function that adds up a set of numbers. *See* **SQL built-in aggregate function**.

Supertype entity: In generalization (IS-A) hierarchies, an entity or object that logically contains subtypes. For example, EMPLOYEE is a supertype of ENGINEER, ACCOUNTANT, and MANAGER.

Surrogate key: A unique, system-supplied identifier used as the primary key of a relation. The values of a surrogate key have no meaning to the users and usually are hidden on forms and reports.

Synonyms: Terms or words that mean the same thing.

System definition stage: The initial stage of the systems development life cycle (SDLC) where the project requirements and constraints are established, and the project team created. *See also* **systems development life cycle (SDLC)**.

Systems development life cycle (SDLC): The five-stage cycle used to develop management information systems. It consists of the following stages: (1) system definition, (2) requirements analysis, (3) component design, (4) implementation, and (5) system maintenance. *See also* **system definition stage**.

Table: A database structure of rows and columns to create cells that hold data values. Also known as a *relation* in a relational database, although strictly only tables that meet specific conditions can be called relations. *See* **relation**.

Tablet: A handheld user device that can run user client applications. Similar to a cell phone but generally larger and without the telephone capability.

Tablet computers: A personal computer (PC) in a tablet format. *See also* **tablet**.

Ternary relationship: A relationship between three entities.

Third normal form (3NF): A relation in second normal form that has no transitive dependencies.

Time dimension: A required dimension table in a dimensional database. The time dimension allows the data to be analyzed over time.

Transaction: (1) A group of actions that is performed on the database atomically; either all actions are committed to the database or none of them are. (2) In the business world, the record of an event. *See also* **ACID transaction** and **atomic transaction**.

Transaction control language (TCL): SQL statements that are used to mark transaction boundaries and control transaction behavior.

Transaction isolation level: The degree to which a database transaction is protected from actions by other transactions. The SQL standard specifies four isolation levels: read uncommitted, read committed, repeatable read, and serializable.

Transaction-level consistency: A situation in which all rows affected by any of the SQL statements in a transaction are protected from changes during the entire transaction. This level of consistency is expensive to enforce and is likely to reduce throughput. It might also prevent a transaction from seeing its own changes. *See also* **statement-level consistency**.

Transactional system: A database dedicated to processing transactions such as product sales and orders. It is designed to make sure that only complete transactions are recorded in the database.

Transitive dependency: In a relation having at least three attributes, such as R (A, B, C), the situation in which A determines B and B determines C, but B does not determine A.

Trigger: A special type of stored procedure that is invoked by the DBMS when a specified condition occurs. BEFORE triggers are executed before a specified database action, AFTER triggers are executed after a specified database action, and INSTEAD OF triggers are executed in place of a specified database action. INSTEAD OF triggers are normally used to update data in SQL views.

Tuple: *See* **row**.

Two-phase locking: A procedure in which locks are obtained and released in two phases. During the growing phase, the locks are obtained; during the shrinking phase, the locks are released. After a lock is released, no other lock will be granted that transaction. Such a procedure ensures consistency in database updates in a concurrent-processing environment.

UML: *See* **Unified Modeling Language (UML)**.

Unary relationship: A relationship between a table and itself. Also called a recursive relationship.

Unified Modeling Language (UML): A set of structures and techniques for modeling and designing object-oriented programs and applications. UML is a methodology and a set of tools for such development. UML incorporates the entity-relationship model for data modeling.

Unique identifier: An identifier that determines exactly one entity instance. *See also* **nonunique identifier**.

Unique key: A key that identifies a unique row.

Use case: In systems analysis and design, a detailed example of how a user interacts with an information system or application.

User: A person using an application.

User account: An account for a specific user on a particular system *See also* **user**.

User-defined function: A stored set of SQL statements that is *called by name* from another SQL statement, that may have *input parameters* passed to it by the calling SQL statement, and that *returns an output value* to the SQL statement that called the function.

User group: A group of users. *See* **user**.

View: *see* **SQL View**.

Virtual machine: A software emulation of a computer system. *See also* **virtualization**.

Virtual machine manager: The software on the host computer that controls the virtual computers running on that host. *See* **hypervisor**.

Virtualization: A technique for sharing the hardware resources of one physical computer by having it host one or more virtual computers (virtual machines).

Weak entity: In the entity-relationship model, an entity whose logical existence in a database depends on the existence of another entity. *See also* **ID-dependent entity** and **strong entity**.

Web (the): A synonym for the World Wide Web. *See also* **World Wide Web**.

Web 2.0: Web sites that allow users to contribute content.

Web browser: The software that is used to connect to and interact with Web pages.

Web sites: Locations on the World Wide Web. *See also* **World Wide Web**.

Well-formed relation: A relation in which every determinant is a candidate key. Any relation that is not well-formed should be normalized into two or more relations that are well formed.

Wildcard characters: In SQL, characters that are used to represent one or more unknown characters in the WHERE clause of a query. Examples include: %, *, ?, and _ (underscore).

World Wide Web: The set of interconnected hypertext objects accessible on the Internet, organized into Web sites.

WWW: An initialism for the World Wide Web. *See also* **World Wide Web**.

XML: *See* **Extensible Markup Language (XML)**.

Index